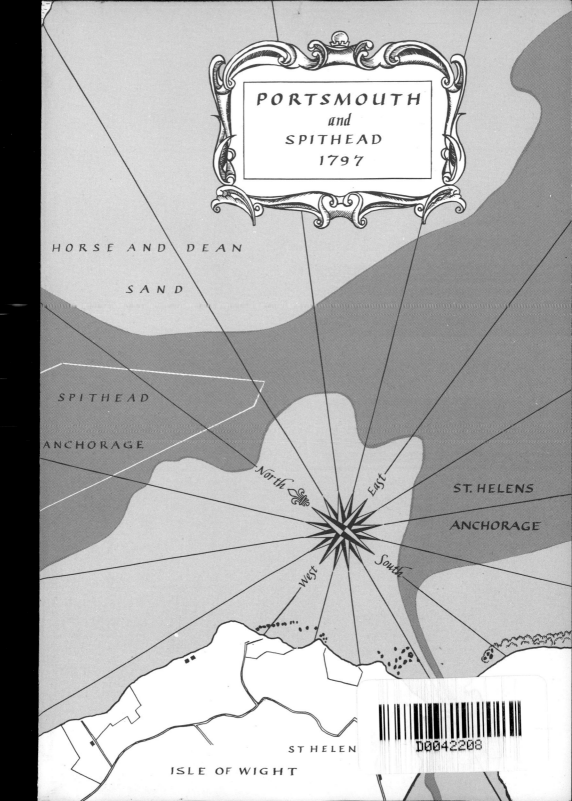

PORTSMOUTH
and
SPITHEAD
1797

HORSE AND DEAN

SAND

SPITHEAD

ANCHORAGE

North

East

ST. HELENS

ANCHORAGE

West

South

ST HELEN

ISLE OF WIGHT

THE GREAT MUTINY

James Dugan

THE GREAT
MUTINY

G. P. Putnam's Sons
New York

Library of Congress Catalog Card Number: 65-22126

PRINTED IN THE UNITED STATES OF AMERICA

For
Professor Emeritus
WILLIAM LOUSER WERNER
The Pennsylvania State University

Acknowledgments

I wish to thank Joan St. George Saunders for generous research contributions to this book. I enjoyed the friendly cooperation of people of the Royal Navy. Helpful advisers on sources were Paul Koston, Peter Throckmorton, Chloe Rome, John Maggs and Professor Melvin Jackson. My wife, Ruth, provided research, spelling, grammar, criticism, typing and reading copy and proofs.

The Meteorological Office at Bracknell, Berkshire, furnished private weather diaries of 1797, which was prior to the establishment of national weather records. June weather at the Nore is from the mutiny log of H.M.S. *Comet*. The Yale University Library gave me access to the uncatalogued letterbooks and papers of Captain John Thomas Duckworth. Most of the information on Georgian sedition and treason trials of John Binns and others came from the Hampton L. Carson Collection on the Growth of the English Common Law in the Free Library of Philadelphia.

This is not a fictionalized account, despite liberal use of quoted dialogue. Speeches and conversations come from court-martial testimony, from personal and state letters, orders and dispatches, from home office field reports, from cabinet and ministry minutes, and from memoirs of principals. I have felt justified in undoing a custom of parliamentary and court reporting, that of changing speech in the first person present tense to the third person past. If a person says, "I am entirely loyal to the crown," the shorthand reporter writes, "He was entirely loyal to the crown." I prefer the original. A little of the dialogue is atmospheric, such as standard navy commands and seamen's vulgate, but I have not interpolated speeches that would alter the documentary evidence, or fill holes in research. I have retained the original misspellings in documents.

I made use of two previous accounts of the Spithead and Nore mutinies by Conrad Gill and by H. E. Manwaring and Bonomy Dobrée, and hope to be forgiven for dilating upon aspects of the affair they did not pursue.

—JAMES DUGAN

Contents

Illustrations will be found following page 256.

The Bastille

> Never perhaps in the long history of England had there been a period when the peril was so great.
>
> —W. E. H. LECKY
> *A History of Ireland.*

IN 1789, the birth cry of our age was sounded. *"Aux armes!"*
The people of Paris were assailing the Bastille, the four-hundred-year-old fortress-prison that the British poet William Cowper called "the house of bondage":

> *There is not an English heart that would not leap*
> *That ye were fallen at last, to know*
> *That even our enemies, so oft employed*
> *In forging chains for us, themselves were free**

The attackers were amateurs, a spontaneous street crowd converging on the Bastille with looted flintlocks and two Siamese ceremonial cannons. Marksmen on the 75-foot towers felled them by the dozen.

"The guards are coming!" The crowd cheered 3,500 Gardes Françaises, the crack military force of the capital, who had been bivouacked in the Palais-Royal without officers, obeying their sergeants, waiting, undecided. The guards pounded up to the Bastille, one company led by a robust, fair-haired youth of twenty-two with gleaming blue eyes and the commanding yet egalitarian manners of a great noble of ancient days. His name was Lazare Louis Hoche, an ex-stable boy, son of a kennelman at Versailles Palace.

Sergeant Hoche and the professionals shot away the chains of the drawbridge. As it crashed down, a roaring hedgehog of bayonets,

---

* "The Task," 1785.

muskets, scythes, axes and newly forged pikes irrupted into the court and faced the towers. Through an embrasure of the fort came a hand holding a piece of paper over the dry moat. *"Cessez le feu!"* The crowd spanned the moat with a plank. It fell short of the reaching hand. People stood on the end to anchor it and a man ran toward the paper. He teetered off and fell screaming. A second volunteer went out on the board and brought back the note.

The defenders had restrained the governor of the Bastille, General the Marquis de Launey, and would surrender if their lives were spared. *"Garde à vous!"* The crowd pulled back and the inner draw-bridge fell across the moat. *"Victoire!"* Hoche and the guards swept into the shadowy inner court to protect the defenders. The crowd swarmed through the prison. Above in a patch of golden evening air, there began a dance of paper, the archives of the Bastille hurled from windows, a history of misery falling.

Dr. Rigby of Norwich, England, was strolling on the rue St-Honoré. He sensed nothing unusual in the shots heard from an eastern suburb; Parisians were always excitably rushing about in bands, shooting off guns. A growing roar came from the east. Rolling toward him, like a tidal bore in the Seine, was a streetwide mass of people, shouting and flaunting banners and trophies. They wore chestnut leaves in their hats.

Rattling from a pole were the huge keys to the Bastille, one of which would be presented to George Washington.

Past Dr. Rigby on an upheld pike went the red-dripping head of the Marquis de Launey.

Hoche and the sergeant's army came by, protecting the survivors of the Bastille garrison. Soon to be renamed the Central Grenadiers of the National Guard under their elected general, the Marquis de la Fayette, Hoche and his men were the cadre of the grand army whose rapid tread would set Europe trembling from Ireland to Holy Russia.

Louis XVI was at Versailles, waiting. He wrote on his diary page for 14 July, 1789, *Rien*—nothing—and went to bed. During the night the Duke of Rochefoucauld-Liancourt awakened his Majesty with the news from Paris.

"But, this is a revolt," said the King.

"No, sire," said the duke. "It is a revolution."

In England, plain folk and intelligentsia hailed the French Revolution with rapture. William Wordsworth, twenty-seven, caroled;

Bliss was it in that dawn to be alive,
But to be young was very heaven.

Dithyrambs to the fall of the Bastille burst from Southey, Blake, Coleridge and Robert Burns. Joseph Priestley, Erasmus Darwin and scores of scientists, including the galaxy of thinkers belonging to the Birmingham Lunar Society, saluted France for ushering in a new age of logic. Calculated praise arose from a new type in British life, the innovating entrepreneur, such as John Wilkinson, the iron-master; Matthew Boulton and James Watt, makers of steam engines; Josiah Wedgwood, the mass potter; and cotton millers—the men who were piling the bricks and hammering the iron of industrial Britain behind the painted Georgian façade. Equalitarian France would create twenty-five million new consumers for British manufactures. The trans-Channel love song echoed back: the French convention made the Englishman Dr. Joseph Priestley, Jeremy Bentham and William Wilberforce honorary citizens of France.

Britons were proud of living in a free country. That did not mean that they enjoyed social, economic or political freedom among themselves, but rather that the country had not been successfully invaded recently. That was the highest freedom that an eighteenth-century European state could boast. The Anglo-Saxon watchers of the dawn thought the revolution lifted the threat of war against England and opened markets for her manufactures, thus making Englishmen feel even more free. Alas, this was not what the French considered freedom. They had not liberated the Bastille to consume Mr. Wedgwood's teapots.

Britain was not changing by a neighboring revolution; but by the passing of her old whiggish hamlet life, shire-minded, spacious and contented, the country of Fielding, Hogarth and Johnson, that shook under the tread of domestic events uncontemplated. As never before, Britons were on the move in a world navy and armies overseas, in shuttling coastal trades, along the new canals, and in great gangs of navigation canal diggers—"navvies"—marching across country; or as wandering radical preachers spreading dissident sects; or as journeymen with "tramping tickets"—a form of unemployment insurance devised by the illegal trade unions with which workless brothers received temporary employment and hospitality from sister guilds. Uprooted Englishmen walked across their land in press gang convoys and, as paupers, were dumped from one township to the next to keep down the poor rates. English farmers ruined by enclosures, and Scottish Highlanders expelled from their crofts to make way for the great Cheviot sheep, were wandering the roads. Youngsters followed the example of Fanny Hill and Joseph Andrews and walked to London to make their fortunes. Engineers were taking people out of the mire that had prevailed since the Roman roads fell into neglect. The well-to-do were now riding in light balloon coaches on dry gravel roads.

Ignorance and illiteracy were attacked by a clomp of presses, disseminating unprecedented bundles of tracts, broadsheets and new town and county newspapers, full of new ideas. Culturally, Britain was being unified and the spirit and substance of the new literacy was egalitarian discontent. Dominating all political prints in circulation and impact were the trenchant, direct, American-trimmed encyclicals of Tom Paine, son of a Quaker corsetmaker in Thetford in East Anglia, onetime collector of his Majesty's customs, briefly a seaman, a writer whom history obeyed. Paine's headlong mixture of political primer, prophecy and journalistic exposé reached literally millions of readers.

In *Rights of Man,* he wrote:

> Never did so great an opportunity offer itself to England, and to all Europe, as is produced by the two Revolutions of America and France. By the former, freedom has a national champion in the western world; and by the latter, in Europe. When another Nation shall join France, despotism and bad Government will scarcely dare to appear. To use a trite expression, the iron is becoming hot all over Europe. The insulted German and the enslaved Spaniard, the Russ and the Pole, are beginning to think. The present age will hereafter merit to be called the Age of Reason, and the present generation will appear to the future as the Adam of a new world.
>
> When all the Governments of Europe shall be established on the representative system, Nations will become acquainted, and the animosities and the prejudices fomented by the intrigue and artifice of Courts will cease. The oppressed soldier will become a freeman; and the tortured sailor, no longer dragged along the streets like a felon, will pursue his mercantile voyage in safety.

Paine demanded maternity relief for poor women, child subsidies and old age pensions, all measures which Britain adopted more than a century later. He called for an escalated income tax, rising in the case of great wealth to twenty shillings on the pound. Paine coolly declared that it would be easy to finance even greater national improvements by taking away the money the British taxpayer expended on armaments and the crown.

The Georgian rich compulsively showed off their gains in country estates, town houses, platoons of liveried servants, coaches, clothing and jewels, and extravagant entertainment. George Macauley Trevelyan said, "Perhaps no set of men and women since the world began enjoyed so many different sides of life, with so much zest, as the English upper class of this period."

To counter crimes of poverty, the Georgians accumulated a system of laws called the Bloody Code, which prescribed death for more than 350 offenses, most of them against property. You could be hanged for stealing an item worth twopence, for carrying a gun or snare on the squire's land, for fishing in his pond, or for cutting down his tree. Convicts were executed in clusters on Hanging Days. If a victim remained alive after the cart pulled away, a compassionate friend or relative might come from the crowd and pull his legs to hasten death.

The more odious offender was still drawn and quartered: that is, dragged head down under the horse's tail to the gallows tree. He was hanged and cut down alive, and his genitalia removed and burned. Some were still living during the next phase of justice, that of disembowelment and ripping out the heart. Afterward the corpse was quartered and hung on a pole in a chain basket as a warning to others. Quartering women was considered indelicate. They were publicly strangled by the executioner before being burned, some still alive if he'd been clumsy.

The crown sometimes included children in public hangings; perhaps a nine-year-old boy who had stolen a Rowlandson cartoon or a ten-year-old scullery drab who had absconded with her young mistress's doll. The judge entered with the black kerchief on his wig and pronounced the death sentence in a clear and even voice, not allowing the wails of the children to upset the dignity of the occasion.

Sir Samuel Romilly, who waged his life (and lost it by suicide) against the Bloody Code, said, "There is no country on the face of the earth in which there are so many different offenses according to the law to be punished with death as in England.*

* Catherine the Great abolished capital punishment in Russia in 1767, Joseph II in Austria in 1781, the Grand Duke of Tuscany in 1786, and in

Britain's king was the third George from the German province of Hannover-Braunschweig to sit over England. The first was brought in by the Whigs in 1714, at the death of the last Stuart, Queen Anne, called "Brandy Nan" by her subjects. The choice was determined by the devout Protestantism of the German house and the Whig party's belief that it would own the monarch. The Hanoverians remained Protestant, but they swallowed the Whig party. The third crown prince of the German line, Frederick, was removed from succession in 1751, when fatally struck on the head by a cricket ball. His father, George II, passed away in 1760 while seated upon the *chaise percée,* leaving the throne to his grandson, George III.

George had been a timid, neurotic, cloistered and disciplined youth. His mother, the former Princess Augusta of Saxe-Gotha, herself cheated of enthronement by the cricket ball, confined his education to court etiquette and the divine right of kings. The boy could not read until he was ten years old. There was a Scottish Rasputin involved, a wily Edinburgh lawyer, the Earl of Bute (pronounced boot), a confidant of his late father's, who had come to fill the same office for his mother. Bute told the boy, "Remember, when you are king, you must be ruthless." When George took the throne, he made Bute his Prime Minister. The rest of his life, George went around asking questions about matters that had been neglected in his education. In fact he always asked twice in rapid succession so that he and the interviewee would, as it were, each have a copy of his Majesty's demand.

The King was a blocky, red-faced country squire type with bulging blue eyes and a tiny black "w" moustache. He wore spectacles to read and worried about getting fat. His mother had taught him to eat alone like the Pope. After breakfast he went out on horseback. On wet days he turned around the ring in his London riding house. Before lunch, he looked after household business in picayune detail. He did not employ a secretary or penman and every day wrote a sheaf of petty minutes and state letters, datelined from his residence of the time, whether Windsor, St. James's Palace, or Queen's House, which was located where Buckingham Palace now stands. He put the exact hour and minute at the top of his letters.

1791 the French revolutionary assembly, the object of British loathing, reduced the number of capital crimes from 115 to 32. Georgian law debased everything except the steady glum pluck of the commoners which has carried essential English humanity like an undiagnosed communicable disease through the centuries.

The King's lunch was almost always the same, roast mutton with caper sauce, a cheese tart and cherry pie. In an era of drunken statesmen—his Prime Minister was no exception and the leader of the opposition habitually sat up all night drinking—the King was a virtual abstainer. His problem was insanity. He lived on the brink and four times fell over it. His first confinement was in 1765. The gentlemanly Thomas Jefferson, while arraigning his Majesty in the Declaration of Independence on 27 counts of "repeated injuries and usurpations" in attempting to establish "absolute tyranny over these states," did not mention that the King was also crazy.

After the American war, in November 1788, his Majesty again departed his reason, this time while driving through Windsor Great Park. He ordered his coachman to halt, got out, bowed to a tree, and greeted it as the King of Prussia. He was removed from state cares for several months, part of the time in strait-waistcoats. During his "normal" periods the King was sternly monogamous and prim of speech. When mad, he shouted out voluptuous fantasies, ran a repertory of billingsgate, and went around singing Handel in a croaking, tuneless voice.

Although he had never visited Germany, as the Elector of Hannover-Braunschweig George believed that everything German was superior to everything British, including discipline and underwear. He wore only German linen, unaware that one suit had been forged in Dublin as a secret joke on a monarch otherwise difficult to link with anything humorous. The King was physically courageous. He had "bottom," a navy term that was carried over to resolute individuals who were good stayers. He devoured agricultural writings and introduced the Spanish merino sheep to Britain.

In the afternoons twice a week his Majesty held a levee, then relaxed at a band concert and went to the nursery to look at his many bewildered children. The heir apparent, called "Florizel," a fat youth, indulged his Oedipus complex by carousing around town at night with Charles James Fox, the opposition politician the King hated worst of all. As a child, the prince learned that his father loathed the radical crowd rouser John Wilkes, publisher of the gadfly paper, the *North Briton*. The King called him "That Devil." When Papa looked into the nursery, the child yelled, "Wilkes and the *North Briton* forever!"

When their proctors administered corporal punishment to his sons, the King came around to watch. Princess Sophia said her brothers had their arms seized up and "were flogged like dogs with a long whip."

When they got out of the palace, the princelings took to whoring and living with women. Afraid that designing jades would entrap them, the King had Parliament pass a royal marriage act, severely limiting the starters and providing punishments for anyone abetting or witnessing a black royal wedding. Elated with this license to remain unmarried, the princes took on women seriatim. Prince Augustus Frederick at twenty mislaid his indulgence in Rome and secretly married Lady Augusta Murray, age unknown. (Even her natural mother claimed she didn't know it. Sir William Hamilton, the British ambassador to the Neopolitan court, who had for some time observed her worldly transactions in that passionate clime, thought Lady Augusta was thirty-one.) The illegal princess gave Frederick a son. The King convened a fossil institution, the Arches Court of Canterbury, and a solemn moot of mitered bishops nullified Prince Frederick's vows. He complained to his father, "Can a man of honor, a man of religious principles, seek to deceive a harmless being by holding out a phantom, by making false promises and having obtained his purposes abandon her because the law is in his favor? Can a man of feeling who, through an involuntary error, has become a father, forsake his child because the law is ignorant of his birth?"

In late afternoon the King customarily held a privy council or a meeting of his principal cabinet ministers, then changed clothes and went to the palace cellars to count the wine stores. If a bottle was shy, his Majesty was ill-tempered at dinner.

In the evening the King really got down to being king. He wrote orders to his ministers, their secretaries, and their commissioners and their superintendents. Runners and riders waited in an anteroom to speed these instructions through the night.

He spent the nodding end of the evening at backgammon, while his musicians played chamber music.

He founded the Royal Academy of Arts and commissioned large oils by its first president, the American, Benjamin West. He formed the core of the present royal family's art collection and fortune in land rents. He gave Britain's prime scientific institution, the Royal Society, perpetual rent-free quarters in Burlington House. He went to bed early, perhaps, if he was at Windsor, stopping to look reflectively at a trophy captured from the French, a small red silk kerchief that had been carried on a pike ahead of Louis XVI on his way to the guillotine.

His mother and Bute had taught the monarch that the essence of statecraft was to pick fawning ministers and give them money to buy off persons who seemed indifferent or dangerous to his policies. These stipends were popularly known as "the golden pills." Methodical degradation of English morals had gone so far since the Restoration that few men in the arcades of influence refused the King's clinking tranquilizers. They were not concerned about government, only about power. "Interest" was the name of the greatest virtue a man could possess in Georgian politics. It meant the influence of your relatives and friends with the King and the ministry.

Out of earshot, members of the establishment called the King "His Nobs" and his wife, Queen Charlotte, "Snuffy Charlotte" on account of her only vice. She fussed a good deal over the upbringing of her thirteen children and sewed their garments to keep within the household budget. Meanwhile her Hessian housekeeper, Mme. Schnellenberg gathered nearly two hundred thousand pounds' tribute from tradesmen and place-seekers.

As Paine and company taught French revolutionary philosophy in the tongue of Bunyan and Milton, the high Georgians became frightened and the King took up his baton against the word. Even before hostilities against the revolution were conceived, his Majesty (1792) issued a proclamation forbidding "seditious meetings and political libels." He called upon his loving subjects" to help prevent disaffection and to suppress dangerous publications." When a regime invites the populace to play policeman and censor, prospects pall for domestic tranquillity. A church-and-king mob promptly burned the home of the scientist Dr. Joseph Priestley, and his library in Birmingham, and outrages occurred against reformers up and down the land.

The duty of preserving Britain from revolutionary sentiments fell to the youthful first minister and Chancellor of the Exchequer William Pitt the Younger, an emaciated aristocrat with blue eyes, a retroussé nose and a long, pale face. His father, the Earl of Chatham, a great and robust Prime Minister, and his erudite mother destined him as an infant for Parliament and ministerial seals. At seven the child was called "The Counselor." At fourteen, as "Mr. Pitt," he went up to Cambridge with a tutor, a nurse and the gout. A family physician had already addicted him to drinking fortified wine and spirits all day for "medical improvement." He was saturated with sticky, head-bursting ports and cordials for the rest of his life and was physically ill much of the time. This frail human bark was held together by dedication, insularity, tenacity and an absence of magnanimity rare among British statesmen.

The prodigy claimed a seat in the House at twenty-one. Lord Rosebery said, "Parliament was Pitt's mistress, his stud, his dice box, his game preserve, his library, his creed." Although Pitt's voice "sounded as if he had worsted in his mouth," according to the banker-poet Samuel Rogers, the fledgling gained attention with his bold maiden speech, the first in which a new member intervened in an actual debate. He opposed increased royal powers during the American war.

The King's men surrounded this potentially dangerous youth whose father's ministry they had ruined. They tempted him with office, and, at twenty-three, the semi-invalid became Chancellor of the Exchequer, next in rank to the first minister. The great liberal, Charles James Fox, went into a thunderous criticism in the House, to which Pitt listened through a crack of the door behind the speaker's chair, while vomiting into a basin.

The sick man put down the basin, took the carpet, and bested Fox in a three-hour speech. The Pitt-Fox debate was to last for a generation and encompass both sides of every measure and misery of Britain during Georgian times.

Pitt's niece, Lady Hester Stanhope, who acted as hostess for the bachelor Prime Minister, recounted how he lived:

> Ah, in town during the sitting of parliament, what a life was his! Roused from his sleep (for he was a good sleeper) with a dispatch from Lord Melville;—then down to Windsor, then, if he had half an hour to spare, trying to swallow something:—Mr. Adams with a paper, Mr. Long with another, then Mr. Rose, then, with a little bottle of cordial confection in his pocket, off to the House until two or three in the morning; then home to a hot supper for two or three hours more, to talk over what was to be done next day:—and wine, and wine!—Scarcely up next morning, when tat-tat-tat—twenty or thirty people, one after another, and the horses walking before the door from two till sunset, waiting for him. It was enough to kill a man—it was murder!

As the French Revolution unrolled its astonishing events and regime succeeded regime by the plunge of the tracked knife, middle-ground English sympathizers decamped. Few were left to praise except resolute republicans and a contingent of intellectuals, who were increasingly put upon by Pitt's government. The climax came in 1793, when the new French national convention emulated an uncomfortable episode in British history and severed the head of King Louis XVI.

Translations of seventeenth-century English exhortations against Charles I were hawked in the Paris throng that watched it fall.

Britain and France went almost immediately to war, the former to restore Louis's head and the latter to take George's.

Pitt did not want the war. He was a cheeseparing conservative who wished revenues to exceed estimates and all things to be tidy. He knew the British army and navy were in sad disrepair ten years after the defeat in America. And France had three times Britain's population and natural resources.

But Pitt was surrounded by war-manic ministers, frightened by the danger to their refuge, the crown. Chief among them was the army minister and Pitt's spokesman in Commons, William Windham, who was elected in Norwich by voters he imported from London. He saw an opportunity, while France was divided in regicidal trauma and helpless before Austria and the Germanies, to lay the axe against the domestic republican movement. Windham called for a simultaneous crusade to crush French "Jacobinism" * and "the revolutionary party at home," which he said was trying to make England "too vile or too dangerous to live in." Another war hawk was the Duke of Portland, Home Secretary and chief of prosecutions, who was still endorsing sentences of Englishwomen to be publicly burned. He considered the war "to be merely grounded on one principle, the preservation of the Christian religion."

Pitt maintained, throughout his war ministry, that Britain sought only to restore the balance of power in Europe, not to regulate the Frenchman's choice of government, and he demonstrated willingness to make peace by sending to France truce missions on several occasions. These varied motives of the cabinet gave the war the character that Benjamin Franklin had charged to the one in 1775, "a ministerial war against us."

Above all, the Pitt ministry did not wish the articles of the proposed French constitution to be adopted in England:

—Every man who pays a tax of 60 sous per annum (35 cents) is an elector.
—The number of representatives for any place shall be in ratio to the number of taxable inhabitants or electors.
—The National Assembly shall be elected every two years.
—There shall be no game laws.

---

* To British Tories a "Jacobin" was a republican guttersnipe. To French peasants a "Jacobin" was an ambitious *commerçant* who owned a carriage.

—To preserve the national representation from being corrupt no member of the National Assembly shall be an officer of the Government, a placeman or a pensioner.

—The right of war and peace is in the nation.

—There shall be no titles.

—There shall be no tithes.

At the beginning of the war with England, France was all but overcome by defection among her generals and panic among her green troops meeting uniformed professionals for the first time. At Lille the French saw the Austrian outposts and broke and ran, crying, *"Nous sommes trahis!"* They killed their Irish general, Dillon, for trying to rally them. The British government thought war against such people would be a field day. George III liberally purchased Prussians, Austrians, Hessians and French émigrés who assailed France from the Rhine, while hired Piedmontese marched from the south, routing the untrained French, slaying wounded and surrendered men.

War *à outrance* produced resistance. By forcing the French to fight for their lives, the coalition taught them war. And the unprofessional army raised new leaders. The most important was a forty-year-old regular engineer corps officer named Lazare Carnot, a gangling mathematical savant with a big nose and thick lips. He saved the broken northeast front and unified the armies. Carnot gained an enormous advantage in communications by constructing a semaphore telegraph system invented by Claude Chappe and was soon able to command the northern front from Paris by means of fifteen telegraph relay stations on elevations along the 144 miles from the capital to Lille. A string of semaphores to Strasbourg and Brest completed Carnot's rapid army control system, while his foes took days to communicate by courier.

Another of the revolutionary captains who made conquerors out of carls and clerks was Lazare Hoche. In the winter of 1793, he showed his mettle by recapturing Landau and part of the Palatinate from the Austrians. He campaigned brilliantly in the north of France and aroused enough jealousy among older generals to be jailed and marked for the guillotine. In his cell, Hoche read military history and tactics. His motto was "Deeds not words." The purge of St. Just on 9 Thermidor of the revolutionary calendar (29 July 1794) saved his head.

The revolution also produced the manpower formula that destroyed caste militarism for good. Carnot put every able-bodied man between eighteen and twenty-five into the army—the famous *levée en masse*. It was like a plague of locusts; it consumed the wealth of the land as it moved, a characteristic that the authors soon felt would serve France best by taking the war to other people's countries. The mass army carried no tents or wagons and hardly any artillery. With it marched political commissars called "representatives on mission," appointed by the Committee of Public Safety to inspire the troops and keep the generals loyal. This frightful juggernaut refined the tactics of war. It brought forth a new infantry book to supercede that of Frederick the Great. The French abandoned the classic route-march cadence of 70 steps a minute, and went as high as 120 p.m. in quick marches. They stopped attacking in line and advanced in columns.

Returning to military duty from jail, General Hoche found the republic beset from within by a threat as serious as any the counter-revolutionary coalition had offered. In the Vendée, a western region of France taking in parts of Brittany, Poitou and Anjou, landlords and priests had raised a peasant army led by professional old guard officers which had won back the province and was gathering to march on Paris and overturn the godless state. It was a civil war of pitiless terror. It was something of an international civil war; the English poet-pamphleteer, John Oswald, and his two sons were killed in action defending the republic in the Vendée.

The Directory offered the field command in the Vendée to young Napoleon Bonaparte. He declined it and was stricken from the army list. Lazare Hoche accepted the appointment.

He took several veteran divisions of the citizen army into the Vendée, and used a mixed art new to Europe, a campaign using both columnar and bushwhacking components. In long, rapid surprise marches, Hoche excited the peasants from the rear and hammered them down from the front. In five months he pacified the region by breaking up the royalist army and treating its wounded and captives humanely. This sort of experience now awaited the defenders of Britain if Hoche were able to penetrate the isles.

The British made a counterattack on Hoche in 1795.

The foremost French royalist sympathizer in Britain, William Windham, began to clamor for recapture of the Vendée. He believed émigré claims that tens of thousands of armed peasants awaited leadership to seize the province, march on Paris and exterminate the revolution. Windham had his way in the cabinet. An expedition was organized under Admiral Sir John Borlase Warren of 300 British marines, 2,000 armed French émigrés under the Count de Puisaye, and 500 French civilians who believed it possible to restore the Bourbons. Windham enlisted most of the French troops from British prisoner-of-war camps. The émigrés took with them portable guillotines to assist in resurrecting the old regime.

The expedition left in June in three battleships, six frigates and fifty transports, headed for Quiberon Bay in southern Brittany, the most favorable landing place in the Vendée. Lord Bridport protected it with the Channel fleet. A slighter French force came out of Brest to disrupt the attack and was beaten off. The troop convoy, however, had been fully protected, and arrived intact in Quiberon Bay. The Marines quickly overcame the resistance of a republican *groupement* on the beach. The landings went off like an exercise. The troops were billeted on villagers and 16,000 stand of arms were brought ashore to equip royalist recruits. The invaders reduced a small fortress and took 600 republican prisoners.

From the interior, Hoche precipitated one of his lightning marches and occupied a ridge that overlooked exit routes from the landing place. He camped among Stone Age menhirs and barrows containing crouched skeletons, among runic granite columns covered with eerie white lichen. He brought up artillery, entrenched, and constructed three lines of earthworks. Below, the British and royalists made thorough and leisurely preparation to strike inland. The expedition "fared sumptuously" on its lavish victuals and passed food out to the villagers and to several thousand recruits who came down to the shore without Hoche making any attempt to prevent them. Three weeks after the landing the invasion force moved off the beach.

The breakout began with a surprise night attack of 5,000 royalists and two hundred British marines on Hoche's right flank. They swarmed up the ridge and swept over two lightly manned republican lines. Cheering wildly, they formed up to take the third and last redoubt. Masked republican batteries opened up with a heavy, accurate, quick-loading barrage of anti-infantry projectiles that fell precisely into the rallying point. It was an ambush. It was a massacre. The surviving invaders ran down the hill in crazed disorder, closely followed by the troops Hoche had held back for the purpose. British launches covered the retreat with twenty-four-pound carronades. The fleeing men crowded into the fort. Sneaking out of it came the French prisoners from Britain who had joined Windham's expedition solely to get out of jail and go home. The men plotted with friends still remaining in the fort. Using the day's royalist password, Hoche invested the place on a night of howling rain. Royalist officers were cut down by their own men who cried, "Vive la République!" Hoche saved as many of them as he could. Two members of the Committee of Public Safety arrived on the scene and marched the prisoner column to Nantes. Most of the royalist officers and a Roman bishop were sentenced to death at courts-martial, while many of the invasion troops joined Hoche.

The British navy evacuated about a thousand uniformed royalists and 1,500 local people who feared republican retaliation. Only a few British marines were left alive after days of shock fighting. Windham's crusade had killed them, delivered 2,000 prisoners-of-war back to France and gained Britain a new batch of exiles to maintain, while awarding Hoche 10,000 muskets, 150,000 pairs of boots, clothing and accoutrements for 40,000 men, and six shiploads of victuals and spirits.

Pitt did not regard this epitome of debacles as a reflection on the competence of his army minister and Windham stayed in office. As C. Northcote Parkinson has observed, "Little progress could be made with the war until Pitt was dead."

Along with their military efforts, Pitt and his Home Secretary moved boldly to suppress the "rising high liberty party" as Lord Brougham called the plebeian movement, which "numbered its supporters out-of-doors by the million and yet is almost unrepresented in Parliament." The government seized the leaders of the principal reform societies for high treason and accused them of "compassing or imagining the death of the King" and, "being moved and seduced by the instigation of the Devil, [having] withdrawn their affection and allegiance from the King."

Among the state prisoners placed in the Tower of London was Thomas Hardy, a Piccadilly shoemaker, who had founded the London Corresponding Society (LCS) in 1792, after the earlier American model by Samuel Adams. The LCS program demanded universal male suffrage and annual parliaments. The others seized were Jeremiah Joyce, a left-wing political tactician; John Thelwall, a magnetic lecturer and editor; and Daniel Adams, secretary of the Society for Constitutional Information, a rather sarcastically christened outfit, since Great Britain had no written constitution (and still gets along without one). The selection was rounded off by John Horne Tooke, a handsome and worldly ex-clergyman who had constituted an open and bleeding stigmata in the left side of the Georgian political corpus for thirty years. Tooke was a learned etymologist, a cutting logician, "without a rival in private conversation, an expert public speaker, a keen politician, a first rate grammarian, and the finest gentleman (to say the least) of his own party," said William Hazlitt.

Horne Tooke, five years before the American revolt, organized the generic Society of Supporters of the Bill of Rights from which the LCS and other protest organs stemmed. He was elected to Parliament and expelled by a king's party stratagem which barred clergymen (and ex-clergymen) from the House of Commons. He forcefully espoused the cause of American Englishmen in 1775 and was tried for libel and given a year in prison. He used that surrogate university of British social thinkers to master the essence of the invisible British constitution, the tests-at-law of rights and liberties entombed in crumbling calf-bound lawbooks, parchment rolls, and sepia scrawls of court reporters.

By the time he was freed, he was merrily equipped to defend himself and his beliefs in new jousts with the crown.

The jury for the big state treason trials of 1794 included two coal merchants, two brewers, two distillers, and Adam Steinmetz, a biscuit baker. Hardy's attorney was an unquenchable Scottish libertarian, Thomas, Lord Erskine, First Baron of Restormel. In pleading for shoemaker Hardy, Lord Erskine managed to read much of *Rights of Man* into the evidence. The jury acquitted Hardy, but the LCS secretary had lost his business while held in the Tower for five months awaiting trial and was rendered *hors de combat* in the coming struggle.

The next chosen "traitor" was Horne Tooke, who acted as his own counsel. His speaking style was unique in that heyday of hypnotic cantors like Burke, Sheridan and Fox. Horne Tooke projected his speech "hardly more animated than the ordinary degree of conversation," according to Brougham. He never roared. He inserted his words into the audience's mind in a slow composed meter, pausing for interrupters, taking up again with a needed repetition, and giving the shorthand reporters time to take verbatim notes. Much of what Burke, Sheridan and Fox said in the House of Commons is either unrecorded or corrupted by shorthand scribes. Horne Tooke knew the value of his words lay in accurate newspaper accounts, rather than in the impressions made upon his audience.

Horne Tooke subpoenaed William Pitt and put him in the witness box. He asked the Prime Minister to describe for the jury the friendly association he'd had with Horne Tooke some years before when they were both trying to overthrow Prime Minister Lord North. Pitt could not recall any of these meetings. The defense attorney dismissed the witness and called the playwright Richard Brinsley Sheridan, M.P. He asked if Mr. Sheridan remembered any meetings between himself, Pitt and Horne Tooke. Sheridan remembered several of them in illustrative detail. His memory refreshed, Mr. Pitt resumed the stand and corroborated Sheridan's testimony. The jury acquitted Horne Tooke in ten minutes and then marched as his honor guard from Old Bailey to the London Coffee House, street crowds applauding and shouting for him on the way. In the tavern "the company, who amounted to about five hundred gentlemen, immediately arose, took off their hats, ranged themselves on each side as they passed through, saluting them with the most animated and expressive tokens of applause," said the *New Annual Register.*

The next man the crown had marked for hanging was John Thelwall, the populist agitator, among whose worst traits, according to the indictment, was that he made his living by selling tickets for his "virulent attacks upon the Constitution." The jury liberated Thelwall and the remaining defendants.

Even had they succeeded, these backfiring show trials could not have solved Pitt's real problems. The country was in grave financial straits. The seizure of India was costing more than it yielded. The adverse balance of trade obliged the exchequer to ship a half million pounds of silver a year to India. Everything cost more. Neutral Scandinavia turned the price screws on Britain for vital naval stores—cordage, hemp, timber, iron, copper, turpentine, pitch and niter, and could do so because the French navy relied on the same source of fleet materials. England had been deforested of naval oak and was bringing in pine masts from America. Wise old admirals strolling in the country took pocketfuls of acorns and punched them into the soil.

The price of candles went up twopence a pound. A Lancashire housewife said, "Dang it! Are they got to feighten by candlelight?" Queen Charlotte wrote to her husband, "I do almost feel ashamed of again troubling your Majesty with my affairs. . . . Every article is so raised in price, even the most trivial things . . . that those who must manage in order to live find their expenses double to what it was a year ago."

Another member of the royal family caught short was "Florizel," the Prince of Wales, on the eve of his marriage. Pitt asked Parliament to give him £125,000 a year, and £13,000 from the Duchy of Lancaster, plus £77,000 for wedding expenses. The lawmakers grumbled left and right. They had already assumed the Crown Prince's debts of £630,000 which amounted to 4 percent of the annual national revenue. Charles James Fox said it was wrong at a time of general calamity that the King should be the only person who did not contribute a farthing to his son's debts. Sheridan added that the government should sell the royal forests and crown lands and abolish sinecures to pay the Prince's creditors. Pitt had an excruciating time getting the money bills through, but he succeeded. (When he was discarded, Pitt had to beg for a modest pension.)

Pitt was between the hammer and the anvil. If the royal family punished him from above, the commoners gave him a hard bed below. Villagers combined with mobile gangs of navvies and road builders to commandeer grain and flour before it could be carted to the city. They auctioned the grain at pre-famine prices, but returned the proceeds to the miller. In Lancashire an old soldier, Thomas Spencer, was hanged for such a day's work. The crown and the judges trimmed the bloody code to the bone. Offenders against property and those hostile to the regime were hanged. Murderers were shipped to Australia.

Pitt taxed theatre tickets, five shillings at Covent Garden opera and a half crown for Drury Lane stalls and a shilling in the pit. Tax collectors sat in the box office. George Otto Trevelyan called it "a serious matter for the peace and order of London." Loyal newspaper proprietors omitted or disguised accounts of demonstrations.

In 1795 his Majesty received a marked impression of animosity among his subjects. There had been a summer of frequent civic disorders, stirring terrifying memories of the Gordon Riots in 1780 when street guerrillas destroyed or damaged a third of London and reduced not one bastille but five—the prisons at Newgate (criminals), the Fleet (debtors), and Bridewell (women), and the King's Bench jail and the Borough Clink.

The agencies of law enforcement were more concerned with the peaceful and orderly rallies of the reform element, which were attracting the greatest numbers of people in British political history. They massed at Hackney and Chalk Farm; at St. George's Fields, the London Corresponding Society moved, and the crowd passed with roaring acclaim, a resolution to the King calling upon him to dismiss his ministers and end the war for his "own personal security and for the happiness of the people." The home office sent Bow Street runners and magistrates to provoke commotions at these meetings.

Meanwhile the London urchinry and alehouse infantry burned army recruiting stations and navy crimping houses and stoned the windows out of No. 10 Downing Street. By late summer it became evident that the harvest would fall short. In the countryside, mutinous militiamen led seizures of granaries. The English were beginning to behave French.

On the eve of the opening of Parliament in October, the LCS held the largest political meeting Britain had ever seen—150,000 people in Islington, near the Copenhagen Tea House. The people passed *viva voce* a *Remonstrance to the King* which asked: "Wherefore, in the midst of apparent plenty, are we thus compelled to starve? . . . Parliamentary corruption like a foaming whirlpool, swallows the fruits of all our labours."

London was under an ominous and sullen pressure as Parliament convened. From the mews at St. James's Palace came the carved and gilded royal state coach, its driver seated between two conch-blowing tritons. Within, the King of England sat with two peers. The carriage body was formed of a carved thicket of golden palms whose fronds supported the roof, atop which cherubs representing England, Scotland and Ireland held up the imperial crown. On the fantail of the state carriage perched two coachmen between high reliefs of tritons holding fasces. Escorted by a corporal's guard of Royal Horse Guards and a platoon of halberdiers on foot, the King's carriage rolled into Pall Mall.

Awaiting his Majesty was a gulf of humanity, London's greatest street crowd, estimated at 200,000 by the *Annual Register*. No person had his hat off or tugged his forelock. There were no cheers or applause. Youths slipped through the horsemen and axemen and ran along beside the coach, hooting and spanking the heavy golden wheels like hoops. The mass gave a hoarse groaning and mourning noise. The King's escorts were carried away in a chop of shoulders and elbows, the horses whinnying in fright. The crowd began chanting.

"No war!"

"Down with George!"

"No Pitt!"

A pellet went through the window by the King's head, missed him, and flew out the open window opposite.

"This is a shot!" exclaimed Lord Onslow, one of the King's companions. But they did not hear the sound of a shot. They thought the projectile came from a diabolical sort of wind-gun or blowpipe.

The coach arrived at Westminster Palace Yard and the indignant monarch went in and addressed Parliament with exceptional firmness. He was prevailed upon to send the golden coach back empty and leave the House of Peers in a private two-horse chariot without escorts. The crowd was still thick in Parliament Street and Whitehall. The news passed like a gale among the throng that the state coach was empty. People inspected the inmates of each carriage coming out of the yard. They found his Majesty again. Hands reached for the reins and stopped the horses. The carriage was blocked, walled up by people.

Stones smashed through the windows.

"No king!"

"Down with George!"

The crowd began rocking the chariot from side to side, closer by the moment to overturning the sovereign.

A small number of brave loyalists fought their way to the carriage, trying to prevent the ultimate disgrace of a mobbed king.

"Bread!"

"Bread!"

"Peace!"

"Peace!"

"No king!"

The Horse Guards arrived shouting and rode into the mass to relieve the King. They found him composed. He picked a stone out of his sleeve cuff and gave it to Onslow, saying, "Milord, I make you a present of this, as a mark of the civilities we have met with on our journey today." He was oblivious to all peril and protest for he was armored with the serene belief that the British people deserved him.

A twenty-seven-year-old journeyman printer from Gosport in "a green coat and black collar" was seized for making an attempt on the King's life. His name was Kid Wake. The crown failed to produce a witness who had seen him propel anything at the coach, so he was convicted of "hooting, groaning and hissing at the King," and sentenced to five years, for the first three months to be taken to Gloucester and pilloried on market days. The sentencing justice suspected Wake would not be pelted in the Gosport pillory, so chose one in a larger town with strong royalist sympathies. The printer was also to put up a thousand pounds' surety for his good behavior for ten years after his sentence expired, or continue in prison until he found the money.* This monstrous sentence was, of course, meant to intimidate publishers, printers and booksellers, and the trade read it as such.

---

* Kid Wake died in jail of abuse.

There were many curious and anonymous handbills, prints and ballad sheets passing around and raising popular passions. One described the guillotine and noted:

> As it is the custom to decapitate and not hang kings, it is proper to have this instrument ready to make death easy for them. England and France have had their regular turns in executing their kings. France did it last.

Incitements like this could harm only the democratic organizations. British social historian, E. P. Thompson, says, "In a sense, the government needed conspirators to justify the continuation of repressive legislation which prevented nationwide popular organizations."

After the King's bad day, Parliament quickly gave Pitt a series of acts providing death for those who incited people to hate the King, the constitution or the government. It outlawed meetings of more than fifty people unless sanctioned by a magistrate and gave judges power to padlock lecture rooms as "disorderly houses." During the month before the royal assent lent these enactments the force of law, the Foxite Whigs and reform societies joined forces to resist the acts and oust William Pitt. The Prime Minister remarked, "Were I to resign, my head would be off in six months." Two hundred thousand people gathered at the Copenhagen Tea House to urge the King to disapprove the acts. He signed them and the reform societies were forced underground against their will.

By the third year of the war, people of substance and interest scarcely needed to have fear induced by Parliament. They were served by two successive crop failures, the rise of republicanism, and the astounding transformation of the war from a punitive expedition to France to a siege of England. They lost patriotic feeling. They took their gold out of the banks. A tide of provincial bank failures rolled toward Threadneedle Street. Lord Grenville, the Foreign Secretary, predicted that Parliament would not be able to vote the estimates for another year of war unless possibilities improved for a negotiated peace. Britain forgot that victory also brought peace. No substantial battle on land or sea had gone her way for more than two years since the Glorious First of June, Admiral Lord Richard Howe's victory over a French fleet in the Atlantic.

Mr. Pitt's artificial method of war-waking was also cock-a-heap. It was infuriating to Englishmen smarting under a grief of taxes, without recourse to the ballot and their petitions ignored, to learn that the

French had shattered another of the King's hired continental armies and that his Majesty was giving asylum to routed Hessians and French royalists at additional expense to his subjects. It did the public temper no good to see two champion consumers of English gold, the Czarina Catherine and the Emperor of Prussia, reel back from a stout French knock and fall upon bystanding Poland and dismember her. The maladministration of the war, the debauch with public money, and the constant new encroachments of Pitt and Parliament upon the liberty of the subject were spread by populist newspapers and orators from the lochs of Scotland to the southernmost smuggler's cove.

In contrast another set of the King's enemies, the former Englishmen across the Atlantic, were enjoying peace and, although the French Revolution excited the United States pro and con, transfer of executive power was orderly there: the U. S. electoral college chose the Federalist John Adams as President, and his opponent, Thomas Jefferson, candidate of the Democratic-Republican party, as Vice-President. That same autumn in London, in the general election of 1796, the opposition leader, Charles James Fox, won a seat in Westminster, the borough of the royal palaces, ministries and the legislature, with assertions that "a more detestable government has never existed in British history. It has destroyed more human beings in its foreign wars than Louis XIV and attempted the lives of more innocent men at home than Henry VIII."

Pitt was too smart to rest his anti-French policy on bayonets and gagging bills; he kept an olive branch to extend when Britain's military fortunes were dim. He sent Sir James Harris to France with a safe conduct from the Directory to open peace talks. During the immediate wave of optimism, Pitt floated an £18 million "loyalty loan" in four bank days. For £100 the investor received a certificate worth £112, redeemable at 5 percent three years after previous loans had been retired, or at par two years after "a definite treaty of peace." Samuel Taylor Coleridge remarked on these events of December:

> To juggle this easily-juggled people into better humor with the supplies* (and themselves, perhaps, affrighted by the successes of the French) our Ministry sent an Ambassador to Paris to sue for Peace. The supplies were granted: and in the meantime the Archduke Charles turns the scale of victory on

---

* The war budget estimate to Parliament.

the Rhine, and Buonaparte is checked before Mantua. Straight-ways our courtly messenger is commanded to *uncurl* his lips, and propose to the lofty Republic to *restore* all its conquests, and to suffer England to *retain* all *hers* (at least all her *important* ones), as the only terms of peace and the ultimate of the negotiation!

In this same month Captain Thomas Pakenham of the Channel fleet warned the First Lord of the Admiralty, Earl Spencer, that sea-men were increasingly discontented at not being paid—some were owed two or three years back wages, and, moreover, thought they deserved increases. Spencer replied, "In the present state of the country, it is not possible to enormously increase disbursements, which are already sufficiently burdensome."

The navy pay office estimated that, as of the end of 1796, the total arrears owed the seamen amounted to £1,408,720/7/11, about fourteen million dollars in today's values.

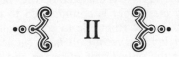

The Rights
of Man

The year 1797, the year of this narrative, belongs to a
period which, as every thinker now feels, involved a
crisis for Christendom not exceeded in its undetermined
momentousness at the time by any other era whereof
there is record.

—HERMAN MELVILLE
Billy Budd, Foretopman, 1891

I N THE kingdom of England the last russet peel of the hunter's moon
sank into the cold and misty nights of Hallowmas, All Saints, All
Souls and Guy Fawkes, and, in the republic of France, the new moon
arose in Frimaire, the month of hoarfrost, in Year IV of the revolution. This winter of 1796-97 inaugurated a year of dread and tor-
ment that would wrack Europe and raise in Britain close expectations of a French conquest, the overturn of her regime and the fall
of the great.

The throne of George III itself was menaced by republicanism,
which Edmund Burke, M.P., called "irrational, unprincipled, pro-
scribing, confiscating, plundering, ferocious, bloody and tyrannical."
The King himself called it "the horrid French fabrick!" The landed
people dreamed of a guillotine in Parliament Square, replacing the
reassuring gallows at Newgate.

British men-of-war, the nation's legendary wooden walls, staggered
to and fro in mountainous seas in La Manche, hanging on for punishing months to intercept French invasion fleets sailing for the British
Isles. Even nature was out of sorts. Baffled watch officers logged

"fresh breezes," while above the circling topgallants, English birds were blown helplessly to France in substratospheric gales. Fish left the surging English Channel and crowded up rivers in The Solent and Brittany.

The English people were agitated, angry and disobedient. Parliament, in the name of "agricultural improvement," was enacting private bills of enclosure, by which influential persons were empowered to condemn, pay for, and divide village communes, in which country folk had traditionally raised food as insurance against hard times. In Scotland, landlords were pulling down rooftrees and burning crofter villages to replace people with profitable sheep pasturages. Robert Burns died, aged thirty-seven, having "alienated many of his best friends by too freely expressing sympathy with the French Revolution, and then the unpopular advocates of reform at home." * The harvest had fallen short for the second year in a row. Women tied black ribbons around loaves of bread, hoisted them on staves, and led marchers on the water mills and granaries.

It was the fourth year of the war against the French Revolution. Britain had entered it overestimating her strength against France, which in popul~*~ was, respectively, one against three. Edmund Burke said, "France contains all within herself. England is an artificial country. Take away her commerce and what has she got?" George III, in his previous martial exploit, had subtracted three million American English people and by now had turned four million Irish irrevocably against England. His war policy consisted of purchasing the armies of European absolutism to exterminate the French Revolution. French citizen-armies had mauled them flat. Now, these out-of-work, hungry and battle-hard French corps were marching to the Atlantic to board fleets at Brest and Texel in Holland to invade Ireland and England.

The British populist and republican movement was headed for a showdown with the monarch and his ministry.

A most depressing aspect of Britain's plight was her naval reverses. There was no longer a British ship-of-the-line in the Mediterranean Sea from the Pillars of Hercules to the Golden Horn. The decrepit southern fleet was repairing and refitting in Atlantic ports of the Iberian Peninsula. (Although Spain had been at war with England since August of the previous year, Britain used neutral Lisbon and hung off belligerent Cadiz.) Her world-ranging fighting seamen had

---

* John W. Cousins, Everyman's *Short Biographical Dictionary of English Literature;* see also Burns article in *Encyclopedia Britannica* by John Nichol.

won Britain two empires, the first of which she had lost by indulging the phobias of George III in America. The men-of-wars-men captured foreigners' wealth and bestowed it upon the British ruling caste. Captain Horatio Nelson described the seamen as "finished at forty-five, double-ruptured, raw with scurvy, and racked with agonizing pains after every meal." One hundred thousand of these sea exiles were now deployed to prevent the French from coming over to plunder the winnings.

In this nadir of imperialism, unsuspected by the government, the last defenders of the home islands, the seamen of the grand fleet and the North Sea fleet, went on strike. Their protest is unparalleled in history. In the four main naval bases of England, about half the lower deck of the navy and five thousand marines hauled down the royal standard and the Union Jack and the pendants of admirals of the red, admirals of the white and admirals of the blue. On more than a hundred vessels they raised the red flag of defiance. They swore oaths of extreme fidelity to their cause, deposed his Majesty's officers, and elected their own. They established the first government based on universal suffrage that Britain had ever seen, afloat or ashore.

At the beginning of the winter British spies in the French naval ministry were sending alarming reports of the invasion fleet shaping at Brest. Neutral voyagers corroborated the danger.

In the mastheads of his Majesty's ship *Indefatigable,* 44, insolently patrolling outside Brest, freezing lookouts counted twelve French sail-of-the-line, ten frigates and dozens of transports, corvettes and auxiliaries in the harbor roads. The captain of *Indefatigable,* Sir Edward Pellew, sent swift craft with serial news of the French to twelve men-of-war, under Sir John Colpoys, that were cruising on the horizon. Afterward the dispatch boats sailed on to report to England, where the main Channel fleet was repairing at Portsmouth to be ready for action when the French came out.

Brest was confronted with the greatest military difficulty of the republic—feeding, clothing and paying its conscripts. They had marched into the port on short rations and had been imprisoned in the orlop and bilges of the invasion ships. After weeks, they were still unpaid and unsure of being fed, and they made mutiny. The revolutionary cure was the same as that of the monarchy: drumhead courts-martial and summary execution.

Pellew watched helplessly as five more French capital ships and three frigates slipped into Brest unmolested. They had come from the Mediterranean, eluding Sir John Jervis' squadron off Cadiz and Colpoys' cruisers as well. Pellew spent his next-to-last frigate to send the bad news home. By now there were about 20,000 massed troops in this *Armee française en Irlande* and one transport full of horses.

Le Moniteur, the official French newspaper, and other gazettes that found their way to Pellew's cabin, published exciting speculations about a great invasion to liberate Ireland. British officials, noting the unanimous announcement of objective, thought the stories were an official ruse to trick the British navy away from an invasion course to the West Indies or even around the Cape of Good Hope to intervene in India.

On 15 December the French force sailed at night, taking a perilous rockbound detour to sea, rather than walk into an unknown number of British sail in the watching grounds. But there was only Pellew at the gate. Two French ships collided in the passage and began firing distress and signal rockets. Their admiral joined in the fireworks, and Pellew sailed close and sent up flares to assist the confusion. The invasion armada anchored until dawn. When it got under way again a 74-gun ship went on the rocks and 1,800 men were lost.

During the first confused night, the French task force split up and was unable to unite in the haze next day. Pellew reported the French movement to Admiral Colpoys by flag signals, and sent a ship's boat with a confirming letter. Colpoys, for reasons never investigated, turned back to England, despite Pellew's taunt that he would fight the French with his own frigate and a pair of Colpoys' two-deckers.

Pellew sent his last lugger to England with word that the big French force was out. His provisions were exhausted. He took *Indefatigable* into Falmouth on 20 December. The Admiralty issued orders to the main Channel fleet to sail from Portsmouth and hunt the French. By 22 December, heavy gales were blowing in the Channel. The French fleet was divided, part of it on the planned course, and the rest, containing the fleet commander and the army commander, falling away in the winds.

Three days before Christmas the secret destination of the invasion fleet was revealed to Irish peasants in western County Cork, who looked out in the blowing rain at eight battleships, two frigates, four corvettes, and a transport coming into Bantry Bay conned by local pilots. The French expedition arrived exactly where the French press said it would arrive. It was the smaller element of the divided force, led by the deputy commander, General Jean J. M. Humbert, a redoubtable civil war specialist. The flotilla anchored and waited for the gale to abate in order to land 6,000 men in advance of the main body which was still out of contact in the ocean. Reconnaissance boats went ashore in high and icy seas and found no sign of resistance. The surprise was complete. A landing would find only three thousand British troops scattered in western Ireland, with two field guns and no reserve ammunition. In the Bantry riding there were only four hundred militia and a troop of light horse. Cork City, the main victualing center for British forces throughout the world, was only forty-five miles away over a dry, fast coach pike. East of Cork, in counties Waterford and Wexford, there were thousands of organized Irish patriots waiting for French arms and orders.

Humbert wanted to land his troops immediately, accepting losses of men in the tempestuous bay, to be sure he held a beachhead when the main force arrived. Admiral François Bouvet demurred, considering that the losses would be too heavy. While they conferred, the weather got worse. An incessant gale enfolded the French ships and even Humbert admitted that a debarkation was inconceivable.

While they rocked, the main force rolled under storm sails, unable to make progress for Bantry Bay. On board the lost flagship was the invasion commander, Lazare Louis Hoche, the onetime sergeant of the Bastille, now a famous general at the age of twenty-nine. He could say of another high-soaring young eagle, "Napoleon has been my pupil, but he will never be my master."

At Bantry Bay on Christmas morning the larger ships were dragging anchor driving toward the lee shore. Admiral Bouvet ordered them to chop their cables and retreat to the open sea for safety. That same morning at Portsmouth, Lord Bridport, the venerable deputy commander of the British Channel fleet, took belatedly to sea, looking for an enemy formation last reported eight days earlier. He did not know of the French arrival in Ireland. The weather remained monstrous for all three elements of the intending battle: Hoche's force blowing apart with several ships in distress; Humbert's squadron now unable to return to Bantry Bay, much less land troops; and Bridport's men-of-war in trouble getting out of Spithead. H.M.S. *Prince* and *Sans Pareil,* a French prize, fouled each other. *Atlas* went aground. *Formidable* crashed into H.M.S. *Ville de Paris.* Bridport collected the rest at St. Helen's, a shelter a few miles away on the east side of the Isle of Wight, which the fleet used to make rendezvous with merchant convoys or to marshal for cruises. Now the wind swung around and set against Bridport and he was locked up at St. Helen's.

Christmas was cruel as fate. In London the cold was fifteen degrees below zero Fahrenheit. It was "Armada weather" for ships at-tempting the British isles.

The strayed French flagships swept farther apart in the Channel winds and confused waves and swells which tormented both adver-saries. In Bantry Bay an easterly gale blew against the tossing French fleet. French scouting boats got ashore and came back an-nouncing that there was still no resistance to the invasion. The fleet was full of seasick and freezing men. Victuals were running out. The rest of the ships did not arrive. After ten miserable days in sight of the Irish shore, Admiral Bouvet weighed anchor and left, overruling General Humbert's protests.

At last, through the beastly weather, dispatches reached London that the French were ready to land in Bantry. Pitt strained the gov-ernment's credit to the limit and scoured London for 50,000 gold guineas that were boxed and sent express to the Lord Lieutenant in Dublin.

That same last day of 1796, Colpoys, the equivocating watchdog of Brest, arrived in Portsmouth to reprovision. Now no British vessel stood near the return passage of the expedition. But the divided French fleet was losing to the storm; twelve ships wrecked, foundered or were captured foundering by British privateers. By the third day of January, when the Channel was full of tired French in various de-grees of distress, Lord Bridport at last pulled out of St. Helen's. He headed for Ushant to picket the stormy strait north and south.

Following the debacle at Bantry Bay, the French Directory had another force for invading the British Isles—1,800 picked men of the Légion Noire (Black Legion), who wore brown-dyed British uniforms captured at Quiberon in '95. One of their generals who saw the legionnaires paraded at Brest remarked, "So these are the ban-ditti intended for England. Sad blackguards they are." Six hundred of the Black Legion were galley slaves who had been marched to Brest in leg irons, and the rest—according to spy reports to Pitt— "the most abandoned rogues" that could be found in the prisons of Brittany. Their officers were fiery young Jacobins, including Sub-lieutenant Barry St. Leger, aged twenty, who was eager to lead them to Ireland. The youngster had been living in Charleston, South Carolina, from whence the year before he sailed in a merchantman that went aground and broke up in the Shannon mouth. Escaping from this he started back to Carolina and was captured by a French privateer. Arriving in Brest, he claimed U. S. citizenship and the

French enlisted him in the Bantry Bay expedition in which the trans-Atlantic lad did not even toe his motherland. Back in Brest, St. Leger joined the Black Legion, whose commanding officer was a fellow Charlestonian, Colonel William Tate. How this skinny, teetotaling, ascetic seventy-year-old American who did not speak French came to be placed in charge of these French rascals can only be explained in Hanoverian terms. Strange messmates often resulted among the rich variety of his Britannic Majesty's enemies. George III made the first world war. It lasted, off and on, from his accession in 1760, for 55 years.

Old Bill Tate had been discharged from the Continental Army at the end of the American war of independence with a bounty of money and virgin land. As an ardent republican and Francophile, in 1794, Tate joined the French ambassador to the U. S., Edmond "Citizen" Genêt, in a scheme to seize Florida and Louisiana from Spain with an "American Revolutionary Legion" of backwoods riflemen—who probably existed largely in the hopes of Old Bill and his fellow commander, George Rogers Clark. President Washington's peacemongering administration asked France to recall her meddling ambassador. The Paris guillotine was currently whacking away at Genêt's Girondiste party, so he resigned, married the daughter of Governor George Clinton of New York and became an American gentleman farmer.

This left Tate destitute and powerless; he had spent his last substance on ballyhoo for the Revolutionary Legion. So while Genêt became an American, Tate became a Frenchman. He took the files of the abortive guerrilla army to Paris and tried to collect his expenses. His most powerful paper was a commission that Genêt had given him as chef de brigade in the French army. General Lazare Hoche inclined a friendly ear to the aged rebel. When laying out his diversionary onslaughts on England to accompany Bantry Bay, he picked the American to lead the galley slaves and convicts on an expedition to capture Bristol. They were to extort a huge tribute from her mercantile wealth by threatening to burn the city. The scheme was not mad. England's second port was almost completely undefended.

The assaults on England were General Lazare Hoche's personal affair; by now his star burned brightest of all the revolution's martial children. So little was known of the invasion plans in the Paris ministries that Pitt's spies did not know the objectives. For French revolutionary designs of the period this was unique. Hoche was enthusiastic about Tate's record and the possibilities of his capturing Bristol. The more subtle mind of Lazare Carnot, now President of the ruling Directory, may have reckoned nothing would be lost either way. Carnot could do without the convicts. If Tate failed, the British would simply have more men to feed and desperate men at that. There would be no extra risk to the vessels that put the Black Legion ashore, for they were to sail immediately afterward.

However, after Bantry Bay, ships were not available to lift Tate's mob to Bristol. The survivors of the Irish expedition were disbanded to reduce the demand on rations in the isolated port of Brest with sullen royalist farmers at its rear. Tate kept the Legion penned up in two island forts.

Finally in late January Colonel Tate was ordered to sail for Bristol with his men locked belowdecks in two frigates. His orders read:

> The expedition under the command of Col. Tate has in view three principal objects; the first is, if possible, to raise an insurrection in the country; the second is to interrupt and embarrass the commerce of the enemy; and the third is to prepare and facilitate the way for a descent by distracting the attention of the English government. . . . In all countries the poor are the class most prone to insurrection and this disposition is to be forwarded by distributing money and drink; by inveighing against the government as the cause of the public distress; by recommending and facilitating a rising to plunder the public stores and magazines and the property of the rich. . . . With an eye to preserving law and order, however, the property of magistrates and even of country gentlemen, is to be respected, but the property of all who fulfilled no civil function, peers, men of high rank and fortune, and the clergy, is to be given up to plunder by picked detachments of the Legion.

The Legion of the lost sailed on 18 February 1797 in *Vengeance* and *Résistance,* the latest big frigates in the French navy, and in a corvette and a lugger. There was a brisk wind from the east to stiffen canvas on a rapid overnight run across the English Channel. The French ships flew Russian flags. The Czar was a British ally and this might fool somebody. No British warship saw the dash. Lord Bridport's blockading squadron was refreshing itself at Spithead between cruises.

The invasion carriers anchored near the mouth of Bristol Channel and waited for the flood tide needed to beat eighty miles to Bristol against the strong easterly. Admiral Castagnier tacked halfway to his destination on ingoing tides, anchoring against the ebbs, before he gave up off Porlock, telling Old Bill the weather was going to get worse. The admiral offered to land the troops in Swansea Bay. Tate expostulated that his alternative orders were for Cardigan Bay, but to no avail. As the French ships sailed northwest, they were closely seen by a sloop bound from St. Ives for Swansea, and expresses rode to warn port captains at Milford and Bristol and the Plymouth command, which would pass the news to London.

No ship passed the north coast of Pembrokeshire without falling under inspection by good glass men—owlers and retired mariners who were out sticking the lens to their good eyes, watching these four vessels. Admiral Castagnier got up to The Smalls, the outer shoaling reef at the beginning of St. George's Channel, and turned the rocks close enough for a band of men on The Smalls to recognize the black hulls as French ships despite their false colors. It was bad luck for the French: men had never stood before on The Smalls. These were working half in and half out of the cold sea at the foundations of the first lighthouse on the most westerly obstacle in the Irish Sea approaches. The construction gang came out of Solva, twenty miles over the sea in St. Bride's Bay. They were bossed by a Liverpool civil engineer named Whitesides.

The French ships were blown briskly along the hilly north shore of Pembrokeshire, while the spyglass men sent riders inland to give progress of the journey. As evening approached, the French squadron anchored inshore two miles around a cape from the town of Fishguard, the economic pursuit of whose several hundred souls is indicated by its name. Castagnier sent the lugger to snoop the town. From the main peak, down came the imperial eagle of the czar and aloft went the Union Jack as the lively boat, close-hauled, skimmed toward Fishguard at candle-lighting time.

The town had just been warned. Its tiny fort with one nine-pounder, a dozen bags of powder and three cannon balls, was freshly manned. The officer of the gun made out British colors and, much relieved, fired a blank salute. The French skipper thought it the opening of hostilities. He took off the Jack, hoisted the *tricouleur,* and went about smartly to report to Admiral Castagnier that the place was alertly defended. Commander E. H. Stuart Jones, RN, historian of the remarkable doings at Fishguard, says, "Unconsciously the [Welsh] bombardiers had saved the town and the shipping, which could have been battered to pieces by the combined fire of the four French ships."

It was a mild evening. The wind died. The sea purred on the rocks. French bad luck with invasion weather had turned. Tate began landing. The Black Legion, wild to get out of the jam of lousy and vomiting men, poured down into the boats, and over the placid beach. They landed amidst boulders that on any other February day would have stoved their boats. They loped up the grassy slope to howl at the setting sun and look down at more brown backs climbing into Wales for authorized rapine. With the Legion were four women, two of them officers' wives. The invaders pulled up gorse bushes and made smoky campfires. The officers put them to their night's logistical duties of bringing ashore two thousand firelocks and bales of captured British army woolen uniforms to equip Welsh partisans whom they expected to join. Up the hill they rolled forty-seven barrels of powder. The unopposed landing cost only a few men drowned. The American commander was ashore with his people and impedimenta in one of the easiest amphibious operations on record. William Tate was the latest inheritor of a rich continental tradition, that of going a-viking in England. Since 1066 there had been forty-two successful military landings in the British Isles.

Before daylight was gone, Old Bill sent Barry St. Leger out to make a command post. A mile or so inland, the patrol found a locked and abandoned farmhouse. They knocked the door in and stared at a trove of food intended for a wedding feast. *"Ne pas toucher!"* said the young officer sternly. "Or you'll be shot." A brown shirt replied, "Then we shoot you, monsieur," and drove the bung into a butt of wine. By the time Old Bill arrived to open headquarters, the advance party was lurching, smashing, and showing tendencies toward pyromania. They even deprived the tired old man of a cozy farm bed. Several of his charges who had landed without seats to their pantaloons had emptied the goosedown mattresses to make trousers of the ticking.

The invading army snuggled down to its best sleep in weeks. The night was warm and airless. Some miles away, doors and windows had been flung open at a dancing party at the manor of William Knox, who had retired to Wales with a fortune gained as Lord North's Undersecretary of State for America. He supported several companies of home guards, known as Fencibles and, according to custom, had made his son Thomas Knox, twenty-eight, their colonel. A rider burst in with the chilling report that the French had landed. Eyes turned to the colonel. He set his jaw, rode for Fishguard and found seventy Fencibles already drilling on the town beach. They wore striped jackets and slouch hats pinned up at one side with cockades of leeks and ribbons emblazoned *Ich Dien* (I serve), the Prince of Wales's motto that had been taken from John, the blind King of Bohemia, killed at Crécy in 1346.

The Fencibles fired an alarm gun and retired to a small fort on a peak above town. Three hours had passed since the landing and it had not occurred to either side to inaugurate hostilities. The French gunners might have pounded Fishguard to ruin and the Fencibles might have slain the brown shirts in their sleep.

Colonel Knox was without military experience and had no veteran to consult. He placed himself in the thinking of the enemy commander and became convinced that a second French invasion was being made on his flank and would soon engulf the flimsy redoubt of the Fishguard Fencibles. He pounded spikes into the touchholes of his guns and began hard-bashing toward Haverfordwest, twenty miles south of the invasion beach, leaving North Pembrokeshire defenseless.

At that time of evening, the revolution incarnate, the homeless American, weary with his seventy years, was sitting up in the burning bush, holding his eyes open on an all-night vigil to guard his powder casks and brandy barrels from his own troops.

Halfway to Haverfordwest, momentarily expecting the French second front to chew into his flank, Knox encountered a force of five hundred volunteers, shire militia, horsemen, and a hundred felons and prest men marching toward Fishguard. The Haverfordwest battalion was led by Baron Cawdor of Castlemartin, a Welsh title Pitt had recently given to a veteran Whig M. P. from Scotland, named John Campbell, for coming over to the King's camp. The politician had no military experience, but he responded alertly to Knox's fears of French envelopment. Lord Cawdor started the whole lot pounding the turnpike back to Haverfordwest. The road was cluttered with carriages and wagons of dames, maidenheads, children and family plate heading for safety in all directions. Back on the undefended heath at Fishguard, *les enfants perdus* slept and coughed and scratched themselves.

It was the first amphibious invasion of Britain since Commodore O'Farrell Thurot had landed a thousand Frenchmen at Carrickfergus in 1760. It was unopposed and the defenders had fled. During darkness some Welsh lads, trained in night maneuver as wreckers and smugglers, carried off two Black Legionnaires for questioning. The boys sent a rider out to find Lord Cawdor with the information that the French force consisted of fourteen hundred desperadoes with a hundred rounds each, four days' rations per man, and arms for Welsh partisans amounting to two thousand firelocks and as many uniforms.

By this time Lord Cawdor had again changed his mind and marched his outfit back to within a few miles of the French.

The invasion planners' notion that the Welsh would join Tate was already flouted. The dingles and hills were astir with duration-only militia and home guard, mobilized and marching to defend Fishguard. At Methyr a thousand ironworkers forged spearheads and shouldered them to go pike Johnny Crapaud. Meanwhile, the French multiplied invisibly. Some west country coasting vessels that had anchored at St. David's Head to wait for the flood tide to Milford (and to amuse themselves robbing fishermen's seines) became another French invasion. In London, Lloyd's Coffee House, whose insurance and cargo brokers sometimes knew of enemy naval movements before the government did, reported to the Admiralty that seven French transports were discharging at Worms Head. Another landing was rumored at Cardigan Bay. The sea lords sent an order to Sir Edward Pellew at Plymouth to collect 500 stand of arms from the vessels in port and cruise the invasion coast, distributing them to the home guard. This made Sir Edward angry. He was in the navy to take prize ships, not to pass out firelocks to Geordie and Meg. Besides his own prosperity, Sir Edward had to look after the fortunes of two relatives in his semiprivate navy, his inept brother Israel and his promising son, midshipman Pownoll Bastard Pellew.*

And so the furies gathered in the unseasonably balmy February night. The French invasion fleet rode peaceably at anchor, and for skittish reasons, Lord Cawdor and Old Bill Tate did not rise to grapple in the dark. Toward dawn, Tate held a council of war and divided his force for the opening of operations. Six hundred men in small detachments were to spread out and forage for provisions and bring them back in expropriated wagons that would be used to carry the arms forward to Welsh insurrectionists. The rest of the Black Legion was to march toward Fishguard and occupy Carn Gelli and another high point overlooking the town and commanding likely salients of counterattack.

As soon as the first foraging party hit the first farmhouse the French Revolution began to lose Wales. Famished after a week of seasickness and gnawing on weevil biscuit and salt junk, raving with fever after sleeping on sloshing ballast stones in the stinking bilges and suddenly free of cells, turnkeys, forts, officers and hell ships, the galley slaves and hard cases plowed into the bounty of Wales. Here,

---

* His actual legal name. The middle name was a tribute to a Mr. Bastard, who was present at his christening. The bowl of cheer must have been flowing.

miraculously, was the liberty that the politicians in France and Britain were prating about. The barnyards were full of fat cattle, pigs and geese. The pantries were redolent with cheeses and butter. Many deserving families had just received a pipe of Madeira or a cask of brandy out of the wreck of a smuggler that had gone aground a few days earlier.

Colonel Tate and his staff went out to *Vengeance* and dismissed Admiral Castagnier and his ships according to the plan that the vessels would depart when the landing was completed. The admiral warily had Tate and his officers sign a paper releasing him without complaint in case he was accused of deserting them when he got home.

Old Bill returned to his hilltop positions. He seemed dazed and confused. Instead of patrols, Tate sent lone officers across the fields waving large banners bearing a tree-of-liberty device. This was intended to welcome Welsh republicans to the army of liberation. None showed up.

By midday, twenty hours after the landings, there was still no contact between Tate and Cawdor. The empty front was the quietest place in Wales. Noise and confusion expanded from it in growing volume.

Engineer Whitesides of The Smalls light went ashore and armed his construction workers and some Solva seamen and marched for Fishguard. As they drew near there was no sign of action or even of defensive forces. Lord Cawdor stood a mile short of the French, preferring to contain them until reinforcements arrived, and did not see Whitesides infiltrating from another direction.

Old Bill saw an unmilitary body numbering possibly two dozen men coming toward Carn Gelli and sent five brown shirts out to chase them. The French dashed out, firing a running volley without hitting anyone. Whitesides said to five of his men, "Take your time. Aim well before firing," and sent them toward the Carn. The first British shots of the invasion killed one Frenchman, wounded two and sent two pelting for cover.

The sight plunged Colonel Tate into audible despair. He wondered aloud what his men could expect from English regulars when besmocked volunteers like these showed such nerve. Hordes of sightseers arrived, including hundreds of farm women wearing the traditional red shawls of Wales. From a distance they looked like Redcoats to the French.

Nothing more happened that day, the second of the invasion. That night Barry St. Leger, the Irish subaltern, came to Old Bill with two other Irish officers of the Légion Noire. They wished to resign. In Brest they had understood the expedition was headed for Ireland. They had been ready to risk their lives in their motherland, but this was Wales and they were less enthusiastic about being hanged as traitors for invading that alien Protestant country. Tate dithered.

Colonel Tate had been thinking. Half his jailbirds were lost in plunderland. It was evident that the Welsh were not going to join him. The calm and deliberate way the enemy commander was playing with him bespoke a coming obliterating assault. He told the Irish officers he had decided to surrender on terms. He sent an English-speaking officer to the enemy commander with a note that said: *The circumstances render it unnecessary to attempt any military operations, as they would tend only to Bloodshed and Pillage.*

While Cawdor was reading the note, Tate's emissary said to Colonel Knox, "We do not wish to fight if we can avoid it as men of honor." What he meant by this, he then confided to the English officer: "Our leader's terms are quite simple. All he wants is for the English to take us back to France."

Cawdor replied to Tate that he, too, wished to prevent "an unnecessary Effusion of Blood which your speedy surrender alone can prevent, and which will entitle you to that consideration it is ever the wish of British Troops to show an enemy whose numbers are inferior." He refused to give terms and told Tate to make up his mind.

Next morning Old Bill surrendered without conditions, and Cawdor selected a theatrical site on the town beach for the ceremonial parade of surrender. The people enjoyed it from housetops and hillsides. The French ragamuffins enjoyed it, too. They drilled smartly as they lay down arms; and as they marched through Fishguard to an unknown fate, they treated the choristical Welsh to booming renditions of *"La Carmagnole"* and *"La Marseillaise."* They larked and sang all the way to Haverfordwest, which apprehensively locked them in the county jail, warehouses and churches.

Another kind of French subversion finally tainted some Welsh persons. Two scullery girls in the jail smuggled in crude implements with which thirty Frenchmen dug a sixty-foot escape tunnel under the wall. Gathering up the kindly damsels, the escapers sailed away in Lord Cawdor's yacht which the victor had thoughtlessly left unattended. The fugitives reached St.-Malo safely. They went home the hard way. The rank-and-file of the Legion was returned to France at Britain's expense as soon as a pretext could be devised. They went as an installment on a four-thousand-man ransom for Captain Sir Sydney Smith, an imaginative officer taken in a dashing cutting-out raid in Le Havre roads. The Directory did not want the Legion back, but got them anyway. Before he was exchanged, Sir Sydney reduced the trade value of the Legion to minus nothing by escaping to England with the help of three French ladies.

A poetical clergyman, Dr. Morgan, was not content with Old Bill Tate's bloodless surrender; he staged a noisy battle in a song called *The Victory of Fishguard:*

> *Hark! how strokes on strokes resounding*
> *Through the distant valleys ring!*
> *Britons, o'er the rocks rebounding,*
> *On their foes with ardour spring.* (Repeat)
> *O'er the trackless sand pursuing,*
> *Round they deal the vengeful steel,*
> *Vanquish'd Frenchmen, humbly suing,*
> *Now before the victors kneel.* (Repeat)

In the Foreign Office, the cynical young George Canning, who was close enough to the rulers to laugh impudently at them, wrote, "The invasion turns out a farce. . . . Pitt, I think, will now certainly get his money. . . . The City are in spirits again, and the Bank in good humour. And in the House of Commons, though we shall have here and there a rat, our majority is upon the whole steady and certain and our cause triumphant." It was only a brief flush of optimism. That month Napoleon whipped the Austrians, and forced the Pope to give up Avignon, Bologna, Ferrara and Rome.

Tate's three captured Irish officers awaited their fate. In any nation's law the indictment most flexible, most discretionary and most subject to expedience is the indictment for high treason. Luckily for St. Leger and his friends, in Britain that year only English-born reformers were eligible for the arraignment, not Irishmen in French uniforms. The Directory held hundreds of French royalists in British uniforms. Hanging St. Leger's trio might have inspired the French to turn off a disproportionate number of royalists. The three Irishmen were sent to France.

This left Britain with no souvenirs of Fishguard save several thousands of pounds in farm damage which the government paid, and Old Bill Tate. He was interrogated personally by Pitt and the privy council. For a while he was free on parole in London, but then, in fear of further invasions, the crown interned him in the filthy prison hulk *Royal Oak,* at Spithead. The cautious new regime of John Adams in Philadelphia would do nothing for such a filibusterer and liberty spouter.

Crushing Satan at Fishguard—the English victory was attributed to divine intercession rather than to Tate's horse sense—raised Lord Cawdor in royal esteem and he assumed viceregal pretensions in the shire. He and his fellow conqueror, young Knox, quarreled and rode out to duel on the field of honor. But then mysteriously, they rode back from the rendezvous unhurt and incommunicative. Cawdor also deemed the time ripe to crush Anabaptists, Tom Paine readers, and reformers on the charge that they had aided Tate's invasion. The peer kept back a half dozen French prisoners as crown witnesses and arraigned two dissenting clergymen and a half dozen other malcontents, none of whom had had intercourse with the French. Of the number, the grand jury indicted John Reed, weaver, and Thomas John and Samuel Griffith, yeomen farmers, on charges of high treason.

Before the trials, the fatuous young Duke of Rutland came to Haverfordwest and Cawdor showed him the French witnesses in the county jail. His Grace reported that they sang "the Marsellois Hymn in quite a polished method." He also wrote that "Lord Cawdor gave some money to the prisoners. . . . The reason of this attention to the prisoners was on account of the evidence they had in their power to give against the state prisoners and which, if ill treated, they might possibly withhold. It was therefore our interest to treat them as kindly as possible."

Crown counsel rehearsed the French captives in Grand Guignol dramas about the Baptists guiding Old Bill's men against the King. When court took up, the defense produced two hundred substantial countryfolk who placed the accused in their usual rounds of life during the invasion. This left much ground to be regained by the chief prosecution witness, Charles Prudhomme, a demoralized American member of the Black Legion. He had been taught a lurid account to hang the nonconformists. He took the stand and refused to say a word. When he was shown his written deposition, the illiterate witness refused to identify the cross with which he had signed it. The judge indignantly ordered Prudhomme taken back to jail. Two more Légion Noire grenadiers were called forth to recite and both remained mute. The last uncooperative Frenchman, Caporal Degouy, even refused to put his hand on the Bible. As he was hustled away, he shouted, "I came over here to fight, not to answer questions." The crown abandoned Lord Cawdor's vendetta. French republicans had, at last, defeated English monarchists on their own territory.

The walkover at Fishguard paradoxically set off heavier runs on English banks. "Every little noise makes the moneyed people quake," Canning noted. The Bank of England had barely more than a million pounds specie left in its vaults. On Saturday 25 February, the official *Gazette* came out with an extra announcing new French landings in Wales. The report was erroneous. That evening Pitt wrote the King at Windsor saying that a bank run could produce "permanent consequences." He declared that "the only possible remedy seems to be to restrain the bank from paying in ready money till the impression has subsided." Pitt said that an Order-in-Council to stop paying in gold was "absolutely necessary." His Majesty went to London and met with the Privy Council on the first occasion that he had ever done state business on the Lord's day.

Extra dispatch boxes piled up at the King's door. "In March most of the counties, cities and towns of the kingdom petitioned his Majesty for the removal of ministers and the consequent restoration of peace," said the *Annual Register*. The King made no replies, nor gave sign that he was concerned with this national remonstrance.

Early Monday morning a crowd gathered before the Bank of England to withdraw gold. The bank distributed copies of the Order-in-Council bearing the King's sign manual and announced that "the general concerns of the bank are in a most affluent and prosperous situation and such as to preclude any doubt as to the security of its notes." However, the notes required more confidence than the bank could impart, even though four thousand bankers and merchants signed a pledge to use only paper during the emergency. A week later the bank started to pay in Spanish gold dollars stamped with a London mint mark. They sold quickly at four shillings, sixpence, and had an unexpected bonus for early birds—when weighed, the coins proved to contain gold worth twopence more than the bank value. The Spanish dollars of course had been taken from vessels captured by the British navy. The kingdom now relied on the fleet even for the cash to conduct its business.

Providentially the navy quickly improved Pitt's fortunes. On 3 March, a frigate arrived with the glorious news that two weeks before, Sir John Jervis' Mediterranean fleet had decisively beaten the

Spanish grand fleet of Don Josef de Cordova off Cape St. Vincent, the southwestern tip of Portugal. Fifteen British warships met 26 enemy vessels, captured 4 and lost none. Horatio Nelson, commanding H.M.S. *Captain,* disobeyed orders to perform an outstanding feat. He pulled out of the battle line and ran his bowsprit over *San-Nicolas,* 80. A marine smashed the window in the Spaniard's quarter gallery and Nelson followed him through the captain's latrine to take the surrender of *San-Nicolas.* While Nelson was congratulating himself, H.M.S. *Prince George* drove the badly riddled *San-Josef* into the surrendered vessel and Nelson stepped over and claimed his second prize.

Admiral Jervis, "Old Jarvey" to the navy, had reduced the triple threat of a junction of the French, Dutch and Spanish fleets to invade Britain or overwhelm her navy in the Channel. The Dons were out of it for a while.

Repairing his battle damage in the *Tagus,* Old Jarvey gave a thought to gold. He decided to send Nelson after some, for the good old Bank of England; to demonstrate to the shaky Portuguese neutral, Britain's last friend in Europe, her naval power; and last, but not least, to benefit Old Jarvey and Young Nelson themselves.

The treasure ship *Prince of Asturias* and an escort had left Manila for Spain via Cape Horn, with the annual Filipino tribute of about seven million pounds worth of gold. Spies had reported that because of the English blockade of Spanish ports, the treasure ships intended to hole up in Teneriffe Island in the Spanish Canaries until the home coast was clear. The old admiral gave Nelson permission to raid Teneriffe and hold the populace to ransom "if they do not put you in possession of the whole cargo of the *Prince of Asturias.*" He added, "God bless and prosper you." The beckoning plunder equaled Britain's annual expenditure in the war, and denying it to Spain could well knock Old Jarvey's tiresome enemy out of the conflict.

"What a strike it would be!" Nelson caroled. He was not oblivious to another attractive feature of the raid. If it succeeded, one-third of the gold would be allotted to the winning officers and men. Of that Old Jarvey would draw a third, or about £777,000, and would hand over a third of it to his flag officer, Nelson—an amount of $1,662,000 at that time, which would represent about fifteen million dollars today. Nelson attached a thousand marines under General (and Admiral) Thomas Troubridge, and took three battleships cruising for gold between Tangier and Cape St. Vincent. While Nelson awaited the right time to swoop on Teneriffe, as a "temporary" war-time measure Parliament passed the Bank Restriction Act, suspending gold payments, and for the first time, the Bank issued standardized £1 and £2 paper notes. The temporary tender has lasted to this day.

III

The Humble Petition

"A ship is worse than a jail. There is, in jail, better air, better company, better conveniency of every kind; and a ship has the additional disadvantage of being in danger."

—SAMUEL JOHNSON
(to Boswell, 1776)

HAVING missed the French expedition to Ireland during the month it was trespassing his jurisdiction, Admiral Lord Bridport took his fleet into the empty Channel early in March 1797 and plowed to and fro in sullen weather. With his dispatches to the Admiralty, Bridport sent a request to be relieved on grounds of ill health. He was seventy years old. He owned a good deal of land. Revolution was a specter in England. During chancy times property owners and investors liked to be in London.

Two French attempts to land in Britain in recent months indicated that more were coming. Surveillance and espionage now focused on a second invasion base across the Channel, the Dutch fleet rendezvous behind the Texel, one of the West Frisian Islands.

Bridport's force was the main reliance of the country. Within the oaken walls of his sixteen sail-of-the-line and two dozen lesser war craft were about 12,500 men. Most of them were serving unwillingly and quite a few had not formed a consoling philosophy about it. They wanted to stay home as much as Lord Bridport did.

The sailing man-of-war was not built to fit men; they were warped to fit the ship. The low overheads bent Jack's head, rounded his back and bowed his legs. Architecture was dictated by armament. Shipbuilders compressed the decks to lower the center of gravity so that the weight of the upper gun deck would not overset the ship in heavy seas.

Queen Charlotte, the flagship of the Channel fleet, was 186 feet long on the lower gun deck, beam 50 feet, "depth of hold" 22 feet. She was a three-decker, displacing 3,500 tons and cost, in today's values, about a half million dollars to build. She was a colossal wooden machine powered by wind and muscle alone. The most intricate mechanisms on board were her chronometer and the yard chain pump, a bucket windlass that reduced water in the bilges. To lift anchor, 280 men shoved the bars around her main capstan. The hemp anchor hawser was 24 inches in circumference, too large to wind on the capstan. It was brought in by attaching a "messenger" about four inches thick which could be bent around the capstan. The job of attaching and detaching the messenger to keep the ponderous main cable falling into the cable tier belowdecks was called "nipping." The nippers were teen-age boys.

The mainmast was 175 feet from deck to top truck, and the main-yard was 100 feet wide. The top deck, or weather deck, was divided territory. Before the mainmast if was called the forecastle, or fore-deck, the domain of the crew or "the people." Abaft the mainmast, it was the quarterdeck, sanctum of the officers. The weather side of the quarterdeck was the solitary precinct of the captain. When he chose to stroll there, lesser officers cleared off to the lee side. The elevated deck at the stern, the poop, was considered part of the quarterdeck and was even more sacred.

The next deck below was the upper gun deck. It held thirty 12-pound muzzle-loading cannons. The poundage was that of the ball, or round. Sufficient natural light entered its hatchways and ports to serve the carpenters, sailmakers, armorers, artificers and cooks at their toil. Beneath it was the middle gun deck with twenty-eight 24-pounders, and under that the actual main deck at the broadest beam and greatest deck length of the vessel. It was not called the main deck, but the lower gun deck. It had the thickest wooden walls and heaviest guns—thirty 32-pounders, each weighing three tons. A 32-pound round shot could penetrate three feet of oak at short range and deal death and destruction to a ship a mile away. The guns on their ponderous-wheeled wooden trucks had tremendous recoil, which if uncontrolled, would hurl the piece through the opposite side. To curb recoil, the gun was reined to stanchions by a massive hempen bridle called a breech tackle.

The big iron naval gun was a man-enslaving machine, forcing him to eat beside it and sleep above it in bumping hammocks.

Below the lower gun deck was a dark cavern beneath the water-line, the orlop deck (from "overlap"). Here the builder did not have to answer human demands at all. Unable to place guns on the orlop deck, he forced your head low in a perpetually foul and dripping twilight. Men ran doubled over on its red-painted decks; in the orlop was the surgeon's cubby, where the wounded were treated by candle-light. Blood was less noticeable on a red deck. In the cockpit of H.M.S. *Victory,* Horatio Nelson died bled white in candlelight against a great ship's knee, with green water sliding past outside.

Below the orlop were cable tiers, shot lockers, powder magazines, the main hold, victual rooms, water casks and spirit room. Here a pale, arthritic tribe called "holders" worked in the dark. Beneath them was the bilge, where a cesspool of leakage and ship's effluvia soaked the ballast gravel, becoming a source of foulness and disease. Troops and prisoners-of-war got to sleep in the bilge and cable tiers. The sick rate in the Georgian navy is not on record. Captains did not care to report a noticeably long sick list and surgeons liked to keep captains happy. If the daily quota was twelve, the surgeon's mate might say to No. 13, "Avast, you bugger. I won't have any more to-day." One doctor dosed all patients with salt water to reduce com-plaints. While drunk, he fell overboard and his mate reported to the captain, "Sir, he drowned in his own medicine chest."

Soap was not issued in the British navy until 1808. Diseases and unhealed ulcers were common on the seaman's skin. Prevailing dampness belowdecks and wet cold work topside produced much rheumatism and joint ailments. The only heat on board came from the galley fires which were doused between meals. The most wide-spread disability was abdominal rupture, mainly caused by working with both hands on the canvas while lying on the stomach across the yards. For ruptured men there were no trusses, no treatments, and little hope of discharge.

The mess was the primary social unit in a man-of-war. The crew of each gun constituted a mess. They ate by the guns from a table and benches that were lashed overhead between meals. They ate with work knives, wooden bowls, leather cans, and tarry hands. Forks and spoons were not fashionable. Each mess was served by a nipper, sometimes as young as ten, who was also the powder monkey in battle. He brought the food in tubs from the galley, a patch of bricked deck with a wood-burning iron range that fed hundreds of men. Navy cooks were enlisted from disabled ranks to lighten the pension roll and often had the classic peg leg. On small vessels the ship's boy, lowest member of the pecking order, was forced to cook. The galley stove furnished the surgeon with a pint or two of distilled water daily.

The people (and the officers) drank water from wooden casks in which, after a couple of weeks at sea, a teeming biota would form. Beer usually went bad early on the voyage. Morning and evening each man was issued a quarter of a pint of West Indian rum. Originally it had been taken neat, but fifty years before this, Admiral Edward Vernon deemed that rum be cut with cask water, a recipe that became known as grog after the green grogram (grosgrain) cloak the admiral wore. Green water was more nearly palatable laced with rum, which perhaps also killed some of the organisms in it.

Since '95, the navy had been issuing lime juice, an anti-scurvy dosage that had been urged on the sea lords for two centuries before that. To retard spoilage, fish oil was floated on top of the lime juice in the casks. The odorous bead was lost to the sensitive nostril by the governing smells between decks: the reek of unwashed bodies in close proximity, and that of tar, rats and rotten bilges.

In the seventeenth century, navy regulations set forth the British seaman's weekly ration:

> One pound averdupois of good, clean, sweet, sound, well-bolted with a horse cloth, well-baked and well-conditioned biscuit; one gallon, wine measure, of beer; two pounds averdupois of beef killed and made up with salt in England, of a well-fed ox, for Sundays, Mondays, Tuesdays and Thursdays, or instead of beef, for two of these days one pound averdupois of bacon, or salted English pork, or a well-fed hog, and a pint of pease (Winchester measure) therewith; and for Wednesdays, Fridays and Saturdays, every man, besides the aforesaid allowance of bread and beer, to have by the day the eighth part of a full-size North Sea cod of 24 inches long, or the sixth part of a haberdine 22 inches long, or a quarter part of the same if but 16 inches long; or a pound averdupois of a well-savoured Poor John, together with two ounces of butter, and four ounces of Suffolk cheese, or two thirds of that weight of Cheshire.

This hearty bill of fare was not entirely illusory for a small coasting navy of a government that paid its provision bills, whose victualers lived by honest measure, and whose ships' pursers had not come aboard solely to steal. By late Georgian times, however, the food in Britain's world navy was short and vile. The victualing department was overextended by a fourfold increase in seamen, by long voyages and establishing depots in far places, and by the Georgian tradition that victualing officials were expected to steal as much as they could. The foodstuffs came aboard, in poor quality and short weight, to a ship's purser who had invested a tidy sum for his appointment. He shortened the weight further and diverted the better provisions for private sale, or as bribes, to the officers. Any or all of these facets of the swindle could have been suppressed by the Lords Commissioners of the Admiralty, but they did not care.

The ship was usually victualed for six months with salt beef and salt pork barreled in brine; dried biscuit, oatmeal, dried peas, vinegar, loaf sugar, cheese and cocoa. The purser brought out the oldest stores from the hold first. Betimes the beef had been below for years in sloshing casks and had been polished into hard black nuggets from which the men carved charms. Pork fat lasted better. The foremost table treat was a tub of "lobscouse" or "sea lawyer," a stew which consisted of salt pork interlayered with showers of pepper and slices of fresh shark, topped off by biscuit. Catching a shark was a gala event in the ship.

Bakers in the Thames and the port towns, grown rich from gigantic fleet orders, got richer adulterating the flour and cheating on weight. Out to sea, ships' biscuits underwent a change of life. One consumer said, "You have to watch very narrowly the bread you eat, or the inhabitant animalcules will walk away, house and all on their backs." In the forecastle and the great cabin alike, the signal to begin eating was a tattoo of biscuits on the table, to knock the worms out. The flour was made by the most advanced milling technology in existence, John Smeaton's colossal hydraulic mills in which the water column was raised by steam-pumping engines. Big war made big industry. By 1797 there were about two hundred water-powered factories in England.

Navy dried peas, after boiling for hours, rattled like shot in the eating tub. Cheese was a rare treat and the suppliers who adulterated it were virtuosi. Without suspicion of cream, it furnished olfactory clues to kitchen scourings, beeswax, rancid fat, glue, and yellow ochre coloring. When the purser's steward brought up cheese you could smell him the length of the deck.

Samuel Pepys, who spent his life as a servant of Admiralty, said, "Englishmen, and more especially seamen, love their bellies above everything else." To fail them on victuals, said he, "is to discourage

and provoke them in the tenderest point, and will sooner render them
disgusted with the King's service than any other hardship that can
be put on them."

The tolerant British historian, G. M. Trevelyan, said of the
Stuart period, "The sailors, famished when they were not poisoned,
seldom clothed, and hardly ever paid, were kept together by flogging,
keel-hauling and other sea tortures, on men-of-war that were often
little better than ill-managed convict hulks and ill-supplied plague
hospitals." Since then keel-hauling had been eliminated.

Food was only one reason why men of the Channel fleet were em-
bittered. Well over half of them were impressed or otherwise forced
into service by economic or political misfortune. Britain had declared
war on France with a navy consisting of 25,000 seamen. Now there
were 100,000 men behind the wooden walls. The impressment service
ranged the coast and waterways, seizing those "water users" who
did not possess "protections"—apprenticeship papers, foreign passports or shipbuilding employment. The press gang also passed over
men who were well-dressed and spoke condescendingly to them.
Originally the press was intended to bring in experienced seamen and
watermen who had not volunteered. By now, after four years of war,
the navy had consumed most able-bodied seamen, and the gangers
took what they could find. The impressment service was made up
of an admiral, 47 regulating captains and commanders, 80 lieutenants, and a force of strong-arm boys. Their town headquarters with
detention cells were called rendezvous, which everyone shortened to
"rondy."

The gangsmen easily detected seamen on the run, even if they
had managed landlubber clothing. Jack betrayed himself by his round
shoulders and stoop, occupational argot, tattoos and rolling gait. By
error, the press took landsmen with occupational bandy-legs—tinkers,
peddlers, and tailors who sat cross-legged on the cutting table; men
who had suffered rickets; liberated convicts who ambled from side
to side after wearing leg irons. The gang rarely corrected these mistakes.

Some seamen were seized by treachery and denunciation. You could
get rid of powerless creditors, rivals for legacies, unwanted suitors of
your daughter, and the opposite faction in a family feud by betraying
them to the gang. Hale men were rarely seen in certain areas: some
were depleted of them, some were hiding them. The impressment
system affected the birth rate. Although it was increasing in the '90s
the removal of scores of thousands of virile males was an appreciable

deterrent. Impressment encouraged unmarried liaisons between resident foreigners and Englishwomen. By law, a foreigner was immune from seizure, but if he married in the kingdom, he could be taken at the church door.

The lunatic *corvée* also had the aspect of a popular national game, a contest longer and more dangerous than cricket, a cross-country match between the wits and legs of the hunter and the hunted. When the press tender entered Spithead with its latest load of victims, those of the previous batch joined veteran seamen in jeering at the wretches and luridly describing miseries to come.

The gangers did not use firearms or cutlasses in taking men. The ship's captain was liable for a dead or ruined captive. They preferred clubs, which gave resolute men a chance to defend with pokers and staves or hardened tar mops which stretched out gangsmen in many a shindy. Counterviolence was the only resource left to men abandoned by moralists and kidnapped by Act of Parliament. The political climate of certain areas put the press off bounds. John "That Devil" Wilkes, when high sheriff of London a generation earlier, jailed or expelled the gang when it attempted to raid the city. In his day, after an unavailing hot press in London, 16,000 seamen came out of hiding.

The town of Pill on the Avonmouth was thronged with prime seamen who had immunity as "pilot's assistants." They were protected by Bristol shipowners in order to relieve merchant crews from impressment upon return to port. The Pill pilots replaced the regular crew downstream and worked the ship to Bristol. Outside Cork City, a thousand evading sailors lived in a colony and went about in armed bands, defying the gang. This was exceptional because skulkers and runaways rarely had means to subsist long ashore. The Cork colony was supported by crimps who procured for the merchant fleet. When they received an order for men from a Liverpool or Bristol ship, they marched members of the colony to a lonely coastal rendezvous with the boat. In 1796 the gang laid on a hot press in Cork and came out with sixteen captives.

When prices for merchant seamen dropped, the crimps sometimes sold to the navy by revealing a man's whereabouts for twenty shillings a head. Informers were paid off secretly. Newcastle-upon-Tyne queered this game by requiring informers to report openly to the customhouse to be paid off. Several sneaks were mobbed and one "nearly murthered."

Scotland was an unhealthy clime for the press gang. Her waterfronts teemed with defiant seamen. At Leith it was almost impossible to snatch a man, and the gang was confined to operating on the waters of the Firth. On one occasion the press picked up several men offshore and, having no floating prison at hand, took them to the town rondy. That evening three respectable-looking burghers were admitted to say good-bye to the men in the cells. They dashed a pot of brandy on the open fire and rescued the prisoners as the place burned down.

The impressment service was not proud of capturing tailors and tinkers; it preferred able seamen, when obtainable. Its prime and prize specimens were crewmen of smugglers, or even better, the finest fighting sailors of England, the men of the privateers and letters of marque. Although they were an active part of the country's naval strength, privateersmen were not exempted from the press. At sea it was a very rare occasion when a press boat could overtake a swift privateer and hove out her crew, so that the attractive quarry was sedulously pursued ashore. One night the Liverpool gang waylaid the Lancaster coach and marched off with fifteen stout-looking seamen, whose value doubled when it came out that they were from the privateer *Stag,* due to sail in the morning.

Captain Spence of *Stag* heard about it and became angry. He led eighty men in a stealthy dark descent on the rondy, burst in and overcame the gangers. He delivered his fifteen men and took eight more for good measure.

By 1797, the gang furnished the fleet with aged, infirm and very young males. Legally youths under eighteen could not be seized, but the service did not tarry to read the parish register. Warrants were issued for boys of eleven, proclaiming them eighteen. Judges had a ready remedy for juvenile delinquency; one turned a boy over to the gang for playing on the village green during divine services.

The principle of impressment was approved by almost every Englishman of that age, if we are to judge from the lack of criticism of it. There were plenty of sermons, petitions and cartoons about individual injustices inflicted by the gang, but almost nothing attacking the grotesque institution itself.

One of the lonely critics was Adam Anderson, a chief clerk in South Sea House, who, in his stupendous history of commerce, in 1764, wrote of "the barbarous and unconstitutional practice of pressing."

One eighteenth-century British admiral who published criticisms of the naval system was Edward "Grog" Vernon, Esquire, Admiral of the White. "Our fleets are defrauded by injustice, manned by violence and maintained by cruelty," said the rough-tongued commoner. The King denied Vernon civil honors and personally struck him off the navy list, and public houses named after him were renamed The King of Prussia for Frederick the Great, an ally of George III. Most commanding officers hated impressment, some disliked flogging and a few governed their own decks humanely. Samuel Richardson sailed on hell ships and happy ones.

He said, "In all my experience at sea, I have found seamen grateful for good usage, and yet they like to see subordination kept up, as they know the duty could not be carried out without it; but whenever I hear of a mutiny in a ship, I am much of the opinion of Admiral Lord Collingwood, who said it must assuredly be the fault of the captain or the officers."

Impressment was introduced in 1378 during the regency of Thomas, Duke of Gloucester, uncle of the boy king, Richard II, as a desperate measure in a war against France that had been going on for a generation. The rebellion of Wat Tyler and men of the home counties three years later was partially inspired by this abuse. The Long Parliament abolished the press in 1641. Later in that century, France manned her navy by a fair and rational conscription introduced by Jean-Baptiste Colbert in his Inscription Maritime, still in business, which registered sailors of every variety, drafted them for set and reasonable terms of service, and then maintained them as a civilian reserve for war.

In 1696, Britain emulated Colbert by establishing a national register of 30,000 volunteer mariners, fishermen and rivermen, who were paid a bounty of forty shillings a year to stand in readiness to serve the fleet. The registered man had preferment in promotion and a double share in prizes. He enjoyed retirement and disability rights at Greenwich Hospital, and if he died in service, his widow and children were cared for by Greenwich. But, like other practical and humane measures of the seventeenth century, the register act was repealed in the eighteenth—in 1711, under Queen Anne.

Child labor was supplied to the navy of George III by the Marine Society, which collected orphans, runaways and boys frowned upon by magistrates. The society scrubbed, clothed and fed these undersized specimens and imparted a little schooling until a ship sent for nippers.

A 1795 Act authorized justices and magistrates to hand over to the fleet "rogues, vagabonds, smugglers, embezzlers of naval stores and other able-bodied, idle and disorderly persons exercising no lawful employment and not having some substance sufficient for their support and maintenance." The land was squeezed to extrude more seamen. Parliament tapped localities for per capita contributions; for instance, 666 men from Bristol and 5,704 from London. Professor Michael Lewis of the Maritime Museum at Greenwich, says, "It suited the Justices of the Peace to conclude that the local poacher could be as destructive to French sailors as he was to British birds." And urban authorities "sent worse types—beggars, minor thieves and pickpockets, or people who looked like they might pick pockets, on this quota scheme. The selectors, being the wrong selectors, selected the wrong people."

Among these "quota men" there was a fractional but sinister and important new strain of navy chattels—tradesmen, teachers, attorneys and clerks, resentful fellows who had lost out in the grabbing game ashore but were superior in education and guile to the run of people at sea. Some had been freed from debtors' jails to collect enlistment bonuses sufficient to keep their families for a year or more. Many "quota men" were politically alert; some were "Old Jacks"— Jacobins the government had pounded underground—and a few were looking forward to sabotaging the King's navy if they could.

Navy professionals despised the quota manning scheme. Captain Edward Brenton thought it "the most ill-advised and fatal measure ever adopted by the government. The seamen who voluntarily enlisted in 1793, and fought some of the most glorious of our battles, received the comparatively small bounty of £5. These brave fellows saw men, totally ignorant of the profession, the very refuse and outcasts of society, fleeing from justice and the vengeance of the law, come on board with bounty to the amount of £70."

A lowerdeck craftsman said of the quota men:

> Them was the chaps as played hell with the fleet! Every grass-combing beggar as chose to bear up for the bounty had nothing to do but dock the tails of his togs and take to the tender. They used to ship in shoals; they were drafted by forties and fifties to each ship of the fleet. They were hardly up the side, hardly mustered abaft before there was, "Send for the barber," "Shave their pates," and send them forward to the head to be scrubbed and sluished from clue to earring afore you could venture to berth with them below. Then stand clear of their shore-going rigs! Every finger was fairly a fish hook; neither chest nor bed nor blanket nor bag escaped their sleight-of-hand thievery. They pluck you—aye, clean as a

poulterer, and bone your eyebrows whilst staring you straight in the face.*

The new conscripts included political heretics, ranging from proponents of enlarged male suffrage and annual parliaments to men bent upon overturning the crown and establishing a Republic of Britain. Their bible was *Rights of Man,* Part the Second, by Thomas Paine, which had gone through editions of hundreds of thousands of cheap copies in the past five years. In his youth Paine had been a revenue collector at Lewes and sailed one voyage in a privateer. While firing his literary carronades against Burke, Pitt and the King, Paine pointed out: "The pay of the army, the navy, and all of the revenue officers, is about the same now as it was about a hundred years ago, when the taxes were not above a tenth part of what they are at present." That was in "the prodigal times of Charles the Second," Paine added. The tremendous influence of Paine's ideas was now transmitted by the quota men to the ignorant Jack, who for the first time saw how long his wages had stood still while the essentials of life had doubled and redoubled in price.**

While the Channel fleet was blockading Brest in February 1797, a small group of quota men met clandestinely on H.M.S. *Queen Charlotte* to make a mighty expression of this long-pent wrong. The leading spirit was a quartermaster's mate of *Royal George,* Valentine Joyce, who had served a sentence for sedition, lost his tobacco shop in Belfast as a result, and had recently come aboard in the quota. Joyce and the self-appointed grievance committee composed an extraordinary petition for redress of inequitable pay. The document departed from tradition and regulations. It was not drawn up by a single crew to be presented to its captain. It was designed for the

---

* Commander C. N. Robinson, quoted by Michael Lewis, *A Social History of the Navy.*

** Pay had been raised by Charles I before his demise. The Commonwealth stimulated the service by distributing prize money among officers and men, and allotting half the value of captured ships to care for the sick and wounded and navy widows and orphans. It also raised wages and divided the sailors into ordinaries and able seamen, the A.B. rating carrying higher pay. There was even a bounty paid to prest men, including mileage money from the spot of detention. After the Dutchman Von Tromp humiliated the Roundhead navy in 1652, the government put up a substantial cash gratuity for volunteers and boosted wages another 20 percent. The result was astonishing. The navy manned sixty ships in six weeks, surprised the Dutchmen, and dominated the North Sea war. M. Oppenheim has observed, "Throughout the history of the navy any improvement in the position of the man-of-war's men is found to bear a direct relationship to the momentary needs of the governing class."

entire Channel fleet to be copied and addressed, presumably separately by each ship, to the Lords Commissioners of Admiralty. It was
the voice of the fleet speaking directly to the rulers of the navy.

Belowdecks, scribes made copies on paper watermarked G(eorge)
R(ex) that had been diverted from official use:

To the Right Honourable the Lords Commissioners of the
Admiralty.
THE HUMBLE PETITION of the seamen on board His
Majesty's Ship.......... in behalf of themselves and all
others serving in His Majesty's fleets
Humbly Sheweth
THAT your petitioners must humbly intreat your Lordships will take the hardships of which they complain into
your consideration, not in the least doubting that wisdom and
goodness will induce your Lordships to grant them a speedy
redress.

It is now upwards of two years since your Lordships' petitioners observed with pleasure the increase of pay which has
been granted to the Army and Militia, and the separate provision for their wives or families—naturally expecting that
they should in turn experience the same munificence, but alas,
no notice has been taken of them nor the smallest provision
made for their wives or families.

THAT your petitioners humbly presume their loyalty to
their sovereign is as conspicuous and their courage as unques-
tionable, as any other description of men in His Majesty's
service, and at the present interesting moment when their
country calls on them so pressingly to advance once more to
face her foes, your Lordships are entreated to reflect with
what additional vigour, with what happy minds, they would
fly to their duty, could they have the satisfaction to think their
families were enabled to live comfortably at home.

That your Lordships' petitioners humbly request your
Lordships will take into consideration the difference between
the time their wages was settled, which was in the reign of
Charles the First and the present; at that time their wages
was sufficient for a comfortable support, both for themselves
and families, but at present, by the considerable rise in every
necessary of life, and an advance of 30 per cent, on slops,
your Lordships will plainly see that they can but barely support themselves.

Your petitioners therefore relying on the goodness of your
Lordships again humbly implore your Lordships' considera-

tion of the matters before stated, and such a complyance of
their request as the wisdom and goodness of your Lordships
shall think meet.

The authors shrewdly confined the master document to the single
issue of wages, supporting the grievance with the irrefutable fact that
the army had recently received a rise and the seamen none. There
was no mention of bad food and short rations, cruel officers, unseaworthy ships, unpaid prize money, or impressment. By concentrat-
ing the whole moral force on wages, Joyce's group gave the fleet
a minimum demand with which none could cavil and all could gain.
It was a unity resolution.

The authors sent copies of the petition to every ship with a letter
of transmittal, signed "The Charlottes." They could afford anonymity.
But addresses had to be named. Joyce's group sent the documents
addressed by name to men of right trusty reputations on other ships.

The *ad hoc* committee risked the petition falling into wrong hands
and even replies from provocateurs. Even more likely would be a
breakdown in transmission. The authors covered broken links by
using an ingenious version of the chain letter. Typical of the stratagem
were the instructions to Seaman Weyman Brown of H.M.S. *Minotaur*: "Send a copy to your acquaintances in every other ship, and
direct them to address replies to any man they know on *Minotaur*."
By "Tuesday 7th (March) . . . there will be sufficient time to collect the sense of the fleet." In this wise busy copyists on *Queen
Charlotte* begat busy copyists on many vessels and a dense fabric
of petitions was woven. The papers went invisibly in the pockets of
captain's boat crews, luggers and fleet tenders. Judging from the
surprise of the authorities when the petitions became public, they
circulated for weeks among the ships without detection by the command.

The *London* ships' company replied to the Queen Charlottes' message: "Messmates, your letter was shown to several and all agree
in returning their harty thanks for your kind intentions. The resolutions is genoures, the intention is noble." The Londons pointed out,
however, that the sea lords did not have the power to raise pay; that
was Parliament's business. They promised every assistance to the
Charlottes if the cause was carried on without disorder or tumult.
"We have no doubt our late glorious commander will step forth in
behalf of his fellow conquers. Please let us know what ships you
would wish us to acquaint with it. Most affectionately. London."

The Minotaurs, the Impétueuxes and the Glorys thought the Charlottes had spoken well and did not rewrite the petition, but other companies were bursting with affliction that they had to express. "At present our wives and families is in a starving condition," said the petition from Mars, "Things is so dear and wages so low."

The seamen resented the fact that not only had soldiers' pay been raised recently but naval lieutenants had received increases by an Order-in-Council, the King cordially approving. An officer had a bargaining position. He could legally withhold his services from the navy, which a seaman could not.

Without waiting for the 7th of March several crews gave their petitions to a man who posted them ashore. They were not addressed to the Admiralty directly but to the absent and ailing "glorious commander" of the Channel fleet, the sailor's friend, Admiral Richard Earl Howe, whom they called "Black Dick." They expected him to be their advocate to the sea lords.

They were delivered to Howe about the first of March at Bath, the famous spa where he was treating a case of crippling gout. As he was to explain later, Howe found them "all exact copies of each other; limited solely to a request *for an increase of pay,* that the seamen might be able to make better provision for their families; decently expressed; but *without any signature.*

"I could not reply to applications which were anonymous; nor acknowledge the receipt of them, to parties unavowed & unascertained.

"About three or four of the petitions first received, tho' a little different in the handwriting, were obviously dated by the same person: and I had therein further reason to think they were fabricated by some malicious individual; who meant to insinuate the prevalence of a general discontent in the Fleet.

"Not resting however on this conclusion, I writ to the Officer at Portsmouth [Lord Hugh Seymour], to whom I was naturally to expect such applications would, in my absence, be addressed. The answer was—that no such appearance had been heard of there; and it was supposed the petitions had been framed for the purpose I suspected.

"On the morning of the 22nd of March, the day after I was able to come to town, one of the Lords of the Admiralty, happening to call upon me, I related these particulars to him; shewed him the petitions, and sent them the same day to his house in the Office, for being communicated to [the First Lord of the Admiralty] the Earl Spencer."

The Lord High Commissioners of the Admiralty had worries more immediate than the petitions. The Duke of Portland was circulating a secret memorandum declaring that the navy could not find victualers to bid on fleet provisions because they had not been paid for earlier deliveries. "Beside that," he said, "the fleet is now becoming incapable of service from death and desertion of the original complement of men."

The fifty-nine-year-old Duke of Portland, as Secretary of State, was responsible for domestic security and justice. Like Pitt and Spencer, he was a political turncoat, having been Whig leader in Commons and that party's prime minister before he crossed the carpet. He owned a Greek art treasure known as "the Portland vase." His name was William Henry Bentinck and he had recently taken out a license to call himself Cavendish in case he needed to.

At the same time he was distressing the sea lords with his secret memorandum, Lord Portland was also sending them reports from his spies that agitators from the London Corresponding Society (LCS) were frequenting the naval bases and royal dockyards. The London Society was the most challenging reform group in Britain. While much of its program paralleled the causes of the Whigs in Parliament led by Charles James Fox, the LCS was less of a parliamentary movement than it was a national membership association. It was a party without M.P.s, while Fox was an M.P. without a party.

The LCS and its local branches throughout the country had a simple, appealing program: universal suffrage and annual parliaments. The Society was loathed and hounded by Pitt and the golden pillmen simply because the attainment of its two goals would have turned them out of power. The LCS membership was made up of artisans, small tradesmen, and innovating entrepreneurs. Their leader was twenty-nine-year-old Francis Place, a self-educated tradesman who had a shrewd insight into what was happening historically in Britain. In the Georgian establishment there was no side entrance by which such talented plebeians could be brought in to replace brave clowns, old fools and venereal bloodstock.

Francis Place began his career by organizing a breeches-makers' union. He was blacklisted and starved out of the trade. He began again with a small tailor shop. When Lord Portland seized the LCS leaders on charges of high treason in 1794, Place joined the organization, feeling it "a duty to become a member now that it is threatened with violence and its founder and secretary prosecuted." He rose rapidly in the Society and was chosen national secretary within a year.

Place's most effective organizers were men even younger than he —John Gale Jones and John Binns. As early as '95, Jones had visited extensively in the naval dockyards in the Thames from Deptford to Chatham. When the King's party tried to induce the shipwrights and dockers on the river to sign a loyal address to his Majesty, hoping to stimulate popular approval of Pitt's policies, the workers refused almost to a man.

John Binns, twenty-five, was a Dublin-born plumber's helper, a disciple of the social mystic, William Godwin, and an extemporaneous orator whom his admirers likened to Charles James Fox himself. In '96, Binns went to Portsmouth and Gosport on LCS business. A friend of the LCS in the home office tipped off Francis Place that Lord Portland had a shadow on John Binns and was getting daily reports on his movements in the naval ports. Place recalled the youth and sent him to Birmingham to help build the United Corresponding Society. (Local societies took variants of the generic name because Parliament had made a law banning nationwide organizations.) John Gale Jones went with Binns, and the two young radicals brought fresh enthusiasm and new members to the United Society. The Duke of Portland sent three agents to observe this activity.

Early in March, Portland had Jones and Binns seized on charges of sedition. Jones' arraignment was based on the allegation that he had asked an audience, "Will the people of Birmingham submit to the treason and sedition laws?" Binns was arrested without a warrant after addressing a meeting at the Swan Tavern. Bail was set at £2,600, equivalent to more than $100,000 today. Jones was tried immediately and acquitted in five minutes. Portland postponed Binns' trial indefinitely and by placing a punitive bail on the culprit's head, he threatened to wipe out the financial resources of the battered LCS.

When Francis Place got the news, he was already in a quandary over the fate of the Society. Under government harassment, the dwindling membership was splitting over the choice of going underground or issuing a loyal address pledging to join the militia if the French invaded Britain. Place thought both directions were off course for a reform movement. He was personally determined to stay away from sabotage, collaboration *and* jail in order to continue working for his ideals. Portland had permeated the LCS with spies, and some of the bedeviled remaining members thought that Francis Place was one of them. Now he had the problem of young Binns, the most valuable organizational asset left to the Society. If the government could convict him, Portland could walk into the wreckage of the LCS and capture the last men left.

Francis Place resigned from the Society and went to Birmingham to save one of its leaders. Once there, he spurred the Society's membership to a tremendous effort. They raised the bail and freed John Binns. They engaged as defense counsel the noted crusader against capital punishment, Sir Samuel Romilly. They arranged to subpoena people who had attended the meeting at the Swan. They heard about three other men who had never been seen before at a reform meeting. The trio had been conspicuous as the only persons present who took notes. Place was not surprised to discover that the three were to be called as crown witnesses. Having drawn up the order of battle, Place and the defendant lay back awaiting the venue of King *v.* Binns, which would be heard when Portland was ready.

On the last day of March, after a month's cruise, Bridport's Channel fleet returned to Spithead, the great naval anchorage at Portsmouth, to "make good defects," take on stores, and lay in four months' victuals including an extra beer allowance to the limit of stowage.

Spithead, the main fleet anchorage, is a fish-shaped area within a ten-fathom contour line. It lies along The Solent for about eight miles between Portsmouth and Isle of Wight. A ship anchored in the middle of Spithead would be three miles from Portsmouth Point, the hard, or pebbled, beach where legions and generations of British sailors had embarked or landed. Across from the Point was the sister sea-town of Gosport. Portsmouth itself was the last ramparted town in Britain, the strongest military position in the isles. North of the fortified neck, in a landlocked harbor, was Portsmouth dockyard, built during the Commonwealth by two Roundhead Commissioners of Admiralty, Francis Moulton and Colonel William Willoughby of the Massachusetts colony, who left his son Francis in charge when he went back to America.

The big three-deckers and two-decked men-of-war coming in to Spithead were the ships that had fought the Battle of the Glorious First of June in 1794 under Black Dick Howe. During Howe's current gout attack, his deputy, Lord Bridport, was in temporary command with his flag in *Royal George,* 100 guns. Lord Bridport was a ruddy, twinkly, grandfatherly type, bald and hook-nosed, whose name was Alexander Hood. He came of a noted naval family. His elder brother was Viscount Samuel Hood who had taken Toulon and Corsica early in the war. Bridport's cousin, also named Alexander, served under him as captain of *Mars*, 74. Bridport had entered the navy as a child lieutenant in the days of Admiral Vernon and had married an heiress. He had a good deal of interest; his wealthy second wife was related to the mighty Lytteltons and the mightier Grenvilles. The King paid one of the Grenvilles £5,000 a year for doing nothing under the title: "Inspector of the Mint." Bridport was rich and stingy, a Knight Commander of the Order of the Bath and a Member of Parliament.

As soon as his ships were at anchor at Spithead, Bridport went ashore and booked a seat on the London coach. Many of his captains also left their posts. But among the seamen, only the elite crews of the captains' boats set foot on land. The rest were not allowed shore liberty despite the fact that many of them had not been on dry land for three years.

From Portsmouth Point, you could "behold a city upon inconstant billows dancing, for so appears this fleet majestical." Sailing wherries tacked toward Spithead, women steering with a yoke-and-rudder while solidly blocked in the stern sheets by panniers of fresh meats, fruit, butter and cheese, and "soft tommy"—fresh bread. The double-ended "Spithead wherry" was a water truck that carried about a quarter ton of goods in a deep, wide bulge amidships. The good-wives were out to win Jack's last pittance. Laundresses and slops sellers sailed with them. Hidden in some of these boats were forbidden flasks of brandy and worse intoxicants—radical tracts, peace pleas, republican propaganda, and works by Thomas Paine. The very royal mailbags for the fleet also contained letters and papers attacking Pitt, the King, and war.

The next wave of wherries contained women with bags and hampers —sailors' wives and sweethearts and public women as well. Since the men were not permitted to go home, wives were obliged to journey to the ports and join them on board during the ship's stay.

Even on the high seas in the midst of war, women accompanied the King's vessels. Warrant Officer Samuel Richardson of *Tromp*, 54, sailed for the West Indies in 1800 with his own wife, and the captain's, the master's, the purser's, the bosun's and the marine sergeants' wives, and those of six others were also on board; and Gunner John

Nichol of *Goliath* said that an Edinburgh woman gave birth on board his vessel during the battle of the Nile.

The boatloads of women going out to Spithead shuddered as they passed a great warship visible only to the extent of ten feet of her main-topmast. *Royal George,* 104, had overset and sunk in 1782 as her crew tried to repair a seacock three feet under the load line. After her brass cannon had been trundled to the other side to raise the damage-point, water came in the depressed gunports, filled her, and sank her, drowning eight hundred seamen and three hundred women and children aboard just prior to her "sailing foreign." Britain lost one of her smartest admirals, Richard Kempenfelt, who went down trapped in his great cabin.

Besides the Channel fleet, there were dozens of other warships in the great fleet base—for refit, awaiting orders, standing by to escort convoys, or waiting for crews to be filled out—press tenders, troopers, and sheer hulks standing alongside ships under repair, guard ships, and prison hulks. The biggest ship ever seen in England was there— *Commerce de Marseille,* 120 guns, a three-decker delivered over by French royalists at Toulon in 1793. The British employed her as a fleet storeship.

The ubiquitous bumboats and wherries passed the Charlottes' model petition to more ships and the natural leaders of the ships' companies contrived to meet each other to discuss the next move. It was now several weeks since the petitions had been sent to Black Dick Howe and there was no reply. Anxiety and disappointment turned to bitterness and resolve. In several forecastles a new stage of the protest developed; the people drew together in the cause and began taking secret oaths to stand by each other and their leaders. On 1 April, 144 seamen, mates and marines on H.M.S. *Garland* signed a statement that they would *not* join "any assembly for the purpose of taking an oath to have grievances redressed but to act with the captain to suppress such meeting or assembly." The fact that these men vowed to repudiate an oath-taking group showed for the first time that one was forming.

The Coming Invasion

Now fair and strong the south-east blew,
And high the billows rose;
The French fleet bounded o'er the main,
Freighted with Erin's foes.

Oh! where was Hood, and where was Howe,
And where Cornwallis then;
Where Colpoys, Bridport, or Pellew,
And all their gallant men?

—*Ballad of the Invasion, 1797*

THAT week in Cologne two of the King's most determined enemies met to forward plans for an imminent invasion of the British Isles, to be launched from the Texel, one of the West Frisian Islands off Holland. General Lazare Hoche, not yet thirty, was incognito in a drab brown coat and nankeen pantaloons—the *sans-culottes* that had given their name to the revolutionary soldier; *sans-culottes* did not mean "without trousers," but applied to those who wore loose plebeian pantaloons instead of aristocratic knee breeches or *culottes*. Hoche had recently taken a saber scar that split one eyebrow and the side of his nose in a picturesque but not unappealing fashion, as a number of wellborn ladies would testify. The ex-stableboy general, newly appointed to command the invasion army, was meeting with the leader of the shock brigade of the landing force, a slim, pale man with rosy cheeks and a beaked nose, thirty-three years old and carrying the credentials of a United States citizen, Brigadier James Smith, who wore a blue coat and a laced-up hat with a *tricouleur* cockade. Smith was a sentimentalist with a realistic grasp of war, an idealist with a saving dash of cynicism.

Hoche and Smith had previously attempted an invasion of the

British Isles in the unsuccessful Bantry Bay affair a few months before. Smith had been with Humbert's division that was frustrated by weather while anchored in the bay; Hoche's ship had never raised Ireland. Since then, Hoche had been serving in command of the army of the Sambre-et-Meuse and was expecting momentary transfer to a new "Army of the Coast" that President Carnot was assembling for him. Smith talked of their next attempt to land in Ireland. "The encampments will be forming in the middle of May," he said, alluding to the emergence of Irish patriots to drill with pikes and muskets in the spring.

Hoche was not surprised at his friend's knowledge of Irish affairs. He was one of the few Frenchmen who knew Smith's identity. He was not an American. He was a Dublin Protestant lawyer named Theobald Wolfe Tone, and a founder of the United Irishmen who were raising partisans to join the French invasion. Nor was Tone a soldier. He was wearing his first uniform. He had suffered alone and incognito through two years of French plans, promises, misgivings, delays and abortions of the Irish invasion. Hoche had shared his fiery purpose, and Carnot, President of the Directory, was a steadfast adherent of the Irish adventure.

Many French leaders thought the coming invasion should be spearheaded by Irishmen captured from the British army and navy. Tone said, "I know the Irish a little. The way to manage them is this. If you intend to use Irish prisoners, let them be marched down under other pretenses to the port from whence the embarkation is made. When everything is ready, let them send a large quantity of wine and brandy, a fiddle and some French *filles*. Then, when Pat's heart is a little soft with love and wine, send in two or three proper persons in regimentals with green cockades in their hats to speak to them—of whom I will very gladly be one—I think in that case it would not be very hard to persuade him to take a trip once to Ireland, just to see his *people* a little."

Because of poverty and anonymity, the gregarious Irish lawyer had known few friends in Paris. Tom Paine was one, or rather Tone was one of the few who would sit up late listening to the old brandy-soaked republican hero. Tone panted for reminiscences of great men Paine had known—Washington, Franklin, Lafayette—but the writer placed himself in the foreground and blotted out these scenes.

Wolfe Tone had been befriended by the American minister to France, James Monroe. The President-to-be and author of a future doctrine forbidding European powers to intervene in pan-American affairs was busily meddling with pan-European affairs. Tone confided to Monroe his plans for the Irish invasion and national rising and told him who was involved in the French government. Monroe said that he was dealing with inferior people. "Go see Carnot," said the American, "and use my name."

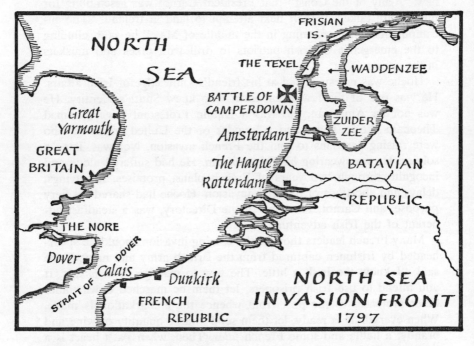

The President of the Directorate, the executive of France, endorsed Tone's invasion plan and sent him to work out details with his foreign minister, Charles de la Croix. Tone left his interview with Carnot and wrote in his diary, "I am a pretty fellow to negotiate with the Director of France to pull down a monarchy and establish a republic, to break a connection six hundred years' standing and contract a fresh alliance with another country."

Charles de la Croix's main distinction was to beget Eugene Delacroix, the painter. Wolfe Tone found him steeped in myths about Ireland. He wanted Tone to indoctrinate Irish captured by the French and stage their "escapes" to England to "cause a powerful revulsion in the Navy of England."

Tone said, "That is flat nonsense."

"Mais, monsieur!" the foreign minister protested. "More than half

the seamen in the King's navy are Irish!" Tone had heard that before. It was the minimum version of a claim that Irish operators had been putting over on the French for years; some French officials assured Tone that 80 percent of the British fleet was Irish.

Nobody knew how many. The King's navy kept no tabulations on nativity of seamen. It did not even know how many dead it had against alive, or how many deserters against recruits.

At the time, the historian Lecky estimates that Irishmen made up 11,500 out of 100,000 seamen and 4,000 marines out of a total of 20,000 in the King's navy. Seventy-four gun ships thus might average seventy or eighty Irish apiece not counting Irish officers who were "plantation Irish," partisans of the King and Protestant enemies of the Catholic plebs. Tone said, "If we ever get to that country, we will humble the pride of that execrable and contemptible corps, the country gentlemen of Ireland."

In Cologne, as the would-be invaders parted, Hoche said he hoped to wind up the campaign in the Meuse in a few weeks and join Tone in Holland for the cross-Channel venture. Reverting to his alias as *chef de brigade* James Smith, Wolfe Tone reviewed an Irish émigré formation in Cologne called O'Donnell's Free Corps which was eager to land home in its green jackets, red *sans-culottes* and white belts.

Tone talked to a picturesque Dutch republican admiral in a red cape with a white ostrich feather curled around his hat brim. The Dutchman told him that at the Texel there were already fifteen sail-of-the-line ready and manned, and many transports. Of course, there were the usual vexations. Some complaining seamen ran away with the frigate *Jason* and there were other mutinous combinations to be dealt with.

Wolfe Tone left for the Texel. In that grim spring all the navies were sore with insubordination. Belowdecks the seamen were listening to messmates reading aloud *Rights of Man* in English, French and Dutch.

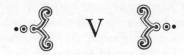

The Spithead Telegraph

THE MUSE'S FRIENDLY AID

A copy of verses on the Seamen displaying their Noble
Spirit in the Year 1797

The Muse's friendly aid I must invite,
Likewise a pen that's taught itself to write,
No wit I boast, but am by fancy led
To search the deep caverns of my hollow head,
If Attic rhyme Apollo there has stored,
I'll here deposit all her favourite hoard

In days of yore when rich and poor agreed,
Poor served the rich and rich the poor relieved.
No despotic tyrants then the womb produced
But mutual all, each loved, and none abused,
But now how dreadful is the scene reversed,
We're blest with birth, but with oppression cursed.

The theme I treat on is our royal tars,
Whose godlike spirits rival even Mars,
From their supineness now their souls are roused
To rod and yoke no longer are exposed.
But all alike, each swears he will be true,
And tyrants ne've their former course renew.

At Spithead first their noble blood was fired;
Each loved his King, but one and all aspired;
To serve each other was their full intent,
And if insulted were on mischief bent,
But still their country's cause they would maintain,
Against the rebels or the power of Spain.

—From a Ms ballad found on
H.M.S. *Repulse* at the Great Nore, 1797

I T WAS Maundy Thursday, 13 April. Parliament had risen for Easter after indulgently listening to a threat of a third party forming to overthrow Pitt and make peace with France under the slogan of "armed neutrality." Although Pitt retained an eightfold majority, he took additional insurance by sending an envoy to consult his ally, Josef II of Austria, about conditions for a negotiated peace.

The day before Good Friday, English sovereigns traditionally presided over a rite called Royal Maundy in St. James's Palace chapel. The Hanoverians, however, had stopped participating in a ceremony that symbolized English poverty and royal mortality. George III was at Windsor Castle for a week of stag hunting while his Lord High Almoner received 59 poor persons in the chapel and handed them 59 purses, one for each year of his Majesty's life. A city teller could envy the poor persons the coins. There was a shortage of hard money. Silver was going to India in John Company's holds to buy moguls or make war on moguls. Mined gold had ceased to flow from America. Minted gold was draining off to hired armies on the Continent. The proprietary was hoarding coin. Tradesmen issued their own scrip. In Norwich, a whimsical Jacobin employer was paying wages in paper *assignats* of the French Directory and creditors were honoring them. The Foreign Secretary advised the Admiralty that the French frigate *Citoyen* had landed a midshipman in Scotland who was touring the country speaking to republican meetings.

In Portsmouth the day was sentimental and sad. Black Dick Howe's command pendant had been struck for the last time. His servants were removing his chattels from *Queen Charlotte*. His successor Lord Bridport, as commander of the Channel fleet was in London on private business. While there, Bridport neglected to call at the Admiralty office and tell the sea lords that lower-deck informants had reported grievance meetings going on daily in many of his vessels and of long writings passing from ship to ship.

Even after he returned to Spithead to take command, Bridport also failed to mention this unrest to his deputy, Sir Alan Gardner, or to the senior political admiral present, Rear Admiral of the Blue, Sir Hugh Seymour, a Commissioner of the Admiralty who operated out of Portsmouth. Bridport did not even divulge the peril to Vice-Admiral Sir Peter Parker,* commanding the Portsmouth base.

Sir Peter, a plump, jowly party of seventy-six, was noted as the

---

* There were two other Admiral Parkers, unrelated to Sir Peter: Sir William of the Mediterranean fleet and Sir Hyde Parker, commander-in-chief of the Jamaica station.

biggest jobber in the navy. He was the son of an admiral and he looked after the naval careers of a number of kinsmen. He made his nephew George Parker a lieutenant at the age of thirteen and his son Christopher, seventeen, was promoted directly from midshipman to post captain. There were plenty of elderly captains in the King's navy who never made post captain, which meant that you had been posted to command a ship. Mere captains languished ashore on half pay, while post captains drew full pay, collected head money for each crew member of a defeated enemy vessel, and received prize money for capturing a ship.

For Sir Peter Parker the visit of the Channel squadron meant another plague of prayers for discharge from seamen declaring that they were foreigners. *Duke* had two who said they were Prussians. Captain Payne, of *L'Impetueux,* opposed another German's appeal by pointing out that the man had volunteered from an East Indiaman for a bounty. This meant that the sailor, about to be abducted without a bonus, had smartly "volunteered" in order to collect one.

Dozens of Americans were trying to get out. One of these Jonathans, Richard Garrick of H.M.S. *San Fiorenzo,* claimed to be "an American subject." (During the early years of the U. S. republic, Americans referred to their "empire.") Captain Sir Harry Neale of *San Fiorenzo* had found Garrick on a British prize retaken from the French and was convinced he had been a British crewman for a long time. Garrick asked permission to go to the Nore, from which he had last sailed, for papers that would prove his U. S. nationality. Admiral Parker denied the request. "If there are such papers at the Nore, many English sailors could pass as Americans," he said.

The King's navy hated these American "protections." It had not accepted U. S. independence and tended to class the separated nation with mass skulking and mutiny. A seaman with American papers usually got himself hurried below with a "starter," a cane or a tarred knotted rope knout. This attitude owed something to the fact that forged U. S. papers lapped like wavelets around the King's ships. At Liverpool and London, printers thrived on fake American documents. British ships calling in neutral New York were met by touts for Patrick Riley, an entrepreneur recently immigrated from Ireland, who naturalized Americans in jig time. For three dollars he took a British seaman before an alderman and swore he had been born on Paddy's own native turf in Manhattan. With this affidavit, any U. S. customs collector would give the applicant a certificate of citizenship.

The present-day blight of passports, identity cards, police *fiches,*

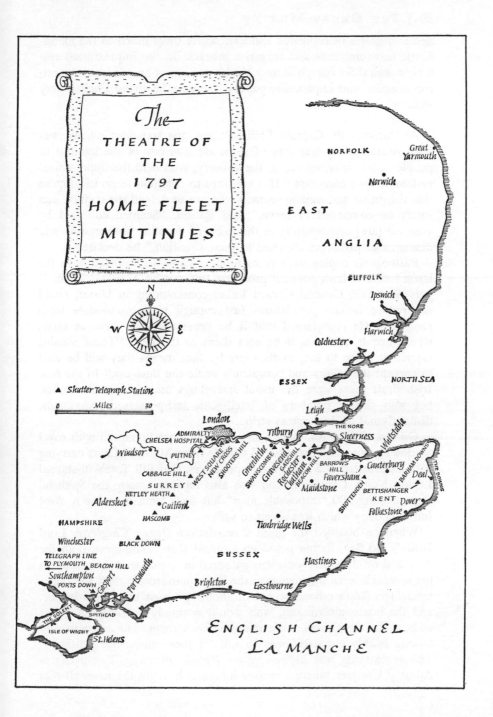

The
THEATRE OF
THE
1797
HOME FLEET
MUTINIES

N
W   E
S

▲ Shutter Telegraph Station

0   Miles   30

NORFOLK   Great
                                 Yarmouth
        Norwich

EAST

ANGLIA

        SUFFOLK

                Ipswich

            Harwich

    Colchester •

                    NORTH SEA

ESSEX

                Leigh

    London   Tilbury
    ADMIRALTY▲   THE NORE   Whitstable
CHELSEA HOSPITAL▲   ▲▲   Sheerness
            SHOOTERS HILL
Windsor   ▲   ▲Greenhithe   BARROW'S   Canterbury   ▲
        PUTNEY WEST SQUARE ▲SWANSCOMBE   HILL   BARHAM DOWNS
                NEW CROSS ▲Gravesend Faversham   Deal THE DOWNS
    CABBAGE HILL ▲   GADSHILL   BEACON HILL   BETTISHANGER
        SURREY   ROCHESTER   SHOTTENDEN KENT Dover
    NETLEY HEATH   Chatham   Maidstone   Folkestone
Aldershot •   •Guilford
        HASCOMB
HAMPSHIRE   Tunbridge Wells
Winchester •   BLACK DOWN
                        SUSSEX   Hastings
TELEGRAPH LINE
TO PLYMOUTH ▲BEACON HILL
Southampton •   Portsmouth   Brighton   Eastbourne
PORTS DOWN GOSPORT
        SPITHEAD
    THE SOLENT
ISLE OF WIGHT
        St. Helens   ENGLISH CHANNEL
                            LA MANCHE

and certificates of residence and nationality owes much to the identi-
fications, exemptions and forgeries inherent in the impressment system. Admiral Sir Joseph Sidney Yorke once prest an educated American seaman with impeccable papers "because he spoke English very
well."

At Portsmouth, Captain Philip Patton, the transport officer, was
also overtasked by transfers of men. He was one of the handful of
people in the navy, indeed in the country, who held the impressment
system in open contempt. "It is contrary to common sense to suppose
that the prime and leading seamen who are to defend the country can
safely be compelled to serve," said Patton. "Seamen collected by
violence [are] consequently in the habit of deeming both mutiny and
desertion as privileges attached to their situation," he declared.

Patton was coping with press tenders come to Spithead with the
latest batch of Irish political prisoners to serve his Majesty. Ireland's
jails were full. General Gerard Lake, commanding in Ulster, could
not reduce inmate populations fast enough to accommodate fresh
roundups. He complained that if he prosecuted the captives juries
would acquit, and that if he sent them to the fleet, "These villains
rejoice at going to sea, as they say by that means they will be able
to corrupt the sailors and completely settle the business." In the new
Irish draft there were the usual starvelings and desperate rowdies,
but also sizable numbers of intelligent, self-possessed individuals,
distinctly not of the impress stripe.

On top of the Irish, there came *Terrible* from Plymouth with royal
marine recruits, and two packed vessels from Milford Haven carrying
1,173 exhausted and sick French prisoners, Old Bill Tate's ill-starred
Légion Noire. Captain Patton was also moving among the Spithead
ships posting 500 "disposable men" left over from manning a West
Indies convoy which was about to sail.

When he boarded the great three-decker *Queen Charlotte,* Lord
Howe's old flag, Patton noted an unusual scene. The crew, both the
duty and off-duty divisions, was gathered in argumentative groups on
the foredeck, even impinging on the holy quarterdeck abaft the mainmast. The ship's officers were not shouting about this impertinence,
and the boatswain's mates, who would normally be swinging rope's
ends at the trespassers, were mingling with them. The seamen were
talking openly about refusing to sail "if they ignore the petitions."
The same thing was happening on *Royal Sovereign,* flag of Vice-
Admiral Gardner, where a marine informer brought the news aft that

if the petitions remained unanswered, two guns would signal a general mutiny.

Patton got down in his boat and sent his crew pulling hard for Portsmouth. Instead of heading upstream for his office in the dockyard, he hastened toward the highest feature in the walled town, the square tower of the church of St. Thomas à Becket of Canterbury, which had served seamen as a landfall, beacon and signal station since the time of Richard the Lionhearted. In the tower was a peal of ten bells which called newly appointed admirals to be reconfirmed in the Church of England before raising their broad pendants in the ships.

The transport officer climbed the tower. On the flat top there was a gilded weathervane, a Tudor three-master blossoming with wind, familiar to seamen as the Golden Barque. Standing high over the gilded ship was a black framework with six windows, in each of which there was a pivoted shutter that could be opened and closed by levers below. A boy stood ready at the manuals as Patton gave the elderly lieutenant in charge of the contrivance an urgent message for the Admiralty: *a mutiny brewing in Spithead.*

The lieutenant lifted a ten-guinea telescope to his eye and looked north across the dockyard and inner harbor at a similar shuttered frame standing on the 450-foot rise of Ports Down.* The boy clacked the shutters and the lieutenant lowered his glass and said to Patton, "Ports Down answers, sir." He and the lad spelled out the mutiny message, using 63 code permutations afforded by opening and closing the six windows. The Ports Down station repeated it across South Downs, ten miles to Beacon Hill.

The previous year the Admiralty, noting the success of Carnot's semaphore lines in France, had adopted a variant system. From the roof of the Admiralty office in Whitehall two main lines stretched east and west. One extended two hundred miles to Plymouth with a spur from Beacon Hill to Portsmouth. The other trunk route ran to Deal, where it could be read by ships standing offshore in the Downs. The Deal line had a branch to Sheerness, a dockyard and garrison town near the huge naval and mercantile anchorage of the Nore in the Thames estuary.

From Beacon Hill the mutiny message winked east twenty miles to a station atop 900-foot Black Down. It ran clucking along through Hanscomb, Netley Heath and Cabbage Hill, to Putney, southwest of London, and leaped the Thames to the top of Chelsea Hospital, from

* In South of England topography, "down" means height.

which it was read by the station keeper on the Admiralty roof. The message took about three minutes in transmission from Portsmouth to London, a distance of 75 miles on the telegraph route. Sometimes the shutter operators passed the routine noon signal from the Admiralty three times as far to Plymouth in three minutes. If it took more than two minutes to reach Deal, it was probably due to Thames fog curling around Shooter's Hill station.

Communications among the disaffected ships would be laborious, oar-creeping subterfuges. The Lords of Admiralty could employ against the dissidents the most rapid long-range signal system in the world.

The Lords of Admiralty were called from their holiday preparations to deal with Patton's warning. The telegraph was shut down for the night and they had nothing further to go on until express letters would arrive next morning, Good Friday. The sea lords canceled their Easter recreations. In the morning a rider brought an express from Lord Bridport written the previous evening, saying that "disagreeable combinations" were forming, especially on *Queen Charlotte*. A morning drizzle obscured the telegraph. It was evening before some particulars arrived by rider from Sir Peter Parker: an informer had told him that the Charlottes, Sovereigns and other ships' companies were going to refuse duty at Tuesday noon, the 18th, if their wage demands were not met. The signal would be made by *Queen Charlotte*, hoisting the Union Jack and firing two guns. Sir Peter expressed resentment that Lord Bridport had not informed him about the seamen's petitions.

Bridport had no reason to think that the Spithead remonstrance was idle talk and that the men would not act. The recent *Bounty*, *Windsor Castle* and *Culloden* mutinies were well remembered. But Bridport's health was poor, he was old, he was distracted by cares of property and investment, and he may well have been discouraged by years of governmental disinterest in paying seamen and by Lord Spencer's nonchalant replies when fleet commanders had warned him about the situation during past months. Moreover, the higher persons, harassed by the crisis of state, did not wish to bother each other about a lesser matter like sailors' grumbling, nor could they recognize that foremast discontent was turning to protest. Six weeks of silence had passed since the seamen had sent their pleas to Black Dick Howe. They could no longer hope for his good offices. They decided to apply directly to the Admiralty and the House of Commons.

Saturday morning was cloudy at Spithead. Unauthorized ships' boats went among the men-of-war without officers in the stern sheets or jacks to the fore. The men were dicing for big stakes. Their officers were marooned in disbelief. *Defense,* 74, not of the Channel fleet and denied access to the planning, received an anonymous letter from *Royal Sovereign*: "FRIENDS, I am happy to hear of your honourable courage towards redress. We are carrying on the business with the greatest expeditions. We flatter ourselves with the hopes that we shall attain our wishes, for they had better go to war with the whole globe than with their own subjects."

The letter announced that when *Queen Charlotte* fired two guns "was the time for taking charge and sending the officers and women out of every ship. The second signal is a red flag at the mizzen top-masthead and two guns; this is to send a speaker from every ship. The petitions is to be ready to go on Monday if possible. You must send them and your letters to Mr. Pink, the Bear and Ragged Staff, as that is our post office. Direct one petition to Evan Nepean, Secretary to the Admiralty. The other to Honourable Charles James Fox, South Street, Grosvenor Square.

"Success to the proceedings."

With the letter was a copy of *Queen Charlotte's* original petition from which other crews could copy their own two drafts.

It was difficult for the seamen to think of a political friend. The only democrat in the House of Peers, Lord Charles Stanhope, Pitt's brother-in-law and political enemy, who called himself "a minority of one," had been driven to retirement by schoolboy insults and assaults from their lordships. (In exile, Stanhope employed himself inventing calculating machines, printing presses, and a microscope lens that bears his name.)

The distinction to Charles James Fox, as recipient of the petitions, was merited. He was leader of the opposition in Parliament and the seagoing navy's favorite politician. He was the great English liberal of the age. Gibbon called him "the Black Patriot." He was a fat man with swollen legs, gunpowder jowls, black hair sprouting through his unwashed stockings, and a sauce-spotted coat of buff and blue, the dress of George Washington whom he much admired. Fox was a spectacular gambler, Lothario and drinker, and the best racing handicapper in London. When one of his own horses was running at Newmarket, he would ride on the other side of the rail for the last furlong to scrutinize its stretch tactics. Once, when he was broke, he ran the house bank at Brooks's Club for a year and came out winners. He loved to play cricket and tennis and swim in the Thames in the morning.

For friend and foe alike Fox had the attraction of a wise and angelic child. Nobody disliked him except Pitt and the King. In the streets he addressed one and all with the sweet eighteenth-century greeting "I give you joy" as he stopped to chat with persons of any station. Discussion groups formed around him. Great ladies stopped their coaches to jest with "Charles" and at balls they would keep their *carnets* blank hoping that Fox would partner them.

This unique individual was the chief and tireless opponent of the Georges and William Pitt. For 40 years Fox and a small shifting following in the House of Commons upheld English honor and liberty, despite, as Hazlitt said, being "assailed with all the engines of power; by nicknames, by lies, by all the arts of malice, interest and hypocrisy; from 'the pelting of the pitiless storm' that poured down upon them from the strongholds of corruption and authority."

Fox's father was a notorious crook, the first Lord Holland, who boasted of being "the most unpopular man in England." As Henry Fox, Papa had been chief purchasing agent for the navy, and cornered stores and provisions that he sold the fleet through dummies to gain a great fortune. He gave his son a permissive upbringing. "Young people are always in the right and old people in the wrong," said the enlightened scoundrel. "Let nothing be done to break a child's spirit. The world will do that business fast enough."

One time Lord Holland promised that the boy could watch him demolish an old brick building with gunpowder, but the pledge slipped his mind and he blew it up while Charles was away at Eton School. When he remembered, Milord had the place rebuilt, and when Charles came home, blew it up all over again. If the youngster was about to fling a wild oat, his father handed him a bushel. One historian actually charges Fox Major and Fox Minor with instituting the notorious licentiousness that marked the late Georgian era at Eton and Cambridge. If so, they stimulated a process already far advanced. Cromwell founded the English public school as a county-supported high school for sons of commoners. Restoration of the crown cut off public funds, and hungry schoolmasters packed off the students and brought in rich men's sons, whose scholastic standing was determined by their rank and precedence in *Burke's Peerage and Usage*. Relieved of overmuch study, the young honorables engaged in gang rumbles and ran in feral packs. The adolescents drank, whored and gambled. The school was deserted during the Newmarket meeting. Eton sprouts were entered on the rolls of the navy as junior officers and were acquiring seniority while absorbed with such school rags as smashing up bordellos in Covent Garden. A twelve-year-old King's navy lieutenant sneaking back to school with a rumfustion hangover was likely, however, to be birched on the bare bottom only slightly less smartly than a man-o-war's man receiving twelve from a boatswain's mate.

There were no school games to soak up youth's awful calories. The first rugby match, which did not come until 1796, was played by Eton *v.* Westminster. It was not arranged by the respective headmasters but by a London publican who expelled two gangs of brawling scholars to fight it out on a field. The Etonians lost. When they got back to Windsor, the headmaster lined them up, had them drop their breeches, and whipped them again.

Such were the happy schooldays of Charles James Fox. They made a scholar of him. He excelled at classics, mathematics and languages. With his unlimited allowance, he dressed like a French macaroni in a lurid tufted coat and lacquered red heels, and when driving his own coach and pair in London, he held a dainty bouquet to his nose to offset the stinks. At sixteen, he matriculated at Oxford University and Brooks's famous gaming club in St. James's Street. Before a night of games and wine, Master Fox turned his coat inside out, pulled sleeve guards over his ruffles, and jammed a wide-brimmed straw hat on his head to contain his powdered curls and shade his beady eyes from the candelabrum. When playing for big stakes he put on a black mask to conceal his uncontrollable facial expressions. Charles cleaned out was a smiling lad who retreated to a corner to read Herodotus in the original. A fond aunt boasted that he was "the most egregious coxcomb in Europe." During his teens, he piled up £140,000 in debts—the equivalent of several million dollars today. When Charles, aged nineteen, was carousing through the Continent, visiting Voltaire, flinging sovereigns and experimenting with passion in Napoli, Lord Holland at last decided the boy needed something to steady him. He purchased for his son the Midhurst, Essex, seat in the House of Commons and settled his debts to the penny.

Most of the 558 seats in Parliament were filled by nominees of landowners and elected by a handful of property owners. In Bath, a city of 25,000 people which loved to talk politics, there were only 31 enfranchised voters. William Adam, a Scottish M.P., who once tried to kill Fox in a duel, represented two electors. Old Sarum had two

M.P.s and no population at all. Aspirants talked of "taking" their seats, not of "running" or even "standing" for Parliament.

Only selected property owners were enfranchised in England. They told the rest that they could not vote because they paid no taxes. But the rest paid nearly all the national revenue through purchase taxes on boots, candles, soap, salt, sugar, coffee, beer, bricks, tobacco, tea, rum, newspapers and windowpanes. In *Rights of Man* Tom Paine pointed out that the tax upon beer brewed for sale "is nearly equal to the whole of the land-tax." A laborer earning eighteen pounds a year paid ten pounds in taxes on his necessities. Not a farthing of state revenue was returned in national benefits such as highways, medicine, poor relief or education. It all went to the army, navy, church and crown.

The King kept a secret of his pension rolls and patent places. He gave individuals lavish salaries and perquisites for life and sometimes for "three lives," in which the treasury was committed for the same amount to sons and grandsons. He bestowed idle offices and active superintendencies which amounted to licenses to steal. They were openly and officially called "offices of profit under the crown." Much of the King's unpublished largesse went to members of the House of Commons. He controlled the House of Lords largely by hidden quarterly doles to peeresses and dependents. When Sir George Saville brought a bill to Commons calling for publication of these "grace and favor" payoffs, the King's ministers resisted on grounds of "delicacy," explaining that "many Lady Bridgets, Lady Marys and Lady Jennies would be much hurt at having their names entered as pensioners of state."

The King not only paid his own parliamentary adherents but personally rigged elections against opponents. When the disfavored Whig admiral, Augustus Keppel, stood for the Borough of Windsor, near the palace, his Majesty moved the royal servants into houses he owned in the town and had them certified as voters. Two courtiers slept in the stables overnight in order to help defeat Keppel by sixteen votes.

On a recent occasion the King's ministers floated a £12.5 million war loan at high rates of interest and allotted shares only to court favorites, mostly M.P.s. City bankers would have subscribed it at fair interest rates, but that would not have served the royal purpose which was to raise cash and, at the same time, purchase favor. The profits to insiders amounted to nearly a million pounds. The Lord Advocate for Scotland was not impressed. "The constant salutation that I meet from friends of the ministers," said he, "is: 'It is damned hard. I have only ten thousand pounds out of it.' "

The majority of Commons was made up of gilded youth or youth that wished gilding. An American Tory, Samuel Curwen of Massachusetts, was dismayed at his first view of the Mother of Parliaments: "that assembly of untutored, inexperienced youths, for half, I believe, have not seen thirty."

Although every safeguard was taken against voting by conscience, Pitt remained uneasy over divisions that he lost by less than four to one and resorted to the royal power to create more dukes, viscounts, earls, marquesses and barons in order to outpoint the foe. In their century, the three Georges nearly doubled the roll of peers made during the previous thousand years of English history. In 1796 and 1797 alone, Pitt had the King invent thirty more players for his side.

Such was the political order and deliberative body into which wandered the brilliant boy wastrel Charles James Fox in 1768. He had a chanting tenor voice and could build extemporaneous sentences that parsed and balanced, and kept people awake. His erudition was immense. There was not a libertine in the House who could match his nocturnal record. He thundered out promptly against the King's anathemas, the Americans, the French, freedom of the press, and the dastardly reformers, and was quickly made junior Lord of the Admiralty. Hearing a mendacious rumor that Fox was to be married, his father said, "I am glad to hear that there is a prospect of Charles going to bed for one night at least."

The dark chanticleer was rising fast and sure toward cabinet rank when the King's men decided to punish the Reverend John Horne Tooke for libels against the House of Commons. He was indicted for accusing the speaker of the House as an accomplice in a theft. Tooke claimed that some of his land had been expropriated by a bill of enclosure connived in by the speaker. The crown did not elect to bring Tooke before a civil jury. He was seized and carried by sergeants at arms to the bar of the House of Commons. The King's political virgin, Charles James Fox, took the floor and to the shocked surprise of the government proceeded to bamboozle the house into declaring the arrest illegal and voting the prisoner over to common law.

Fox was immediately removed from the Admiralty. Overnight he had found his métier, always to speak for principle. He became the perennial "tribune of the people." Gibbon said, "Depend on it, Billy's [Pitt's] painted galley will soon sink under Charles's black collier."

Fox, of course, was not a revolutionist. He upheld the French Revolution without demanding the end of British monarchy. He denied the existence of a deity without attacking religion. He demolished a minister's policy in Parliament and went swimming with him afterward. He married the Prince of Wales's former mistress, an ex-madam, and lived with her in monogamous bliss. Fox was the supreme liberal. Edward Gibbon thought that "Perhaps no human being was ever more exempt from the taint of malevolence, vanity or falsehood." One time during the American Revolution, Fox flayed the war secretary, after which Prime Minister Lord North whispered to him, "Charles, I am glad you did not fall upon me today, for you was in full feather."

When Parisians tore down the Bastille, Fox said, "How much the greatest event that has ever happened in the world! and how much the best!" He never wavered in his admiration for the revolution, although he was often alone in a parliament bent on destroying it by arms. Edmund Burke, his erstwhile patron, railed against the new French military code which gave every soldier and sailor full civil rights, whether or not he had enjoyed them prior to enlistment. Fox said that Britain would do well to copy France, where "a man, by becoming a soldier, does not cease to become a citizen." Burke never spoke to him again. British soldiers and sailors however, marked Fox's words.

When Britain went to war against the revolution, Fox pledged his support to the King in "repelling every hostile attack against this country." That was not the same thing as approving an invasion of France, and Fox's distinction found an echo among seamen. The Black Patriot insisted at the outset that the navy should be increased to 40,000 men and these men should have new ships. "The neglect of building a single ship that could possibly be built is a neglect highly criminal," said he. Fox's idea was at variance with that of the government, which preferred to send out British seamen in disintegrating ships on the chance that they would bring back new French ones.

He was the political favorite of the serving navy; among officers and seamen for his denunciations of thieving suppliers and cynical ministers, and among higher ranks for his defense of the good admirals under political attack. He loved to visit Spithead and was invited, on one occasion, to sail against a French fleet that was rumored to be out. He was disappointed when it proved to be a false alarm. In 1792, merchant seamen in several Scottish and East Anglian ports demonstrated for better pay. The King, in a speech to Parliament, called it an "insurrection." Fox replied, "I ask the gentlemen if they believe that in each of these places the avowed object of the complaints of the people was not the real one; that the sailors . . . did not want some increase of their wages, but were actuated by a design of overthrowing the constitution."

The day before Easter, with the Spithead petitions asserting themselves as open secrets in command circles, Lord Bridport did a curious thing. The admiral now ordered his captains to invite the seamen to send in more of them and be specific. His motives may have been cathartic: to bring all these boils to a head and lance them; and they may have been cautionary: to amass enough evidence to impress the sea lords with the need for sweeping reforms. At any rate the lower deck replied with a will. Admiral Parker got a box of grievances.

The Marlboroughs charged Captain Henry Nicholls and his first lieutenant with cruel and oppressive behavior, citing the recent death of Seaman John Mulvanin by flogging at the gangway. Parker dispatched a commission to investigate, consisting of Admiral Sir Alan Gardner, and two captains. While on board *Marlborough,* Gardner pronounced that the charge "was not founded in facts," which the Marlboroughs greeted with "a degree of dissatisfaction," as he noted. As Gardner bound up the tablets of justice to debark, "five of the ship's company deputed by the rest, came up to me and declared that they were determined not to proceed to sea without the Captain, First Lieutenant and Master's Mate being removed." Citing this accumulation of incidents, Bridport wrote a letter to the sea lords in which he hoped they would "not direct the squadron to proceed to sea, before some answer is given to these petitions, as I am afraid it could not be put in execution without the appearance of serious consequences, which the complexion of the fleet sufficiently indicates." While he was sanding the letter, an Admiralty express rider was on his way with orders to Bridport to "hold himself in instant readiness to put to sea at the shortest notice." He was also directed to send eight men-of-war under Sir Alan Gardner down to St. Helen's, the departure anchorage off the east side of the Isle of Wight.

It was a day of tense waiting, that Saturday eve of Easter. Boats went to and fro, carrying petitions and speakers, or flag lieutenants and admirals' secretaries. Express riders were galloping. Forecastle penmen were writing:

To the Right Honourable the Lords Commissioners of the Admiralty. THE HUMBLE PETITION of the seamen on board His Majesty's ship *Terrible* in behalf of themselves and all others serving in His Majesty's fleets Humbly Sheweth THAT. . . .

THE HUMBLE PETITION of the seamen on board His Majesty's ship *Royal Sovereign*. . . .

. . . on board His Majesty's ship *London*

. . . His Majesty's ship *Mars*

. . . *Pompée, Glory*

. . . *Defiance*

. . . *Impétueux*

. . . board his Majesty's ship *Advice, Argo, Cleopatra Concorde, Fly, Hornet, Hind, Jason, Juste, Latona, Marlborough, Melpomène, Minotaur, Nimble, Nymph, Penguin, Plover, Pompée, Porcupine* . . .

. . . On board His Majesty's ship *Megara, Melampus, Monarch, Ramillies, Robust, Royal William, Speedwell, Stag, Success, Syren, Telemachus, Triton, Unite, Venus* . . .

On behalf of themselves and all others serving in His Majesty's fleet HUMBLY SHEWETH

With increasing confidence the ships' companies elected "speakers" who were to transform ship democracy to a fleet republic. In a handful of days British naval peasantry traversed political ground that the nation had not yet crossed in a millennium. The all-fleet committee had no inspiration from the national Parliament or other legal organism in Britain; it derived its laws and precedents from the United States Congress and French Assembly, the Irish underground, and the forbidden British reform societies. The thing was unbelievable.

The Georgian plutocrats had invented a character for the British sailor—mentally inferior, simple, jolly and loyal. He was by nature lazy, so the boatswain's mate used a knout to send him up the shrouds. He was improvident; therefore pay only indulged his weakness. He was a drunkard, so he must not be allowed ashore. He was a child who looked to the captain and the admiral as his father. It was precisely the myth that the Southern white in the United States attached to Negro slaves. The mutiny—with its skillful planning, determination and discipline—wrecked the jolly jack tar mystique. It was hard for most officers to believe in the new man who had come so unexpectedly on deck. It was hard for some of the men, too.

The industrious, watchful, preoccupied eve of Easter was elevated

by a thrilling and ominous sound. On a ship, someone started three
cheers and presently the throats of thousands of men were lofting
hurrahs. Portsmouth was accustomed to regulation morning duty
cheers at 8, but not to this doubled volume rolling over evening
waters. People were inspired or frightened, according to their apprehension of coming events. Portsmouth slept restlessly.

On Easter Sunday morning the Whitehall express arrived in spring
showers, bringing Lord Bridport the order he feared: make ready to
sail. Dictating from bed, he sent a message back to the sea lords, referring to his afore-stated qualms: he was convinced that his crews
would not sail. He was obliged, however, to convey the order to
Admiral Gardner to drop eight ships down to St. Helen's.

Sir Alan Gardner followed orders. He was an excitable, black-
browed man of fifty-five with flaring nostrils, missing upper teeth and
a protruding jaw. He had been in the navy for 42 years and was a
major general of the marine corps. In earlier wars he made a reputation for bellicosity. He fought under Howe at the Glorious First and
put in five years as a Lord Commissioner of the Admiralty. He was a
Member of Parliament for Westminster. Sheridan and the Whig back
bench loved it when Sir Alan attended the house; when the sailor
sounded off, he was fine foil for quips.

Admiral Gardner issued orders to the Royal Sovereigns to hoist
in boats and make ready for sea.

Not a man moved to the boat falls.

No one took up capstan bars.

The nippers did not come forward with stoppers for the anchor
cable.

In the rest of the squadron, the drummers beat to quarters. The
men did not move.

The seamen had planned this universal disobedience to take place
two days from then. Guns would boom, flags would flutter, bands
would play. Now it happened in silence, precipitated by a blind order
from London.

Sir Alan ordered his company to fall in on the quarterdeck and
bawled them out for their "impropriety," the "disgrace and mischief
you are about to bring upon yourselves and your country" and the
"encouragement you are giving to the enemy."

The company just stood there.

Gardner picked out "all the good and leading men" and exhorted
them to deliver the rest to a sense of duty. "We are fully determined,

sir, not to go to sea until the petitions are attended to and complied with," was their answer.

"The petitions were not sent in due form. It is impossible for the Admiralty to answer anonymous letters. But I tell you, their lordships will take them into consideration."

"That answer will not be satisfactory to the fleet."

Gardner reported to Bridport, "My admonitions and friendly advice was rejected in a manner which has hurt my feelings exceedingly."

The Queen Charlottes swung out a boat, which was joined by a Royal George boat. They visited the ships, addressing the crews. In the Royal George boat was the principal leader of the seamen, Valentine Joyce. He had made the plan during long patient months with several messmates, including, according to legend, an attorney named Evans, whom misfortune had also contributed to the navy. Evans was serving under an assumed name which has not survived. Or perhaps he never existed save as a convenience to Valentine Joyce or journalists who required a devil at Spithead.

Joyce spoke firmly and moderately to the seamen. All officers were to be permitted to remain on board. Every man should obey orders as before, except one order that was to be ignored until their grievances were remedied; they were not to weigh anchor. He called on each crew to pick two delegates and send them to a meeting of a fleet committee that evening on *Queen Charlotte*.

Joyce and the leaders hailed *London,* 98, and came by the ladder. Looking down from the gangway was the grim face of Vice-Admiral Sir John Colpoys, who had the reputation of being "the most experienced disciplinarian in the navy." Colpoys bellowed that they were not going to board his ship and he sent the marines to points of vantage. The Londons yelled down that the delegates were welcome aboard. The delegates declined to try the bayonets of the lobsterbacks. While the opponents faced each other, Bridport's dispatch boat came and handed up a message for Admiral Colpoys, ordering him not to resist intrusion by delegates.

Joyce and the lower-deck leaders went on board and addressed the 850-man crew in equable and careful terms and went below to speak as messmates out of hearing of the great disciplinarian and his disciples. Colpoys' nephew was captain of *London*.

Lord Bridport sent Rear Admiral Sir Charles Morice Pole on horseback to London to give the Lords of Admiralty firsthand descriptions of these ominous quarterdeck dramas. Hearty, pink, blue-eyed

Pole was a brave and unlucky officer. In 1780, with the pay chests of the British troops in New York aboard, he lost *Hussar,* frigate, in Hell Gate, and divers are still looking for it. A couple of years later, he took an ill-gunned storeship, H.M.S. *Vernon,* into close combat with a 34-gun Spanish frigate, *Santa Catalina,* and captured her. His men were refitting the Spaniard to take along when they spied ships bearing down on them from the horizon. Pole ordered his men to burn *Santa Catalina.* The newcomers turned out to be British.

Pole carried a letter from Bridport to the Admiralty: "Their lordships desire me to use every means in my power to restore the discipline of the fleet. Would to God I had influence sufficient for this important object, which nothing in my opinion will be able to effect, but a compliance with their petitions." Pole also took an intercepted message from the seamen of *Minotaur* to Charles James Fox, M.P., which the sea lords did not send on to Fox. Bridport advised his employers: "I see no method of checking the progress of this business but by complying in some measure with the prayer of the petitions." He predicted it would be impossible to "get the better" of the Spithead men by "vigorous and effectual measures" or to capture the leaders by force. He reminded their lordships that the men had "no objection to go to sea, provided an answer is given to their petitions."

Lord Bridport had been acting all day to avert bloodshed. He had curbed Colpoys in time, and now he advised the captain of *Queen Charlotte* to raise no objection to a meeting of the fleet delegates in the great cabin.

That evening backs bent and oars delved as ships' boats carried delegates to the parliament of the fleet aboard *Queen Charlotte,* their grins revealing missing teeth, checked shirts scrubbed in salt water,*

---

* British naval seamen dressed as they pleased (until 1857), or within the choice afforded by the slops chest on board and the bumboat in harbor. In the nineties they no longer wore cocked hats, but affected a variety of round, narrow-brimmed bonnets in straw or wool. Some wore beaver hats resembling astrakhans. They knotted kerchiefs around their necks, preferring black silk ones. Short brass-buttoned blue jackets and striped or flowered double-breasted waistcoats were fashionable. The tarred pigtail had not yet appeared. They wore their hair in shoulder-length tresses, gathered in back with a ribbon. Some trousers were knee-length, either open or gathered at the bottom, but most men wore French-style pantaloons. The trousers were often striped red or blue. The men went barefoot except in cold weather or on formal occasions when they pulled on stockings and slippers with buckles. They had no proper foul weather gear, but could reduce the discomfort of a storm with canvas aprons.

great tarry feet shoved into blacked shoes, hair tied, manhood proclaimed. It was the first expression of universal male suffrage that Britain had ever seen.

They openly signed their names on the Queen Charlottes' petition, unanswered for all these weeks. When a man did not know how to spell his name, the penman guessed it, and handed him the quill to make his mark.

Royal George: Valentine Joyce, John Morice
Royal Sovereign: John Richardson, Joseph Tate Green
London: Alexander Harding, William Riley
Queen Charlotte: John Hudelstone, Patrick Glynn
Glory: Patrick Dugan, John Bethell
Duke: Michael Adams, William Anderson
Mars: Thomas Allen, James Blythe
Marlborough: William Senator, John Vassil
Ramillies: Charles Berry, George Clear
Robust: David Wilson, John Scrivener
L'Impétueux: William Porter, John Whitney
Defence: George Galloway, James Berwick
Terrible: Mark Turner, George Salkeld
La Pompée: William Potts, James Melvin
Minotaur: Dennis Lawler, George Crosland
Defiance: John Saunders, John Husband

About a third of the names appear to be Irish, a considerably higher percentage than there were Irishmen in the British navy.

The forecastle government was ruled by delegates; there were now two from each ship's company, without regard to the number of constituents, as in the United States Senate. They did not, however, elect a chairman, but, by general confidence, Valentine Joyce was their speaker. He continued to sign documents as a delegate of *Royal George*.

The Spithead parliament enacted three measures:

—All of its orders were to be written.

—On the basis of signed charges, designated officers could be expelled from ships for extreme cruelty, after being respectfully notified. On *Marlborough,* the death floggers were nominated along with Captain Henry Nicholls.

—The seamen of the fleet were to swear an oath to be true to their cause. This was copied from English and Irish reform, radical and republican societies. The Admiralty did not compel seamen to swear allegiance to King or nation. Men who had never before been dignified by a solemn compact with a higher cause took the oath on Holy Writ and kept it devoutly.

The oath proved useful in committing people who were not enthusiastic, or feared the consequences. Royal marines, traditionally the policemen of seamen, one of whose duties was to prevent mutiny, took the oath, some under duress but most with approval of the cause. The marines wanted better food and more pay, too. Bridport wrote the Admiralty that the lobsterbacks took "a decided part in favor of the seamen."

Most of the petty officers, masters' mates, boatswains' mates, gunners' mates, carpenters' mates, quartermasters, stewards, trumpeters and cooks took the delegate's oath, but on a few ships they remained aloof.

From Lord Bridport down, officers who commented on the Spithead rising said that the delegates were "the best men aboard," "the good and leading men," and "the best-behaved and reliable." There were reasons why this should be so. With a central planning group offering a levelheaded program and giving him a choice of a leader, the seaman voted for the messmate he respected most and had known for some time. He did not elect a wild-talking English radical or Irish agitator who had just been dumped off a press tender. Even when the better men were reluctant to serve on the fleet committee, force of opinion drafted them. Several delegates accepted office partly because they recognized the need for a core of moderates in the fleet government.

As the solemn seamen met, holiday audiences ashore were hearing the first performances of a Georgian popular song hit, "The Snug Little Island." In the Easter gala at Sadler's Wells, it was sung by an entertainer billed as "Jew" Davis, and at Maidstone by its author, Thomas Dibdin, a protégé of Pitt and the King. The first verse went:

> *Daddy Neptune one day to Freedom did say,*
> *If ever I lived upon dry land,*
> *The spot I should hit on would be little Britain!*
> *Says Freedom, "Why that's my own island!"*
> *O, it's a snug little island!*
> *A right little, tight little island!*
> *Search the Globe round, none can be found*
> *So happy as this little island.*

The Spithead Cause

The law doth punish man or woman
That steals the goose from off the common,
But lets the greater felon loose,
That steals the common from the goose.

—Anon, eighteenth century

BRIDPORT's emissary, Admiral Pole, arrived at the Admiralty office
at midnight on Easter Sunday and described to their lordships
the seriousness of the situation at Spithead. It was a concerted action
of the whole fleet, following the unanimous refusal of eight big ships
to weigh anchor. The officials refused to consider the petitions or the
reality that Pole spread before them, dismissed him, and took their
own brief counsel. At one A.M., they sent another order to Bridport
to sail.

The fleet commander relayed it to his ships Monday morning with
a lame postscript. "The Commander-in-Chief trusts this answer will
be satisfactory, and that the different ships' companies will immediately return to their duty, as the service of the country requires
their proceeding to sea." It was no answer at all. The anchors stayed
down.

The men-of-wars-men had precedent of a successful protest to remove brutal officers. In November 1794, when at anchor in San
Fiorenzo Bay, Corsica, the men of *Windsor Castle*, 98, broke into
"a most alarming mutiny," according to William James, the British
navy historian. They demanded replacement of their admiral, Robert
Linzee; their captain, William Shield; and two other officers. Admirals
Lord William Hotham and Sir Hyde Parker made personal appeals
for them to return to duty "without the necessity of resorting to the
extremities." The men "positively refused." Since there was nothing

in standing instructions to help an officer faced with solid intransigence, Shield demanded a court-martial to resolve the issue and clear himself. His brother officers, not inclined to find him guilty of charges laid by mutineers, acquitted him honorably. The crew would not yield. Admiral Hotham stopped the shadow play, replaced Shield and pardoned the mutineers.

At Spithead this Easter Monday a merchant ship convoy was due to leave for Newfoundland with H.M.S. *Romney* and *Venus* as escorts. Their crews refused to hoist anchor. The delegates of the fleet sent a message:

> To the Seamen on board His Majesty's Ship *Romney*. It is the desire and earnest wish of the fleet that you will proceed peaceably and regularly to sea with the convoy you shall have under your charge, as we would in no wise wish to bring the injury of our country in our cause; and we shall proceed on your behalf in a regular way; and we are fully satisfied of your loyalty in our cause, and remain yours, H.M. Ship *Queen Charlotte*.

The Romneys still refused to leave, but night talks persuaded them that their messmates would hold the line while they showed the country that seamen would not interfere with Britain's trade. The two warships joined the convoy next morning. The delegates also permitted H.M.S. *Porcupine* to sail to Plymouth for refit.

Aboard the ships, as a reminder that self-government was no license for riot and debauch, lower-deck committees hung ropes from blocks at the end of yardarms. Classically, the yard rope was the preliminary rig for execution by hanging; to its dangling end the prepared halter was spliced in an actual punishment. Yard ropes became the sign of a ship that belonged to the cause. Ashore, it was mistakenly thought the ropes were meant to intimidate officers, but they were an expression of rigid self-discipline by the men.

When the startling event came to H.M.S. *Glory,* Lieutenant Fitzpatrick ordered the marines to fire on the ship's company. The lobsterbacks refused. The Glories posted their disciplinary regulations by the ship's bell and the officer tore down the bill. The seamen petitioned the Admiralty to remove Fitzpatrick, "for he has in every means behaved tieranicaly to the People." The company of *Duke* applied to be relieved of their captain, Charles Rowley, who was accused of shaving heads for petty offenses and withholding a thousand gallons of rum from the crew.

After his first reactions to Pole's mission on Sunday night and refreshed by Monday morning's overnight dispatches from Portsmouth, Lord Spencer entertained second thoughts about the affair at Spithead. His cogitations did not have the benefit of advice by his Majesty, who was crashing about in wet thickets at Windsor Great Park, yoicking after stag, and unaware of trouble in the fleet, nor were they subject to the opinions of the Prime Minister, who was at "Hayes," his villa in Putney, for the long weekend. He was ill and upset over the termination of his engagement to Eleanor Eden, the only love affair of his life. Parliament was in recess and the other ministers were absent from London, too. Fox was out of town. There was no opposition outcry to influence Spencer's reconsiderations.

But Spencer, Monday morning, arrived at a decision that he was going to Portsmouth to settle the matter himself. He sent Admiral Pole ahead hot-hooved to inform Bridport. The sense of the message was that the sea lords "were well inclined to the prayer of the seamen's petition and were coming down to decide upon it." Spencer sent a note to Windsor, in which the King received his first intimation of the mutiny and replied at 6:15 P.M., "I think [Lord Spencer] is perfectly right in proceeding thither."

Spencer and two other commissioners and the undersecretary of the Admiralty left their office at five, just before Fox arrived to inquire about the alarming news of Spithead. "Uninformed as I was," said he, "I thought we should have the transaction with all possible speed." An Admiralty official assured the opposition leader that Spencer was going to handle it that way.

Admiral Pole arrived in Portsmouth in the evening and Bridport wasted no time sending the grand news out to the ships that the First Lord himself was coming, favorably disposed to redress the grievance. The men were wonderfully surprised and shook their heads in smiling admiration over what delegates could do. Black Dick Howe they thought had failed them, but the petitions had produced something more than they had dared to dream—the distant and mighty First Lord was coming uninvited to wait upon them. It seemed like a grand opportunity to air all their wrongs, not merely the wage issue. Accordingly the delegates went into deliberation to prepare a larger list of grievances to hand the sea lords when they arrived.

The Spithead parliament was elated, but cautious. It was to be involved in negotiations with great nobles whom none had ever seen, who sat in inner rooms ruling the highest men the ships ever encountered, a fleet commander or a port admiral. The delegates resolved that they had to secure from these mighty men not only agreement to redress the grievances, but a pledge that Parliament would give it the force of law. Moreover, they needed a royal pardon for every man in the fleet so that there could be no victimization of the leaders when the officers returned to power. The men in the great cabin were keenly aware that they had violated more than half of the 36 articles of war. Twenty-one of the articles provided the death penalty.

George John, Second Earl Spencer, thirty-nine, was a rich sophisticate who knew nothing about naval life. He was a King's man with strong Whig connections. His sister, the ravishing Duchess of Devonshire, campaigned scandalously for Charles James Fox by swishing silkily through the Westminster markets, bussing butchers and poulterers. His beautiful wife, Lady Lavinia Spencer, sister of a great Whig landowner, held the wittiest drawing room in London. Her admirers included Samuel Johnson, Edward Gibbon and Horatio Nelson.

At the age of twenty-two, Spencer had taken a seat on the opposition side of the House, but concurrently with his accession to the earldom and the execution of Louis XVI, he had gone over to the King's party. He was one of the great bibliophiles of England, specializing in Italian *incunabula*. He worked hard at the Admiralty office, for in addition to the cares of a world naval war and feuding admirals, he had to sweep out the slutswool left by his predecessors, the ineffable Earl of Sandwich and the Prime Minister's brother, Lord Chatham.

Spencer tried as hard as anyone in the regime to make objective decisions. He was able, on one occasion, to flout the rule that King's men made good admirals and Whigs made bad ones. In 1795, with the precarious Mediterranean fleet crying for a leader, he appointed Admiral Sir John Jervis, who, as a Whig M.P., had voted against declaring war on France. Spencer was drawing credit from Old Jarvey's recent smash-'em-up victory over the Spanish at Cape St. Vincent.

At five in the afternoon of Easter Monday, the deputation of sea lords set out in a coach in the rain for Portsmouth. With Spencer was his colleague, Sir Richard Pepper Arden, a bright lawyer who was a close friend of Pitt's. The third Lord of Admiralty was Rear Admiral William Young, Spencer's closest naval adviser. At the beginning of the war, Young had captured a round Corsican tower at Mortella

Bay, the design of which became the "Martello" Towers that dotted British coasts during the Napoleonic wars. With their lordships rode the deputy secretary of the Admiralty, William Marsden, a well-known Orientalist who supported his studies by working for the sea lords.

The great ones reeled through the night for a rendezvous with unknown members of the lower orders who had suddenly usurped their control of the grand fleet. The coach stopped only for fresh horses. Next morning, the 18th, they rode into Hampshire in fair weather, the sight of which also pleased his Majesty, downing his breakfast burgoo* at Windsor and snorting for stag. The King's Easter hunt had already ridden two horses to death. One stag had been brought down beyond Reading after a 260-mile chase.

The sea lords rattled into Portsmouth at noon. Apart from a royal naval review, the descent of such a galaxy on a mere naval base was unprecedented. The Lords Commissioners expected their presence would overawe both factions and that their prepared offer of settlement would unknot all issues. It did not turn out that way. Hearing from Bridport that a body of white wigs was hastening to cope with his protests, poor foolish Jack only "felt [his] power over the country and over the government," as W. J. Neale put it in his 1842 book on the affair.

The delegates of the fleet would also have been proud could they have heard what the King was saying about them in a letter to Henry Dundas: "The spirit seems to be of a most dangerous kind, as at the same time the mutiny is conducted with a degree of coolness it is not arid of method. How this could break out at once without any suspicion before arising seems unaccountable."

Waiting for Lord Spencer in Portsmouth was a letter from Captain Willet Payne of *Impétueux* who saw "secret Jacobin springs" behind the mutiny. He suggested that every cannon in the area be pointed at the fleet. He proposed two schemes to divide the seamen: that fake news of rising national indignation against the sailors be printed in their favorite paper, the *Star*; and that the Admiralty should create a new bottom grade in the service called "landsmen" in order to arouse fears of demotion among the seamen.

Spencer adopted Payne's ideas and the opponents began exchang-

---

* Oatmeal porridge. Burgoo was introduced to the navy by Rear Admiral Sir Cloudesly Shovel, who was lost in 1707 when he led four warships to doom on the Bishop and Clerk Rocks in the Scilly Islands. He is buried in Westminster Abbey and in former days the face on his marble effigy was stained with tobacco juice sprayed by sailors who did not like burgoo.

ing broadsides—by letterpress. A proclamation appeared in Portsmouth, addressed to the seamen as "Friends, Countrymen and Fellow Subjects." It complained of "your very extraordinary conduct," "strong circumstances of aggravation," "your refusal to weigh anchor," "your sending of deputations from Ship-to-Ship," and "your public procession through the Fleet in a line of boats at the time appropriated for Divine Service"—during a "crisis *the most momentous* in the Annals of Naval History." The poster declared the seamen had caused "the most poignant grief" among "your Gracious Monarch's *well-affected* subjects." It likened the sailors' behavior to "the ravenous offspring of the Pelican [craving] for the last drop of their affectionate mother's blood, though not in want!" The petitioners were advised, "Make known your wants in an official and respectful manner, and be assured the love your King and Country bear you, will dispose them to give you every comfort and reward a grateful Country can bestow, consistent with its existance as a Nation."

This exhortation was signed, *The Spirit of Kempenfeldt,* the good admiral whose bones lay in the anchorage in the wreck of the *Royal George.*

The delegates replied with a carronade, *From the Living to the Dead,* and a little wig-pulling, "Art thou a Spirit of Earth, or Goblin damn'd?" They protested their loyalty and the "official and loyal manner" in which they had presented their complaints to "that Honorable Earl, [Howe] who wore the Laurels of the Glorious First of June, and who was in the Hearts of British Seamen represented as their Friend, but sorry to say that we found to the contrary, in his not representing our Petitions to the Lords Commissioners of the Admiralty." They invited Kempenfeldt to "come forth in your real and corporeal State and try for one Week the scanty Allowance on which we are obliged to Subsist."

Two elderly well-wishers gazed at the troubled ships. Old Bill Tate, the invader of Fishguard, was languishing in the prison hulk *Royal Oak* at Spithead, along with a group of French officers and the four Frenchwomen who had accompanied the landing in Wales. Peering down from a villa on the Isle of Wight above St. Helen's was "a merry, cockeyed, curious-looking sprite, dressed in a fashion now forgotten quite," * the tempestuous nemesis of George III,** John Wilkes; now seventy, a self-described "extinct volcano," Devil Wilkes was still leering at the ladies with his crooked grin and squinted eyes.

---

* Lord Byron
** "I love my king so well," said Wilkes, "that I never hope to see another."

But he was no longer championing the seamen, as he had twenty years before, when, as a London magistrate, he'd declared impressment illegal.

Lord Spencer and his party got down to business at the Fountain Inn. The Lords of Admiralty summoned Sir Peter Parker and Lord Bridport and listened to their description of the events of the five days since Maundy Thursday. The London chieftains wasted no time dissecting history. They had come with concessions to settle with the delegates of the fleet.

At this juncture, the new enlarged petition of the delegates was handed to the commissioners:

> To the Right Honourable the Lords Commissioners of the Admiralty.
> My Lords,
>   We, the seamen of His Majesty's navy, take the liberty of addressing your Lordships in an humble petition, shewing the many hardships and oppressions we have laboured under for many years, and which we hope your Lordships will redress as soon as possible. We flatter ourselves that your Lordships, together with the nation in general, will acknowledge our worth and good services, both in the American War as well as the present; for which good service your Lordships' petitioners do unanimously agree in opinion, that their worth to the nation, and laborious industry in defence of their country, deserve some better encouragement than that we meet with at present, or from any we have experienced. We, your petitioners, do not boast of our good services for any other purpose than that of putting you and the nation in mind of the respect due to us, nor do we ever intend to deviate from our former character; so far from anything of that kind, or than an Englishman or men should turn their coats, we likewise agree in opinion, that we should suffer double the hardships we have hitherto experienced before we would suffer the crown of England to be in the least imposed upon by that of any other power in the world; we therefore beg leave to inform your Lordships of the grievances which we at present labour under.
>   We, your humble petitioners, relying that your Lordships will take into early consideration the grievances of which we complain, and do not in the least doubt but your Lordships will comply with our desires, which are every way reasonable.
>   The first grievance we have to complain of is, that our wages are too low, and ought to be raised, that we might be the better able to support our wives and families in a manner

comfortable, and whom we are in duty bound to support as far as our wages will allow, which, we trust, will be looked into by your Lordships, and the Honourable House of Commons in Parliament assembled.

We, your petitioners, beg that your Lordships will take into consideration the grievance of which we complain, and now lay before you.

First, That our provisions be raised to the weight of sixteen ounces to the pound, and of a better quality; and that our measures may be the same as those used in the commercial code of this country.

Secondly, That your petitioners request your Honours will be pleased to observe, there should be no flour served while we are in harbour, in any port whatever, under the command of the British flag; and also, that there might be granted a sufficient quantity of vegetables of such kind as may be the most plentiful in the ports to which we go; which we grievously complain and lay under the want of.

Thirdly, That your Lordships will be pleased seriously to look into the state of the sick on board His Majesty's ships, that they may be better attended to, and that they may have the use of such necessaries as are allowed for them in time of sickness; and that these necessaries be not on any account embezzled.

Fourthly, That your Lordships will be so kind as to look into this affair, which is nowise unreasonable; and that we may be looked upon as a number of men standing in defence of our country; and that we may in somewise have grant and opportunity to taste the sweets of liberty on shore, when in any harbour, and when we have completed the duty of our ship, after our return from sea; and that no man may encroach upon his liberty, there shall be a boundary limited, and those trespassing any further, without a written order from the commanding officer, shall be punished according to the rules of the navy; which is a natural request, and congenial to the heart of man, and certainly to us, that you make the boast of being guardians of the land.

Fifthly, That if any man is wounded in action, his pay be continued until he is cured and discharged; and if any ship has any real grievances to complain of, we hope your Lordships will readily redress them, as far as in your power, to prevent any disturbances.

It is also unanimously agreed by the fleet, that, from this day, no grievances shall be received, in order to convince the nation at large that we know when to cease to ask, as well as to begin, and that we ask nothing but what is moderate, and may be granted without detriment to the nation, or injury to the service.

> Given on board the *Queen Charlotte,* by the delegates of the Fleet, the 18th day of April 1797.

It was signed by the same delegate list as on the original petition.

Lord Spencer appears to have been dumbfounded by the document. Moral bruises followed. Here he had come with the best of intentions to adjust wages after a humble and correct, if anonymous, petition by the seamen, only to be confronted with a rattle of further demands by an illegal group of men calling themselves "delegates of the Fleet" and having the audacity to sign their names.

Their lordships refused to consider the new petition. They proceeded with an answer to the original unsigned plea on wages only. They could not, of course, acknowledge the existence of such an infamous body as "the delegates of the Fleet." The thing had to be done by regulations: seamen could only transmit complaints through a chain of superiors to the fleet commander. Therefore Bridport could legally represent them to the Admiralty. So the negotiations were officially conducted between Bridport and Spencer. The delegates would not get to lay eyes on the great sea lords, after all.

The Admiralty offered to raise the pay of petty officers and able seamen from 22 shillings, sixpence a month to 26s/6d; ordinary seamen from 19 shillings to 22; and landsmen should have a two-shilling raise. Wounded men would receive full pay until return to duty or discharge, and if then disabled, would be pensioned or hospitalized.

Bridport sent his flag officers, Colpoys, Gardner and Pole, out to the *Queen Charlotte* to dictate this to the delegates. The errand-running admirals were politely received. Their hosts said they would reply at ten next morning.

The strikers dared to raise the King's commissioners. They wanted one shilling, sixpence more than the Admiralty bid for all ratings and marines. They reiterated the grievance on rations and required a real poundweight instead of fourteen ounces, full measure on beer and spirits, and better quality victuals. They wanted more vegetables and no more flour to be issued as makeweight for their rightful share of meat. They asked that pensions be raised to £10 a year. They declined to bargain for landsmen, saying, "There never has existed but two orders of men in the navy, able and ordinary, therefore the distinction between ordinary seamen and landsmen is totally new."

The reply made the sea lords exceedingly angry. Over their after-dinner port and pipes, they composed a rigid and menacing counter-blast. It said the delegates' reply had "not even any relation to the situation of seamen in his Majesty's navy"; that "it has been and ever will be our intention that provisions shall be of the best quality"; and that "the quantity now served is sufficient." It repeated the original wage offer, including that for landsmen. Their lordships ordered Bridport to have his captains read this to the company of every ship. If the men remained "insensible to the liberal offers now made to them, and persist in their present disobedience, they must no longer expect . . . any smart money or pension," and there might be other "dreadful consequences." The Lords Commissioners gave the fleet one hour to accept this ultimatum. Ships companies that returned to duty immediately would receive "perfect forgiveness."

Their lordships signed it and then decided not to send it. Into their reluctant minds seeped the suspicion that bluster would not serve. They considered that they were pitted against a devilish canny clique of villains who had deluded and intimidated the great body of loyal, contented men. Bridport and his flag officers could have corrected this impression, for they had seen everywhere in the anchorage crew unity and vaulting enthusiasm that could not have been forced on the people. Spencer decided on a council-of-war and summoned the senior officers of the fleet to meet next morning at the Fountain Inn.

Four admirals and fourteen post captains reported early Wednesday morning to their lordships. Spencer proposed that they return to their ships, rally their officers and loyal seamen, and while the delegates were absent at meeting, slip cables and take their vessels around to St. Helen's. This would leave *Queen Charlotte* and the fleet delegates isolated, to be overcome by force. Admiral Sir John Colpoys and the captains argued heatedly against the scheme. Bridport was the only one to speak for it. He was not insane, had no sense of humor, and was not kowtowing to the First Lord, so his reason must have been to afford Spencer an illustrative slice of real life should he order this harebrained attempt. Spencer relegated his naval maneuver to the dead file along with the discarded ultimatum.

The possibilities narrowed down to negotiation with the delegates. Spencer posed it rather sarcastically, and the line officers sounded off to a man in favor of giving the seamen most of their demands.

Spencer wanted to know where it would end. If the government yielded, what was to prevent the seamen from making new outrageous demands and refusing to sail until they were met? Suppose they wanted to abolish flogging? The seagoing officers said they believed their people would abide by an honest settlement. Their lordships grudgingly turned to this avenue. They decided to give what the delegates asked, a straight increase across the board of 5s/6d per month for petty officers and able seamen, 4s/6d for ordinaries, and—they stuck to their guns on this—3s/6d for landsmen. Now a boatswain's mate with twenty years' service was going to receive a shilling a day in the King's navy.

The sea lords refused to discuss pensions, rations, and shore leave. They added another ultimatum: this offer had to be accepted immediately. As Conrad Gill put it, "The Lords of the Admiralty felt that they had done their part in conciliating the seamen, and that, to save their self-respect, they must make some show of firmness."

Thursday morning the captains beat for general quarters and read the Admiralty resolution to all hands. The men were pleased. However, on *Duke,* when Captain John Holloway finished, a voice from the back of the crowd sang out, "Wait and see what is done on the *Queen Charlotte.*" The seamen would not move without an order from the delegates. None of the captains was so unwise as to order anchors brought in. Spencer's ultimatum on immediate acceptance was simply forgotten. The delegates left the ships for a meeting on *Queen Charlotte.*

The settlement was going to be postponed for perhaps another day because of their lordships' pretense that there existed no such power as the delegates of the fleet. The remonstrance might have ended, and much worse to come might have been avoided, if the sea lords had sent their reply to the sailors' parliament instead of reading it on each ship in the fashion of a thankful address to his Majesty. Spencer was not acquainted with the etiquette of representative organizations.

As delegates John Richardson and Joseph Tate Green left *Royal Sovereign* for the fleet assembly, Sir Alan Gardner called, "I want you back here promptly and return the lads to duty." But the boats remained clustered alongside *Queen Charlotte* for hours. Gardner could not stand the suspense. Gathering up Admirals Colpoys and Pole, he went to *Queen Charlotte* to harangue the delegates to accept the Admiralty terms.

The three admirals entered the great cabin of *Queen Charlotte* and found that the meeting had not even started. The delegates were waiting for their principal leaders, Valentine Joyce, John Morice, John Hudelstone and Patrick Glynn, to return from a trip ashore. Sir Alan thought their absence gave him an even better opportunity to steer these misguided men back on course. He referred to a fresh command memorandum:

That the effect already produced by the liberal offers of the Admiralty in the several ships' companies is evidently such that they will be ultimately accepted by the fleet; and therefore that if the men from the several ships now assembled in the *Queen Charlotte* do not immediately accede thereto (they being all well known) they may rely upon it that they will be brought to condign punishment and suffer the utmost vengeance of the law. But, on the contrary, should they submit with alacrity, they will experience the forgiveness for which the Board of Admiralty have publickly and solemnly pledged their faith to them.

The delegates did not appreciate the tone of this message, but admitted they liked the terms the sea lords had offered. Sir Alan proposed that they send a letter of thanks to the Admiralty. Nobody objected, so the admiral sat down and began to write it for them. While he was bent over his composition, Joyce and his three henchmen entered. A ripe exchange of extemporaneous oratory took place. Joyce exclaimed that the delegates would be fools to accept any agreement, or submit to their officers, until they had a pardon signed and sealed by the King.

The verbal tempest moved out on the quarterdeck and Joyce appealed to the Charlottes on the forecastle, "How do we know these admirals did not come here to deceive us? Remember the *Culloden!* They hanged the delegates on the *Culloden* after they promised them a pardon." He was bringing up a black article in the sailor's soul.

The *Culloden* mutiny occurred at Spithead in 1794. The ship was old and crank from going aground. When Captain Thomas Troubridge ordered anchor weighed to return to sea, 250 men and six marines unexpectedly barricaded themselves belowdecks, declaring that they would not resume duty until they got a new ship or *Culloden* was drydocked and made seaworthy. Troubridge, who was also a colonel of marines, called out the marine garrison and threatened to swab out the forecastle with bayonets. The challenge failed to bring even the six delinquent lobsterbacks out on deck.

Admiral Lord Bridport went aboard and shouted appeals down to the fortified men. They repeated their demands. Lord Cornwallis addressed the Cullodens, without avail. Several days passed in deadlock. The great disciplinarian, Admiral John Colpoys, was called out to lecture the recalcitrants, but they were deaf to his charms. Captain Troubridge applied for a mutiny court-martial on ten of the protestors.

Lord Bridport received a letter from between decks. It said the demonstrators would "surrender" on condition that they got "a new ship or the old one docked." Or they would settle for "all the people present between decks draughted on board different ships, or as your lordship shall think proper; and your lordship's word and honour not to punish any man concerned in the present business, or to mention or remember it hereafter." The letter was signed "A DELEGATE."

Delegate was a sinister borrowing from the American and French revolutions. It had never been heard before in the British navy. Lord Howe said, "I can hardly imagine consequences more necessary to be guarded against than those not unlikely to be expected from the introduction of *delegates* amongst us."

Apparently there was an Irish complexion to the defiant Cullodens, for on the eighth day of the holdout, the command sent a "Paddy captain," the popular and witty Thomas Pakenham, to entreat with them. (After the First of June battle, another captain had hailed him, "Tommy, d'ye have many killed?" Pakenham yelled back, "Damme if I know. They won't tell me, for fear I should stop their grog.")

What Captain Pakenham said to the men belowdecks is not on record. The Cullodens took down their barricades and obeyed a call to general quarters. Then Captain Troubridge "with great resolution and firmness seized the [ten] principal mutineers," as naval chronicler Isaac Schomberg has it, and tried them on his standing court-martial order. Two were acquitted, three were pardoned, and five were hanged. It was widely believed among seamen that Pakenham had pledged the Cullodens that their leaders would not be punished.

Now Joyce's reminder of the *Culloden* affair brought the men of *Queen Charlotte* aft to give support to the delegates. Sir Alan Gardner lost his mainmast. "You're a damned mutinous blackguard set that deserves hanging!" he bawled at the seamen. "Poor skulking fellows. You know the French are ready for sea and you're afraid to meet them!" He grabbed a man by the collar. "I'll hang you, and I'll hang every fifth man in the fleet," the ex-peacemaker cried. The Charlottes hissed him. The admiral ranted on. The hissing stopped and the Charlottes, shouting in anger, surrounded Gardner and his two colleagues. There is no valid evidence of a laying on of blackened hands on the person of a vice-admiral of the White, but the three admirals were soon sitting in a boat departing *Queen Charlotte.*

Even Paris heard about Admiral Gardner's adventure. A fortnight afterward *Moniteur* said that *"L'amiral Gasner"* had been menaced to be thrown into the sea for having reproached the English *matelôts* with fear of encountering the *français."* The French snickered at the latest odd happening in the land of Jack Rosbif.

Sir Alan Gardner's tribute to the Admiralty lay unsigned in the great cabin while the aroused delegates voted to ignore the counter-offer of the sea lords. They resolved to hold out until his Majesty's pardon was in their hands. Gardner's rampage had divided command and seamen by darker suspicions than had prevailed on Maundy Thursday, now a week in the wake. The glass was falling on "the breeze at Spithead."

The "utmost vengeance" threat referred to by Sir Alan inflamed open sores. Captain Henry Nicholls of *Marlborough,* whose company was trying to prefer court-martial charges against him and three officers for brutality, called his crew forward and read it to them.

"Now, my lads, I ask your answer!"

"No!"

Nobody in the front ranks had opened his mouth. The company went to the forecastle, and presently two delegates approached Nicholls.

"Sir, we request a boat to go to the *Queen Charlotte."*

"Why? Why do you wish to go to the *Charlotte?"*

"Captain, they hung people on the *Cullodon* after they promised to forgive them."

"NO!"

The delegates took the boat.

Late in the afternoon on shore, an officer idly watching the fleet with a telescope exclaimed, "Look at her!" On the fore halyard of *Royal George,* a stopped flag darted aloft against a pewter sky and snapped open on the forepeak. It was a red banner with no device. At the news, white hands trembled in the Fountain Inn and hard brown hands in The George, frequented by senior officers. In the Star and Garter, lieutenants stared unbelievingly at each other, gulped their drinks and ran out to see. Midshipmen crammed buttered rolls at the Blue Posts and mates drained their cans at the Duncan's Head.

The red flag was out of the locker.

It was raised only when the fleet entered battle.

Off in the anchorage, guns were being loaded and run out the ports of the men-of-war. At Portsmouth Point, a boatmen leaped out announcing, "They say Admiral Gardner come out to sow division and mistrust."

When Gardner dined with the sea lords that evening, he evidently did not allude to his behavior on *Queen Charlotte* but gave Spencer the impression that nothing but an actual royal pardon paper with the King's seal and sign manual would induce the fleet to resume obedience. Spencer decided to return to London immediately and ask it of his Majesty.

The fleet delegates convened again that evening. They passed a resolution to Lord Bridport apologizing for replacing his pendant with the red flag and invited him as "father of the fleet" to return to *Royal George*. They told him if it had not been for Gardner's acts, "every tittle of the business would have been settled; but at present it is the resolution of all not to lift anchor till every article is rendered into an Act of Parliament and the King's Pardon to all concerned." They composed "a total and final answer" to Lord Spencer, who was now on the road to London.

> To the Right Honourable the Lords Commissioners of the Admiralty.
>
> We the seamen and marines in and belonging to His Majesty's fleet now lying at Spithead, having received with the utmost satisfaction, and with hearts full of gratitude, the bountiful augmentation of pay and provisions which your Lordships have been pleased to signify shall take place in future in His Majesty's royal navy, by your order, which has been read to us this morning, by the command of Admiral Lord Bridport:
>
> Your Lordships having thus generously taken the prayer of our several petitions into your serious consideration, you have given satisfaction to every loyal and well disposed seaman and marine belonging to His Majesty's fleets: and, from the assurance which your Lordships have given us respecting such other grievances as we thought right to lay before you, we are thoroughly convinced, should any real grievance or other cause of complaint arise in future, and the same be laid before your Lordships in a regular manner, we are perfectly satisfied that your Lordships will pay every attention to a number

of brave men who ever have, and ever will be, true and faithful to their King and country.

But we beg leave to remind your Lordships, that it is a firm resolution that, until the flour in port be removed, the vegetables and pensions augmented, the grievances of private ships redressed, an act passed, and His Majesty's gracious pardon for the fleet now lying at Spithead be granted, that the fleet will not lift an anchor; and this is the total and final answer.

This document followed Lord Spencer who arrived in Whitehall at nine A.M., Saturday, 22 April. He found Pitt in town but his Majesty was at Windsor, looking after private business. Parliament had voted the King an act of enclosure to expropriate part of the village green of New Windsor and today he transmitted the condemnation fee of £700. He also instructed his agent to inspect another common at Winkfield Manor and report whether it would be suitable to seize "for the convenience of the dog kennels." Resentful former users of common lands thought twice about pulling down enclosure fences; it was punishable by death.

The Prime Minister called the cabinet. For a fair spring Saturday, the attendance was good. Pitt's brother, Lord Chatham, the Lord President of the Council and former first sea lord (who was trying to undermine Spencer and get the job back); the Lord Chancellor, Lord Loughborough; the home secretary, the Duke of Portland; Marquis Cornwallis, Master-General of the Ordnance; Foreign Secretary Lord Grenville; and Henry Dundas, Secretary of War and treasurer of the navy.* They approved Spencer's last offer to the seamen and addressed a minute to the King: "It is agreed humbly to recommend to your Majesty forthwith to issue your Royal Proclamation offering your gracious and full pardon to all seamen and marines serving in the [Spithead] fleet, and on such proclamation being notified to them, return to the regular and ordinary discharge of their duty according to the rules and practice of the navy." Pitt, Spencer and Loughborough left for Windsor to secure the royal pardon without delay.

At Spithead, Bridport advised the delegates of Spencer's mission and they settled down to wait. The delegates authorized *Concorde,* 36, and the sloop *Scourge* to sail with a merchant convoy, and re-

---

* There were two "war" ministers in the cabinet, the Secretary *of* War (Henry Dundas), who was the actual war minister, and the Secretary *at* War (William Windham, M.P.), who was merely secretary of the army.

leased *Niger*, 32, to accompany freighters bound for London. When the freighters were safely in the Thames, *Niger* would drop off in the great miscellaneous fleet anchorage of the Nore off Sheerness where her men would be able to give the first eyewitness accounts of the business at Spithead to interested brother seamen.

Pitt and the ministers arrived at Windsor Castle at nine o'clock. They were relieved when the King agreed readily to the pardon proclamation. While compositors were setting type for a hundred copies, Spencer wrote to Bridport on how to use them to best effect. He wanted the captains to read the pardon to the ships' companies and to dramatize the end flourish, "God Save the King"; "in order, if it yet be possible, to secure in the minds of these deluded people that loyalty which it may be too much apprehended the late melancholy events have damped." The First Lord asked Bridport to return to *Royal George* and hoist his flag during the ceremonies. If the seamen insisted on removal of certain officers, the captains were to reply, "After your complete return to your duty in the terms of the King's royal proclamation, if there is any real grievance or complaint that can be fairly and properly stated through your commander-in-chief, all due attention shall be paid to it. But no officer can possibly be removed in any other manner than what is proscribed by the established rules and invariable practice of the service."

Night riders brought the pardon proclamations to Portsmouth by early Sunday morning. The captains read them to their companies. Lord Bridport gave the text on *Royal George* and added his personal pledge of complete righting of the wrongs. The Royal Georges cheered and removed the yard ropes, the mace-of-office of the Spithead parliamentary navy. Now that it had triumphed, the commissioned officers of the King could resume power.

The officers held up the pardon paper, but the people in the back of the crowd pointed out that the delegates still had not received a reply to their Total and Final resolution. They had no settlement in writing on wages, victuals, pensions, treatment of the sick, or officer abuses. If the agreement was to have any value, it had to be enacted by Parliament. And where was the answer of the darling of the fleet, Charles James Fox, to whom their resolutions had been sent?

Admiral Pole read the royal pardon on *Queen Charlotte*. There was no applause. Their delegates challenged him to show a pardon signed and sealed by the King, not the printed version. Fortunately Bridport had received the holograph copy and it was exhibited to the Charlottes. They made dutiful cheers and unreeved the yard ropes.

With the indomitable Charlottes voluntarily returning to obedience without even waiting for a reply to the total and final demands, the breeze at Spithead seemed to be over. Tomorrow or sharply thereafter, Bridport could take the Channel fleet out and confound the French invasion menace.

Monday morning Bridport marshaled the Channel fleet for sea. During the unusual fortnight past, the ships had been provisioned as though nothing were happening. The Marlboroughs, the Minotaurs, and Ramillies and the Nymphes were still testy about unpopular officers. Some of their charges against officers were: Surgeon Bell of *Minotaur* for inattention to the sick, not being qualified, and being drunk when he went to the sick bay. Gunner John England was accused of punching a man in the mouth, calling one an Irish rascal, overturning washtubs, and "what gives more offence, he advised the company to be moderate in the attempts they were engaged in." The Nymphes charged their captain and lieutenants with cruel punishment: they had given three dozen stripes to a boatswain's mate for "not turning the people up quick enough," to a seaman for "pissing in the manger," and to another for "being extremely filthy and dirty." Lieutenant Lawrence of *Nymphe* was accused of having a man beaten by the boatswain's mate and then beating the mate for "not punishing the man more severely."

The Admiralty had not answered these charges, so Bridport left the four aggrieved ships lying at Spithead under the command of Sir John Colpoys in H.M.S. *London,* while he took six sail-of-the-line to St. Helen's to await immediate sailing orders.

In the evening the sea lords sent down their reply to the Total and Final demand of the sailors' parliament of three days before. According to regulations, it was couched as a message from Nepean to Bridport.

The sea lords refused to institute honest measures of provisions or to stop substituting flour for meat, saying that there was a general meat shortage, but, "it has always been their Lordships' intention to cause the full proportion of fresh beef to be supplied."

Claiming that the fleet received more fresh vegetables while in port "than was ever served in any former war," their lordships thought the men "should be most thankful for that . . . instead of unreasonably asking for more."

There would be no appropriation to increase the out-pensions at Greenwich Hospital.

There would be no removal of officers without application through channels for courts-martial, and "as the character of officers are not to be lightly attacked, the seamen should be admonished not to prefer any complaint against them without having good cause for so doing."

Finally, their lordships saw "a favourable change" and "were inclined to hope that all animosities have ceased and that the complaints which were brought forward in a moment of ill-humour may now be suffered to drop."

Presented with this adamant reply, the Portsmouth command simply suppressed it. It was not transmitted to the seamen. It was too explosive. Most of the ships had returned to discipline and were ready to set to sea. If the Admiralty reply got out at St. Helen's, who knows but what the delegates would seize the ships and take them over to the enemy? If the men knew nothing of the paper, the unsolved issues could probably be dissipated by hard discipline on a long cruise or erased by battle.

Spencer wrote Bridport congratulating him on the "termination of the mutiny and to express the great additional satisfaction that I feel on hearing by the Telegraph that a part of the fleet was actually in motion this morning."

But a treacherous element prevented Bridport from leaving St. Helen's. The wind shifted. It was too strong to venture into, although, sheltered by the Isle of Wight, the rest of the fleet was able to slip down from Spithead, leaving only Admiral Colpoys aboard *London* to police *Marlborough, Ramillies, Nymphe* and *Minotaur*. The first sea lord wrote Bridport that these ships were held "in order if possible to get the better of the separate complaints of some of those ships or to bring them into a state of regular Enquiry."

Whitehall yearned to place as many ships as possible in the Channel. The Prince de Bouillon, a British agent in the Bureau de la Marine in Paris, had sent a long report of troops massing at Brest and an invasion fleet growing. The Lord Lieutenant of Ireland had sent "a most secret and confidential" letter to Portland, stating that the Irish rebels were intensively recruiting with "an assurance that the French are likely to come to Ireland immediately." On 25 April, Lord Spencer wrote privately to Bridport, to accompany urgent sailing orders: "The uneasiness that prevails in London on account of the fleet remaining at Spithead [and St. Helen's] and still more the very great alarm in Ireland on the expectation . . . of an almost immediate attack from the Enemy, make it a matter of absolute necessity for your lordship to shew yourself at sea with as large a squadron as the general state of things will admit of."

Bridport could do nothing about Whitehall's emergencies. A whistling gale swept St. Helen's on Wednesday, 26 April. The fleet parliament had voluntarily dissolved; when was the Westminster Parliament going to honor Spencer's pledge of a pay rise? The sad fact was that the nation's Parliament had not been approached yet. Only today, five days after he left Portsmouth, did Spencer submit the "proposed increases" of fleet provisions and pay to the first echelon of the lawmaking process, the privy council, an appointed body which initiated money bills for Parliament. The council named a subcommittee to study the matter and the subcommittee, hearing that the disturbance was over, saw no urgency in it. The seamen's demand was considered ill-timed.

Pitt was presenting the legislature with a punishing national budget, which included £5½ million for the Emperor of Austria, Britain's last ally left in the field against the French Revolution. The increased revenue was to be raised by vaulting the taxes on consumer goods and doubling the tolls on turnpikes. The Prime Minister told the King that Fox had spoken against the estimates, "chiefly to aggravate the difficulties," and his Majesty replied sympathetically that it should "convince every impartial man that from personal pique at me and my administration, he has become the open enemy of his country."

By the last week of April, two weeks after the original manifestations, the privy council had still failed to send the fleet pay bill to Parliament. On the 26th, in the debate on the budget, Pitt promised that the pay increase "will become the subject of a specific discussion upon an early day." He had not yet heard of an outbreak of mutiny at Plymouth that morning.

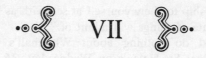

VII

The Liberty at Plymouth

> I believe that the peak of British culture was reached in
> the latter years of George III; that the rot began to set
> in with the "Romantics"; that the apparent prosperity
> of Victoria's reign was autumnal not vernal; and that
> now we are done for.
> —T. H. WHITE
> —*The Age of Scandal* (1950)

IN PLYMOUTH SOUND, Cawsand Bay and the Hamoaze, the lake-like estuary of the Tamar River at Plymouth, there were a dozen men-of-war and many smaller craft in from channel patrols or foreign stations. One was *Porcupine,* which had left Spithead several days after the protest began. She had brought the first lower-deck version of those events to Plymouth. At eight A.M. on the 26th, the ship's company of *Atlas,* 98, in Plymouth Sound, assembled without orders and gave three cheers, which were returned from the neighboring two-deckers *Saturn* and *Majestic.* The first lieutenant of *Atlas,* acting for his absent captain, Matthew Squire, called the Atlases to the quarter-deck and asked their intentions. A gnomic voice hidden in the crowd said, "We will show all respect to officers and obey every command except in going to sea, unless proofs appear that the enemy's fleet is at sea."

A voice asked the first officer to read out some articles to the ship's company, "which," he said, "I thought prudent not to deny." A paper came into his hand from the crowd:

> We the Ship's Company of HM Ship *Atlas* have unan-
> imously resolved to stand to the following Articles
> 1st That every person on Board pay due respect to his Offrs
> as before, & discharge the Ship's duty in every respect as for-

merly, excepting in going to Sea, before going to Spithead—
unless proofs appear of the Enemy's fleet being at Sea—
2nd That no person belonging to the Ship be admitted to go
on Shore excepting Officers & Boats Crews on duty—
3rd That no liquor be admitted on Board & any person or
person's being Intoxicated and behaving in a Contemptible
manner shall be liable to such punishment as the Ship's
Company shall find meet—
4th That we being unacquainted with the requests of the fleet
at Spithead we are willing to comply to the terms which may
be accepted of by them—
5th Any person or persons deviating from these Articles,
shall be punished as the Majority of the Ship's Company shall
find meet—
NB   In case of Weighing Anchor for Spithead a Blue flag will
be shewn at the for(e) topgall Masthead, & a Blue flag, at the
Mizenpeek for a Boat every morning at 9 O Clock for the
squadron to come on Board the *Atlas*—

The first lieutenant asked for the original and the Atlases let him
have it. A spokesman said, "We ask permission for a boat to go on
board the *Saturn, Majestic* and *Edgar,* to make known the resolution." The lieutenant said, "I advise you to pay particular respects
to the officers of his Majesty's ships that you board." After the boat
had left, the acting captain found that the ship's company had already
broken the marine corporals and sergeants and replaced them with
privates, and had changed the sentinels. When the delegates' boat
returned, the lieutenant said, "They have deviated from your first
article." A delegate replied, "If that was done, it was not the voice
of the ship's company. It shall be immediately countermanded."

The *Atlas* delegates had made quite a stir on *Edgar*. The leader
mobilized the lower deck and asked Captain John McDougall if he
might read the articles. "No," said the captain. Before he could speak
further, a seaman bounded past him and took possession of the
arms chests on the poop deck and descended to secure the powder
magazines. McDougall "judged it prudent to yield" in order to be
free to report to the Admiralty.

That morning in the Hamoaze lay *Leviathan,* 74, recently in from
the West Indies. Her captain, John Thomas Duckworth, a tall bony
man with an enormous nose and a small quirky mouth, was ashore
in the dockyard office writing to the Admiralty for things needed to
restore his ship to fitness. He had already requested a remedy for

"the very great hardship we [captains] labour under from our salary's being quite inadequate," and was now listing cordage, spars, and naval stores. He signed impressment warrants to replace yellow fever deaths in the crew on the Jamaica station. He made out Dead Tickets, which would entitle the mothers or widows to a year's pay and unmarried orphans to a third of that.

Five U. S. citizens petitioned Duckworth for release. Richard Mumford of Providence, Rhode Island, had been in forced servitude for four years. The other unwilling Leviathans were Anthony Sneel of Dighton, Massachusetts, John Canby and William Clark of New York City and Walter Pearce, another Rhode Islander.

The Leviathans had not been paid for two years, going back almost as far as their conspicuous part in winning the Glorious First of June battle. Now they were not permitted ashore after more than a year in the tropics. They had not yet received fresh rations and were eating what was left in the holds after the long cruise, mainly "rotten cheese, rotten beef and sour beer."

While Captain Duckworth was prosecuting his paper work ashore, delegates from *Atlas* boarded his ship. He heard a stir in the dockyard office and looked around to see his commissioned officers standing mournfully behind him. The Leviathans had put them ashore, and his first lieutenant, William Buchanan, had the painful duty to impart the news that the crew had also "disbanded" Captain Duckworth.

The worthy commander was dumbfounded; his first reaction was to marvel at the ingratitude of his people. Then he exploded properly. He sent Buchanan back to the ship to bring the men back to their senses. They responded to general quarters. Buchanan said, "Captain Duckworth has resolved never to command such a set of villains till he has proved to the world through a court-martial your baseness and his innocence." An unidentified voice from the crowd said, "The captain may prove it to the world but not to us. He may command the ship but not us."

The distraught Duckworth suffered audibly and got some advice from an admiral. "Have your officers apply for courts-martial and challenge people from the crew to come forth with charges. If the charges are unfounded, it might possibly expose them to at least a risk of punishment." The Leviathans recognized this as a trap for their leaders, and left Duckworth and their officers on the beach. The captain began writing private and official letters to London, protesting his virtue.

Later that morning the royal proclamation of pardon for the Spithead mutineers was read on the Plymouth ships. At the same time, from parties and by means unknown, a rank-and-file letter arrived from Spithead and was rapidly communicated among the ships' companies. Captain Squire of *Atlas,* who did not see the letter and was not on board to hear it, left the only gloss: *"If you do not support your comrades at Spithead, you will be treated 'very ill' when we meet again."* *

A rider came into Plymouth with an Admiralty letter sent two days earlier to Admiral Sir John Orde, the officer commanding at Plymouth: "The business at Spithead is at length terminated and the ships have returned to their duty." This was slightly vague; there were four big ships still holding out. Before daylight closed, Orde received a message by shutter telegraph from Portsmouth that some of Bridport's crews had obeyed orders to weigh anchor and were moving under regular discipline to St. Helen's. Admiral Orde spread this among his ships. The men did not respond. Voices in the rear insistently called for confirmation from the Spithead delegates.

The next morning, the 27th, the Plymouth fleet representatives met on *Atlas* and designated her as "the Parliament Ship," with two delegates from each vessel. They asked the authorities to permit them to send two or three men from each vessel to Spithead. The forecastle senate emphasized its authority by taking down mainyards and topgallant masts. Individual ships' companies were busy in the meantime drawing up disciplinary codes, such as this one nailed to a mainmast:

> An Act passed amongst the Crew of His
> Majesty's Ship *Saturn* which will be
> strictly and severely enforced.

1st   Every Man or Men who shall deviate or turn their Coats to their Brethren in the present case engaged shall suffer death.

2nd   Any Man or Men who shall treat any Officer with the least contempt shall suffer two dozen Lashes and further punishment if the case require.

3d   If any Man or Men shall at any time hear any Master's Mate or Midshipman, for whose benefit our Brother Sailors have stood as well as their own, utter any words tending to say the Ships Company is in any

---

* The letter does not sound like one from the Spithead delegates, whose surviving documents to new ships are couched in cordial and brotherly tones.

state of mutiny, and does not make the same known, shall suffer if convicted the like punishment as the offender.

4th   Any Man who shall disobey his superior officer on any part of the Ship's duty, shall suffer one dozen Lashes, besides three times ducking at the Yard Arm.

5thly   We do hereby unanimously one and all heart and hand agree that no Man or Men shall be pointed out as the Chief or Chiefs Instigators, or to suffer any punishment whatsoever for this case, or shall we suffer ourselves to be separated on this account to any Ship whatsoever, and we do hereby further agree that there shall be no Man reflected upon for this case, and when it is proved that our Brothers are doing their duty as before at Spithead, we shall immediately comply with our Captain to carry the Ship to any place where he may receive his orders for.

SATURN'S

The first sea lord, acting from his belief that the Spithead remonstrance was over, wrote Bridport suggesting that he sail his squadron to Plymouth, saying, "Your lordship's appearance off Plymouth would be a very strong confirmation that all has happily terminated at Spithead." Bridport, in his rocking, wind-beset cabin, could do nothing about this latest helpful hint from London.

Admiral Orde reported from Plymouth to the sea lords that his people were appointing new petty officers and flogging transgressors. The admiral could not yet make up his mind about permitting delegates to go to Portsmouth. Court-martial, relegation, or, at best, retirement on half-pay awaited a commanding officer who assisted fractious seamen. On 28 April an officer of *Saturn* showed his crew a letter from a lieutenant on H.M.S. *Terrible* at Spithead, which declared that every grievance of the seamen had been redressed. "I wish to God they could prove to us that everything is settled," a *Saturn* delegate remarked to Captain James Douglas before taking a boat to visit *Atlas*. The *Atlas* delegates came over to look at the letter. They took it off to show to the Edgars. This two-decker, first to respond to *Atlas*'s initiative, was dominated by voices in the crowd rather than by elected delegates:

"The letter is false!"

"Why won't they let us send people to Spithead?"

"The delegates go to Spithead, or we hang the delegates!"

The *Edgar's* delegates were happy to go down the side along with their legislative colleagues. That night the Plymouth parliament resolved to enter no negotiations before its emissaries had been allowed to visit Portsmouth and report back. Captains Squire and McDougall pleaded with Admiral Orde to let the delegates go. They reminded him that all women had been sent ashore from *Atlas* that day and that the strikers were capable of carrying the ships off to sea. Orde called a captains' meeting and all of them recommended that he let the delegates go. Orde adjourned the meeting and then told the captains privately that he would look the other way if a few people left the ships. The captains of *Atlas* and *Saturn* requested funds to pay their crews. They believed the men would sail if paid back wages. Orde refused: it would make trouble with other captains. And he didn't have the money. The captains went to Captain Robert Fanshawe, commissioner of the Admiralty at Plymouth who was Orde's superior, and he gave them the wages.

Orde wrote to the Admiralty, tattling on the captains and the commissioner. He said, "The poor deluded men are in the hands of artful wicked advisors," and that, by paying them, the captains and the commissioner had only "turned the [sailors'] heads and increased the commotions." Eight delegates left that afternoon, cheered by the ships and primed by travel expenses contributed from the flush of money suddenly come aboard. They were able to hire a fast coaster for Portsmouth.

Sir John Orde received an Admiralty order to board all refractory vessels, muster the companies, and *"state to them distinctly that all is settled at Portsmouth."* He was to serve a one-hour ultimatum to return to duty. For the chore he sent Captain John Pakenham of *Gibraltar,* 80; Duckworth of *Leviathan,* and the commander of *Magnanime,* not to their own resentful ships, but to *Atlas, Saturn, Edgar* and *Majestic.* The captains came back ruffled. The Edgars had treated them with "utmost contempt." Aboard *Atlas* "the marines mixed on the forecastle with the seamen," and when the captains started to speak, the company went below, leaving only indifferent listeners.

The Plymouth delegation sailed into St. Helen's, boarded *Royal George* and talked with Joyce and Morice, the leaders of the dissolved forecastle assembly, who assured them that the government had complied with all their demands and that the remonstrance was over. The men from Plymouth then proceded to Portsmouth and put the good news into a letter which they entrusted to a steward named

Glover to take back to the Plymouth ships. They dismissed their charter boat and decided to treat themselves to a ride back on a stage-coach. As a protection against the press gang they requested over-land passes from Sir Peter Parker. The admiral replied, "You have no passes from Admiral Orde to come here. Make the best of your way back."

The most distant ocean force engaged in defense of the home islands, the Mediterranean fleet, on station off Cadiz, showed signs of deteriorating morale. This was nothing new to its admiral, Old Jarvey, soon to be proclaimed Lord St. Vincent for his victory over the Dons at Cape St. Vincent. Although no word had yet arrived to command or men of the Spithead rising. Old Jarvey's frowning eye fell on "a state of licentiousness" in *Britannia*. He reported it to London, attributing it to "the notorious imbecility of Sir Charles Knowles," her captain. The First Lord replied, "You will have heard of the sad work of that kind we have had here," and told him about Spithead. Immediately, Old Jarvey acted to head off troubles that might come rippling from the home anchorage. He called the squad-ron's marine captains and covered the unusual event with a buzz that he was lecturing them on smart dress and drill. He said, "I gave them some sense about keeping a watchful eye, not only upon their own men, but upon the seamen. I directed that a subaltern should visit [the marines and seamen] at their meals; I exhorted them to keep up the pride and spirit in their detachments; to prevent conversation being carried on in Irish, and to call the roll at least twice a day."

Old Jarvey also issued a general order to his fleet. It is a souvenir of the great mutiny still observed in the Royal Navy: the marines to parade every morning at 8:30 on the poop, to descend to the quarter-deck at nine and present arms as the entire company stands at general quarters with hats off and the band plays "God Save the King." Old Jarvey put on his full dress uniform every morning for his anti-mutiny ritual and once jumped from the poop onto the back of a midshipman who forgot to remove his bonnet.

In Holland, Wolfe Tone, returning from his meeting with General Hoche, was sailing from the Hague for Amsterdam in a *trakschuyt,* a passage boat, to take up his post with the invasion fleet. He en-countered Citizen van Amstel, a deputy of the Batavian republic, who said, "I suppose you have heard that there has been a mutiny in the English fleet. The seamen nearly threw the admiral overboard."

"This is too good news to be true."

"They have tried, condemned and hanged one of their comrades for opposing their measures."

"If this be true, I regard it as scarcely less important than the peace with the [Austrian] emperor."

The surrender of Austria left Britain without an ally in Europe by May Day. The main shield of the kingdom, the Channel fleet, lay helpless, deactivated by its own seamen. Fortunately for Britain, Lazare Hoche was still occupied on the eastern front; and until he could turn his energies and influence to the invasion force, there was a breathing spell in the Channel.

At the Texel, with the coming of spring, the Dutch amphibious fleet grew larger in the Waddenzee. Just outside in the North Sea, seventeen British sail patrolled endlessly, boringly, sending luggers home with periodic reports of enemy strength. This British North Sea squadron had been scratched together from near-carcasses two years earlier after the French invested Holland in a wild winter campaign that included such feats as infantry winning battles on ice skates and cavalry capturing ships frozen in the Waddenzee.

When the immediate necessity of creating a deterrent North Sea fleet fell upon the Admiralty, Lord Spencer, who was new to the First Lord's job, asked the help of Henry Dundas, the experienced navy treasurer, in picking a commander for the crucial seafront. Going down the list, Spencer said, "What can be the reason that Duncan has never been brought forward?" Dundas replied, "I think he would like employment. He married my niece." And so Spencer, the renegade Whig, and Dundas, the King's man, chose Adam Duncan, an unregenerate Whig, because of the dominant ties of blood and interest. It proved a good choice. Duncan was a robust, determined and magnetic man of six-foot four, who, figuratively as well, stood head and shoulders above the crowd. When he got to know his ships he warned Spencer that the people of the patched-together squadron were grumbling bitterly over their outworn, cranky vessels, bad food and absence of pay. Spencer blithely replied, "It will hardly make a difficulty for so short a cruise, and the ship's company may be paid as soon as she returns."

Duncan asked the Admiralty to issue his people trawls and fishing lines and hooks to catch fresh fish "for the preservation of their health." He requested a wine issue for the sick and a daily ration of lemon juice for each seaman. In some cases, the big Scotsman was more demanding than his most disgruntled hand. He wanted the

Admiralty to issue the men free tobacco and soap, pay ships regularly even when on foreign station, make a more equitable and prompter distribution of prize money, and render the purser strictly account- able to the captain. He also desired swearing punished in the old way by laying a hot spike on the offender's tongue. Finally, he delivered himself of the supreme heresy: "As to pressing, if possible [it] should be put an end to [and used] only in emergency."

Admiral Duncan had once experienced a mutiny over tardy pay; at Spithead in 1779, when he was captain of *Monarch,* 74, his men refused to weigh anchor until paid. Duncan himself had twice refused to serve in the West Indies on medical grounds, but insubordination among captains was not called mutiny. They were merely put on shore on half pay until a new crisis came and the Admiralty needed everybody.

On his left hand Duncan wore a curious double ring connecting his ring finger and little finger. He had rendered the smaller digit permanently numb and limp on the skull of a member of a mob in a street fight in Edinburgh in 1792. He was defending his Majesty's honor on the occasion.

Duncan's ships were stepchildren of Admiralty. While they were drawn from the major fleet base of the Nore at the mouth of the Thames and were paid and provisioned there, they sailed from Great Yarmouth, a hundred miles closer to the Texel. Yarmouth was near Norwich, a busy center of reform and republican feeling.

While mutiny simmered on Duncan's cranky cruisers on the out- side, it was boiling in the Dutch fleet inside the Texel. Most Dutch seamen preferred the prewar rations, pay and nonbelligerency of the House of Orange, to the short rations, slow pay and fight talk of the French-sponsored Batavian republic. Desertions kept the invasion ships under strength. The situation at the Texel was such that Dun- can and his opponent might come to solve their common labor prob- lems by pitting the malcontents in battle.

One of Duncan's ships was an old 64-gun, *Director,* with a crew of 491 men. Early in April, while "exercizing the great guns," some of her crew suddenly became derelict. Six men were flogged for shirk- ing their duties. The captain gave the customary punishment of eight to eighteen lashes apiece. During the following days he ordered five more men to be whipped for neglect of duty. This flurry of punish- ments was unusual for *Director.* Her captain, forty-three-year-old William Bligh, was not a persecutor, although out of hearing his sailors called him "The Bounty Bastard."

He was the famous Bligh of the epic mutiny near Tofoa Island eight years before.* After the *Bounty* business, when he returned from his second breadfruit voyage and paid off his vessels at Woolwich, *The Kentish Register* noted, "The high estimation in which Captain Bligh was deservedly held by the whole crew, was conspicuous to all present. He was cheered on quitting the ship . . . and at the dock-gates the men drew up and repeated the parting acclamation."

The stocky brown-eyed Cornishman was one of the most accomplished professional officers in the service and a fellow of the Royal Society. He came out of the scientific cult of Captain James Cook, under whom he had served at the age of twenty-two as the sailing master of *Resolution* on the tragic third circumnavigation. Bligh drew the first accurate coastal charts of Hawaii and acted as expedition cartographer throughout the 1776-79 global rounding. After Cook was killed in the surf at Hawaii, Bligh led a party that recovered what was left of his body. He brought Cook's ships home and helped to edit the journal of the voyage. The Admiralty often employed Bligh as a hydrographer of bays and harbors, an art blending the highest navigational skills—triangulating land features, constant celestial fixes, and a running correlation of log speed, soundings, and draftsmanship.

Captain Bligh and *Director* returned to Yarmouth Tuesday, 25 April, with the rest of Duncan's neglected and apprehensive ships. They had been out seven weeks. For an unexplained reason, Duncan had disregarded an Admiralty order to return ten days earlier. By now the North Sea wind had turned westerly and as long as it prevailed, the Dutch could not come out. When the squadron dropped its hooks in Yarmouth Roads, news of the Spithead mutiny quickly spread among the crews. Duncan distributed Admiralty reassurances that the fleet's grievances had been remedied. Bligh read them to his company, which listened without evident emotion.

The Directors may have known of the Channel fleet's resolve as early as February when the Charlottes were drawing up the initial

---

* Bligh's reputation has suffered less from three English mutinies than from two American movies. He is also mistaken for two other contemporaneous Captain Blighs in the King's navy. Captain Richard Rodney Bligh of *Alexander*, 74, was captured by the French in 1794. He was exchanged, routinely court-martialed for losing, and acquitted. Captain John Bligh was involved in the 1797 mutiny. A mutinous ship from Spithead, the *Latona* went around to the Nore sans her captain. John Bligh was appointed captain. The Latonas expelled him, too.

petition. Bligh's rickety ship had spent January and February at anchor in the Humber River and Yarmouth Roads. Eleven whippings for insubordination on *Director* from 10 to 17 April may have had some connection with the Spithead outbreak the 16th, a conjecture that gains interest from Duncan's staying on billet ten days after ordered home: did he know mutiny was brewing and remain at sea to reduce the infection? Was there an agreement between seamen of the Channel fleet and the North Sea fleet to strike simultaneously on 18 April? If so, did Duncan abort it by cruising on and past the date? Duncan knew more about the thoughts of his men than he reported to the Admiralty.

In London, the spring social calendar went on as usual. Sheridan's *The School for Scandal* had just closed, freeing the leading lady, Miss Warren, for her marriage to the Earl of Derby. Elizabeth O'Connor received the death sentence for shoplifting. The same was meted out to James Andrews for returning from transportation to Australia. The Newgate hangman was looking forward to inheriting the clothing of six housebreakers, two highwaymen, a forger and a man convicted of stealing wine.

Throughout the kingdom the Lent assizes had been busy. One hundred and ten persons were sentenced to death and forty-six were executed, the balance consisting of souls commuted for years to solitary, the hulks, hard labor, or transportation. The crown was stocking Australia with the sturdy breed that was to return in later wars and uphold the monarchy. English juries acquitted many capital offenders, almost outscoring the King's bench in the hanging game. The veniremen may not have been permitted to vote for representatives to Parliament, but they voted liberally against the bloody code.

Two future heads of state took brides in London that season. John Quincy Adams, son of the U. S. President, married an American girl, Louisa Johnson, at Great Tower Hill. And the capital was looking forward to the wedding of Charlotte, the Princess Royal. Due to Papa's Royal Marriage Act and her sheltered life in the queen's sewing circle, Charlotte had waited a long time for Lochinvar. He was a screened selection from Stuttgart, his serene highness the hereditary Prince of Württemberg. He was a round, swarthy little man who owned the world's largest collection of Holy Bibles, 9,000 of them in various editions and tongues. He turned up in London a month before he was expected with his suite, Baron Goerbitz and Count

Zippelin. In the secretariat of state, George Canning drew the chore of amusing and edifying the unexpected visitors. He fobbed them off on Sir Joseph Banks, president of the Royal Society, who just as promptly dispatched them on a tour of Bath, Bristol, Birmingham, Oxford and Portsmouth. Württemberg received the diffident civic honors of Portsmouth while the port was locked in mutiny, and the red flag was borne through the streets. Bridport barged him through the fleet and the mutineers gave him three hearty cheers.

Canning complained over the royal wedding papers, which took "as much care and attention as the most serious and important negotiation in the world. The Treaty of Peace, whenever that comes to be made, will not be half so much trouble—not to mention that there is rather more satisfaction in bringing the nations of the world to a good understanding with each other than in coupling all the Princes and Princesses on earth for their own private convenience and satisfaction."

George Caning wrote to Evan Nepean, secretary of the Admiralty, as an oblique reminder that the sea lords had better get the ships back into service since the Prince of Waldeck, another state visitor, was headed for Portsmouth "to take passage on a frigate for Lisbon."

Pitt's spy De Bouillon, who had journeyed to Brest to observe the fleet preparations, reported to London "redoubled activity" in constructing sixty-foot infantry landing craft.

Aboard *Mars*, at St. Helen's, Samuel Nelson, ship's watchmaker, took surgeon's mate James White aside and said, "What a state the ship's company is in, Mr. White."

"What do you mean?"

"Why, sir, I will assure you the company is very dissatisfied."

"Why?"

"They say the Admiralty is trifling with them in regard to their allowance of victuals."

"Why, Nelson, I thought everybody was satisfied."

"O dear, sir, not by any means. . . . Sir, if you will not say anything, I will tell you something that will surprise you."

"Let it be what it will, I shan't trouble my head with it."

"Well then, Mr. White, the ship's company has agreed that if the Admiralty has not complied with everything they proposed before they go to sea, they are determined to take the ship to Brest."

"Why, is there a man in the ship who can take her to Brest?"

"O dear, sir, many of the forecastle men could."

"In what manner would they take the ship into Brest?"

"Under French colors, sir. And you may depend on it, sir, it is not our ship in particular, but the fleet."

"Is every ship the same way of thinking?"

"Yes, sir. Nothing is transacted aboard any ship, but what the others know."

James White reported this conversation to Captain Alexander Hood of *Mars,* who passed it on to his cousin, Lord Bridport.

On Sunday afternoon, 30 April, at Yarmouth, Admiral Duncan was in his cabin on *Venerable,* 74, when he heard his people give three rousing cheers at the wrong time of day. He stepped out on the quarterdeck. The Venerables were massed on the forecastle and shrouds. Duncan sent for his officers and the marine detachment. The marines formed a menacing line on the poop rail. From across the water cheers rolled back from *Nassau,* 64.

Duncan went to the mainmast, "What is the cause of this?" he demanded. There was no reply. He pointed to five men in the front rank and ordered the others to disperse. The crowd broke up. The five men stood attentive to Duncan. The admiral had the drummers sound general quarters. The Venerables reassembled. Now that the gathering was constitutional, Duncan spoke loudly to the five men he had chosen. "Why have you come against me?"

"We thought there was no harm in it," said one of them, "as our friends at Spithead have done so. We wish to know when our increased pay and provisions is to commence."

Duncan proclaimed that they need not fear; the pay and provisions were secured and on their way. The crew appeared to believe him completely. "Having satisfied them on this head," said Duncan, "I pointed out the enormity of the crime of mutiny and pardoned the offenders. Good order was again established." Before he let them go, Duncan publicly thanked the marines for their loyal support.

Duncan's facedown with the Venerables was the best news the Admiralty had received since the business began. Lady Spencer was moved to write him her regrets "that we do not have more Adam Duncans. However, since we can't cut him up into several pieces (tho' there is certainly enough of him to make many reasonable-sized men), we must be contented with having one of that name who will keep the North Sea fleet in good order. God bless you, my dear Admiral."

The same day Lady Spencer's husband, the first sea lord, was writing privately, "The Channel fleet is now absolutely lost to the country as much as it was at the bottom of the sea. The blow . . . is in its effects incalculable." Spencer's despair may have influenced an extraordinary Admiralty general order that he sent out next day, the first of May. Or Pitt may have forced it on Spencer.

The order went to the world-girdling commands:

—The Right Honble. Lord Bridport, Admiral of the White, St. Helen's
—Adam Duncan Esq., Admiral of the Blue, Yarmouth
—Sir John Jervis K.B., Admiral of the Blue, Lisbon
—Sir Hyde Parker, Knt., Vice Admiral of the Red, Jamaica
—Henry Harvey Esq., Rear Admiral of the Red, Leeward Islands
—Peter Rainier Esq., Rear Admiral of the White, East Indies
—Thomas Pringle Esq., Rear Admiral of the Blue, Cape of Good Hope

It began:

Whereas by the dispositions lately shewn by the seamen belonging to several of His Majesty's Ships, it has become highly necessary that the strictest attention should be paid by all officers in His Majesty's Naval Service, not only to their own conduct but to the conduct of those who may be under orders.

It ordered that:
—Officers frequently muster the crews
—Captains' and officers' shore leaves be limited to 24 hours.
—Officers wear uniforms at all times, afloat and ashore.
—Officers read the Articles of War to the men once a month.
—Officers keep the marines' "arms and ammunition in good order and fit for immediate service."
—Officers be "very careful to rate their ship's companies according to the merit of the men, in order that those who may not be deserving thereof, may not receive the pay of Able, or Ordinary Seamen."
—Officers pay "particular attention to the regulations relating to the cutting up of fresh beef, that choice pieces be never purposely selected for the officers from that which is cut up for the ship's company, and that choice pieces of salt meat be never taken for the officers out of the tub or vessel from which it may be served the ship's company."

—Officers not pick out the best casks of wine or spirits from ship's provisions, or trade any of their own for them.

—Captains were to "strictly enjoin" surgeons from pilfering medicines or necessaries.

And finally:

> That the captains and commanders of His Majesty's ships be particularly attentive to the conduct of the men under their command and that they be ready on the first appearance of mutiny to use the most vigorous means to suppress it, and to bring the ringleaders to punishment.

Admiral Bridport seems to have regarded the general order as a disaster. Next day, or the one following, he wrote a secret letter to Spencer, which has not been preserved, but, judging from Spencer's reply of 4 May, must have been a wail of impending doom. After imparting it to their officers, most captains tried to forget the document, but corners and slants on it were talked of when the men saw officers minding their uniforms, inspecting the marine battle chests, and inventorying surgeon's stores.

To men who had just won a great contest over their employers, the general order was bound to increase resentment. It tightened up intimidation, surveillance and distrust. The advice to disrate "undeserving" people would seem to be adding the threat of pay cuts to the snarl of the lash. It singled out "ringleaders" for condign punishment, while dozens of ringleaders were still waiting for Whitehall to make good a nonretaliatory agreement.

The officers disliked being told to limit themselves to overnight leaves and to stop nobbling food and wine. Surgeons were inferentially accused of stealing. Everyone knew many of them were dishonest, but to have it officially from the Lords Commissioners of Admiralty was a novelty.

The order embarrassed captains in front of their staffs by tacitly criticizing their lengthy shore leaves. It annoyed captains to give up mufti and it alarmed them to think of the rancor this order would cause throughout the ship's hierarchy. Nobody appreciated Lord Spencer's gasconnade except the author. Even the great meddler Sir Alan Gardner wrote Nepean that it was "an unfortunate order."

To quarantine Spithead fever, the Admiralty sent warnings to all commands to keep an eye on ships that had been with the Channel fleet. *Bellerophon, Audacious* and *Theseus,* although they had not participated in the remonstrance, had been with Bridport's blockade squadron during the winter and were now on the way to join Sir John Jervis at Lisbon. The sea lords told Old Jarvey, "You may take the most vigorous and effectual measures for counter-acting any attempt that may be made by ill-designing persons to excite the spirit of mutiny among the crews of your squadron."

The same caution went to Vice-Admiral Sir Hyde Parker, commanding in the West Indies. His ships were at St. Nicholas Mole, Haiti, in ambuscade for French and Spanish in the Windward Passage. Parker was a quick signer of impressment warrants and, to offset his staggering yellow fever death rate, he took blacks, Jonathans and other neutrals without compunction. Sir Hyde did not especially need a mutiny warning: the crew of one of his auxiliary schooners, H.M.S. *Antoinette,* had just killed their captain and first officer and handed the ship to the French. Another of Hyde Parker's charges was the frigate *Hermione*. Before the summer of discontent was done, she was to enact the very epic of bloody mutiny.

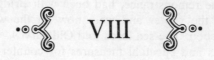

VIII

The Rule
of Delegates

George the Third
Ought never to have occurred.
One can only wonder
At so grotesque a blunder.

—E. C. BENTLEY

WHILE the fleet difficulty excited the press, public and Whitehall, Parliament itself maintained a stoic silence, awaiting the pay bill to filter down to it. On 3 May, the King approved the privy council's recommendation and the bill went to the Prime Minister. That day a brash young radical Whig peer, the Duke of Bedford, brought the issue into the open in the House of Lords: "I should like to ask," said he, "whether any of his Majesty's ministers have it in charge from his Majesty to make any communication upon the recent important transactions in the marine department?"

Spencer replied that the King had not instructed him to communicate to them on the matter, nor did he expect that his Majesty ever would. Lord Howe tried to cover Spencer's arrogant reply. "My name has been mentioned," he said. "I have anxiously awaited . . . to explain to your lordships . . . the part acted in this business . . . any censure attached to my professional character I shall look to another quarter for inquiry. . . . I wish that for the sake of the service, the business had never been brought under discussion . . . for the legislature will be placed in a most delicate situation."

In arabesque language, Howe tried to have the House understand that debate on Spencer's concessions to the seamen would turn up embarrassing facets and might result in a vote denouncing Spencer's settlement as made "under the pressure of the moment."

Bedford replied that he knew it would be fruitless to try to debate the matter if the ministers did not wish to. "But," he added, "if I could conceive of any terms in which I could couch a motion for the production of the papers connected with it, I would make the motion now. The transactions are without parallel in history," said he. "I know of no instance but the present, in which the ministers of the King had entered into correspondence and negotiation with any body of his Majesty's subjects. . . ."

Howe, no doubt concerned that some puzzled country peer should follow Bedford with more questions, decided to drop the occult language. He gave their lordships a straightforward recital of receiving the fleet petitions in March and thinking them the work of a "malicious individual." To dispel any doubt he had consulted "an officer in Portsmouth" (unnamed, but Lord Hugh Seymour), who had assured Howe there was no trouble in the fleet. Howe then turned the petitions over to the Admiralty.

The result of this frank exposure, as Lord Howe hoped, calmed the breeze in the House of Lords. But it became a hurricane in the streets. The royalist and Whig press did not report Howe's remarks, but reform newspaper and pamphleteer publishers did. They pointed out that the noble lord admitted that the Admiralty had received the seamen's petitions at least two weeks before the Spithead remonstrance began and that two more weeks had since passed without action from the government. A handbill to this effect quickly appeared in Portsmouth. It also alleged that the government was breaking the pledges that Lord Spencer had made to the fleet.

"Our bill has been hove out!"

"The man-eaters went back on us."

Fierce emotions surged through the forecastle. Originally the seamen had backed their leaders to gain something, now they united in towering anger to preserve the gain. Public sympathy for the Spithead cause also became warmer after Howe opened up the case.

Spencer advised Bridport: "I think it extremely essential that, if possible, the men should be convinced that every thing what was promised them not only is intended to be performed, but actually has been, as far as it possibly could be, carried into execution." The First Lord pointed out that form required the lengthy deliberations of the privy council and its committee and that estimates of the cost of the pay rise were now being drawn up in several offices. "Mr.

Pitt means to lay it before the committee of supply tomorrow [5 May] in the House of Commons."

As to "augmentation of victuals," Spencer wrote, "the weights and measures necessarily take a considerable time in making, but I am assured by the Victualling board that a considerable number of weights will be ready to be sent down Tuesday or Wednesday next" [10 May]. Here was an oblique admission of the venality of victualers and pursers; they had been stealing the seamen's food so long that they had standardized lighter weights and smaller measures than were legal in Britain.

In closing, Spencer bade the admiral have his officers "see & feel the utmost vigilance in being beforehand with any commotion or disturbance. This wind is very unfortunate for us, as I am persuaded being at Sea would be the best prevention against further disturbances." He added that another French invasion was expected during the month.

In Westminster a number of politicians considered the possibility that Pitt could not survive the shocks of spring. The nation's finances were in an alarming state. The war on the Continent was lost. The victorious French armies seemed about to descend on the Isles. Navy discontent had been badly bungled; now, perhaps the seamen would refuse to fight the French expedition.

An undisciplined Irish member of the House of Peers, Francis Rawdon-Hastings, the Earl of Moira, secretly began planning a new coalition to take over the government. He had intimate access to the King, having been useful to his Majesty in patching up an imminently scandalous separation of the Prince and Princess of Wales. He considered going to the King and urging Pitt's removal. "It is impossible to prevent the storm if the King do not himself become thoroughly sensible to the nature of the exigency," Moira noted.

Reform papers were reaching the anchorage. At Spithead a boat from *Mars* threw a bundle of newspapers through an open gunport on *Queen Charlotte's* lower gun deck. From the beginning the seamen held popular sympathy, which was reflected to a surprising extent in the press. The evening London *Courier* and the *Morning Chronicle* reported the business fairly. The *Publican's Advertiser* was friendly toward the seamen. The young provincial press was generally sympathetic to them. Conservative papers took the line that the sailors deserved more pay and better food but mutiny was not the way to obtain them. The traumatic event had come so suddenly and was apparently settled so soon that the King's journals had not been able to form an editorial attitude. Now they would have more time. Lord Bridport received unmistakable notice that another general strike was imminent. He got a note from the Queen Charlottes retracting their agreement to return to duty:

> We are still to a man on our lawful cause. . . . We have come to an understanding of parliament, finding there is no likelihood of redress to our former grievance. Therefore we think it prudent to obtain the same liberty as before. So, until our matters are comply'd with we are determined not to go to sea.
> P.S. There is *Marlborough* and *Nymphe* in a wretched condition. If Admiral Bridport does not comply with these measures and forward them, we will take the speediest methods.

Although the weather was still rough at St. Helen's the crews were exchanging letters. *Pompée* wrote to *Royal George:*

> Our opinion is that there [is] not the least reliance to be placed in their promises. . . . Our oath of fidelity is broke, if we do not remain unshaken until the whole thing is sanctioned by an act of Parliament. Now, brothers, your steady friends the Pompées beg of you to give them a final answer, and whatever may be your proposals, we one and all will never deviate from being determined to sink or swim.

A more sophisticated framing of the suspicions appeared in a letter from the Ramillies to the Royal Georges:

> They mean to lull us into a supposed state of security . . . by granting us a temporary increase of provisions, which 'tis true they have already done, with no other view than to keep us in the dark as to their intentions respecting the main point of view. If they once divide us and get us upon different stations, be assured they think they can then make their own terms. They know we are no politicians, but at the same time our late proceedings have convinced them that we are not entirely bereft of rationality.

The Ramillies had it on good authority that the seamen's bill had been thrown out, largely at the instigation of Lord Spencer. "If you receive this letter and approve of it," they told the Royal Georges, "let a pair of white trousers be hung from the sprit-sail arm as a signal of approbation."

Lord Spencer, "truly happy to find that at length tranquillity and order seemed to be perfectly reestablished," wrote privately to Bridport:

> We have had a very severe Lesson in this Business, & I trust all the Officers in the Fleet will feel the Effects of it; A relaxation of discipline will sooner or later produce mischief & the only way to remedy what is past will, I am full persuaded, be by a very steady & invincible adherence to the strictest Rules of the Service. It has ever been my desire to make the Service as far as I thought consistent with its Interests, as agreeable as possible to all engaged in it, & I may perhaps have been misled by this principle in some degree to give a little more indulgence than could in strictness be justified; the Example which the late Events have exhibited to us, must necessarily produce more caution upon this head, & I trust that the Effect of it will be what we must all most sincerely wish it to be.

Although Pitt had expected to present the estimates for the seamen's wage bill to Parliament on Friday 5 May, the calculations were not ready in time and the legislators went home for the weekend, oblivious to the mounting crisis of national safety. Before they reassembled on Monday afternoon two omens and a thundercrash took place in politics and war.

At Yarmouth several of the seventeen vessels of Adam Duncan's rueful North Sea fleet had not been paid for more than a year, among them *Standard,* 64. During the predawn hours of Saturday her crew wheeled out four guns and pointed them at the aftercastle. Admiral Duncan went aboard and found the men barricaded between decks. They sent him a note:

> Honoured Sir—We are sorry to have recorce to this method of disclosing our minds to you, but nessesety demands it to clear ourselves from the infamous imputation of mutney being thrown upon us meaning no sutch thing but the common cause of the British Navy we being already the jest and redicule of this whole fleet likewise our boats cannot go on shore but the men are exposed to the scoffts and jests of others and accounted as men that cannot stand up for their own rights threatned that whenever the blessings of peace shall be re-

stored to revenge themselves upon us wherever they meat us for our cowerdliness as they term it. . . .

In this oozing communique, the Standards were requesting their commander-in-chief not to think them mutinous for training cannons on their officers; they were only keeping up with the Joneses. Unit pride and intership rivalry was a binding force in navy morale and figured just as much in the mutiny bond. Duncan called them to the afterdeck and made a speech:

"Surrounded as Britain is with enemies, still we have nothing to fear if the fleet strictly adheres to their former character which never shone with more brightness than during this war. I hope and trust you and others will ever support that character, which in due time will bring the blessings of peace now so particularly desirable. The regard we owe our country and our families, I think, should animate us to exert ourselves in a particular manner and not flinch at the appearance of danger."

Although Duncan courted the popular peace sentiment, he saw no mockery in the idea of alluding to families the men could not visit or support.

The admiral's speech restored an appearance of the *status quo ante* on *Standard*. But he found that many other companies were hesitating on the edge of revolt. He visited each ship and gave patriotic talks to the men.

In London that weekend his Majesty was obliged to countenance a weighty protest. For several months the lord mayor, the sheriff and the Corporations of London had been trying to deliver a petition to his Majesty against continuing William Pitt's ministry. They had sent their Remembrancer to court in March to address the King on his throne, but the envoy was turned away on a technicality. Finally on this Sunday, 7 May, they delivered a petition praying that his Majesty "dismiss from his presence and councils his present weak and wicked ministers as the most likely means of obtaining a speedy and permanent peace." The petitioners represented the principal mercantile and banking powers of the kingdom.

The King was highly annoyed at the presumption of the City businessmen, but his day improved when Portland "begged leave to lay the draft at his Majesty's feet" of the Message that the lord lieutenant of Ireland was sending to the Irish Parliament to provide a £5,000 lifetime annuity to the Princess Royal. After Pitt's difficulties in extracting funds from Parliament to pay the Prince of Wales's debts, it was felt that his sister, the intended bride of the German prince, had better be kept by Ireland.

But these pressing concerns of Sunday paled before the wild stutter the telegraph brought slowly through the rain from Portsmouth. The Channel fleet was again under the bloody flag.

During the previous night the imprisoning wind had turned around from west to east and at dawn, the commanders listened for Lord Bridport's signal gun ordering the fleet to sail. But the admiral did not make the order. He believed the men would refuse to take up the capstan bars. He sat in his cabin writing the Admiralty, "I intended to have made the signal for the fleet to weigh this morning, as the wind was easterly; but I am compelled to remain here unless the vote of supply in the House of Commons for the increase of seamen's pay and provisions should arrive, and give the crews of the fleet satisfaction."

At nine o'clock the ships' companies at St. Helen's set up the extra hearty cheers that characterized their own cause. Ropes reappeared on the yardarms. On *Pompée,* 80, the former delegates, James Melvin and William Potts, resumed their powers and informed Captain James Vashon that they wanted their rights confirmed by Parliament. They began launching a boat. The captain ordered them to stop. They put the boat into the water anyway, the first one launched in the new outbreak, and visited the ships, one after another. The crew of *Defiance,* 74, Captain Theophrastus Jones, cheered, reeved the yard ropes and dropped a boat to join the Pompées. They visited *Defence,* 74, whose men held back and refused to produce delegates. There was a trundle of cannons on the flanking ships, *Pompée* and *Glory,* 98, and the Defences looked into the round black eyes of 32-pounders. The Defences quickly put up yard ropes, cheered and picked delegates. The marines accepted the order to take up arms, but the captain, Thomas Wells, wary of the guns of *Pompée* and *Glory,* had the lobsterbacks stand down. The delegates seized all small arms aboard and put the captain and officers in a boat.

When Captain Alexander Hood of *Mars* left his cabin, the marine sentry at his door stopped him. "Sir, you are not to go on the quarterdeck. Ship's company orders, sir." Captain John Holloway of *Duke* received a note: "Gentlemen, you are desired upon the receipt of this that the undermentioned persons quit the ship never to return again, except the persons with a mark against their names, who is to return when everything is settled to the satisfaction of the fleet." Holloway's name led the list of those not wanted back.

Captain Robert Campbell of *Terrible,* 74, who was a cousin of Lord Cawdor, the conquerer of Fishguard, resisted Melvin's demands until *Pompée* rolled some ordnance in position to rake her. The delegates seized the small arms on board and sent the captain and all officers except a middie into a boat with jeers and whistles. *Minotaur,* 74, Captain Thomas Lewis, ran up the red flag immediately. So did *Ramillies,* 74, despite pleas from Captain Sir Richard Bickerton. Throughout the fleet the men justified their fresh insubordination by referring to what Lord Howe had reported in the House of Lords. The circulation of radical papers had been thorough. But at Spithead, several ships' companies flatly refused to join the cause and were not molested. The strikers called them "The King's Party." *Eurydice,* "a happy ship" under genial Captain Sir John Talbot, did not participate in either Spithead mutiny, nor did the port admiral's flag, *Royal William.*

When the delegates' flotilla came up to *Queen Charlotte,* her acting captain, Walter Lock, ordered the *Pompée* boat to fend off; he wanted none of them aboard. But his marines refused to take up position to repel boarders and Lock had to stand aside.

By noon Sunday all the vessels at St. Helen's were under forecastle discipline. Bridport was writing the sea lords, "I have endeavored to prevent this mischief by every argument in my power, but without effect; and I cannot command this fleet, as all authority is taken from me. My mind is too deeply wounded by all these proceedings, and I am so unwell that I can scarcely hold my pen to write these sentiments of distress."

The St. Helen's parliament rowed to Spithead to bring *Marlborough* and *Nymphe* and other major vessels into the demonstration. The delegates had a new scheme, adapted to the new situation. They had decided to move all the capital ships to St. Helen's, away from the shore batteries of Portsmouth and to an anchorage from which they could escape to sea if other ships were sent against them.

In the dockyard there were many anxious thoughts about sabotage. The Portsmouth dockyard had been burned in 1760 and 1770, and in 1776, the ropewalk was burned in a famous conflagration caused by an incendiary machine set by an aged American known as John the Painter, by real name James Aitken. Apprehended on the road to London, Aitken readily explained that he had acted in a private patriotic capacity to avenge the burning of his home in New Jersey by British troops. He added that, having destroyed the ropeworks, he was on his way to London to kill King George. John the Painter was convicted and hanged. His body hung high in chains over the dock-yard until decay blunted the warning.*

The morning the second Spithead mutiny broke out, the officers had received another reminder from the Admiralty about tightening discipline. In *London,* 98, at Spithead, Vice-Admiral Sir John Colpoys had his glass on the movements of ships' boats at St. Helen's and saw the yard ropes go up again. Colpoys's nephew, Captain Edward Griffith of *London,* assembled the crew and read the Articles of War. Afterward Colpoys had the company brought aft and he spoke to them from the poop rail.

"Do you know what is happening at St. Helen's?"

"No, sir." It came in a ready chorus.

"Well then, let me know if you have any grievances remaining."

"No, none," voices replied.

"Have you not had everything granted, nay more than you ex-pected, by the Admiralty?"

"Yes. Yes. Aye. Aye."

"That being the case, I now pledge myself, if you will follow my advice, that you shall not get into any disgrace with your brethren in the fleet, as I shall become responsible for your conduct." Their father had spoken.

"All hands below!"

"House and secure the guns!"

"Close the gunports!"

Colpoys was buttoning up his ship to prevent the delegates from talking with his men through lower gunports or boarding through them. His marine company obeyed orders to take stations to repel boarders and his officers drew side arms. The crew was not allowed to come back on deck.

The Spithead boats arrived alongside *Marlborough,* 74. Captain Henry Nicholls raised no objection to boarding. Delegate Melvin requested the company to move the ship to St. Helen's and to put ashore officers who had mistreated seamen. Removing unwanted offi-cers had come late in the first strike; now it was the first order of the day. Captain Nicholls was sent from the ship. He was in the habit of hitting men with his fists, spyglass or speaking trumpet.

The seamen retained belowdecks in *London* improved their time by holding a meeting. They had been a strong element in the original

---

* Harper's *Encyclopedia of American History* edited by Woodrow Wilson.

test. A quantity of hidden rum came out and many Londons got drunk. It was the first time liquor had entered the fleet crisis. The seamen started yelling to be allowed topside. Armed officers guarding the hatchways called to Admiral Colpoys, "Should we fire?"

"Yes, certainly," he replied. "They must not be allowed to come up until I order them."

The men started to rush the hatchways. The officers opened fire. And it was returned from small arms among the seamen.

Colpoys called to his marine captain to bring his men into action; the seamen were pouring out and would run over the officers.

"Marines! You may fire at will."

No shots sounded. A marine dropped his musket on the deck. The others threw down their weapons. The lobsterbacks mingled with the sailors. Two foreign marines on the poop obeyed orders and fired on the seamen. Colpoys quickly recognized that, without the marines, resistance was folly. "Cease fire!" he bellowed and the officers roared it around the deck. The admiral and the officers retreated to the poop. "All hands aft!" the admiral cried.

The Londons looked at men who lay bleeding on the deck. Sailors ran toward the poop ladder, gathering up abandoned marine muskets, and yelling, "Blood for blood!" Other men grappled with them to stop further mayhem. The seamen seized the boyish first lieutenant, Peter Bover, who had mortally wounded one of the Londons in the fight in the hatchways. They hauled Bover to the forecastle, lowered one of the yard ropes, and put it around his neck.

Mr. Smith, the ship's surgeon, pleaded with the would-be lynchers to desist and listen to what the admiral had to say. The hard hands on the end of the yard rope slacked off, the block squeaked, and Lieutenant Bover found himself still with an upright head connected to his spine. At this point, the St. Helen's delegates, for whom Colpoys had arranged this hostile reception, came aboard without hindrance.

The surgeon had committed Sir John Colpoys to a difficult extemporaneous occasion; he had to talk the noose from his first officer's neck. The Londons gave him a grimly quiet audience. "I take the responsibility for all my officers may have done," the admiral began. "Lieutenant Bover, in firing, was carrying out my orders. And, I myself, was only doing my duty. I was bound to resist any attempt at mutiny, particularly at this time."

Then, to underscore this line of hopeless obedience to superior power, Sir John Colpoys said, "I have received very recent instructions from their lordships for the conduct of officers towards the men."

"Orders?"

"What orders, sir?"

"Let us see the orders!"

A committee escorted Sir John to his great cabin, where, thinking it might help Bover, he stalled for time, hunting for the keys to his desk. On the forecastle the debate over young Bover's fate resumed. The captain of the maintop was against hanging. He called Bover "a brave boy." The fleet delegates moderated the passion of the crowd and Valentine Joyce spoke up for the lieutenant under whom he had served on another vessel. They decided to confine Bover to his cabin. "And what about the bleedin' hadmiral?" By unanimous acclaim, confinement was also voted to Admiral Colpoys and Captain Griffith.

At last Sir John found his keys and extracted the document from his desk. He returned to the crowd and read the Admiralty general order of 1 May, which the officers of the fleet had been trying to swallow and forget.

"The captains and commanders . . . be ready on the first appearance of mutiny, to use the most vigorous means to suppress and to bring the ringleaders to punishment."

As the ringleaders heard this, it seemed to them the final irrevocable proof that Spencer had betrayed them. A week ago while sending reassurances through Bridport that everything was going smoothly, the first lord had issued this secret order to "suppress and bring the ringleaders to punishment." The delegates took his copy of the order from the admiral and escorted him below, past hundreds of hard faces, to a junior officer's cabin.

Surgeon Smith had been dealing with the men shot in Sir John's proof of obedience. He sent the six most seriously wounded to Haslar Hospital in Gosport, where three of them, all rebellious seamen, died.

If there was any further difficulty convincing men that they must stand out again and hold firm, the delegates simply read the Admiralty general order to them and their qualms disappeared. And the cause had its martyrs.

It appeared to the forecastle leaders that they had been traduced by the Admiralty, rejected by Parliament, and menaced by crafty hidden orders. And they had three dead men. No officer could be trusted now. That night the delegates ordered the ships to send all officers ashore. During the following three days, the seamen turned them out, keeping deference to superior rank, often saying, "Good luck, sir," and "Hope you'll be returning aboard soon, sir."

On *Royal Sovereign,* the leaders took control of the arms chests and ammunition and walked into Admiral Sir Alan Gardner's cabin.

"I demand an explanation of this!"

"We are deceived, sir. The government has thrown us over the side."

Sir Alan spluttered in disbelief.

"Alls we know, sir, there is an order out to punish the delegates."

Gardner left the ship, promising retribution. He went ashore and wrote to Bridport: "I desire that I may be allowed to quit the place and proceed into the country to reestablish my health which has greatly suffered by the fatigue and anxiety of mind which I have lately experienced." Bridport, who had just been denied the same request, did not approve.

Most ships gave sufficient notice for their officers to gather up gear, but the crew of *Glory,* 98, hustled Captain James Brine and his officers into a boat with a departing slogan, "For an Act of Parliament and an honest three pounds of pork!"

Next morning a northeaster was blowing. On *Hind* frigate, whose company had earlier protested her unseaworthiness, both divisions of the crew massed on deck at dawn. Lt. James Anthony Gardner turned out and found Capt. John Bazely "in the most impressive manner, requesting them to return to their duty, but all to no purpose. Had we been the only ship we should have soon driven the scoundrels to the devil; but as we were situated, surrounded by line-of-battle ships acting in the same disgraceful manner, it would have been little use to resist."

The captain received an unsigned note: "Gentlemen, It is the request of the ship's company that you leave the ship precisely at eight o'clock. As it is unanimously agreed . . . we would wish you to leave it peaceable or desperate measures will be taken."

Seamen armed with cutlasses brought the barge alongside and men handed down the officers' trunks. "Don't carry anything ashore for them," a delegate warned the boat crew, "or you'll be punished severe." This was a dreadful humiliation. An officer never carried anything; seamen sprang cheerily forward to tote his belongings on all occasions, or were sent for and ordered to port them. Lieutenant Gardner was in foul temper. He stuck two loaded pistols in his greatcoat and did not regain his equanimity during a sweating spray-swept four-hour row to the Point.

The boatmen ran the barge on the hard, passed the officers' chests above the dry line, and began to shove off. Lieutenant Gardner, reported, "I desired the bowman and one or two more, who I knew to be great scoundrels, to take [my chests] to Turner's, only a step from the boat, shewing them at the same time my pistols and saying 'You understand me.' " The sailors "most reluctantly" obeyed. Gardner said, "The others having reported them, those fellows got a fine ducking the moment they got on board."

H.M.S. *London* moved to St. Helen's with Admiral Colpoys and Captain Griffith still detained on board. The delegates seem to have considered giving them a trial. Captain Milne of *La Pique* was invited on board *London* as a witness or member of the court. Whatever was intended, a flag officer and a commanding officer were now prisoners of sailors and would soon be considered hostages by both sides.

The delegates of the fleet went to Gosport that Monday morning and viewed the bodies of their messmates who had been killed on *London*. A coroner's jury reached a verdict of "justifiable homicide." One of those wounded in the affray, Alexander Sutton, reported that the patients in the hospital wanted to take part in the fleet protest. The delegates appointed Sutton to organize them along approved lines.

The bodies were rowed in *London*'s barge to the Common Hard at Portsmouth and were carried from there in a procession to Kingston churchyard beyond the ramparts. Each coffin was led by a color-bearer with the Union Jack at half staff and flanked by twelve women in black. Behind them marched fifty seamen of H.M.S. *London* and dozens of veiled women, through a large respectful crowd lining the route.

In Westminster, government people received the first overnight expresses from Portsmouth. Pitt and the sea lords were astonished at the fresh outbreak of mutiny. *Men wounded, some believed dead. An admiral held prisoner. Ships all moving to St. Helen's, as though intending to leave for France. All officers removed.*

His Majesty's grand fleet lay at a sailing point, provisioned for a long cruise, fully manned and disciplined, with almost no commissioned officers aboard save the commander-in-chief, Admiral Baron Bridport of Cricket St. Thomas. The delegates did not wish to show disrespect to the father of the fleet.

The Prime Minister rushed to the Admiralty office. He could not do anything more positive until midafternoon when Parliament resumed after the weekend. One of the commissioners of Admiralty, Sir

Charles Arden, greeted Pitt with an anguished cry, "Total destruction
is near us!" He went on in great agitation, "Deterioration of the
service has gone so deep . . . apprehends national defeat . . . can
only be forestalled by exposing all naval matters in Parliament!"

Pitt and Spencer argued with the disturbed man. The last thing
Pitt wanted was a parliamentary debate. As it was, when Parliament
heard the Spithead news it, too, might break into panic and turn Pitt's
ministry out. Arden would not be calmed. He broke off and started
writing his resignation. An open split over principle in the board of
Admiralty would exacerbate public opinion and Parliament and furnish dramatic new arguments to Fox and the mysterious "party of
armed neutrality" in their crusade to replace the cabinet. It took Lord
Spencer forty-eight hours to persuade Arden to withdraw his resignation.

That afternoon the lobbies of Parliament were gloomy and ex-
pectant when Pitt arrived to present, in his capacity as Chancellor of
the Exchequer, additional estimates for the navy. The House fell
silent to hear what Pitt had to say about the calamity at Spithead. He
presented a resolution, calling for £900,000, and spoke for ten
minutes without mentioning the navy, seamen or even water. Then
he asked "the silent judgment of the committee on the proposition."

Charles James Fox got up.

"I shall certainly vote for the resolution, but I cannot do it in the
manner which the right honourable gentleman proposes, namely, to
give it silently. . . . He seems to deprecate discussion upon this subject at this moment, as being likely to increase our difficulties. It is
not to discussion but to silence, we owe that difficulty. This house
should not have been the confidants of the minister, and remained
silent so long upon this subject. Had this house interposed upon the
commencement of the matter, instead of indulging the ministers for
the scandalous delay of a fortnight, I verily believe we should not
have heard anything of the misfortunes which recently happened."

Fox accused the government of trying to bargain the seamen down,
which only increased their suspicions. He continued:

"This house might on the Monday or the Wednesday following the
notification of the discontents, have voted that which is now proposed. It is inexcusable in ministers to have delayed it so long. But
most extraordinary indeed it is, that silent confidence in ministers
should be demanded of this house. . . . It will be criminal to repose
trust and continue power in the hands of men whom we know by

bitter experience, to be unfit to conduct our affairs; who have shown a degree of guilt or incapacity, or both, that has led us to the brink of destruction."

Fox blamed Pitt and not Spencer for delaying the remedy. "Knowing and valuing as I do, the private character of the First Lord of Admiralty, I cannot but wonder that a man with feelings like this could suffer a fortnight to pass without suggesting to his friends the necessity of haste." Fox complained that he did not know the cause of the Spithead mutinies. "All I know is what I have seen in the papers," he said. Here was the answer to disappointed men in the fleet who were wondering why the great liberal had done nothing about their petitions, sent nearly two months earlier.

Fox had never received the petitions.

They had been addressed to him at "South Street, Grosvenor Square," which was not a bad hit at 46 Clarges Street, Fox's house in Mayfair. There were two possible ways to intercept letters in the royal mails. The home secretary (then Lord Portland, an old crony of Fox's and cofounder of Brooks's gambling club) had the power to issue a specific warrant to stop or open letters in the post office. Portland knew nothing in March about rebellious sentiments in the navy, and, unless he had already been secretly checking Fox's mail for political reasons, had no motive for the act. The other interception point could well have been Portsmouth dockyard, where the ordinary personal mail of the fleet was transferred to and from the royal mails. That the stop occurred here seems proven by the fact that several original 1797 petitions from the fleet addressed on the obverse fold to Charles James Fox are to be found today among the Admiralty documents in the Public Record Office in Chancery Lane. At least one petition addressed to Fox was sent to the Admiralty by Lord Bridport. The seamen never knew why Fox let them down.

Concluding his speech on the navy estimates, Fox predicted that if the House did not look into the reasons for Spithead, "what has happened may happen again." None of his prophecies was more quickly or liberally fulfilled.

Nearly half the members of the House of Commons were absent from the sitting. The vote was unanimous and, at eight o'clock, an express rider spurred away for Portsmouth. The resolution, however, approved spending the money but not what it was to be spent for. That would still have to be brought before both Houses of Parliament in the form of an act. Pitt sent a runner to the King with a note, "From the critical state in which things seem to have been left by the last accounts from the Fleet today, it may become necessary, on receiving further accounts tomorrow, to resolve on further measures, which may require a Message to be submitted to your Majesty tomorrow, with a view to its being presented the same day in the House." He asked the King to stand by until midafternoon Tuesday for the latest news from Spithead, at which time they could make up the King's orders to Parliament. Apparently the Prime Minister still believed the mutiny might dissolve. Instead of giving Parliament both the resolution and the enabling act that day, Pitt was putting off the earliest reply to the men until Wednesday morning, four days after the delegates had seized the grand fleet for the second time. At the end of this strenuous Monday, the cabinet met.

Subject to changed circumstances that might be advised from Spithead next morning by express or telegraph, the ministers decided to put the act confirming increased navy pay and rations before both Houses next day. Pitt knew that while Fox, Sheridan and their cohorts were trapped into voting for the navy pay bill they would continue to flog the ministry for concealment and tardiness.

Pitt requested that his Majesty remain in town next day to preside over a court ceremony essential to British law-giving. To seal an enactment of the House of Commons, a "commission for giving the Royal Assent" carried the bill from Commons to the King and when he inscribed "G.R.," the commissioners brought the bill before the House of Lords, if it was in session. Pitt would have to see that the peers were still seated at the end of tomorrow's process. The King responded considerately to Pitt's stage directions. He proposed that the Assent commission be unique and particular for the seamen's pay bill. If the retinue came to him with the usual mixed bag of enclosure acts and other exactions of Parliament that he liked to pore over with his glasses on, the business might be further delayed.

After the cabinet session, Lord Spencer wrote a private letter to Lord Bridport, whom he had left to transform shortcomings of state into victories of discipline. "The unanimous vote of the House of Commons today will remove all the difficulties," said the earl, soothingly. "Being at sea," said he, "will bring them back into their old habits of regularity and obedience to their officers." There were virtually no officers left in Bridport's ships. Spencer said he understood that several officers had been removed from *Marlborough:* "If you shall be enabled to sail before you hear further from us," he privately advised Bridport, "it will be advisable for your Lordship to appoint others to act in their room."

One of Fox's friends in Parliament, Thomas Grenville, brother of the foreign secretary, wrote of the mutiny to another brother, Lord Buckingham, "I cannot help fearing the evil is deeply rooted in the influence of Jacobin emissaries and the Corresponding Society."

Next morning the cabinet members returned to 10 Downing Street to conduct business while waiting for the overnight couriers from Portsmouth. The shutter telegraph was closed down by a violent squall. The ministers discussed how to most effectively present to the refractory fleet the enabling acts on seamens' pay and provisions, which they hoped to obtain that afternoon from Parliament. Forgotten was the fact that the seamen had not yet seen Spencer's last answer to them, in which he refused to consider complaints against abusive officers, or to grant shore leave or better treatment to sick and wounded. The legislation going to the two Houses in a few hours was confined to pay and victuals.

The cabinet decided that some forceful and magnetic person should take the acts personally to the fleet, and, by the trust sailors had in him, win immediate settlement. Nobody mentioned Charles James Fox. Nor was Lord Spencer considered. The man selected was Admiral Richard Earl Howe, the retired commander of the mutinous fleet.

As the cabinet adjourned to attend Parliament, Spencer sent a note to the King requesting approval of Howe as government emissary and asked for an audience that evening. The King invited him immediately and said to Spencer complacently, "It would be idle to lament that the measures for increasing their pay have been delayed for two weeks coming forward in Parliament."

Lord Howe had partially recovered from a fit of gout at Bath and was back in his London house in Grafton Street. There Lord Spencer repaired to ask him to save the fleet. The old admiral accepted the mission. Spencer wanted to know whom Howe wished to accompany him. "Lady Howe," said the admiral. The aged couple prepared to leave immediately the bills had received the royal assent.

Howe agreed to attempt the mission of pacification despite the fact that his high esteem among seamen had been compromised by Admiralty neglect of their petitions. In the exchange of propaganda bills that played with Kempenfeldt's ghost, the forecastle writer had criticized Howe for "not representing our petitions to the Lords Commissioners of the Admiralty." Another lower-deck penman had written the *Sun* newspaper, saying that Howe had lost his place "in the harts of British seamen."

But Richard Howe's sense of duty had always been larger than fealty to the King and regulations. He walked through the mire of Georgism with clean boots. No matter what had happened to his personal trust in the fleet, he intended to try to set things right.

In the House of Commons the big guns of the opposition opened fire on Mr. Pitt. They were led by Samuel Whitbread, a rich, handsome Foxite, who typified the rising industrial entrepreneurs who were going to shatter Georgism and create a government in their own image. Whitbread's father had risen from an articled clerk to ownership of a great brewery. He gave the son an exotic grounding for life in the nonconformist creed, Eton, Oxford *and* Cambridge, as well as the Grand Tour. Whitbread deplored military inefficiency, sedition bills, and rural distress. He championed Negro emancipation, religious and civil rights, national education and peace with France.

"In consequence of what passed last night, and considering the impressions on men's minds relative to the disturbances at Portsmouth, I now rise," said Whitbread, "not to enter into the causes of that affair, but to press upon the Chancellor of the Exchequer, a question which was distinctly proposed to him [Pitt] by two of his honourable friends last night, and to which no answer was made. I beg to ask, therefore, why the proposition moved last night was not brought forward on an earlier day?" If Pitt had no satisfactory explanation, Whitbread served notice that it was his intention "to move a direct vote of censure against the Chancellor of the Exchequer, for gross neglect of duty."

Pitt answered firmly, "I am responsible for what I have done in my official capacity. Whenever the vote of censure is proposed will be time to state to the House of Commons the circumstances upon which I shall be ready to rest my justification." He said the Lords of Admiralty had made their recommendations to a committee of the privy council on 26 April. The committee had submitted a report to his Majesty. "All these forms, which the regular conduct of business requires, necessarily consume some time," he said. "Delays till the opinion of the privy council was taken!" roared Fox. "Good God!"

Fox reminded Pitt that the Admiralty and seamen were reconciled on 23 April. "Was it not the duty of ministers after they had recognized the delegates with whom they treated; after they had made a promise, to have lost no time in completing the transaction? Even after the council had taken its 'tedious steps' by 3 May," Fox said, five more days elapsed before Pitt brought the matter to the House.

In the House of Lords, the Duke of Bedford called for a parliamentary investigation of the ministers' delay which would "convict them of odious treachery, or the most shameful incapacity." The Duke of Grafton added, "The present is one of the greatest calamities with which the country was ever afflicted, and it arises chiefly from procrastination." Lord Loughborough, the lord chancellor, defended the government. He begged their lordships to cease wasting time in debate, which "might be putting in peril the lives of the best and bravest men in the country." He meant the seamen.

The opposition, having registered its protests, could do nothing but join the unanimous vote for the bill. The result was run to the House of Lords. Commons remained seated until the peers had voted for it and the Royal Assent commissioners had obtained his Majesty's signature at the Queen's House, and sent it on to Lord Howe.

The day's lashing rains had turned into a nightlong downpour as Lord Howe and his lady arrived in chairs at Lombard Street to board the night mail for Portsmouth. It was past eight o'clock and the mails were being loaded from the general post office into a double file of chocolate-colored royal mail coaches with gilded G.R. crests on the doors. Even in the wet, there was a small crowd out to see the ceremonial departure of flying coaches to the ends of the kingdom. The horses were splendidly groomed, their harnesses waxed, brass glistening, and seated on top in storm cloaks covering their king's scarlet livery were the heroic guards and coachmen. The flying coach was a marvel of light, strong, uncluttered construction. Every morning postal servants took down each carriage and laid out the individual parts—wheels, axles, linchpins, even windows—for official inspection. Admirers called them "balloon coaches" after the lightest and speediest vehicle of the age, the French aerial balloon.

Passengers took the four inside places in each coach as it moved forward in the queue to receive the mailbags. The crowd applauded Lord Howe as he climbed laboriously into the Portsmouth coach on his gouty feet. He let the glass down and nodded to them. A painful grimace was engraved on his face. The famous "Black Dick" Howe was coming out of retirement by urgent royal command after 58 years in the nation's service, fighting the King's wars at sea and his policies at home.

"Edinburgh!" bawled the post office majordomo. The Edinburgh coach drew up, received mails, and charged away.

"Gloucester!"

"York!"

"Portsmouth!"

Overhead the lids slammed shut on the mailbags. The horses sprang and ran. The guard blasted his trumpet. The crowd cheered. The city reverberated with the clatter of ironshod horses and carriage wheels, and the syncopated workings of the flexible carriage. On the edge of the city, passing from cobblestones to the open road, the mail gathered speed, bestriding the crown, until it was singing along at ten miles an hour. Mail coaches "first revealed the glory of motion," said Thomas de Quincey, who started riding them at this time. He was excited by the "power and beauty of the horses and the conscious presence of a central intellect"—the imperial postal service. The glory was not due, however, to the postal service. A Scottish engineer, John L. McAdam, had built the necessary dry gravel-topped pikes on rock beds. And the flying coaches had been introduced by John Palmer, a theatre owner in Bath, for the purpose of bringing Londoners to his plays in sixteen hours. What H.M. government had contributed was ever-increasing turnpike taxes.

Black Dick Howe was the victor of the most important fleet battle so far in the war, which he fought in 1794 with an equal weight of French guns under Admiral Louis Vilaret de Joyeuse 450 miles southwest of Ireland at 47° 48′ north and 18° 30′ west. Lacking identification with a cape, it was called "The Battle of the Glorious First of June." The mutinous fleet consisted principally of ships and men Howe had commanded there. When Howe came back to Spithead with all of his ships and six French men-of-war in tow, thousands converged on Portsmouth, and London caroused with pride and relief. Pitt ordered three nights' illuminations and for a period the victory took people's minds off the national dilemma. There was no public manifestation when it was established that Vilaret de Joyeuse had sacrificed the warships to keep Howe away from a convoy of 116 vessels from America bringing food that guaranteed that France could eat and fight if the next harvest should fail.

Lord Howe was also an adroit opposition politician. Years before, when the American English were being pushed inexorably to revolt, he attempted to avert it by private accord with Benjamin Franklin, the colonies' agent in London. He acknowledged that Franklin had been "very ill-treated" by the ministry and offered to negotiate confidentially between him and the ministers.

Franklin said he had confidence in Howe's "decent intentions," but the King's belligerent speeches and harsher decrees by "the present ministry" held no encouragement for reconciliation.

When the American war came, Howe left Spithead for New York

in command of a battle squadron and a fleet of troop transports. He held a dual royal commission with his brother, General Sir William Howe, field commander in North America, as military and civil governor of the colonies. His own hope for the mission was that he could avoid hostilities and use his viceregal powers for peace. He arrived at Staten Island on 4 July 1776 and immediately sent a private letter to Franklin in Philadelphia. Franklin turned it over to the Continental Congress, which authorized him to reply in kind—he said he was sorry to read Howe's offer of pardon upon submission, "as it must give your lordship pain to be sent so far on so hopeless a mission."

In their military capacity the Howe brothers were not so frustrated. They ran Washington's amateur army off Long Island to a temporary refuge on Manhattan. Instead of pressing on, Lord Howe again tried to treat with Congress, although he could not, as H.M. governor-general, admit the existence of the outlaw body. He invited some people up from Philadelphia in "their private characters." The Congress found legal means to send Franklin, John Adams and Edward Rutledge as a credentials committee to ascertain the extent of Howe's royal warrant. It was too late. Howe could not deceive himself or the emissaries that his employer desired anything but punitive war. He and his brother decided to resign. When more commissioners arrived in America, Black Dick went home and entered Parliament to sit the war out.

Now as the Portsmouth mail coach clattered along the macadam, it was bringing to the striking fleet a man much experienced in dealing with upstart delegates deriving sovereign powers from people rather than kings.

Nor was Howe attending his first mutiny. While he was acting briefly as First Lord of the Admiralty at the close of the American war, the fleet revolted at Spithead, Plymouth and the Nore. The mutiny was touched off by the arrogance or blundering of the previous board of Admiralty. The seamen, who had been away from home for years, expected to be paid off and discharged now that the war was over. Instead they were kept aboard and ordered to work some of the vessels into dockyards. At Portsmouth, *Janus,* 44, from the West Indies, was told to refit for sea. Forecastle indignation flamed into action. The men locked up their officers. The captain was ashore. When he returned, armed men prevented him from boarding.

At length, he was allowed to come up and proceeded to read the Januses a lecture, in which he confirmed their suspicions: *Janus* was being kept in commission and was returning to America. The crew broke in, "That's enough! We'll listen no more!" They went to stations and shotted the guns. The powder boys lit slow matches. The captain went ashore and reported to the port admiral that they threatened to fire on any ship that interfered with them. The rising spread to other vessels of uncertain status, while hundreds of men who had been paid off frolicked around the beaches, demonstrating sympathy and liquidating their terminal pay. The port admiral wrote despairingly to the Admiralty and Black Dick Howe decided to go to Portsmouth and treat the business. He went alone.

He notified *Janus* that he was coming aboard and approached in a boat with no special show of arms. The sideboys were turned properly, the boatswain was tweetling, men rigged hand ropes, and fifes and drums played "Hearts of Oak," as Howe went up the side and faced all hands on the quarterdeck. He said:

"I am much grieved to hear of such mutinous conduct in British seamen. I have always found you orderly and obedient. I hope you know the deep interest I have always taken in your welfare. I have always been, and am now, more than ever, as becomes the high and responsible situation I have the honor to hold, ready to listen to any complaints you have to make, and to comply with any reasonable request you might address to me. You are acting under the influence of a false report. The *Janus* will be paid off, although my predecessor decided she be kept in commission.

"It is with great reluctance that I part with so fine a ship's company as that now standing before me. Again I assure you, she will be paid off."

Upon hearing Howe countermand the sailing order, the Januses erupted in three sounding cheers. The mutiny was over. There were no punishments. That navy generation passed on the report—Howe was "the sailors' friend."

Howe blamed ships' captains for much lower-deck discontent; he especially criticized them for refusing the crew shore leave in home port while the captains themselves spent most of the time at home or politicking at the Admiralty. When he was a commander, Black Dick gave his men liberty in a fair rotation. He disliked the way the Admiralty usually dealt with complaining crews by transferring the most vocal men to other ships, as had been done two years before on *Caesar* at Spithead. "It exposes their former captain to an imputation of misconduct," said Howe, "while it gratifies the desire of [perhaps

misbehaving] men to change their situation." It also distributed malcontents from one ship to several, which might well increase the disaffection.

While Lord Howe's old bones were being jarred on the long ride
through the rainy night, the home secretary, the Duke of Portland,
concluded some thoughts about the mutiny. He suspected that it had
been caused by Jacobin agitators.

Among the republicans, Jacobins, radicals, reformers, Irish revolutionaries, chapel orators, pantisocrats, clubbists, Paineites and agitators on Portland's suspect list, the name of John Thelwall led all the
rest. For three years Portland had been trying to hang this dumpy little thirty-one-year-old tailor, versifier, anti-Pitt lampooner, and cam-
paigner for a British republic. Thelwall was an orator and debater
who stirred the populace, and a cunning publisher. The crown had
failed to turn him off in its attempt on the core of the opposition in
1794 state treason trials. Free as a cat, Thelwall was going about
turning unhappiness into protest and resistance. Portland sent shorthand reporters to his lectures and forwarded their transcripts to the
King along with the number present and descriptions of the class
composition of Thelwall's audiences.

The duke was obsessed with Thelwall, perhaps because he was
one of the rare revolutionaries his grace had met personally. The
place was the privy council chamber, the time 1794, the occasion, the
night Portland's constables dragged Thelwall out of his house and
removed three carriageloads of his books and papers. Led before the
privy council, Thelwall refused to submit to questioning. Pitt exclaimed, "He does not know what is against him? Here, let him see
this paper. Read it to him. What does he say?" Thelwall replied to
the Prime Minister, "It is no part of the law or constitution of this
country that I should answer the questions of the privy council." He
turned his back on Pitt and looked at the paintings on the walls.

The state confined Thelwall in the Tower without copy of the
charges for three months. He never did get his library back from the
government. Then for two months before trial he was confined in the
dead hole in Newgate Prison with corpses of disease victims awaiting
removal. Although Thelwall was acquitted with Hardy and Tooke in
the state trials, Parliament passed harsher treason and sedition bills,
"the Pitt and Grenville Acts," which declared that "no one should
deliver discourses on or concerning any supposed public grievance
or any matters relative to the laws, government or policy of the
kingdom."

Thelwall hired halls in London, staging debates, he taking the reform position. Government harassment scared off his patrons and
audiences and closed his paper, the *Tribune.* He tried lecturing on
Roman history with Aesopian slants on England but this, too, failed
in the choking atmosphere of intimidation.

Thelwall took to the road. Provincial dissidents arranged lectures
in the Midlands and East Anglia. At Great Yarmouth the hall was
invaded by seamen from the frigate H.M.S. *l'Espiègle,* armed with
clubs and cutlasses. They pummeled the audiences, wrecked the hall,
and made off with shawls and overcoats. Town magistrates and naval
authorities refused to register complaints.

During Thelwall's provincial tour, the Duke of Portland lost track
of him. Britain had no national police and officials had to rely on
casual reports. In April the newspapers gave Portland a clue from
Derby. A loyalist mob broke into a Methodist chapel and menaced the
speaker, Thelwall. He pulled a pistol and the King's supporters departed.

Now a naval officer advised the duke that John Thelwall had been
seen aboard a mutinous ship at Spithead. This was stirring news. If his
grace could surprise a leading radical on board a rebellious vessel, it
promised that another round of high treason trials could finish the
agitators for good. But who could he send to Portsmouth to arrest
Thelwall on the basis of solid evidence of complicity in the mutiny?
The duke had call on what the government called "missionaries," a
pool of informers paid by the piece, who were recruited in debtors'
jails. The Fleet Prison in London was the principal spy academy.
A missionary's basic interest was to supply salable anecdotes but
the home secretary did not care to entrust the Thelwall job to such
low-grade auxiliaries. He selected his agent, not from the missionaries but from their severest critics, the judges who often failed to
urge juries to convict political prisoners on the evidence of the home
secretary's narks.

The duke picked as his hunter, a clever and thoroughgoing London
magistrate, Aaron Graham of Hatton Garden, a street of jewelers and
goldsmiths not far from Newgate Prison. Near Graham's court was
The Bleeding Heart, a resort of Irish rebels. Recently London gallows
had been moved from Tyburn* to Newgate, padding Graham's docket

---

* Tyburn was at Marble Arch, at the western end of Tyburn Street, now
called Oxford Street. Civilians were hanged there. Refractory soldiers were
shot at Marble Arch or were flogged in the Tilt Yard at the east end of St.
James's Park. Their shrieks so much upset clerks in the treasury, foreign and

with pickpockets charged with picking pockets of people gaping at the hanging of pickpockets. In the neighborhood the night before hanging day you could hear the bellman of St. Sepulchre's pass the prison walls chanting,

> *"All you that in the condemned hold do lie,*
> *Prepare you, for tomorrow you shall die;*
> *Watch all, and pray, the hour is drawing near,*
> *That you before the Almighty must appear;*
> *Examine well yourselves, in time repent,*
> *That you may not to eternal flames be sent,*
> *And when St. Sepulchre's bell tomorrow tolls,*
> *The Lord above have mercy on your souls.*
>   *—Past twelve o'clock"*

In selecting the magistrate, the Duke of Portland remembered that Graham had aided the naval prosecution by examining two of the mutineers of H.M.S. *Bounty,* Joseph Coleman and Thomas McIntosh, prior to their court-martial in 1792. (After the two men were acquitted they complained to Captain Bligh that Graham refused to return their mutiny narratives.) The magistrate also had a son who was a midshipman in the navy.

In Commons the Foxites did not let Pitt get off with his mechanical vote on the navy estimates. Samuel Whitbread brought a motion of censure against Pitt for "omitting to press forward measures with extraordinary haste, in matters of such vital importance to the safety of the state." A government member pleaded with Whitbread to withdraw since "the country had suffered so much from untimely discussion." Whitbread refused. "I regret," said he, "that on the day the estimates were taken into consideration a vote of censure was not passed upon his conduct, which might have accompanied the other vote to Portsmouth, for the purpose of convincing the sailors that the House of Commons had not been party to that delay, to which all the subsequent calamities are to be attributed." The brewing heir reminded the House that on 23 April the sea lords had promised the seamen ratification of their agreement by Parliament. "What were the seamen naturally led to expect?" he asked. "Certainly that an immediate message would be sent by his Majesty to the two houses of

---

India offices and in No. 10 Downing Street, that they were muffled by drum pounding.

Parliament recommending the subject to their consideration. But was any message sent? No! Nor has there been one to this day."

Pitt charged that his critics misrepresented the executive government, "and to this species of misrepresentation I, in part, ascribe the mischiefs which have arisen."

Playwright Sheridan supported the vote to censure Pitt. The ministers, said he, "postponed consideration of the seamen's demands . . . to such objects as the imperial loan and the marriage portion of the Princess Royal." Sheridan called for a joint parliamentary inquiry into conditions in the navy. But few supporters of Fox and Sheridan wanted the navy's morale problems aired in the midst of war. The House went into division on the resolution of censure and defeated it 237 to 63. Pitt was still in the saddle, but the anti-administration vote was growing.

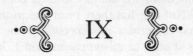

IX

Black Dick Howe

All hail, brother seamen, that ploughs on the main,
Likewise to wellwishers of seamen of fame,
May Providence watch over brave British tars,
And guide them with care from the dangers of wars.

Good Providence long looked with pity at last
For to see Honest Jack so shamefully thrashed,
But still held his arm for to let Jack subdue
The pride of those masters whose hearts were not true.

At Spithead Jack from a long silence was roused,
Which waked other brothers who did not refuse
To assist in the plan that good Providence taught
In the hearts of brave seamen that 'ad long been forgot.

All Hail Brother Seamen
Forecastle ballad, 1797 mutiny

WHILE Lord Howe was en route to Portsmouth, Spencer notified the commander-in-chief of the Channel fleet, Lord Bridport, that the former commander was coming to supercede him in the mutiny negotiations. Spencer wrote, "His Majesty's Servants had determined to advise the King to send down Lord Howe with Instructions under the Sign Manual to communicate with the Fleet . . . in order to bring them back to their duty and a proper subordination to their officers." And, "It had been decided that the circumstances of your being their commanding officer on the occasion suggested many Reasons against your being personally charged with the Execution of this Measure." Spencer hoped that Bridport would appreciate "the very extraordinary Mark of Attention which the Legislature has paid to the Wishes of the Seamen by passing through all the Stages [of the act] in one day."

Pitt also sent a placatory letter to the forsaken admiral. Bridport replied tartly to that one, "I have always considered peevish words and hasty orders detrimental . . . I wish that rule had guided the conduct of those in higher situations." He assured Pitt of "my Loyalty to the King and my devoted attachment to your [*sic*] excellent Constitution."

Black Dick Howe arrived in Portsmouth in the morning of Wednesday 10 May. Dropping his lady at the house of the garrison commander, General Sir William Pitt,* Howe gathered up Sir Peter Parker, Sir Alan Gardner, and a number of beached officers, and set out by barge for St. Helen's. He made for *Royal George,* Bridport's flagship, where that worthy still sat in his great cabin. Spurning assistance, Howe went up the side of the three-decker on his gouty feet and paid his respects to the admiral. He and Bridport had despised each other for years. Then Howe had the ship's company called to the quarterdeck. Scores of these men had fought under him on the Glorious First of June. There were sailors who had been wounded there who remembered Howe's coming down to the orlop after the battle, bringing his own wine to them and talking with every man.

Black Dick dispensed with the official attitude that they were children, that they were wicked, and that they were misled. He said he was empowered to treat between them and the King, to reach a state "of pardon and oblivion for all that had happened, upon conditions that were just and necessary to the future order and strength of the service." Now that their demands for pay increases and full rations had been officially enacted by Parliament, pardon and forgiveness proclaimed, all that was necessary was a pledge through their own ship's delegates that they would again submit to their officers and cooperate with them in enforcing discipline and checking the first appearance of mutiny. After three hours, Howe won an amiable agreement on these points. However, the Royal Georges said they could not answer for other crews. The man was now obliged to visit in turn the major vessels of the grand fleet and speak with each company.

He went to his old flag, *Queen Charlotte,* and talked to the crew. Black Dick remained as they remembered him, reasonable, manly, his manner conceding an equal intelligence to his listeners. Even before they saw him, the simple news of their old commander's presence

---

* General Sir William Pitt, K.B., was not related to the Prime Minister. He was a sixty-nine-year-old Hampshireman whose career went back to the Seven Years' War. His wife was a cousin of Lord Howe's.

relaxed distemper in the fleet. The ship's company of *London* voted to release Admiral Colpoys and Captain Griffith, whom they had detained below for three days following the fatal shooting of their messmates. The officers were respectfully shown to a boat and as it pulled away, a seaman called out amiably, "Come back soon!"

Lord Howe did not berate the men for insubordination and mutiny. Instead he expressed his amazement that they should have struck a second time on the basis of false reports and suspicions. Here! He held up the printed Act of Parliament, and the Royal Pardon, all engrossed "G.R." These sincere fulfillments of the Admiralty pledge had been undergoing the procedures of constitutional government while the sailors acted on false and malicious rumors.

By the end of his first day's work, Black Dick had caused the red flag to be struck and the yard ropes unreeved on *Royal George, Queen Charlotte* and *Duke*. However, it was done as much by the admiral's prestige as by forecastle belief that the government had changed its ways. The *Times* newspaper reported that the seamen were more impressed by Fox and Sheridan's attacks on ministerial delay and duplicity than they were by the Act of Parliament.

The night following Howe's departure from London, Magistrate Aaron Graham, inflated by ministerial preferment that could lead to power and affluence, took the Portsmouth mail carriage. At breakfast in a seafront inn, with a chop in one hand and a pen in the other, he dashed off an express to the Duke of Portland announcing his arrival.

His first order of business was to enlist aid from his colleague, Sir John Carter, crown magistrate for Portsmouth. Sir John does not appear to have been out of bed for Graham's call and to have yawned at his queries about republican agitators. The London man went off disappointed and visited the mayor of the town, who would not even see him.

Portsmouth was fed up with Mr. Pitt's government and his war. As England's main naval base, the town had unwillingly received thousands of inland wives, sweethearts, mothers and children of seamen not permitted to leave their ships. Unpaid tars could not send their families home and they fell on the pauper rolls of Portsmouth and other harbor parishes. For several years the mayor and aldermen had petitioned the government for relief, but got nothing. In the prevailing mood of the townsmen, a fleet run by seamen seemed no worse than one run by the Admiralty. In fact the shopkeeper and publican were doing somewhat better than usual since the delegates permitted the men to come ashore to parade and speechify.

This, however, was not the story that Magistrate Graham had been sent to hear. The Duke of Portland wanted treason, quick and flagrant. The Londoner gave up on the town officials and went to the waterfront. And there they were! Live mutineers strolled about, bold as bells, wearing red cockades and gilded ribbons on their hats. Graham spoke to a man whose ribbon said SUCCESS TO THE EIGHT UNITED ROSES. The sailor proudly explained that the motto referred to his squadron, which had just run up the red flag at Spithead. The seaman showed Graham the shop in which he had bought the ribbon; it was busy selling garish hatbands with other encouraging slogans. Publicans, ribboniers, cockade makers and printers were catering to the mutiny. Graham returned to Sir John Carter and demanded that he enjoin the sale of treasonable ribbons. The local judge was not interested.

Graham went out and struck up conversations with people in the street. He met a voluble cordwainer named William Shapland who asserted that a Portsea slopseller, Charles Brassett by name, included books among the wares he sold from his boat in the fleet anchorage. The informer hadn't seen the books close and did not know whether or not Tom Paine had written them.

The Hatton Garden magistrate loitered around groups of idle seamen. We can fairly picture him, a forty-four-year-old cushioned city type, somewhat forcibly suppressing his judicial scowl and assuming a matey expression as he lent his ears to a black-pawed, gin-fired foretopman delivering himself of blasphemies upon all that Graham held dear. Getting only fleeting bits of information, the magistrate decided that he needed assistant spies.

As a home office representative, Graham delicately refrained from asking the port admiral, Sir Peter Parker, for help. He went to Sir John Carter again and asked for the loan of a town constable, a man who had been an admiral's steward and was now running a public house at Portsmouth Point, through which everyone passed to and from the Spithead ships. Graham said his nominee "would be admirably calculated to frequent the ale houses and gin shops to find sentiments of landlords and whores who have great influence among seamen." But the local magistrate would have nothing to do with this, either. Vexed, Graham wrote to the duke that Portsmouth officials showed "a great deal of party spirit," which was a King's party epithet for Whiggery and Foxism, and were "lukewarm in their endeavors to put a stop to this most dangerous conspiracy."

On the chance that the political weather was better in Gosport, Graham hired a waterman to row him across the harbor. When he presented himself at the rooms of Magistrate Curry of Gosport, a servant said, "His honor is absent on business. He did not say when he would return." Curry had simply left town until the fleet disturbance was over.

Failing on the beaches, Graham took to the water and was rowed, sometimes by strapping wenches, from Portsmouth to Gosport to Spithead. He swanned around the towering wooden walls, gammed with gangway watches and hung around when delegates' boats came and went. He learned the names of two important delegates, Valentine Joyce of *Royal George* and James Melvin of *Pompée*. He sounded for information about the two men and heard from "a lady of the town" that Joyce's aged parents and a sister were in Portsmouth, the father a member of the garrison invalid corps and the mesdames Joyce apparently stranded on parish charity. The London magistrate had experience dealing with police familiars such as the lady of the town. He most likely paid for her assistance; his next letter to Portland says, "I assume I can spend money freely."

The woman promised that she would have Mother Joyce plead with her son to abandon the rebellion. Graham hastened to write Portland that he had "completely the possession" of Mrs. Joyce through whom he would take the leader of the mutiny under his power and "trace the incendiaries (if any there are) who have been wicked enough to stimulate the seamen." Leaving the conspiratorial Cyprian to arrange the confrontation, Graham crossed to Gosport for high tea. He overheard a remark at the next table that sent him hurriedly back to Portsmouth to talk with an oracle named Bridgeland, who was full of inside gossip about the fleet and warned Graham, "Even if the present grievances are redressed, the next time the fleet comes in the men will stand out for their arrears of prize money."

Since his rebuff by magistrates and the mayor, the Londoner had been seeking a confidant in Portsmouth and hit upon Bridgeland. "Citizen Dean, a surgeon at Haslar Naval Hospital [in Gosport], is one of the most violent democrats in this part of the country," Graham disclosed. Bridgeland said, "Yes, he has already been sent out of the hospital." Graham passed on the charge that slopseller Brassett had been distributing books to the fleet. Bridgeland took his allegation down in writing and abruptly left the room. He went directly to Brassett and told him of the accusation and about the London agent who was looking for him.

Among the ships, Howe's presence improved the atmosphere and inspired mutual acts of magnanimity. Bridport withdrew a court-martial order for three men of *Duke* who had been charged with mutiny (insubordination) before the fleet strike. The crew of *Royal Sovereign* invited Sir Alan Gardner to come back aboard. He went out in a boat and saw the yard ropes were still up. "I shan't come aboard until you remove those disgraceful appendages!" he bawled. The next day the men again asked him back. But the ropes were still hanging and he departed in another roaring sulk. He complained to Lord Howe, who issued him a direct order to return to *Royal Sovereign,* yard ropes or no yard ropes. Gardner obeyed, griping about Howe and bitching at Bridport for denying his application for nervous leave. The Royal Sovereigns took him aboard with befitting honors and gave him three cheers. The yard ropes were still there. He gave the people a harangue. "I hope that your future good conduct will be the means of obliterating from my memory all that has passed," Sir Alan warned the people.

Howe reported to Spencer, "The discussion [seems to be] approaching to a desirable issue; but there appears to be some watchful agents, not yet to be traced, who neglect no opportunity to start fresh difficulties for obstructing the desirable accommodation." Howe patiently and painfully visited and spoke on ship after ship, showing the sailors that there had been no deception in Whitehall and that the parliamentary acts were in motion when the second strike occurred. With these points established, Howe got down to the bargain: if the seamen "generally" would express contrition to him and make up a petition praying for Howe to interpose his good offices for forgiveness, then the royal pardon would surely be forthcoming.

Most of the hands were willing, but they stuck with "unalterable adherence" to removing cruel and obnoxious officers. This was awkward; Howe could not accept from seamen a list of such officers and their offenses. It would necessitate courts-martial which would advertise to the service and to the world that the British Admiralty permitted menials to presume to select their masters. It was a dilemma in the French style.

Howe turned it inside out and split it as fine as possible. He requested special petitions from each plaintiff ship, listing not the names of objectionable officers but posts they held, "praying that his Majesty would indulge them with the appointment of other officers to those ships."

During his ship visits, Lord Howe patiently parlayed over the same ground with each company, observing the Whitehall pretense that a fleet legislature did not exist. The pose became most difficult when the negotiations reached the question of which, if any, officers were to be removed. Spencer had not faced this forecastle demand. The seamen, however, held scores of officers in loathing. If Howe's latent purpose was to be achieved, that of returning the fleet willingly to sea to meet the French, he had to sit with the sailors' parliament and go over its total blacklist. Accordingly, Black Dick violated a dozen articles of war and committed high state treason by asking the delegates of the fleet to duly assemble with him on Saturday 13 May on board Sir Peter Parker's office, H.M.S. *Royal William,* whose clerkly company had declined to join both mutinies. Lord Howe did not choose *Royal George,* flagship of the mutinous fleet. *Royal William* was the nearer of the two vessels to Portsmouth Point, but Black Dick may have had other reasons. Perhaps he wanted to keep Bridport out of the settlement and perhaps it amused him to bring the delegates aboard a vessel that had remained loyal throughout the risings.

Next morning Magistrate Graham, who had been unable to flush an agitator in Portsmouth, got up early to cross to the Isle of Wight and look for John Thelwall. But there were heavy rollers in The Solent and he postponed the voyage. While he was standing irresolutely at the Point, his friend, the lady-of-the-town, came up with news that the plot against Valentine Joyce was ripe. The mutiny leader was being lured ashore by word that his mother was dangerously ill. The old woman was primed to plead with her son that she would be cured only by his renouncing the mutiny. Graham and his female nark repaired to Mother Joyce's sickroom to await Delegate Joyce.

Boots galore pounded in the corridor and Valentine Joyce entered with eight shipmates, of hard and suspicious mien. The mother began her recital. The seamen broke in with jeers and demanded to know why she was with this strange gentleman and the well-known waterfront bawd. "The language became very violent," Graham noted. Joyce and his friends went back to the ship, leaving the magistrate with the ruins of his intrigue.

Aaron Graham persisted. He found a man who knew James Melvin, the leading delegate of *Pompée.* The middleman, however, would not produce the delegate until Graham consented to guarantee Melvin a navy discharge for deserting the cause. Although Graham was not able to detach Melvin, he wrote Portland, "I assume I have the power of discharge." He added that he was willing "to spend the better half of his private fortune" to end the business.

He added:

> I mix with and converse a great deal with seamen upon the beach and it is no small degree of consolation to me under the misfortune which they have brought upon the country (but which I am persuaded they do not sufficiently understand to be sensible of) to find that there is not a man in the fleet whose attachment to the King need be doubted or who would not rejoice in an opportunity of meeting and fighting the enemy.

Aaron Graham may have been green at snooping but he was not a fool.

In the Spithead anchorage as the great peace conference approached, goodwill swelled like Lord Howe's tortured feet. Several crews sent people ashore to invite their exiled officers to return. The Robusts handed a written address to their captain:

> The favours and goodness our officers confer upon us, are such as can be equalled by few officers in the fleet; and that is our just and grateful sense of the officers of his majesty's ship *Robust*. Is there a man so poor in spirit, that praises such as we have without imitating the actions worthy of them?

Preparing for Saturday's decisive meeting, each ship's company drew up petitions setting forth in detail their final demands, expressed with the best penmanship and grammar it could command. After the delegates arrived aboard *Royal William*, Black Dick and Sir Peter Parker embarked on a barge at the Point and were rowed in pomp to the ship. They were received aboard with full honors and entered the great cabin. It was empty. The delegates were below in the gun-room settling on the list of officers they wished removed. They kept the admirals waiting while they weighed degrees of obnoxiousness. Then they went up the hatchway in a body to meet Lord Howe.

The forecastle wanted to finish this conference with a purge of officers and the great cabin wanted to finish it with solid assurances that discipline would be restored and maintained. Howe brought out a theme never before heard in the service, that these elected representatives of the seamen would share with the officers responsibility for preventing mutiny. The delegates pledged it to the old admiral.

There may have been some unspoken reservations. Howe's inter-disciplinary idea was so novel that the men did not think of the *quid pro quo:* if the lower deck was to help discipline itself, it should also be represented on naval courts.

Then the meeting considered the officer blacklist. On this matter Howe's instructions were not firm. No one in authority knew which, or how many, officers the seamen wanted removed, or how insistent they would be about it. However, that same morning the sea lords had left to Bridport the decision of replacing the commanding officers of *Terrible* and *La Nymphe* and he had sent a new man to the latter. By this time, one of the commissioners of Admiralty, William Young, had come down to Portsmouth and was available as an adviser to Howe. Young carried great weight with Lord Spencer. But it remained Howe's risk.

The delegates handed him a list of about 75 names, or rather of specific positions on vessels. And, lo, Sir John Colpoys' name led all the rest. Thereupon, an admiral-of-the-fleet, ex-vice-admiral of England, general of marines, former member of the House of Commons, member of the House of Lords, Knight of the Garter and former first sea lord, coolly removed a brother admiral from employment at the insistence of an illegally constituted cabal of mutineers. Probably Howe gave them Sir John's pendant without much inner remorse. Then he resisted name after name, and they insisted. Howe found the delegates the "most suspicious but most generous minds I think I ever met with in the same class of men."

That morning they agreed to vacate about fifty appointments. Although Black Dick held the power to remove them formally, he decided to telegraph Spencer about the situation, in case there was strenuous objection in Whitehall; that is, from the Prime Minister. He also told Spencer he hoped to conclude negotiations next morning. He sent a horseman with amplification: "I must beg leave to confine my present intimations to the necessity of replacing a greater number of officers than I flattered myself would have been desired." He asked Spencer for replacements with "all possible dispatch. However ineligible the concession, it has become indispensably necessary." This would give Spencer time to object by telegraph before the settlement next morning.

When the delegates of *Duke* and *Mars* returned aboard and reported the day's proceedings, their ships' companies refused to join the general submission. While the other vessels were hauling down the red flag, the Dukes and Marses nailed it to the foretop. These crews had been suspected of conducting "traitorous" correspondence with persons ashore. Although the delegates had won every point in its bill of demands except shore leave, here were controlling groups on two capital ships that could defy the delegates and the agreement. Suspicion pointed to political, pacifist or Irish motivations that had been previously frustrated by the delegates.

The two recusant companies lowered boats and toured the fleet, trying to pull the rank and file in with them. No other crew would allow them on board. Hisses and abuse poured down on them. They went back to their ships and the delegates sent guard boats to cordon them off.

The ships at Plymouth still remained in a mutinous state but since they had voluntarily taken their cues from the Spithead delegates, Howe could be confident that they would observe the agreement he was about to conclude. At this juncture eight men-of-war came in The Solent flying red flags and yard ropes. This was a squadron belonging to Sir Roger Curtis, who was a prisoner aboard his flagship while seamen navigated and commanded his ships on a passage from Torbay. The men had learned of the cause from Plymouth seamen and decided to go to Spithead, ships and all, to have their wrongs righted. Lord Howe made his way to St. Helen's and visited the newcome vessels. He made known the parliamentary warranties, and the crews cheered. But when it came to signing the agreement, the Torbay squadron refused flatly until it was revised to throw out some of their officers, too. They had a longer list than Spithead, although they had many fewer ships. Howe heard the names and charges. The admiral's busy day ended with voluntary submission of the truculent men on *Duke* and *Mars*. They declared that "no set of men in his Majesty's service are more attached to their sovereign and their country," or more prepared "to shed the last drop of their vital blood" than the respondents.

But all was not quiet at Plymouth. Furious bellows issued from the fighting frigate captain, Sir Edward Pellew, who had returned from a cruise to find that his brother Israel, captain of *Greyhound,* had been put ashore by his crew on an accusation of tyranny. And Israel had been advised to ask for a replacement. Sir Edward protested to Lord Spencer, who replied that he and their lordships felt "the utmost indignation" over Israel's troubles, and he would "feel it his duty to find a situation for Capt. Pellew on board some other ship as soon as I can." Spencer was accepting the ouster. Pellew waxed even more wroth at this compliant attitude toward Israel's exile and assailed the First Lord again with a letter threatening to resign. But Spencer did not order *Greyhound* to take back its rejected captain and Sir Edward did not resign.

Pellew's own crews, however, made no move toward collective disobedience. The reason is given by Sir Edward's biographer, C. Northcote Parkinson: "It is clear that such men never thought in terms of pay. A frigate's crew thought only of prize money. Wages were to them a secondary consideration. They did not want more pay. They wanted to be transferred to a more lucrative station. And, as they and their officers wanted precisely the same thing, there was no need for them to quarrel."

Sir John Orde at Plymouth informed the Admiralty that the seamen would not take back the officers they had sent ashore. Their lordships replied:

> If this point should be strenuously opposed and remain the only obstacle to an accommodation and the return of the seamen to their duty, it must be conceded to the seamen at Plymouth as has already been done to those at Portsmouth on the ground of the officers themselves, disgusted at the unjust accusations brought against them by their crews, having requested to be superceded.

Every day during Howe's negotiations the Admiralty had been sending Bridport urgent sailing orders. On Saturday the sea lords told him to get away immediately even if he had to leave disaffected ships behind. More alarms had reached London of the French sailing from Brest. At the same time that the Admiralty expected the old admiral to move ships still under mutineer control, Lord Howe presented Bridport with a list of more than a hundred officers he would have to replace. And he was hearing from other officers who had been put ashore who did not want to return. Lieutenants John Cramer and Edward Clarributt of *Terrible* begged not to be forced back to their ship, "knowing the sentiments of the ship's company toward us since their final determination."

Sunday morning, 14 May, exactly four weeks after the thing began, the formal reconciliation of his Majesty's government and his seamen was enacted in the great cabin of *Royal William*. It was a beaming day for all save the 114 officers who were removed, led by Admiral Colpoys, and Captains Griffith, *London*; Nicholls, *Marl-*

borough; Campbell, *Terrible* and Cook, *Nymphe*. With them went 29 lieutenants; 8 commanders of marine detachments; 3 sailing masters; 4 surgeons; a chaplain; 17 master's mates; 25 midshipmen; 7 gunners, boatswains and carpenters; 5 noncommissioned marine officers and 3 masters-at-arms.

More than half of them were from Sir Roger Curtis's squadron. Not all went unwillingly. Admiral Colpoys had realistically appraised his situation several days earlier and his request for relief had already reached Whitehall. Captain Campbell and several others had also technically forestalled embarrassment by submitting applications for transfer.

Closing the conference, Admiral Howe pledged his honor that future petitions, properly drafted and signed, would receive prompt and serious attention.

The scene in the great cabin of *Royal William* represented an exceptional event in naval history. Men with no legal rights, kidnapped men, oppressed and disease-ridden, for the most part ignorant and illiterate men, subjected to the most rigid discipline, had organized secretly, set shrewd demands, maintained democratic as well as naval discipline, and won most of their aims from a great autocracy. If an earlier English confrontation was called Magna Carta, surely this was Minima Carta, a compass card for the future of a maritime people.

The delegates thanked Lord Howe for his "conciliatory behavior" and asked his permission to publicly thank him ashore next day for the happy result. Deeply fatigued and aching, Black Dick nevertheless acceded to the request. "Away all boats!" the word passed around St. Helen's. Fiddlers, fifers and drummers struck up "Hearts of Oak" and "Rule Britannia." A huge water procession formed and escorted Howe to Portsmouth Point. The church bells were ringing noon as Black Dick stepped ashore to the hails of "an immense multitude," and the smiles of Lady Howe. Together they walked to General Pitt's house. Valentine Joyce, ex-president of the delegates of the Whole Fleet, stepped up to Howe and said, "At what hour tomorrow morning would your lordship be pleased to embark?"

Howe said, "Your time shall be mine."

"At seven? The tide will serve at that hour, your lordship."

"At seven, then."

Joyce turned to Lady Howe. "I beg to know whether your ladyship will honor us with your company? I assure your ladyship of perfect safety and freedom from apprehension."

Lady Howe replied, "Nothing will give me greater pleasure than to accede to your request."

Lord Howe said, "Joyce, come along and have a glass of wine with me." The admiral and the mutineer walked into the military governor's house and toasted his Majesty.

That evening Howe received copies of the Admiralty orders confirming the King's pardon. George had signed it three days earlier. It had been promised three weeks earlier. The pardon extended to "all such seamen and marines on board any ships of the fleet who may have been guilty of any act of mutiny, or disobedience of orders, or neglect of duty, or who have returned, or shall, upon notification of such his Majesty's proclamation, return to the regular and ordinary discharge of their duty." It confirmed Howe's pledge that there was to be no recrimination but a "total oblivion of such offenses."

Commissioner Young told Hugh Seymour, "I am afraid much mischief has been done by the mode in which the mutineers at Spithead were treated by Lord Howe; but the concession made, by letting the officers be sent on shore, was not entirely to be attributed to him. The ministers were so anxious to get the fleet to sea, that they directed it to be done, rather than protract the settlement of the business." Young's reference to "ministers" could only mean that Pitt himself approved sacking the officers. Other admirals severely criticized Howe for surrendering the careers and honor of brother-officers to mutineers. Black Dick wrote Portland how the thing had gone and cited Bridport for helpfulness "in my endeavours to promote the benefit of his Majesty's service upon this most intensely interesting occasion."

At Portsmouth, Monday was given up to public rejoicing for peace between the forecastle and quarterdeck and honors to the great pacifier, Admiral Howe. The delegates came ashore at dawn and marched behind a band of music to General Pitt's house, where they serenaded Black Dick. At that hour the tired old man may have preferred some other form of approbation, but he came down and invited them all in to splice the main brace for the military governor's sideboard. Then he conducted them to a balcony and townspeople collected to applaud him and the successful mutineers. A number of ships' bands and the fleet marine band arrived and swelled the grand effect. Lord and Lady Howe came down with the delegates and started walking to the Point, nobody in step, all chatting amiably, while the musicians raced ahead, took up marching order, and blasted away. At the water's edge it seemed that all the men and boats in The Solent waited to make up the triumphant progression through the fleet. The first barge contained musicians and flags, the second Lord and Lady Howe, the next ones delegates, and then came admirals, lords and ladies. They were escorted on either side by a line of captain's boats with crews duked out fit to kill. They were the only seamen in the Georgian navy who wore uniforms and it was a point of vanity with a post captain to outfit his private crew with original and sometimes eye-popping livery.

Valentine Joyce, the forecastle leader, was sending the boats off when a seaman brought him four strangers who had inquired for the head of the delegates. They wore landsmen's clothes, but they were unmistakably seamen, Charles MacCarthy, Thomas Atkinson, Matthew Hollister and a man named Hinds. They had come overland as elected delegates of the Nore, the great fleet base at Thamesmouth, to offer support to their messmates' cause at Spithead. Joyce put them aboard his boat as honored guests to accompany the review of the fleet that marked the triumph of the cause.

During the long pull to St. Helen's, the Nore party told their story. Atkinson was the captain of the forecastle in the command ship, *Sandwich,* 90, at the Nore. MacCarthy was his shipmate. Hinds came from *Clyde,* 38, and Hollister from *Director,* 64, Captain William Bligh's ship.

Four days ago Admiral Duncan of the North Sea fleet had detached *Director* to go around to the Thames for refit. She had arrived last Friday, when, without warning, Hollister and the company had gone to Bligh and ordered him to put ashore Lieutenants Ireland and Church and Mr. Birch, the sailing master, on grounds of "ill usage" of the men. That same day many other ships raised the red flag and sent their captains and unpopular officers away. Captain Bligh, however, had not been expelled. "The Bounty Bastard," moreover, circumvented the expulsion of his odious juniors by taking them off the watch list and sending them into hiding on board.

The Nore delegation regaled Joyce with their perilous overland odyssey. To endow the journey, their unpaid messmates on *Sandwich* contributed £2/6/10, and the rest of the Nore fleet chipped in sufficient coppers for them to obtain two ten-pound notes in Sheerness. They took the cheapest coach to London and bought seats on the Portsmouth stage, due to depart in three hours from Charing Cross. During the layover the quartet, which had not been allowed on land for quite a while, split up and visited friends and relatives in the city. MacCarthy and Hinds, walking back from the East End, were collared by a press gang on Tower Hill. The Nore delegates were by law deserters, by circumstance mutineers, and by nature eloquent men. MacCarthy actually induced the impress officer to let them go free.

Now the men from the Nore had come to St. Helen's just in time to witness the victory of justice and unity that everyone thought would also pacify the fleets of Yarmouth, the Nore and Plymouth.

As the procession of the boats passed the ships in Spithead, thousands of men in the yards, fighting tops, bulwarks and shrouds shouted in unison for Black Dick and the delegates.

But as the flotilla tracked toward Sir Roger Curtis's flagship, *Prince,* 98, it was noticed that she wore no flag and not many sailors in the top hamper. His companions tried to divert Howe's attention from *Prince,* but the old man ordered his bargemen to go alongside her. He grabbed the receiving ropes and dragged himself up the wooden cliff. The seamen on deck were carrying arms, which the rest of the fleet had returned to the chests the day before. The boatswain bounded forward, sounding his whistle. Black Dick's official party clambered aboard and the fleet delegates had a frowning word or two for the Princes. The holdouts contritely ran the Union Jack aloft.

Howe made a ceremonial stop at Bridport's flagship, *Royal George,* that afternoon and read the original copy of the royal pardon to the company. He held it high, turning it about for everyone to see the King's initials and great seal. All over the fleet, the union flag was restored and the red jack was folded in the locker until it next should be brought forth for battle.

Black Dick heard that seamen from the Nore were aboard and had them brought to the great cabin.

"I have heard there is a disturbance at the Nore," he said. "What is it all about?"

MacCarthy answered, "My lord, we just want the same treatment as the Spithead people."

Howe gave them each a print of the royal pardon, and MacCarthy a copy of the Act of Parliament. The concessions applied to all seamen in the King's navy. "Show these to your people."

When the boat parade got back in the evening, it was received by the largest crowds in Portsmouth since Black Dick came in with the French frigates after the Glorious First of June. The delegates of the fleet carried him on their shoulders to the governor's house. Not to be outdone, Lady Howe asked the delegates in for supper.

Historians call it "the respectable mutiny."

Admiral Lord Bridport, shunned during the pacification of his

fleet and not consulted by either Howe or Spencer on the humiliation
to scores of his officers, was now nonchalantly advised by the first sea
lord "to supply the deficiency of officers which may occur by availing
yourself of the services of any Captains or other Officers belonging to
ships in a state of refitting or on Half Pay who may be proper for the
purpose and within reach." What Lord Bridport needed was a press
gang that captured officers.

Howe went back to London and talked earnestly with Spencer
about the future of the dislocated officers. He urged that they be
continued on full pay. "It was justice due them, as it was not deemed
expedient to call them to account for their imputed misconduct."
Spencer agreed. The old peacemaker reflected that the times might
continue to be perilous if "the assumed right of rejecting their officers
will go through the fleet at home and abroad." He had, at Spithead,
in his own judgment and the approval of the cabinet and the sea lords,
contributed directly to this dangerous prospect.

Edmund Burke, who was heading into terminal insanity, wrote
Secretary-at-War Windham:

> But among all the parts of this fatal measure the Mission of
> my Lord Howe has been by far the most mischievous. Had a
> great naval commander been sent down—*Gravem pietate et
> meritus virum quem*—To awe the seditious into obedience, it
> would have been the best thing that could have been thought
> of; but to send the first name in the Navy, and who had been
> but lately a Cabinet Minister and First Lord of the Admiralty,
> at upwards of seventy years of age, to hunt among mutineers
> for grievances, to take the law from Joice, a seditious clubist
> of Belfast, and to remove by his orders some of the principal
> Officers of the Navy, puts an end to all hopes forever. Such
> mischief need not to have been attended with such degradation.

Lord Bridport wanted to resign. He had wanted to resign before
the disturbance started and now he wanted to resign the more. He
wrote for sympathy and advice to Lord Chatham, the former first sea
lord, Spencer's enemy who agreed with Bridport on "the delicate
situation in which an Officer is placed who is to carry this Fleet to
sea. . . . I foresee difficulties in any long and arduous services.
With a view however to the Publick, I should consider any change in
the Command of the Fleet as most unfortunate." This was also the
Admiralty's position. Lord Bridport had succeeded by failing. To
save faces all around he was sentenced to go back to sea with the

Channel fleet. The Admiralty office telegraphed him to sail immediately. It was an impossibility. He did not have enough officers, and fifty of his boats and 500 of his best seamen were still ashore ringing the welkin. Next morning Bridport tried to leave. The crews obeyed the order to unmoor, but toward the flagship came hails, flag hoists, and boats protesting that too many people were missing. Most of the boats and 400 men remained at Portsmouth. Lord Bridport rescinded the sailing order.

The four delegates from the Nore were also sleeping off the celebration. In their pockets were the vital peace documents that might have ended their mutiny. It took MacCarthy and Hollister twenty-four hours to get started on their two-day journey to the Nore. Atkinson stayed a week in Portsmouth and was the object of a local fund drive to get him out of town. Hinds woke up, recognized that he was a free man, and hit the road for the interior, deserting King and mutiny alike.

The unwilling Admiral Bridport sailed at dawn 17 May in thick weather, short dozens of officers and hundreds of hands. There were so many leading men still at liberty in Portsmouth that Magistrate Graham extended his researches into the cause of the mutiny for an indefinite period.

After Bridport left, the Admiralty received a folk missive signed only, *"Thou unknowed,"* which asserted that "One of the dilagates of the fleet told me that there would allways be a private corryspondence carried on between them by letters" and that, before the committee of delegates was dissolved, it designated Valentine Joyce and a man named Watkins of *Defence* as shadow leaders, to be prepared to reconvene the delegates if necessary.

The King also received a note:

> Earl Spencer has the honour of laying before your Majesty a letter received from Lord Howe this morning, together with a message just come up by the telegraph, in consequence of which he flatters himself he may congratulate your Majesty on the termination of the disorders on board the Fleet under the command of Lord Bridport, and it is to be hoped that the other divisions of your Majesty's Fleet which have been affected by the contagion of their bad example, will now follow them in returning to their duty.
>
> Earl Spencer likewise lays before your Majesty the letter received from Vice-Admiral Buckner subject of disturbances at the Nore and Sheerness which he hopes will very speedily

be terminated, as the persons concerned in them do not appear
to have any specifick object of complaint.

The King replied:

I receive with pleasure Earl Spencer's report of the well-
grounded hopes that the Channel Fleet, by the cool conduct
of Earl Howe, is returning to reason. As soon as it is known
what officers have been obliged to quit particular ships I desire I may have a list of them and of those sent to relieve them.
I trust the disturbance at the Nore, as it seem[s] ungrounded,
will, when it is known that the Channel Fleet has sailed, will
cease.

But the disturbance at the Nore, now three days old, was bigger
and more violent than the breeze at Spithead.

X

Mutiny at the Nore

"Let death be shared like prize money—the lion's share to the officers."

—*18th-century British seaman before a battle*

THE SEAT of the big new mutiny, the Nore, was the most populated naval and merchant ship anchorage in Britain. It was in the lower Thames estuary at its confluence with the river Medway. Tens of thousands of wooden vessels a year passed the Nore up the seariver to imperial London or to the shipyards and docks along the way, or into the meandering Medway at the head of which lay a major naval dockyard at Chatham. At this period, in the infancy of canals and conception of railroads, Britain's domestic bulk cargo was carried mainly in coasting sail. In the coal trade alone there were about two thousand colliers rounding her dangerous shores.

The King's navy resorted to the Nore more than to any proper base including Portsmouth, the grand fleet base. At the Nore, frigates rendezvoused with merchant convoys for the Baltic and the western ocean, ships came in to be provisioned, paid or repaired, or to be sheltered from the stormy Channel, and ships came down from the big Thames yards on builders' trials. Ships wandered or blown in from squadrons lay by for orders or were sent out to reinforce the blockaders—Adam Duncan at the Texel, or Bridport at Brest or Old Jarvey at Cadiz. There was as well a clutter of prison hulks, guard ships, receiving ships, sheer hulks, captured bottoms, storeships, and all the lesser watercraft required to serve the big ones. The Nore was a catchall.

The Great Nore anchorage was about a half mile wide and four miles long, marked out from the prevailing mud shoals by a depth contour averaging six fathoms. It lay in the mainstream, northwest of the town of Sheerness, which jutted into the junction of the Thames and Medway. A pocket anchorage off the town was called the Little Nore.

Sheerness was a small, drab garrison reclaimed from tidal mud by a bulkheaded landfill which gave it the appearance of a fortress. Nominally the Sheerness guns dominated the invasion course to London, but the town had a feeble claim in the military estimates. It usually got burned and sacked the first day a hostile fleet raised the English shore. Its role was delaying, not deterrent. The next day the invaders got swamped in the lascivious curves of the Medway trying to get at Chatham or started the discouraging voyage up the Thames against many ships and forts in the thirteen coils of water that moated London from enemy keels.

Sheerness had some scruffy soldiers' barracks and a small dockyard. The dockyard workers' families lived in three old two-deckers, propped upright on the flats and covered with shanties, children and washing lines.

"The Officer in Command of H.M. Ships and Vessels in the River Medway and at the Buoy of the Nore," to give his full title, was a troubled old Vice-Admiral named Charles Buckner. Unlike his Spithead counterpart, Sir Peter Parker, who usually dealt with fleets and squadrons under central command, Buckner had a welter of individual ships. He was the admiral of everything and nothing. Everyone complained to him. The company of H.M.S. *Blanche,* for instance:

> We are imployed from morning to two or three o'clock in the afternoon washing and scrubbing the Dicks and Every Day Ourer Chest and Bags is ordered on Dick and not down till night nor ourselves neither Even so perticlor as to wash the Dicks with fresh watter and if we gate wett at aney time and hang or spread our cloas to Dry our Captain thros them overboard by which we Big the favour of an other Commander or an other Ship we still remain your most Worthy Subjects. (Signed) BLANCHES CREW

Petitions to redress grievances had been coming in since the war began. Some of the earliest were from captains, begging the Admiralty to pay their private servants instead of their having to foot £11/8/2 per annum from their own pockets. Among the signers were Sir Roger Curtis, Alexander Hood and Sir Charles Pole of the

Spithead drama. Crews complained: "We want another ship or removal of officers" (*Crescent*); "kindly remove our first lieutenant for drunkenness and cruelty" (Sloop *Weazle*); protests on flogging and short rations (*Amphitrite*); for removal of a cruel captain (*Nassau*); "Captain a tiriant," enough to "make the sparites of the Englishman to Rise and Steer the Ship into an Enemies Port" (*Shannon*); "Captain stops our grog if our shirts aren't clean, but we have only salt water to wash in" (*Reunion*); "We are very inhumanly used" (*Emerald*). Among these petitions there were several from crews begging the sea lords *not* to take away their captain or first officer, or else transfer the company with them to the new ship.

Many months before the Spithead mutiny, Admiral Buckner had received petitions that were no longer prayerful but defiant. The previous winter the Reunions had declared, "We one and all do solemnly protest that we will neither fight nor sail away any more with the said Captain and Third Lieutenant." And two years earlier the ship's company of *Ceres* frigate had petitioned their lordships for relief from their captain, John Peyton, and his first officer. Evan Nepean, secretary of the Admiralty, instructed Sheerness "to take any steps that can prudently be adopted to ascertain whether there are any grounds for complaints." He asked Buckner for a report "but not in the shape of a public inquiry."

This was one of the rare occasions that Whitehall paid attention to pressures on Buckner from below. Nobody in London seemed interested in the fact that the marine company on *Barfleur* had been more than two years without shore leave. The Admiralty poured people on Buckner and did not care to hear about what happened then.

His own flagship, *Sandwich,* 90 guns, was being used as an emergency receiving ship for impressed men. In addition to her normal complement of 900, she had more than 500 coerced supernumeraries. The navy was scraping deep into the manpower of England. Admiral Buckner complained to the Admiralty about 80 men that Rochester magistrates had sent him, "Fifteen are absolutely unfit on account of old age and various diseases. Thirteen are fit only for second class boys." Surgeon William Snipe of *Sandwich* wrote a letter to his captain, James Robert Mosse, about conditions on board. The men were "dirty, almost naked and in general without beds, having lost them by either their own insolence or by the villainy of their companions. . . . I feel myself peculiarly called upon to point out the little avail of prescribing medicines to unhappy sufferers who are so bare of common necessities and compelled to mix with the throng by laying on the decks."

Snipe found that sores and scalds degenerated into ulcers which he could not cure in the jumble of befouled misery between decks. "The air is so impregnated with human effluvia," said the physician, "that contagious fevers must inevitably be the consequence. Untoward fortune has often placed me in situations where I could not practice my profession agreeable to its principles or the feelings of my conscience, but I never was in a situation more replete with anxiety than the present as surgeon of the *Sandwich.*"

The letter was forwarded to Nepean who ordered the ulcer cases to a hospital ship, or if it was full, to another unarmed vessel. Buckner reduced the congestion by sending able-bodied extras to *Latona.*

Among the quota men thrown in *Sandwich* at the time Snipe wrote was a handsome, robust, dark-eyed thirty-year-old named Richard Parker, who was to become the most famous mutiny leader in maritime history, excepting perhaps Fletcher Christian. Parker had just come from Perth, where he had accepted £30 to transfer from a debtors' jail to H.M.S. *Sandwich.* He had been a carpenter, schoolteacher, a midshipman and a lieutenant in the King's navy; he knew it from head to quarter gallery. He was a magniloquent speaker with an appealing personality, and he had been court-martialed for disobedience. Parker did not consider himself inferior to anyone. Except for this flaw, he was a perfect Georgian hero.

During their struggle the Spithead seamen wrote and sent envoys to the Nore to solicit support and to carry their regulations as guides. The men in the Thames estuary recognized that, if their messmates at Spithead succeeded, they, too, would benefit. The trouble was that there was no forecastle organization at the Nore. They could not translate feeling to acts until they had united the lower deck in a miscellany of vessels.

After Sir Alan Gardner's tantrum and Sir John Colpoys' bloodletting, the Nore seamen suspected perfidy. They could no longer remain passive. It was time to demonstrate real unity with Spithead. Individual ship's companies produced leaders. On 6 May, midway in the second Spithead remonstrance, they circulated a resolution for a delegates' meeting on *Sandwich* to adopt a fraternal oath, which would be given to all sailors at the Nore and which imitated the Spithead oath:

I, A.B., do voluntary make oath and swear that I will be true in the cause we are embarked in and I will to the laying down of my life be true to the Delegates at present assembl'd, whilst they continue to support the present cause, and I will communicate to them at all times all such things as may be for the good of our undertakings and all conspiracies that may tend to the subversion of our present plan. I will also endeavour to detect and suppress as full as in my power everything that may lead to a separation of the unity so necessary [to] completing our present system.

The first Nore delegates' meeting on *Sandwich* was handled with effective secrecy; the command took no notice of it. It would take the delegates quite a few days to win the ships over to their oath and administer it, and not before then would the Nore be strong enough to act on its own. Word quickly came that the grand fleet at Spithead had again gone over to delegate control. The Nore committee redoubled its organizing activity to reach strike capability as soon as possible. The delegates named 9:30 in the morning of Friday 12 May as the time for the Sandwiches to give the opening cheers and the delegates to take over the anchorage. Not a suspicion of this plot reached Admiral Buckner. He, in fact, unwittingly made the seizure easier by scheduling a court-martial on the appointed morning, which removed many captains from their ships, William Bligh among them.

The court-martial was duly convened aboard H.M.S. *Inflexible,* 64. On *Sandwich,* after breakfast, all hands were turned out to work. Without warning, the Sandwiches left the waist and thronged to the foremast and fore shrouds.

"Now altogether. Hip! Hip!"

"HURRAH!"

"Hip! Hip!"

"HURRAH!"

"Hip! Hip!"

"HURRAH!"

Seamen Peter Holding, Black Jack Campbell, and Thomas McCann led a crowd that gathered around 3rd Lt. Nicholas Platt. Holding said, "Sir, we desire the keys to the magazine. We want to load the signal gun." Platt said, "Why, Holding, Mr. Justice has taken the keys ashore with him." The delegate cried, "Damn my eyes! We must go down and break it all open, then."

As the cheers boomed through the anchorage, the officers of the court-martial looked at each other. The hurrahs of mutiny sounded from ship to ship. Buckner adjourned the court and the captains hastened to their vessels. They found that "Reeve yard ropes!" had already been ordered. Admiral Buckner went ashore to be closer to the Admiralty by telegraph and rider, calling for Captain James Robert Mosse of *Sandwich* to deal with the situation on the flagship. Mosse, who had been ashore nursing an attack of gout, went to his ship and sent a report to Buckner:

> I shall just describe to you the state I found the *Sandwich* in. The people all quiet, but had taken the command of the ship, planted sentinels with cutlasses both on the decks and gangways, were in possession of the keys of the magazine, store-rooms, etc. . . .
>
> The master [William Bray] is their chosen commander, and who conveys all messages between me and them. Delegates have come on board from some of the other ships, and at present their council-chamber is the starboard bay. Their steps exactly copied from their brethren at Portsmouth. They sent soon after I got on board, demanded and almost instantly seized all the arms, which, I am told, are lodged in a store-room below. They are strick in their discipline and look-out, and have a watchful jealousy throughout. . . .

While Captain Bligh was away at the trial, the Directors elected their delegates and voted to expel his two lieutenants and sailing master on charges of "ill usage." The leading delegate, Able Seaman John Hulme, had formerly served with Bligh in H.M.S. *Calcutta* where he had won a promotion to master's mate. Now, after taking over *Director,* Hulme went to *Swan,* 16, which had not yet joined the cause, and hailed the watch officer. "Sir, ask permission to come on board to see my brother." He was allowed on the ladder and went below. After a bit, the first officer of *Swan,* Mr. Marshall, sent for Hulme and said, "I have heard of the doings on the *Director.* I have sent word to Captain Bligh. His boat is coming to pick you up." Hulme said, "But, I'm not finished with my visit." The officer said, "We are busy at work here. You must return to your own ship." Hulme protested. Marshall put him in one of his boats and delivered him to *Director.*

William Bligh returned to his ship and found his men obeying Hulme and delegate James MacLaurin, and learned that they had "discharged" his officers. Bligh controlled his famous temper and scorching lexicon. The crew was obeying all routine orders. There was no hint from the company of putting Bligh himself off the ship. He decided to play the waiting game and the first move, when he could make it, was going to be against Messrs. Hulme and Mac-Laurin.

Bligh continued to control the side arms on *Director* and retained the keys to the chests. Delegate Thomas McCann of *Sandwich* came aboard, cutlass in hand and a brace of pistols in his belt, and exhorted the Directors to put out an armed boat to rescue delegates detained on another ship. A *Director* spokesman said, "Captain Bligh, we request arms and leave to take a boat." The Captain replied, "No." McCann yelled, "If I was on the *Director,* I'd have the arms!" He overlooked the fact that he *was* on *Director,* with pistols, with which he might have attempted Bligh's keys. But McCann went over the side without trying. He returned to *Sandwich* and went to the cockpit to have an infected leg dressed. "If the people of *Director* would have been willing to help, I'd have thrown Bligh overboard," he boasted.

McCann was suffering from unhealed ulcerated wounds and debility. Surgeon Snipe ordered him ashore to hospital, with approval of the ship's committee. McCann climbed the hospital roof and hoisted a red flag. He complained that the hospital beer was no good and returned to *Sandwich.* They tried to put him in the sick bay in H.M.S. *Spanker,* but McCann refused, explaining that he had helped duck the butcher on *Spanker* and feared revenge. The committee regarded him as hotheaded.

The delegates made a second attempt to enlist *Swan* in the cause by sending a boat of delegates led by Charles MacCarthy, the eccentric supernumerary from *Sandwich,* who was about to be sent in the liaison party to Spithead. First Lieutenant Marshall was on the alert. He called out *Swan*'s marines and forbade MacCarthy to come aboard. The ship's company "all jumped up," according to Boatswain William Parr, and "cried out with one voice, 'Let them come!'" MacCarthy said to the lieutenant, "Remember what happened to Admiral Colpoys. We have got charge of the *Sandwich* and the *Director* and we have come to see your people righted. They have lodged a complaint with the committee." He came up the side. The officer did not resist. The delegate handed him a list of complaints from the Swans.

Admiral Buckner explained to the Admiralty that the seamen did not believe Parliament had passed the act and alleged that "their brethren in Portsmouth had been ill used." Secretary Nepean replied,

"As affairs are now however in so favorable a train, their lordships hope and trust that a happy termination will be put to these matters in the course of a few hours." The sea lords were determined to instill optimism in the troubled commands.

On the first day of the Nore stoppage, the delegates laid out an organization varying from that of Spithead. The individual ship elected twelve committeemen to decide its affairs and sent two men to the fleet committee. The ship committee elected a captain, whose functions were similar to those of a post captain with his Majesty's commission, except that he could be overruled or removed by the committee on board.

The fleet committee drew up preliminary regulations and sent them to the ships:

Art. 1. Unanimity the only means of gaining the end in view.
Art. 2. Strict discipline to be maintained. No private liquor allowed.
Art. 3. Respect to superior officers. Duty to be carried on as before.
Art. 4. An early communication with all delegates, to bring about a speedy remedy.
Art. 5. No master or pilot to go ashore.
Art. 6. All unsuitable officers to be sent ashore, as at Spithead.

An added article went, "Any regulation which may occur among yourselves for the preservation of good order, you will add them to the above." The copy of these orders received by the fireship *Comet* was dated 11 May.

Several of these bylaws came from Spithead, but the intent of No. 5 could be interpreted two ways: navigators would be retained aboard for immediate sailing against the enemy, or for sailing to a destination decided by the mutineers.

A set of *Rules to be Observed* by the seaman, preserved only in the *Comet* papers, included:

5) That he will observe the directions of the Boatswain's Mates, not considering them in their former Characters (as Soul Drivers) but as Men desirous of having the Duty of the Ship carried on in a Manlike and Proper Manner.

Another rule provided that:

A committee of not less than seven or more than thirteen People at a time shall be held on board every Morning between

the Hours of Seven & Eight O Clock to take into Consideration the Transactions for the Day and also to decide in all
Cause of dispute & and to endeavour to comprimise all of a
trifling nature & punish such as are of an improper kind.

The Nore rules applied to feminine company as well:

That for the better Support of the Rules, Women the time
they are on board are Subject to such Punishments as the Committee may find necessary to Inflict and Proof from three Witnesses attesting their Misconduct but it is to be observed that
her husband is not admitted as Evidence [witness] against her.

The internal ships' committees chose officers to be sent ashore.
Sandwich delegate William Gregory demanded that the first lieutenant, Philip Justice, be expelled for removing screens that were
placed around the hammocks of married and visiting couples between
decks. Gregory objected to having "our women exposed as brutes
in the field or common prostitutes." Other witnesses said they had
heard Justice boasting to a yacht captain, "I have taken the screens
down." The committee voted unanimously to put the officer out. His
sea chest was thrown into a boat and he followed.

Admiral Buckner ordered *Champion,* 20, out of Sheerness harbor
to the Little Nore, but the crew forced the pilot to the Great Nore
and sent their captain ashore. The ship's marines, however, refused
to put their officers off.

The seamen of the frigate *Clyde,* 38, were reluctant fellow travelers
in the cause. Their captain, Charles Cunningham, was a fine professional officer who ruled his ship humanely. He appreciated the over-
whelming odds against a crew that refused to join the mutiny and did
not oppose—in fact may have covertly encouraged—his men to go
through the motions of cheering, hanging yard ropes, and attending
meetings. Still in command of his ship, he withheld exercise of this
power until the proper time.

The second morning of the stand-out the frigate *San Fiorenzo,*
Captain Sir Harry Neale, arrived at the Buoy of the Nore under orders
to await the newlyweds, the Prince and Princess of Württemberg, and
carry them to Germany. The *San Fiorenzo* crew was also disinclined
to join the mutiny. Hearing this good news, Admiral Buckner moved
his court-martial from the hostile *Inflexible* to the loyal ship. He was
doing his best to pretend that nothing was happening. Whitehall encouraged the attitude. Nepean thought this minor petulance in the

Thames would be over as soon as Lord Howe settled things at Portsmouth, which was expected next day.

The military court moved into the great cabin of *San Fiorenzo,* which had been tastefully furnished as the nuptial bower of their highnesses. Buckner and the captains were trying a man for mutiny. The hearing was interrupted by shouting. Sir Harry Neale went out. On the quarterdeck stood the massed delegates of the fleet, earnestly addressing his men on the advantages of joining the cause. The Fiorenzos remained reluctant. Perhaps because of irresistible curiosity on both sides, Sir Harry conducted the mutineer delegates into the military court. According to Conrad Gill, a historian of the mutiny, "The delegates wanted to take charge of the prisoner themselves."

When Captain Neale asked his uninvited guests to leave, the delegates got into their boats without demur. They rowed over to *Inflexible.* She weighed anchor and slid past *San Fiorenzo* on the tide. There was a puff of smoke from the two-decker, and a shocking sound —the boom of a twelve-pounder, and a whistling cannon ball cut the footrope on the jib boom of *San Fiorenzo.* The ex-loyalists obediently gave three cheers and rove the yard ropes. The shot, even if a warning, differentiated the Nore from Spithead. This was not a respectable mutiny.

Officers who remained on board ships by sufferance of their companies were treated with respect and their orders were obeyed—if they chose to give them. Some juniors discovered that things went on as usual without orders, so spent their time improving their minds. The seamen worked up a running joke with a thousand variations with which they twitted the officers. A man would approach an officer with complete deference and wait to be recognized. "Begging your pardon, sir. Request permission, sir. Would you be so good, sir, as to authorize each man a bottle of gin for breakfast?" Lt. Edward Birch of *Director* described these jests as "illegal or atrocious."

The second day, the delegates raised twenty pounds to send Matthew Hollister, MacCarthy and two others to Spithead to show their material support and bring back latest strategies from the authors of it all. The mission carried no suggestions of its own. The Nore was a holding action, without separate ambitions. Its hastily drafted regulations imposed no policy on shore leave, the liberty book was open at the gangway, and tickets were handed out generously.

The morning liberty boats carried demonstrators and musicians, including a deafening brass band which swaggered at the head of frequent sailors' street parades, blasting out a true blue repertoire of "God Save the King," "Rule Britannia" and "Britons Strike Home." The marchers wore blue hatbands with golden legends, *Success to the Delegates of the fleet.* At the head of the march was McCann, the sick man of *Sandwich,* carrying a large Union Jack. He said he was "determined to stay and see it out."

The afternoon liberty boats carried some ships' committees ashore to deliberate in taverns. They adopted The Checquers public house as the official rendezvous in Sheerness. The fleet delegates continued to meet on *Sandwich.* Both sides, the Nore parliament and Admiral Buckner's command, indulged parading and high jinks in town while waiting for Black Dick to make peace. There was no strategic urgency. Here there was no battle fleet pinned down as there was at Spithead.

On Monday evening, 15 May, the telegraph brought a welcome message to Admiral Buckner: Admiral Howe had reached a complete settlement at Spithead. Buckner sent the news to *Sandwich* and it was spread in the fleet. *Sandwich* refused to accede until documentary proof was produced. When orders were given on the storeship *Grampus* to weigh anchor, the crew disobeyed.

Buckner complained to London that he needed more than a telegraph message to persuade his men to duty. The Admiralty replied that he should "convince [the seamen] of the enormity of their offenses, particularly the death of Mr. Saffray, occasioned by their misconduct."

Saffray was one of the two surgeons at the naval hospital in Sheerness. The first day the delegates had gone to the hospital to see how their messmates were getting on. The patients charged Saffray and his colleague with maltreatment and the delegates threatened them. One doctor ran away and Saffray committed suicide. No other surgeon would take charge. During the rest of the Nore affair the sick aboard and ashore were treated by surgeon's mates and the hippocratist Doctor Snipe.

The Sheerness commissioner obtained cash to pay the crews of *Champion* and *Inflexible,* but it did not induce them to return to captain's orders. The seamen found themselves in almost complete charge of ship's husbandry. They did a thorough job, especially in inspecting the victuals aboard. Edward Mehan, a delegate of *Inflexible,* appointed a committee to examine the bread stores. Out of 8,400 pounds aboard, they condemned more than half.

The days imitated all days in home port. Requisitions went ashore for supplies and victuals; the pursers looked for slops to sell the seamen; the crew lowered the yards and repaired them, and restored standing rigging.

Quartermaster William Thursby of *Sandwich* wrote a personal letter to a friend on *Inflexible* in which he referred to the fleet delegates as "members of parliament." A committee censor read it and turned the letter over to the fleet delegates, who reprimanded Thursby "for speaking so lightly of them."

Richard Parker blossomed rapidly in the combination. Two days after the strike began, he was in the chair of the *Sandwich* company. He called in the reluctant petty officers to persuade them to join the cause. He said, "I have been a petty officer and I know petty officers labor under many grievances. Am I right?" They did not answer. Parker invited them to take the oath. Charles Ryan, schoolmaster of the ship, said it was unnecessary since an Act of Parliament had granted a pay increase. Parker said, "I beg your pardon, not an Act, an Order-in-Council." The bashful mates questioned that and Parker called for the official text and read it. It was an Act of Parliament, all right, but Parker said, "It isn't permanent. It's only good for 365 days and a few hours. Now, my friends, this oath is voluntary. . . ." He made no converts.

Although the gravity of the Nore demonstration was not yet appreciated in Westminster, Pitt's position was growing weaker. Lord Moira continued to promote a combination to oust him, while disclaiming interest in succeeding to the office. His lordship flaunted a "formidable body of members, violent against Pitt, though they vote with him, but they will not bear the Opposition as a party." This group was not "the Armed Neutralists," said Moira, "but an association of much greater weight," whose existence was not suspected. They wanted to parry "the impending anarchy." Evidently Moira's braves were formed of everybody in the House with any reason to dislike Pitt. Moira appealed for aid to a silly old gent called the Duke of Northumberland, who had quarreled with Pitt, had been turfed out of the army as a hindrance and who owned three members of the House, including Joseph Richardson, a Foxite Whig.

The duke was poaching his rejected carcass at Bath when Lord Moira's flattering appeal arrived. The old peer thought Moira was nominating him for prime minister and in the great tradition of politics replied, "No power on earth should ever have persuaded me to accept a place in cabinet, when there was one moment's doubt whether I should be admitted or not. People seem wonderfully to mistake my character, and appear to imagine that I am anxious to hold office. I have an ample fortune and the general good opinion of the country to satisfy me if I wish to be quiet; a numerous and hardy race of men, my tenantry, to back me and support me in troublesome times; and so far from wishing to seek for office, it would require much persuasion indeed to prevail upon me to accept of any." Having said that, Northumberland stated his conditions for accepting the prime ministry: first, Fox would not be allowed in the cabinet; second, Moira was to tell him who was in on the plot and what policies they wished him to embrace; and third, his employees and followers had to be given powerful posts near his side.

Both the duke's Whig M.P. and Moira passed this secret memoire to Charles James Fox, who kept a straight face and agreed to act as Northumberland's stalking horse until such time as the duke rejected him for office.

The Nore delegates had enacted a demand on the Admiralty which they put in force experimentally:

> That every man on a Ship Coming into Harbour shall have Liberty a Certain Number at a Time, so as not to injure the Ship's Duty to go and see there friends and Families a Convenient Time to be allowed Each Man.

The relatives came and made seaside holidays of the mutiny. The navy had invented a fearsome amount of unnecessary work in port to keep jack's mind off women and home. Now it was dispensed with. Frolic and parades reigned at Sheerness.

For Admiral Lord Bridport, and squadron leaders and port admirals on the south coast, life held less joy. During the greater part of the mutiny, Sir John Borlase Warren had been sailing a small squadron off Brest. When word reached his men of the settlement at Spithead, they were indignant that they had had no opportunity to rid themselves of their undesirable officers. These companies united while at sea and forced Sir John to return to Plymouth, the first instance in the lower-deck rebellion in which the men left a position facing the enemy. While some persons in high places believed, or at least tried to induce others to believe, that the seamen wanted to turn the ships over to the French, these men, who could have sailed right in to Brest, instead returned to England to get rid of a few officers. Captain Richard Goodwin Keats of *Galatea,* 32, headed the list.

Sir John Warren disembarked from his flag, *La Pomone,* 40, at Plymouth dock to get his dispatches off to London, requesting, among other things, that Captain Keats be replaced and that amnesty be extended to the Galateas. While he was ashore, the Pomones seized Admiral Warren's belongings and his purser, Mr. Prynn. They sent a letter ashore to Sir John:

> We are sorry to inform your Honour that each day affords a strange uneasiness in our unsettled minds. . . . Your humble petitioners hopes you will take into consideration by granting them a general certificate for the Prizemoney [sic] Due to the *La Pomone* trusts you'll forward the Payment of such Prizes as are payable to be paid as soon as possible, . . .

The Pomone's letter speaks of an abuse often inflicted on prize-taking crews. Months and years went by before courts of Admiralty condemned captured vessels for sale, before sale was completed to the navy or merchant, and before the proceeds were sent by the agent of the commanding officer for division among officers and people. During this length of time, the captain may have gone to another vessel and his old company to some distant station. Dead men did not enjoy a share, nor their families, and the discharged man rarely discovered how to collect.

Lord Bridport had been at sea only a few days when misfortune returned to the Channel fleet. Due perhaps to his dearth of officers and men, accidents became epidemic. *Royal Sovereign* and *Defence* sprang their fore-topmasts, whereupon *Incendiary* collided with *Defence*. Bridport went into Plymouth for cure, also hoping to scrounge fresh provisions and seamen. There his eye alighted on unhappy Sir John Warren's squadron, its officers marooned until prize money was forthcoming. Bridport got off a fast request to the sea lords: "As I shall very much want frigates off Brest, I hope your Lordships will be able to send his [Warren's] squadron to me . . . and five boats and fifty of his men still at Portsmouth." (The latter were forecastle delegates sent to confirm Howe's treaty; by now they had been celebrating in Portsmouth for more than a week.) Lord Bridport added piously, "I hope my appearance [in Plymouth] has restored quiet to the several crews of His Majesty's ships there."

Dublin Castle advised London that E. J. Lewins, an Irish republican leader, had left for France and that the French fleet could be expected off the British coast within a week. Bridport was ordered hurriedly to sea. Soon a lugger brought Lord Spencer a private letter from the old mariner. The handwriting was mutilated, with some words unintelligible but suggestive:

> I believe your Lordship must allow that no Flag Officer ever carried a Squadron to Sea under similar circumstances since the Navy of England has been Established.
> It had not been but a few days out of a general and unexampled Mutiny, before I quitted St. Helen's and I no sooner joyned the ships off the Lizard, that I am informed of the recurrence of one in the *Pique*. Since which, the most dangerous one broke out in the *Pompée,* which ship, I hope is now safe in Spithead, instead of being carried into one of the Ports of France. Some disturbances have also appeared in the *Royal Sovereign, Proserpine* and *Ramillies*. The *Royal George*'s crew have been pretty quiet and I have had them before me three times and I hope with good effect.
> My Constitution is so shook by my attention & feelings that I have not spirit left to do my Duty as I ought, in these awful times, unsupported by a proper staff of Flag officers. I am given to understand, by . . . the Intelligence sent to me, that I may expect the French fleet at Sea in great force, and Commanded by four Admirals, [while] I have (only) Sir Alan Gardner under me. . . .

Things were going better for Captain Sir John Thomas Duckworth at Plymouth. His men were back on duty, reassured by documentary evidence of Howe's Spithead treaty and by Duckworth's diligently going about correcting past and fresh grievances. He sent his delinquent pay books to the Admiralty and made repeated demands for crew arrears. His letter books, preserved at Yale University, contain dozens of protests over rotten food from the victualing yards, and even of a barrel of bad shoes, which was pretty good for a commander in a barefoot navy. During Captain Duckworth's enforced sessions of paper work ashore, kidnapped foreigners found the time and temerity to put in applications for discharge. He pushed the pleas and discharged dozens of Americans and Danes, unfit Englishmen, and even two apprentices prest illegally. With his other hand the Captain issued more press warrants to replace them.

Disciplinary woes even came to fortune's favorite, Admiral Lord Hugh Seymour, born Hugh Seymour Conway, friend of the Prince of Wales, and a Lord Commissioner of the Admiralty. Seymour had an envied assignment. He sailed independently out of Spithead, with four sail-of-the-line and two frigates, hunting homebound Spanish treasure ships from Havana which reputedly contained five million dollars. The Chancellor of the Exchequer needed the coin. Seymour had been at sea during both Spithead stoppages and perhaps still believed what he had told Howe back in March, that there was nothing wrong with morale at Portsmouth. When he returned there, three of his ships boiled over. The crews of *Stag,* 32, and *Révolutionnaire,* 38, demanded dismissal of their first officers for "violent and cruel behavior." The Stags agreed to return to duty on Seymour's pledge that their lieutenant would be court-martialed "and if cleared, never sent to the *Stag* again." Lord Hugh reproached the Révolutionnaires: "Officers are not to be removed according to the caprice of a ship's company but only after regular charges are proved."

With his third ship, *Triumph,* 74, Lord Hugh could do nothing. The people flatly insisted on the removal of Captain Sir Erasmus Gower and several officers. Sir Erasmus was a small, fair man with large blue eyes, a cherry nose and full lips. Seymour could do nothing for him; the Triumphs had put Captain Gower ashore and taken oaths never to have him back. Lord Hugh told the sea lords they would not "derive any advantage from the services of that ship" until she was purged like the rest. "Sir Erasmus Gower's feelings are so deeply wounded," he added, "by the ingratitude of the people, whom by his own account he has treated as if they had been his children, that he won't come back." The next day the Triumphs contritely asked Gower to return, but he kept his pledge not to.

The fleet example was spreading in the civil shore establishment. From Portsmouth, Magistrate Graham reported to the Duke of Portland, "The police of the place is in so weak a state that government can hope but for little assistance from it. There is to be a meeting of the shipwrights to consider an application for an addition to their pay *in time of peace* [Graham's stress]. They are to appoint delegates."

The seamen did not allow Lord Howe's pledged right of petition to fall into disuse.

Left behind at Spithead for repairs were Sir Roger Curtis's Eight United Roses. On Curtis's flagship, *Prince,* the marine company sent him a plea:

SHEWETH

That your petitioners are put to much trouble and expense
by the uniform cloathes now used and humbly take the liberty
to represent that they should be changed to:

—Blue coats faced with red
—Red waistcoats
—Blue pantaloons edged with red
—Half gaitors
—Round hats.

The President of the Fleet

A dog starved at his master's gate
Predicts the ruin of the State

—WILLIAM BLAKE
Auguries of Innocence

ALTHOUGH the stoppage at the Nore was a week old, the sea lords
regarded the Spithead treaty and Lord Bridport's successful attempt to weigh anchors in the Channel fleet as the conclusion of "the
late interesting period," as Nepean termed it in a letter to Admiral
Duncan in Great Yarmouth on 18 May. This letter crossed in the
Norfolk mails a report from Duncan admitting only one of the current series of outbreaks in the North Sea fleet.

> Sir—Be pleased to acquaint the Lords Commissioners of
> the Admiralty that the crew of His Majesty's sloop *Albatross*
> were very riotous and disorderly last evening, but the deter-
> mined and officer-like conduct of Captain Scott, who presented
> a pistol at the first man that appeared, and of Lieutenant
> Lambert, who cut down another with his hanger, the business
> was soon settled, and she sailed this morning to put in execu-
> tion my order of the 15th instant to proceed to Hull and take
> the "Trade" from thence to the Elbe.

Duncan was dealing with a passive mutiny. His ships' companies
were not putting forth delegates or flying the red flag or expelling
officers, but they would not sail. It had taken two days of bluster and
cutlass thrusts to force a sloop to go on convoy duty to neutral Hamburg. Duncan forwarded to the sea lords a statement of grievances
from the Nassaus, which said that they had "nineteen months' wages

due" and were "in general in want of almost every article of wearing apparel that may conduce to render our lives comfortable."

But Whitehall offices and ears were closed. It was the wedding day of the Princess Royal. The city was extremely hot and humid and receiving sullen showers of rain. The month had been the hottest May in many years, averaging 78° F. For his wedding, the Hereditary Prince wore a peach velvet suit, deeply embroidered, and the bride was in white and silver with a crimson mantle and coronet and a large plume of diamonds. His Majesty wore a richly embroidered dark brown suit. The unmarried princesses wept and "their majesties also discovered an excess of parental feeling," according to the *Annual Register*. The royal party drove to Windsor Lodge for dinner.

The London Corresponding Society, meeting that evening at the Crown & Anchor, failed to toast the nuptials. A leading reform M.P., Sir Frederick Burdett,* spoke for repeal of the sedition acts, and the assembly passed several resolutions:

1. That nothing but a full, fair and free representation of the people can preserve this country from incumbent and impending calamities.
2. That no good to the country can arise from a change in administration, unless their successors pledge themselves to sort out the corruptions of the State, and to restore to the people their due weight in the Legislature.
3. That those who have opposed the present war, in opposition to the corruption of Administration, shall be requested to pursue the same system, in compliance with the principles laid down in the second resolution.

Before he drove to Windsor for the marriage ball, Pitt sent the Admiralty a fresh espionage report for Duncan's attention: "There are now lying in the Texel ready for sea—18 ships of the line; 22 frigates, sloops and brigs, from 44 to 10 guns; 42 large transports fitting out for the reception of troops. There is little doubt of a descent upon this country being in contemplation."

The wedding weekend had been relieved of heavy cares by the treaty at Spithead and the reliance that Admiral Duncan was ready to sail from Yarmouth against the Dutch as soon as the wind changed. He had been assuring their lordships that his crews were "perfectly orderly and quiet." Actually, Duncan's seventeen ships were on the

---

* He was the son-in-law of the King's banker, Thomas Coutts.

brink of riot. On his own flagship, *Venerable,* 74, the marines were guarding the main halyard, lest the crew run up the bloody flag.

From H.M.S. *Nassau,* 64, Midshipman Alexander Hardy wrote his family in Ireland that "we are in a bad state here as you are at home —mutinies almost every day. We remained quiet for some time, but have broke out again." He said that Yarmouth was "in an uproar; the seamen are committing great depredations, beating and evil treating all the inhabitants and breaking windows etc., so that no people venture out after dark. Our ship—I believe all the fleet is the same— in a state of intoxication from two to eight o'clock."

Admiral Duncan thought that the foremen—the captains of the tops, the mates, the skilled veterans—were forcing his troubles. He restrained his fleet from open mutiny by a strenuous lecture tour from ship to ship, warning the leaders by telling the companies, "I will venture to say you was misled by a few designing men . . . I shall keep a strict eye on them. Nor can they expect to be longer petty officers in this ship." When the gigantic admiral found an attentive crowd (inattentive persons he would offer to fistfight) he would dispose of the sin of mutiny and rip into drink and profanity. "I shall take this opportunity," he thundered at his own browbeaten company, "of mentioning a thing that has often offended my ears in this ship; I mean the profane oaths, and I will say blasphemy, that too much prevails, and, I really believe, often without meaning. But, if there is a God—and everything around us shows it—we ought to pay Him more respect."

The Venerables got up a smarmy reply to his harangues, thanking the admiral "for so graciously forgiving us the rash step which we took on that fatel day," which was due to "some misguided circumstance or other while in the state of intoxication which is the ruin of thousands." They blamed supernatural powers for making them truant: "As far as we can learn no one knows what unforeseen deamon possest our minds to act as we did." They said they were going to be Christians from then on, but did not promise to stop drinking or cussing.

Duncan had urged the Admiralty to send money to Yarmouth to pay his crews. His patron, Lord Spencer, replied privately that sending money would be "impracticable, without very great inconvenience to the service," but suggested Duncan send his neediest ships to the Nore to be paid.

Duncan's "quiet and orderly" period at Yarmouth included his lurid pastoral visit to *Adamant,* 74, the flag of his vice-admiral. The

Adamants had held a defiant demonstration two weeks before. Duncan climbed aboard, saw to it that his flag was hoisted, and had the company to general quarters. "My lads," he bellowed, "I am not in the smallest degree apprehensive of any violent measures you may have in contemplation. And, though I assure you I would much rather acquire your love than incur your fear, I will with my own hand put to death the first man who displays the slightest sign of rebellion."

The admiral asked if anyone disputed the authority of himself or the ship's officers. A man stepped forward and said, "I do." Duncan looked down at him, grasped his collar and lifted him toward the rail with one hand. "My lads, look at this fellow!" he said, pantomiming dropping the man overboard. The stunt brought Duncan a personal note from Lord Spencer, congratulating him on "the very dextrous manner in which you contrived to get rid of the rising disturbance on board the *Adamant*."

"The Dutch fleet is under sailing orders at the Texel and only waiting for a fresh breeze of Easterly wind to proceed to sea," reported John Mitchell, British consul at Hamburg, to 10 Downing Street, on 19 May. The Admiralty required and directed Adam Duncan to go to the Texel since it "appears that the enemy's fleet is in every respect ready for sea." He was to lose no time "if the wind should continue easterly." Duncan continued to conceal from the sea lords the strong probability that his men would not sail until their complaints were looked after, or unless the Dutch came out to offer battle.

On the eighteenth, delegates MacCarthy and Hollister returned from Spithead with the papers that Lord Howe had given them to bring the Nore demonstration to an end. The delegates of the fleet heard the Royal Pardon of a week earlier and the text of Howe's settlement dated the fourteenth. MacCarthy and his fellow envoy thought they had delivered the peace in these official papers that they had seen solving the Spithead remonstrance. To their surprise, the delegates sneered at the texts. Richard Parker held them up and cried, "You've brought three pennyworth of ballads for our twenty pounds."

Although the royal proclamation forgave "all seamen and marines on board any ships of the fleet who may have been guilty of any act of mutiny . . . and who have returned, or shall, upon notification of such of his Majesty's proclamation, return to . . . duty," they declared that it did not protect the men of the Nore because of the prior dating. And what about discharge of tyrants? other delegates wanted to know. Someone yelled, "Run MacCarthy up on the yard-arm for disloyalty to the cause!" William Bray, the sailing master of *Sandwich,* who was working for both sides, as elected ship's captain and informer to Buckner, said, "MacCarthy, the people are going to hang you for going to Portsmouth and spending their money idly." They voted to put MacCarthy in irons overnight.

The delegates did not proclaim the Act of Parliament and the royal pardon to the ships' companies. The people went on thinking they were standing out in order to support their brethren at Spithead. To inquiries from men who had heard about the proclamations from other sources, the delegates claimed the act was only an Order-in-Council, or that it would be in force for only one year.

MacCarthy and Hollister told of hearing Lord Howe discussing matters man-to-man with the Spithead delegates, and of participating in the victory celebrations ashore. They had dined with lords and ladies in the governor's mansion. Now, what were the sea lords doing for the men of the Nore? Was the fleet committee simply to apply for pardon and go meekly back to the starter and the lash? Then there was the question of officers to be removed. When was Lord Howe coming to receive their blacklist and replace oppressive officers? And, while the seamen had the government at their mercy, why not show the lads at Spithead a thing or two and gain more than they did? The delegates began drawing up demands on the Admiralty, consulting by means of emissaries with the men of the North Sea fleet at Great Yarmouth.

In their anxiety to have the Spithead fleet return to the Brest blockade, the sea lords paid little attention to the week-old Nore disturbance, although newspapers were reporting it in this vein:

> The delegates go regularly every day to Sheerness, where they hold their conferences. They then parade the streets and ramparts of the garrison with a degree of triumphant insolence, and hold up the bloody flag of defiance as a mark of scorn to the military. At the head of these men marches the person who is considered the admiral of their fleet.
> *—Annual Register*

The "admiral of their fleet" * was Richard Parker, the quota man, who had emerged as head of the *Sandwich* committee two days after

---

* There is no evidence that Parker styled himself "admiral" or that the delegates addressed him as such. Out of earshot, some seamen may have done so.

the sympathy strike began and was now the elected President of the Delegates of the Whole Fleet at the Nore.

The dynamic orator with flashing black eyes came from Exeter, where his father was a grain merchant and baker. Parker attended Exeter Grammar school. He was apprenticed in the building trade but ran away to sea, serving as a midshipman during the war against the American English. His second time out, Parker was said to have challenged his captain, Edward Riou, to a duel. He himself claimed to have been a petty officer in H.M.S. *Mediator* in 1783. At the end of the American war, he was reported to have shipped as a master's mate in a Mediterranean trader and to have led a mutiny over bad food. The short curriculum vitae has got some unverified entries: after he became famous, Parker did not find time to write his autobiography.

In 1791 he married Ann McHardy, the daughter of a farmer at Braemar near Aberdeen. When the war with France began, he appeared on the navy books as an officer in H.M.S. *Assurance* in Lord Howe's Channel fleet. A few months later a court-martial found him guilty of disobeying a superior and he was demoted to ordinary seaman. Throwing ex-officers in with men they have ordered around is not healthy, and such men are hard to transfer. But his captain readily found another willing to take Parker and he entered H.M.S. *Hebe* at Gosport as a foremast hand. In April 1794, Parker was sent to Haslar Hospital at Gosport with severe rheumatism. For that, he missed the Glorious First of June battle and was working as a supernumerary on Sir Peter Parker's flag, *Royal William,* at Spithead, when Black Dick came in with the six French prizes. Rheumatism sent Parker into hospital again that summer and he was discharged on medical grounds in November.

Parker returned to his wife in Scotland, after which there is a blur of two years during which it has been said that he taught school. The documented pages begin to turn again early in '97 when he was sentenced to the debtors' prison at Perth. Thence came in February the magistrates looking to fill the navy quota for Perthshire. They gazed on the strong, intelligent, experienced seaman and offered to spring Parker if he would swell the quota. The prisoner had a queer sort of bargaining power that the blameless innocent outside did not have when a procurement drive was on. Parker dickered. He got thirty pounds for his body, enough to pay his debts and leave something for his wife. On 9 April he entered *Sandwich* at the Nore.

The emergence of Parker as President of the Delegates led to assertions by the King's men a while later that the Nore mutiny was a Jacobin plot and that Pitt's opponents had sent Parker to direct this embarrassment to the ministry. There is no evidence for the notion, and all the circumstances are contrary to it. Conspirators would hardly have placed Parker in jail, trusting to luck he would be purchased and sent to the Nore, rather than to a half dozen other naval bases. The easiest way to place him in a selected ship would have been to tip off an impressment officer that she could use a choice hand like Parker. The President of the Fleet made dozens of forceful speeches in none of which was there any reported reflection of revolutionary ideas.

Parker was intelligent, discontented, vain and enthusiastic. The seamen picked him to lead because he was comparatively well-educated, literate, attractive and officially a gentleman for having held the King's commission. In the negotiations with the great lords from London, they desired a man smart enough to see through their tricks. And no small part of Parker's testimonials with the sea peasantry was the fact that he had been court-martialed for insubordination and did not even get his stripes for it. Above all, Parker was willing to be president, which most of the other delegates were not. At Spithead, leaders looked for people: at the Nore, people looked for leaders.

Seeking to restore order in his command, Admiral Buckner sent a message to "the delegates from the different ships in this port" announcing that he would meet them on *Sandwich* to "notify his Majesty's pardon upon the terms expressed in their lordships' direction." The delegates naturally felt that Buckner was going to play Black Dick Howe's role and negotiate with them; they had no reason to think otherwise. The Admiralty had made no pronouncement about the Nore and its last act toward seamen had been the concession at Spithead to expel the officers.

The delegates answered Admiral Buckner that they would come ashore next morning and escort him in a procession of honor through the fleet, as had been done at Portsmouth for Lord Howe. They went into extra session and produced additional demands to give themselves more bargaining power with Buckner. The meeting lasted all night and into the morning of 19 June. It was 2 P.M. before they arrived at Sheerness to receive the admiral. They handed him their reconsidered demands, consisting of eight articles, which he and his entourage might read while the boats skimmed over the calm sunswept waters to H.M.S. *Sandwich*.

Admiral Buckner looked at the paper and refused to get into the boat. He said, "I discussed with them and endeavoured by every means in my power to shake their resolution" for the unexpected and shocking demands. The delegates were considerate about his agitated state and agreed to postpone the talks for twenty-four hours. Buckner said, "They expressed that they had no doubt the whole would be satisfactorily settled."

Early the next day, lower-deck envoys arrived from Great Yarmouth with the endorsement of a dozen of Adam Duncan's North Sea ships to the eight articles. In terms of supporting manpower this more than doubled the weight of the demands.

Next morning at nine the procession of honor delivered on board *Sandwich* Admiral Buckner, her captain, Mosse, and Captain James Dixon of *l'Espion*. The delegates were in session and no one on deck had the presence of mind to accord the admiral the boarding honors of his rank. Several junior officers stood around the quarterdeck, without acting. There has never been an explanation of President Parker's absence on board for this appointment. A delegate came out of the meeting and notified Admiral Buckner that they still had something to settle which they "would lay before [you] in half an hour."

Admiral Buckner waited on board his own flagship on the will of an illegal body of underlings usurping his own great cabin. Almost two hours passed before the delegates came in a body to the quarterdeck and handed the admiral the formal signed copy of the eight articles.

> Article 1. That every indulgence granted to the fleet at Portsmouth, be granted to his Majesty's subjects serving in the Fleet at the Nore, and places adjacent.
> 2. That every man, upon a ship's coming into harbour, shall have liberty (a certain number at a time, so as not to injure the ship's duty) to go and see their friends and families; a convenient time to be allowed to each man.
> 3. That all ships before they go to sea shall be paid all arrears of wages down to six months, according to the old rules.
> 4. That no officer that has been turned out of any of his Majesty's ships shall be employed in the same ship again, without consent of the ship's company.
> 5. That when any of his Majesty's ships shall be paid, that may have been some time in commission, if there are any pressed men on board, that may not be in the regular course of payment, they shall receive two months advance to furnish them with necessaries.

6. That an indemnification be made any men who have run, and may now be in his Majesty's naval service, and that they shall not be liable to be taken up as deserters.

7. That a more equal distribution be made of prize-money to the crews of his Majesty's ships and vessels of war.

8. That the Articles of war, as now enforced, require various alterations, several of which to be expunged therefrom; and if more moderate ones were held forth to seamen in general, it would be the means of taking off that terror and prejudice against his Majesty's service, on that account too frequently imbibed by seamen from entering voluntarily into the service.

The Committee of Delegates of the whole Fleet assembled in council on board his Majesty's ship *Sandwich,* have unanimously agreed that they will not deliver up their charge until the appearance of some of the Lords Commissioners of the Admiralty to ratify the same.

Given on board his Majesty's ship *Sandwich,* by the Delegates of the Fleet, 20th May, 1797.

It was signed by delegates from *Sandwich,* 40; *Montagu,* 74; *Director,* 64; *Inflexible,* 64; *Belliqueux,* 64; *Standard,* 64; *Lion,* 64; *Nassau,* 64; *Repulse,* 64; *Monmouth,* 64; *Isis,* 50; *Tisiphone,* 12; *Swan,* 16; *Inspector,* 16; *Grampus,* 20; *Proserpine* 28; *Brilliant,* 28; *Champion,* 20; *Comet,* 14; and *Pylades,* 16.

As Admiral Buckner took the document, the mutineers "declared with one voice *that they would not resign the charge they now had in their hands* till the conditions therein . . . were complied with, and satisfied *by the personal attendance of the Board of their Lordships here,* which they insist they have a right to expect, there having been a precedent for it at Spithead." (The italics are Buckner's in his report to the sea lords.)

At the same time the delegates disclaimed any "disrespect or want of confidence towards me," said the admiral. He was not authorized to concede or even discuss points with the delegates, but he assured them that he would mention to their lordships the idea of giving impressed men advance money.

A swarthy young man in a beaver hat, blue coat and half boots came up the side of *Sandwich* and addressed Admiral Buckner. "Sir, it was a mistake you was not treated with proper respect when you came aboard. But, if you will excuse it, the crew will give you three cheers." The Sandwiches gave a feeble accolade. Admiral Buckner did not recognize Richard Parker. He had never heard of him and did not even know there was a "president of the fleet." The papers he had received from the mutineers were signed by the delegates with no distinctions of office. The only thing the admiral and his two captains remembered of the first meeting with President Parker was that the man had failed to remove his hat when addressing them.

As the president chatted with the admiral, Delegate Charles MacCarthy came over to them, cupped his mouth at Parker's ear and whispered so as to be heard by all, "Settle with him!" After the admiral went ashore, a posse of Sandwiches grabbed MacCarthy, strung a greased halter around his neck and dragged him along the gangway. He clawed at the noose to breathe and shouted, "What have I done? What do you do to me!" Hating the cruel joke, other Sandwiches leaped in and bloodied the noses of MacCarthy's tormentors. The master-at-arms had to come out and calm the people.

They court-martialed MacCarthy for sedition. The judges found him guilty, but showed mercy and remitted his sentence to transportation. They threw MacCarthy in a boat, amidst yells of "Put him in the *Inflexible!*" Already MacCarthy had worn out his welcome on that militant ship and the Inflexibles had served notice that if he came again, they would fly him from a yardarm. The boat put him on *Brilliant.* The Inflexibles kept the rough joke going by picking him up and rowing him to the diffident ship, *Pylades.* "Ahoy, *Pylades!* Here's your new captain." The torpid Pylades accepted MacCarthy as their mutineer captain.

Admiral Buckner sent the delegates' eight articles to the Admiralty and the next day received their lordships' reply, which categorically refused to alleviate or negotiate any grievance. "All that could reasonably be expected by the seamen and marines has already been granted them," said the answer. "Their lordships cannot accede to any further requests."

Admiral Buckner simply could not bring himself to forward this unbending reply to the delegates. He pocketed the paper. The rest of the port admiral's bad day is rather blurred. He appears to have accosted a party of seamen with red cockades and exhorted them to accept his Majesty's pardon. Without exposing the iron document from Whitehall, he apparently made it vividly clear to them that nothing but hostility could be expected from the fathers of the fleet. And he gave them a brief period—one description says ten minutes— in which to convince the delegates to submit.

The red cockades hurried to the delegates with the message. By resolution of the Inflexibles, the delegates sent a man to haul down

Buckner's pendant, which had been left flying on the flagship as a mark of respect. Up went the bloody flag in its place.

The delegates sent crews rowing to Sheerness harbor, where they seized eight gunboats and sailed them to the Great Nore. As they passed the fort the gunboats each whistled a round at the ramparts. They were not courtesy salutes.

The fleet parliamentarians went on full alert and began defensive alignments. They pulled the ships in the Little Nore out to the main anchorage. They moved the fleet into two businesslike arcs with the gunboats at either end.

Nervous seamen got a message to Admiral Buckner begging him to do something to mollify the extremists of the committee. Buckner appealed to the sea lords by express, saying that the fleet was "clamorous to have the pardon notified to them in a more solemn manner."

The delegates were saying to the men, "Lord Bridport's fleet were thought worthy of the presence of the board to investigate their complaints; are we of less importance to our country in the hour of danger, or are our grievances more insignificant?"

In London, Prince Augustus Frederick, the King's second son, attended a general staff meeting with Secretary Windham. The land forces had come home from Europe with no foreseeable prospect of returning and were bored, tainted with republicanism, and jealous of the seamen's new pay rise. In a way, Frederick had incited the sailors by increasing army pay two years before. Now the general staff decided to ask Parliament to raise the soldiers' pay by twopence a day, the bill to be introduced in four days' time, in contrast to the eighteen days that Pitt had claimed essential to producing the seamen's wage bill.*

The generals also did something for the admirals, by ordering Major General Edward Fox to march two militia regiments from Canterbury to reinforce the Sheerness garrison, and by sending another regiment from Chelmsford to Southend to protect the Essex shore from an irruption of rebellious seamen.

When the soldiers arrived at Sheerness, the seamen greeted them with "violent proceedings" and threats to bombard the fort. President Parker wrote Admiral Buckner that the militia intervention was "an insult to the peaceable behavior of the seamen through the fleet at the Nore." The presiding delegate did not understand that the gov-

---

* The bill was passed five days later.

ernment was correcting mistakes made at Portsmouth and had not singled out his regime as especially odious. Westminster was in the position of a man whose purse had been lifted before he could cock his pistol, only to have a second highwayman ride right up to the muzzle. Valentine Joyce had taught the government much and the lessons were applied to Parker.

Neither Buckner, Parker nor the Admiralty interfered with the seamen's demonstrations in Sheerness. There were no clashes between the two arms of his Majesty's services. The sailors marched alongside the soldiers, shaking hands, and leading them in patriotic songs. Mutinous sailors mingled with shipwrights in the dockyard and vessels came in under the red flag to be repaired. The commander-in-chief of southern England, General Sir Charles Grey, thought it was "a most perfectly new and strange and an uncommon method of crushing rebellion in the bud." He expostulated to Secretary Dundas that the mutineers could blow up the dockyard any time they chose.

Thinking of the Irish active in the mutiny, the Admiralty asked a Roman Catholic priest to go to Sheerness and exhort them to submit. The clergyman did so, despite the Georgian "test and corporation acts" that denied civil rights to his religion. No Catholic could hold public office or a commission in the King's navy.

On *Proserpine*, 28, the senior officer left aboard was Junior Lieutenant Henry Hawes. The delegates asked him to swear an oath that he would not bring any man to punishment for participation in the cause. Hawes said, "You have already been pardoned by the King. All you need to do is accept the pardon." That meant returning to discipline immediately. The reply was, "But, sir, every officer in the fleet is taking the oath. The *Sandwich* is waiting on us to finish it." Hawes submitted to the pledge, then learned that no other officer had been obliged to take such an oath. He went to the *Proserpine* delegates and declared that he would not be bound to the oath, due to the false premise. They released him from the pledge.

Now at the Nore, for the second time in his career, Captain William Bligh experienced the rare indignity of being put in a boat by a mutinous crew. He described it to Nepean:

> You will please to inform my Lords Commissioners of the Admiralty that this morning about nine o'clock, soon after the return of the delegates from Spithead, they came on board and

declared to me they had seen Earl Howe, who had told them all officers were to be removed from their ships who they disapproved of;* they were in consequence to inform me in the name of the ship's company that I was to quit the command of the ship & for it to devolve on the first Lieutenant, who they in the same breath ordered to supercede me.

Being without any resource I was obliged to quit the ship. I have stated the whole transaction to Admiral Buckner, and now wait their Lordships' directions, being ready to meet any charge that can be brought against me or such investigation as they may think proper to direct. I have reason to believe the whole has originated with the *Sandwich*'s crew—hitherto never did a ship's company behave better or did ever a ship bear more marks of content and correctness.

Mr. Purdue, Mr. Blaguire, and Mr. Eldridge, Midm. are also turned on shore for being too much noticed by their Captain & Mr. Purdue particularly because he did his duty like a spirited young officer—I know of nothing dishonourable they can be accused of.

I have the Honour to be, etc.,
WM. BLIGH

Delegate Thomas McCann went to *Director* and disarmed her marine company, a feat he had not been able to accomplish upon the single person of Captain Bligh.

The fleet parliament passed new internal regulations for the emergency:

1. Every ship shall diligently keep a quarterwatch; and every man found below in his watch shall be severly punished.

2. Every ship shall give three cheers morning and evening.

3. No woman shall be permitted to go on shore from any ship, but as many may come in as please.

4. Any person attempting to bring liquor into the ship, or any person found drunk, shall be severely punished.

5. The greatest attention to be paid to the officers' orders. Any person failing in the respect due to them, of neglecting their duty, shall be severely punished.

6. Every seaman and marine shall take an oath of fidelity, not only to themselves but to the fleet in general.

7. No ship shall lift their anchors to proceed from this port, until the desires of the fleet be satisfied.

---

* Howe had told them no such thing.

8. That there be no liberty given from ship to ship till all are settled.

—No private letters to be sent on shore.

President Parker wrote Buckner, "The Lords of the Admiralty have been remiss in their duty in not attending when their appearance would have given satisfaction." Until the proud commissioners came to Sheerness, there could be no settlement. To convey the decision to the admiral, Parker and William Davis, chief delegate of *Sandwich*, led a deputation ashore and knocked on the door of Commissioner Hartwell's house. Hartwell was holding a hearing on two marines who had been arrested for drunkenness by militiamen.

Parker asked, "Can the commissioner be spoken with?"

"Yes, I suppose so."

"What is the reason the soldiers brought the marines here?"

Commissioner Hartwell referred it to Parker's employer. Admiral Buckner said sternly, "What right have you to make such an inquiry?"

"I am not to be intimidated," said Parker. "Your flag is struck, sir. You have no authority here. We command the fleet."

He picked up a pencil and sheet of paper and questioned one of the marines. One of the captains present yelled, "I'll kill the insolent bugger!" Another officer hauled him back into his seat. Parker finished his quiz and announced, "You men are under arrest to be tried by the fleet," and took the marines along with him.

When the first sea lord heard of this latest outrage, he wrote the King:

(Eton College, 23 May 1797, 9:55 A.M.) Earl Spencer has the honour of laying before your Majesty the accompanying dispatch from Vice-Admiral Buckner, received here this morning at 9 o'clock, and is concerned to find that so extravagantly mutinous a spirit should exist in the minds of the seamen at the Nore. Whatever may be the result of this unfortunate business, and whatever it may be necessary to do, Earl Spencer feels that he shall best perform his duty to your Majesty's service by going immediately to London where he may be more on the spot to receive information and give directions, than by attending your Majesty at Windsor with this dispatch which he should in any other case have the honour of doing.

The King replied:

(Windsor, 23 May, 2:30 P.M.) I was out on horseback when Earl Spencer's box arrived, and on returning home lose no time in approving of his having instantly returned to town to take such steps as he may, on consulting the Board of Admiralty, seem most conducive to restore subordination in the ships at the Nore, which farther concessions would render impracticable.

The King received that day other indications of the mood of his subjects:

(Burlington House) The Duke of Portland most humbly begs leave of your Majesty to express his concern at laying before your Majesty the account of symptoms of disorder & outrage having appeared in a part of Ireland which has hitherto been considered to be perfectly sound & untainted, or where that spirit had been thought to have been totally subdued & extirpated.

Nepean wrote to Adam Duncan at Great Yarmouth:

(Private and confidential.)   Admiralty: May 22
MY DEAR SIR,—The ships at the Nore are in the most complete state of mutiny, and it seems to be very difficult to bring them to any reason without submitting to conditions which would be highly disgraceful. You know the state of your fleet, I believe, as well as anyone can do, and what use could be made of it. Do you think that you could depend upon any of the ships if you were to bring them up to the Nore, if it should be necessary to employ them in bringing the two or three ships of the line over there to reason?
You may give me your private thoughts on this head, but the less they are communicated to other people the better.
         Yours ever most sincerely,
         EVAN NEPEAN

Admiral Duncan replied with realistic discretion:

         Venerable, May 23, 1797
MY DEAR SIR,—Your two letters of the 21st and 22nd was yesterday secured. The last required some delicacy to answer. The fleet continues to behave well, and I am sure will refuse no common service. At the same time, to call them who have kept in order to chastise those at the Nore, in my opinion

would subject them to a disagreeable jealousy from all other parts of the fleet who engage in this unhappy business; but for all this I don't shrink from the business if it cannot otherwise be got the better of. . . . Much harmony is in this fleet, which I think has kept us right. I hear that people from the ships at Sheerness go ashore in numbers and play the devil. Why are there not troops to lay hold of them and secure all the boats that come from them? As to the 'Sandwich,' you should get her cast adrift in the night and let her go on the sands, that the scoundrels may drown; for until some example is made this will not stop.

God bless you and send us better times, not that I despair. This chastisement is sent us for a warning to mend our ways.

I always am most truly and faithfully yours

ADAM DUNCAN

To EVAN NEPEAN, ESQ.

P.S. I have met with so many interruptions I fear you will not be able to make out my letter.

Duncan also sent Nepean a cryptic protestation of loyalty he had received from his own forecastle:

It is with the utmost regret we hear of the proceedings of different ships in the squadron, but sincerely hope their present grievances will be redressed as soon as possible, as it would appear unnatural for us to unsheath the sword against our brethern, notwithstanding we would wish to show ourselves like men in behalf of our Commander, should necessity require.

It was signed by eight seamen "for the ship's Company in general."

Admiral Buckner could do nothing but speculate on what next would go bad at the Nore. He requested the Admiralty not to send any more ships or men there. This was effected in the London reaches, but vessels at sea, if Thames-bound, continued to arrive at the Nore, including press tenders. The command vacuum had to be filled and, as was the case at Spithead, the idle seamen filled it with suspicions of the government. The delegates struck more dramatic poses and their legislative machinery progressed. By now their votes were marked on ship lists, rather than by show of hands. John Blake, leader of *Inflexible,* moved to establish a battle chest by contributions from the men. It would cover printing, travel of delegates and hiring a lawyer to plead the cause. Among influential people, there were no voluntary voices raised for the Nore seamen.

The egalitarian British intelligentsia, which in sunnier times would have espoused the sailors, had been silenced. Thomas Holcroft, actor-playwright and leader of the Society for Constitutional Information, had been gagged by a high treason indictment and was biding his moment to escape to France. The philosopher of radicalism, William Godwin, who had stood by the LCS men booked for high treason in 1794, said nothing about the men of Spithead or the Nore. His ardent humanitarian wife, Mary Wollstonecraft, was carrying a child (whose birth would kill her). The mystical poet-engraver William Blake, who had helped Tom Paine flee to France from a treason indictment and had been himself arraigned for joking about the King, was secluded in a drab house in Lambeth, illustrating Young's *Night Thoughts.*

Tom Paine was in Paris sitting in the assembly of the King's enemies, unaware of the crisis he had helped to create in the British fleet, and unable to do anything about it if he had known. Bristol-born Robert Southey, well-versed on living conditions at sea, and who had been expelled from school for writing against flogging, was making his *Minor Poems* during the mutiny. The most realistic literary observer of Georgian misery, George Crabbe, unsuccessful surgeon and opium eater, was preaching blameless sermons in his Dorsetshire parish church. William Cobbett, later to be England's great popular agitator, was in Philadelphia publishing a paper called *Peter Porcupine.* During the mutiny, a nine-year-old scholar at Harrow, George Gordon, succeeded to the title of Lord Byron. Distant were the days when he would write a book about the mutiny on H.M.S. *Bounty.*

At this juncture of Britain's fate, the Admiralty ordered Buckner to send H.M.S. *San Fiorenzo* and *Clyde,* the loyal ships masquerading as mutineers, up the river to Gravesend to take the royal newlyweds on their honeymoon. Their lordships thought "it probable when the purpose for which those ships are intended shall be known that no opposition will be offered by the crews to their proceeding upon this service." The delegates did not permit the two ships to sail.

The King was enraged. His day was not improved by Charles James Fox's asking for a royal audience. They had not spoken to each other for decades. His Majesty granted the appointment.

The Black Patriot had decided that, in view of the extreme danger to the state from mutiny, invasion, rebellion and bankruptcy, it was his unpleasant but exigent duty to go to his enemy, the King. Fox reported later, "After having stated the situation as it appears to me as well of this country as of Ireland, I told his Majesty that many persons wished a change of Ministry who would not like that I should be one of the new Administration, and therefore I begged I might not stand in the way of a change which might prove beneficial to the public. On the contrary, that if a ministry could be formed that could save the country it would give me the more satisfaction by my not being part of it. The King heard me attentively and seriously, but said not one word."

Fox went away, hoping that Moira or another peer in the peace bloc might prevail on the obdurate King. "Nothing but peace can allay the irritation and ferment in the minds of the people," Fox wrote. "The French can make peace with a new administration in three weeks' time, but never with the present but on the most humiliating terms. Why should the King and the country be sacrificed to preserve the characters of the present ministers from degradation?"

Without Fox's knowing it, at that moment there was a critical struggle going on in the French government over peace or war. The recent general elections in France had placed a majority of counter-revolutionaries in the benumbed legislature, emboldening the rightist Paul de Barras to take control in the Directory. President Carnot and the revolutionary minority wanted immediate peace in order the check the counterrevolution and palliate the miseries of the country. In the cafés of Paris they were singing a song called "Dying of Hunger, Dying of Cold," by François Babeuf, "the first socialist," who had recently been guillotined for high treason. But Barras and a new crowd rising on the coattails of Bonaparte did not want to conclude hostilities for the same reason William Pitt did not wish to. Peace would overturn the right in both countries.

But in Westminster, Lord Moira felt so certain of Pitt's dismissal that he broke the news to the Duke of Northumberland that he was not to be Prime Minister. The new party had chosen Fox.

Members of Pitt's cabinet began equivocating. Henry Dundas privately announced that he saw "the possibility of events that would make it uncreditable for me to stay in." The foreign minister, Lord Grenville, talked about resigning. This would be a calamity for the court party. The ministry might survive the defection of Dundas by opening a random page in the book of scandals involving the wily Scot. But if Baron Grenville resigned, Pitt was finished. Lord Liverpool, chancellor of the Duchy of Lancaster and President of the Board of Trade, was a follower of Grenville. And William Windham, Secretary-at-War and Pitt's leader in the House of Commons, owed more to the Foreign Secretary than to the Prime Minister. The predicament was so serious that the King himself came out to plead with Grenville to stay. The minister had several relatives on royal pensions. He was devoted to restoring the civil rights of Roman Catholics, and he went along with the King's men, indulging his dream that his Protestant Majesty would agree to Catholic emancipation.

In Sheerness, Sir Harry Neale, captain of *San Fiorenzo,* unable to fulfill his orders to go up to Gravesend and take their highnesses aboard for Germany, was stopped by several delegates who complained about the refusal of the sea lords to come to talk with them. Their tone was respectful and the spirit mutual, as if Sir Harry's detention was due to the willfulness of the Admiralty. Buckner noted that the delegates seemed "hourly to assume more confidence and act with more decision."

On Thursday 25 May, the Admiralty sent a telegraph message to Buckner asserting that order had been restored in all the other fleets. Vainly he told Nepean of his "infinite concern" and "doubt of a return to order among the seamen and marines at this port." On the basis of reports from informers, Admiral Buckner notified London that the delegates were talking about blockading commerce in the Thames and Medway.

XII

The Twenty-sixth of May

That the King can do no wrong is a necessary and
fundamental principle of the English constitution.

—SIR WILLIAM BLACKSTONE

A T BREAKFAST Lord Spencer found an upsetting letter from Lord
Chancellor Loughborough, the ranking law official in the kingdom: the pardon offered at the Nore was not valid. It applied only
to offenses committed before the Spithead settlement and not to those
of the last ten days. The delegates were justified in distrusting anyone who spoke of pardon, from Buckner to Spencer. The First Lord
went dolefully to his office.

The sea lords gathered around the green cloth-covered table in
their board room in Whitehall. It was an airy Palladian chamber with
a coffered ceiling, Corinthian pilasters and a large clock with points
of the compass in place of numerals. Their lordships were sore
troubled. They could not think what to do about the Nore mutiny
now two weeks old.

Visibility was good that Friday morning and traffic began early on
the Deal & Sheerness shutter telegraph. The spyglass man on the roof
of the Admiralty office read a message on the West Square station
across the river in Southwark and sent a boy below to their lordships with a sinister word from Sheerness: longboats full of armed
mutineers were pulling toward London.

Their objective, said Sheerness (by guess or informer), was to
seduce four warships, including *Lancaster,* 64, that were anchored in
Long Reach about halfway to the capital. The Admiralty was in an
awkward position to warn *Lancaster* by telegraph. The nearest relay
station, Swanscombe, on the south bank, was invisible from the ship.
Nepean sent an express rider from London to Long Reach: "The

mutineers at the Nore have sent up a party of their comrades to bring your ships to the Nore," he notified the captains. "You are to take most vigorous means in your power preventing them on board."

A slow match was burning toward the magazine. Two boats from *Isis* and *Brilliant* came sweeping lustily into cannon fire from Tilbury Fort downriver from Long Reach. They passed through the thumps and splashes without harm and landed nearby at Gravesend. Hostile people on the waterfront sent them scuttling back aboard. The mutineers resumed stroke toward London. The Admiralty express rider arrived at Long Reach ahead of them and warned the ships. Nevertheless, the delegates boarded *Lancaster* without bloodshed, although there was "greatest confusion" on deck. During the yelling, Captain John Wells of *Lancaster* popped through a porthole into a rowing boat, made it ashore, and spurred for the Admiralty office. The red flag was now flying fifteen miles from the Court of St. James.

In London the news from Long Reach set off a pother recalling the great fright of 1667 when Michel de Ruyter, the Dutch admiral, came crashing into the Thames with 66 vessels, many of them manned by English deserters who had gone over to Holland when they were paid off in worthless script. They came back, yelling to English ships in the Nore, "Ye fight for tickets! We fight for dollars!" The raiders blew up the forts and powder magazine at Sheerness and cut the chain across the Medway River which led to the naval base at Chatham.

Going up the meandering Medway to destroy Chatham, the unpiloted Dutch ships cracked up on Grain Spit, Stangate Spit and Stoke Ooze, but their revenge-crazed crews burned the wrecks and pressed on, the ship's trumpeters blasting mocking tunes across the marshes, "The Roast Beef of Old England" and "Joan's Placket Is Torn." They burned three of his Majesty's largest warships, *Royal James, Royal Oak* and *Loyal London* and de Ruyter contemptuously towed away the largest one, *Royal Charles*. The rumble of cannon was heard in London.

Eight hundred invading Dutch and English seamen marched as far as Gillingham Reach, led by the exiled Commonwealth soldier, Colonel Dolmen. Admiral de Ruyter called them back before they clashed with royal troops who had hastened to the north bank of the Medway.

Frightened people in London on 26 May 1797 thought of the de Ruyter raid and considered it quite possible that Parker was coming all the way to town with a force London could not match.

The King awakened at his customary hour of seven and took his customary breakfast of oatmeal porridge, the same burgoo his men-of-wars-men ate. He had stayed overnight at the Queen's House after attending her Majesty's regular Thursday Drawing Room.

While the alarms were sounding, the King wrote a letter to the First Lord of the Admiralty. Having been balked at obtaining two frigates from the Nore as honeymoon barks, he required three from Great Yarmouth.

> Queen's House, 26 May 1797, 9:49 A.M.
> The Earl of Spencer, to avoid any delay in my waiting untill he comes to St. James's this day, is to send an express to Yarmouth that three frigates may be prepared for the reception of the Princess Royal, one for the Hereditary Prince of Wirtemburg and his suit, the third for Lord Cathcart, Col. Gwynn, the Clerk of the Green Cloth, and any part of the suit that cannot be accommodated in the two others.

The King's rider dashed down the Mall to the Admiralty and was back in forty minutes with Spencer's reply:

> Earl Spencer has had the honour of receiving your Majesty's commands on the subject of ordering three of Admiral Duncan's squadron to be prepared to receive on board her Royal Highness the Princess Royal & his Serene Highness the Prince of Würtemberg with their suite, and will send an express off immediately for that purpose; but he humbly presumes to suggest to your Majesty whether it would not be more adviseable for the embarkation to take place at Harwich which is a much more convenient port for the purpose, and is at an easy day's journey from London. The ships destined for this service must be two-deckers, Admiral Duncan not having any frigates with him at present.

His Majesty sent a rider back:

> Queen's House, 26 May, 11:05 A.M.
> I have just received Earl Spencer's note. Harwich, I know, will please the Hereditary P. of Wirtemburg better than any other port. I desire orders may therefore be given for three two-deckers and any additions as an escort that may be judged right. I have already sent orders to the kitchen and stables that Harwich will be on Wednesday evening the place of embarkation.

While the King was deploying his ships for the nuptial voyage, along the lower Thames there was a racket and lather of cavalry and express horses, galloping in the dust. They rode not only to check the menacing encroachments of the naval mutineers but to forestall a threat as old as Wat Tyler, a rising by the politicalized artisans of the river—tanners, watermen, dockers, and workers in the country's principle shipbuilding complex at Blackwall, Gravesend, Deptford, Woolwich and Chatham.

The Thames shipwrights belonged to an illegal trade union called the St. Helena Benefit Society. The ship caulkers had formed this concealed union in 1794 under the motto *Main et Coeur.* Parliament had outlawed trade unions and they existed very much as did the proscribed political organizations—by sacred oaths of brotherhood. Many shipyard guildsmen were members of the London Corresponding Society and a few belonged to the republican United Englishmen. A familiar speaker and counselor in the gray world of muck and pilings in the Thames reaches was John Gale Jones, the bold field organizer of the LCS whom the Duke of Portland had tried on charges of sedition a few months before.

The Nore delegates showed no hand in the bankside stir. After dispatching the boats to Long Reach, they tidied up their watery precinct. The sham-mutinous frigates, *Clyde* and *San Fiorenzo,* lay in adjacent berths apart from the rest, like virgins in a brothel. President Parker boarded *Clyde* and exhorted the company to work the ship upriver into the main formation. The Clydes declined, so he sent *Pylades,* commanded by the exiled *Sandwich* delegate Charles Mac-Carthy, to move in between the faithful pair and keep guns on them.

During the morning, pilots were called aboard many of the capital ships at the Great Nore. No one was told what intention of Parker and the delegates this implied. It could mean they were taking the fleet to France or Ireland, or even that they were going to attack London. As this heart-fluttering news clicked on the telegraph to Whitehall from the theatre of mutiny, from the other quarter the long line from Plymouth warned that grave news in Dublin dispatches was coming up by express: the French invasion fleet was reported to have sailed from Brest. But his Majesty's servants heard this story every other day from some source or another. They confined their worries to the known and immediate.

In the afternoon a fresh alarm came from another discontented element in his Majesty's service. Soldiers at Woolwich Arsenal began acting queer. The arsenal, twelve miles downriver from London, was the largest artillery base in the British Isles and the principal defense of the city. Now, swelling the national discord and the seeming menace to the government from mutinous seamen, the Royal Artillery Company began uttering disobedient cries. The arsenal commandant, Colonel Congreve, was obliged to report them to the Master-General of Ordnance, General the Marquis Charles Cornwallis, the loser in the American war and a recent victor in India. Lord Cornwallis was at his command post in the Horse Guards barracks in Whitehall, which was near the Admiralty office, a situation which brought army express dispatches and navy telegraph signals quickly to governmental focus. With Cornwallis was one of the best generals in the King's employment, his second son, Prince Augustus Frederick. Although Lazare Hoche had run Frederick into the water at Dunkirk in 1795 with the apparatus and personnel of his father's coalition of European pensioners, the Prince had much good sense and was excited at once again maneuvering troops. Following the forced annulment of his marriage to Lady Augusta Murray, he had found happiness in an unsanctified liaison with the actress Mrs. Clarke, whom he set up in Gloucester Place with a packet of blank army commissions. Her sales were confined to age limits Frederick had recently set when he retired lieutenant colonels under twenty years of age and captains under twelve.

To the colonel's alarm from Woolwich, Cornwallis and Frederick sent an order for him to forward the gunners' complaints in writing. He obeyed too fully. Frederick complained to the King, "Colonel Congreve rather imprudently sent the paper into the different barracks in order to ascertain whether it contained everything which they meant, upon which they immediately ordered more demands [including] the restoration of the rank and pay of first gunners, which had been abolished in 1783." As Cornwallis departed in haste for the scene, Frederick thoughtfully ordered the Seventh Light Dragoons to proceed from Croydon to Lewisham, there to stand ready within a few hours' march of Woolwich, if Cornwallis required help.

Sensations of fear and hope crossed Westminster like the changing play of sun and cloud shadows on that ominous Friday in May. Among the hurrying up-riders going to and from London was a new stakeholder in the dangerous game, General Sir Charles Grey, Commandant of Southern England. He was a volatile old soldier who had entered combat with Wolfe at Quebec in 1759. In the American War of Independence, Sir Charles beat Anthony Wayne at Paoli and was victorious in small fights at Germantown and Tappan. He and Old Jarvey seized the West Indies in '94, but Grey had recently refused the command of Ireland. He and his son Charles, who was a Member of Parliament, were advocates of Roman Catholic emancipation. Charles Major sat on his Majesty's privy council, and Charles Minor was the closest follower of H.M. *bête noire,* Charles James Fox.

General Grey had stiffened the brummagem defenses of Sheerness as best he could in the event that Richard Parker tried to take the town. Now he was racing to London with an anti-mutiny strategy to propose to the government. By the time he rode into Whitehall, Pitt had called an emergency cabinet meeting and the general was invited to attend. If his Majesty's ministers had earlier been remiss in appreciating the mutiny, they were compensating for it now. The seamen were the subject of the top-order papers of the secretariats at 10 Downing Street, navy, interior and now the army. In fact, his Majesty was going to sit up past his bedtime to have latest reports. The sea lords were in continuous deliberation. And there was to be a night session of Parliament. The word went around town that Charles James Fox intended a major speech against the ministry.

Commons would be full. When Fox spoke, the King's men appeared in numbers, not only to crush him with votes but to relish the artistic way he piked the front bench and held ministers high to wriggle before their followers.

Pitt called a cabinet meeting for eight o'clock and left Downing Street at five to place himself under Fox's barrage. The Prime Minister had no fear for his majority, but hated to see any votes flaking away. He intended to answer forcefully: Fox had made a special occasion of the evening by urging all his friends to attend. To Thomas Coke, a mild agrarian reform member from Norfolk, he wrote, "It is of great importance that the lead in such a business should be in the hands of persons who mean well, and not of Corresponding Societies."

Fox was near to complete despair for English representative government. In the evening before him, he could only hope to advance the cause of liberty and suffrage and try to lead more centrists into the cross-bench coalition that Moira and Northumberland were forming backstairs. Fox was bringing in a bill to give the right to vote to all householders paying "scot and lot," a kind of parish assessment. It would broaden the base of parliamentary representation and perhaps finish the dictatorship of the golden pills and the political career of William Pitt the Younger. Fox had discussed the bill with his and Moira's men and they had assigned speakers to promote its various

aspects. The Duke of Northumberland was enthusiastic about it.*
The old lad envisioned that the unveiling would call forth from the
shadows his Anti-Pitt Legion "to publicly show themselves and strike
their premeditated blow."

The Foxite chosen to introduce the bill was thirty-three-year-old
Charles Grey, whose father, the general, was at that moment waiting
at 10 Downing Street for Pitt to dispose of the factious business and
come deal with the mutiny. Young Grey arose and moved for "Leave
to bring a bill to improve and amend the representation of the people
in the House of Commons." In expatiating on it, he did not flinch
from defending the ideals of the French Revolution, which he predicted "in the end will tend to the diffusion of liberty and rational
knowledge all over the world."

The motion was seconded by Thomas Erskine, the iconoclastic
Scot barrister, who was followed by the eloquent, witty and inebriated
Richard Brinsley Sheridan. There was no sign of Lord Moira's center
army.

Fox took up the argument in what a government supporter, Lord
Morpeth, said "was the finest and most impressive speech I ever
heard him make." The *Times* of London, which held Fox's bill "objectionable by introducing too numerous a description of voters,"
nevertheless said his speech was "a *chef d'oeuvre* of eloquence, of
sound reasoning and of mature reflection. It is acknowledged by everyone that he never spoke with greater ability in his life."

Fox struck again the chord touched by Grey: adopting French
principles of liberty and manhood suffrage would embolden the
Englishman to feel "he is fighting for himself and not another; that
it is his own cause, his own safety, his own concern, his own dignity
on the face of the earth and his own interest on the identical soil
which he has to maintain."

At candlelighting time Fox was still commanding a quiet and re-
flective audience, which heard him bring to a close his last address of
the century:

> "And now, Sir, before I sit down, allow me to make a single
> observation with respect to the character and conduct of those
> who have, in conjunction with myself, felt it their duty to op-
> pose the progress of this disastrous war. I hear it said, 'You
> do nothing but mischief when you are here; and yet we should

---

* He had not given it much thought. If enacted, Fox's bill would remove
two of the duke's three pocket M.P.s.

be sorry to see you away.' I do not know how we shall be able to satisfy gentlemen who feel toward us in this way. If we can neither do our duty without mischief, nor please them with doing nothing, I know but of one way by which we can give them content, and that is by putting an end to our existence. With respect to myself, and I believe I can also speak for others, I do not feel it consistent with my duty totally to secede from this House. I have no such intention; but, Sir, I have no hesitation in saying that after seeing the conduct of this House, after seeing them give to Ministers their confidence and support, upon convicted failure, imposition and incapacity; after seeing them deaf and blind to the consequences of a career that penetrates the hearts of all other men with alarm, and that neither reason, experience, nor duty are sufficiently powerful to influence them to oppose the conduct of government, I certainly do think that I may devote more of my time to my private pursuits, and to the retirement which I love, than I have hitherto done; I certainly think I need not devote much of it to fruitless exertions, and to idle talk, in this House. Whenever it shall appear that my efforts may contribute in any degree to restore us to the situation from which the confidence of this House in a desperate system and incapable administration has so suddenly reduced us, I shall be found ready to discharge my duty."

The Black Patriot was leaving the House of Commons in disgust and sorrow. Gibbon's prophecy in the salad days of Pitt and Fox had been reversed. Billy Pitt's painted boat had crushed Charles's black collier. The Prime Minister sailed through Fox's shattered timbers. Pitt delivered a scathing attack on extension of male suffrage, which he said came from "modern reformers and borrowed principles, from the novel doctrines of the rights of man, from French proselytes, from Paine, from the Jacobins and affiliated societies, and from that shallow philosophy, which, under a specious mask, had endeavoured to impose on the world one of the wildest species of bigotry which had ever existed."

Pitt hurried back to Downing Street without waiting for the division. Fox's motion was defeated 256 to 91. It was the highest protest vote he had generated since his resolution terminating the American war. The new opposition bloc did not show its face.

It was a day of irresolution at the Admiralty. It seemed to their lordships that Adam Duncan was the remaining hope for putting down the Nore mutiny, but what was the actual situation in his North Sea fleet lying at Yarmouth? Spencer had reason to suspect that his dear friend Duncan was not telling him all his troubles. On the one hand, the big Scotsman would assure him, as he had three days earlier, that "much harmony is in this fleet," and on the other hand, Spencer had a petition from the Nore prior to then with the signatures of delegates from eleven of Duncan's ships. Their lordships decided to send a confidential emissary to Great Yarmouth to learn the true situation. They picked an officer who had been an "eyewitness to all the transactions" at the Nore, Captain William Bligh. Secretary Nepean wrote Duncan, asking that he confide in Bligh "whether in the event of being reduced to the necessity of resorting to extremities you have reason to think that [your] crews can be depended on, should they be called upon, to act [to reduce] the ships of the Nore to submission." He also twitted Duncan on whether or not he knew that four Nore delegates under Mathew Hollister had visited his ships and secured signatures for the eight articles.

Duncan had not detected them, but through an intelligence coup of his own he knew something Nepean did not know—that eighteen Nore delegates were headed in the fast cutter *Cygnet* for Great Yarmouth. Duncan sent south two gunboats under Lieutenant Reddy. He seized *Cygnet* inshore without resistance, but three delegates were already meeting in Yarmouth town with North Sea legislators. Lieutenant Reddy waited for the trio. They came aboard nonchalantly and showed him a letter purportedly written by the Yarmouth delegates advising the Nore that "all" Duncan's people "are perfectly satisfied and are going to sea." They said that it was imperative that they be permitted to return to the Nore with this message which might put a finish to the business there. Reddy was impressed. He released them and their cutter and even escorted them partway home. The letter had been prepared as a ruse in case they were captured and they were taking the real substance of the Yarmouth meeting verbally to the Nore.

With the Admiralty's orders to Bligh, still on the beach at Sheerness, went a note to Duncan: "We send you Captain Bligh on a very delicate business. . . . The welfare and almost the existence of the country may depend upon what is the event of this very important crisis. But till we know what we can look for from your squadron it will be very difficult for us to know how to act."

Spencer wrote a report to the King on Bligh's mission and hurried to Downing Street for the night cabinet meeting. There he was embarrassed to find that Pitt had heard of his blunder in offering an inoperative pardon to the mutineers. The Prime Minister had drafted a new one, already at the printers, that forgave violations of the articles of war up to the time of a Nore submission. He gave Spencer the responsibility of soliciting the royal signature to the revised document.

In contrast to indecisive meeting of the sea lords, there was a positive atmosphere in the cabinet room at Downing Street where Charles Grey, the old soldier, expounded on how to solve the navy's troubles. "I am decidedly of the opinion that the business ought not to be allowed to remain longer on its present footing of suspense," said he, "but ought without delay to be brought to the point." At midnight Henry Dundas reported to the King that General Grey

is strong impressed with an opinion that there is still a misapprehension prevailing among the mutineers as to the former pardon not being applicable to them, and he urges strongly the expediency of the Board of Admiralty going down, not to make any further concessions, but to declare the new demands inadmissible, and if they did not immediately return to their duty, to publish to them distinctly the extent of the outrages they had committed and that they had forfeited the promise of pardon offered to and accepted by the rest of the Fleet. This is thought to be expedient for the purpose of separating the cause of the Sheerness mutineers from those who have returned to their duty. Sir Charles Grey is perfectly confident of the fidelity of the whole troops under his command.

The King replied, "If it upon the whole should be thought right for the Lords of the Admiralty to go to Sheerness it must be to explain the danger to individuals if they do not return to their duty, not with a view to make the smallest concession."

Pitt liked General Grey's recommendation. With variation, it resembled the formula the Prime Minister used in the war with France. When Pitt's war-making capability and influence with his own people were at their lowest he would send an envoy to France to see what the republic would give in a quid pro quo—island for island, colony for colony—in a peace treaty. The longer such trucial talks dawdled, the more quiet and hopeful things became at home and the more time Pitt had to gather a military blow. Actually, he was presently arranging such a truce flag with the Directory, by which Sir James Harris* was to go to France in six days' time.

Such a coquettish stratagem was now shaped against President Parker. He was to be waited upon at Sheerness while Adam Duncan came around from Yarmouth to overcome him. Although the sea lords had refused an invitation from the delegates to come to Sheerness three days before, Pitt ordered them to proceed there with all dispatch. He also rescinded Admiralty orders to Duncan to return to the Texel, and instead summoned the North Sea fleet to come to the Thames for the ultimate test.

Thus arose in prospect the apotheosis of Hanoverian Admiralty. Following Old Jarvey's precept that "manly resistance to mutineers is the most meritorious of all military services" and the equally intransigent delegates' oath, in the offing hung the spectacle of forty British warships sinking each other in the approaches to the imperial capital.

What the sea lords thought about usurpation of their business by a soldier and the Prime Minister is not known. They prepared to leave for Sheerness next afternoon. The day's decisions were formed without consulting Black Dick Howe, who had settled the Spithead mutiny. He was in London and he had analyzed the new rising. He wrote to an old crony about "the extravagance of the seamen at the Nore." He thought the port command "highly erroneous" and the ships' officers nearly as addled as the sailors. "I almost think that some attempts upon our coasts, commencing by the enemy, seem to be the last hope we have for recovery of our senses," he said. Howe imputed the neglect of the seamen's complaints to "the incompetency of the persons who have the immediate superintendence in the department." He declared that "preventative measures rather than correctives are to be preferred for preserving discipline in fleets and armies."

This long apprehensive day in Westminster had closed two doors to the delegates of the fleet. With Fox abandoning Parliament there was little further hope that it would inquire into their grievances. The seamen might think the sea lords were coming to Sheerness to hear and consider complaints as they had done at Spithead. But Spencer was under plain orders from Pitt: "Any new claims which may be

---

* Harris was to receive the gratitude of his sovereign and claim the beautiful name, Lord Malmesbury.

brought forward by the seamen should be absolutely and explicitly refused."

Riders galloped into the night with defense dispositions for to-morrow. General Sir William Howe, brother of Black Dick, headed for Chelmsford with orders to march the Warwickshire Militia Regiment to reinforce Purfleet and the East End of London. From Woolwich arsenal, Lord Cornwallis sent an express to London evincing a "strong desire" for more troops to prevent outbreaks of seamen or dockers. At Gravesend and Tilbury forts, furnaces were fired to make ready red-hot cannon balls for President Parker if he came up the river.

Prince Frederick received word that, in addition to the artillery-men, three companies of militia were disaffected at Woolwich and the most unruly was being posted elsewhere.

Prince Frederick sent Colonel Nesbitt, an aide-de-camp of the King's, to take command at Gravesend on the south bank of the river, which post had been vacated by a major general moved to defend Chatham. Gravesend, lying opposite Tilbury Fort in the first narrow place in the Thames, was the outer interception point for hostile craft coming to London. During the night Colonel Nesbitt discerned a ship's boat sweeping up the river and ordered it to halt. The oarsmen hesitated and a musketeer whistled two balls across their bow. The boat came in and six delegates from the Nore materialized in the rays of a candle lantern.

"Sir, here is our demands to the Lords of the Admiralty," said one of them, handing the officer a copy of the eight articles. "We never received any answer to them."

"I promise you to forward this paper to the Admiralty," said Nesbitt. "And now, my good lads, I advise you to return to your ships." The boat shoved off and went dutifully downstream.

The delegates curtailed shore leave and sent search parties on board passing merchant shipping to prevent desertions from their ranks.

The next morning the cabinet met and completed its instructions to Lord Spencer's mission.

The commissioners shall take all precautions to get the officers ashore previous to the necessity of resource to measures of force.

The commissioners shall on no account go on board of any

ships unless order should have been completely restored there. If not, His Majesty intends that Duncan shall act against the mutineers with such part of his force on which he may think he can rely. The great object with a view of this will be to shew to the crews of H.M. Fleet that the mutiny at Sheerness rests on grounds different than those complaints or applications which were originally preferred by the seamen at Spithead.

The cabinet sent orders to Duncan, authorizing him to detach on a separate cruise any vessel he deemed undependable.

The sea lords—Spencer, Arden, Young and Marsden—left for Sheerness in the afternoon and slept at Rochester. While they were on the road, Admiral Buckner sent to the fleet the latest statement he had from the Admiralty. It had been drawn up before Pitt reversed his orders. In it, their lordships denied the sailors better food, shore leave, advances to impressed men, removal of cruel officers, and all other demands. Buckner told the ships that "Although their Lordships thought proper to go to Portsmouth [to obtain] more perfect information of the grievances . . . and [to grant] such further indulgences as might render their situation more comfortable, and enable them to better provide for the support of their families, no similar reason exists for taking such a step on the present occasion."

The delegates replied through Parker:

> To the Lords Commissioners for executing the office of Lord High Admiral of Great Britain and Ireland, &c.
> I am commanded by the delegates of the whole fleet assembled in council, on board his Majesty's ship *Sandwich,* to inform your lordships, that they have received your letter from Admiral Buckner, which informs them that it is not your intention of coming to Sheerness: the same has been communicated to his Majesty's ships and vessels lying here, and the determination of the whole is, that they will not come to any accommodation until you appear at the Nore, and redress our grievances.
>
> RICHARD PARKER, President
> By order of the Committee of Delegates of the Whole Fleet

Scarcely had Parker sent this ashore when he heard that their lordships, despite last night's refusal, had just arrived in Sheerness.

XIII

Mutiny of
the North Sea Fleet

Old Neptune made haste, to the Nore he did come,
To waken his sons who had slept for too long.
His thundering loud voice made us start with surprise,
To hear his sweet words, and he bid us arise.

"Your brothers," says he, "has all firmly resolved,
To banish all tyrants that long did uphold,
Their crewel intentions to scourge when they please,
Sutch a set of brace villians you must instantly seize.

"So away, tell your brothers, near Yarmouth they lie,
To embark in the cause they will never deny.
Their harts are all good, their like lyons I say,
I've furnished there minds and they all will obey.

"And when they arrive, which I trust they soon will,
Be steady and cautious, let wrangling lay still,
And love one another, my favour you'll keep,
Sucksess to King George and his glorious fleet."

All Hail Brother Seamen
Forecastle ballad, 1797 mutiny

WHILE the Lords Commissioners of the Admiralty were en route to Sheerness, General Grey had returned there and was tidying up the town. He stopped all parades and sent the militia to their barracks to spare their lordships the sight of his men fraternizing with theirs.

For the second consecutive night, Colonel Nesbitt stopped a boat from the Nore that was trying to run the Gravesend-Tilbury gauntlet.

This one contained two delegates from *Sandwich* and fourteen from *Lancaster,* the newly defected two-decker lying farther upstream. Despite the fact that his soldiery was acting queerly, Nesbitt took the seamen to Tilbury Fort. The Lancasters claimed they would never have joined the mutiny if they had known of the loyal protection of the river forts. First thing in the morning, Nesbitt received a strongly worded demand from the Nore delegates that he return his captives to their ships. The colonel ignored it and went about looking for some authority to charge the seamen with something.

The day—Sunday 28 May—was cloudy. It found Lord Spencer's coach wending through Chatham toward Sheerness, while in London, his ministerial powers were being assumed by Henry Dundas, the War Secretary and Admiralty treasurer, and by the renascent generalissimo, Prince Frederick, who was writing his father:

> . . . by the advice of Mr. Pitt and Mr. Dundas, I have sent directions to Colonel Nesbitt not to allow the *Lancaster* to go down to the Nore, nor any suspicious vessell to proceed up the river without being examined, in which I trust I shall have full-filled your Majesty's intentions—and I have written to Marquess Cornwallis to send if possible some guns to any place which can command the *Lancaster,* in order to force her into subjection, in case the negotiation of the Lords of the Admiralty does not succeed at Sheerness.

The Commander-in-Chief of the Army, it may be noted, thought that Spencer was going to the Nore for the purpose of negotiating with the mutineers.

The sea lords arrived in Sheerness in the afternoon and constituted a board in the dockyard mansion of the resident commissioner, Captain Francis John Hartwell. A large body of seamen marched on the house, led by Richard Parker. The sailors wore red ribbons on their hats. "Their behavior was quiet and orderly," said Lord Spencer, who watched from a curtained window. "There was no huzzaing or musick." Parker approached the door and Admiral Buckner opened it. "Good evening, sir," said the head mutineer. "We should like to ask whether these are the same lords who have been at Portsmouth."

"They are."

"We respectfully request their lordships to come aboard the *Sandwich* and settle the business."

"No. Their lordships will not do that."

Buckner stepped inside to receive instructions from the invisible Spencer, and came to the door again.

"You may see their lordships only for the purpose of declaring that you will return to duty and accept the King's pardon."

"But how are we to have our grievances taken into consideration?" Buckner withdrew for another tête-à-tête.

"All of your grievances have been redressed. No discussion can possibly take place with their lordships."

Rumbles from within.

"If you accept his Majesty's most gracious pardon you will be allowed to declare it personally to their lordships. Their lordships will then pronounce to you the pardon in the King's name."

Parker and his people turned away, undemonstrably, and walked to a tavern at which they were holding meetings. Lord Spencer's party went back to discussing forcible strategy with Buckner, Hartwell and Grey. Buckner now had an informer, a marine sergeant named Collins, sitting with the delegates of the fleet and people were bringing him tales from the lower-deck juntas. Collins had reported "a division and much agitation" in the fleet congress.

The republic at the Nore was fragile. These unattached casual ships did not share squadron pride as at Spithead. Their leaders had risen overnight and had created no program except for an increasing sentiment to demand shore leaves and prize money payment—two articles that had been abandoned at Spithead. Morale was being maintained by demonstrations but discipline was often upheld by intimidation. There was a good deal of mutual distrust between the fleet committee and the rank and file.

The consensus of Buckner's spy reports was that "the smaller ships are all well disposed" to return to duty, and "the *Director* is wavering." The Directors were ready to secede, but were "completely under the influence of terror" by *Sandwich* and *Inflexible*. General Grey impressed the less fervid sea lords with his spirit and optimism: "It is time this temporizing system should be at an end!" Still, Spencer wrote Nepean, "I have but very slender hopes. . . ."

Printed copies of the revised royal pardon legally absolving the Nore people arrived in the saddlebags of a special courier. The sea lords sent Captain Mosse to *Sandwich* to distribute them and pronounce an ultimatum to the delegates: unless they capitulated and accepted the King's pardon by noon the next day, their lordships would strike the Admiralty pendant from the commissioner's house, return to London, and leave the mutineers to their fate. Of course, wrote Marsden to Nepean, "We shall not be precise to that hour," on account of the many ships involved. Captain Mosse was to sleep on *Sandwich* to follow overnight developments.

Lord Spencer glanced at the latest letters forwarded from Adam Duncan and went to bed gloomy. They contained unmistakable evidence of organized conspiracy in the North Sea fleet. Thomas Barnes, chief boatswain's mate of *Adamant,* who was opposed to the lower-deck combination, had turned over to Duncan a paper the delegates had sent him. It was titled "The Outlines of ye Articles of H.M. Ships *Belliqueux, Montague, Standard, Monmouth* and *Adamant,*" and included some interesting legislation:

> . . . That no assembly whatsomever shall conveen in the Gally after nine at night where there might be any reason of suspecting that a mutinous or disorderly mind reigned in us more than our ship-mates at Spithead to maintain which we here pledge ourselves [unanimous] by oath one and all. . . .
>
> That as many women may come on board as please, none to go on shore unless in a bad stat of health and no hopes of recovery. . . .

The other regulations duplicated many of the internal rules at the Nore and served as further confirmation that the Nore and Great Yarmouth were in close liaison. It was evidence that the forecastle controlled Duncan's ships, despite the big Scotsman's soothing reports to the Admiralty. But Bligh should be that day in Yarmouth and factual reports would be coming from him in a few days' time. However, what Bligh was to report of events occurring that very evening in the North Sea fleet was not going to improve Lord Spencer's morale.

Duncan had not yet received Pitt's order to come round to the Nore prepared to battle the delegate fleet. He was still under instructions to go to sea and rendezvous with two antiquated reinforcements from Spithead, *Russell,* 48, and *Ganges,* 74, and proceed to the Texel. He was keenly aware that most of his ships were under delegate discipline, although none were flaunting symbolic nooses, crimson banners and rebel cheers, and no officers had been anathematized. However, *Nassau,* 64, was so near to an outbreak that Duncan removed his vice-admiral from her to *Adamant,* 74, a vessel that he kept in order by constant preachings.

On one of Duncan's two-deckers, *Standard,* 64, Captain Thomas

Parr was accosted on his forbidden quarterdeck by William Wallis, captain of the forecastle, one of the steadiest seamen aboard, a man who had actually volunteered for the navy and who had served well with Parr for five years.

"Captain Parr, I have been elected a delegate of the ship's company. We wish a boat to visit the *Lion.*"

"No, Wallis, you shall not have a boat."

"Very well, sir." Wallis turned to a gang on the fore hatch that was rigging the ship's boats to go over the side so that the weather deck could be scrubbed down. The first lieutenant, John Buller, was bossing the job. The captain of the forecastle assumed Buller's authority.

"Drop them out astern," ordered Wallis. The men obeyed the delegate.

"Captain Parr, I must ask you again to permit us to take a boat."

"Wallis, you will carry a midshipman in the boat."

"No, sir," said the delegate as he told off oarsmen. They went down to the boat. "Avast bo-o-o-o-at!" the captain yelled. The first lieutenant amplified the order with his speaking trumpet. The boat pulled away.

"Arm the marines!"

Slowly, dragging their feet, a handful of marines came out of the hatchway. Marine Captain Mackintosh dashed across the quarterdeck and tackled the marine sentry at the gangway. The ship's company drained into the forepeak, augmented by men bouncing out of the gun decks. *Standard*'s unwashed boards rumbled under the fore carronades. The men shoved the bullfrog-throated guns inboard and wheeled them to point at the aftercastle.

"Stand clear of the guns!" These gaping muzzles could blast the whole poop. Parr and the officers retreated to the great cabin. Barefooted topmen were running out on the yards with blocks and ropes.

"Mackintosh, you're going out of the ship!"

"Put the sawnie bugger ashore!" The Scottish marine officer stayed out of sight.

Delegate Wallis returned from the sister two-decker and disappeared in the crowd at the forecastle. The mass moved aft, with the delegate hidden in its midst. "We want our pay!" Wallis shouted from the crowd. "We must have our pay and his Majesty's pardon or we will not go to sea." Captain Parr tried to talk over the hubbub. "Captain!" said another voice. "The Captain of the *Lion* has issued soap and tobacco to his company." Parr, deadlocked, retired and wrote an urgent requisition on the victualing office for soap and tobacco.

Admiral Duncan fired one gun and loosed his fore topsail, the signal to prepare for sea. The men in the North Sea fleet were roused out to put their backs to the capstan bars, let down canvas, cat the gigantic anchors and lay the cable in the tiers. *Standard,* to the admiral's astonishment, obeyed orders, but the companies of *Venerable,* 74, *Montagu,* 74, and *Nassau* climbed the shrouds, waved their bonnets and lofted the huzzas of the people. Duncan heatedly reproached his own Venerables and shamed them back to duty, but the other two ships remained at anchor. They said they would refuse orders until their back wages were paid. *Montagu* had been paid a few weeks before and could hardly cavil on that score. But Duncan was forced to leave *Montagu* and *Nassau* at Lowestoft Sands as he sailed on with the dozen vessels that he still had. In the afternoon he anchored twenty miles at sea at his prearranged meeting place with the Spithead two-deckers.

An officer came over from *Belliqueux,* 64, and told him that her crew was in a state of mutiny and demanding use of boats to visit other ships. In order to shut off further fraternization among the ships' companies, Duncan gave orders to recommence the voyage to the Texel. *Belliqueux* acknowledged with a signal flag meaning "unable to comply with order" and went about on a course for Great Yarmouth. *Lion* trooped in behind her, revealing that *Belliqueux* was the parliament ship.

The Standards weighed anchor. Out of the corner of his eye, Captain Parr noticed a boat approaching. "Let a reef out of the topsail and set mainsail!" he ordered. Lieutenant Buller bawled it to the tops. Another delegate unveiled himself. Seaman William Holdsworth came to the edge of the captain's holy ground and said, "Captain Parr, we must heave to and wait. We must speak to that boat."

"But why, my lad?"

"I don't know, sir. We are deceived."

The seaman turned and shouted to the waist, "Furl mainsail!" High above, along the mainyard, the row of men pivoted on their bellies, held on to the take points, hesitating whether to continue paying it out or to reef it in.

"Set mainsail!" the first officer repeated.

"Furl mainsail!" yelled Holdsworth, joined by delegates Wallis and Henry Freeman. The topmen obeyed their elected leaders. *Standard* fell back from the squadron. Captain Parr tried to reason with the delegates, but they kept saying, "It's no use, sir," and "We are deceived." Delegate Holdsworth walked on the quarterdeck and the ship's company followed him there in a rush. Captain Parr said to Lieutenant Buller, "Signal inability to the flagship." The crowd shouted, "No signal!" They took over the color chest. The boat came up and put aboard delegates from *Lion*.

The mizzen topsail backed in the drifting ship. "Shiver the mizzen topsail," Holdsworth ordered. "Damn your bloods! Haul in the weather forebrace." H.M.S. *Lion* passed and the two companies cheered each other. Holdsworth said to *Standard*'s pilot, "The ship should go in to Yarmouth." The pilot replied, "I can't carry her in tonight." The delegate said, "I'll make you carry her in." Lieutenant Buller intervened. "Holdsworth, it's not possible. Let her be brought to." The delegate did not insist and the men high in the yards obeyed the officer's order to set the main topsail.

"I must have the keys to the magazine," Holdsworth announced.

Captain Parr asked, "Are you taking my ship from me?"

The mutineer did not reply. Captain Parr said, "Mister Buller, go below and talk to them." On the way, the lieutenant encountered Quartermaster Brice Gilliland,* a friend of his, and was disturbed to find him sympathetic to the men. There was a meeting going on in the upper gun deck, led by delegates from *Standard* and *Lion*. Lieutenant Buller asked them what was the matter. "We have been deceived about the Dutch fleet being out," was the answer. "We'll go to Yarmouth Roads in the morning. Have our pay and his Majesty's pardon. Then nothing will prevent us from going out to meet the enemies of the country."

On H.M.S. *Leopard, 50*, anonymous commands sounded forth from the waist and break of the forecastle. "All hands! Ahoy!" The company pounded out on deck. The captain of the forecastle, Thomas Starling, came aft, and said to Captain William Hargood, "The ship must go to port and leave the fleet." The commander attempted to dissuade the company from disobedience. He wanted to send a boat to Admiral Duncan. "No!" the seamen replied. "No!"

He went forward and spoke with the men crowded into the peak. "No!" they yelled. As the captain absented the quarterdeck, seamen gathered around the wheel. And when he ran aft, the topman let fly the foresheet. "Starling, can't you make these people obey orders?" Hargood demanded. The delegate said, "Captain, I'm only one man and can do nothing." Hargood's ship was hauled about on the other tack, despite the efforts of loyal boatswain's mate Thomas Norman to

---

* Killed in action on *Royal Sovereign* at Trafalgar as a lieutenant.

hold the helm on course. The two-decker headed for Great Yarmouth. Captain Hargood went into his cabin and fainted.

Forecastle government was quickly instituted on board. The yard ropes were let down and the main conspirators, Starling, William Welch, James Robertson, Joseph Fearon (captain of the maintop), William Ross and George Shave, set up headquarters in the prisoners' berth under the larboard bay. They had bound their own association by kissing a Bible and now brought the crew down one by one to swear allegiance to the delegates and the sacred cause. Some of the men already sported red cockades. As they anchored at Yarmouth Roads, the committee administered twelve lashes to Norman for defending the helm. This rapid exercise of sovereignty was intended also to impress "the King's party," seamen with misgivings about the business. The committee decreed an extra issue of rum and the company cheered the cause. Individual swearing of sailors went on, until the oath-takers were in majority, after which men were inducted three or four at a time. Seaman John Habbigan was awakened at three in the morning to file into the prisoners' bay. In the candlelight, the taking of the first oath for which he had ever been asked in his life left a strong impression.

In the evening, *Leopard* was visited by a boat flying a vice-admiral's pendant, and a heavy one-legged admiral clambered aboard. He was Sir Thomas Pasley, who had lost his limb at the Glorious First of June. He exhorted the Leopards to rejoin Duncan and go to the Dutch coast to stop an invasion of the country. He was heckled by delegate George Shave, who was assuming Captain Hargood's functions. Shave called off demands of the seamen and challenged the admiral to talk about them. The orator did not rise to the occasion. Admiral Pasley went ashore without swerving the Leopards. That night delegate Starling left for the Nore in a cutter.

The ship's internal committee was filled out. Of the twelve members only William Ross was literate. He was drafted as secretary and worked very hard. The committee demanded documentation in inverse proportion to its ability to read and write. Ross had to write down what they said to each other and read it back to them. They also ordered him to compile a roster of the entire ship's company, although why they did not simply appropriate the ship's muster roll remains a mystery.

That evening aboard *Monmouth*, 64, back of the Yarmouth Sands, the crew assembled in the starboard bay and drew up articles. First Lieutenant Charles Bullen went below and demanded, "What do you mean, so many assembling here? I order you to go directly on deck."

"We are going into port to look for the Belliqueuxs who insulted our boat's crew two evenings ago by throwing shot at them."

"I order you on deck!"

"No!" said William Vance, a quartermaster.

"Don't leave your admiral, who is going in search of the Dutch fleet. Stay with the admiral and when we return to port, he will redress your grievances."

"We have no grievances. We like our officers. But we are going into port to search the Belliqueuxs."

With that, the Monmouths bounded up on deck and into the fore-rigging. They raised three roaring cheers and nimble topmen raced out on the quarters and passed ropes through the yardarm blocks. Seamen picked up the small arms chests from the poop and carried them below.

The captain of H.M.S. *Monmouth,* the Earl of Northesk, returned aboard after supper. He was a humane officer and the Monmouths were not dissembling when they said they liked him (and Lieutenant Bullen). "Mr. Bullen, will you be so good as to have the boatswain pipe the hammocks down?" Lord Northesk said. It was the practice on British warships in the morning for each man to roll his hammock tight, bring it up to the weather deck and stow it with the others in the antiboarding nets along the bulwarks. In battle the hammocks stopped many a bullet, shell fragment and splinter.

The boatswain tweetled. Not a man touched his hammock to take it below. Quartermaster Vance gathered the *Monmouth* company and told them to take no more orders from the officers. Lord Northesk heard this from the break of the poop and considered that Vance was assuming his post. At dawn the captain sent for his first officer to come topside and witness the quartermaster's latest affront. Vance was standing illegally on the quarterdeck, giving commands to men swaying up the gallant and topgallant yards. Northesk said to Bullen, "Make a signal of inability to Admiral Duncan." Vance barred the color chest. "Sorry, Lieutenant, there will be no signals. Orders of the ship's company." Instead of turning back to Yarmouth to chastise the Belliqueuxs, the mutineer captain astonished Northesk by getting under way for sea. His lordship addressed his men, without inter-ference from Vance, and after pleading with them to accept only lawful orders, asked what their grievances were. Many men told him in great detail. Northesk was left with a troubled conscience. His ship was headed for the Nore.

At the North Sea rendezvous, Adam Duncan saw mutiny disintegrate his fleet. The sixty-four-gun ships, *Repulse* and *Ardent,* turned back for Yarmouth Roads, followed by the fifty-gun frigates, *Isis* and *Glatton.* The finest 64-gun ship in the navy, Commodore Horatio Nelson's favorite, *Agamemnon,* built at Buckler's Hard by Henry Adams, master shipwright, showed her stern galley to the admiral. Little ones slipped away, frigate *Vestal,* sloops *Hound* and *Inspector,* cutter *Ranger,* and the fireship *Comet.* Some hoisted red flags against the lowering sun as they sailed away.

Adam Duncan was left with *Venerable* and one cranky sister, *Adamant.* He decided it was infeasible to go to Holland with 124 guns when the Dutch, according to his latest intelligence from Downing Street, had 18 sail-of-the-line, 22 frigates, sloops and brigs, and 42 large transports with perhaps 1,200 guns. He anchored at the rendezvous to await the brace of two-deckers from Spithead that had been promised him.

Captain Bligh arrived in Yarmouth by coach, too late to find Duncan, but in time to see most of his fleet coming back to the Roads, the companies cheering like men in possession of a great victory. They cheered all night. In the morning, Bligh took a boat out to the mutinous anchorage. The new officers-of-the-watch were short with the Bounty Bastard. "Fend off there, sir. Only ship's boats permitted." The Glattons, however, impressed Bligh with their "remarkably loyal and good character." He found guns were loaded on *Montagu.* He got aboard *Nassau* and had a candid conversation with her people. When he asked whether they would resist mutiny in other ships, a delegate answered cryptically, "Every captain should keep his own ship quiet."

Bligh summed up to the Admiralty, "It appeared to me very doubtful and hazardous what would be the conduct of the favorable party of seamen if employed against the other." Taking some dispatches Duncan had sent ashore, Bligh hastened overland to London.

That morning, Admiral Duncan, waiting in his lonely post for the Spithead ships, saw "the *Montagu* a long way to windward of us, standing to the westward. I therefore conclude she is going to the Nore."

Monday, 29 May, the morning that Spencer had appointed for surrender, was gray and blowing at the Nore, obscuring the fleet and preventing its boats from coming up to Sheerness. It happened to be Restoration Day, commemorating the return of kings to Britain in

1660, after the nation's brief, awkward encounter with commoner rule. Their lordships, settling in to wait on the weather, heard the rumbling of repeated salvos of naval guns. But it proved no occasion for alarm. His Majesty's worshipful mutineers were firing a nineteen-gun blank salute to Charles II, and, for the occasion, had hoisted the red flag at the main and the royal standard at the fore.

Before noon, the limit of Lord Spencer's toleration, it was raining thickly and the Thames estuary heaved with green and white dragon scales. *Niger,* 32, came into Sheerness dockyard wearing a red flag and requesting repairs. The shipwrights had a cause of their own which they did not care to prosecute under the bloody rag, and although sympathetic with the sailors, they took off the red flag and raised the loyal standard. The *Niger* delegates protested, and soon seamen and workers were milling in the rain. The row ended with red noses, puffed eyes, handshakes and an understanding that there would be no more red flags brought into the yard. Significantly, quite a few Nigers fought for the loyal flag.

The gunboats that the delegates had brought out to anchor in the Great Nore were in distress from the gale, and Parker let them go back to shelter in Sheerness. Twelve noon rang in town, and eight bells jingled in the invisible fleet, ending the logbook day. The sea lords received no word from their emissary, Captain Mosse, or from the mutineers. They waited. At two o'clock a pair of sodden seamen came to the commissioner's house and knocked. Admiral Buckner recognized one of the best men in his forecastle, John Davis, mutineer-captain of *Sandwich,* a moderate man who had been trying to reduce the delegates' demands in order to arrive at a bargain with the Admiralty. He said, "Admiral Buckner, we cannot make up our minds until we know truly what was done for the seamen at Portsmouth. We most humbly beg their lordships to inform us of that." Buckner gave them a copy of the Act of Parliament on pay and rations. It did not, of course, mention removal of officers. There was no official document on that Spithead concession. Davis thanked the admiral and left.

The delegates of the whole fleet were quarreling. There were hot and profane arguments between legislators who wanted to take the pardon and get the thing over with and those who insisted on forcing the Admiralty to negotiate. The mutineers could still sway the pardoneers by invoking the suspicion of official treachery. "Remember the *Culloden!*" The body voted to send a delegation ashore to notify Lord Spencer that the fleet continued to abide by its demands.

Both Admiral Buckner and Commissioner Hartwell came out of the mansion to see the delegates, while their lordships listened from the interior. The encounter was brief. Hartwell took a letter from the delegates formally rejecting Spencer's latest pronouncements and reiterating their grievances. He went into the house and closed the door. The seamen went to their tavern. Cannon fire grumbled from the Great Nore and ceased after a few minutes. A boatman came in and reported to their lordships that one of Parker's gunboats had spied the blue flag on *Niger* and opened fire to bring her back in line.

At six in the evening a seaman carrying a large red flag appeared at the commissioner's house. Behind him was Richard Parker with a party of delegates. The president knocked on the door and said, "Good evening, Admiral Buckner, have their lordships given an answer to our letter?"

"No! There will be no answer. It is out of the question. And if this firing on one of his Majesty's ships is repeated, every man on the offending vessels will be excluded from pardon."

The President of the Delegates made a low bow and the seamen marched away.

Lord Spencer said, "Gentlemen, we have failed in our attempt to restore order and obedience. Let us return to London." He held in his hands telegraph briefs of the news that Bligh had brought to London posthaste from Great Yarmouth: DUNCAN'S SQUADRON ALMOST ALL IN A STATE OF MUTINY. Marsden said, "The people here have almost certainly been encouraged to hold out by the prospect of assistance from the disaffected of Duncan's squadron. *They know as well as we do that some ships were left at Yarmouth.*"

General Grey remained optimistic and full of fight. He thought their lordships' visit had shown "the whole inhabitants how desirous government were [*sic*] to set the misguided seamen right, and to bring them back to a just and proper sense of their duty and allegiance." That was precisely the effect upon the public that Pitt desired.

The sea lords slept at Rochester, three hours up the road, and sent a courier ahead with dispatches. Marsden wrote Nepean, "Mr. Parker's letters will amuse you. I shall not be surprised to hear that they have hanged him from one of his own yardropes." He added, "Now it remains to be seen what effect vigorous measures will produce."

At that hour of the night the vigorous measures were already in motion in Sheerness. Buckner ordered ashore officers still in the ships. Sir Charles Grey received an additional infantry regiment to secure

Sheerness and guard the ferry and the town well. He embargoed mail to and from the anchorage. He issued orders to seize every boat that came in from the Great Nore and send its occupants to jail in Chatham. He ordered batteries to fire on any armed vessel under delegate control that came into their range. He took over, as additional harbor defenses, the gunboats that Parker permitted to come in from the storm.

These were mere annoyances compared with the resounding stroke the Admiralty brought down on the delegates. The order went out to storeships, victualing yards, slops agents, dockyards and commands to stop furnishing any stores or provisions to ships at the Great Nore. Until this time the ships had been supplied as (inadequately as) usual —but now they were totally cut off and would have to make do with what was aboard. Unlike the ships at Spithead, which had been provisioned for a long cruise when the mutiny began, those at the Nore were quite unequally stocked. Some companies were already living hand to mouth. Shutting off food from the ships was calculated to discourage further resistance. Instead it inflamed the seamen and pushed moderates toward the militant faction. The men regarded it as "treachery" and "highly improper." Most of the seamen were innocent royalists. *How could the King inflict this on his humble and loyal subjects?* Or, *Why did the King permit wicked ministers like Pitt and Spencer to starve his loving subjects?* Some men blamed Henry Dundas instead of Spencer.

The tender from Leith arrived with a fresh supply of prest and quota men. Boats with armed sailors surrounded the tender and gave her company an ultimatum: "Come with us or be sunk!" Lieutenant Watson, in command of the floating prison van, had no cannon and advised his men to "mutiny for your own safety." Muttering vows of fidelity to their commander, his men grudgingly rebeled. Their dilemma did not affect the passengers belowdecks.

Parker called Lieutenant Platt of *Sandwich.* "You are ordered, sir, to receive one hundred and eleven men from the Leith tender, and to give a receipt for them as usual, and we are answerable for what we do." The lieutenant said, "Sir, I have no orders to receive them from Admiral Buckner, and my receipt, having no command, is of no use." Parker said, "We are answerable for what we do." Platt accepted the men and signed the receipt.

The company of the tender was obliged to elect delegates, who went sullenly to the fleet parliament on *Sandwich,* where they were called upon to prefer charges against Lieutenant Watson. They refused, saying that he was a good captain. Richard Parker spoke up in agreement; the Leith tender had delivered the head mutineer to the Nore on her previous voyage, and Parker testified that Watson was one of the finest officers he had encountered. The lieutenant was held blameless and left in command of his vessel.

Two young sloop captains who had been put ashore, Robert Honeyman of *Swan* and Adam MacKenzie of *Pylades,* had time to ponder on the true nature of the mutiny and on realistic ways to end it. Bluster and persuasion were not solving it. The prospect of British ships under the Union Jack battling sister ships under the red flag did not appeal to them. They stripped away the emotional issues; neither patriotism nor the British naval system was involved. The seamen were ready to fight any invader, and they had not condemned impressment or flogging. Despite rumbling among the Irish and some of the quota men, there was little political content to it. What was it, then? Honeyman and MacKenzie decided it was exactly what the petitions said it was, a matter of English rights and for better food, pay and treatment under the King's standing regulations. It was an economic cause. Therefore, the answer was economic. When the war was over, the majority of seamen, not having another trade, would depend on the merchant marine for employment. The young officers went to Benjamin Stow, Admiral Buckner's secretary, and proposed that the shipowners and mercantile powers of London publicly resolve not to employ in the future any seamen who held out at the Nore after a given date. Stow passed the blacklist idea to Nepean at the Admiralty.

Ship-keeping went on at the Nore. The lower deck conducted its own courts-martial and dealt punishments. The trials aped quarter-deck justice with "Clerk of Arains," "Defense Counsel" and "Council for the Crown." On *Repulse,* Midshipman Smith was charged with kicking a "brother," Seaman William Johnson. The court finding went:

> Mr. Smith, on account of your good character and the intercession of William Johnson, the principal evidence, the jury has thought proper to mitigate the sentence that might be entail'd upon you. You are to [be] confin'd to your cabin for twenty-four hours, and ast Mr. William Johnson's pardon.

In Portsmouth, things were quiet. Magistrate Aaron Graham continued to hunt English republicans as instigators of the mutiny. He was sure, he told Lord Portland, that he had discovered "all the dangerous characters" in the port area, including two persons at Gosport who had distributed books and handbills aboard ship. But, Graham lamented, "I am very much surprised that neither the magistrates nor any of the officers of the fleet are able to procure me a single copy of either."

Seeking the daring radical John Thelwall, Graham traced the rumor of his presence to the original storyteller, Captain the Honourable Sir George Berkeley, who declared that Thelwall had been aboard his ship a short time before. "Do you know him?" asked Graham. "No," said the officer. "Then how can you be certain it was Thelwall?" "Why, some of my people told me so." "Did they know him personally?" "No, but they believed it to be him and I believed them." Graham concluded that Thelwall had not been in Portsmouth since the business started. His assumption was correct.

That destitute, sore-used citizen of the dream was trudging the roads west. Pitt, Parliament and magistrate had trodden on Thelwall's last fingerhold in London. While trying to provide for his family as a tramping lecturer in East Anglia, he had been beaten up and robbed four times by King's mobs. He could think of only one place to turn. He was trekking to a remote part of Somersetshire to seek asylum with William Wordsworth and Samuel Taylor Coleridge, who had written Thelwall praising his verses of protest. They had never met, but Thelwall believed he would find good comrades in these ardent republicans living in the tiny village of Nether Stowey. Coleridge was the writer of:

> *Shall France alone a despot spurn?*
> *She she alone, O Freedom, boast thy care?*
> *Lo, round the standard Belgia's heroes burn,*
> *Tho' Powers blood-stain'd streamers fire the air,*
> *And wider yet thy influence spread,*
> *Nor e'er recline thy weary head,*
> *Till every land from pole to pole*
> *Shall boast one independent soul!*
> *And still, as erst, let favour'd Britain be*
> *First ever of the first and freest of the free!**

---

* Samuel Taylor Coleridge "Destruction of the Bastile," 1789.

Coleridge enjoyed painting battle scenes:

> *Red from the Tyrant's wound I shook the lance,*
> *And strode in joy the reeking plains of France!*

It compensated for a personal military disappointment. He had run away from Cambridge in 1791 and joined the 15th Dragoons under the name "Silas Tomkyn Comberbacke," but could not stay on a horse and was bought out by his family.

The poet was a thick-haired young man with flushed cheeks and grey-green eyes. He had started taking laudanum, a tincture of opium, the previous year. The East India Company was introducing cheap opium as a light and profitable return cargo from the Orient. Neuresthenics and disappointed intellectuals were taking to the poppy for solace and inspiration, among them Coleridge, Thomas de Quincey and George Crabbe.

William Hazlitt said, "It was a misfortune to any man of talent to be born in the latter end of the eighteenth century. Genius stopped the way of Legitimacy, and therefore was to be abated, crushed, or set aside as a nuisance. The spirit of the monarchy was at variance with the spirit of the age. The flame of liberty, the light of intellect, was to be extinguished with the sword—or with slander whose edge is sharper than the sword."

Lately in Mr. Pitt's intimidating clime, Coleridge's appetite for politics and gore had gone flat. So had Wordsworth's, who jested that he had "snapped his squeaking baby trumpet of sedition." As the uninvited Thelwall limped toward the dales elysian, Coleridge and Wordsworth were getting up a dual collection, *Lyrical Ballads,* on scenic topics and "mute, insensate things." Of all that has been laid in tribute to William Pitt the Younger, why has no one thought to salute him for founding the English school of nature poets?

Coleridge greeted the weary traveler and gave him a bed, thinking about embarrassments that Thelwall brought. Coleridge was being supported by a tanner named Thomas Poole, and, as the prime intendant of a literary living,* was disinclined to bring another writing bird into the nest. Nor was Nether Stowey as remote from strife as it had seemed to Thelwall. It was five miles from the Bristol Channel with its invasion scares. Cloddish peasants knew the black alphabet, F for Fox, P for Paine, T for Thelwall. Moreover, in this sweet recess

---

* A Poole-bright.

of arcady one of the Duke of Portland's spies was piecing out a living watching Coleridge and Wordsworth.*

In the morning, Coleridge took Thelwall for a ramble in the Quantock Hills. They paused in a lovely glen. "Citizen John," said the rimester, "this is a fine place to talk treason in." "Nay, Citizen Samuel," the mobbed poet replied, "it is rather a place to make a man forget that there is any necessity for treason."

Coleridge made a gesture toward finding a cottage for Thelwall, but the villagers were scared to rent him the meanest ruin. The spy followed the poets, trying to record their animated chatter, but succeeded in conveying little more than Thelwall's appearance, "a stout little man with a dark crop of hair and wore a white hat." That Portland already knew. The white hat was the bonnet of the English revolution, and Thelwall had put stiffening in his to take the shock of loyal cudgels.

Coleridge fidgeted for several days over his guest and then braced Thelwall. "At present I see that much evil and little good could result from your settling here." Coleridge also needed thinking time; in the midst of the great fleet mutiny he was full of a mystical narrative verse, encrusted with glosses, called "The Rime of the Ancient Mariner."

Thelwall shouldered his bindle and bade the famous versifiers farewell. You will have to shout loud in the poets' corner of Westminster Abbey to hear a whispered echo of John Thelwall. He walked twenty miles to Bridgewater. There, on his thirty-third birthday, he ignited his inward fireworks of despair:

> . . . *my soul*
> *Is sick of public turmoil—ah! most sick*
> *Of the vain effort to redeem a race*
> *Enslav'd because degenerate; lost to hope,*
> *Because to virtue lost—wrapp'd up in self,*
> *In sordid avarice, luxurious pomp,*
> *And profligate intemperance—a race*
> *Fierce without courage; abject and yet proud;*
> *And most licentious, tho' most far from free.*

---

* The incumbent poet laureate of England was Henry James Pye, who wrote loyal verse for Mr. Pitt.

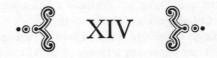

The Red Flag

In Yarmouth next old Neptune reared his head,
Awake my sons, the watery monarch said—
The torpid vapours from your souls remove—
Inspire yourselves with true fraternal love.
Unto the Nore repair without delay,
There join your brothers with a loud Huzza.

—"The Muse's Friendly Aid"
Ballad found on H.M.S. *Repulse*, 1797

ON TUESDAY, 30 MAY, the morning after their lordships went back to London, President Parker and the moderate delegate, John Davis of *Sandwich,* went to Sheerness to induce the authorities not to cut off victuals from the fleet. They found the houses shuttered and women and children being evacuated. Townsmen threatened to take them as hostages. Others cried, "Hang them!" Parker left a note for Commissioner Hartwell requesting that, if he was to be seized, it be done in the proper form of arrest. The two delegates went to the navy yard and addressed the workers, calling for support. There was little response.

The command was busy that morning smuggling the King's pardon and the Acts of Parliament through fog and drizzle to the ships. Buckner's informers said that several crews were ready to turn out their delegates and submit for pardon. The papers reached the captains of *Iris,* 32, and *Brilliant,* 28, who were still aboard as quasi hostages. Patient Captain Charles Cunningham of *Clyde,* 38, read them to his crew. Four companies that were shamming mutiny, those of *San Fiorenzo, Firm* (a floating battery), *l'Espion,* and *Niger,* heard the documents. Even on *Grampus* storeship, which was controlled by aggressive committeemen, the papers were read. The reversible Charles MacCarthy allowed the Pylades to hear them.

As soon as the reading was finished, a half dozen crews rushed their delegates and grabbed the halyard to haul down the red flag. Melées of varying intensity broke out on the ships. *San Fiorenzo* and *Clyde* rapidly took off the red flag and ran up the white flag of surrender, although *Pylades* was sitting between them with guns shotted. As the two ships under white flags made move to get under way, MacCarthy shouted threats from *Pylades* and the Inflexibles bent a spring on their anchor cable to bring their broadside to bear on the schismatics. The loyalists on Bligh's ship *Director* hailed for *San Fiorenzo* to come to their aid in a raging deck brawl for control of the two-decker, but the mutineers prevailed. The two white flags came down. The delegates' party overcame the pardoneers on the other vessels. No ship escaped.

Although it failed, the counter-mutiny of nine ships showed the worried middle people in the fleet that a great many men wanted to take the pardon rather than continue defiance. When he got back to *Sandwich* from his feckless mission to Sheerness, Parker, too, was impressed by the extent of this sentiment. The implacable men on the central committee belittled the pardon faction, but to their amazement, Parker called out the *Sandwich* company and asked them if they wanted to stop or carry on.

"Give it up!" the men cried. "Give it up!"

After his impulsive appeal to the Sandwiches, Parker was no longer trusted by the zealots. He aroused the suspicion that he had entered into a private bargain with their lordships. The realists were convinced that most or all of the central committee would be hanged if they submitted; therefore no man true to his oath would trifle with the idea of surrender, as Parker had just done. *Unless they have promised him his life in return for ours.*

Parker had merely let the command know that he was attempting to swing the delegates toward ending the mutiny. He thought that if he could bring the wild men around to ending the mutiny, the Admiralty would recognize it as an act of goodwill and pardon him and the central committee. After all, not a man had been punished at Spithead or Plymouth. The president must have felt that there was hope for a peaceful adjustment at the Great Nore.

The intractables on the fleet committee lowered the boom on Parker. They devised and passed one of the most unusual constitutional safeguards of a legislature against an executive in parliamentary history. They decreed that the President of the Fleet was to be elected each morning. Power-for-a-day would prevent Parker from concluding any agreement the delegates did not desire. Now he was strictly a servant of the delegates, allowed to retain the appearance of decision, but subject to discard or worse the moment he displeased them. Ironically the King's men were calling him "Admiral" Parker, thinking he was in sole command.

Sheerness was preparing to withstand a siege. The energetic Captain James Dixon of *l'Espion* and his faithful crew succeeded in taking her to Sheerness. There he joined the frigate *Niger,* which had finally overthrown its delegates while in the yard for repair. Dixon constructed booms across the mouth of the Medway, denying entrance to Chatham, Rochester and Sheerness. His sailors dragged guns from the frigates overland to commanding spots on the shoreline. They set up a mortar battery across the Medway on the Isle of Grain. Red-hot cannon balls glowed in furnaces in the dockyard. One infantry regiment refused to heat the shot that might be fired at fellow countrymen. Two more militia regiments arrived to double General Grey's garrison. He sent the disobedient regiment away.

The soldier-sailor lark was over. The delegates of the fleet closed the liberty books. To go ashore now required a pass from President Parker and a truce flag. The agent victualer at Chatham stopped all boats to the Great Nore and the magistrates there and in Rochester looked for accommodations "for many prisoners" by request of Lord Spencer.

In the midst of these British differences, a Swedish packet sailed through the Nore for London, with a party of wounded Polish officers released from Russian prisoner-of-war detention. They were victims of Georgian geopolitics. King George's hired Russian army, sick of the unfair way the French fought, had mutinied toward the rear. The Russian command encouraged them to loot and rape neutral Poland. These Polish patriots, captured in the affair and lately liberated, were on their way to America, led by their gallant general, Tadeusz Kosciusko, who had been an aide to General Washington and held an honorary U. S. citizenship. Kosciusko wore a bandage over a suppurating saber cut on his head and favored his healed wounds— three bayonet thrusts in the back and a thigh partially shot away. He sat on the poop sketching scenes of the river. In London the Poles were to receive much unofficial sympathy, but would away soon in flying coaches for Bristol and a ship to New York.

For the first time since the crisis began, the Admiralty lost its communications advantage over the mutineers. There was no shutter telegraph line to Great Yarmouth and it was an eleven-hour journey for an express rider. Lord Spencer wrote Admiral Duncan, "The wind seems inclined to come round to the eastward. It is highly important that every practical means should be exerted, without holding out anything that can be in the least degree be construed to lead to an expectation of further concessions, to induce the crews of the ships at Yarmouth to put to sea, in whole or considerable part to Texel." Duncan should assure his people they would be paid at the Nore "the moment the public service would admit." Pay would be delayed only "by the unfortunate state of the ships now there," said the first sea lord. Six days later, when he got this, Duncan may have wondered what prevented his ministerial friend from sending the money to Yarmouth.

That morning, 30 May, only two ships stood between the British Isles and the revolutionary invasion fleets, Adam Duncan's *Venerable* and *Adamant*. They remained at anchor out in the North Sea for twenty-four hours, waiting for two sail-of-the-line that had been ordered to him from Spithead. They did not arrive because of adverse winds. Duncan felt it his duty to proceed to the Texel. He was still ignorant of Pitt's countermanding orders for him to go to the Nore and attempt to break up the mutiny by force. It was just as well, for now the government did not wish Duncan, with two ships, to attack the overpowering force in the Thames, and fresh orders were on the way for him to go to Holland.

The gigantic Scotsman sailed to the West Frisians and looked over the sandbars at the Dutch invasion fleet. He counted fourteen sail-of-the-line, eight frigates, "and a number of other vessels amounting in the whole to 95." His vice-admiral, Richard Onslow, came over from *Adamant* and said, "Admiral, I suggest Leith Roads as a retreat of security against either an attack from the Texel or an encounter with the rebels from the Nore."

"No!" said Duncan. He taunted his deputy, "Homesick for the wife and family, eh, Onslow? I have a different plan. The duty I am charged with is to keep the Texel closed. I intend to do that with ships or without ships. Would you be so good as to ask Hotham to come over?"

Captain William Hotham of *Adamant* reported to the flag. Duncan said, "Hotham, you'll fight her till she sinks and I intend to do the same with *Venerable*."

"Yes, sir."

Duncan assembled his ship's company: "He told them plainly what lay before us," Hotham recalled. The admiral said, "The *Venerable* is going to block the Texel. The soundings are such that my flag will continue to fly above shoal water after the ship and company have disappeared. And, mark you, if she survives this performance of duty here, she is going to sail to the Nore and reduce those misguided men to obedience. Do you understand that?"

"Aye, aye, sir!" The chorus sounded genuine.

Duncan tacked *Venerable* and *Adamant* to the outer Dutch buoy of the Texel Channel and anchored them in a narrow berth that physically discouraged the exit of any vessel larger than a sloop. The wind veered to straight out of the east. It was perfect invasion weather for the Dutch. Duncan sounded general quarters and announced that every man would be on duty day and night until further orders. The British navy had nailed its wooden walls over the enemy's front gate.

Back at Yarmouth the 14-gun fire ship *Comet* sat among Duncan's defected two-deckers. Little *Comet* left the only surviving ship's log kept by the mutineers. It began:

Remarks, *Comet,* Moord in Yarmouth Roads. Tuesday, 30 May 1797. Winds variable. P.M. Hoisted a red flag at the Fore topgnt Masthead seeing his Majesty's ships laying here had the same—viz. the *Standard, Lion, Nassau, Inspector,* etc, etc, etc. AM [Wednesday, 31 May] light airs at 5 the Delegates from HMS *Standard* came on board & desired to know if we did not mean to go to the Nore in Company with the rest of his Majesty's Ships that were going there with an expectation of being paid their Wages, etc. They told us if we wanted hands, they would send us a gang to assist us round— gave charge of the ship to the Pilot Mr. Williams. Weighed at 7 Captain [Henry] Duncan desired the hands to come aft and after addressing some time told them if they liked that he Capt. Duncan with the assistance of the rest of the Officers of the Ship would take charge of the ship and carry her round to the Nore, the Ships Company answered him they hoped he & his Officers would not conceive that they had ever meant to take any charges from them—made sail in Company with the Squadron—At 11 fresh breezes & squally with showers of rain—Reefed the Fore & Main Topsails—Opened a cask of Pease 5 Bushels.

That night the moon was full over the English Channel, saturating the mist with mournful light. On the night flood tide at the Great Nore, the people of *Clyde* chopped her cables and she drifted upstream undetected by watches in the fleet until she was beyond gunshot. *Clyde* put on canvas and worked into Sheerness at dawn, where the townsmen cheered the anti-mutineers as fervently as they had cheered the mutineers a few weeks before. The feat encouraged the eight ships' companies that had failed to escape from the Nore the day before. Admiral Buckner, whose flag had been taken off *Sandwich*, raised it on *Clyde*, as a symbol of the counter-mutiny.

San Fiorenzo sneaked an Admiralty pilot aboard and tried to join *Clyde*'s resignation from the mutiny. But the pilot missed the flood tide and had to wait twelve and a half hours for the next one in broad daylight. Then, he miscalculated and cut away into the ebb, and a northwest breeze blew the frigate through the midst of the fleet. Ships opened fire on the secessionist but nobody was hit and the torn rigging was spliced in short order. A merchant captain led *San Fiorenzo* to safety in the English Channel as she made for Spithead.* On the way, the lookouts called "Sail, ho!" The officers put their glasses on a squadron headed for the Nore. What they saw led Sir Harry Neale to order the red jack returned to his foretop. The oncoming ships wore the flag of defiance. They were Admiral Duncan's defectors coming from Great Yarmouth, led by *Montagu*. Sir Harry ordered his crew out to cheer them as the ships passed.

The North Sea ships arrived at the Great Nore at five in the afternoon of the last day of May. They came in through the rain, volleying cheers. The companies in the anchorage roared back in a mighty revival of hope and enthusiasm for the cause. The pardoneers were downcast. The ailing mutiny was miraculously cured. In twenty-four hours the delegates had lost four weak ships and gained eight strong ones.

Comet, the little fireship, dropped anchor, awed by the sight of dozens of men-of-war with red at the main "and many merchant vessels," her logkeeper noted. Now seven two-deckers from Duncan's fleet were at the Nore: *Montagu, Director, Belliqueux, Repulse, Standard, Lion* and *Nassau*, plus *Comet* and the sloop *Inspector*. Their tonnage, ordnance, and personnel more than doubled the fleet strength of the delegates.

---

* On the way, she captured a French privateer. Her captain, Sir Harry Neale, came to the Nore to conduct a German honeymoon and left it with a French prize.

As *Standard* came in, a delegates' boat met her and hailed orders: "Before you anchor, drop your yard ropes and cheer every ship as you go along." Chief Delegate Wallis of *Standard* ran to a lower gunport and talked to the boat out of earshot of Captain Parr and the officers. He came back and told them, "You are not to do any duty on the ship from the time of anchoring."

When Midshipman Hardy on *Nassau* heard the whole Nore fleet cheering mutiny he went below to his cot and cried for hours, "thinking to what a pitch our men had got in defiance of their King and Country." The Nassaus put another midshipman ashore. Young Hardy tried to provoke the sailors to get himself expelled, but they smiled at him and said, "Oh, you are too well liked. You'll be one of the last turned out of the ship."

Three delegates boarded *Comet* and asked the crew to elect two representatives to the central committee and send them to a meeting on *Sandwich* when they saw her raise "the meeting flag," the Union Jack, at the foretop masthead. *Comet* was to acknowledge by hoisting the red jack to her mizzen peak. The Comets elected William Webb and Robert Bennington. The flag courtesies were exchanged and the delegates went off.

The North Sea delegates had previously signed the eight articles drawn up by the Nore committee, but in the exhilaration of the first combined meeting of both elements, which took place aboard *Sandwich,* they advanced four additional demands. Optimism prevailed despite the fact that the original eight articles had been flatly turned down by the government.

The first extra demand was that court-martial boards for accused seamen be made up of seamen instead of officers. When a sailor was being tried, the court was to be composed of nine seamen and four marines. When a marine was on trial, his judges were to be nine marines and four seamen. This would be introducing English trial by jury of one's equals into the military service.

The bill called for wages of tenpence a day for marines; and asked immediate payment of bounties. It demanded that three-fifths of prize money be distributed among seamen and petty officers, and two-fifths to the quarterdeck.

President Parker and delegates Widgery and Wallis took the four new articles ashore under a white flag. It was dark when they reached Captain Hartwell's mansion in the dockyard. Parker said, "Commissioner, I hand you the final determination of the North Sea fleet."

"It is out of my power to go to London with these articles you produce."

"Sir," said Parker, "these are the final determinations. We shall ask no more." Hartwell was silent. The president said, "Commissioner, the *Repulse* is badly in need of ground tackle. We wish to obtain anchors and new cable from the yard."

"Nothing will be taken from the yard without the express permission of the Admiralty," said Hartwell. "And not even necessaries will be issued at night."

When Parker returned to *Sandwich* with these hard lines, he found a spree under way in the great cabin. William Gregory had moved benches in for the augmented fleet parliament, roused out the flagship band, and the leaders of the mutiny were dancing and singing to celebrate the renascence of the cause.

Admiral Buckner also felt that the arrival of the North Sea ships had restored the advantage to the mutineers. He wrote an overnight express to the Admiralty questioning whether he should read the government proclamations to the newcomers, telling their lordships that "this great increase in the mutinous force" made it advisable to rescind their orders to stop supplies and intercourse with the seamen. The sea lords were annoyed with Buckner. They replied that of course he should read the proclamation and that there was no need for alarm: Duncan's ships had come round to the Nore to be paid; in fact some vessels had official orders to make the call.

Their lordships chided Buckner, "You have permitted [Parker and Davis] to return on board [after visiting Commissioner Hartwell]. Their lordships are by no means sanguine in the expectations that any advantage will be felt from the influence they [Parker and Davis] have promised to exercize to induce their deluded brethren to return to duty." This statement demonstrated that the sea lords were aware that Parker and Davis were trying to induce the delegates to end the mutiny.

While this admonition was on its way down the Canterbury road, Buckner had another letter headed back: "I am uncertain whether their lordships may approve any conference held with the mutineers. Under consideration of the great increase of force that has lately joined the mutinous ships, I wish to know their lordships' pleasure how far it would be expected to enforce the last orders . . . with absolute rigidity under all the present existing circumstances." Secretary Nepean replied that he might receive a boat from the fleet, taking care that the delegates have no rendezvous ashore.

The Admiralty decided to sack Buckner without saying so. He was to remain port admiral, as in the case of Sir Peter Parker at Portsmouth, while his powers were assumed by another man, nominally his deputy. The sea lords pondered on whom to send.

Buckner, unaware he was to be deposed, sent a letter "to the Respective Captains and Commanders of His Majesty's Ships at the Nore," without addressing anyone by name or signing his own. The message read, "The Dutch fleet is ready."

But the British fleet had its mind on other things. Between decks, balladeers reaped inspiration from the augmentation of the cause and sang to fiddle and fife:

> *Then at the Nore the lions boldly roused*
> *Their brethren's cause of Spithead they espoused.*
> *Each swore alike to King he would be true,*
> *But one and all the tyrants would subdue,*
> *Their gallant hearts the chains of bondage broke*
> *Not to revolt, but to evade the yoke.*

Aboard his ship John Blake, president of *Inflexible,* found a chained seaman, a deserter from *Repulse.* Blake sent him back to his ship with a note, "According to our discipline, prisoners are liberated when a gun is fired in anger. I have therefore to inform you that several guns was fired from on board this ship at the *San Fiorenzo* frigate, which in our opinion the prisoner is entitled to the benefit therefrom."

In London, a volunteer cavalry unit that had been formed to harass LCS gatherings turned out with standby orders to oppose the mutinous fleet in the Thames. Lord Colchester (Charles Abbott), a member of Commons, was one of the volunteers. Royal condemnations of the refractory seamen regularly poured forth. After *Clyde* and *San Fiorenzo* escaped, his Majesty's proclamation criticized the men who had "by terror of their force, compelled two frigates to desist from executing a particular service"—the royal honeymoon duty. Another dire royal utterance was posted conspicuously throughout the Thames counties, and copies were smuggled into the Great Nore.

His Majesty condemned the seamen's "perseverance in rebellious and treasonable attempts against our crown and dignity," and found it necessary "to call on all our loving subjects, that they in their several stations do use their utmost endeavours, according to law, to suppress all such mutinous and treasonable proceedings." He enjoined and commanded all his loving subjects whatsoever "not to give any aid, comfort, assistance, or encouragement whatsoever, to any person or persons concerned in such mutinous and treasonable proceedings, as they will answer the same at their peril."

The delegates recognized that the King's roarings were frightening many men and countered by circulating an anonymous *Address to the Seamen of the Fleet*. (The *Address* turned up among the *Comet* papers that had been copied by Lieut. William Price Cumby at the time of the mutiny and which were held privately until 1963.)

> Our conduct is represented on shore as disorderly & that everything we undertake is done in a State of Drunkenness. How egregiously are they mistaken! How will they be surprised to find that altho' every species of Liquor is at our disposal, that we can refrain when the Interests of our Country is at Stake. Brothers! I am certain that nothing has ever been further from our Principles than *Jacobism*. No people can be more devoted to their Sovereign & Laws. But an abuse of these laws by wicked & designing Men have imposed upon our gracious Majesty's good disposition have been the cause of all our discontents. . . .
>
> You saw in what a base Manner you were deserted last Night by one ship [*Clyde*] of our Party. So far from being mortified at such proceeding we ought to rejoice that we have got rid of so many traitors, who might at a future time have done us more mischief than at present. If I would have my wile [*sic*] every wretch would be sent ashore who would not willingly lose his Life's Blood sooner than depart from his Interests. Unity is our only resource in the present juncture. I shall conclude by taking notice of the excellent Comparison of the Romans— the People are likened to a Number of Rods, which when tied together in a Bundle cannot be broken, but if separated may be taken singly and destroyed.
>
> May all the Blessings of good fellowship attend you—
>
> A BROTHER SEAMAN

That night H.M.S. *Maria,* a victualing ship for Old Jarvey's fleet at Lisbon, came down the river from Deptford, and was stopped in the Great Nore. The delegates told the captain that his food stores were worse needed at the Nore than in Spain. During the night, Buckner heard about the seizure and, in first light, telegraphed the signal relay station at New Cross to stop further sailings of food ships from the nearby Deptford Yard.

Little *Comet*'s second day of self-rule, the first of June, began at eight with all hands turned out to join the morning cheers of ten thousand men at the Great Nore. The Comets swung out their cutter and sent their delegates to the fleet committee deliberation on *Sandwich*. Ships' committees came by the fireship and read her people resolutions and encouraging words.

As Captain Henry Duncan of *Comet* listened, he lost whatever illusion he may have entertained that the purpose of the trip to the Thames was to collect back pay. This was a mutiny. He feared that he would be laid open to charges of abetting mutiny under naval law and treason under civil law if he did not protest. He told the assembly that he and his officers would take no further responsibility. The Comets were perplexed. They were not rebelling against the captain or his staff, but demonstrating for better conditions. The company sent to *Sandwich* for instructions. Back they came: "The committee of delegates desires the ship's company to appoint certain persons on board for the better preservation of His Majesty's ship and stores." This did not depose the King's officers, but created what might be called a committee of public safety following the abdication of Captain Duncan. A ship is a model of a state.

To guard their little England, the people of the fireship elected Thomas Wilkinson, James Graham, Charles Downey, Thomas Mills, William Fatheringham, Joseph Penrose, Martin McCarty, William Whiting, William Williams, Bryan Nowlen, James Fletcher, Michael Bonnatt, James Black and Samuel Turner. *Comet*'s chosen deputies, instead of convening a political debate, "employed people overhauling the rigging and cleaned ship," according to her mutiny log.

Ship-keeping, the *Comet* book shows, went on as usual, perhaps intensified by the novelty of democratic decision. Throughout the fleet, forecastle courts heard a large number of indictments for intoxication. The surviving scraps of illegal court-martial records do not show, however, any flogging more severe than twelve stripes, the limit allowed to a captain's discretion by King's regulations. But, the "gentlemen of the jury," as the sailor veniremen called themselves, sentenced people to ducking, including several petty officers of *Sandwich*. In a ducking the victim was trussed up in his hammock with an eighteen-pound bar-shot made fast to his feet. The ever-menacing yard rope came swaying down and was spliced to the back harness. In a parody of hanging, the man was run up to the yardarm block, and, as the saying was, "dropped souse in the sea." This was repeated three times "until he was half dead," before he was let down on deck and upended to help him choke water from his lungs.

Aboard *Standard* the talk was that you would be ducked if you did not wear a red cockade to exhibit your sworn devotion to your delegates, who wore green cockades. A *Standard* committeeman, Quartermaster John Rowland, was informing on the internal committee to Captain Parr and passing him copies of "seditious books" coming aboard. He was not detected at this game, but ran afoul of the committeeman for sleeping on watch. The court found him guilty, dismissed him from the committee, and bound his outstretched arms on an upended hatch grating in the classic fashion to receive a dozen of the King's best. The surgeon's mate protested that Rowland was physically incapable of taking the lash. "They sang out from the forecastle that I should not be forgiven," said Rowland, and the nine knotted answers to disobedience were imprinted twelve times in red on his naked back.

Several of Adam Duncan's capital ships were still sitting in Yarmouth Roads under delegate control, their companies arguing whether to join him at the Texel or follow the main part of the North Sea squadron to the Nore. The parliament ship was *Isis,* 50, from which the delegates issued a public proclamation saying that they wished to send four delegates from each ship in a cutter to the Nore to "enquire into the reason or cause why the said ships deserted the fleet." (As if the delegates of *Isis* had not known exactly why, since they had signed the eight articles eleven days before while she was at the Nore.) This buttery paper proclaimed "every wish for the general good" and said the delegates "would act with the oeconomy [*sic*] which men in our critical situation should do. . . . Every obedience would be paid to Officers in command when the ship's duty is required." It requested the public to regard them not "as ringleaders of a Mutinous Assembly, but as men appointed by the majority of each ship's company in order to prevent confusion and obtain as speedy a regularity of affairs as possible." The Yarmouth delegation went to the Nore that night and slipped into the anchorage without interference.

The Admiralty was covering many saddlebags with dust and rain, striving to keep abreast of the state of ships at the Nore and Great Yarmouth. Curiously, the sea lords did not reemploy the services of its proven field men: both Bligh and Lord Howe, who were in London, were not consulted on the new stage of the business. For the second time, Lord Spencer sent one-legged Sir Thomas Pasley to Yarmouth to address the recusants, although he had not achieved anything on his first visit. Their lordships encouraged Sir Thomas to expect an easy settlement because the Yarmouth seamen had not "alleged any sort of grievance, but have been separated from the Admiral [Duncan] merely because other ships of the squadron have so done."

Considering the fact that almost a dozen of Duncan's ships' companies had signed the eight articles of the Nore the week before, why was Lord Spencer trying to deceive Sir Thomas? *Isis,* the parliament ship at Yarmouth, where the envoy would be taxed for his utmost persuasiveness, had been at the Nore when the crews first struck there.

Spencer's fib was part of a pretense that the government was weaving for the benefit of home and enemy onlookers; that the North Sea fleet was merely going to the Nore to be paid. And the sea lords carried it so far as to diddle their own confidential agent, Sir Thomas. A new peak of alarm had been reached in Westminster, both over Pitt's unsafe government and the national security. It was feared that if the French found out how many disaffected ships there were in the Channel and North Sea, they might fall upon Britain immediately. French privateers were snapping around English ports, perhaps compiling the effective strength of the King's navy. Talebearing neutral ships—Danes and Jonathans—crossed freely from the Texel to Yarmouth, from the Nore to Brest. The British navy relied on their reports of enemy activity, and certainly the French and Dutch were also quizzing the skippers.

The official Paris newspaper *Le Moniteur* had a London correspondent who prudently remained anonymous, but whose fairly accurate news appeared in the week or two that it took horses, luggers and hand typesetters to place the paper fresh before the wetted forefingers and half spectacles of the mutineer ministers of France. Another compelling reason for the North Sea fleet hoax was diplomatic: Pitt was warming up Sir James Harris once more to go to France and start dickering. His hand would be weak on court cards if the French knew the plight of the British navy.

In this hour of deepening gloom, Lord Spencer received a cheerful telegraph clicking from Deal: five of his double-deckers from Spithead had appeared in the Downs and none were wearing red cockades. The Downs was a fleet rendezvous in the Strait of Dover that was protected from shore winds by the chalk cliffs and from Channel rollers by the Goodwin sands. In fair weather the telegraph station could read flag signals from ships in the Downs and transmit shutter code to them. This afforded the Admiralty the ultimate in eighteenth-century naval communications. Lord Whitewig at Admiralty could send a command from his roof in London and receive in perhaps a half hour a *very-well-sir* from Admiral Whitewig on his quarterdeck, Downs. The original purpose of the shutter telegraph was as a rapid command channel between London and ships in the Downs. There was an intelligence advantage as well: the cliffs overlooked anybody's ships that passed through the Dover Strait. From Deal, the shutter mosaic went to stations at Bettishanger, Barham Downs, Shottenden and Tong Beacon Hill (where the Sheerness spur branched off) and thenceforward on the London main line that Deal shared with Sheerness.

On this first of June, through intermittent showers, the Deal station passed word from Admiral Joseph Peyton, C-in-C, Downs, that he had with him in a perfect state of discipline, awaiting orders, H.M.S. *Sans Pareil,* an 80-gun ship Howe had captured on the Glorious First of June exactly three years before, and four two-deckers, *Caesar, Russell, Ganges* and *Bedford.* None of these vessels had been involved with the mutinies. With the choice of sending the five virtuous crews into the Nore to attack the mutineers or dispatching them to the Texel, the sea lords chose to reinforce Adam Duncan.

The big Scot, with his two sail-of-the-line, was still staked out in the exit channel of the Dutch invasion fleet, his sleepless crews hauling and paying lines on the anchor hawsers according to the swing of tide, always confronting the Dutch with broadsides. Duncan mystified his people by ordering his color officer to run meaningless signal flag strings up and down.

An American brig skimmed out the Waddenzee and hove to. The admiral received her skipper on the gangway. The Yankee told Duncan, "The Dutchmen say your ships only came in here as decoys. They know you have a large fleet in the offing. They can see you making signals to them."

Duncan received some small helpers, the frigate *Circe* and sloop *Stork,* which he sent to patrol a few miles out. If the Dutch broke out and sank him, the sloop would take the news home and the frigate would follow the Dutch convoy until its general destination seemed evident. Duncan, standing in irons, as it were, in the Channel, could do nothing about a fantastic quandary in which H.M.S. *Circe* found herself.

Captain Peter Halkett of *Circe* and his first officer sat back to back on the quarterdeck with loaded carbines and pistols, defending the helm in unsleeping vigil while a minority of the crew and officers sailed the ship. Most of the ship's company was barricaded below-decks in a state of mutiny, besieged at the hatchways by the marine company. Although the sloop, running alongside *Circe,* was not under delegate control, she could not interpose because the mutineers held the gun deck of the frigate. A ship in an almost perfect state of mutiny continued to do its duty.

His Majesty asked both chambers of Parliament to pass stricter acts on mutiny. Pitt tinged the proposals with his political vendetta, asking that "persons who should endeavour to seduce either soldiers or sailors from their duty . . . should be deemed guilty of felony and should suffer death," which was less a preventative for mutiny than bait for the radical hunt, assisting the Duke of Portland to hang John Thelwall—if he could find him. Commons passed the bill with one dissenting vote by Charles Grey.

Still unappeased, Pitt brought in a bill next day, 2 June, to provide death "without benefit of clergy" for anyone who communicated with a person on a mutinous ship. This was too much for John Nicholls, Member for Tregony, who pointed out that "intercourse with a person guilty of high treason is not, by law, even a misdemeanour, provided it is not accompanied by open acts of aiding or abetting." Another Member said that family letters could be denied to mutineers under Pitt's proposal. The Prime Minister emphatically agreed, "If they value intercourse and connection with a parent, a wife or other relatives and friends, they ought, before they were permitted to enjoy the sweets of those endearing connections, reconcile themselves to the offended country, by returning to it the allegiance they owe it."

Sir Francis Burdett, the radical M. P., spoke against the bill. He asked the members to consider the real causes of the mutinies. "First they may, without hesitation, be ascribed to the popular maxims prevailing everywhere, of the right inherent in all men to require an equitable treatment, and, if it be denied them, to obtain it by force, if the means appeared insufficient." He spoke of Spithead, where "the systematic order and moderation of the sailors and their cheerful return to obedience, illustrated the mighty advantage of a free government, in which men could assume the manly air of freedom without abandoning themselves to the licentiousness and phrenzy [sic] of slaves broken loose from bondage."

1797. "That year was one of the darkest and most perilous in English history." —Prof. Conrad Gill

1. King George III, whose dictatorial policies forced the Americans out of the British Empire, has pushed four million Irish to the brink of a national rising.

2. William Pitt, prime minister of eight million Britons, has made war on 25 million Frenchmen. Gallic revolutionists have driven the King's armies out of Europe and his navy from the Mediterranean.

3. In Britain angry subjects stone the King's carriage as vast crowds shout "Bread!" "No war!" "No Pitt!" "No king!" Reform and republican societies grow rapidly. A run on gold forces the Bank of England to issue its first paper notes.

The King and Pitt had picturesque enemies

4. Thomas Paine, "the writer whom history obeyed," infused spirit in the American and French revolutions and now gives voice to one that is gathering in his native England. Millions read *Rights of Man*.

5. Eloquent opposition to the domestic injustice and foreign wars of Pitt and the King comes from a handful in Parliament, led by Charles James Fox, "The Black Patriot," England's greatest liberal.

6. Wolfe Tone, Irish leader, is on the Continent, coordinating French and Dutch invasion forces with Irish rebels to overthrow the British crown. An American-led French legion lands in Wales.

7. Tone's strongest ally is a 29-year-old revolutionary general named Louis Lazare Hoche, an ex-stableboy who has already routed British forces in France and Holland, and has mastered civil war methods.

In the darkest hour, a mutiny in the King's navy

8. More than half the seamen in the swollen war fleet were forcibly impressed (above) or recruited from debtors' jails. Radicals and republicans among them read Tom Paine aloud in the forecastle and circulate grievance petitions. Jolly Jack Tar is angry.

9. From Spithead, the main home fleet base at Portsmouth, ships' companies send petitions to Parliament and the admiralty through two champions of the seamen, Charles James Fox, and the recently retired Admiral Black Dick Howe, "the sailor's friend." On Easter Sunday, with no answer after six weeks, the crews refuse to take orders.

The sailors protest low pay and bad food

10. Sea cooks are obliged to serve rotten meat, wormy biscuits, rancid cheese and sour beer. Fresh shark stew is regarded as a great treat in the King's navy. Grog is often short.

11. Pursers (who buy their appointments) cheat on food rations. Victualing contractors make fortunes with crooked weights and measures and share the loot with courtiers and M.P.s.

12. In port, seamen are confined to ship. Women are permitted to live on board. Some crews have not been ashore or paid their wages for three years. The high command does not curb unworthy officers, tyrants and some death floggers. But the mutineers' demands do not criticize the government, impressment or the punishment system.

The Spithead mutiny astounds the government

13. When the amazing news arrives in London via the shutter telegraph from Portsmouth, the first sea lord, the Earl Spencer, calls an emergency meeting of the lords commissioners of the admiralty in their Whitehall board room. For weeks their lordships have ignored the seamen's petitions. Now they decide to ignore the strike, even after an agitated admiral arrives from Portsmouth and confirms the largest naval mutiny in history. Lord Spencer sends an express rider back with orders to the home fleet commander, Lord Bridport, to force his men to sail next morning and resume their watch on Hoche's invasion fleet at Brest. Bridport gives the order but the men refuse to weigh anchor.

14. George John the Earl Spencer, M. A. Oxon, first lord of the admiralty.

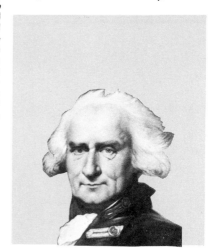

15. Alexander Hood, Baron Bridport of Cricket St. Thomas, vice-admiral of Great Britain, vice-admiral of the Red, Order of the Bath, commander-in-chief of the Channel Squadron.

The government links its opponents to the mutiny

16. The Duke of Portland, in charge of domestic security, suspects that the mutiny was incited by the London Corresponding Society, a reform group seeking male suffrage and annual parliaments.

17. The main suspect is a republican poet and lecturer, John Thelwall, whom Portland has long tried to silence. The duke sends a London police magistrate to Portsmouth to nab Thelwall.

18. But the poet is tramping the country roads to seek asylum in Somerset from two young colleagues with revolutionary sympathies, William Wordsworth (above) and Samuel Taylor Coleridge (right).

19. But, in the oppressive situation, Wordsworth has "snapped his squeaking baby trumpet of sedition" and Coleridge has dropped politics to write *The Rime of the Ancient Mariner.* Thelwall finds no home.

The striking seamen win government concessions

20. For a month the delegates of the fleet hold firm, forcing the sea lords to send Black Dick Howe (right) to Portsmouth with power to negotiate. He grants a pay rise, better rations, but the delegates will not yield until cruel officers are removed. With Pitt's approval, Black Dick ousts a hundred of them, including an admiral. Lord and Lady Howe join the mutineers in a gala celebration of unity in the fleet.

21. At Portsmouth Point, the bustle of sailing day is resumed. Lord Bridport is taking the Channel Squadron to sea. The mutineers have been pardoned by his Majesty.

Hardly noticed in the rejoicing, a worse mutiny

starts at the Nore . . .

7

"The mutiny at the Nore still strikes awe into those who study past history." —The Earl of Camperdown

22. Toward the end of the Spithead stand-out, sympathetic seamen at the Nore, the fleet anchorage at the mouth of the Thames, immobilize more ships than at Spithead, and set up a fleet parliament. The government does nothing, expecting that the Nore will accept the Spithead settlement and royal pardon. But the men refuse until their unwanted officers are removed. The delegates claim the Spithead pardon does not cover them.

23. Alarms and rumors spread in England about a wild supernumerary seaman at the Nore, calling himself "Admiral of the Fleet." He is supposed to be hanging loyal men and planning to turn the ships over to France.

The Nore sailors' parliament
demands more than the one at Spithead

List of Grievances
1st Three fifths of Prize Money
2d Trial by Jury
&c &c .

24. Admiral Buckner, C-in-C the Nore, goes to his usurped flagship *Sandwich*, where the rebel delegates are meeting in his great cabin. The President of the Fleet hands him eight articles of navy reform proposed by the lower deck. Although Parker is respectful toward the admiral, courtesies to his rank are omitted.

25. Richard Parker, 30, is an educated ex-naval officer from Exeter. He was broken in rank for insubordination and medically discharged. Recently he accepted £30 to exchange a debtors' jail for a sailors' one.

True Blue an old Song

Hearts of oak are our ships
Jolly tars are our men
we always are Ready

Aye, Aye, we are at the bottom of it

The DELEGATES in COUNS

ADMIRAL BUCKNER   CHARLES JAMES FOX

Government propaganda: cartoonist Cruikshank places

RICHARD PARKER

or BEGGARS on HORSEBACK

Fox where Pitt wants him — under the mutineers' table.

But Fox has left in despair for his rural retreat

27. Fox has never seen the seamen's petitions because of postal interception. At the height of the mutiny crisis, now a state crisis, the great liberal loses a vote in Parliament for electoral reform, and "secedes" from Commons to seclusion with his mistress at St. Anne's Hill.

28. Suspecting that the Nore mutineers are tampering at Great Yarmouth with seamen of the North Sea fleet, Britain's last shield against invasion, the admiralty sends "The Bounty Bastard," Captain William Bligh, to check up. Bligh arrives at Yarmouth to find the ships gone to join the Nore mutiny.

Mutineers blockade London, Portland hunts radicals

29. John Horne Tooke, unfrocked pastor, learned philologist, magnetic republican agitator, three times elected to Parliament and three times ejected by the King's men, is a prime suspect.

30. Samuel Whitbread, M.P., a radical brewer, upholds the seamen and quietly confers with the mutineer-captain of H.M.S. *Lancaster*. Whitbread is too rich and popular to be seized.

31. John Binns (at age 88 in 1860), radical organizer, frequenter of navy towns, is tried for sedition. His shrewd and fearless defense hashes Portland's case and Binns goes free—into more mischief.

32. Afraid that President Parker will bring his 1,300-gun fleet to London and overthrow all that they hold dear, the peerage and gentry form ward volunteers and light horse troops.

Hunger, desertion, Pitt's tenacity, defeat mutiny

33. After a month of delegate control, the Nore ships surrender one by one to Admiral Lord Keith. The last to haul down the red flag and hand over delegates is Bligh's *Director*.

34. Sir Thomas Pasley heads Parker's court-martial board. The president of the Nore, denied counsel and access to the transcript, is swiftly sentenced to death. Parker hangs from the yardarm of his parliament ship; 35 more delegates are executed and hundreds flogged or exiled.

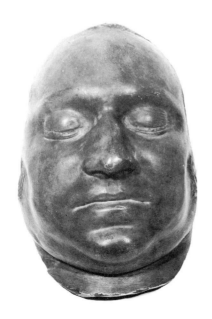

35. Parker's death mask, taken during the macabre travels of his body from the Nore to a vault in London.

Pitt saved by ex-mutineers and opposition admiral

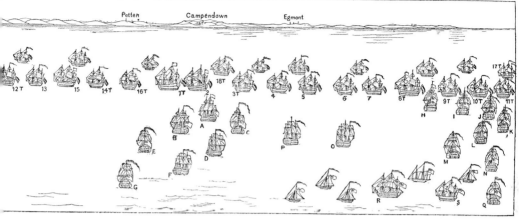

PLAN OF THE ACTION OFF CAMPERDOWN

36. Duncan sails two ragged divisions abreast into the Dutch line and hammers the enemy to pieces with heavy carronades. The victory lifts the invasion threat and pressure for Pitt's resignation. His Majesty rejoices with Duncan at St. Paul's. People stone Pitt's carriage going to the thanksgiving service.

KEY TO CAMPERDOWN BATTLE

ENGLISH	GUNS		DUTCH	GUNS
A Venerable	74		1 Vryheid	74
B Ardent	64		2 States General	74
C Triumph	74		3 Wassenaer	64
D Isis	50		4 Cerberus	68
E Bedford	74		5 Beschermer	56
F Lancaster	64		6 Leyden	68
G Belliqueux	64		7 Batavier	56
H Monarch	74		8 Jupiter	74
I Powerful	74		9 Haarlem	68
J Russel	74		10 Alkmaar	56
K Monmouth	64		11 Delft	56
L Veteran	64		12 Gelykheid	68
M Agincourt	64		13 Mars	44
N Adamant	50		14 Admiral Devries	68
O Director	64		15 Brutus	74
P Montagu	74		16 Hercules	64
Frigates			*Frigates*	
Q Beaulieu	40		17 Munnikkendam	44
R Circe	28		18 Ambuscade	32
S Martin (sloop)	16			
Four Cutters and a Lugger.				

Three more Frigates, names unknown, and five Brigs.

Those marked T taken.

37. The ex-Nore mutineers under Admiral Adam Duncan, who is politically at odds with Pitt, go back to North Sea guard duty. A lugger brings Duncan word, "The Dutch are out!" He pursues immediately and comes upon the Dutch line in dangerous shoal water off Camperdown in the West Frisians.

15

Mutiny rolls on and Old Jarvey beats it down

38. Admiral St. Vincent, "Old Jarvey" to his men, handles petitions and complaints in the Mediterranean fleet by quick mutiny trials and immediate hangings. Later, when he succeeds Spencer as first lord of the admiralty, Old Jarvey gets sacked for trying to abolish dockyard corruption.

39. At the end of the Napoleonic wars the officers and men who won at Camperdown and Trafalgar are put ashore on paltry pensions, amidst unemployment and political unrest. Thousands of begging seamen roam the streets and highways. George III is insane, the government more repressive than Pitt's. Sailors ask, "What did we win?"

(Picture credits in Appendix x)

The House attached a provision to Pitt's bill, limiting the force of the act to one month. There was one dissenting voice, that of Charles Sturt, a retired naval officer. Since nobody would act as teller of the Noes, Sturt did and thereby lost his right as a Member to vote Nay. As a result the bill was passed unanimously.

In the debate Sheridan, who in past years had introduced several bills for navy reform, said that events had moved too far for him to bring in a scheme to set up a parliamentary inquiry into naval abuses. The House must unite behind his Majesty. Sheridan now believed that "a rooted spirit of disobedience had taken the place of those manly and loyal sentiments" of old time seamen. "If there is, indeed, a rot in the wooden walls of Old England, decay and ultimate ruin cannot be far distant," he concluded. With Sheridan, their last sympathizer in Parliament, approving Pitt's line, the seamen could expect no further comfort from public opinion.

Buckner sent the delegates the latest royal proclamation and a letter calling on them to submit. Since they had struck Admiral Buckner's flag and no longer recognized his authority, the delegates replied with a letter to the Lords Commissioners of Admiralty. In reckless bitterness it went beyond anything the seamen's representatives had previously issued:

My LORDS,
We had the honour to receive your Lordships Proclamation (for we do not conceive it to be His Majesty's) accompanied by an insipid address from Adml. Buckner. They met with the fate they justly deserved. How could your Lordships think to frighten us as old women in the Country frighten Children with such stories as the Wolf and Raw head & bloody bones or as the Pope wished to terrify the French Republic by his famous Bull at the Beginning of the Revolution. Know Gentlemen, that we are Men—Men long tried for Courage & Perseverence in a Cause not altogether so interesting to ourselves as the Present. Shall we then now be induced from a few Paltry threats to forsake our Glorious plan & lick your Lordship's feet for Pardon & Grace, when we see ourselves in possession of 13 sail of as noble Ships as any in His Majesty's Service, and Men not inferior to any in the Kingdom? Do we demand anything but what Justice Licences and Preservation Approves? The few reasonable Articles we have presented to your Lordships should have been attended to in a respectful Manner, otherwise by your deferring it a few days longer, some others

may Pop up their terrific heads, to stare your Lordships in the face. We have nothing more to say, but hope you will take the necessary steps to save your Country from a Civil War, which may end in the ruin of yourselves and Uneasiness of our most Gracious Sovereign, to whom we have ever been and will be loyal whilst there is a probability of our Grievances being re-dress'd.

With regard to our having fired at the *Sn. Fiorenzo,* be it known to you, that we are very sorry that we could not sink her, as without regard to the League she had entered into with us, she basely deserted.

We wish your Lordships likewise to observe that the Article No. 6 shall extend to all Persons Condemn'd to Imprisonments or any other Punishment by the Sentence of the Court Martial as well as to Prisoners who have not been tried, and that all Persons now on Board labouring under any such Sentence be from this time entirely free.

We have to Honour to be
My Lords
Your Lordships' very humble Servts.
THE SEAMEN OF THE FLEET AT THE NORE*

Just about everything in this letter infuriated their lordships and stiffened their backs. The delegates were trying to bait the Admiralty into direct exchanges, bypassing the local command. For the first time they invoked the dreadful words "Republic," "Revolution," "Civil War." They boasted "possession" of the ships, of adding to their demands if the Admiralty did not settle, hinted at the ruin of their lordships and declared they would be loyal to the King as long as there was a probability of getting what they wanted. The state-ment of intent to sink a vessel of their own navy was the final note of outrage.

At St. James's Palace that morning, the King advanced Lord Brid-port's Irish title to "the dignity of a peer of Great Britain" and per-sonally invested Lord Howe with the Order of the Garter for his labors at Spithead. His Majesty did not ask Black Dick's advice on what to do about the Nore, where the latest royal stricture was being distributed. After dismissing Howe, the King went into the courtyard to say good-bye to the Prince and Princess of Württemberg, who were setting out by post chaise for Harwich from whence three British naval vessels were to be employed to carry them past the Texel to

* *Comet* papers 13-14.

Germany. The royal couple was glowing with devotion and security. The British Parliament had voted the holy bibliophile a marriage portion of £80,000, and the Irish Parliament had acceded to his Majesty's request to settle £5,000 per annum on the princess. The son-in-law expressed to the King his hopes that "a general peace will come forward" and that the father-in-law would continue to "support the interest of his family," no doubt alluding to other members of the fresh German connection that would come hopefully to England.

The post chaise rattled away and his Majesty turned from paternal sentiment to the cares of state which awaited him in increasing numbers of dispatch boxes. Several contained bulky petitions signed by provincial mayors, city fathers and townsfolk by the scores of thousands, begging him to dismiss Pitt and make peace. There was a letter from Benjamin West, his Majesty's favorite artist, who had been painting an expansive canvas sequence for the King's chapel at an annual retainer of a thousand pounds. The American-born painter begged his Majesty to pay him for the last two years' work, even if by installment. West had drawn the money from the King's banker, Thomas Coutts, who had now advised him that the funds had not been secured and was threatening to take West to court.

The King read an advice from Lord Portland to say that the Home Secretary was circulating a plan to the Commander-in-Chief and the lord lieutenants of the home counties to coordinate the army, the Fencibles and the magistrates to deal with the mutineer landings and run down fugitive seamen.

Another letter from Portland enclosed two others like a nest of Chinese boxes. His grace explained that a delegation of "several respectable gentlemen" had called upon him a week before on the day of the extraordinary night session of Commons and "strongly requested" Portland not to leave the city. "I had a conversation with many of them on the dangers that appeared equally to all of us to approach with formidable rapidity. A common & anxious sense of those perils has produced connection among these gentlemen to the length of uniting in the earnest representation which they entreat me to lay at your Majesty's feet."

The representation at H. M.'s feet was from Lord Moira's centrist cabal. It was couched as a letter to Lord Moira from members of his group, requesting him to advise the King that "there is at present very great uneasiness in the minds of an extensive number of moderate men concerning the situation of public affairs . . . they think the public will not . . . be satisfied without a change of administration . . . the moment is critical."

"Irritation and alarm" prevailed in the populace, said the letter. Pitt's government was not "likely to extricate the country from the difficulty in which it is involved . . . every hour is pressing. . . . A considerable number of respectable Members of Parliament" concur —enough "to [assure] that a dissolution . . . would not be necessary." The note ended gloomily: "We fear there is but a short interval left for applying the remedy. . . . It may very speedily be too late to apply any remedy whatever—if, in truth, it be not already too late."

The portentous declaration was signed by five M. P.'s not noted for kicking at the traces—Sir George Shuckburgh-Evelyn, Bryan Edwards, Sir Christopher Hawkins, Joseph Foster Barham, and Sir John Sinclair, a Scottish agricultural-improvement zealot who corresponded with the King on this common interest.

The political King must certainly have been alerted that an alternative ministry was forming, or had been formed, and that Portland was ready to remain aboard should the captain of state be sent over the side by cabinet mutineers. There was the odor of catnip for the King in the claim that the writers spoke for "a number [of respectable members] so considerable . . . that a dissolution of the Parliament would not be necessary." It promised that Pitt could be retired and the ministry reshuffled without a general election. But the stubborn King refused to discharge his stubborn first minister. His Majesty's problem was to discover the strength of this new opposition in terms of numbers and talents, and then deal with them in the accustomed manner.

The storm was gathering also in the House of Lords. The King received "a solemn address" from a group of peers whose signatures are missing in the archives. "The enormous and accumulating debt in our opinion will be the cause of some convulsion in the Empire," they predicted. "The war . . . presses severely on the country. . . . We think its continuance in the highest degree alarming.

"Under the present Minister the country can neither treat with dignity or advantage" since Pitt's conduct "must have made him peculiarly obnoxious" to France, said their lordships. "If your Majesty is determined at all hazards either to continue the war" or to insist that Pitt negotiate peace, the petitioners advised the sovereign that unpleasant alternatives would be necessary: "retrenchment of publick and private expense, the burthen of which every individual in the country must endure, especially the higher and richer classes. . . .

"It is our duty to state that your Majesty and family must set the example" of "retrenchment" or the plight of the nation would become "intolerable," the statement went on, and "the country must be undone."

This foreboding, obviously emanating from Moira's rump in Lords, did not alter the King's course a single degree.

Friday morning, 2 June, there arrived in the rain at Sheerness the Admiralty's appointee as commander of the counter-mutiny, Viscount Keith, Rear Admiral of the White, né the Honorable Charles Elphinstone, a fifty-year-old Scot with a ruddy complexion, half-lidded eyes, bristling brows and a clamped mouth. He had been given English and Irish peerages in 1780 for taking Fort Moultrie and investing Charleston, South Carolina, the pillage amounting to more than a million dollars; for outstanding performance at Toulon in '93 for which he received the Order of the Bath; and two years later for the capture of the Cape of Good Hope from the Dutch, for which he received £64,000 in prize money. His wife, Lady Hester (née Thrale), who had been privately schooled by Dr. Samuel Johnson, was a mathematician and Hebrew scholar.

Lord Keith brought printed copies of the latest royal proclamation against mutiny, which were inserted in newspapers and given to bumboatmen to pass into the ships. By now some newspapers were crying vengeance as loudly as his Majesty and Parliament.

The pretense was maintained that Admiral Buckner was still in charge, and Keith's written orders went out under his signature. Verbal orders did not. The new hope of the sea lords inspected the Sheerness defenses, which the hardworking General Grey and Captain Dixon had made respectable, although not strong enough to long withstand a naval attack by a force as large as the delegates' fleet. In the sick quarters, Lord Keith found no surgeons or mates on duty, and the place full of "disorderly and mutinous seamen." He shipped them out to H.M.S. *Union,* a hospital ship occupied by ailing Russian sailors.

There was another defection that morning. The floating battery *Firm* left a hole in Parker's line and filled one in Keith's formation, which consisted of two undergunned frigates and two sloops stationed at the Medway defense boom.

Aboard *Sandwich* the delegates unanimously reelected Parker president. They debated what to reply to the Admiralty's stoppage of food, water and their access to Sheerness. Rough estimates on their total food stocks showed that if dry and cask stores were shared out of the amply supplied North Sea ships and the victualers, the fleet might operate for ten weeks. Fresh water was a more pressing need and there was a candle shortage. Cooks with dwindling stove wood were eying the carpenters' lumber stores.

The delegates' indignation over the Admiralty quarantine was inflamed by an appreciation of their fresh increase of power—the two-deckers from Great Yarmouth. They controlled thirteen sail-of-the-line and many support craft, more ships than had won some of Britain's greatest fleet victories. The sea lords would not listen to words and papers; the answer was ships. The emotion of the great cabin swung to retaliation, a show of might that would force Lord Spencer to restore their supplies.

The delegates passed a motion to institute a partial blockade of London:

> The Delegates of the Whole Fleet Assembled in Council on Board H.M.S *Sandwich* Having Information that the Dutch Fleet are ready for Sea have resolved that as it is the Determination of the Delegates that on Friday the Second Day of June if the Weather Permits that such Ships shall be Stationed in the Entrance of the River Thames as may be sufficient to stop all Vessels passing and departing until we have our Grievances adjusted that they may be able with the more Expedition to face the Enemies of their Country.
>
> Signed by Order of the Committee
> On Board H.M.S. *Sandwich*. Nore*

The order went out, "Detain all vessels to and from the port of London, those excepted whose cargoes are perishable." To pass through the blockade a ship must have President Parker's signed permission. Thomas Jephson, the fiddler of *Sandwich,* exulted, "We will get what we ask or all London will be in an uproar Saturday night!"

During his first hours on the job, Lord Keith was presented with an unexpected escalation of the mutiny—a blockade of the imperial capital. At the anchorage there was a squeal of capstans that had not turned for weeks and a reel of fiddlers making rhythm for capstan

---

* *Comet* papers.

gangs who turned faster and faster with the increasing beat of the falling pawls. Great weed-covered sea serpents of anchor cables entered the hawseholes and sloshed and reeked through lower gun decks, laying trails of muck, oyster shells, and ship's refuse. Strong bodies went into the boats with towing lines for small ships and for big ones, anchors to place ahead of the stream anchor to warp the ships intc new berths. They transformed the double crescent formation into a line of ships anchored a half mile apart across the navigable channel of the Thames. The frigates *Standard* and *Brilliant* and the sloops *Swan* and *Inspector* were told off to patrol the line, arrest ships, and conduct them to anchor within range of fleet ordnance. As the delegates' new disposition became evident in Sheerness, Keith telegraphed the Admiralty about the blockade and the sea lords telegraphed the Downs, ordering Admiral Peyton to halt victualers coming from Ireland and not permit them to sail into the mutineers' net.

The weather turned squally in the afternoon and there came upstream in the chop Adam Duncan's 64-gun ship, *Monmouth,* captain the Earl of Northesk, and sloop *Hound,* shifting their colors from blue to red. Huzzas ran up and down the blockade front. In the forecastle ballad Old Neptune had advised them "unto the Nore repair without delay," and now:

> *The worthy god's advice the heroes took*
> *Each broke his chains and off the panic shook*
> *Unto the Nore their gallant ships they steered*
> *Whilst brethren cheered them as each ship appeared.*
> *Oh Britons free, usurp no tyrant sway,*
> *Protect your tars, and then they'll you obey.*

For the first time in the great fleet mutinies an overt political act occurred and it occurred aboard the parliament ship herself. The Sandwiches made effigies of William Pitt and Henry Dundas and ran them up to the yardarms. Playful seamen took musket shots at the dummies. Lord Keith telegraphed the Admiralty that two men had been hanged aboard H.M.S. *Sandwich.* Lord Spencer quickly passed this incorrect report to his cabinet colleague Lord Grenville, who was most unhappy about the way the Nore, and just about everything else, was being handled.

The forcible act of the fleet parliament was part blockade and part ambuscade. It set a net for navy victualing ships coming down from Deptford or entering the Thames from Cork, while admitting perishable cargoes for London so that she would not starve. By demurring dry cargo vessels, colliers, grain boats, American cotton ships, West Indian sugar schooners, and the like, the delegates expected to send City merchants shouting to the sea lords to replenish the seamen and induce them to lift the blockade.

London would not starve, but she would vary her diet according to the recipe of the Nore. There would be less starches and carbohydrates. Potato boats from Cornwall and grain ships from America were stopped. Salmon was landed at Billingsgate fish market as usual from ice-holds of Scottish smacks a week out of Inverness or Aberdeen. Big salmon that were caught in the Thames arrived in straw-packed carts. From Barnstable, Whitstable and the Cheyneyrock Ground at the Great Nore, oyster boats went unhindered upstream.

Fishermen passed to Billingsgate from Faversham, Malden, Rochester, Colchester and Dover. Kentish market-farm boats delivered fruits and greens for Covent Garden. There was no disturbance of produce coming downriver from the western home counties or of Middlesex hay and fodder that was sold on the curb at Haymarket and in the slaughterhouse district in Whitechapel. The pretty sight continued of Berkshire market-garden wherries coming down to London—"Arrived at Hungerford, ten sail of apricot boats."

Nor was the Roast Beef of Old England imperiled by the mutineers. Meat came to London on the hoof, not on the deck. Stockmen started the weekly cattle drive to the capital on different days, depending on marching distance from the city, all aiming to arrive in the outskirts on Sunday. At dark on the Sabbath, London's streets were given over to barbaric processions of steers, complaining sheep, lowing oxen, barking herd dogs, thumps of staves and shouts of drovers, throwing up fogs of dust and horse-leavings that formed haloes around the men's flaming torches. At dawn in back of Whitechapel road the animals were pushed down chutes into cellars where butchers, wading in blood, adeptly killed and skinned and hoisted back the whole carcass to be carted to Smithfield market.

The blockade, however, would certainly hurt some powerful people —coal-factors, Mark Lane corn brokers expecting foreign grain to make up for the short English crop, timber merchants, wharfingers, tackle house and city porters, cotton factors, potato warehousemen in Tooley Street, wine and spirit importers, suppliers of Scandinavian naval stores to the Admiralty, and dealers in sugar and tobacco. Fortunately, there was no concern over tea. Pitt had taxed it so dear that most of the nation's requirement was supplied by the south coast smuggling industry.

When the exchange realized London was blockaded, "three per cents," the famous bedrock stocks of the country, fell to 47½, the lowest quotation on record.

XV

The Blockade of London

The enduring courage of [English] mariners [was] responsible for the gradual transformation of a poor country into one of wealth and predominance.

—E. KEBLE CHATTERTON

AT THE Great Nore the third of June was a rainy day. The Inflexibles held an early meeting and passed a resolution calling on the fleet committee to distribute food stocks from the storeship *Grampus* among ships that were running short. The message ended, "We are not to surrender our command here until every article of our grievances is redressed. President John Blake."

The delegates of the whole fleet endorsed this proposal. To the threats pouring out of Westminster, they made angry reply:

> I am commanded by the Committee of his Majesty's Ship *Sandwich* to inform you that they have this Day taken the Opinion of the Delegates of the Whole Fleet, who are universally of Opinion that the Conduct of the Administration has been highly improper in stopping the provisions by Government allow'd to the Seamen. And that the *foolish* proclamations which we have receiv'd are only fitted to exasperate the Minds of a Sett of Honest Men, who would never be more happy then in realy serving their Country.
>
> RICHARD PARKER, *President*

Rather than send a messenger ashore in the downpour, Parker mischievously hailed an old bumboatman, whom he knew the port admiral was using to smuggle messages to officers on the ships, and handed him the paper to deliver to his employer.

A seaman sent his own opinion to their lordships:

Damn my Eyes if I understand your Lingo or Long Proclamations, but in short give us our due at once & no more of it
while we go in search of the Enemies of our Country.

(Signed) HENRY LONG
Belonging to H.M. Ship *Champion,* Great Nore
June 3ᵈ 1797

To the Lords Commissioners
of H.M. Board of Admiralty

The writer of the *Monmouth* committee, Maurice Fitzgerald, fifty-
two, "a sick and weak old man," as a messmate described him, had
been at sea three months as a quota man. The mutiny was a tonic
for him. He wrote a letter to the elected captain of the ship:

Captain William Vance, *Monmouth*
SIR,

When I came aboard the *Monmouth* I had the pleasure of
your being one of my first acquaintances. Ever since I have
always found you a worthy respectful one in consequence of
which I think it my duty to sound the praise in a few verses
as far as my poor abilities will enable me of your good conduct and the rest of your brother officers that merit encomiums.

The notes I intend with your permission to take down will
enable some able writer hereafter to comment on the business,
which noble exertions I hope will be recorded in all the annals
of Europe which will redound to the honour of future ages.*

President Parker went ashore that Saturday afternoon and stayed
away all night. There is nothing in the official correspondence to
indicate that he met with anyone in authority. That evening in
Rochester, three hours from Sheerness by post chaise, an Anglican
priest, standing on the bridge over the Medway at dusk, was approached by two seamen. One asked, "Are you the gentleman in
black?" The cleric disavowed it, but thought the incident curious
enough to report to a magistrate.

Historian E. P. Thompson suggests that "the gentleman in black"
may have been Dr. Richard Watson, whom Francis Place had just
pushed out of the London Corresponding Society for conspiring at a
French invasion of Britain. Watson was arrested later in the year on
the charge of conveying information to France, and jailed for two
years.

---

* Fitzgerald's notes, if made, have not been found.

Another whom Professor Thompson suggests may have been linked to the mutiny was one of the few open advocates of insurrection, Thomas Spence, who sold anarchist tracts and sassafras tea from a London street barrow. He was five feet tall and had invented a phonetic alphabet in which he published his own writings. Spence was simple and candid, "unpractical in the ways of the world to an extent hardly imaginable," said Francis Place.* The borrowman stood left of the French revolution; he predicted that, after ingesting his writings, to "suitably prepare the public mind," Englishmen would have "only to declare the land to be theirs and form a convention of Parochial Delegates." They would dismiss their lords and squires and elect delegates "and thus would a beautiful and powerful New Republic instantaneously arise in full vigour," said Spence. He asserted that this would render tyrants "weak and harmless" and being "Scalped of their Revenues and the Lands that produced them, their Power would never more grow to enable them to overturn our Temple of Liberty." This little philosopher had a following too, and Portland had spies on him.

Spence broadcast his ideas on all planes—pamphlets, broadsides, discussions and chalk talks on the sidewalk. He wrote and published a paper called *Pig's Meat* "by one of the Swinish Multitude"—the last a regretted epithet Edmund Burke had applied to common English people. Whether or not Spence had connection with the naval mutineers his "beautiful and powerful New Republic," organized by "Delegates," had the colors of the Nore, where the delegates won the ships one by one, as Spence thought the parishes would respond.

Sunday morning the *Comet* logkeeper recorded that "Delegates from this ship read the Intelligence of the Day to the Ships Company." On *Sandwich,* the outlawed men rigged church and welcomed Chaplain Hatherall aboard for divine services. He took as his text Job xxvii,5:

> God forbid that I should justify you; till I die I will not remove my integrity from me.

His vestments flapping in gusts of rain, the padre extolled loyalty to the crown in a lengthy discourse to which his flock listened with nods of approval.

When President Parker returned from his mysterious overnight absence, he was called to *Montagu* to adjudicate a problem. When the

---

* Place was wrong. Spence had a metal press with which he stamped reform slogans into The King's pennies and halfpennies.

ship had suddenly left Yarmouth three days before, it carried off Mrs. Knight, the captain's wife, who was aboard on a day visit. The lady was "in distress." She had nothing to wear. Captain's ladies did not approve of being kidnapped and forced to live amongst mutineers. She desired to return to her family in London. And if they did not let her go, she would show them a thing or two about mutiny.

Parker gave John Knight a parole to conduct his wife to London. As the seamen swung out a boat with a white flag, Parker asked Captain Knight to make known to all ashore that, "Every delegate has sworn himself that he has no communication with any Jacobins or people of that description." And he repeated the patriotic theme of the blockade order: "Captain Knight, I will lead the fleet to Texel if the Dutch are still there."

Admiral Buckner sent the *Montagu* boat back immediately Knight and his wife were ashore; he was concerned over "constant boats between the Nore and the coast of Essex near Leigh." At night the mutineers were slipping into the estuary villages of Hartrey, Whitstable and Faversham. Nor could President Parker control the boats; that day Delegate Samuel Penny of *Sandwich* seceded by way of the Leigh sands.* As more merchant vessels were detained at the Great Nore, more promiscuous boatwork took place. Buckner suspected that Parker was landing emissaries on the wooded shores and ooze of the Thames north bank, where the cover was good and the going hard for light cavalry patrols.

In Sheerness Lord Keith, in command of the counter-mutiny, had his men hopping to it. He mustered the deposed ships' officers and gave them duty on the boom, in the dockyard and commanding newly emplaced shore batteries, the heavy guns of the frigates *Niger* and *l'Espion* dragged overland by their companies through sand and marsh. After a few days of it, the Nigers and Espions presented a petition, humbly begging to know what extra pay might be expected for seamen so employed. They were pledged the same bonus that soldiers got for engineering labor.

Round from Spithead to the Downs came H.M.S. *Glatton,* the equivocal ship that had deserted Adam Duncan at North Foreland and then deserted her sister mutineers going to the Nore. C-in-C Downs telegraphed London that the Glattons were submissive and had put up £100 for "detecting a seducer" on board.

Up and down the Thames blockade line, picket ships stopped merchantmen and collected them in an anchorage, whose masts soon

* He was at large five months.

outnumbered those of the fleet. Parker authorized expropriation of gunpowder from one vessel. The Champions demanded that he punish some fleet boats that had ventured out and plundered the Folkestone cutter.

Transactions declined in London dockland, usually the most raucous and chaotic scene outside of Bedlam Hospital in Lambeth. Even in wartime, Britain's waterborne trade had increased to a point where the wharves groaned with goods waiting to be taxed. Crown excisemen, who were as badly paid as seamen, never missed a Hanging Day or other festivity that would, in the Mediterranean fashion, offset poor pay with an off day. A shipmaster attempting to unload Madeira and finding his wharf covered with previous shipments would dump his casks on two other piers. The anguished consignee would have to hunt for them and try to grab an exciseman at the same time. It was exactly like passenger baggage inspection on a steamship pier today.

Open-air factory operations compounded the uproar on the waterfront. Virginia leaf tobacco was taken from hogsheads, stripped, taxed and cut on the pier.* Coopers went about smashing barrels open and smashing others shut. Hundreds of thieves—both of the starving and vocational varieties—flitted through the cornucopia.

But now, two days after the blockade, the wharves were becoming clear and the watermen, lightermen, carters, porters and coopers were scowling in the direction of the Great Nore from whence their deprivations came.

On Tower Hill the mutiny brought an unusual number of salty-looking gentlemen in and out of a new building adorned by portrait medallions of his Majesty and Queen Charlotte, navigational devices and the arms of "The Master, Wardens, and Assistants of the Guild, Fraternity or Brotherhood, of the most glorious and undivided Trinity." The government had enlisted the aid of the Elder Brethren of Trinity House, the ancient royal guild that planted and maintained Britain's lighthouses and buoys, licensed her pilots, and sat with the Admiralty court on cases of collisions at sea.

The Trinity House Brethren took a hand after the sea lords had considered a number of counterstrokes against the blockade. One notion was to sink hulks in the Channel below the Great Nore and imprison the rebellious vessels. It was abandoned because if and

---

* It was illegal to enter tobacco in a container weighing less than 450 pounds. This was meant to deter smugglers.

when Parker was overcome, the hulks would have to be removed in order to have use of the ships, the anchorage and the big river.

The Admiralty decided instead to remove navigational marks below the blockade line, which automatically concerned Trinity House. The Brethren organized the blackout rapidly in order to prevent any more defected naval vessels from coming in to join Parker, particularly the hovering delegate ships at Great Yarmouth.

At Hollesley Bay between the Nore and Yarmouth, the Spithead two-deckers *Sans Pareil* and *Russell* were wind-locked on their way to join Duncan at the Texel. Admiral Sir Thomas Pasley told their captains they could not expect any vessel to join them from Yarmouth, where he was cajoling, shaming, and thundering at the Agamemnons, Ardents, Leopards and Isises, who persistently refused to weigh anchor until their delegates returned from the Nore. Sir Thomas had gone over the side, his second mission as fruitless as the first, and rode back to London. He predicted to their lordships that the four Yarmouth men-of-war would pick up and sail to join the mutineers at the Great Nore.

Lord Spencer had better news from Portsmouth. Sir Roger Curtis, whose arrival at Spithead had revived that mutiny, was now taking nine disciplined ships to join Adam Duncan. Indeed, Curtis's crews gave their superiors an address to "such of our brethren who are still in an unsettled state" at the Nore:

"Brother sailors," it began. "It is with utmost concern we see that several ships' companies continue in a state of disaffection, and illegal proceedings, notwithstanding every demand made by our brethren in Lord Bridport's fleet have been most graciously granted to us, by his Majesty and both Houses of Parliament assembled." The United Roses said they had been "actuated by no bad principles" or disaffection, and had made "no fresh demands" at Spithead, while at the Nore "there is no doubt but evil-minded and designing men, a set of men from on shore, wish to take advantage of our honest openness . . . to subvert our most excellent constitution." The writers suspected that "French principles and their agents" were now at work, but, "we have full reliance that all our brother seamen, who labour under any grievance, will make no unreasonable demands, nor delay an amicable settlement by standing out for trifling objects."

It was signed by two delegates each from nine ships. Only one of the virtuous vessels, *La Juste,* had actually participated in the Spithead mutiny. The argument was the same that the King's party was using to turn public opinion against the Nore delegates: that Spithead had been a respectable affair while mysterious subversive agents were behind the current strike.

Moreover, the sea lords did not seem to think that Curtis's men were such monuments of virtue as their address claimed. They ordered Admiral Curtis, before he joined Duncan, to look in at Great Yarmouth but "do not approach even near the anchorage" or expose any of his men to the delegate ships. He was to stand at an antiseptic distance and signal the commanders, asking, "Disposition of crews?" before sending a cutter to invite approved ships' companies to rejoin Duncan in Holland.

The first three days out, the company of the flagship *Prince* was happy with fresh-killed beef, soft tommy and good beer. Then the boys brought them tubs of salt pork. Two captains of the forecastle marched to the mast and asked to speak with the ship's captain. "Sir, we're been short-weighted. Three pounds of salt pork ought not to equal two pounds of salt beef."

Admiral Curtis came out. "My lads, wait until we join the North Sea squadron and you'll see you're getting the same as they are."

"Aye, sir. We'll belay, sir, until we see what measure Admiral Duncan gives."

Next day salt pork was served again and the Princes would not touch it. The marine drummers rolled out general quarters. "All hands! Smartly now. The admiral wishes to see you."

"My lads, I advise you to take the pork. Take the pork, my hearties. I assure you I have sent to their lordships about the matter. If Admiral Duncan's men are getting more, the difference will be made up to you."

At the Texel, Adam Duncan's pair of two-deckers still plugged the fairway of the Dutch invasion fleet. His crews had now been without sleep for two nights. Offshore stood loyal *Stork* and disaffected *Circe*, her majority penned up below, guarded by nodding officers and marines, the captain and first lieutenant in a stupor of fatigue beside the helm. The mutineers were sleeping in normal divisions between decks. Duncan's forlorn patrol was endangered by a Dutch onslaught or a rush of mutineers. As the breeze came up toward the third morning, a watchkeeper shouted joyously, "Damn my eyes! It's come round westerly!"

It was anti-Dutch wind, sharply reducing the probability of the invasion fleet coming out. Duncan lifted his ground tackle from the bottleneck, moved a league to sea, and piped most of his people below to sleep.

He did not make a move against the mutineers on *Circe*. They controlled her guns and he did not seek civil war in his tiny squadron within eyeshot of the enemy. Trying to force the issue could result in disabling even his small deterrent threat over the Dutch. The Circes would come back either when his main fleet arrived or when the Dutch issued forth; Duncan felt sure the Circes would fight the enemy.

In the North Sea, his Majesty's cutter *Rose* spoke to the American brig *Eliza*, out of the Waddenzee by another passage. The master of the brig said that the Dutch invasion fleet had received sailing orders several days before while the easterly wind had favored an expedition. "But," said the American, "the sailors would not go until they got their pay."

Adam Duncan had been spared from battle by an enemy mutiny.*

The American skipper added that the Dutch seamen had been paid before he left and were now obeying orders. Duncan's only friend was the wind.

In the Thames estuary, after a three-day spell of rain and wind, Monday came fair with light airs and the *Comet* committee busied her people at housekeeping. They swayed up the lower yards and topgallant after repairs. H.M.S. *Sandwich* sent them four pounds of candles and a note announcing that the delegates were preparing "An Address to the People of England," to be printed and distributed in London.

To block the river channel upstream, the delegates ordered H.M.S. *Lion* out of the blockade line to a point nearer Gravesend. Admiral Buckner reported to the Admiralty, "There are now 100 merchant vessels detained at the Nore and the number is hourly increasing by fresh arrivals from sea." The sea lords telegraphed the Downs to send a cutter to stop merchantmen from entering the river channel, "as they are absolutely certain to be detained by mutineers." The inbound skippers anchored outside in Herne Bay, off Whitstable, or in the Warp, where their cargoes were denied to London as surely

---

* The ferocity with which the Dutch fought when they came out later indicates that Duncan's unequal force would have been annihilated if he had been given battle at this time.

as if they were in Parker's net. This action by the Admiralty for the first time shut off perishable foodstuffs. It was a deep cut into the city's day-to-day food supply.

Buckner received a visit from an agitated captain and an interpreter from the Russian frigate *Narva*. The allied vessel had abstained from the English quarrel, but now feared it was turning into a battle. *Narva* was anchored between the Sheerness fort and the delegates' big guns. Buckner gave the Russian permission to take refuge behind the Medway boom.

There was something ominous to whisper about in command circles that day. On secret evidence furnished by General Grey, Admiral Buckner arrested two beached navy lieutenants on blank charges and sent them to confinement in Chatham. This turned out to be nothing more serious than indiscretion in assigning boats, but the way it was done enlarged anxiety.

Captain William Bligh arrived in Sheerness with Captains John Blake and Lord William O'Bryen under Admiralty orders to assist the anti-mutiny command. They were welcomed, particularly Bligh with his experience in the subject.

The day, 5 June, was the official birthday of King George III. His actual advent had occurred on 4 June, but in 1797, that fell on a Sunday. Profane events, however grand, were not permitted on Britain's Sabbath and the celebration was put over a day. His Majesty was at Eton College, which kept his anniversary as its annual school fete.* The gathering of children, parents and equipages at picnic in bright sunshine on the green uncorked his Majesty's sentimental vapors. He went about with a half grin, rumpling the locks of little honorables and squirelings, inquiring, "Any rebellions of late? Any rebellions of late?"

At one o'clock on this sparkling day at his Majesty's Buoy of the Nore, the sailors of the mutinous fleet turned out in white trousers and blue jackets (or risked the delegates' displeasure). They covered the shrouds and lined the yards and gunwales. Picked crews wadded the guns and fired a twenty-one-gun royal salute with the speed and precision for which British gunners were famous in battle. In the drifting gunsmoke, the fleet raised three cheers for the King. The fort at Sheerness also fired a loyal salute which caused some of its walls to fall down.

Having joined in the common sentiment, the two sides resumed

---

* And still does.

hostilities. The delegates sent seventy sick men ashore and Lord Keith sent them right back.

An extraordinary official *Gazette* was published in London, announcing Parliament's new acts that provided death without clerical solace to any person communicating with a mutineer. Not to be outdone in propaganda, lower-deck polemicists reduced the stocks of G. R. foolscap in reply:

The Delegates of the different ships at the Nore assembled in Council, to their fellow-Subjects:—COUNTRYMEN,

It is to you particularly that we owe an explanation of our conduct. His Majesty's Ministers too well know our intentions, which are founded on the laws of humanity, honour and national safety,—long since trampled underfoot by those who ought to have been friends to us—the sole protectors of your laws and property. The public prints teem with falsehoods and misrepresentations to induce you to credit things as far from our design as the conduct of those at the helm of national affairs is from honesty or common decorum.

Shall we who have endured the toils of a tedious, disgraceful war, be the victims of tyranny and oppression which vile, gilded, pampered knaves, wallowing in the lap of luxury, choose to load us with? Shall we, who amid the rage of the tempest and the war or jarring elements, undaunted climb the unsteady cordage and totter on the top-mast's dreadful height, suffer ourselves to be treated worse than the dogs of London Streets? Shall we, who in the battle's sanguinary rage, confound, terrify and subdue your proudest foe, guard your coasts from invasion, your children from slaughter, and your lands from pillage—be the footballs and shuttlecocks of a set of tyrants who derives from us alone their honours, their titles and their fortunes? No, the Age of Reason has at length revolved. Long have we been endeavoring to find ourselves men. We now find ourselves so. We will be treated as such. Far, very far, from us is the idea of subverting the government of our beloved country. We have the highest opinion of our Most Gracious Sovereign, and we hope none of those measures taken to deprive us of the common rights of men have been instigated by him.

You cannot, countrymen, form the most distant idea of the slavery under which we have for many years laboured. Rome had her Neros and Caligulas, but how many characters of their description might we not mention in the British Fleet—

men without the least tincture of humanity, without the faintest spark of virtue, education or abilities, exercising the most wanton acts of cruelty over those whom dire misfortune or patriotic zeal may have placed in their power—basking in the sunshine of prosperity, whilst we (need we repeat who we are?) labour under every distress which the breast of inhumanity can suggest. The British Seaman has often with justice been compared to the Lion—gentle, generous and humane— no one would certainly wish to hurt such an animal. Hitherto we have laboured for our sovereign and you. We are now obliged to think for ourselves, for there are many (nay, most of us) in the Fleet who have been prisoners since the commencement of the War, without receiving a single farthing. Have we not a right to complain? Let His Majesty but order us to be paid and the little grievances we have made known redressed, we shall enter with alacrity upon any employment for the defence of our country; but until that is complied with we are determined to stop all commerce and intercept all provisions, for our own subsistence. The military have had their pay augmented, to insult as well as enslave you. Be not appalled. We will adopt the words of a celebrated (Dieu et mon Droit) and defy all attempts to deceive us. We do not wish to adopt the plan of a neighbouring nation, however it may have been suggested; but we [will] sell our lives dearly to maintain what we have demanded. Nay, countrymen, more: We have already discovered the tricks of Government in supplying our enemies with different commodities, and a few days will probably lead to something more.* In the meantime,

> We remain, Dear Countrymen,
> Yours affectionately,
> YOUR LOVING BROTHERS
> RED FOR EVER!

Delegate Patmore provided three guineas to have the declaration printed and posted at the Royal Exchange and other public places in London with a packet of copies to be sent back to the fleet. Delegate Gregory went aboard an American ship that Parker had given a pass to London, gave the money to the river pilot, and asked him to carry out the commission. The London public never saw the proclamation. The pilot took it to the Admiralty and pocketed the three guineas.

---

* English merchants continued trading with France during the war.

On the other hand the Comets, and presumably other companies, regularly received exhortations from the outer world, such as a letter datelined "The British Fleet off Brest 28 May 1797," addressed to "Fellow seamen at the Nore."

> We have heard of the mutinous spirit which is among you with great concern. We have declared ourselves satisfied and we are resolved to maintain the Glory & to fight the Battles of our Country as becomes British Seamen. Do not disgrace yourselves any longer. Your Conduct will bring upon our whole Body the curses of Our Country, who we know (from the best Authority) are to a Man against you . . . Consider you are Britons & that our Country is yet dear to us all, While its numerous Enemies threaten its Destruction in which our Wives & Children will be involved. *Fly to its Assistance like Men,* by returning (as we have done) to your duty. A Voluntary Submission may, perhaps, yet procure for you an Extension of the Royal Mercy. But if you persevere, we must be compelled to assist in subduing you. And, Painful as the Duty may be, a regard to our own *Characters* & to our *Wives, Children & Country* will compel us to do it.
> (Signed) SEAMEN OF THE FLEET OFF BREST*

This document carried no weight at the Nore, because of its lack of signatures. Nore emissaries to Spithead had met and knew the names of many leaders of the previous affair. If the authors of the paper could not secure a single signature for a declaration of loyalty, it indicated that the sentiments of the Spithead men were exactly opposite to the burden of the letter. Moreover, its threats to help subdue the Nore mutiny sounded very queer at a time when a sister blockade fleet, Duncan's North Sea command, was joining the stand-out. The missive was placed in the category of bright young thoughts from the wardroom.

Mutineer-Captain William Vance of *Monmouth* rounded up five messmates for "conspiracy against the ship's company" and convened a lower-deck military court, which found them guilty and sentenced each to three dozen strokes. One was William Dawson, master's mate, whose job it was to flog people in the regular course of things. Vance held out the cat-o'-nine-tails to Dawson and said to the four other culprits, "Is there any of you gentlemen who wishes to take a dozen off Mr. Dawson?" Dawson refused to take

---

* *Comet* papers.

the whip. "Then, Mr. Dawson, you will please strip." The mate took off his shirt and was seized up on the gratings. Vance handed the cat to Boatswain's Mate Stevenson, who flailed Dawson's back twelve times. "I hope, gentlemen, that you are all satisfied that Mr. Stevenson has done his duty," said Vance. Boatswain's Mate Benson took the lash and cracked it several times in the air, shortening its knotted tails to reduce Dawson's injuries. After Dawson collected his three dozen, the seamen tied up a midshipman named Tomlinson. The ship's company agreed with the man who yelled, "Take one dozen off his punishment!" and Tomlinson received less lacerations than Dawson. The whipped men were then drummed around the fleet, the oarsmen calling to the ships, "Rouse up and show yourself! Here is a bloody midshipman!"

At last Admiral Duncan was joined in Holland by the Spithead 74s *Sans Pareil* and *Russell*. The wind went around northeast and blew against Duncan, raising the sailing chances of the Dutch. He put his reinforced squadron at anchor six miles out.

By this time the siege was lifting on *Circe* frigate. The recalcitrants confined belowdecks were now permitted topside in exchange for badly needed labor to keep her cruising. But the people stuck to their organization and their grievances. The *Circe* company was holding a meeting on the forecastle when *Sans Pareil* and *Russell* arrived. Mr. Richardson, the first officer, thought the ships were from the Nore. Therefore the mutiny was over and full strength was coming to the blockade. Richardson cocked his pistol, ran into the seamen's meeting, and dragged the chief delegate below. Officers and non-striking people overcame halfhearted resistance from the rest. Captain Peter Halkett of *Circe* gave a couple of dozen lashes to the ringleaders but did not apply for court-martial, and never reported the mutiny. Neither did Admiral Duncan. There is no record of further troubles on *Circe*. Happy is the ship without a history.

On this day, the revolutionary avengers, Lazare Hoche and Wolfe Tone, were back in Germany. Hoche was plaguing the Directory for a transfer to the invasion coast and the Minister of Marine for immediate sailing of a huge expedition to the British Isles from Brest. Tone evaluated the current situation. "The sedition continues aboard the English fleet and had reached the Army," he wrote. "For the present, however, they seem to be appeased, but at the expense of dismissing a number of officers of the Navy who are obnoxious to the seamen, and increasing the pay of both seamen and soldiers. When a government is forced to such concessions it seems to me an inevitable symptom of decaying empire."

The Paris naval ministry told Hoche that a huge expedition would take two months to organize. "That means six," said Tone. "The time to profit from the state of mutiny and absolute disorganization of the English navy is at this moment." He told Hoche that 5,000 men now were better than 25,000 in three months' time, "when we might find ourselves again blocked up in Brest. Remember that the mutiny will most certainly soon be quelled. There is not one minute to lose. If we are lucky enough to arrive in Ireland before it takes place, we might gain over the seamen. They have already spoken of steering the fleet to Irish harbors. And settle the business without striking a blow."

"I see everything in precisely the same light as you do," Hoche said. "I shall press the Directory and the ministry in the strongest manner."

The following morning, Tuesday 6 June, the Nore parliament was one month old. In the traditional first order of business, Richard Parker was reelected president. Then, with a chord from the *Sandwich* band on the quarterdeck, the swelling accents of "God Save the King" sounded through the fleet. One musician refused to play —Thomas Jephson, an Irish violinist who received republican literature from a London shoemaker, and who maintained, "If the people of England had an equal spirit to that of Ireland, their wrongs would have long since been redressed."

The music greeted an approaching gig containing Captain the Earl of Northesk (William Carnegie) of *Monmouth* and two delegates of that North Sea two-decker. Since his ship had been embezzled at Great Yarmouth, Lord Northesk had been trying to understand why, rather than howling and sulking like so many other commanders. The investigation led his lordship to think the mutineers were not seditionists and traitors. They were men in a dilemma. He spoke with *Monmouth*'s delegates, who arranged the noble lord's visit to the delegates. Of course Northesk notified Admiral Lord Keith, who interposed no objection to this unauthorized meeting at his own risk with the inner ring of mutineers.

After formal boarding courtesies, his lordship was conducted to the great cabin, where the delegates affirmed their allegiance to the crown. Parker finished drafting an inspired letter to "The King's

Most Excellent Majesty," and requested Northesk to take it personally to the sovereign. Northesk said he would take the letter first to
his immediate superiors, and, if they approved, he could carry it
on to London. He glanced through the text and said, "I warn you,
Parker, do not expect a favorable answer. These demands seem
unreasonable."

To the King's Most Excellent Majesty
    May it please Your Majesty,
    We your Majesty's faithful and loyal subjects serving on
Board Your Majesty's Ships and Vessels at the Nore, with the
greatest humility beg leave to lay our Petition before you, and
hope as you have always avowed yourself to be the Father of
your People, that our Petitions will be attended to. We have
already laid a State[ment] of our Grievance before Your
Majesty's Board of Admiralty, which Grievances we have
reasons to imagine, were never properly stated to you, as we
are sorry to have reason to remark the conduct of your present Ministers seems to be directed to the ruin and overthrow
of your Kingdoms, and as their Duty to its good and advantage, a particular instance of which is the Council they have
given Your Majesty with regard to us in proclaiming us
Rebels, traitors and Outlaws. This Council if we had not been
men particularly attached to Your Majesty's sacred person
and Government, moderate but firm in our demands, and
resolved with our lives to oppose your enemies by land and
sea, would before now have driven us to some acts of Outrage and Revenge that might have shaken the very foundations of this Kingdom. We here give you a list of our Grievances, which List is accompanied by a simple but true Statement of the reasons we have of demanding them, and after
thus making our Wants known to Your Majesty, we cannot
longer ascribe a non-compliance with those Wants to Ministry, with you it now rests to determine whether you will or
will not get a Redress of our Suffering. Your Majesty may
depend that in Your Kingdom there is no more loyal and
faithful Subjects than we are, but at the same time we must
assure Your Majesty till all those disgraceful Proclamations
which proscribe Outlaws are contradicted, till we have all our
Grievances redress'd and till we have the same supply from
and communication as usual with the shore, we shall consider ourselves masters of Nore Shipping. We have already
determined how to act, and should be extremely sorry we
should be forced to repose in another Country, which must

evidently be the case if we are denounced as Outlaws in our own.

Your Majesty's Ministers seem to build their hopes on starving us into a compliance, but this is a wrong Idea. We have as much Provisions and Stores as will last Six Months. We were aware of their Intentions, and provided against them, but were it the reverse, and that we had but two days Provisions, we would sooner die in that state than give Up the least article of our Demands.

We shall trust to your Majesty's prudence in chusing such Councillors and Advisors in the present and other affairs as will have the good of their Country in view, and not like the present Ministers its Destruction. And with respect to our own Grievances, we shall allow 54 hours from 8 o'clock on Wednesday June the 7th 1797 to know Your Majesty's final Answer. We shall likewise make known to our fellow-subjects on shore the particulars of the Address and Your Majesty's answer, so as to justify to them any Measure we may take in consequence of a Refusal.

> With loyalty we remain,
> Your Majesty's dutiful Subjects,
> SEAMEN AT THE NORE

Recognizing that this was a historic ultimatum to the King, Admirals Keith and Buckner sent Northesk to London to lay it before Lord Spencer for decision.

That morning the Trinity House Brethren moved secretly from ports flanking the Nore to scuttle the buoys in the ship lane. The surprise was smartly organized, but the Trinity men were chagrined to see a squadron of two-deckers wearing red flags enter the Channel for the Nore before they could remove the seamarks. These were the very ships that Trinity House was trying to cut off—*Agamemnon,* 64, *Ardent,* 64, *Leopard,* 50, and *Isis,* 50, from Great Yarmouth. It seemed that every time the government hacked the dragon it grew another arm.

There was an unhappy social situation aboard the newcomers. Despite the loyalty of her marine troops and the distaste of the mass of seamen for the cause, *Agamemnon* was controlled by a dozen strong-willed committeemen. They menaced the rest of the company with the guns of *Ardent, Leopard* and *Isis.* The unwilling *Ardent* company was frightened by the guns of the other three. And so it went.

Unaware of this corked state of morale, the men of the Nore skylarked into the shrouds and unloosed rejoicing at the advent of the new warships. Grinning again, the delegates congratulated each other. "Every time we're hove out by the man-eaters, more ships come over to us!"

The telegrapher on the roof of the Admiralty office quickly received the word from Sheerness that Trinity House had failed to erase the trail in time to prevent the four North Sea ships from reaching the delegate fleet.

President Parker and the delegates now commanded seventeen sail-of-the-line and a dozen smaller vessels, a larger fleet than Old Jarvey had deployed in the country's last naval battle at Cape St. Vincent.

It seemed now that all preconditions had been met for hostilities to commence. Parker was embayed. If he went to sea down unmarked lanes, many ships would go aground. If he should try to crash into the Medway, the makeshift defenses there would inflict much damage before they were knocked down by his superior firepower. The only way open was upstream to London.

Pitt's racing mind plunged ahead to what frightful things Parker might do next. He sent a note to Spencer: "I cannot help thinking it very probable that if the buoys being taken up prevent them [from] going away, their next idea may be to force their passage up the river. . . . Probably if any attempt is made by the mutineers it will be on the first occasion that the tide serves after the term of fifty-four hours from this morning is expired."

Considering the recent contemptuous and radical texts Parker had been sending the Admiralty, their lordships considered him capable of trying to force the river forts and come to the Pool of London with his 10,000 men and 1,300 guns. On the way, he might gather up *Lancaster, Naiad,* and several smaller vessels still under delegate control in Long Reach.

Their lordships considered throwing a boom across the river above the Nore, but were advised that it could not be done in less than two weeks. They sent out for experts to find how long it would take to assemble enough colliers to string a barrier across the river. While waiting on this study, they wrote to Adam Duncan that Admiral Mackaroff of his Imperial Russian Majesty's service was coming to his support from Yarmouth with three two-deckers and a frigate. As a quid pro quo, Lord Spencer asked his good friend Duncan to detach some of his small craft to cruise the North Sea and warn all merchant shipping away from the Thames. Duncan was writing him, "The delegates seem strict disciplinarians, and if we was to adopt some of their regulations, it would not be amiss."

At the Nore, the delegates of the newly arrived *Leopard,* wishing to establish a belligerent reputation right away, hung an effigy of Pitt at the yardarm. But her sister 64, *Montagu,* arrived the previous week, had lost heart for the new system. The Montagus held a meeting and sent a message to the central committee, mentioning the "unprobible [*sic*] state which our affairs stands at present." They momentarily expected a proclamation of peace, after hearing that "a gentleman went over to France investigated with full authority to treat for peace." They urged the delegates to settle the affair quickly and signed, "We are your most sincere and loving brothers until death."

Desertion corroded the cause. Four seamen of *Grampus* made it ashore and when they inquired where they might apply for the King's pardon and give information on the mutiny, were jailed in Chelmsford. They petitioned the Admiralty for release and Nepean said that when *Grampus* returned to duty he would investigate their case.

Marine Corporal William Wheeler was on sentry duty in the poop of *Standard* when his illiterate sergeant, Thomas Lunniss, came by and requested that he write a petition to the committee. Lunniss was proud of an idea that had come to him and felt it worthy of sanctification in writing. Wheeler took it down:

> For preservation of the whole fleet in order to defend the just and honourabl caus that we has taken in hand I think it requisite and necessary that discipline with small arms should be kept up in every ship of such a number of men including marines according to the rate of each ship as we know not how soon there may be need of them.

Sergeant Lunniss' only literary composition was to cost him his life.

On *Monmouth*, the committee seized Marine Sergeant Watkin Jenkins for attempting to assemble the marine company under arms and take over the ship. The sergeant was taken to the forecastle with a halter around his neck. A seaman spliced a noose to the yard rope and a gang took hold to hang the lobsterback. Several men protested that Jenkins should be heard before execution. He did not deny the charge. He said, "I was doing no more than my duty. If I omitted doing my duty, I was liable to be hanged. And to be hanged for doing my duty and to be hanged for not doing my duty is placing me in a very ticklish situation.

"Have I no chance to live?"

"He was only doing his duty," the would-be lynchers told each other. The hanging was postponed and Jenkins was tried, instead. He received three dozen. They shaved his head and drummed him around the fleet, shouting, "Here's your bloody sergeant." They left a topknot on Jenkin's head, by which, as a humorist in the boat explained, "Mahomet might have an opportunity when he is sinking to haul him up to learn."

Johnson, the president of *Repulse*, congratulated the Monmouths on the punishment. On the back of his letter a forecastle scribe practiced spelling the popular new word,

> *Pertit*
> *Pertisin*
> *Perti*
> *Petision*
> *Petition*

From the beach an exiled captain wrote to Lieutenant Carew on *Repulse*, "I wish our lads would have the fear of God before their eyes. I shall send you a paper if I can get one. All the country are in arms and detest them."

Mutineer intercourse with Sheerness was finished and was becoming impossible on the north shore. Mail was embargoed. Forecastle representatives had to run the Gravesend-Tilbury batteries at night to slip through to and from *Lancaster* and *Naiad* in Long Reach. All means of public appeal were closed to the delegates. The nation was subjected only to the raging campaign against them. Nothing was published on the stubborn issues that kept the cause going—direct negotiations with Admiralty commissioners empowered to remove officers and extension of the Spithead pardon. The average Briton was forced to Mr. Pitt's designed conclusions that it could be only Jacobins, French agents, or traitors who would continue a rebellion that no longer had a cause.*

Oddly enough, quarantine of the mutineers was not effective at Long Reach, the nearest point to London that insubordinate vessels

---

* A British naval historian told the author in 1963, "Ah, the Nore! Nobody will ever understand the Nore!"

lay. Purfleet on the north bank was eighteen road miles from the palace of Westminster.

Captain William Pierrepont of *Naiad*, ashore in Purfleet with time on his hands, was passing a tavern when a fast, elegant chaise pulled up and out stepped "a certain political character in the opposition," none other than the wealthy brewer and social reformer Samuel Whitbread, who had spoken sympathetically of the Spithead cause in the House of Commons. The captain followed the legislator into the pub and saw him sit down with James Wilson, captain of the foretop in H.M.S. *Lancaster* and now her elected ship's captain.

Pierrepont pelted off for the Admiralty to report this astounding incident. Under the new acts, Whitbread could be hanged for making this rendezvous.

The captain of the foretop did not regard meeting with an M.P. anything to be kept secret. Back on deck next day, Wilson's first lieutenant pointed to newly erected shore batteries trained on *Lancaster*. "You see all the country is against you," he said. "Even the opposition is joining the ministerial party to repel you."

"I know that," said the sailor. "I had a half hour's conversation with Mr. Whitbread the other day."

"He's a strong opposition man."

"Yes, sir," said Wilson, "and he is a good friend of ours." The mutineer-captain got into a jollyboat and rowed toward Purfleet. The lieutenant swept the shore with his glass and thought he recognized Samuel Whitbread waiting on the bank.

The night flood tide pulsed through the Great Nore. On the store-ship *Serapis*, whose merchant crew was not involved in the cause, men waited for the blockade ships to swing on their cables until their stingless aftercastles pointed upstream, then they cut her away. Many ships opened fire, but *Serapis* made Sheerness with only one wounded man. During the noise, another storeship, *Discovery*, broke clean to safety at the Medway boom.

XVI

The Loyal Ensign

"We must all hang together, or assuredly we shall all hang separately."

—BENJAMIN FRANKLIN on signing the Declaration of Independence.

DURING the night (6-7 June) Parker's officers of the watch noticed that the lightship at the Buoy of the Nore was dark. At dawn they saw that both the light and the buoy were missing. On *Sandwich* the meeting flag streamed aloft and the delegates hurried to the parliament ship. They set up a "secret service" of four good men from each ship to defend the buoys, under the command of Quartermaster Hockless of *Sandwich*. Hockless gathered them on the cutter *Ranger* and sailed down the Queen's Channel. There was not a navigational aid left in the estuary. Trinity House raiders had sunk the channel markers and moved the Nore buoy and lightship to Whiting Sands and darkened the coastal lighthouses at Harwich, Orfordness and North Foreland. Hockless returned to *Sandwich* and told the delegates not to worry. "I can take the fleet out without the marks," he said. Observing *Ranger*'s cruise, the Trinity Brethren suspected the sloop intended to deposit new seamarks, and called on the Admiralty for gunboats to defend the empty patches of water where the buoys had been.

The disappearance of the buoys led men's thoughts at the Great Nore to escape and entrapment. Buckner's informers in the forecastle said the marine companies were wavering, but did not want to challenge superior numbers of armed seamen. On *Leopard*, John Habbigan found "things turning out very comical." He said, "Everyone of us in the ship began to grow very tired of it."

The *Nassau*'s resolution was cracking. Midshipman Hardy reported, "Our men came aft and one and all said they were ashamed of their conduct, begged the officers' pardon and hoped that they would get the King's pardon likewise, and were so sincere that most of them shed tears." The next morning *Nassau* delegates visited the other North Sea ships that could be considered as having come round to the Nore to be paid rather than as adherents of mutiny and pleaded with them to stop taking orders from *Sandwich* and sail as soon as paid. The other ships from Yarmouth refused; they intended to stick to President Parker until the complaints were settled. The Nassaus rowed off dejectedly and resumed discipline under the red flag.

> (Admiralty, 7 June, 9:45 A.M.) Earl Spencer has the honour of laying before your Majesty a sealed paper brought up this morning from the Nore by the Earl of Northesk, Captain of your Majesty's ship the *Monmouth*. Earl Spencer understands that it is a petition to your Majesty from the persons styling themselves delegates of the Fleet; and will, with your Majesty's permission do himself the honour of attending your Majesty at St. James's before the Levée to receive your Majesty's pleasure upon the subject.

George Rex read the attack on his ministers, the talk of "acts of Outrage and Revenge that might have shaken the very foundations of this Kingdom," of "repose in another country" and the 54-hour time limit on his Majesty's "final answer."
"NO!"
Spencer went back to the Admiralty and gave the definitive result to Lord Northesk. Perhaps the kindly Northesk was distressed that the King had not considered granting the men something, or perhaps Spencer did not want to give the appearance of any further pourparlers with the mutineers; at any rate, the First Lord ordered the emissary to remain in London and sent Captain John Knight, who had been paroled by the mutineers, to take the refusal back.
At the Royal Exchange "a numerous & respectable meeting of merchants, shipowners, insurers & other inhabitants of London" approved the proposals of the Nore sloop captains, Honeyman and MacKenzie. The merchants acclaimed a resolution:

> First, that the disorderly and mutinous proceedings of part of the fleet at the Nore are witnessed with extreme concern, indignation and abhorrence; secondly, that no seaman who

has taken part in the disturbances should henceforward be employed without a certificate of his having returned to his duty; thirdly, that a public subscription should be raised, to detect and bring to public justice such lurking traitors as may have excited and fomented the mutiny at the Nore.

A public reaction had now been aroused. Somebody called for roundups of the mutineers' wives and children to transport them to Botany Bay. Others wanted to mobilize the press gangs to kidnap enough men to put down the mutiny. Some thought the government should offer a pardon and bonus to navy deserters to come forward and suppress those who had not deserted. Lord Portland said sailors' letters from home "found to contain good advice and exhortations to return to duty should be forwarded to them . . ." but those with "different sentiments should not be allowed to proceed."

Merchants thronged the Marine Society hall to thank the ships that had escaped from the Nore and voted to pay their loyal seamen a guinea each and foremen two guineas. They also voted a £100 reward for apprehension and conviction of a mutiny leader.* The same sort of indignation bee was going on in mercantile circles of Leith and Aberdeen, which voted to raise volunteers to quell the mutiny. The Admiralty pledged to release volunteers as soon as the mutiny was suppressed.

Now, at the Great Nore, ten thousand men of flesh and blood who had fought his Majesty's battles and preserved the merchants from French rapine were threatened by three shadow navies, one manned by the Impressment service, one by paid and pardoned deserters, and one by volunteers to be discharged after their first engagement. The mutineers asked much less than that of the government.

The tired and outnumbered defenders of Sheerness heard the noise in London. Lord Keith challenged the city to back its fighting resolutions with some people willing to fight. "There are enough loyal vessels in the Thames to suppress the mutiny." he steamed. "But they cannot be manned! Here are five thousand of the best seamen in the kingdom—in revenue, ordnance, East India company, the watermen's company, the press gang, the tenders, the victualing office, the bargemen to the public offices. Many are protected by noblemen at high pay. When I ask them to volunteer they say, 'We are not fighting men. We have families to provide for.' "

---

* There is no record of a seaman receiving a sixpence either for being good or for arresting a delegate.

Volunteers who did appear, largely Trinity House people, were sent to Long Reach to board the loyal ship *Neptune*, commanded by Sir Erasmus Gower, who had been put off his ship at Spithead. *Lancaster* and *Naiad*, cut off from the main body of the fleet, left the mutiny and came under Sir Erasmus' care. It is not impossible to think that Samuel Whitbread advised Mutineer-Captain Wilson of *Lancaster* to yield.

The Nore delegates debated what to do if their ultimatum to the King expired without answer at 2 P.M. two days hence (9 June). To give their London emissary sufficient time, they voted to put the expiry forward 24 hours. With three days left, the central committee divided into two sections to better accomplish its work. President Parker took a group of delegates on a gala morale-building tour of the fleet with the flagship band. The presidential party intended to visit and harangue every ship, reading the latest documents to their companies, including the nth royal anathema and the condemnation of the London merchants.

On *Repulse*, Parker said to the company, "Brethren, I am obliged for your conduct. We have grievances which we wish to have redressed; we applied for the Lords of the Admiralty to come to the Nore. They only came to Sheerness, and we were not admitted to see them. Lord Spencer and his Aide de Camp only spoke to us through Admiral Buckner, which was no better than a speaking trumpet. We sent to Captain Knight to get our grievances redressed, but he returned without anything satisfactory. He brought us news that we were all declared rebels to our country.

"Is there a rebel among you?"

"NO!"

"Then, if we are not rebels to our country, our country are rebels to us."

Parker told the Monmouths, "I say we are all honest men. I and my brother delegates are all united and acting in the cause of humanity. And while life animates the heart of Dick Parker, he will be true to the cause."

John Blake of *Inflexible* stayed behind looking after the particulars of making a fleet ready for sea without a dockyard, water tenders, or a victualing yard. Blake had no way of knowing that his opposite number, Lord Keith, was in worse straits. The agent victualer at Chatham had no more beer and insufficient bread for the Sheerness defense force. The fleet brewers in Chatham, large creditors of the Admiralty, were reluctant to furnish more beer on tick, and for security reasons Keith did not want to issue his men spirits and laced wine. The nearest bakeries capable of producing fleet tonnages were located up the Thames and their delivery boats were inconveniently barred from Sheerness by the delegates' fleet.

Secretary of the Admiralty Evan Nepean scraped together carts to haul bread to the Chatham yard from Gravesend. Nepean folded up three inches of the back corner of the demand for bread and beer and wrote a slanting minute that Second Secretary Marsden could expand into ministerial prose: "He must issue spirits if no beer can be furnished at Chatham . . ."

On his part, mutineer John Blake wrote orders to acting pursers asking them to give him each ship's inventory of stores, water and provisions in excess of a ten-weeks supply, or, if short of that, a list of what was needed to make up ten weeks. A fleet with a ten-week range could reach haven in neutral or friendly parts of the Americas, or it could seal up the invasion fleets in Brest or the Texel for two months.

The errant 64-gun ship *Repulse*, which ten days before had been fully supplied for about 500 men, returned the following list of stores in hold:

WEEKS	PROVISIONS	(in pounds)
10½	Bread	34,724
13½	Beef (1,684), Flour (8,747)*, Suet (1,760)	
13	Pork	3,075
9	Butter	1,620 good, 200 bad
4½	Cheese	1,750 good, 1,092 bad
4	Sugar, 721, Rice, 1,563	
8	Pease	150
8½	Oatmeal	182
12	Molassas	2,300 gals.
13	Spirits & Wine—Brandy, 1,800 gals; Wine, 600 gals	
10½	Vinegar	480 gals
16	Candles	1,312
	Water, 150 tons	
	Slops wanting: Hats, 3 cases; frocks, 2 bales; stockings, 1 bale	

President Parker's inspirational tour of the fleet was not wholly successful. On *Director,* a lieutenant named Roscoe tried to read the

---

* One of the mutiny complaints: "Flour is not Beef!"

entire text of the Parliamentary acts to his company, but was prevented by Delegate Houston, who gave a short interpretive version and claimed that a promise of pardon was "no pardon at all." The Ardents listened to Richard Parker without response. Lieutenant Young shouted, "He misrepresents the Acts of Parliament!"

William Gregory of *Sandwich* read the documents on H.M.S. *Brilliant*. Of the Act of Parliament he said, "None of your grievances have been redressed! But, this can be altered in four hours. Don't go ashore. You are liable to be shot or hung." He read the blacklist resolution of the London shipowners and brokers. Many Brilliants talked of surrender.

Thomas Wood, a *Leopard* seaman, asked Committee Secretary William Ross where the ship would go if the delegates removed the fleet to sea. Ross named Bantry Bay or Madeira as possible rendezvous, according to Wood's later recollection. Ross's fellow committeeman, William Welch, told Seaman John Copey, "The ship should go to France." Copey replied, "No ship of ours shall ever go to France!" He was in favor of going to the West Indies, where there was plenty of wine, wood and water.

Charles James Fox, the great liberal, who had abdicated the opposition leadership of Parliament midway in the Nore mutiny, was lazing in the sun at his retreat on St. Anne's Hill near Virginia Water with his wife, whom he represented as his mistress. Perhaps with a tic of conscience, Fox wrote to a friend, "Here I am with Liz, enjoying the fine weather, the beauty, and not its least beauty, the idleness of this place, as much as these horrors were not going on. When one has done all one can, as I think I have, to prevent mischief, one has a right, I think, to forget its existence."

Conscience certainly induced young Lieutenant Henry Hawes of mutinous *Proserpine* to send a letter ashore to his captain, telling how the delegates of his ship had tricked him into taking an oath not to punish any of them afterward, and how he had denounced the pledge and had been released from it. He was one of the two commissioned officers in the mutinous ships of '97 who had given the word of a gentleman to rebels of lower social orders. The command placed Hawes on the list of those to be arrested when the mutiny was defeated.

During the three-day period of ultimatum and preparation for sailing, the weather favored the delegates. There were fair skies and moderate to fresh breezes. On the second morning, Friday, 9 June, the fleet legislature submitted a plan for the next day's action to the companies of all the ships. In doing so, the members admitted for the first time that they no longer had enough agreement among themselves to maintain their power of giving orders to the fleet. They were obliged to ask what each ship wished to do: and they listed five choices covering every point of view that had been expressed:

—The fleet was to be parted into five divisions.

—The first would consist of those that wanted to surrender. It would remain at the Nore.

—The second division would sail to the Texel, win over the crews of Adam Duncan's ships, and proceed to Cherbourg to join the French Revolution.

—The third division would sail to Cromarty Firth in the North of Scotland, presumably for temporary haven while deciding its own destiny.

—The fourth division would sail north, round Scotland, and go to Shannon. Evidently, this choice was provided for Irish seamen, who could either form a shamrock navy, join a French invasion, or sell the ships and vanish inland, as the spirit moved them.

—The last division would sail for "the New Colony." This could have meant the United States, or unsettled areas of North America, or the establishment of an actual new colony the way the Brothers of the Coast, buccaneers, and pirates had made settlements in the Caribbean and Gulf of Mexico in the previous century.

While leaving the decision to each ship's company, the delegates offered recommendations of the makeup of the divisions. They made no nominations of ships that would stay and submit. Since *Champion* was low on supplies, they urged her to "go to the Humber & make prizes, then sail to the Texel, then petition the French convention for protection as the only government that understands the rights of man." The Champions turned this down flatly.

Standard was to proceed alone to Cherbourg, probably to set up protocol with the French for turning over the other ships. Since French royalists had handed over a fleet to the British at Toulon in 1793, the republic would no doubt appreciate this return courtesy of the Nore delegates. The crew of the sloop *Swan* leaned toward going to France.

Monmouth, Lion, Nassau, Sandwich and *Director* were slated to proceed to Cromarty Firth. The mixture was shrewd. *Nassau* and *Monmouth* were on the point of surrender. *Director* and *Lion* were still militant and could police them and the flagship. The majority on

Sandwich was for giving up. Their delegate, William Gregory, was placed in the embarrassing situation of having to admit this to his colleagues. He submitted lamely that the mother ship should stay with her weakest ones. Gregory was overheard talking with an American merchant captain about wanting to visit Ireland and America.

When the Nassaus were told off for Cromarty Firth, their spokesman replied, "No! We'll be damned if we leave old England no matter what happens to us!"

There is no record of a ship's company opting for Shannon.

The provisional plan called for *Inflexible, Hound, Proserpine* and little *Comet* to sail for the New Colony.

John Blake, tending to business while Parker showed the red flag up and down the blockade line, tried to synthesize the wishes of the ships' companies and produce a sailing order that made sense. He was having difficulties with his own ship, *Inflexible,* the reddest of them all. Six of his men petitioned Blake to put them ashore; they wanted nothing more to do with the cause. Had Blake been willing, it was now almost impossible to get ashore. The north bank of the river and the convenient Leigh sands were closely patrolled by volunteers and light cavalry. The active hostility of the populace seemed general.

Yet some Nore seamen did go ashore right under the muzzle of Lord Keith's battery on the Isle of Grain. A farmer reported to Sheerness that they had stolen his sheep. Seaman McCann plundered a barge of flour. Some men from *Monmouth* appropriated the catch from a fishing smack. The *Repulse* company witnessed the theft and wrote to the *Monmouth* committee, "We humbly beg that you will endeavor to find out the perpetrators of the atrocious act." The Monmouths tried the men and flogged them, and *Repulse* wrote in gratitude for prompt justice upon "those wretches which ought to be exterminated from the face of the earth." Discipline was breaking down. Brotherly love was being tried.

Apprehensive men tried to stow away in the captive fleet of merchant ships, which now numbered about 150. The lower deck of the traders had arrived generally friendly to the naval seamen, but that cordiality was at an end. Civilian hands vied with their officers in throwing off navy men who sneaked aboard. Adding to John Blake's urgent lists of cares (*"Director* must have five tons of water") came protests from merchant captains who were running out of food and water.

The company of *Sandwich* was eating short rations of biscuit and small, monotonous hunks of salt pork. The water was rank and so scarce that two sentinels were posted at the butts to conserve it.

President Parker honored the smallest vessel of his command with an official visit. The *Comet* log says:

> At 4 o'clock come on board the President of the Committee of Delegates of the Fleet attended by numerous Procession of Boats with Colours flying and Band playing Martial and Loyal tunes the time he remained on board. Regaled him & the Boats Crew with Bread & Cheese & small grog, having no small Beer on board. Mr. Parker, after reading several Papers & Instructions to the Ships Company left the Ship, forming a regular Procession of Boats, Drums Beating etc.

Lieutenant Caley of *Comet* was very ill. The committee asked the delegates to permit the officer to go ashore. They agreed. The Comets gave their first lieutenant a written testimonial.

> The ships Company in general wish to convince you how much they are satisfied with your humane Conduct towards them during the time they had the honor to sail with you.
> They have no other way of expressing their Sentiments on that head than by assuring you that there is no man in His Majesty's Service they would sooner receive as an Officer than yourself. If his Majesty should at any future time have occasion for their Services, they wish you all the Comforts this World can afford you.
> In the Name of the Ship's Company
> THE COMMITTEE OF H.M.S. *Comet*   9 June 1797

A post captain wrote Lord Spencer, offering to kill Parker: "I have so completely made up my mind to the result of the assassination that your Lordship can be assured that I will be happy in performing that which appears to me of such public advantage." It was one of the few suggestions from beached officers that Spencer turned down.

Lieutenant Buller of *Standard* asked some Lions what they would do when the business broke up. "Well, we'd rather go ashore, than go abroad," said one. William Bray, sailing master of *Sandwich,* encountered Delegate Peter Holding on the quarterdeck watch.

"What are you going to do now?" Bray asked.

"We shall take the ships to sea," said Holding.

"All the buoys are taken away. We will get all the ships on shore before you get down the Channel."

"We will get on shore as well as we can and save our lives."

"If they catch you on shore, every soul of you will be hanged."

"We can go with the ships to many islands I know."

Bray said, "It will be peace soon with all Europe, and each power will send out squadrons after you and take you up as pirates and hang you without mercy."

Bray let this sink in, then asked, "Are you married?"

"Yes, I have a wife and three children at Lynn."

"How can you go and leave your wife and children to starve? Certainly they will perish in the streets."

Holding said, "We have embarked in this glorious cause and we will go through with it."

The President of the Fleet returned from his exhaustive naval review and met with Blake and the central committee. They had boiled down the five-division plebiscite to something more practical for tomorrow's momentous 2 o'clock action deadline. They issued the order that night:

Memo.

It is determined by the Delegates of the Whole Fleet to go & cruise off the Texel, to see if the Dutch Fleet is out and Cromarty in the North of Scotland is appointed for the place of rendezvous.

All who wish to desert the Cause to be left in the Sandwich Down the Queen's Channel.

By Order of the Delegates of the Whole Fleet on board H.M.S Sandwich 9th June 1797

Ultimatum day, Saturday the tenth, came without a reply from his Majesty. At two P.M. the sailing order would be in force unless the government sent a counterproposal to the fleet. At many of the internal ships' committee meetings, which were held before the fleet parliament convened, a petition to the government drawn up by the Montagus was introduced. The signers agreed to abide by existing wages and bounties and would return to duty if dilapidated ships were docked and repaired, objectionable officers removed, and no seamen were charged with treason. The formula was approved by the committees of *Agamemnon, Lion, Standard* and *Inflexible*. When it was presented to the fleet delegates, President Parker endorsed it. The scribes began writing multiple copies.

John Blake was redistributing ships' stores to reach ten-week cruising capability. *Comet*'s purser broached a cask of No. 82 rum and gave the ship's committee two gallons to "make grog for strange Boats Crews." There was much ship-visiting. Blake, beset by hungry and thirsty howls from the 200-odd detained commercial vessels, made a motion that ships held five days or more be liberated, and the delegates passed it. Parker's executive order excepted navy victualing ships. A welter of cargo carriers departed the Great Nore for London in a crash and din of fouled ground tackle, tangled yards, collisions and screams and imprecations hurled upon the men-of-wars-men. The Sheerness telegrapher was able to tell London THAMES REOPENED, although scores of captive vessels remained at the Nore.

On several naval ships awaiting the oncoming signal to sail, forecastle boards were trying men for "perjury," which meant violating their oaths to the cause. On *Monmouth,* punishments meted out to "perjurers" took on the scale of those inflicted by deposed officers. Several mates and a marine sergeant received three dozen strokes, heads were shaved, and a midshipman was lashed twenty-four times. The committee of *Brilliant* punished four men for deriding the delegates. In other companies first-and-cudgel fighting expressed policy differences.

The fleet sat down to dinner. There were unhappy messes with puffed eyes and bloody noses, swollen jaws and broken fists. From belowdecks came the moans of men with backs like bloody washboards, the "perjurers." Among them were boatswains' mates who had stood behind a hundred men crucified on the grates, had swept the cat back full, and laid it on ten thousand times. The only thing that could be done for them was the thing done for their victims, to rub salt in the wounds. There was no other antiseptic in the King's navy.

After the noon meal the President of the Delegates of the whole Fleet of his Majesty's Navy in the River Medway & the Buoy of the Nore came out of the great cabin of H.M.S. *Sandwich.* A sailing breeze was blowing and the afternoon was clear. Parker could see Sheerness. There were no boats approaching the Nore.

"All hands!"

The boatswains tooted into the hatchways. The marine drummers dinned general quarters. A delegate-officer reported to Parker, "The ship is in every respect ready for sea." Men climbed to the foretop yard of the parliament ship prepared to slack the fore-topsail as a signal of departure and then set it as the first sail to catch the breeze for ports and fates unknown.

"Is the signal gun shotted?"

"Yes, Mr. Parker."

"Well then, fire."

As the departure gun resounded, some ships let the topsail go and a ragged salvo answered Parker, acknowledging his order to weigh anchor. Quartermaster Hockless, who claimed he could navigate the Queen's Channel without buoys, stood by Parker.

"Mr. Hockless, you may proceed to take the ship to sea."

The ship's boys held their nippers ready to bend on the messenger rope to the great anchor hawser, but their bare feet on the messenger felt no strain from the capstans two decks below. From the main hatch came the noise of fierce argument in the lower gun deck.

Not a capstan turned in the Great Nore. Some did not have enough manpower. Militant companies able to produce capstan crews held back, unwilling to move without *Sandwich* and the others.

In a few minutes it was over. Everyone recognized that the fleet was not going to sea. The scraps of fore-topsails were handed and furled, the masts and spars stood gaunt, and the whistles piped return to at-anchor routines.

Lieutenant Robb, senior officer on *Leopard,* moved surreptitiously between decks looking for men to help him retake the ship and escape from the Nore. He recruited boatswain's mate Thomas Norman, who had demonstrated his loyalty in the tussle for the helm for which he had been flogged by the committee. Norman named men who had expressed private sympathy with him. Quartermaster James Slater joined the counter-mutiny and became its forecastle leader. Others abjured their oaths of loyalty to the cause and came into the secret cell. They made a plan for seizure when the right moment came. Unknowingly, they enlisted a man loyal to the ship's committee.

From Sheerness came a boat toward *Sandwich,* the sullen mutiny flagship. Captain John Knight had returned from London. He came aboard and met with the delegates. Although he bore an absolute rejection of their latest demands, the "final answer" they had demanded of the King, Knight entered into another undertaking with the mutineers. President Parker signed a "commission" to Captain Knight to proceed to London and offer peace on a single condition:

—The delegates would accept the Royal Pardon if undesirable officers were not returned to the ships.

The circle had turned full. The Nore delegates had first met to support the Spithead demands and when they proved to include removal of abusive officers, they wanted the same. Now they stripped off all subsequent demands and asked only that the officers go. But Black Dick Howe and the government had been too cagey to put anything in writing about expelling officers. There was no precedent.

A buzz went around the anchorage that negotiations were opening at last. The rumor became inflated to pathetic size. The *Comet* logkeeper noted, "Captain Knight's promising [on board the *Sandwich*] our grievances being redressed by His Majesty."

As Knight's boat was pulling ashore, *Sandwich* lowered her red flag and hoisted the St. George's ensign and the Union Jack. Every ship in the fleet followed suit. There was joy in Sheerness. The telegrapher winged the great news to Barrow Hill and Tong and it clicked at record speed up the Thames valley to the Admiralty office. But the flag change did not mean surrender. It was the delegates' act of cordiality toward men of good intent on the other side.

The Admiralty sent a telegraph signal to the Downs ordering out gunboats to stop and search an outbound Danish ship in which Parker was rumored to be making his escape. The Dane proved exclusively full of Danes. President Parker was still at the Great Nore, concerned with a round of ship visits, paying special attention to demoralized companies. Around four o'clock he boarded *Ardent* with a party that included *Leopard's* two delegates. Concurrently there was a forecastle meeting on *Leopard*, attended by two hundred men who were listening to readings by Secretary William Ross, delivered in his singular fashion from the back of the crowd. This did not confer anonymity on a committeeman as conspicuous as he, but he held to it as though he were the tongue of a tongueless mass. The secretary read the revenge resolution of the London merchants and the Royal Pardon, which the delegates considered as "altogether a take-in."

In this situation, with the mutinous faction gathered in one lump and their delegates away, Lieutenant Robb decided to let loose his counter-mutiny. Scattered about the ship, there were about a hundred Leopards absent from the meeting out of disinclination or duty and Robb expected them to join the coup. But the delegates' spy betrayed the take-over plot.

The ship's committeemen ordered all hands turned up. The captain's clerk went to the wardroom and told the junior officers, "I think the business is going to begin. It has come to a crisis." The officers went to the quarterdeck.

Lieutenant Robb trumpeted, "Set fore-topsail!"

From high above came a shout, "I'll blow the brains out of any man that comes up to loose the sails." They looked up. Foretopman Alexander Lawson, one of the committee, was on the top yard with several other seamen.

The marine lieutenant handed a firelock to the quartermaster, who fired two shots at Lawson. Others started shooting at the foretop. Lawson and one of his party loosed a few ineffective pistol balls at the deck, according to later testimony, which Lawson denied. He had witnesses who stated that he was not armed. Loyalist Quartermaster Slater took a loaded pistol and went up the fore shrouds. Lawson shouted down, "You bugger, I'll kill you!" Slater kept on going up, cocking his pistol. Lawson and his crew ceased resistance. They cast off gaskets and the sail billowed down on the restraining clew lines, buntlines and slablines; these were let go and, below on the deck, seamen at the sheets and braces trimmed the canvas. The fore-topsail drew. H.M.S. *Leopard* was ready to weigh anchor.

But a scrimmage still raged on *Leopard*'s deck between mutineers, officers and marines, Committeeman Joseph Fearon grabbed a boathook to enter the fray and was shot down by the marine lieutenant. A midshipman fell at Robb's side. Committeeman John Habbigan ran to the color chest, got out a Spanish jack and raised it to the mizzenpeak, a signal for the ship's boats to return. "You are not to raise that flag unless ordered to!" a midshipman shrieked. The *Leopard* delegates, already alarmed by the shots, rapidly returned to the ship. By the time they got there the mutiny was over. Quartermasters were at the gangway with leg-irons, and they were sent below to join the ship's committee in the prisoners' bay that they had been using as mutiny headquarters.

Robb struck the red flag, raised the loyal standard, cut away anchor at 5 P.M.* and started upriver for Gravesend. He had no pilot on board and it was a gray and showery day. There was a loud boom and the delegates' ships opened up on *Leopard*. She ran the gauntlet of anchored vessels, edging away from the fire, trying to lose herself in the wet.

Several *Standard* gun crews fired rounds at the drifting ship. "Stand fast guns!" Lieutenant Buller trumpeted. "Stand fast, you hear!" came the endorsement of Delegates Holdsworth and Freeman. The gunners stepped away.

The first lieutenant invaded the empty moment of the excitement.

---

* As entered in the *Comet* log.

"My lads! You see the *Leopard* is getting away. What's the reason we can't follow? What say you now, my brave fellows?"

The captain's coxswain, half crazy with excitement, slapped Buller on the back and screeched, "Never fear, Mr. Buller! We'll get her up!" Some of the crew started laughing.

Captain Parr cried, "If you please, Mr. Buller! Get her under way! Follow the *Leopard!*"

"Oh, no, you don't!" The delegates forced the captain into his cabin and took Buller below to the wardroom. Holdsworth said, "Mr. Buller, I will not give over this ship. I will not entrust my life to any man, or set of men, until the ship's company has the King's pardon." They brought the remaining officers into the wardroom and retired to the perpetual committee meeting behind tarpaulins on the sweltering half deck.

Sporadic fire was still ranging toward *Leopard* as she shrank close to the northern shoals. She thudded to a stop on the Leigh sands, still within range of some vessels. A "brisk fire" riddled her sails and stripped off rigging. English gunners had suddenly adopted the French style of cutting away top hamper, leaving a sound hull to capture. Not a man on *Leopard* was injured.

Lieutenant Robb started kedging off *Leopard*. All hands fell to, including Committeeman Welch, who slipped out of confinement. Quartermaster Slater, leader of the loyalist coup, was in charge of the kedging boat. He took the enormous bower anchor into it and noticed getting a most willing hand from John Habbigan, one of the ship's committee. They took the anchor into the navigable Channel and heaved it in. When the boat returned, Habbigan was put in chains. The human moloch leaned on the capstan bars and pulled the ship off the shoal. Robb sailed the *Leopard* out of gun range.

Earlier in the afternoon, unknown to the delegates, the ship's company of *Repulse* had surrendered to their first lieutenant. When *Leopard* began her break for freedom, he ordered his pilot to take *Repulse* into the Medway.

"The tide is against us."

"Take her anyway."

Repulse got under way and the fleet opened heavy fire on her. According to two witnesses, Parker left *Sandwich* shouting, "I'll go aboard the *Director,* get a spring on her cable. If my father was aboard that ship," he cried, pointing to *Repulse,* "I'd blow her to hell, for that's where she belongs!"

The president boarded Bligh's ship and ordered the company to let go the anchor cable and move in beside *Repulse*. The Directors refused to comply with his order. He called for a boat to go to *Repulse* under a white flag. They would not give him a boat.

Now, as the pilot had warned, *Repulse* ran upon the Middle-ground Shoal and lay helpless before the delegates' guns. *Sandwich* happened to lie stern-to the stranded ship. Delegate Gregory went below and knocked out an after bulkhead to train a cannon on *Repulse*. People restrained him.

Director's militants began working several guns against *Repulse*. President Parker left the ship and went to *Monmouth,* which was also pounding at *Repulse*. Later he was accused of joining a gun crew in firing several rounds. The firing went on for an hour, while *Repulse* struggled to pull off the shoal. Her impromptu commander ran her lower-deck guns over the side and floated off. Lieut. George Augustus Delanoe lost a leg in the barrage. No one else was injured and the only damage was to canvas and cordage. *Repulse* reached safety in the Medway.

After putting down a counter-mutiny that day and confining their officers, the Standards consulted each other again and resolved to ask Captain Parr to help them find a solution. They invited him to the mast and Delegate Holdsworth opened the wardroom door and said to the officers he was detaining there, "Gentlemen, you may go wherever you please in any part of the ship. I hope everything will soon be settled." They went out on deck. The red flag was down and blue was snapping at the main. Commercial traffic was moving out of the Nore. Captain Parr, hoping to win over his irresolute crew completely, drafted a letter to the Admiralty, requesting their arrears in pay and the King's pardon. He read this to the company and gave the signature as "Captain Thomas Parr, H.M.S. *Standard,* under my command." A delegate said, "I don't call this ship under your command," and the phrase was deleted.

At 11:30, H.M.S. *Ardent* slipped her cable and made for Sheerness. The *Comet* log says: "Several ships fired at her which she returned." *Ardent* made the Medway almost unharmed.

That night one of the Duke of Portland's men attended the meeting of a democratic society in London, at which Horne Tooke was present. The spy's report gives an impression of the mood in anti-government circles as the tide set against the rising at the Nore.

"Horne Tooke and Honest Men," the chairman opened, according to the agent. "May the sailors prove that they are men and will not be lashed or goaded. I heard yesterday that the ship Parker is on board would be between two fires, and there was not choice to the crew, without they submitted, but to be blown up in the air or sunk in the water—horrid fate for oppressed men.

"Fearful times. It will be serious indeed if there is a want of fresh water at Sheerness. Heaven keep the garrison from a serious distemper. These may be the beginning of sorrows, but who can say what will end them? Surely the beacons being destroyed may be as much inconvenience to one side as the other. As the navy affair had a sudden rise, perhaps some other matters may have [as] sudden a fall."

Down the Norwich road into Colchester limped a haggard and ruined seaman, Isaac Bowstead, sixty, late of H.M.S. *Belliqueux,* now discharged unfit for service from hospital at Yarmouth. He was raving drunk as he tramped into the market square on Saturday night, walking toward his messmates at the Nore. "I can speak the dead languages as well as any man!" he declared to the people. "Now gather round and damn the King and country!" This had the opposite effect to that of gathering a crowd. He howled across the bare cobbles, "Damn the King! Damn the country! This town should be burned to the ground!" As Mayor William Mason and the constables carried him off, the ancient mariner croaked, "Listen to me! I led the mutiny on the *Culloden!*"

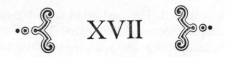

XVII

The White Flag

It is almost a definition of a gentleman to say that he is one who never inflicts pain.

—JOHN HENRY CARDINAL NEWMAN (B. A. Oxon 1820)
The Idea of a University Defined, 1873

THE SUN came up bright at the Great Nore, promising a hot Sunday, the sort that captains sometimes declared a "ropeyarn day" in which the people could loaf most of the time after divine services. But this was no such lazy Sunday. The delegates took assignments to visit recanting companies to keep them in line. There were twenty ships still holding out. Merchantmen demanded food, although they were free to leave. Many were reluctant to sail out in an unmarked lane. The seamen's congress passed a curious resolution to remind those on shore and in London that they were waiting for Captain Knight to return with an answer to the reduced demand: they ordered the flags on all ships to be lowered to half mast. The telegraph reported this to Whitehall, where nobody understood why it was done.

Outbound neutral ships released by the delegates were stopped and searched by cutter in the North Sea. The Admiralty was determined that deserters and mutiny leaders should not escape. Lord Keith went through surrendered ships, gathering incriminating documents for use in trying mutineers. Although *Leopard* had voluntarily escaped, Keith was determined to arraign her committeemen and delegates. A lot of men did not want to be regarded as mutineers. Some of them revolted on the *Hound* sloop, but were put down by delegates' men, who sent thirty "perjurers" to be confined on *Sandwich.* On the sloop *Swan,* the delegates piped up the crew and ordered men true to the cause to go to starboard and men opposed, to the larboard. The majority of feet voted for the right. The "King's party" was put in boats and forbidden to return aboard. The castaways feared gunning from both sides if they attempted to make Sheerness. They rowed to *Isis* and hove to some distance from her side, when they saw that a wild general fray was taking place aboard the frigate, the officers and marines pitted against most of the ship's company. In the fight three men were killed. The delegates' party won the fight on *Isis,* and the *Swan* loyalists sadly rowed away, looking for asylum. No merchant-man would have them.

The *Sandwich* internal committee issued a general appeal for peace and order while awaiting Captain Knight. The Inflexibles retained the character of their name: 337 men took a renewed oath of fidelity to the cause that Sunday morning. Marine Sergeant Joseph Morris wistfully petitioned the delegates to be permitted to go ashore and apply for pardon. He was a ten-year man, and if he remained on a proscribed ship his wife and child would lose their sustenance and his death benefits. There is no record of what the delegates did about the sergeant, but evidently they would not take an individual resignation when whole ships' companies wanted out.

At the outer end of the Queen's Channel, a sailboat full of Nore seamen under full press of canvas ran past a revenue cutter so smartly not a shot was laid on her. The sail headed for France. The telegraph blinked steadily between Sheerness and the Downs on the subject of ships' boats. The anchorage looked like a regatta, as seamen passed back and forth. Fearing that a large-scale escape to France in boats was imminent, Lord Keith sent Lieut. Philip Justice of *Sandwich* pell-mell to Great Yarmouth to find more gunboats to stopper the channel.

Captain John Wood of *Hound* believed the moment was ripe to remind his company of the baneful literature from Westminster. He went ashore, collected specimens and read his people the condemnations of the King, the Commons and the countinghouses. He was interrupted by the arrival of a boatload of delegates led by Thomas Appleyard, captain of the maintop in *Sandwich*. Appleyard took over the attentions of the company. "Why did you let Captain Wood go ashore without permission of the President of the Fleet?" he demanded.

Appleyard took the pardon print out of the captain's hand. "This is a pack of flummery," he said. "We have wagonloads of these on board the *Sandwich*." This implication—that the delegates, in their superior wisdom, were withholding delusive literature from the men—did not register well with the Hounds. Appleyard cited the clause excepting ringleaders from pardon. "Why, this part will hang you all! You have nothing to do but stick true to the cause you embarked

in and we'll bring you through it!" The Hounds stared silently at him.
That shivered Appleyard's timbers. He bellowed, "You're a set of
damned rascals, led by your nose by your captain!" He stalked to the
gangway. "I'll go back to the *Sandwich* and they'll sink you!" declared the undiplomatic envoy. Seaman John Driscoll of *Hound*
jumped off a gun and struck the delegate. Appleyard went down to
the boat, shouting threats of firing on the Hounds. "You cowardly
rascals . . . that swore to be true . . . and now you run. . . ."

Lord Spencer wrote privately to Adam Duncan. "I have no doubt
of their giving way soon, but perhaps not without some bloodshed.
Some examples must be made for the good of the service. . . ." But
he warned the admiral, "I fear from some hints I have received . . .
that you have now got with you one or two ships which contain a good
deal of mischief. If our enemy was only a little more active, it would
be more likely to keep us right than anything else."

At Plymouth on this beautiful Sunday afternoon a marine drummer
boy was daydreaming under a furze bush in Stonehouse Hill above the
victualing yard when he spied some odd behavior. A recent Irish
recruit, a lawyer named Lee, came up the hill leading a file of marines.
Lee placed a book on the grass and called on a man to step forward
and lift it. As the marine complied, the Irishman swore him to
secrecy on something that would be revealed to him later in the
backroom of a public house called The Long Room. Lee directed
the man to place the book on the ground exactly where he found it
and proceeded to swear in others.

The drummer boy crept away and told his story to Sergeant
Andrew Gilborn, who hid in the bushes on Stonehouse Hill until the
ceremony was finished. Gilborn went to the officers' mess and called
his colonel from dinner. The commandant armed his officers and
had general assembly sounded. "Ground arms," howled the sergeant
major. "Three paces forward." The NCOs gathered up the muskets.
Gilborn identified four men as the main plotters: Lee, Branham,
Coffee and McGinnis, all under thirty, all recently sworn into the
corps, and all Irish.

Under interrogation, Lee stated that he was a member of the United
Irishmen. His plan was to fire the powder magazines at the barracks
and Keyham Point, set the French prisoners free, and "do everything
in their power to overthrow the government." He claimed that the
marine coup was to be assisted by the 58th Regiment and the crews of
two men-of-war in the harbor. Lee said he had read Paine's *Age of*

Reason. Here was the summer's first attempt at mutiny for outright political reasons. It seemed unconnected with the seamen's cause. Preparations were made for executing Lee and his confederates as soon as a military court could be assembled.

In London, Captain Knight waited at the Admiralty office with his "commission" from the Nore delegates to offer his Majesty immediate return to duty on condition that obnoxious officers were relieved and that no one would be punished for the stand-out. The proposal was to be heard by the privy council that evening. In the afternoon, Lord Spencer was gratified to receive an express from Duncan that both the squadrons of Sir Roger Curtis and the Russian admiral, Makaroff, had joined him. The Scotsman had formed them in a line and led them past the Texel gate where "they had seen the Dutch fleet." What they saw still heavily outweighed the British counterinvasion force, even though Duncan's squadron now consisted of eleven two-deckers, and a half dozen auxiliaries. President Parker had more guns than that.

The Russian squadron was England's last ally still in the field on land or sea. Among the Russian admirals was a Scot named Tate. Duncan was surprised that the Czar's ships, long out of the breaming yard and without copper on their bottoms, could outsail his. "I am the first British admiral that ever was ordered on service with foreigners only," he complained.

It was a balmy evening in London. Portland's spy was attending a meeting of reformers, all of whom were aware that someone in the room was reporting to his grace. The talk was full of quaint deceits and quips for his benefit. Discussing the governmental crisis and Foreign Secretary Grenville's foresworn temptation to resign and overturn Pitt, a man said, "I need not read Lord Grenville's answer. I know without his declaration that he meant to keep his place." Another remarked, "I heard at the last [London Corresponding Society] meeting, Mr. Horne Tooke was suffered to speak but little. I was glad to hear it, for his enemies would be too much for him in case a spy of good repute like Upton had tickled the ear of Portland, Loughborough or Dundas."

His Majesty's privy council also met and considered the Nore proposal briefly. They handed down their decision and Captain Knight dashed off a breathless night express to his first officer on *Montagu:*

I this moment returned to my house from the Council Chamber who with his Majesty and the people at large are resolved not to accept the proposals I was authorized to make, as nothing short of unconditional submission & trusting to the Generosity of a benevolent Sovereign will now after the late shocking atrocious Crimes have been committed will be listened to. If these terms are acceptable to the Ships or even to the *Montagu,* I recommend their making one early acquainted with it, who knowing them also know how to make a proper distinction. . . . This goes by Mr. Butler, Lieut. of the *Standard.* . . . Peace is talked of—best respects to your shipmates & let me know the state of things as early as possible.

Monday morning there were only two red flags at the Nore, apparently on *Inflexible* and *Montagu. Agamemnon* was missing. She had slipped into Sheerness at night. The delegates of the fleet convened on *Sandwich,* a ship now generally hostile to them. Richard Parker was reelected President of the Fleet, the post he had now held four weeks. John Blake proposed to release all officer hostages and let them go ashore. The motion was carried. Then, in view of the threatening behavior of the *Sandwich* people, the delegates voted to take the meeting flag to *Montagu,* Captain Knight's ship. An informer sent word ashore to Lord Keith that Parker and the delegates intended to escape to sea in *Pylades.* The word was telegraphed to the Downs, which dispatched *Revolutionnaire,* 38, *Melampus,* 36, *Virginie,* 40, and *Ariadne,* 24, to lay in wait at the Channel's mouth for the 16-gun *Pylades.*

At noon the answer to the delegates' last entreaty to London arrived in Sheerness, brought by Evan Nepean, Secretary of the Admiralty, Sir Thomas Pasley, Captain John Knight and Mr. Canant, the magistrate of Great Marlborough Street, London. Before answering, the assembled whitewigs determined which vessels were still laying at the Great Nore and which had abandoned the mutiny. Penmen worked up copies of the government's reply for each ship. The documents were ready at three and Sir Thomas Pasley set out to read the proclamation on each vessel.

The government made no concessions.

It required unconditional surrender. The Admiralty would neither discharge commissioned officers nor forgive elected ones.

The statement said that after the ships' companies had submitted without terms, "the question of recommending them or any of them for his Majesty's pardon rests with the Discretion of the Board." An Act of Parliament had declared the crews of all mutinous vessels had forfeited their wages and prize money and would take a special deed to restore them to a ship. The legislature had moreover pronounced by law an anathema on certain of his Majesty's ships' companies by name and had given a parallel list of those which had been "discharged" by virtue of abandoning the mutiny. However, being on the discharged list did not absolve any seamen from prosecution for mutiny:

DISCHARGED	CONDEMNED	CONDEMNED
Agamemnon	*Sandwich*	*Grampus*
Leopard	*Montagu*	*Proserpine*
Isis	*Director*	*Brilliant*
Vestal	*Inflexible*	*Iris*
	Monmouth	*Champion*
TO BE PAID	*Belliqueux*	*Comet*
Ardent	*Standard*	*Tisiphone*
Repulse	*Lion*	*Pylades*
	Nassau	*Swan*
	Inspector	

As the flat rejection of their last hopes was heard, a dozen ships ran the bloody flag of defiance aloft again. This started a round of yard rope humor. The *Comet* watchkeeper noted a quarter of beef hanging under the Union Jack on the Sheerness garrison flagpole. *Monmouth* hoisted an empty bread bag to her mizzen peak.

Pylades stopped a galliot "richly laden with bale goods etc etc from London bound to Dieppe in France," according to the *Comet* log. British sailors may have been expected to whip France but British merchants were not neglecting French business.

The Standards received a reply to the letter Captain Parr had sent on their behalf. It expressed their lordships' "approbation at your intention of returning to duty, but you must give up the command of the ship to the officers unconditionally."

There was no mention of royal pardon for all or for any. Captain Parr urged them to submit. His crew was in "a violent agitated state" about holding on or surrendering. It was now evident that submission meant that some of the Standards would hang, certainly the three bold delegates, Wallis, Holdsworth and Freeman, among them. Captain Parr and Lieutenant Buller, having been aboard all the time, would have a list of other leading men. Now the question among five hundred men of H.M.S. *Standard,* and in all the companies, was whether they would sacrifice their leaders or continue to resist in the hope of bringing the government to terms as was done at Spithead.

Tuesday was another fair day in southern England. In the morning the red flags were gone from the Nore. All the ships wore blue and *Sandwich* had a huge Union Jack at her maintop. At nine the escaped ships in the Medway started upriver on the tide for Gravesend. The delegates realigned their ships to close gaps left by the departed.

On H.M.S. *Standard,* Lieutenant Buller shouted to the crew. "You have a choice to give over to the officers or put the officers ashore. Anyone found aboard this ship from now is a rebel!"

A loyalist seaman named Higgs cried, "Those for giving up the ship, hold up your hands!"

Many hands were raised.

"Those for going on!" The show of hands seemed about even.

Committeeman Joseph Hudson was resigned. "We may as well go up to Gravesend, for if we are to be hanged, it is as well at first as at last."

Another delegate was unwilling to surrender. Freeman said, "But, can't we go on board the *Lion*?" Part of the crew sang back, "No!" The fleet parliament was blowing toward a lee shore.

As the Standards vacillated, Thomas Cheeseman, captain of the forecastle, a ship's committeeman, asked them if they would rather go to sea. Most men were willing, but none spoke for going to France. Cheeseman then reported to Captain Parr and offered to testify against his messmates. He was accepted and promised a pardon.

Lieutenant Buller promptly asserted his authority. He raised his trumpet and the men went to stations.

"All hands!" The signal officer went to the flag locker, the mates went to their places with their canes and starters, the orders rang out, and the men obeyed. *Standard* sailed in perfect discipline to Gravesend, where the gunners wormed the rounds and powder bags from their guns, cleaned the barrels and tapped tompions into the muzzles. The crew surrendered small arms and returned keys.

When at anchor in loyal grounds, Captain Parr confined his people belowdeck and asked Sir Erasmus Gower what the Admiralty now wished done. He was told to draw up charges against the leading mutineers and hand them over to the provost marshal. Captain Parr took the list to the main hatch and shouted the names down into the gloom.

"William Holdsworth."

"Aye, aye, sir." The delegate came up, and his hands were gyved behind his back.

"William Wallis."

From the orlop came the shout "Here I come!" and a shot. The chief mutineer of *Standard* had put a pistol to his head and killed himself.

Back at the Nore, Richard Parker addressed the Sandwiches, recommending submission, and asked, "Are you willing to accept his Majesty's pardon?"

"Aye!"

"Hands to lower a boat," Parker called.

None came forth.

"Come, hands ahoy to lower a b——"

He went toward a boat in the center gangway. Men barred his way. They were not going to compound their felonies under the new Act of Parliament by giving "aid, comfort, assistance, or encouragement whatsoever, to any person concerned with mutinous and treasonable proceedings." Parker made no further attempt to leave.

Next to *Comet,* the smallest vessel present was the cutter *Ranger,* belonging to the North Sea fleet. She had not dared disobey the Great Yarmouth sailing orders of the big two-deckers and she had been sitting prisoner to them ever since, except when loaded with mutineers for her reconnaissance of the missing buoys. Now it was getting late. The Rangers smuggled an almost tearful appeal to Admiral Buckner to recognize their virtue and their inability to escape.

Captain Henry Duncan of *Comet,* after disclaiming command responsibility, had remained on board in amicable circumstances ever since the little fireship had arrived. He requested permission to go ashore. The fleet delegates let him go under a white flag to avoid being fired on by the fort.

Several more ships left the anchorage for Gravesend.

The next morning, Wednesday 14 June, the *Comet* logkeeper wrote "A.M. Light Airs & Fair. Washed the ship throughout." It was the last entry in the mutineer log of H.M.S. fire ship *Comet.* She surrendered that morning in a cleanly state. One of her delegates, John Watts, escaped. His name does not appear in the ship's list of delegates in the Cumby MS, but Captain Duncan furnished Admiralty man-hunters with a detailed physical description of Watts:

Five ft 6½ inches high—with black short hair and dark swarthy complexion—a large cut over his left eye—with large white teeth and great openings between them—generally wore a blue greatcoat with blue pantaloons, trouzers and seems of the same trimed with white edgings.

Lord Keith made rounds to take surrenders. He boarded *Pylades,* the delegates' guard ship, and three times called for unconditional surrender. The men came aft and handed over Mutineer-Captain Charles MacCarthy and their delegates. Keith went to *Brilliant* and came off with its surrender and its delegates. The Champions bowed to his lordship and gave up their leader James Tippett, captain of the foretop.

First Lieutenant Charles Bullen reclaimed *Monmouth* and raised loyal flags. Mutineer-Captain William Vance refused to give up the ship, and the seamen rejected orders to make sail. Bullen got a loyal faction to cut the anchor cables and *Monmouth* drifted toward Sheerness fort. Under cover of the shore batteries, guard boats boarded the ship and removed Vance.

An Edinburgh girl, Ann Southerland, was one of the many women who stayed on board the mutinous vessels throughout the Nore affair. She had arrived in H.M.S. *Tisiphone* in April. This morning, as the ships fell one after another to Lord Keith's stentorian advance, she transferred to *Proserpine* with Seaman George Ricketts, an act hinting that one or both bore organizational guilt in the business. Or perhaps she was only loyal to her man; that has been going on longer than mutinies. Lord Keith's convoy bore down on *Proserpine*. Southerland and Ricketts hailed a smack, owned by William Everett, and ordered him to take them to *Inflexible*. The Inflexibles would not allow them on board, but they found asylum on *Belliqueux*. There they met John Smith, mutineer captain of *Proserpine*. At the moment, the surrendered company of *Proserpine* was looking high and low for Smith in order to give him to Lord Keith.

Boatman Everett passed *Belliqueux* and was hailed again. The Scottish girl, the mutineer-captain and the seaman got into the smack. Everett was frightened; it was plain that he was dealing with escaping leaders of the great mutiny. Parliament had made it a capital offense even to speak to a mutineer and had widely advertised the act. He tried to put the trio back aboard the two-decker, but they threatened to seize his boat.

"Stay here till high water, then proceed to France," he was instructed.

At night, the smack flitted through the warships and guard boats at the mouth of the Channel and by daylight, arrived in the Downs. The boatman claimed he didn't know the way to France, but would ask it of a passing lugger. It was a simple ruse. He whispered his story to the skipper, who sent his seamen bounding into the smack to overcome the two men and the girl. They were taken to prison in Chatham.

The next morning copies of a proclamation were exhibited in Sheerness and the Thames counties:

> WHEREAS, there is reason to believe that Richard Parker, now or late a supernumerary seaman on board his Majesty's ship *Sandwich,* at the Nore, and who stands charged with divers acts of mutiny, treason and rebellion, will attempt to make his escape from said ship, his Majesty, for the better discovering and apprehending of the said Richard Parker, is hereby pleased to promise a reward of five hundred pounds, to be paid by the lords commissioners of his Majesty's treasury, to any person or persons who shall apprehend, or cause the said Richard Parker to be apprehended, and brought before some of his Majesty's justices of the peace or chief magistrates of the county, town or place where he shall be apprehended, so that he may be dealt withal, and proceeded against according to law.

PORTLAND

The significance of this piece of Portlandiana seems to have escaped the Admiralty. Here was the Home Secretary, who did not have an indictment of Parker for any of the crimes mentioned, making a substantial bid for the offender in order to bring him under civil, not naval, justice. Portland was still hoping to establish a link between the reformers and the mutineers, despite the fact that his field agents had not yet found any such connection. Some counsel of prudence told Portland not to make charges against Samuel Whitbread, M.P.

Richard Parker was still on board *Sandwich* when the reward offer was circulated in the fleet. The president made no move about it except to politely request Third Lieutenant Nicholas Platt, the senior officer aboard, to return to confinement in the wardroom after several days' liberty.

Through the morning, Lord Keith and Sir Thomas Pasley cut ships out of the delegate line and carried their leaders off to captivity. They filled the *Aeolus* hulk to capacity with eighty Nore committeemen and taxed the extra jail quarters that had been arranged at Chatham. About fifty delegates were landed at Sheerness, where the chapel was already full of captives. Admiral Buckner put them in a receiving hulk with prest and quota men, the mutineers under special guard. He complained that they were near disaffected ships and could be liberated by their friends.

With the removal of more than half its membership, the fleet parliament dissolved and the remaining delegates returned to their ships. Parker could not control *Sandwich* any longer. He went below and released the two junior officers, Platt and Mott, from the wardroom. He was still carrying the keys of the flagship. The ex-President of the Fleet said, "Gentlemen, you may come upon the deck but do not talk to the people." He called the crew together and announced, "Mr. Mott is going ashore to bring off his Majesty's pardon. Are you willing that Mr. Mott should go?" They were, vociferously.

"Hoist the white flag!" a voice demanded.

"No!" said Parker. "There are three ships astern of us. If we change the colors they'll fire into us." *Inflexible, Director* and *Belliqueux,* three of the six bitter-enders, sat back of *Sandwich.*

Lieutenant Platt called out, "Don't change the colors until Lieutenant Mott returns." The people agreed to this. The big Union flag rippled at the maintop and blue at the mizzen during Mott's journey. He came back and gave the pardon to a purser's clerk to read.

Parker called out, "Are you willing to accept his Majesty's pardon and let the officers remain with us?"

"Yes."

"Hoist the surrender flag!" came the demand from the crowd.

Parker and the delegates warned again that they would be fired upon.

"Fire and be damned!" said the third lieutenant. Up went the white flag. There was no hostile reply from their neighbors. The parliament ship of the Great Nore mutiny had surrendered without violence.

"We will give three cheers," said Parker, a leader to the end. He joined them, full voice.

Lieutenant Platt said to Parker, "I'll have the keys to the magazine and the small arms." Parker handed them over, saying, "The charge of the ship I give to you as senior officer." Platt knew the Admiralty wanted surrendered ships moved promptly to Gravesend, but Parker warned him of retaliation from *Inflexible* if he lifted anchor. "I don't care," said the third lieutenant, giving his orders. "I suppose I shall soon be confined," said Parker. Platt was busy with Sailing Master Bray getting the ship under weigh. "I'll order you to a cabin and put sentinels over you," the lieutenant said casually as he attended to more urgent business.

The unemployed President of the Fleet went below, took a capstan bar, and helped walk the anchor out of the water. As *Sandwich* moved cautiously toward Gravesend, her commander consulted Fourth Lieutenant Mott about the Parker problem. The head mutineer was lounging on the quarterdeck as had become his habit. The two officers went over and Mott collared Parker. They took him, unresisting, to an officers' cubicle in the lower gun deck and put two marine sentinels on the door.

The *Sandwich's* retired ship's committee was still sitting in the great cabin, a congress without a constituency. Delegates William Gregory and George Taylor, the latter quite drunk, went to see William Bray,* the sailing master who had remained aboard serving the delegates and reporting to Buckner as well. Bray said to the delegates, "I hope everything is now settled and peace and quietness will ensue." He could hardly hear himself speak for the noise in the great ship. The rising at the Nore was declining in sad sprees, arguments, songs, and tears. Gregory grabbed Bray's hand and said, "If the buggers hadn't deserted me, I'd have carried my point." Bray went into the great cabin via the admiral's steerage door and said to the ship's committee, "My good lads, now that you have delivered the ship into our hands you may enjoy yourselves with a drop of grog. You may spend an hour sociably together and then retire like good fellows." The committee sent money out to buy mackerel from a fishing boat. Gregory said, "Some people got a little mellow" at the last supper. Bray ordered them into the outer steerage and locked them up. When they were taken out of the ship, a wailing woman and child clung to James Jones, an illiterate ship's corporal. His wife and infant had lived through the mutiny aboard *Sandwich*.

As the redeemed ships arrived at Gravesend, an Admiralty board sat in the dockyard looking for delegates and restoring order and command. Expelled officers fingered mutiny leaders for the board. A company of the West Yorkshire-militia was placed at their lordships' disposal to control the vessels while complete physical surrender was

---

* His spiritual affinity with the Vicar of Bray may be remarked.

accomplished. There was no consistency to it. One captain would name only a handful of mutiny principals, out of ignorance, honest doubt, or disinclination to lose many of his best hands. Another, full of pique, would wave fifty men off to confinement. There were several cases of mistaken identity. Innocent Thomas Brooks was arrested instead of Delegate Thomas Brooks from the same forecastle. Irishmen who looked alike, such as McCann and MacCarthy of *Sandwich,* were assigned each other's misdeeds.

Admiral Buckner used the last of daylight to telegraph the Admiralty the day's list of nine surrendered ships and wrote to ask instructions what to do "with a great quantity of flour taken out of a vessel at the Nore."

Lord Spencer jubilantly wrote Adam Duncan, "I have pleasure of announcing the approaching termination of the Mutiny at the Nore in as desirable a manner as could under all circumstances be wished. . . . In a few days we shall be able to send you out some ships and frigates, but there must be some purging and purifying first."

It was getting lonely at the Great Nore. The squadron officer-of-the-guard, a boatswain's mate, rowed the guard as usual that night, going round the handful of ships, receiving the hail of the gangway watch, "Boat ahoy!" and replying, "Guard boat." At that hour the week before, there had been 250 vessels of all description plashing and slatting there, with late songs and laughter, and eight bells sounding a giant dinning fugue. Now at midnight, under a sickle moon, the dwindling bells dinged mournfully aboard the last half dozen ships remaining loyal to the cause. *Inflexible,* the hard center of defiance, and *Inspector* were the only survivors of the original Nore insurgence. The others were Adam Duncan's ships, *Montagu, Belliqueux, Lion,* and *Director.*

Sandwich reached Gravesend in the middle of the night and Lieutenant Platt sent ashore to ask higher instructions on what to do with Richard Parker. Back they came. "Put him in the bilboes." The lieutenant went below, awakened his prisoner, and shackled his legs to an iron rod.

In the morning the drive against the diehard mutineers took up again. Captain Wood of *Hound* induced the surrender of *Montagu.* The night before, the company had restored command to the first lieutenant and confined their committee and delegates, but the ship was by no means quiet. Nor were *Belliqueux* and *Inflexible,* upon which orders rang out.

"Up ports!"

"Run out guns!"

Intransigent men, led by John Blake, seemed prepared to go down in blood and smoke.

But *Belliqueux* hauled in her guns and her company seized their delegates. *Inflexible* did not fire on the resigning ship. Wave after wave of condemnations by crown and Parliament had rolled over these ships; they had come near starvation; they were abandoned by all the rest. The last of the delegates' fleet was capitulating. They had food left for a day or so.

Lord Keith went to *Montagu* and faced the people.

"Under what terms are you bringing her in?"

An officer called, "Come, now, handsomely. 'Unconditional submission.' "

"Unconditional submission," rumbled uneasily from the men.

"Not good enough. Under what terms are you bringing her in?"

"Unconditional submission."

"Very good. Now once more."

"Unconditional submission."

"Captain, dismiss your men. Tell off the ringleaders."

In the morning a company of the West Yorks boarded *Sandwich* to remove ex-President Parker. Hands tied behind his back, he was downed in the stern thwart of a longboat, the coxswain above him pinning Parker's shoulders with his legs, militiamen pointing muskets at him, and a *Sandwich* lieutenant standing over him with a drawn sword. The boat stairs at Gravesend were surrounded by soldiers, and a dense crowd which reviled the prisoner. Parker called out, "Don't hoot me. It is not my fault. I will clear myself."

The militia marched him through the dockyard and stuck him in a dark cell under the garrison chapel for several hours. A one-eyed deputy Provost Marshal of Admiralty took charge of the prisoner and placed him in a carriage, surrounded by troops, who stomped out cadence and escorted the carriage to the Maidstone jail, the most secure place of confinement in the region.

As the morning wore on, Lord Keith took the surrender of *Lion* and *Inspector*. They moved off for Gravesend, leaving *Inflexible* and *Director* alone to represent the "present cause" and "final determinations." Delegate Joseph Cox read the King's proclamation again to the Directors and proclaimed, "It's no pardon at all."

John Blake and the central controllers of the mutiny on H.M.S.

Inflexible kept their wits to the end. The people broke into an in-
choate rush for the leaders. Blake and eleven henchmen made themselves invisible in the lower gun deck. The crew ran up the white
flag and waited for Lord Keith. Blake's party got out one of the lower
gun ports into three small boats and slipped out of the Nore in a
southeasterly direction.

The last stand was made by Bligh's *Director*. Lord Keith gave his
submission catechism, secured ten of her mutiny leaders and went
ashore before noon. He telegraphed the sea lords asking to be relieved.
"The mutiny is quite extinguished," he said.

On each ship Keith had instructed the senior officer present to
arrest "the ten most guilty men" and deliver them to Admiral Buckner. Ignorant of this, Buckner issued an arrest order of his own, asking the officers for a "minute state of the crews and vessels [and] so
far as possible the different degrees of guilt that may be imputed to
particular men, and stating the good conduct of such men . . . as
have evinced same."

These conflicting instructions started the wheel of justice spinning
at a distinct list to larboard. For instance, Blake and eleven of the
"guiltiest" Inflexibles were at large, and men of lesser degrees of
responsibility were picked to make up Keith's quota of ten.

When Captain Bligh returned to *Director,* he found that his first
lieutenant had followed Keith's order and sent ten men away in irons,
and had also obeyed Buckner's order and dispatched nineteen more.
William Bligh, a strict man with his inferiors, was not correspondingly
servile to his superiors. He protested hotly to Lord Keith, "I considered from the moment you went on board in my absence [and the
officers pointed out] ten most active men in the mutiny, that the remaining persons were to expect pardon," he said. Bligh was notified
a few days later by Buckner's replacement, Vice-Admiral Skeffington
Lutwidge, that thirty-one Directors were to be tried for mutiny. The
Bounty Bastard went and fought him too. "All but ten of my men
and two deserters have a faith that they will receive his Majesty's
pardon from the assurance given them," he declared. Admiral Lutwidge dropped the charges against the nineteen.

While *Inflexible* and *Director* were leaving the empty mutiny ground
at the Great Nore and trooping to Gravesend, Delegate John Blake's
escaping boats were rowing southeast in waters too shoal for the
intercepting frigates and gunboats stationed at the mouth of Queen's
Channel. The desperate boatmen headed directly for Whitstable, presumably to land and strike inland for a hideout. If they were seen from

a King's ship, the spyglass holder could be confident that twelve such obvious tars would not long go free in a countryside of aroused farmers and cavalry patrols.

Already Captain Ferris of *Inflexible* was giving their descriptions to be spread ashore:

—John Conner, 22, Ware, Herts
—John Edwards, 22, Liverpool
—Thomas Ryley, 30, Dublin, 5'5" ruddy, carroty hair, blue eyes, freckles
—President John Blake, 23, 5'6" dark brown complexion, long brown hair tied up, blue eyes, small mouth. Born County Clare
—James Ross, 26, Newcastle
—George Lewis Bryant, 26, Dublin
—Thomas Williams, 27, Bidfordhaven, Wales, pocked, deaf
—James Lloyd, 20
—Joseph Grant, 27, squints, Irish
—Joseph Turner, 19, Durham, black short hair, very dour look
—William Reed, 35, Shields
—Richard Ryan, 29, Waterford, Ireland, 5'½' tall, ruddy red hair, long large whiskers, freckled

Ten miles from the Nore, when the three boats had passed out of the frigates' sight and were about three miles off Whitstable, they turned hard right and stroked into the river Swale, almost doubling back toward Sheerness. They went four miles up the winding Swale to the fishermen's anchorage of the village of Faversham. There the dozen mutineers overcame two boys who were minding the sloop *Good Intent*. Without alarming the town and taking the only two witnesses with them, Blake's party emerged from the Swale in a boat unconnected with mutiny or King and made sail for Calais.

In appearance Portsmouth, seat of the original Spithead mutiny, was back to normal. The magistrates were trying to reduce the populations of the workhouse and poor rolls of women and children who had come to see husbands and fathers during the mutiny. Many ships had sailed without being paid, and Westminster's castaways crowded Portsmouth's charity.

H.M.S. *Prompte,* 28, came in from two years on the West Indies station, her people unaware of the mutinies. As they came up to the flagship *Royal William,* at Spithead, the Promptes turned out to give the customary three cheers. A lieutenant in a boat trumpeted, "You are not to cheer at all!"

"Why not!" shouted *Prompte*'s amazed first officer.

"There has been too much cheering already."

The Duke of Portland moved his Spithead investigator, Magistrate Aaron Graham, to Sheerness, saying that "government are well informed that some of the London Corresponding Society, particularly Galloway and Beck, have had intercourse with the mutineers at the Nore. . . . This perhaps is the most favorable moment for collecting much information from what may be learnt from the mutineers or such parts of the several crews, whose submission or return to their duty have been accepted."

Graham arrived in Sheerness the day after the mutiny was overcome. He found "the place in a state of absolute siege" and fleet delegates still "going at large about the town." Instead of the chuckling, sardonic Whig gentry who ruled Portsmouth, this place was in the hands of jumpy military persons. "The Admiralty is at a loss to know what to do with prisoners who are continually coming in from the different ships," he wrote Portland. About five hundred men were held on the charge of mutiny. "The captains are very apprehensive of serious consequences from so many being put into confinement and suffered to remain here without any plan being laid down for the disposal of them," said Graham. General Sir Charles Grey had boasted a few days before that "the people would hang every man that came on shore, if they had their will," but Graham found no civic urge toward lynching.

To Graham the chaos seemed so dangerous that he used his powers as a magistrate, without consulting the military, to issue a proclamation forbidding strangers to enter Sheerness. This order prevented Messrs. Galloway and Beck of the London Corresponding Society, had they wished to agitate there, from entering Sheerness to utter the seditious utterances which Aaron Graham had been sent by the Duke of Portland to hear, to record and to copy into charges.

There was enough terrific talk without the LCS. Graham came upon three vociferous tars haranguing a knuckle of townsmen on wrongs to the seamen. He stepped in and arrested the mariners. Since the local lockups had overflowed into the taverns, the Hatton Garden jurist had to transport his prizes fifteen miles to the Maidstone clink.

His captives were John Hulme and James MacLaurin, the *Director*'s delegates who had been put ashore almost a month before by

Captain Bligh, the day he was sent from his ship. The third man was Thomas McCann, the sick, hotheaded delegate from *Sandwich*, who had been last on the hospital ship *Spanker* where Admiral Buckner discovered he was a delegate and sent him ashore. The King's Pardon had never been read on *Spanker*, so McCann had applied for it and was now in a state of purgatory.

Magistrate Graham puzzled over what crimes he could prefer against the three tars. He committed them without charges at Maidstone and sent an express to Lincoln's Inn, London, requesting a legalism to cover his impulsive act of loyalty. The law lords sent him an opinion: Since two of the prisoners had left one of his Majesty's ships at a time when his Majesty's most gracious forgiveness applied to those separating themselves from mutineer allegiance, the navy had no claim on them and it was perfectly in order for Graham to arraign them at the Maidstone assizes for seditious utterances made ashore. As for McCann, the opinion was that he belonged to the Admiralty and had best be discharged to the Provost Marshal. So it was that Magistrate Graham, who had journeyed to the seaboard to apprehend civilians corrupting seamen, ended up by capturing seamen corrupting civilians.*

But the adventitious trail that led Magistrate Graham to the Maidstone jail also led him to Richard Parker, the most famous man in England, who had arrived there with his military retinue a short while before. Admiral Lord Keith had made a serious error after Parker's arrest. Considering him too dangerous and important to be thrown in with his followers in a prison hulk, Keith had Parker conveyed to the strong jail at Maidstone, where he was booked for "piracy and high treason." These happened to be civil offenses, not included in navy articles.

In his anxiety, Lord Keith had unwittingly turned over the Admiralty's prize trophy to the home office and the Duke of Portland who had bet a mere £500 on the possibility and now did not even have to pay that. His grace was not slow to exploit his prestigious captive. Next morning, Magistrate Graham and a colleague spent three hours in Parker's cell, questioning him on civilians who may have aided the mutiny. Graham darted after any pebble that could

---

* Graham was even cheated of that. A naval party came to the Maidstone jail, applied literal habeas corpus, and carried off Hulme and MacLaurin. He was left without a single seditionist to offer the Home Secretary. Needless to say, his Majesty conferred no recognition on the author of these unsuccessful labors, as Magistrate Graham and Lord Portland had dared to hope.

serve as a cornerstone of one of Portland's treason edifices, while Parker vehemently denied contriving with anyone ashore.

He insisted that everything had been invented and performed by the seamen themselves. He ranted against the Inflexibles. He said they had rejected his counsels of moderation and forced the others into reckless politics. (As he spoke, John Blake and the eleven Inflexibles were nearing Calais in *Good Intent*.)

"I expect an impartial trial," Parker told Magistrate Graham. "I hope to establish that I prevented wild men from doing worse injury to the country." This was not an unreasonable hope. In sedition cases, English juries were notoriously disobedient to the desires of the crown. Here in the Maidstone assizes, not too long hence, a jury made up of Men of Kent was to acquit a flagrant Irish revolutionist and his English accomplice of a high treason indictment that Pitt and Portland had all but earmarked with Rawhead & Bones.

While Parker was giving his lengthy interview to Magistrate Graham, Mr. Pitt presided over a shorter cabinet meeting at No. 10 Downing Street. Portland announced that he had made up a commission to go down to Maidstone and arrange Richard Parker's trial for treason.

It was the first time the Prime Minister had heard that Portland held title to Parker. Pitt vehemently rejected the duke's commissioners; he wanted no jury deliberations in this case. He ruled that Richard Parker was to face a regular navy court of thirteen judges of captain's rank or higher. He specified that no officer involved in the Nore mutiny was to sit on the court-martial board.

It would have taken weeks to find thirteen captains not connected with the mutiny. The sea lords picked several dubious qualifiers. The president of the court, Vice-Admiral Sir Thomas Pasley, had formerly held a command in the mutinous Channel fleet and had been a loyalty pleader to refractory crews at Great Yarmouth and the Nore. He enjoyed a £1,000 pension for his leg lost at the Glorious First of June. He was an uncle of Midshipman Peter Heyward, one of the ten *Bounty* mutineers that had been brought to justice. Heyward had received a death sentence, but was pardoned and resumed his navy career.

Sir Erasmus Gower was placed on the trial board. He had been expelled by his crew at Spithead and Lord Howe had confirmed it. Captains Wells of *Lancaster* and Sir Thomas Williamson of *Agincourt* were absolved from participation in the Nore mutiny by ministerial magic despite the fact that their ships had been under delegate control for nearly three weeks. Captain John Pierrepont of *Naiad*, which had been held by delegates at Long Reach for several weeks, was also appointed a judge.

Still another member of the court was a personal enemy of Parker's —Captain Edward Riou, who had commanded the sloop-of-war *Bulldog* on which Parker had served as a midshipman and whom he had reputedly challenged to a duel.

The trial board formed, Secretary of the Admiralty Nepean sent a box of papers down to the President of the Court to prepare him with evidence before the proceedings started. Among the documents were Admiral Buckner's in-letters to the Admiralty "to make you better acquainted with the various stages of the mutiny," Nepean told Sir Thomas.

He added, "Captain Mosse [*Sandwich*] will of course prosecute Parker and the people of *Sandwich*. The captains of all the ships in the river which have been in mutiny should be summoned. In short, you may prove anything you wish against him for he has been guilty of everything that's bad."

Four days after his arrest, the President of the Fleet received a visit in the Maidstone tombs from Admiral Lord Keith, who sought to impress him with the swift approach of justice. Parker asked for time to consult counsel. Keith advised him to apply promptly because he "could only be allowed eighteen hours after the charge."

Parker said, "I have never seen any charge against me."

The prisoner, for all his notoriety, was the loneliest man in England. His wife had not yet heard of his arrest. Parker's father and brother apparently could do nothing. He was isolated from the rest of the imprisoned delegates. He could not obtain defense counsel. No libertarian lawyer came forth to defend the "monstrous and wicked" President of the Fleet. Parker had not got access to the smallest solicitor in Maidstone, or the money to pay him. An advocate, feeling a duty of professional conscience to represent Parker, could well run afoul of Mr. Pitt's new fatal felony of even "communicating" with a mutineer. The Lords Commissioners of Admiralty debased even Georgian military justice by failing to assign counsel to the defendant.

Across the moat that set off England from the revolution, John Blake and the *Inflexible* mutineers landed in Calais. To their surprise, the French authorities locked them up. There were day-to-day expectations of armistice between France and Britain and the French did

not want the shadow of escaped mutineers to fall across the conference table. The twelve Inflexibles heard that Johnny Crapaud was
going to hand them back to the British government in the next
prisoner-of-war cartel. John Blake cast about for a way out of this
new trap. The mutineers were quietly released to take up service in
French privateers. If the long arm of the King's navy reached for
them again, they would be able to fight back.

Wolfe Tone was at The Hague, waiting for Lazare Hoche, who
was in Paris pushing Minister Truguet and the government for the
earliest invasion of Ireland. They met in the Comedie Theatre at The
Hague, Hoche incognito with unpowdered hair and a plain regimental
smock. They took a private room at the Lion d'Or tavern. Hoche was
in great good spirits. The massing of ships and men for the invasion
was nearly completed. And for the operation from the Texel they
were going to have an experienced and audacious naval commander
in Admiral Jan Willem de Winter.

The Dutchman, lean and dark as Quixote, was forty-seven years
old and had entered the navy at twelve. Despite the fact that navies
nurture political orthodoxy, de Winter was a convinced social revolutionist. The Bastille had been his decision day. He left the Dutch
navy and joined the French revolutionary army in which he gained
the rank of brigadier. With the establishment of the States General
government in Holland, de Winter returned to her navy as commander-in-chief. Revolutionary regimes usually have to settle for
poor hand-me-downs of professional military talent, but in Jan de
Winter the Batavian republic had a sea officer the peer of the big
Scotsman looking to fight him outside the Texel.

The Franco-Dutch invasion force in the Waddenzee consisted of
sixteen sail-of-the-line and eight frigates with 15,000 Dutch infantry,
eighty pieces of horsedrawn ordnance, funds and provisions for a
three-month campaign in Britain, and three thousand muskets to pass
to British partisans. In addition, President Carnot had offered the
Dutch five thousand hardened front fighters to storm enemy shores.
With de Winter as naval commander and Hoche as supremo and
army chief, the expedition was the most formidable amphibious force
yet assembled against the British Isles.

There were, it was true, certain administrative matters to settle.
Hoche found the Dutch unwilling to share with France the glory of
conquering Britain. They wanted to restore "the Dutch national
character." However, the French general was optimistic about solving

the problem as he and Wolfe Tone attended the Dutch Committee on Foreign Affairs, where the touchy final arrangements on command responsibilities for the invasion of Ireland were to be made. The Dutch had the strongest hand, since they were furnishing all the ships and wealth. Naturally, they did not say so. An elderly Dutch minister explained to the foreign youths, Tone and Hoche, "The discipline of our navy is very severe. French troops would not submit to such hard regulations. The result would be that all discipline would be relaxed."

The Dutch braced themselves for the reply. Hoche got up and said mildly, "I agree with what the Citizen-Minister has said. On behalf of my ministry, I withdraw the French troops and my own nomination as military commander." The Dutch practically cheered. In the genial atmosphere General Daendels, who would now command the invasion army, said all would be ready in ten days.

But, said the leader of the Dutch republic, Citizen Hahn, "the English squadron appears every day at the mouth of the Texel. When we are about ready to sail, it would be well if our French friends would take their fleet out of Brest and draw the English off our ships."

Hoche said, "Unfortunately, our fleet will not be ready for two months."

"If we sailed out and got into a fight, we would have to come in for refit," said a Dutchman.

"Both the British and ourselves refit at sea after a battle," said Hoche.

Admiral de Winter entered with, "I want to go to sea immediately and engage the enemy!"

Tone said to Citizen Hahn, "His only business is to bring his troop convoy safe to its destination!"

After the meeting, Hoche said to Wolfe Tone, "You must remember they are venturing almost their entire army and navy. They are like a man stripped to his britches who has two sous left. He throws them in a lottery in the hope of being able to buy a coat." He added, "You are wondering about my retreat. I am honestly glad to get the Dutch moving. That is more important than whether I command or not. The instant the Dutch get to sea, Truguet's vanity will be piqued and he'll move heaven and earth to follow them. So, if you reach Ireland, the French army will be there a fortnight after you."

Lest Wolfe Tone be left out of this all-Dutch expedition, Hoche arranged with General Daendels to make the Irishman an adjutant general of the Batavian republic and gave Tone a copy of the military lessons from the conquest of the Vendée. So the Irish patriot, who had never heard the screech of an enemy bullet, became an officer in his second foreign army. Hoche returned to Paris and gave Minister Truguet the news of de Winter's departure in ten days. As Hoche had predicted, Truguet drove the navy apparatus into furious activity to be ready to sail in a fortnight.

By the happiest of coincidences for William Pitt the conclusion of the Nore mutiny saw the parallel collapse of Lord Moira's rump of respectable members who had threatened to turn him out. Moira explained privately that "the whole of this political negotiation is completely extinct," and was embarrassed when this confession was bandied about. The Irish peer disclaimed starting the shadow government, saying that Sir John Sinclair and other respectables had called upon him "to form an administration in the principle of excluding persons who had on either side made themselves obnoxious to the public." Moira denied that his friends had acted secretly. "Indeed," said he, "I know that some of them declared their intentions very openly to the *persons most concerned, the Ministers.*" [His italics]

Pitt did not relax in his tent while Moira and the mutineers were removed from the field. He got a bill through Parliament increasing the taxes on all paper transactions by as much as 300 percent. The exaction on each copy of a newspaper was raised from halfpence to three halfpence, which increased the exchequer and reduced the circulation of populist journals. The *Norfolk Chronicle,* for instance, was obliged to boost its price from fourpence to sixpence. A one-pound loaf of fine white bread cost twopence in Norfolk that week, in a lean year.

Order was restored in the Channel ports. At Plymouth the four Irish marines who had intended mutiny against the British government were found guilty. The ringleader, Lee, and two others received death sentences, and a less guilty accomplice, McGinnis, was let off with one thousand lashes and transportation to Botany Bay. One morning, before 30,000 people on Plymouth Hoe, a marine punishment detail tied McGinnis to halberds, gave him five hundred strokes and carried him, still alive, back to the barracks in a chair to await the second round. His three guiltier compatriots suffered less. The crowd waited four hours to see it. Through the sally port to the Hoe came two marines bearing a black coffin, followed by Lee, gyved, surrounded by a heavy guard. Two more coffins were brought on, followed by Privates Coffee and Branham and their escorts. The Irishmen, indulged in prayer by reverend clergy, were blindfolded and made to kneel on their coffins. The volley missed Lee. A member of the firing squad was sent in to kill him at close quarters.

And to be sure, all was not well with Lord Bridport out in La Manche. As had often been the case before, he found he would have to return the Channel fleet to Spithead. The crew of H.M.S. *Defiance* had forced the purser to condemn tons of rotten cheese and butter; *Nymphe* was out of biscuits; and *Medusa* had seventy people laid up sick. Before the mutiny no doubt the Defiances would have eaten the cheese, the Nymphes would have done without bread and the Medusas would have been started up the shrouds.

A bud from the buried naval mutiny came forth in Scotland, where the Leith press gang petitioned for a wage rise.

Sir James Harris (Lord Malmesbury), Pitt's retractable peace negotiator to France, was very confident that a truce was near. On the strength of it (and their unpaid bills to the Admiralty), navy baking factories stopped production.

Mr. Williams, a bookseller in Holborn, London, was found guilty of blasphemous libel for publishing *The Age of Reason* by Thomas Paine. The Lord Chief Justice, seeing persons taking notes during the trial, addressed the audience:

> I hope no part of this shocking detail will be published. No man who has the least regard to decency or pays the smallest attention to his own interest, would endeavour to disseminate among the public doctrines that no serious Christian would hear.

Magistrate Graham returned to London and submitted his report on the Nore to the Home Secretary. It dispelled hopes in Whitehall that social reformers could be inculpated. It said:

> Mr. Graham and Mr. Williams [Graham's fellow magistrate] beg leave to assure His Grace that they have unremittingly endeavoured to trace if there was any connexion or correspondence carried on between the mutineers and any private person or any society on shore and they think they may with the greatest safety pronounce that no such connexion or correspondence ever did exist.
>
> They do not however mean to say that wicked and designing men have not been amongst the mutineers; on the contrary

they have proof sufficient to found a belief upon that several
whose mischievous dispositions would lead them to the furthest
corner of the Kingdom in hopes of continuing a disturbance
once begun have been in company with the delegates on shore
and have also (some of them) visited the ships at the Nore
and by using inflammatory language endeavoured to spirit on
the sailors to a continuance of the mutiny without, however,
daring to offer anything like a plan for the disposal of the Fleet
or to do more than insinuate that they were belonging to clubs
or societies whose members wished well to the cause but from
which societies Mr. Graham and Mr. Williams are persuaded
no such persons were ever deputed.

In their police capacity, the two London magistrates had attended
orderly meetings of the London Corresponding Society which in no
way resembled, "the wild and extravagant conduct" of the Nore seamen "which was not reducible to any sort of form or order." To
account for the pandemonium, they thought the seamen were "therefore capable of no other mischief than was to be apprehended from
a want of the Fleet to serve against the enemy." In other words, the
seamen were brassed off with cruising two years at the Texel and
wanted to get into a battle. This finding of Graham's was prophetic.

The magistrates saw no sinister blockade plot in the stopping of
merchant vessels. "The want of beer and fresh beef prompted them
to revenge and that and nothing else induced them to interrupt the
trade of the river." Graham believed "it was done on the spur of the
occasion and with a view of obtaining a supply of fresh provisions."

The Duke of Portland had his men out looking for Richard Parker's
relatives and friends. On the day the mutiny ended, they found his
wife, Ann, twenty-seven, in Fife, Scotland. They brought her and
her papers to Edinburgh where she was interrogated by the board
of magistrates. Mrs. Parker "appeared totally ignorant of the causes
which influenced her husband's conduct," said a contemporary account, "not having received a letter from him since the beginning of
May, which letter only stated that he was on board the fleet and
well."

Mrs. Parker told the judges that her husband must have been insane
when he assumed direction of the mutiny. She said he had previous
spells of madness, one of his sisters was in bedlam, and his earlier
discharge from the service was on account of insanity. Under English
law, insanity was no excuse for crime, but Mrs. Parker may have felt

that his Majesty's example might be taken into consideration. The magistrates examined her papers and found no evidence of Richard Parker's affairs, nor did they find a record of his '94 discharge on account of rheumatism.

Mrs. Parker told the judges she wanted to go to London on her husband's behalf, but had no money to pay the passage. Their lordships avowed no interest in her problem. Without funds in the strange city of Edinburgh, Ann Parker somehow managed to raise three or four pounds to take the passage boat to London, where she learned of her husband's arrest and death arraignment.

Nobody knows any more how Ann Parker managed in her second strange big city, but she found friends capable of drawing up a petition to the Queen—not to his Majesty—praying for royal clemency toward all prisoners of the Nore mutiny. The friends also provided her with dress "becoming her unhappy situation" to wear on her novel and unconstitutional mission to the Queen.

Mrs. Parker, carrying her petition, alighted from a hack in front of the Queen's house on 23 June. She was wearing a white petticoat, black silk gown, purple plaid, and a black chip bonnet, her face heavily veiled. The Earl of Morton came out to receive her. He was also Scottish. She asked permission to present the petition to the Queen. Morton said that her Majesty did not intervene in matters of state. But he took the paper and went into the house. Mrs. Parker left with hope that perhaps the Queen would be touched.

Inside, Lord Morton alleged that Mrs. Parker had offered him a bribe of a thousand guineas for the life of her husband.

Mrs. Parker went every day to the Queen's house and waited for an answer to her petition.

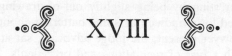

XVIII

The Trial
of Richard Parker

*Oui, je vous l'ai déjà dit, ils commencent ici pas faire
pendre un homme et puis ils lui font sont procès.*

—MOLIÈRE, *Monsieur de
Pourceaugnac*

(Yes, as I have already told you, here they hang a man
first and try him afterwards.)

O N THURSDAY, 22 June, a week after Parker's arrest, his trial
opened aboard *Neptune,* 98, Sir Erasmus Gower's new flag,
which for convenience of visitors was moored near Greenhithe on the
south bank of the Thames in the eastern crook of Long Reach. The
Swanscombe station of the shutter telegraph was a mile away over a
firm road, so the moralistic proceedings could be quickly imparted to
seamen at the ends of the line and to Whitehall.

At a green baize-covered table in the great cabin of *Neptune,* their
powdered hair aureoled against an arch of mullioned windows, sat
Parker's thirteen jurors and judges in full dress—blue coats with
bracketed white facings, white breeches and stockings, and silver-
buckled shoes. The newly adopted French insignia of rank, bullion
epaulets, glistened on the shoulders of the veteran post captains,
while captains with less than three years in the rank wore only one
epaulet. In the center of the table sat the peg-legged president of the
court, Vice-Admiral Sir Thomas Pasley with two silver stars on each
shoulder board. He was a big square-set man with a long bony nose
and a level gaze with a hint of irony in his eye. His face was rendered

the more interesting by being slightly out-of-drawing, its symmetry perhaps marred by a midwife or some battering-about in the service.

The only lawyer present, the judge advocate, sat at the end of the long table with a fuss of regulations and precedents. At ten A.M. Sir Thomas ordered the prisoner admitted. The one-eyed deputy Provost Marshal of Admiralty entered holding a drawn sword. Parker walked beside him with a respectful but unintimidated air. He was wearing a threadbare blue coat, buff waistcoat and half boots. His neck-length black hair was loose which, in Hanoverian England, marked the seaman, artisan, trader or dissenter.

The sword pointed the ex-President of the Fleet to a place next to the judge advocate's chair where Parker and the policeman would be required to stand throughout the trial. "Admit the witnesses and strangers!" There was a scrimmage of journalists and shorthand reporters for the front seats. Britain's infant popular press sucked its milk from trials of rebels and dissenters and social miscarriages. It had not yet discovered murder and sex. The judge advocate read off seaman, artisan, trader or dissenter.

> For causing and endeavouring to cause mutinous assemblies on board his Majesty's Ship *Sandwich,* and others of his Majesty's ships at the Nore, on or about the 12th of May last, for disobeying the lawful orders of his superior officers, and for treating his officers with disrespect.

The court dismissed the witnesses to await individual summons to testify. Captain Mosse of *Sandwich* called Admiral Buckner as the first witness for the prosecution.

"Do you know the prisoner?" he asked. "I do," Buckner replied.

Q. Did he belong to the *Sandwich?*
A. He did; but in what capacity, I do not know of my own knowledge, he was reported to me.
Q. State to the court what you know of the prisoner's conduct relative to this charge, on or about the 12th of May, or during the time the mutiny existed.
A. The first time I observed anything particular in the prisoner's conduct, farther than parading about with a vast number of people with red flags on shore, was on or about the 20th of May, when I went on board the *Sandwich* for the purpose of making known

to that ship and others his Majesty's proclamation of pardon, on their returning to their duty, on the terms granted to their brethren at Spithead, which they—I mean the delegates—with Parker the prisoner among them, had previously declared they would be satisfied with. On my going on board with my flag in the boat, there was no respect shewn me whatever: the officers were without their side arms, and had no command of the ship. Unwilling to return on shore till I had an opportunity of speaking to the people of the ship, I waited a considerable time, when Parker, with some others, came on the quarterdeck and said that none others but themselves, meaning the ship's company, should be present. The prisoner then tendered me a paper containing what he and the rest called a list of grievances; saying at the same time, that until these were redressed, and they had the personal attendance of the Admiralty to ratify it, they would not give up the power they held in their hands. Finding anything I could say of no effect, I then went on shore. About the 23rd my flag was struck on board the *Sandwich*. On that day, while I was examining into the complaints alleged against two marines that were brought in by a party of the military, the prisoner, a man whom they called Davis, with, I believe, three or four others, came abruptly into the commissioner's house at Sheerness and demanded why those men were in custody? —that my flag was struck—that I had no authority—and that the power was in their hands. They then took the men away, as they said, to try them—Parker being the spokesman, and telling me that he was not to be intimidated. About the fourth of June, I received a letter from Parker, to the best of my recollection, styling himself president, signed with his name. The letter stated that Administration had acted improperly in stopping the provisions from the fleet; and that the foolish proclamation was calculated to enflame the minds of honest men.

I have nothing more to state as a narrative. I have had frequent conferences with Parker, at the head of many others, with the hope of bringing them to a sense of their bad conduct, without any good effect. He in general took the lead as spokesman, with some degree of insolence in his manner, appealing to the others if he was not authorised by them; and even prevented one man in particular from answering a question I had put to him, with threats. While I was on board the *Sandwich*, I expostulated with them about having those disgraceful ropes, called yard ropes. Their answer was,

that the ship's company would not suffer them to be taken down.
Q. In the different conversations you had with the prisoner, was there any insolence in his conduct?
A. Frequently so; and at other times a great degree of modesty and apparent respect.

Acting as his own counsel, Richard Parker examined Admiral Buckner. He opened with:

"You have said that you had no respect shewed you when you came on board the ship on the 20th of May: was you or I on board first?"

"I was," said the admiral.

Parker asked, "Did you believe me to be the person who caused you to be received with no respect?"

"I was on board before the prisoner, therefore I cannot suppose that he caused it," said Buckner.

Parker said, "Do you recollect whether, when I came on the quarterdeck, I did not inform you that it must have originated in a mistake that you was not treated with proper respect, but that if you would excuse it, the crew would give three cheers?"

Buckner admitted, "He did come to me and say that it was a mistake, that no disrespect was intended me—I believe some attempts were made to man the yards, but it did not succeed."

Lieut. Philip Justice was called. He had been the acting captain of *Sandwich* on the day the mutiny began. Captain Mosse asked him if he knew the prisoner. Justice said he knew nothing about him until Parker come aft with a letter, and "his behavior was then respectful."

Richard Parker asked Lieutenant Justice, "You have already said you know nothing of me." The witness said, "I do not." The prisoner said, "Then I have no questions to ask the gentleman."

The prosecution called Captain Edward O'Brien of *Nassau*. "Do you know the prisoner?" he was asked. "I never saw him in my life," O'Brien answered. "Was he ever on board the *Nassau*?" O'Brien said, "Not to my personal knowledge."

"That will be all," said the prosecutor. "I wish to call Captain Robert Devereaux of the *Agamemnon*."

"Do you know the prisoner?"

"I never saw him before today."

"Was he ever aboard the *Agamemnon*?"

"Not to my knowledge."

Parker said, "I have no questions to ask Captain Devereaux."

Captain Charles Cobb of *Lion* was sworn. He had never seen Parker before and did not know if he had ever been aboard *Lion*. Captain Thomas Parr of *Standard* had never seen Parker, nor had Captains Robert Watson of *Isis* and William Hargood of *Leopard* seen him aboard their vessels. After each of these incomprehensible blank witnesses for the crown was heard, Parker said, "I have no questions to ask this gentleman."

The audience was watching a very strange opening of a trial that had held every promise of a fast death verdict and a quick hanging. Parker was scoring against the parade of captains. The reason for the muster of non-witnesses was, of course, Nepean's instructions to the court to summon "captains of all the ships in the river that have been in the mutiny." The Admiralty, in its eagerness to make example and get post captains back to sea, had not time to prepare its case.

Surgeon John Snipe of *Sandwich* was sworn and drew out a sheaf of notes. He knew the prisoner "but not before the fourteenth of May." He recalled:

> "On the afternoon of the fourteenth of May, Mr. Bray, the master, who said he was then commanding officer, came to me and said it was committee orders to punish a seaman [Black Jack] Campbell. I found Parker on the gangway with Campbell tied up. Parker addressed the company, saying Campbell had violated the regulations on drunkenness. He got beastly drunk on small beer."

The boatswain's mate gave Campbell, a Negro crew member, two dozen. The surgeon continued:

> "Later I was called below to visit a sick man in irons. I wanted him freed. I had to report in person to the committee. They were in the starboard bay of the lower gun deck with a vast crowd. Somebody said, 'Take off your hat.' I asked whom I should address. Parker desired me to address him. He said, 'It is not our intention to interfere with you. You may do whatever you think proper with the sick man.' "

These glimpses of the sociology of the business were not helping the President of the Fleet. They were establishing Captain Mosse's case that Parker had usurped the powers of an officer. Snipe recounted another visit to the committee, which was this time sitting in the great cabin. The surgeon asked permission to remove a sick man. Parker led the other delegates to agree and asked Snipe, while he was ashore, to request Admiral Buckner to permit all the sick to be landed.

Captain Mosse asked Snipe, "Did you ever see Parker give an order?"

"I never saw him give an order, but I did see him with a hat on remonstrate with Captain Mosse on the quarterdeck, pointing to the yard ropes."

Parker interjected. "I was pointing to the yard ropes and saying that I was sure no man would shrink. If they did, they would go to the yardarm. Do you suppose I meant anything else than that, if the people called delegates were to propose such a thing to the ship's company that the delegates would themselves be the sacrifice alluded to?"

A member of the court said, "You will be cautious not to put questions that may injure yourself."

"I will beg leave to withdraw the question," said Parker. "I will ask Mr. Snipe no more questions. I will reserve myself for the defense."

The prosecutor at last produced a captain who had seen Parker before, Thomas Surridge of *Iris*. He described Parker's visit ashore at the close of the mutiny and told of his handing a paper to Commissioner Hartwell, who read it and said, "I am sorry to find it contains so much fresh matter that I could not think of going to London with it."

Parker, defending himself, broke in: "The fresh material was demands of the North Sea fleet. I was trying to get the commissioner to recognize that it was not further Nore complaints. Is that not so, Captain Surridge?"

The witness said, "That is so."

Captain James Dixon of *l'Espion* took the oath. He confirmed Admiral Buckner's testimony about discourtesy to that flag officer aboard *Sandwich*.

Parker asked, "Do you remember my apologizing to Admiral Buckner for not cheering him, as I was not on board the ship?"

Captain Dixon said, "I do."

Pasley, the president of the court, told Parker, "Take care what you ask. That is acknowledging that you had the command of the ship."

The trial adjourned at four in the afternoon, to resume next morning.

In London, Henry Nicholls, the deposed captain of the Spithead ship, H.M.S. *Marlborough,* shot himself to death in the waiting room of the Admiralty office.

The government desired that Parker's trial and execution be the prime, exclusive opening event of a round of punishments. But two days earlier there began at Spithead a mutiny trial in some ways more serious than Parker's. The accused men were charged with trying to seize the *Pompée* man-of-war on the high seas and, as their captain, James Vashon, put it, "prevail on the fleet to return to Portsmouth and petition the King to make peace, and if it was not immediately done, to compell him to do it, to change the ministry and to have a new parliament. If they had not succeeded in bringing the fleet into their traitorous proceedings, then the *Pompée* was to have been taken to some point in France."

The Pompées had taken the initiative in the second Spithead organization and had been forgiven by Black Dick Howe's peace. Lord Bridport charged that "eighty-six young inexperienced men" had not been satisfied with Howe's redress and the King's pardon. The former *Pompée* delegates, James Melvin and William Potts, were not among them. This new outbreak on the ship occurred on 4 June, after Bridport had managed to leave mutinous Plymouth in sufficient repair to cruise his blockade station. A glint of the passion in *Pompée* was furnished by Bridport's demand to have beer sent to the ship "as serving grog or wine is attended with unpleasant disputes." The new remonstrance began with seamen being conducted belowdecks to a committee headed by Robert Johnson. On a table lay a watermarked sheet of his Majesty's foolscap, under which, said Johnson, was another sheet with five hundred signatures on it. He did not uncover these names but exhibited a list called "The Living and the Dead," consisting of messmates who were to be punished in various degrees when the committee had taken over. "An example must be made of some," Johnson explained. "Young yard ropes are growing."

James Callaway, another committeeman, told the inductee that the object of the new business was "to obtain an immediate peace on the return of the ship to port." Moreover, peace could not be obtained without the dismissal of Pitt and the ministers. Seaman John Broghan (apparently one-third of the committee was Irish) added that he would hang any man who would not take the oath to join their cause. Callaway placed the man's hand on the Bible and Johnson administered the oath:

I swear to ever stand true till death in promoting the cause
of freedom with equity, while any probability of furthering
its progress remains. To stand true to the ship's company, and
not to divulge the secret to any of the officers. So help me
God.

Most of the men in *Pompée* considered that their grievances had
been met by Howe or were not susceptible to schemes to overthrow
Mr. Pitt. Seaman James Addison, when brought before Johnson, told
him off and spoke to the rest of the crew against the plot. A marine
sergeant took the initiative from his officers in securing the loyalty
of the lobsterbacks. Fierce arguments broke out in the forecastle.
Someone split to the officers and the story reached Captain Vashon.
He reported to Lord Bridport, who ordered *Pompée* to return to
Portsmouth. On the passage the majority of Pompées controlled the
disaffected men.

The French navy would have welcomed *La Pompée* back. She
was an elegant ship delivered to Britain by French royalists at Toulon
in '93.

Lord Bridport received an address from the majority of *Pompée*:
"With the greatest concern, we have received the information respecting the misconduct of the seamen of the fleet at the Nore. . . . It is
our final determination by every means to suppress the conduct of any
persons who may by any means be guilty of tending to injure the
Honour of the British Navy." It was signed by 510 men, who intended to have it printed when they got back to England.

At Spithead the six ringleaders were hastened to trial while their
followers were distributed among various ships. Using the tightly
screwed new regulations, the Admiralty charged Johnson's group with
"making, or endeavouring to make, mutinous assemblies," for "inducing, by various artifices and threats, a part of the crew to be true
to them, and to aid them in carrying their unlawful designs into
execution." Broghan was tried separately for "mutinous and threatening speeches" and given a year in solitary. One man was acquitted.
Two of the death sentences were remitted. Johnson and Thomas
Ashly were hanged.

The *Pompée* court-martial demonstrated that there had been a
political strain in the original Spithead protest, but that longer heads
had confined the issue to bread and beef.

For the second day of his trial Richard Parker had summoned
Lord Northesk, captain of *Monmouth,* and Captain John Knight of

Montagu, the last command figures he could remember dealing with, as witnesses to his past good behavior. When the court met, however, Parker said to Sir Thomas Pasley, "I do not wish to give Lord Northesk and Captain Knight the trouble of testifying on my behalf." The non-lawyers in charge of the trial suspected a trick and discussed it audibly up and down the bar of justice. *Suppose he passes them over now, would he have the right to call them later on, when they'll be at sea, and he can delay the trial?* Sir Thomas bethought himself to banish the spectators while this was argued, then called them back and announced that Parker had said he *would* dispense with the evidence, but did not claim that it would be *useless.* Therefore the evidence *might* be essential, and the two captains *should* continue to attend the trial.

Parker inquired if he had the right to call fresh witnesses as the trial proceeded. The prosecutor, Captain Mosse, answered, "I shall produce no witnesses who have not been summoned before the trial. But at the same time, the opposite course would be perfectly legal." Pasley and the Admiralty solicitor put their heads together and endorsed Mosse's opinion, saying, "Also the same privilege would be extended to the prisoner."

After this symposium in the law education of Richard Parker, Captain John Wood, *Hound* sloop, was examined. "I know the prisoner perfectly," he declared with relish. "He was in the *Hound* in April last and was transferred to the tender in the ninth of that month. I saw nothing of him subsequently until the second of June on which day he came on board the *Hound* upon her arrival at the Nore. He then told me he had the honour of representing the whole fleet, an honour which he should never forget. He understood that I had been very violent with some of the delegates, and advised me not to be so violent, or I must take the consequences."

Parker cross-examined this telling witness. "Captain Wood, you said I advised you as a friend," he began. "I now desire you to recollect whether I did not say, upon coming aboard the *Hound,* 'Captain Wood, the differences in the fleet are of a very unpleasant nature. I feel myself in some degree under an obligation to you, therefore I would advise you to do nothing at present, but to suffer the *Hound* to proceed in the same manner as the rest of the ships, for I have no doubt but, that, in the course of a day or two, the officers will resume their command.' " Wood confirmed that Parker had spoken of an obligation to him but "did not recollect any expression about the officers resuming their command."

The next witness was Nicholas Platt, third lieutenant of *Sandwich,* who had remained aboard by sufferance of the company throughout the mutiny, only part of the time confined to quarters, as the senior officer aboard. "When Parker went over the side," he testified, "the hands were piped and the side men and boatswain's mate attended." He testified that Parker had called him to starboard on 2 June, and said, "You are ordered to receive one hundred and eleven men taken out of the Leith tender and to give a receipt for them as usual, as we are answerable for what we do." Platt protested that he had no orders from Admiral Buckner, but complied. The young officer had been confined by Parker's orders on 9 June and released by the fleet president on the fourteenth. He described the crumbling of the cause and how he had personally put the irons on Parker after he surrendered *Sandwich.*

The court went fishing for "Admiral" Parker by inquiring of Platt, "In the course of your evidence you distinguish the prisoner by the name of President; do you know if, during the existence of the mutiny, the prisoner ever assumed any other title, or if he ever was addressed by the crew by any particular mark of distinction?"

Platt answered, "No, I do not, he called himself President."

The prosecution fetched lower-deck witnesses. William Livingston, boatswain of *Director,* testified on Parker's implication in the cannonading of *Repulse.* "The prisoner ordered the guns of the *Director* to be pointed at the *Repulse.*"

Parker asked him, "Do you recall my addressing the ship's company of the *Director,* and pointing out to them how dreadful a thing it would be for one brother to fire upon another; that if they would allow me a boat I would take a flag of truce in it, and repair to the *Repulse,* which I did not doubt would stop the effusion of blood? What might happen to myself I should not consider of any consequence, even if I lost my life to save so many."

Livingston remembered this in substance and detail.

Samuel Hilliard, carpenter of *Director,* corroborated this testimony: "I heard Parker ask for a boat to carry a flag of truce to the *Repulse,* which was denied by the general voice of the ship's company," he said. "I cannot say that the people of the *Director* fired upon the *Repulse* in consequence of the prisoner's orders."

Thomas Barry, seaman, *Monmouth,* was sworn. He declared that Parker had taken command of *Monmouth*'s forecastle guns and fired on *Repulse* six or seven times. "He was not content with nine-pound shot," said Barry, "but seized a crowbar and put the thick end in first. I took it out of his hand, but he gave me a shove on the breast and I fell over the heel of the spare topmast."

Parker spoke to the witness: "I had not fired any gun myself when I first saw you on board. The quarterdeck guns were fired before the forecastle guns."

The President of the Fleet paused. "Have you been promised promotion or money for advancing this hellish account?" he asked.

"No, I was never promised anything," Barry answered.

The next witness, a boatswain's mate of *Monmouth*, John Summerland, was asked, "While the *Monmouth* was firing on the *Repulse* did you see the prisoner in any way active in pointing the guns or otherwise directing them to be fired?"

Summerland answered, "I did not."

The prosecutor told the court, "I have more witnesses but I do not think there is any necessity for calling them." It was Friday afternoon.

"Richard Parker!" said Admiral Sir Thomas Pasley. "The evidence for the crown is closed. You now come upon your defense. The court will meet tomorrow morning to know when you will be ready for your defense."

"It will take some time to prepare," said Parker.

"What time will you want?"

"It will be necessary to have some extracts of things that may have slipped my memory."

"You can have no extracts from the minutes," said the President of the Court. "I cannot part with them out of my possession."

Parker said, "It will be impossible for me to get ready tomorrow. I have no person to assist me in any respect."

The judge advocate said, "Will you be ready Monday morning?"

"I think I will."

Sir Thomas said, "We will hear your defense Monday morning."

"I will be ready Monday morning," said the deposed President of the Fleet.

Parker was taken below, shackled and confined in solitary gloom, the circumstances under which he was obliged to devise his defense. A few days before he had been rowed behind a triumphal barge of music, cheered by ten thousand messmates.

Next morning Parker was brought before a brief session of the court to hear a carefully deliberated opinion on why he might not see the trial record. The judge advocate had found that this matter was not merely discretionary: it would be *illegal* to let Parker see the foregoing testimony.

At his request for witnesses, the court agreed to send an express for several gunners from *Monmouth* and delegate Matthew Hollister of *Director,* who was in the *Eagle* prison hulk awaiting trial. Parker's narrow choice of witnesses indicated that he judged that the case against him turned on the contradictory testimony about his directing the firing on *Repulse*. Without transcripts of what had gone before, he was forgetting some other points developed by the crown.

Parker thanked the court for providing witnesses and requested a copy of the lengthy deposition he had given the civil magistrates in the Maidstone jail.*

Sir Thomas gave Parker a list of crown witnesses, pens, ink and paper, and reminded him that he had "two whole days at his command, by the intervention of Sunday. The trial cannot be delayed one moment longer than Monday morning." The President of the Court bade Parker to be properly grateful for past favors and "the greater indulgence of the present postponement, by which the country was still deprived of the services of so many important persons." Parker bowed and thanked him and the post captains in "a respectful manner."

The foremast witnesses from the Nore were on deck for the resumption of the trial on Monday, 26 June. Lord Northesk and Captain Knight were still there in obedience to their unvacated defense subpoenas. Parker did not call them. He chose instead to read a handwritten manuscript:

> "It is a circumstance well known to one member of this honourable court [Captain Riou] that I have been bred to the sea from my early youth. I cannot be expected to dress up my defence in the pompous language of a lawyer, could I have been assisted by a lawyer. Nothing can be expected of me but a plain simple statement of facts. Such as it is, I am now ready to submit it to the court. I thank the court for the indulgence

---

* I do not know whether or not Parker got this deposition. One 1797 transcript of the trial said he did. Neale, using a mishmash of contemporary newspaper accounts in his book fifty years afterward, writes "The president [of the court] said they had nothing to do with such a paper, although the prisoner had clearly a right to it." The original Admiralty holograph trial reports from shorthand notes do not mention the matter at all, nor do the abridged trial accounts in newspapers. The four court-martial transcripts I used differ in quite a few details. I tried to select the most reasonable variant.

of time granted me, by which I have been able to make my defence perhaps more accurate than it would otherwise have been.

"Nothing but a consciousness of my own integrity and the rectitude of my intentions could have supported me in the trying situation in which I was placed. I only entered it after it commenced with a view to endeavouring to stop the fatal spirit I saw too predominant in the fleet. I did all in my power to prevent the bad effects that were likely to arise from this bad temper of the seamen. All my measures were adopted with that view. The proceedings of the fleet would have been much more alarming had I not acted the part I did."

He asserted, "I never waited on Admiral Buckner without being ordered to by people called Delegates of the Fleet." Parker then entered a question that the court had not opened: "I may be asked how I came to be the person pitched upon as President of the Committee. The answer is that the Delegates of the Fleet insisted. As an individual, in the state the Fleet was in, it was impossible for me to refuse the commands. But again I solemnly declare that I knew nothing of the mutiny being intended until it broke out." Here, for the first time in the entire record of Spithead and the Nore, was a seaman using the word "mutiny."

Parker continued: "In the course of two days afterward I saw with pain a most fatal spirit creeping into the breast of the seamen. I then got myself introduced for the purpose, as far as in me lay, to stop the further progress of it. However melancholy the termination of the mutiny has been, I am convinced that if I had not taken an active part in it, the consequences would have been ten times more dreadful."

The defendant reviewed the testimony, touching most of the main points without access to the transcript. He asserted that when Admiral Buckner came aboard *Sandwich,* "some people were telling the crew that Buckner was incompetent to settle things. *Inflexible* sent word that if the *Sandwich* cheered the admiral she would come alongside and sink the *Sandwich.* The same day, Captain Mosse asked Mr. Bray, master of the *Sandwich,* why the *Inflexible* was beating to quarters. The *Sandwich* committee sent two men to the *Inflexible.* They found the tompions out and matches lighted. They said there would be hostilities if matters were settled on the *Sandwich.*" The Inflexibles called a delegates' meeting themselves to prevent the

Sandwiches from yielding. The Inflexibles began holding daily meetings and sending proposals to meetings on the *Sandwich*.

"All measures originated on board the *Inflexible*," Parker insisted. "There is not a man this day in custody who does not attribute to the conduct of the *Inflexible* that morning the melancholy consequences that have since happened."

The President of the Fleet denied an allegation that he had ordered Captain John Wood off his ship *Hound*. "Captain Wood did not produce a witness," Parker declared. "His testimony was hearsay." The idea of a seaman equating his word with that of a post captain did not go down well with the court. The defendant denied firing a gun from *Monmouth,* and said of Seaman Barry's testimony to that effect, "Every word was false!"

Parker concluded his rebuttal with:

"However my conduct may have been misrepresented in the public prints and otherwise, I trust I shall soon be cleared from such aspersions. My intentions were good, and I have prevented much evil. Justice is allowed to me by my country, and I hope that justice will now be done to me."

Sir Thomas Pasley said, "Richard Parker, you may call upon evidence in support of your defence, but after that evidence shall have been given, you cannot be permitted to make any observation upon it."

The prisoner bowed. His first witness, the Earl of Northesk, was sworn. Before Parker could put a question, Sir Thomas asked from the bench, "Was you on board the *Sandwich,* milord?"

"I was on board on the sixth of June," said Northesk.

"Did it impress your lordship, that, notwithstanding the existing circumstances of the fleet, the seamen were loyal?"

"Yes," the witness told the court.

Parker asked Captain Northesk, "Does your lordship recollect a mark of loyalty in me, when coming into the cabin, that I ordered the band to play 'God Save the King'?"

"I recollect that, on my coming into the cabin, the prisoner did so."

Sir Thomas took over again. "What situation did the prisoner appear to be in when you came to the cabin?"

"He appeared to be the principal of the delegates," said Lord Northesk.

"Was he their chief?" the court inquired.

"He was."

Captain Mosse handed Northesk a letter and asked, "Did your lordship receive from the prisoner this letter now produced?"

Parker broke in, "I thought the prosecution was ended for the crown."

The judge advocate said, "When the prosecutor produces witnesses, the defendant has a right to cross-examine them. If the defendant produces evidence* on his behalf the prosecutor has a right to cross-examine those evidences. This is most clearly the practice by land or by sea."

Parker accepted this without pointing out, if indeed he was aware of it, that opposing attorneys may not break in on each other's examinations, even under military law.

Lord Northesk identified the letter:

Sandwich at the Nore 6th June Three P.M.
To the Most Right Honourable the Earl of Northesk My Lord:
 You are hereby required and directed to proceed to London with such papers as you are entrusted with to lay same before our most gracious Sovereign, King George III, and to represent to our most gracious Sovereign that the seamen at the Nore have been most grossly misrepresented to his Majesty: at the same time that if our most gracious Sovereign does not order us to be redressed in 54 hours after 8 o'clock of the morning of June the seventh, 1797, such steps by the fleet will be taken as will astonish their dear countrymen and your Lordship is further requested to send us accounts in the specified time by your purser who is allowed to attend your Lordship. I am my Lord, your lordship's most humble servant, Richard Parker, President by order of the Committee of Delegates of the Whole Fleet.
 My Lord. I am further to acquaint your Lordship that an oath has been taken by the delegates of the fleet that they never have had any communications with Jacobins and traitors.

"Was your lordship present at the writing of that letter?" Parker asked.

"Yes, at the part beginning with the word 'my Lord' and ending the word 'president.' "

Parker said, "I would wish to withdraw the question."

The judge advocate said, "You cannot now."

---

* Throughout the mutiny trials witnesses are called "evidences."

"You might have withdrawn it, before it was answered," said Sir Thomas Pasley, "but you cannot afterwards."

Parker asked of Northesk, "Does your lordship recollect seeing a show of hands from the delegates, expressive of their wish that this part of the letter should be inserted?"

Northesk said, "I remember it was their wish that it should be known that they were not Jacobins or traitors."

Northesk stood down.

The prosecutor had appropriated Parker's first witness to establish damaging evidence against him, that he had signed a paper "requiring" a captain of the British navy to carry out a mission "by order" of mutineers.

The next defense witness was Captain John Knight, the last emissary between the seamen and the King. He testified hearing Parker say, "If the enemy's fleet is at sea the delegates will put to sea and attack them. Or, if the Dutch fleet comes out of the Texel, we will go to meet them, and prove to the world that we are neither rebels nor traitors."

Captain Mosse cut in with questions to Captain Knight on use of the red flag at the Nore. Knight saw on *Sandwich* on the King's birthday the Loyal standard at the foretop masthead, a red flag at the main and the Union Jack at the mizzen. The prosecutor asked, "On all loyal days, is it not the practice and custom to hoist the Loyal standard at the main-topmast?"

"Yes, it is," said Knight.

Both the bench and the prosecutor employed the new defense witness to establish that Parker's war cry against the French and Dutch was made while he was standing under the red flag instead of the King's pennant. Captain Henry Stanhope,* another of the judges, addressed a question to Captain Knight:

"How do you reconcile the expressions of loyalty you have mentioned with the treatment you received, by the total annihilation of your authority, the breach of the laws of your country, and the imprisonment of your officers?"

Knight answered demurely, "They are certainly irreconcilable."

Parker said, "I wish to know if I can ask Captain Mosse a question?" The President of the Court replied, "It cannot be allowed, unless Captain Mosse is regularly sworn." Parker did not call Mosse as a witness.

When the trial opened, the prosecution had called a half dozen

---

* He was a kinsman of Prime Minister Pitt.

captains who had contributed nothing to convicting Parker and now the defense had called two who damaged him below the waterline.

Parker summoned his forecastle witnesses to repair the breach. Jacob Swanson, *Sandwich* gunner, took the oath. Captain Mosse permitted Parker to interrogate him.

Q. Do you recollect the day on which Admiral Buckner's flag was struck on board the *Sandwich?*
A. I do not.
Q. Do you know any person or persons who were aiding or assisting in striking the flag?
A. No.
Q. Do you recollect Captain Mosse's having said on the quarterdeck that, as the mutiny unfortunately had commenced, he thought it fortunate I happened to be on board the *Sandwich,* to keep down the spirit of it, as I seemed perfectly moderate?
A. I do not recollect that Captain Mosse said anything of the kind.
Q. Do you recollect, during the mutiny, to have informed me that such conversation had taken place between Captain Mosse and his officers?
A. I do not.

Gunner Swanson was no comfort to Parker. Mosse queried him on what Parker had said when *Repulse* went aground. The witness replied, "I heard him say that, if his father was aboard that ship, pointing to *Repulse,* he would send her to hell, for that was where she belonged." Beyond that, Swanson proved generally unhelpful to Mosse: he swore he had never heard Parker giving an order and knew nothing about the significance of the red flag.

Parker, with confidence imparted by these exchanges, interrupted the prosecutor to ask the gunner, "Do you recollect if I ever told you it was a great pity the *Inflexible* should have been in the fleet, and that, if it had not been for that ship, things would have been settled amicable long since?"

Swanson said, "I do."

The captains' table fired questions at the gunner about the cannonading of *Repulse,* but Swanson remembered nothing further. Edward Allen, seaman, *Sandwich,* sworn, had no material evidence for either side.

Between witnesses Parker was handed a letter from his brother, who said the best help he could give was a five-pound note enclosed. There was no five-pound note in the fold. It had been lifted, according to navy regulations, by Captain Stanhope of *Neptune,* who would decide how best the money should be spent on the prisoner's behalf.

Parker took up the allegation of Seaman Thomas Barry that he had directed cannon fire against his Majesty's ship *Repulse* after she had cast off to abandon the mutiny. The fallen President of the Fleet apparently considered that rebutting Barry would establish his innocence of the main material charge left in the indictment. Parker sought to establish the hour *Repulse* had decamped and show that he could not have physically participated in firing upon her. His handicap was that the Admiralty had placed no ship's logs in evidence, although, during the mutiny, systematic logs had been kept as usual. (This is not an assumption based on the orthodox ship-keeping of the mutineers, but on the reappearance in 1963 of a hand copy of the mutineers' log and delegates' papers of the *Comet* fire ship.) Parker tried to reconstruct the time sequence from recollection of those present.

Matthew Hollister, delegate of *Director,* was brought in wearing leg-irons. Parker asked him, "Do you recall what time I left his Majesty's ship, *Director,* the day on which the *Repulse* went ashore in attempting to get into Sheerness harbor?"

"I cannot speak as to the hour or minute, but it was late in the evening," said his fellow delegate.

Parker said to the court, "That is the only question I have to ask the witness as he is in confinement for trial. I do not wish to ask him any question that many tend to accuse himself."

Parker had done well with a single question to Matthew Hollister. Earlier testimony had been that *Repulse* got off the ground at 5:30 P.M. Hollister said Parker left *Director* "late in the evening." On this date the sun sets after 8 P.M. GMT in the south of England.

Now Parker was to have his innings with Thomas Barry, the *Monmouth* seaman, who was the only witness to testify that he had fired a *Monmouth* gun at *Repulse* after he left *Director.* He asked the witness, "What time of day was it that you stated me to have fired the forecastle guns of the *Monmouth* upon the *Repulse,* as she was endeavouring to get into Sheerness harbor?"

Barry replied, "At four o'clock in the afternoon, to the best of my knowledge."

The forecastle witnesses from *Monmouth* that Parker had summoned to his defense, William Hobbs, James Nicholls and Samuel

Beer, swore on the Bible they had never seen him before. Parker detained Beer.

"Look at me. Do you know me?" he demanded.

"No, I do not," said Beer. "I never saw the prisoner before, to my knowledge."

Sir Thomas Pasley interjected, "In what part of the ship were you placed during the firing of the *Monmouth* upon the *Repulse?*"

"On the forecastle part of the time," said Beer, "and between decks for the remainder."

The President of the Court continued: "At what gun of the forecastle were you stationed?" The seaman answered, "At the second gun. I remained on the forecastle about a quarter of an hour after the firing commenced."

Parker asked, "During the time you were on the forecastle, did you observe a crowbar being introduced into a gun?"

"No," said the witness.

"How long did the firing last?"

"About an hour," said the seaman.

"May it please the court," Parker said. "I have no more witnesses to call. But I request that I might be permitted to put a few more questions to Matthew Hollister."

"Permission granted," said Sir Thomas Pasley.

The shackled *Director* delegate waddled in again. He said that *Repulse* was off the shoal and afloat before Parker left *Director* for *Monmouth*. This, too, contradicted Seaman Barry's testimony. Captain Mosse took Hollister through a quiz and elicited a more precise recollection of when Parker had left *Director*—"between seven and eight, but I cannot be certain." Mosse asked, "Was it before or after sunset?" Hollister replied, "It was some time near sunset."

The fact of the matter was not brought out in court. The *Comet* log states:

> At 6, H.M.S. *Repulse* slipped her cables & got on shore—
> on the Sand—and the Ships of the Fleet fired upon her for
> endeavoring to get away. . . .

The Admiralty witness had Parker coming aboard Monmouth at four o'clock, knocking him down, and firing a cannon at a ship that did not get under way for two more hours. Nevertheless, it may be true that the President of the Fleet had overtly—as against oratorically—opposed the secession of *Repulse*. But that the crown did not prove.

Parker told the court, "I have no more witnesses to call." Sir Thomas said, "The charges exhibited against you are of the most weighty and serious nature. If you have any more witnesses upon whom you can now call, for God's sake avail yourself of their testimony."

The defendant said, "Could the court allow me to consider further till the morning?"

"That is impossible. You have had two days to prepare your defense," said the President of the Court.

"Then I have done," said Parker. "I hope the court will place the most favourable construction on my actions and recollect that I have been moderate in the whole of my conduct and willingly assisted in delivering up the ship."

It was half past one. Sir Thomas Pasley ordered Parker to be locked up and cleared the great cabin for the captains to deliberate the verdict. They were ready at four o'clock. Parker was brought back.

The judge advocate read the original order from the Lords of Admiralty and the charges against Richard Parker.

> "The court has heard witnesses on the part of the prosecution to support these charges, and witnesses on behalf of the prisoner for his defense. And having maturely weighed and considered same, the court is of the opinion that the whole of the charges were fully proved against Richard Parker.
>
> "The court, therefore have determined that the said Richard Parker shall suffer death, and that he be accordingly hanged by the neck until dead on such day, and on board such ship, as the Lords Commissioners of the Admiralty shall appoint."

Parker listened stoically and read from a paper he had just written in his cell.

> "My Lords, I shall submit to your sentence with all due submission, being confident from the clearness of my conscience that God who knows the hearts of all people will favourably receive me. I most sincerely hope that my death may atone to the country and that all the rest of the fleet may be pardoned and restored to their former situations. I am convinced they will return to their duty with steadiness and alacrity."

Listening outside the great cabin, awaiting their trials, were John Davis, mutineer-captain of *Sandwich,* and others to be tried as a group, now that the "admiral" was disposed of. The one-eyed deputy Provost Marshal brutally clanked the bilboes on Parker's legs. The condemned man shouted to him, "Mark me, you dam'd Polyphemus-looking bugger. When you put the halter around my neck, I'll give you such a kick in the guts . . . as shall send your soul to hell!" He turned to the officers and apologized "for using such language in your presence."

Delegate Davis said to his group, "If they condemn me, I would ask to die with him." "Aye." they said, the chains rattling. As Parker clanked below, the *Sandwich* committee entered to face the spliced persons of their commanders, accusers, judges, assizemen and executioners.

The shorthand reporters and journalists scampered down Neptune's sides. In Greenhithe, express riders waited to gallop the dispatch to Whitehall. In a few minutes the votive news was spread by telegraph to the Admiralty office and Horse Guards to St. James's, Downing Street and the home office.

Secretary Nepean received a caustic letter from Sir Thomas Pasley: "The conviction of this villain Parker must have been so very dear to you at the Admiralty that the place and time of his execution might have been previously settled." The presiding judge added that the naval court had not hanged him immediately out of deference to their lordships, but expressed a wish that the corpse "could be hung in some conspicuous place as an example."

> (Admiralty, 27 June) Earl Spencer has the honour to lay before your Majesty the proceedings of the Court Martial on Richard Parker, together with the sentence passed on him, and thinks it his duty at the same time to submit to your Majesty's consideration the propriety of ordering his body after execution to be hanged in chains in some conspicuous situation within view of the ships at the Nore, with a view of more effectually deterring others in future from following so pernicious an example. This suggestion your Majesty will please [*sic*] is made in a private letter from Sir Thomas Pasley to Mr Nepean, the Court not having thought it right to include it in their sentence lest it should create a doubt as to the legality of that sentence; and Earl Spencer, in submitting it to your Majesty's pleasure, only does it in case such an order shall appear to be warranted by the Law, for which purpose he has directed an opinion be taken. It appears by a document which Earl Spencer has also the honour to lay before your Majesty that there is a precedent for such an order in a case of murder.

In his cell in the orlop, Richard Parker wrote a letter to a friend he had known since childhood, in which he analyzed his part in the mutiny. The letter was intercepted by the Admiralty:

"The only comfortable reflection that I at present enjoy," he said, "is that I am to die a Martyr to the cause of humanity. I know the multitude think hard things of me, but this gives me no uneasiness, for my conscience testifies that the part I acted among the seamen has been right, although not to be justified by prudence." He went on:

Yes, prudence urges *that I ought to have known mankind better* than blindfold to have plunged into certain destruction. Long since I had learnt that the miseries under which the lower classes groan are imputable in great measure to their ignorance, cowardice, and duplicity. . . . However severe this reflection, still I preserve my fortitude, and I am able to do this by considering that as a human being I stand subject to human passion, the noblest of which is a tender *sensibility at every species of human woe.* Thus influenced, how could I indifferently stand by, and behold some of the best of my fellow creatures cruelly treated by some of the worse.

Upon the word of a dying man, I solemnly declare that I was not an original mover of the disturbances among those men, who have treated me so very ungratefully. Also, that I was elected by my Shipmates their Delegate without my knowledge, and in the same manner by the Delegates their President. I was compelled to accept those situations much against my inclinations by those who pushed me into them. . . . I further declare that from the aggregate body originated every plan, and that during the time the Delegates held their perilous situations, they always acted pursuant to, and obeyed the instructions of their constituents . . . The only instances in which the Delegates acted of themselves were in those of checking the violence and turpitude of their masters, and this God knows we had hard work to do, but considering all circumstances, those who know anything of sailors will readily allow that we preserved much better order than could reasonably have been expected upon such an occasion. For not according with the preposterous ideas of the seamen, I and many more must suffer death.

Owing to the Delegates moderation, they have been overcome, and for my own part I cheerfully forgive the vanquishers the bloody use they intend to make of their victory; perhaps it is policy in them to do it.

At the pressing applications of my brother shipmates, I

suffered humanity to surmount reason. . . . I am the devoted scapegoat for the sins of many, and henceforth when the oppressed groan under the stripes of the oppressors, let my example deter any man from risking himself as the victim to ameliorate their wretchedness. . . . Remember never to make yourself the busybody of the lower classes, for they are cowardly, selfish and ungrateful; the least trifle will intimidate them, and him whom they have exalted one moment as their Demagogue, the next they will not scruple to exalt upon the gallows.

It is my opinion that if Government had not been too hasty the Portsmouth Mutiny would have been as readily overcome as that at Sheerness. A very trifling forbearance on their part would have occasioned the Portsmouth Delegates to have been delivered up like those at Sheerness. . . . The Mutineers have been accused of disloyalty, but it is a false accusation. They were only so to their ill-fated tools, the Delegates.

I have reason to think the Civil Power would have acquitted me, but, by the Articles of War, my destruction was irremidiable, and of this Government was well aware, or I should not have been tried by a Court Martial. By the Laws of War I acknowledge myself to be legally convicted, but by the Laws of Humanity, which should be the basis of all laws, I die illegally. My judges were respectable, but not totally disinterested, for one of the demands had for its tendency the abridgement of their emoluments in Prize Money.

O, pray for me . . . that when I am on the point of being offered up, that I may be inspired with a charity sufficient to forgive those for whom I am sacrificed. The moment my body is suspended the spectators will behold a wretch who is exposed as an example of his own frailty, and of the disgrace and dishonour of those men for whom I met so ignominious a death. . . .

Captain Henry Stanhope entered Parker's cubby and gave him two guineas of the five-pound note Parker's brother had sent. "Well then," said the prisoner, "I shall have a roast goose before I die." He wrote a farewell letter to his wife:

MY DEAREST ANNA:

Unhappy as the news I have to communicate will make you, still, if I have the power of finishing this letter, it shall come from no other pen but my own. I am my dearest Anna, at this time in the most trying situation any man can possible be in.

Sentenced to death, despised by my country, yourself liable to be stigmatized by the vulgar on my account; my father and brother, consequently, the most unhappy beings, myself excepted; your family naturally not excepted from the general storm; would, if it were not for a firm and thorough reliance on God, who knows the heart of all men, and who can bring good of evil, throw me into a state of despondence. . . .

I trust in Jesus Christ, our Blessed Redeemer, that my being cut off is to the glory of God and to the salvation of my own soul. —my dearest Anna, before you receive this, in all human probability, I shall be no more! . . . In whatever I may have offended you, give me your forgiveness, as I freely from the bottom of my heart do you, any thing that might have taken place to ruffle our tempers, while we were united together. . . . I die in charity with all mankind—Give my love to all your family, and believe me to be,

Your affectionate and loving,
Though unhappy, Husband
RICHARD PARKER

To Mrs Ann Parker
Bromair, Aberdeenshire.

Parker did not know that his wife was in London. She was still vainly awaiting a reply from the Queen. The Earl of Morton, who had taken her petition, was invested by his Majesty, a few weeks later, with a royal order, which may or may not have been connected with his treatment of Mrs. Parker.

Parker's execution morning was announced for 30 June. The afternoon before, his wife gave up her vigil at the Queen's house and took a coach for Rochester, arriving at eleven o'clock. Despite the hour, she roused out a market gardener who agreed to take her to Sheerness with his boatload of vegetables at dawn.

XIX

The Yellow Flag

"Seamen are neither reckoned among the living nor
the dead, their whole lives being spent in jeopardy. No
sooner is one peril over, but another comes rolling on,
like the waves of a fullgrown sea."

—SAMUEL KELLY
An Eighteenth-Century Seaman, 1786

THE SHIPS were brought down from Gravesend to the Medway
for the execution. They lay at anchor past Sheerness with *Sandwich,* the former parliament ship, now the gallows ship, standing at
the head between Queenborough and the Isle of Grain. Spectator
stands had been erected on the island. A flotilla of yachts and sightsee-
ing craft crowded in to points of vantage. Heavily armed guard boats
rowed round the ships.

The Sheerness garrison tumbled out early and marched out of
the sally port with fixed bayonets and flying colors—three non-
mutinous infantry regiments, the East Yorkshire, the West Yorks
and the West Norfolks. They were followed by walking invalids
from the hospital and an artillery train. The column marched to
Queenborough and formed ranks facing *Sandwich.*

Belowdecks in the flagship, the one-eyed Provost awakened
Parker. The marine guards said he had slept soundly. The prisoner
asked for a barber and got a clean shave. A friend of his named
Templar had indulged a wish of Parker's to have an all-black cos-
tume to die in. The prisoner put on the black suit, silk stockings
and silk neckerchief. He sat down to breakfast, chatting with the
marines. He assured them that the ships would have been carried
off to enemy ports if he had not prevented it.

On deck, sentinels saw a market boat pushing through the sight-seers to the side of *Sandwich*.

"Shove off!"

"Ahoy boat, shove off!"

From the boat, a woman in black shouted, "I want permission to speak to my husband, Richard Parker."

"You shove off. If you don't we must fire into you!"

The gardener backed his oars despite Mrs. Parker's pleas. "The yellow flag is not up," he said reassuringly. "There will be no execution today." He took her back to Sheerness. The Scotswoman hired another boat at the garrison stairs and asked to be put aboard *Sandwich*. As the waterman pulled up to the flagship, a signal gun sounded on *l'Espion,* and the yellow flag, sign of capital punishment, ascended to her foretop. *Sandwich* answered with a yellow hoist. Mrs. Parker grabbed the receiving ropes, crying to see her husband. The marines put her back in the boat and ordered the waterman away. He had a party waiting ashore that had booked him for the hanging. Once again Mrs. Parker was landed. She went looking for another boat.

Ships' boats, commanded by lieutenants and full of armed marines, drew up to *Sandwich* to witness punishment. Her chaplain, the Reverend Mr. Atherton, called Parker to the quarterdeck. He came up blinking in the dazzling morning sun, wearing his elegant black suit of mourning. He was pale, near to fainting. He bowed to the ship's officers and asked for a chair. He sat and looked around the silent, suspended scene, at what he had commanded. The marine company stood at ramrod attention in a hollow square, which framed the deck from the poop rail to the mainmast, the *alta crux* of ship's society. He looked at the Sandwiches massed in the forecastle and the other companies ranged fore-and-aft and in the shrouds, and at the yellow flag above his head. He said nothing.

The chaplain came to him. Parker thanked the officers for the chair and agreed with the clergyman on two psalms appropriate to the occasion. He knelt with the Reverend Atherton and gave the responses in a clear voice. He said, "Now, with your permission, sir, I will add a psalm." They read from the 51st Psalm of David:

PRIEST

Have mercy upon me, O God, according to Thy loving kind-ness; according unto the multitude of Thy tender mercies blot out my transgressions.

PRESIDENT

Wash me thoroughly from mine iniquity, and cleanse me from my sin.

PRIEST

For I acknowledge my transgressions: and my sin is ever before me.

PRESIDENT

Against Thee, Thee only, have I sinned, and done this evil in Thy sight: that Thou mightest be justified when Thou speakest, and be clear when Thou judgest.

· · · · · · · ·

Deliver me from bloodguiltiness, O God, thou God of my salvation: and my tongue shall sing aloud of Thy righteousness.

· · · · · · · ·

For Thou desirest not sacrifice; else I would give it; Thou delightest not in burnt offering.

PRIEST

The sacrifices of God are a broken spirit: a broken and a contrite heart, O God, Thou wilt not despise.

PRESIDENT

Do good in Thy pleasure unto Zion: build Thou the walls of Jerusalem.

PRIEST

Then shalt Thou be pleased with the sacrifices of righteousness, with burnt offering and whole burnt offering: then shall they offer bullocks upon thine altar.

Parker was still on his knees, praying in a low voice, when the preparatory gun sounded from *l'Espion.* He finished without showing visible concern for what was coming.

He got up and said, "Captain Mosse, may I be indulged with a glass of white wine?" His commander and prosecutor sent a steward to the great cabin. Parker took the wine, looked aloft, and cried aloud, "I drink first to the salvation of my soul! And next to the forgiveness of my enemies!" He drained the glass and said to Captain Mosse, "I hope you will shake hands with me." The officer took his hand. "I desire to be remembered to my companions who are awaiting trial aboard the *Neptune,*" the ex-President of the Fleet said, "and my last dying entreaty to them is to prepare for their fate and refrain from unbecoming levity."

They bound Parker's hands behind his back and the final procession paced deliberately toward the forecastle, led by the boatswain and mates—his followers become his hangmen. Next came the provost with drawn sword in one hand and the halter in the other, the captain's clerk with the warrant of execution, and the chaplain, Parker, and the master-at-arms holding a cutlass. Bringing up the rear were Captain Mosse, officers and several gentlemen privileged to watch the event.

That was the scene Mrs. Parker saw as she drew near *Sandwich* on her third attempt to speak with her husband. She fainted.

The progression passed through a double file of marines and halted at the starboard cathead, upon which a special platform had been rigged that extended high out over the side for wider public visibility. Parker and the padre knelt again and the condemned man produced several fervent cries of "Amen!" to the parting orisons of the state religion.

The chief clerk enunciated the execution order to Captain Mosse. Parker listened and nodded his head. He said to Mosse, "May I be allowed to speak?" The captain hesitated, loathe to permit him to harangue the largest and most attentive audience the president had ever commanded. Parker said hastily, "I am not going, sir, to address the ship's company. I wish only to declare—" and he shouted it to the whole fleet, "I acknowledge the justice of the sentence under which I suffer! I hope my death may be deemed a sufficient atonement, and save the lives of others!" *

"I wish a minute to collect myself." said Parker. Captain Mosse nodded. The former President of the Delegates of the Whole Fleet of his Majesty's Ships at the Buoy of the Nore knelt by the cathead. The slack tide was dissolving into the ebb and the parliament ship swung round her moorings, bringing the starboard yardarm and cathead to a position in front of the spectators on the Isle of Grain and the yachts in the Medway.

"I am ready," said Parker. He held his head with officer hauteur

---

* That Parker, in his last chance to speak publicly, elected to appeal solely for mercy to his fellow delegates should dispel any lingering suspicion that he was a Jacobin or an agent of the reform societies. John Binns, John Thelwall, Horne Tooke, and other jacks and revolutionaries never missed an opportunity to declaim political hot gospels when the enemy gave them a forum.

and said to the boatswain's mate, "Take off my kerchief." The mate unknotted the black silk scarf.

The one-eyed deputy provost marshal stepped in with a greased halter, a rope passed through a metal thimble around which an eye had been spliced in the end of the hemp. The provost hated Parker and was naturally clumsy. Parker had threatened him that, when they went on the cathead, as the last shot out of his locker, he would kick the guard. The provost put the noose over Parker's head and got it wrong.

The prisoner said to the boatswain's mate, "Do *you* do it, for he seemed to know nothing about it."

The mate set the noose expertly so that the weight of the metal eye would come up against the occipital, behind the left ear, simultaneously strangling, rupturing the jugular and snapping the spine. The mate looked up at a topman who let down a yard rope. The mate took a splicing fid and rapidly worked a union of the halter and the yard rope. On deck, a mate of the gang of hanging mates took up the hauling end of the yard rope and belayed it on a cleat.

The one-eyed marshal tried to pull a hood over Parker's head, but he protested. The embarrassed guard told Parker he was disobeying regulations. The ex-President of the Fleet submitted, but before doing so, gained the single concession of his contest with Admiralty. "I request that you do not pull the cap over my eyes till I desire you to," he said. Mosse gestured to the marshal, who turned up the cap so Parker could see.

The man in the mourning suit had been facing aft toward the officers, clergy and executioners. Now he turned to his messmates packed in close to him in the forecastle, "and with an effectionate kind of smile, nodded his head, and said, 'Goodbye to you,' " according to an eyewitness report.

"Captain Mosse, is the gun pointed?" Parker asked.

"It is."

A crew stood by the brass signal gun.

"Is the match alight?"

"All is ready," Mosse replied.

Parker, the noose around his neck, took several steps aft and said to the officers and guests, "Will any gentleman be so good as to lend me a white handkerchief for the signal?"

A guest placed a handkerchief in one of Parker's hands gyved at his back. The prisoner nodded his thanks and started up the precarious flight of stairs that had been built high and overboard from the cathead. The marshal stumbled after him to complete his duty of pulling the hood over Parker's face.

In the boat, Mrs. Parker recovered consciousness, saw him on the cathead and lowered her eyes. Parker called, "Is the signal gun ready?" A lieutenant sang out, "All is in readiness." The yard rope was still belayed, with the mates standing by to take the hitch off quickly and run him up when the gun sounded. The surly provost yanked the hood down over Parker's eyes and fled down the stairs. Parker did not try to kick him.

Parker did not know that his wife was present. Now he never would. Mrs. Parker could not bear to watch it. She lay in a half-faint over the gunwales of the skiff, her vision encompassing only green-gray water, twinkling in the sun.

The crew at the execution gun stared at the black figure on the pulpit. They were ready to fire at the drop of the handkerchief.

Parker bent his knees and sprang toward the water. The handkerchief fluttered away like a snowy petrel. The yard rope went bar-tight, still belayed, still untouched by the hanging gang. The crowd's death gasp sawed the air.

Mrs. Parker saw "nothing but the sea, which appeared covered with blood."

The death gun boomed. The mates raised the President of the Fleet slowly to the yard. Midway aloft the body seemed to convulse, which may have been only the elastic rope contracting after the sudden strain. Parker had taken his own life, denying their lordships that much gratification and absolving his messmates of the deed.

The waterman rowed the unconscious widow to Sheerness.

The Sheerness telegrapher took a long look through his glass at the unmoving black figure hanging from *Sandwich*'s starboard main foreyard. It was 9:30 A.M. on a clear summer's day. The death notice flickered rapidly along the telegraph line to London.

The body was left hanging for an hour according to law and custom. There was speculation among the witnesses about where Parker would be gibbeted, as had been demanded by the President of the Court Martial. But no order came down the telegraph from the Admiralty. The King had decided against exhibiting the body.

Ashore, the widow Parker revived and engaged a fourth boatman to take her to *Sandwich*. From a distance, she saw the body lowered and swayed inboard. The yellow flag came down. The spectator fleet scattered for dinner. His messmates placed Parker's body in a wooden coffin, and removed the hangman's cap. His eyes were open. They made no move to sew the body in his hammock and weight him for sea-burial, because of a taboo against polluting estuarial waters with corpses. Instead, they payed out the last yard rope of the unrespectable mutiny and lowered the coffin into a boat. The oarsmen did not head for shore, but swept down the Medway, past Sheerness, into the Thames and turned toward the Dover Strait. They were trying to throw off inquisitive persons spellbound by "Admiral Parker," and now avid for his necrology.

Mrs. Parker got alongside the lower gunports of H.M.S. *Sandwich* without being driven off; hanging day was over. Seamen said the body was being taken around to the sea side of Sheerness fort to be landed surreptitiously and carried through the Red Barrier gate to a specially prepared burial ground.

She went ashore and laid siege to Vice-Admiral Skeffington Lutwidge, Buckner's successor. He was overloaded with work—deciding which of the five hundred Nore prisoners should be tried for their lives and assailed by angry captains who questioned his judgment on their people. Lutwidge put Mrs. Parker off all afternoon, but she waited and she had her word with him.

"But, my good woman, why should you propose to remove his body?"

"To have him interred like a gentleman, as he was bred."

"That will not be permitted. And now if you will allow me . . ." Vice-Admiral Skeffington Lutwidge departed for supper.

Mrs. Parker went out and asked people in the evening streets how to get to the burying ground. It was "out there toward Minster, but you won't get in. They've got a new stockade fence ten feet high around it."

"Who has the keys?"

"It's not properly consecrated, I suppose. No sexton, that's sure. Now, who *would* have the keys?"

Mrs. Parker walked to the new burying ground. At ten o'clock in the lingering light of summer in that high latitude, she descried three women near the stockade. "My name is Ann Parker, my husband is buried in there. Richard Parker." After a brief talk, a female mutiny was mounted at the new burying ground.

Ann Parker climbed the gateway, gave the others a hand up, and the four women dropped into his Majesty's postmortem prison. With their hands they scooped the loose, sandy soil from Parker's shallow grave, and lifted the coffin out.

Somehow they passed it over the ten-foot wall and sat on the coffin to conceal it when the sentries at the Red Barrier gate walked by. Toward dawn the drawbridge clanked down and a filth cart came out of the garrison on its way to replenish Rochester market-gardens. For payment of a guinea, Mrs. Parker prevailed upon the driver to conceal the coffin in his cargo. And so the famous Richard Parker, who may have clandestinely sought a political "gentleman in black" on Rochester bridge, crossed it in a dungheap on his way to London.

The day Parker was executed, men at sea who knew of his capture and certainty of death were circulating "inflammatory papers," signed "United Brothers of the Fleet." On the Spithead two-decker *Mars,* Captain Alexander Hood's crew remained disorderly, "despite advice from officers and all the punishment my instructions allow me to inflict." When he read them the King's pardon proclamation they evinced "contempt and indifference." William Heather, carpenter's yeoman, who had been a delegate of *Mars* at St. Helen's, brought Captain Hood some letters he had found under a storeroom door. They were petitions to the Admiralty asking prompt and fair payment of prize money before ships were paid off and men scattered. Hood reported this to Cousin Bridport, who ordered him to take *Mars* out of the squadron to keep the "United Brothers of the Fleet" away from the rest. Hood charged David Lambeth, seaman, and Patrick Dunlavey, marine, with circulating the petitions and ordered them tried at Spithead. They seem to have been sent there in *Triton,* which Bridport detached from the fleet to take two of her own—cook, John Todd, and landsman, David English, ashore to be tried for mutiny.

Parker's posthumous voyage continued. After his wife smuggled the corpse to Rochester in the dung cart, she engaged a driver of a caravan, a large canvas-covered goods and passenger wagon, to take it to London for six guineas.* She gave the caravan driver a door key. It opened a room she had hired in the Hoop and Horseshoe public house in Queen Street, Little Tower Hill, where he was to deliver the coffin. She took a stage which arrived in London earlier than the plodding wagon.

The cold remains of the President of the Fleet arrived on Saturday night in the city that three weeks before had quaked over the threat of his hot presence with a thousand cannons. Mrs. Parker locked the

---

* Contemporary accounts do not explain how, after arriving in London penniless, Mrs. Parker raised at least £20 to carry out her resurrectionist raid on the sealed graveyard.

body in the tavern until she could arrange burial in consecrated ground. The news of its arrival drew crowds to the Hoop and Horseshoe. Strangers implored Mrs. Parker to view the body. She would not permit it. They represented themselves as interested in helping her find decent interment. She let them look. They let others look, and next morning when Mrs. Parker returned from a vain effort to find a grave, there was a long queue of people passing through the pub, looking at Richard Parker. Constables came to control the crowds. More people pressed into Queen Street late Sunday night and arrived in greater numbers Monday morning to see the President of the Nore.

Mrs. Parker was summoned to the Lambeth Street police office. The magistrate asked, "What were your intentions in removing the body of your husband from Sheerness?"

"To take it down, either to his own family at Exeter, or to mine in Scotland, to bury him like a Christian."

The magistrate said, "Is it true that you have suffered him to be shewn for money?"

The widow burst into tears. "Do I appear like a monster so unnatural?" she said.

She was allowed to resume her quest for Christian burial.

The home office was disturbed by the mass veneration of Parker's clay. ("The dead advance as much as the living advance," said Walt Whitman.) The Duke of Portland regarded the queues at the Hoop and Horseshoe as an LCS plot. He suspected that "the disaffected societies" were planning a public funeral, which would be transformed to demonstrations against the government. Dead and pious Parker had become a Jacobin.

Home office people descended on the Hoop and Horseshoe, removed Parker's body and hid it in a workhouse in Nightingale Lane in dockland. All visitors were barred, including the widow. The home office arranged to bury the mutineer clandestinely in the churchyard of St. Botolph Aldgate as soon as a grave could be dug, which requisite determined that he would be safely below ground at eleven next morning, Tuesday, five days after the Admiralty had attempted same.

The secret was out on Monday evening. In the Minories, a cheap commercial street of weavers, vociferous Whigs, cryptic Jacobins, Jews, Irish laborers, and outdoor philosophers, thousands gathered that fine evening and did not disperse. The Minories was the direct route between the Nightingale Lane workhouse and St. Botolph's church.

It seemed to the magistrates that the crowd in the Minories planned to blockade Parker's last voyage. At one in the morning, constables slipped the coffin from the workhouse and carted it through tortuous streets back of the royal mint to Whitechapel road, where it was put in the burying vault of St. Mary Matfelon, the original of which church had been the headquarters of Wat Tyler's mutinous encampment in 1381.

When the coffin did not appear at St. Botolph's next morning, Ann Parker resumed the search for her husband. By afternoon she discovered what the magistrates had done with the body and went to St. Mary Matfelon. The church authorities were civilized people. The sexton took her to the vault and unscrewed the coffin lid. The rector performed the official Christian ritual for the dead and gave the widow a signed certificate to that effect.*

Soon after the posthumous exhibition of Parker, the country was captivated by the disinterment of an older cadaver. Masons rehabilitating Worcester cathedral struck the vault containing King John the First, John "Lackland," who was forced to sign the Magna Carta in 1215. The skeleton measured five feet, six-and-a-half inches long. His boots and part of his sword were preserved, and gray hairs stuck out of a tight cap buckled under the chin. King John was exhibited for a week.

Opportunistic printers hurried out trial reports and discrepant lives of Parker. Street vendors hawked them with lurid epithet. Several who cried "Parker the Traitor!" were set upon and beaten by persons unknown who also scattered their wares.

A home office spy attended a political club where the opening toast was "Marmontel!" to the venerable French historian and educator who was writing children's textbooks for republican schools. The discussion turned to the subject all London talked of that week. "It would have been better if the widow Parker had let her husband's body rest where it was first laid in the earth."

---

* St. Mary Matfelon was also called Whitechapel Church. It was gutted by fire in 1874 and 1882 and rebuilt, but was not replaced after virtual destruction by German fire bombs in World War Two. There survives a physical trace of the President of the Fleet in his death mask taken at St. Mary Matfelon, which was given to the Royal College of Surgeons in Lincoln's Inn Fields a century after his death by Dr. Charles Davies Sherborn, F.R.G.S. (1859-1942), author of the *Catalogue of British Fossil Vertebrata*. Parker's effigy is in the Human Osteological Collection of the Surgeon's College Museum, which also includes the skeletons of the Irish Giant Byrne (7'7") and the Sicilian Dwarf, Caroline Crachami, twenty inches high.

"I rejoice that she recovered it for her peace of mind, though to have saved herself the fatigue she underwent, I wish she had demanded it from the executioners after his death."

"Could she have lawfully done that?"

"It seems they have no power to have refused it to her."

"However, it is perhaps better as it was, as she now owes nothing to their good will."

"If they had thrown his body into the sea, it would have spared her a great deal of anxiety of mind."

"You believe, I suppose, that the different retailers of his dying speech were insulted by the swinish multitude out of affection to Parker?"

With the seamen of the Nore wholly submitting to the power of their officers, the government thought it wise to withdraw condign threats against the whole fleet and pardon all except those who had been arrested. All but 42 people on *Leopard* were forgiven and all but seven on *Vestal*. Every man on *Beaulieu* and the sloop *Hound* was pardoned. General Sir Charles Grey was alarmed by these "indulgences." Naughty soldiers might see that there was not so much risk to mutiny after all.

The Nore parliament ship *Sandwich* was condemned and broken up as unseaworthy.

The Heat of July

At the time when half Europe was intoxicated and the other half terrified by the new magic of the word citizen, the English nation was in the hands of men who regarded the idea of citizenship as a challenge to their religion and their civilization; who deliberately sought to make the inequalities of life the basis of the state, and to emphasize and perpetuate the position of the work-people as a subject class. Hence it happened that the French Revolution has divided the people of France less than the industrial revolution has divided the people of England.

—J. L. AND BARBARA HAMMOND
The Town Labourer

ADMIRAL ADAM DUNCAN tried a ruse to learn the strength of the Dutch invasion fleet behind Texel Island. He sent an ambiguous letter to its commander, Jan de Winter, by an officer under a truce flag. The Dutchman scented the trick, detained the Briton, and sent one of his staff back to Duncan under a white flag with an equally unimportant letter.

The Dutch officer came back to de Winter with a long face. There were eleven British sail-of-the-line, including a trio of three-deckers.

The mutiny was over.

A most favorable opportunity to invade Britain was lost.*

It was 26 Messidor, the eighth anniversary of the storming of the Bastille. Theobald Wolfe Tone, stepchild of revolution, was waiting patiently in the great cabin of the Dutch flagship, *Vrijheid* (Free-

---

* The historian W. E. H. Lecky estimated, "If an invasion of Northern Ireland had been undertaken in these critical weeks, it could not possibly have been prevented."

dom), at anchor behind the Texel—waiting as only the political exile must learn to wait. "My sole amusement," he entered in his journal, "is reading Voltaire."

Into the great cabin, the first officer of *Vrijheid* brought a boatman with information for Admiral de Winter: Admiral Duncan had been obliged to detach five ships to the Medway to participate in the ceremonial execution of Richard Parker. De Winter thanked him. When the spy left, the admiral said to Tone, "I think he's a double agent."

The winds blew foul for days on end and the invasion fleet rolled and groaned on its cables in the Waddenzee. Downwind of *Vrijheid* the bored and surly Dutch seamen heard the sound of flutes as de Winter and Wolfe Tone played duets to while away the time. During an hour of clear visibility, Tone counted nineteen English sail outside. De Winter tried to cheer up his moody companion by passing him an espionage report that three of Lord Bridport's ships were still in revolt. Tone brightened. "And they'll have to try all the rest of the Thames mutineers before they can trust the ships to sea." he said.

The King's navy was doing just that, and doing it swiftly by batches in *Neptune* at Long Reach. The accused seamen acted as their own attorneys against their captains as prosecutors.

George Shave, the *Leopard* committeeman who had interrupted Sir Thomas Pasley's appeal for obedience at Great Yarmouth, was brought into the great cabin to stand trial for his life. Sitting as president of his judges was Sir Thomas Pasley. Captain Hargood of *Leopard* stepped out of his role as prosecutor to testify that Shave was "particularly active" in the mutiny. When the *Leopard* company revolted, Hargood asserted that Shave came to the gangway and said, "The country has been oppressed for five years. The war has been too long. Now is the time to get ourselves righted. We must go to our fellow creatures." Shave was sentenced to die.

John Lapthorn, master-at-arms of *Leopard,* testified against Dennis Sullivan, one of the committeemen:

> "On the day the ship was taken from the Nore, I heard a conversation between the prisoner and [Committeeman Alexander] Lawson. He said there was something more than common about to take place, by the manner in which the officers were hurrying backwards and forwards; he thought it would be best to confine the officers until the delegates came on board, and should anything happen before [then] the best way would be to jump down into the magazine, blow up the ship, and go all together."

"You have sworn my life away, Lapthorn," said Sullivan. The prisoner was sentenced to hang.

When *Leopard* committeeman John Habbigan was put up for his life, he made a weak, confused defense. He interrogated Quartermaster Slater, as a defense witness. Slater introduced nothing that helped the prisoner, but suddenly broke off and said to the judges, "I have something to say in the prisoner's favor if you please." Slater said:

> "This man and I were never friends since we have been in the ship. Mostly his temper and mine never agreed. That day we retook the ship I was determined—and looked out for him on purpose—to kill him if I came athwart of him. When I came athwart of him he was as active as anyone in lending a hand to get the boat out and got into the boat as well as us and lent a hand to get the anchor out at the time the ship was aground. I asked him in the boat how he thought of this affair. He thanked God and said he was as glad as if someone had given him a thousand pound."

The court found Habbigan guilty but recommended him to the King's mercy.

Charles MacCarthy, the erratic delegate who had been shunted from one ship to another, was tried. Lieutenant Platt of *Sandwich* testified that MacCarthy had demanded the keys to the magazine from him. The defendant interrogated Platt:

Q. Do you know a man who was on board on the twelfth of May by the name of McCann?
A. Yes, I have seen the man but have a slight knowledge of him.
Q. Is he not a man of about my size?
A. He is, nearly, but his long hair is tied, if I am not mistaken.
Q. Were there not many persons round you at the time you were asked for the keys, and considerable noise?
A. There were a good number of persons but there was not much noise.
Q. Isn't McCann an Irishman and his accent much like mine?
A. I do not know. I never examined what countryman he was and I have not particularly observed his accent.

The court said, "Could you have mistaken one for the other?" Lieutenant Platt said, "I could not."

The next witness was Henry Dobson, the captain's clerk. He testified that McCann was standing near Lieutenant Platt when the keys were demanded. "McCann had a very bad black eye at the time," the clerk recalled. The court inquired, "Was MacCarthy there?" The witness replied, "I did not see MacCarthy there."

MacCarthy got his opportunity to plead for his life. He said, "I desire that those who are to determine upon my fate will do unto me as they would expect, were our situations inverted, that I would do unto them." The court did not choose to apply the golden rule. It found MacCarthy guilty and sentenced him to death.

On the other hand MacCarthy's double, the sick, hotheaded Thomas McCann, by the criteria of the court equally as guilty or more so, successfully pleaded that he had never been read the royal proclamations and had applied for pardon while not aboard a proscribed vessel. This puzzle was referred to the solicitor-general, who advised against capital punishment. McCann received "his Majesty's gracious pardon on condition of being transported to Botany Bay for life."

During the trial of the Sandwiches, the mass executions began. Seven leaders of *Leopard* were hanged at the Nore: Dennis Sullivan, Alexander Lawson, William Welch, Joseph Fearon, George Shave, Thomas Sterling and William Ross, the only one who could read and write.

To the bar of military justice came William Davis, mutineer-captain of *Sandwich,* the moderate who had attempted with Parker to reach a compromise in the last days of the Nore mutiny. He was an impressed man who had previously served in the navy for three years. Commissioner Hartwell gave Davis a good character, saying, "He always took his hat off before me or other officers on shore." Captain Henry Blackwell of *Brilliant* testified that Davis was "very polite," but he had seen the prisoner walking arm in arm with Parker in processions through Sheerness. A crown witness, Seaman Robert Morty, said that Davis's office in the mutiny he "understood was from Parker."

CAPTAIN MOSSE: You understood?
WITNESS: From public rumor.
Q. You only heard that Parker had given these orders?
A. Nothing further.
Q. Who informed you?
A. I cannot remember the name of the man, but he has since drowned.
Q. Were you not one of the committee?

A. No, I never understood myself as such.

Q. Did you ever sit at the committee?

A. Yes, l did by command.

Q. By whose command?

A. By command of three or four persons.

Q. Name them.

A. I do not recall them. There was an extra committee appointed, strangers to me, whose names I do not know.

PRESIDENT OF THE COURT: You must tell the whole truth. If you prevaricate here, the consequences will be bad for you. You cannot criminate [*sic*] yourself. You are safe from any consequences.

Q. Who ordered the prisoner [Davis] to command the ship?

A. I understand Patmore did—

Q. Did he drown?

A. Patmore, the person whose name I did not recall before.

The court had much of this sort of difficulty with each of its own witnesses. The seamen knew that three leaders were already dead, Parker by hanging, Wallis by suicide, and Patmore by drowning, and when the prosecutor cornered them on who had assumed officers' functions, it turned out to be one of that three.

William Davis was sentenced to hang.

Quartermaster William Thursby of *Sandwich* was questioned by Captain Mosse:

Q. Where were you born?

A. I am not positive because I never knew father or mother.

Q. What religion are you of?

A. Presbyterian.

Q. You are not Roman Catholic?

A. No.

Q. Are you a foundling?

A. The first country I knew was America but there have been several disputes whether I was born at sea or in America.

Q. Where were you bred?

A. Brunswick in North Carolina is the first place that I ever knew.

Coxswain Charles Chant was accused of saying, "Damn and bugger the King. We want no King." He was among those hanged.

Some of the Nore seamen were being tried at Spithead:

Admiralty, 14 July 1797. Earl Spencer has the honour to lay before your Majesty the proceedings and sentence of a Court Martial held at Portsmouth on six [*sic*] men belonging to the *Grampus* for mutiny, and at the same time to accompany it with a secret letter from Sir John Orde, the President of the Court, representing the different degrees of guilt which appeared to him to attach on each of the five men whom they have condemned, and Earl Spencer humbly submits to your Majesty that in consequence of the circumstances alluded to by Sir John Orde it may be proper to order the three first-named men, viz: Smart, Crosskell and Preston for execution, & that the two last, Taylor and Hardy may be respited for the present, in order hereafter to obtain your Majesty's most gracious pardon upon such conditions as may seem proper.

Earl Spencer also humbly submits to your Majesty that upon reconsideration of the case of Meldrum who was ordered for execution in the Council on Wednesday on the report of Sir James Marriott for serving on board a French privateer, it appeared rather more adviseable that he should be recommended to your Majesty's mercy on condition of his being transported to Botany Bay for life, for which direction shall be given, if your Majesty should be pleased to approve it.

The King answered to these feats of jurisprudence:

Windsor, 15 July, 7:55 A.M. Agreable to the recommendation of Sir John Orde I consent the law may take its course on Smart, Crosskell and Preston, and Taylor and Hardy respited for the present. As to the fate of the man whose case was reported on Wednesday, I will not on the present occasion refuse my assent to his not being executed, though there certainly is no reason for reports being made if the decisions taken there are to be reversed at pleasure afterwards.

The Nore mutineers sentenced to transportation missed an eventful voyage to Australia in the convict transport *Lady Shore,* which left Spithead early in July before the mass trials produced extra passengers. There were 119 civil convicts and a scattering of political prisoners in the hold. British manpower was so drained by the navy that the party of guards over the convicts was made up of French residents of Britain emigrating voluntarily to Australia and even by French prisoners-of-war released for the purpose.

On board were Chief Quartermaster Selis and Pilot Thierry, who had been captured in the French corvette, *Bonne-Citoyenne* in 1796. They had been imprisoned at Petersfield, but escaped. They were retaken by Fencibles near Portsmouth and jailed there. The town fathers regarded these two extra mouths with lack of enthusiasm and the French mariners swiftly found themselves in a hulk at Spithead. They recruited six compatriots and vanished again. The next time they were picked up, they found themselves in the *Lady Shore* for Botany Bay.

At sea, bound for the Cape Horn passage, an international ship's committee was formed of the convicts, including three Germans and a Spaniard, French sentries, and disgruntled members of the English crew. The cabal swore in a majority of the seamen and rushed the quarterdeck. The officers and male passengers resisted, but a petty officer got into the arms chests and passed out decisive weapons to the mutineers. The new command put 29 people in a longboat, including women and children, about seven hundred miles east of Cape Sta. Maria, Brazil. They made land alive. The mutineers sailed to Montevideo, sold *Lady Shore,* and were free men.

In the trials at Long Reach, Elias Bradbury, a purser's steward, accused James Lurar, a writer on the *Sandwich* committee, of saying during the blockade, "I wish everybody was of my opinion, to unmoor all the ships and the merchant ships as well, and carry them on France." The informant said he had reported this to Parker, who took him and Lurar into the great cabin, where "There was a gentleman from London of the name of Calvert." Parker said, "Mr. Calvert, this gentleman has come to lodge a complaint against the prisoner by which I hope you will be fully satisfied that we are true to our King and Country." The accused Lurar asked Parker, "Will I be allowed to speak?" Parker said, "Yes." Lurar said, "Mr. Parker, I have heard you and Gregory and most of the committee say as much."

This vignette of a trial within a trial brought a nodding of loyal heads: everybody in the anecdote was a villain save the crown witness. The court called James Lurar and asked him if he wished to say anything to the accusation. "Yes," said the writer, "I was a prisoner-of-war in France and escaped in a small boat to return to duty. How could I have said anything like that?" Lurar received three years' hard labor.

Now came the turn of the *Sandwich* fiddler, Thomas Jephson, who refused to play "God Save the King" * while President Parker was entertaining mutinous ships' companies and loyal visiting admirals. An American supernumerary, Thomas Hewson, testified against Jephson, claiming that he heard the musician say of the mutiny, "A glorious thing it is, and it shouldn't end until the head is off King George and Billy Pitt!" Moreover, when Lord Northesk came aboard, and the bandleader said, "Gentlemen, 'God Save,' " Jephson announced, "By Jesus, that's an old stale tune! I care nothing about kings. Bad luck to the whole of them."

The American said Jephson wore a red cockade and read to the Sandwiches an address from the people of Ulster to the people of England, calling for dismissal of the ministers. Jephson, he further alleged, belonged to a society in London "where a member threw down a note of ten thousand pounds to buy arms." A whisper went through the court-martial audience: the scuttlebutt in London was that the very rich and radical young Duke of Bedford was financing an insurrection.

The King's American witness charged more blasphemies to Jephson than had been attributed to any of the mutineers, including Parker. The fiddler's lame rebuttal was that he had never lived in London, but belonged to a Masonic lodge there which he attended twice a year. And the drowned Patmore had ordered him to wear the red cockade. He did not deny any of his lurid utterances against the crown and ministry. He was sentenced to 100 lashes.

His Majesty paid prompt attention to his duties of enforcing the judgments of the naval courts:

> Kew, 27 July, 7:08 A.M. Agreable to Earl Spencer's proposal, I approve that of the men belonging to the *Sandwich,* Gregory,

---

* Many English people regarded "God Save the King" as a ministerial rather than patriotic anthem. The song was new and the King's party was promoting it assiduously to replace the quondam national hymn, "The Roast Beef of Old England." For example, at Lincoln a large church-and-king audience watched an effigy of Tom Paine hanged, gibbeted and burned to ashes "with great solemnity," while "a great band of music played "God Save the King." A chorus of it goes:

> *O Lord our God, arise!*
> *Scatter our enemies*
> *And make them fall*
> *Confound their politics*
> *Frustrate their knavish tricks*
> *On Thee our hopes we fix*
> *God save us all!*

Hockless, Hughes, Appleyard, Holding, Chant, Gaines, Davies, McCarty [Charles MacCarthy] and James Jones shall suffer death, James Lurar and Henry Wolfe be pardoned on condition of being confined for three years to hard labour, Porter, Whitly, Brady and Taylor to be pardoned on condition of being confined for one year to hard labour, and Thos. Brooks, who has (been) condemned under a wrong Christian name, to obtain a free pardon.

The men of the *Beaulieu* to be executed agreable to sentence, and the two recommended to be kept for two year to hard labour.

The men of the *Calipso* to be pardoned on condition of hard labour for three years.—G.R.

In Paris an Irishman broke the news to Tom Paine that his old enemy, the great reactionary Edmund Burke, had died insane and heartbroken over the death of his son, who opposed Burke's politics. Paine downed a *fine a l'eau* and rasped, "Not at all, sir! *Rights of Man* broke Burke's heart."

In the midst of the proceedings against the seamen, Lord Portland opened an important civil trial that had been pending for three months. The sedition case against young John Binns, the lion of the London Corresponding Society, came up in Birmingham. Francis Place, the defense strategist, had laid careful plans to thwart the Duke of Portland, for if the Home Secretary could convict Binns, he would be closer to destroying the democratic leadership of the country. The crown was expected to make much of Binns' visit to Portsmouth prior to the mutiny.

Among Place's arrangements was a mute prompter, to condition the jury's emotional responses. He seated a respected old Whig schoolmaster, Samuel Parr, in a full-bottomed chair facing the jury box. When the prosecution climaxed an argument, Dr. Parr would grimace and shake his head in disbelief. When the defense made a point, the pedagogue would smile and sparkle and gaze at the author with admiration.

The crown's first witness was Joseph Mason, threadmaker, one of the three home office missionaries who had taken notes during Binns' speech at the Swan Tavern. He opened with the line Place feared, claiming that Binns had boasted of being in Portsmouth "to read some resolutions of the Plymouth Corresponding Society." This connected the LCS agitator with two navy towns at the outset of the trial.

Crown counsel let this impression simmer and led the threadmaker to the next thrust point. Mason asserted that Binns had harangued the crowd at the Swan Tavern to issue forth and "reform Parliament by force." The threadmaker accused John Binns of slurring the King. He read from his meeting notes a passage that sounded like Binns: "His Majesty and his ministers are well convinced that annual parliaments and universal suffrage are most conducive to the happiness of the people and have granted them to Corsica! Although, he has refused them to his natural subjects."

Dr. Parr led the public outburst of laughter. People knew the story: a Corsican named Pasquale di Paoli, who was taking King George's golden pills, had helped the British navy separate the island from France in '94, but the island assembly, created by the revolution, refused to take an oath of allegiance to his Britannic Majesty unless he permitted male Corsicans to keep their voting privileges. By accepting, George, in effect, was elected King of a Corsican republic and acquired its natural-born citizens as subjects, including Napoleon Buonaparte.

The two remaining crown witnesses read off damaging allegations against Binns from their notes of the meeting. Neither mentioned his visits to navy towns, which was a relief to Francis Place. Defense counsel Sir Samuel Romilly cross-examined the note-takers. He gave a demonstration of editorial archaeology. He showed that Portland's trio, listening to the same man in the same meeting, had produced notes so contradictory that they could not be reconciled except by an elaborate synthetic reconstruction. And that, Sir Samuel demonstrated, was exactly what the crown had composed. By picking a phrase here and there from the three variants, the prosecution had turned lawful speech into an indictment for sedition.

Having demolished the prosecution, Romilly declined to call defense witnesses, thus denying the crown further opportunity to exploit testimony. Sir Samuel's summation was brief and often punctuated by Dr. Parr's gestures of approbation. Halfway through the speech, Binns pulled his sleeve, and Romilly broke off to consult his client. The lawyer began again:

"Gentlemen, were I to exercise my own judgment, I should rest my defence here. I think it would be setting a bad precedent to examine a single witness on the part of the defendant, but he is not satisfied to obtain a verdict of acquittal on the contradictions of the crown evidence, but desires—I speak to Your Honour—to be acquitted solely on the merits of his cause, the justice of his principles, and the purity of his intentions. He desires me to repeat exactly what he said. I shall therefore call all the witnesses."

This unheard-of piece of cheek left the crown servants gasping. And also Francis Place. Two schoolmasters, an anvil maker, an auctioneer's clerk, and a freight agent for the Birmingham & Liverpool Waggons thereupon recited the program of the corresponding societies to the court. A jury composed of seven squires, three yeomen, a farmer and a builder, acquitted Binns.

Binns and Place promptly got out a book, *The Trial of John Binns,* from a shorthand transcript, "Published by the Defendant," and with a Dedication to the jury: "The men who have given me liberty to publish and who have delivered me from the hands of my enemies."

The Trial of John Binns became popular reading throughout the country; the author put the addresses of the booksellers on his title page. He also ran a nose-thumbing footnote, advising one and all that he was a member of the Portsmouth Corresponding Society. Binns returned to London and became a bigger pang in Portland's angst: he hired a hall in the Strand and packed them in for political debates at a shilling a head.

Off Cadiz, Lord St. Vincent's fleet was feeling the first long swells of the earthquakes in the home fleet. Old Jarvey tightened discipline and surveillance and handed down rules against such lapses as officers appearing in his presence in round hats and laced shoes. All was quiet, cocked and buckled, when *Romulus,* 36 guns, returned early from a patrol in the Azores. St. Vincent demanded the reason from the captain: *Romulus* had met some Spithead-tainted ships in the mid-Atlantic and his people forced him to return, after securing his word that no punishments would be given. Old Jarvey put five Romuluses up for mutiny court-martial and divided the rest among his ships. He was in a precarious situation on a distant seafront. If disobedience spread he intended to use his privilege of hanging people without referring the death sentence to the King for approval.

The captain of *St. George* applied to St. Vincent for a military trial of two seamen found in the same berth. In the navy the most common and mildest epithet was "bugger," but homosexual acts were capital offenses like cowardice, mutiny and touching an officer. Ordinarily in such male prisons, sodomy was overlooked, but these two were accused of muttering "sedition" as well. The men were declared guilty and the admiral set Hanging Day for 3 July.

On the first of that month Captain Shuldham Peard of *St. George* was in his cabin when the ordinary hum of work faded out. Against the workings of the vessel and rigging, he heard the shuffle of hundreds of bare feet coming up on the quarterdeck. He sent his lieutenant out. From the front rank of the St. Georges, Gunner John Anderson and Forecastle-man Michael McCann stepped forward and handed a letter to the lieutenant. "This is a petition for mercy on behalf of the prisoners sentenced to death," said the spokesman. "We request you to give it to the captain."

When Peard saw the paper he said to his first officer, "I desire you to tell them that I am surprised at the indelicacy of their application and that I disapprove of their coming aft in this manner." When this was relayed to the company, the leaders said that they would come back in a body next morning to have the captain's answer. Peard took the petition to Old Jarvey, who ordered the executions to be performed on schedule.

Next morning, when the St. Georges came unordered to the quarterdeck, Peard read the Articles of War, and announced, "Admiral St. Vincent has given me a warrant to carry out the sentence of the court. The guilty men will certainly suffer at nine o'clock tomorrow morning. I will caution you to be on your guard and not let yourselves be seduced by a few villains among you that I am acquainted with." The chaplain delivered a sermon and prayed for his Majesty's ship *St. George*.

The captain sent a mate below to warn Anderson and McCann, the crew spokesmen, that they would be held responsible for any disturbances. That evening a lower-deck informer told Captain Peard that the men planned to seize the ship that night. He doubled the sentinels, ordered out the marines and stationed a company of infantry on the poop, to cover the main hatch. He sent an armed party below to seize Anderson and McCann, and he shipped them to Old Jarvey on *Ville de Paris*.

On Hanging Day, St. Vincent executed the two homosexuals early in the morning. The yellow flag was barely down before the red flag went up on *Ville de Paris*. Old Jarvey ordered the fleet into battle. He sailed inshore and bombarded Cadiz. The military justification was to provoke the Spanish fleet to come out and give battle. Part of it did. The larger purpose was, as St. Vincent wrote, to "employ the minds of the seamen and divert them from following the mischievous example of the ships in England" and "to divert the animal from these damnable doctrines which letters from England have produced."

St. Vincent secretly put officers to work reading all correspondence to and from his ships and was pleased to hear this extract from an outgoing letter: "Blockading is a stupid kind of work, but it is enlivened by a pleasing variety of hanging and praying, flogging and fighting."

Captain Peard convened a mutiny court for Anderson and McCann and tried two others with them. Three of the four had Irish-sounding names. Two were deserters with "R" for "run" opposite their names on old crew lists. McCann had actually served on a French republican privateer, from which he had been captured but not tried for taking up arms against his sovereign. Two fleet chaplains visited with the prisoners and placed considerations of Admiralty above those of the state religion by reporting that Anderson and McCann had confessed to hatching a mutiny plot six months before. It was alleged to include men on the great men-of-war *Britannia,* 100, *Captain,* 74, *Diadem,* 64 and *Egmont,* 74.

The death sentence was pronounced after dark on Saturday night. Old Jarvey desired rapid execution. It was not considered conducive to spreading moral lessons to hang men in the dark, and Sunday had never been profaned by the most righteous strokes of the King's justice. Nonetheless, the old disciplinarian ordered Anderson and McCann run up on Sunday morning.

Vice-Admiral Sir Charles Thompson protested executions on the Sabbath. Old Jarvey shipped him to England and sent out a general order:

> *Ville de Paris,* 8th July 1797
> Every ship of the squadron is to fend two boats, with an Officer in each, and two Marines, or Soldiers properly armed, in the Stern Sheets of each Boat, on board His Majesty's Ship the *Saint George,* at half past seven o'Clock tomorrow morning (Sunday) to attend a Punishment.
> The Sentence is to be carried into execution by the Crew of the *Saint George alone,* and no part of the Boats Crews of other Ships, as is usual on similar occasions, is to assist in this painful Service, in order to mark the high sense, the Com-

mander in Chief entertains, of the loyalty, fidelity, and Sub-ordination of the Fleet, which he will not fail to make known to the Lords Commissioners of the Admiralty, and request their Lordships to lay it before the King.

This Memorandum is to be read to the Ships Companies *before the Execution.*

After hanging the four St. Georges in this unprecedented manner, St. Vincent prodded the Admiralty to promote Captain Peard and other officers zealous in scotching organized representations from the forecastle. He told his officers that "there is much greater merit (in stopping a dangerous conspiracy) than in taking a ship of war by force from the enemy." This was a blunt statement of the policy that now dominated the King's navy, common to a Whig like Old Jarvey and to a Pittite like Sir Alan Gardner. Putting down protesting British sea slaves was more important than defeating the enemy.

Horatio Nelson, serving restlessly under Old Jarvey and waiting since March to be unloosed in his big gold raid, did not agree with the doctrine. He said, "I shall give Johnny his full scope for fighting. It is good at these times to keep the devil out of their heads. I had rather see fifty shot by the enemy than one hanged by us." The shorter survival odds Nelson wished for his men soon became operative. Old Jarvey gave the little commodore a thousand marines led by General and Admiral Thomas Troubridge, and Nelson sailed for the Canaries to grab the Spanish treasure.

While he was gone, Old Jarvey continued to hang seamen. He ordered their shipmates to run up petitioners from *El Corso,* 18, *Alcmene,* 32, and *Emerald,* 36. The Alcmenes especially grieved Lord St. Vincent; this ship had been at Spithead throughout both mutinies and had refused every plea and taunt to join the stand-out.

"Why do they send me mutinous ships?" cried Old Jarvey. "Do they think I will be hangman to the fleet?"

When Nelson's gold raiders reached Teneriffe Island in the Canaries, the seas were high and the winds unfavorable. Because of extensive shoals, the British ships could not draw close enough to cover the marine assault landings with cannon. The enemy also refused to play his role in Sir Horatio's drama. Spanish resistance was brave and dominant. The marines withdrew in fair order.

Nelson would not be appeased. He ordered a night amphibious

assault, although he felt it "a forlorn hope." He led it himself. Before he got in the boat he wrote St. Vincent, "The honor of the country calls. I never expect to return. This night, I, as humble as I am, command the whole, destined the land under the batteries of the town, and tomorrow my head will probably be crowned by either laurels or cypress."

He led a night landing of a thousand marines in raging surf that smashed boats and men on the rocks. Spanish church bells were tolling the alarm as the first attack craft reached the harbor mole and Sir Horatio stepped ashore with his sword raised. A grapeshot shattered his right arm above the elbow. He took the sword in his other hand and fell back into the arms of his stepson, Josiah Nisbet, who put on a tourniquet. As oarsmen carried Nelson back to the boat, Spanish cannon sank the cutter *Fox* with 98 men. Nelson stopped his boat to search for survivors in the dark sea and then climbed the side of the *Theseus* without assistance and called for the surgeon to amputate his arm.

Troubridge, whose record was obscured by serving under Nelson,* led three hundred marines into the plaza at Santa Cruz. By dawn their situation was hopeless, but the cocky Troubridge served notice on the Spanish governor, Don Juan Gutierrez, that he would burn the place unless he was permitted to remove his entire party under arms in their own boats. Don Juan magnanimously agreed, although he could have slaughtered Troubridge's surrounded force. The governor's sole condition was that the British would swear not to molest the Canary Islands again. The raid ended with Troubridge's color-bearers leading the marines smartly to the jetty, where Don Juan even gave them back the boats he had captured; with Nelson in agony from a bad amputation in which a ligature had been twisted around an artery; and with Nelson's stepson given command of a ship whose captain had been killed in the affair. Nelson practiced writing left-handed; to St. Vincent, "I am become a burden to my friends and useless to my country," and to Don Juan, "I beg Your Excellency will do me the honor to accept a cask of English beer and a cheese."

The Spaniard sat on his gold and ate the cheese while Nelson sailed away in gloom, wracked with pain and self-pity. But Old Jarvey forgave him the lost men and treasure and sent him to England to recuperate. The heroic egoist regained his *amour-propre* in the acclaim of the country. Nelson's fiasco became Nelson's luck. The

---

* St. Vincent considered Troubridge a better officer than Nelson. Disciplinarian appealed to disciplinarian.

King gave him the Order of the Bath and a thousand pounds a year. It was the best pension investment George III ever made. Nelson was through losing.

The British reform movement continued its battle. In contrast to the despairing gesture of the Foxites in withdrawing to their country seats and Lord Moira's deferral, the London Corresponding Society remained in contempt of Pitt. The LCS called an alfresco mass meeting on the last day of July to move another petition to the King to dismiss his ministers and make peace. Complying with the act requiring meetings of more than fifty people to be approved by the police, the LCS had put in for a license at Bow Street, but it was refused without a hearing. The Society went ahead and advertised a peaceful remonstrance on a field next to the veterinary hospital in St. Pancras. Three rostrums were erected from which the throng could hear simultaneous readings of the resolution. From all London they came on foot with wives and children, always a feature of the LCS meetings, and as they packed into the green, slow cavalry hoofs sounded behind them. Crying "Make way!" a large posse led by Sir William Addington pushed through the crowd toward the main tribune. The disturbers consisted of magistrates and constables from Bow Street, Shadwell, Whitechapel, Union Street, Queen's Square, Lambeth Street, Worship Street, Marlborough Street and Hatton Garden.

The like of it had never been seen before. For the first time the London police were gathered in a front. The Duke of Portland was answering the metropolitan democratic organization with metropolitan police. It was the germ of Scotland Yard, formed, it may be noted, for political, not criminal, reasons.

Sir William Addington stood under the LCS convener Alexander Galloway, a maker of mathematical instruments, and bawled, "This meeting is illegally convoked! I intend to read the riot act." He unreefed the document and began reading. "I ask the magistrate to tell us what is illegal about what we are doing," Galloway shouted.

Sir William did not reply.

Galloway continued. "I propose Citizen Tuckey as chairman." The audience gave this vocal acclaim. Tuckey began reading the petition to the King, joined by the orators on the other stands, John Gale Jones and John Binns. The statement reminded his Majesty that the right to petition and remonstrate was secured for the British people in the 1688 revolution and that a condition of bringing the Hanoverians to the British throne had been their commitment to defend that right. "It was solemnly recognised by your predecessors," the statement told the King.

"The riot act has been read!" shouted the Bow Street magistrate.

"I didn't hear it," a man on the tribune yelled back.

"We didn't hear it," came from the crowd.

"Then my fellow citizens," Sir William pronounced, "we are bound to disperse in peace within an hour. I conjure you to depart. I believe it will shortly be seen whether Bow Street magistrates are to be interpreters of the laws of England."

The constables pulled Galloway, Binns, Jones and Tuckey off the stands. People left the grounds. The horse soldiers rode at lingering knots of them. The posse took the men to Bow Street court where Sir William set bail at a hundred guineas each and additional sureties of fifty guineas per man for keeping the peace. When the Corresponding Society leaders came out of court, the people seated them in carriages and hauled them through the streets.

His Majesty was not interested in reading the LCS petition, but rather in how Portland broke up the meeting.

Whitehall, Monday 31 July 1797, 3:15 P.M. The Duke of Portland humbly begs leave to acquaint your Majesty that an account is this moment received from the meeting of the London Corresponding Society that they were dispersed without resistance by the Magistrates, but that four persons who persisted in speaking after the orders given by the Magistrates for the dispersion of the meeting were apprehended & were bringing away in custody.

The Duke of Portland begs leave to add for your Majesty's information that he has reason to believe that no other meetings will take place in any part of the kingdom except at Nottingham, & that he is well assured that cannot consist of more than two or three hundred people at most of the lowest & most contemptible description.

Thus Pitt and the King stumbled on in the summer of their greatest peril. In mid-July they ran into some luck; there occurred an event in France that bore out one of the aphorisms of Sun Tzu, the fifth-century B.C. Chinese military sage:

> *To secure ourselves against defeat lies in our own hands, but the opportunity of defeating the enemy is provided by the enemy himself.*

A French domestic crisis hatched a military blunder that reduced the invasion menace to Britain and may have changed the direction of European history. Lazare Hoche had wound up his victorious campaign in the east and was marching to the Atlantic with six thousand crack troops to board the transports and sail for Ireland from Brest. In Paris the energetic navy minister Truguet had almost completed arming and provisioning the amphibious strike force. But, in the Directory, the right-wing Vicomte Paul de Barras had just about overcome Lazare Carnot's forces of the left. There was a division over the Irish operation; Carnot upholding Hoche's master plan and Barras opposing the invasion. At the critical moment, Hoche's all-conquering legions bivouacked at Ferté-Allais in the outskirts of Paris, and the general rode in to confer with the Directory. Hoche intervened passionately on behalf of the blow that he and Wolfe Tone and Truguet intended to deal Britain. But Barras was more impressed with an immediate danger to himself: the most powerful army in France, resting unopposed at the city gates, and its young general the darling of the people. All Hoche needed to do was issue a proclamation, ride in at the head of his soldiers, and sweep away Barras and the new carrion feasting on the dying revolution and the loot of Napoleon. Barras moved to put Hoche into perpetual check. He replaced Admiral Truguet with an ancient oceanophobic admiral, Georges Pléville-le-Pelley, known as *"l'Amiral à la jamb de bois"* (Admiral Peg-leg). The new minister promptly rescinded Truguet's current manning and supply orders for the invasion fleets.*

Instead of bringing in his army and kicking the plotters out, Hoche kept on arguing for invasion. The young general had no power ambitions; all he desired was to invade England and overthrow another king. He planned to foster a British republic, in which the home secretary would be Thomas Hardy, founder of the London Corresponding Society.**

Barras was greatly relieved when the army of the Sambre and Meuse continued to loll in the *banlieue*. He tested Hoche again, by offering him supreme command of the Brest invasion force while it was being reduced to impotence. Hoche replied, "I do not intend to play Don Quixote on top of the sea for the pleasure of some men who wish to see me under it." †

---

* Admiral Peg-leg was constitutionally indisposed to sending ships to places where they might be lost. He resigned the next year in protest against Bonaparte's taking the fleet to Egypt.

** Hardy knew nothing of the honor awaiting him.

† *"Je n'irai plus faire le Don Quichotte sur les mers pour le plaisir de quelques hommes qui voudraient m'y voir au fond."*

Hoche left in calm disgust and marched his men around the city, the only army that ever touched Paris without investing her.

Admiral Peg-leg defeated the Brest invasion fleet more thoroughly than the British Channel fleet could ever hope to do. He disarmed nineteen sail-of-the-line and discharged their crews. He sold several frigates at public auction. They were snapped up as privateers. The state was poor and shipowners were rich. Admiral Pléville-le-Pelley made a victor out of Lord Bridport.

XXI

The Mutineer-Surgeon

We will deny justice to no one, or delay it.

—Magna Carta, 1215

THE WEST wind whistled through the Waddenzee. Wolfe Tone, alone in the great cabin of *Vrijheid,* looked through a glass and saw twenty-two English sail at anchor beyond the Texel. Below-decks the Dutch troops, packed like herrings for more than a month, were being forced into a mutiny of sheer desperation. The sick had not been removed and provisions were running short. It was early in August.

Tone had now been twenty-five days aboard *Vrijheid* without moving, "at a time when twenty-five hours are of importance." He wrote:

> There seems to be a fate in this business. Five weeks, I believe six weeks, the English fleet was paralysed by the mutinies at Portsmouth, Plymouth and the Nore. The sea was open, and nothing to prevent both the Dutch and French fleets to put to sea. Well, nothing was ready. That precious opportunity which we can never expect to return was lost; and now, that at last, we are ready here, the wind is against us, the mutiny is quelled and we are sure to be attacked by a superior force.
>
> At Brest it is, I fancy, still worse. Had we been in Ireland at the moment of the insurrection at the Nore, we should beyond a doubt have had at least that fleet, and God only knows the influence such an event might have had on the whole British navy. The destiny of Europe might have been changed forever. But, as I have already said, the great occasion is lost and we must now do as well as we can. *Le vin est tiré, il faut le boire.*

Tone played host to two Irish revolutionaries, Francis Lowry of County Down and John Tennant of Belfast, who said persecution of dissidents was rising at home and that republican morale was ebbing. The people were losing confidence in their leaders because the French invasion had not materialized. Lowry said, "They ground their suspicions on the mutiny being suffered to pass by without the French government making the smallest attempt to profit of it." The visitors claimed that "The [Irish] militia was to revolt to a man in June" and that 800 men in the Dublin garrison had been prepared to start it by seizing their barracks and magazine, all keyed to the French advent.

It was heartbreaking news, but Tone did not permit himself to collapse. Pacing the great cabin, he composed a new, decisive invasion plan. The Dutch fleet would land its troops at Harwich and march directly on London. He pictured 100,000 English forced into a last hollow square in Hyde Park: *General Tone sends a truce flag with the ultimatum: "You have the choice of surrendering now or we shall fire the four quarters of the city."* He sent the plan to General Daendels, who was not impressed.

Meanwhile the Irish underground was losing its hoarded weapons. In the last month the authorities had seized 10,000 illegal muskets, 2,000 bayonets and thousands of pistols, swords and pikes.

In the great cabin of H.M.S. *Neptune,* Mutineer-Captain William Vance of *Monmouth* stood before the court. He had been twenty years in the King's navy and had been impressed twice. He had a wife and four minor children. The damning evidence of Captain Northesk, who was prosecuting him, and Lieutenant Bullen, as main witness, could not be challenged. Vance's farewell speech before the sentence to death, was brief:

"As for the evidences they have all spoken more than the truth. The name of a captain in a state of mutiny is horrible in the eyes of the ignorant but not in the eyes of God. I give myself up to God Almighty, the honourable court and his Majesty King George the Third. I hope Lord Northesk will look after my wife and children."

The King was at Weymouth, on his customary August bathing holiday in the Channel. He was drawn into the water concealed in a bathing machine, accompanied through the surf by wading musicians playing "God Save the King." He kept up with affairs of state. He wrote Lord Spencer:

> I approve of the minutes of the court martial of the muti-neers of the *Monmouth* not having been [sent] because they are so voluminous, but the sentence [only?]; I consent that Vance, Earle, Frith, Brown and Dunn may suffer death agre-able to it; that Holmes and Callaghan be pardoned on con-dition of being confined seven years to hard labour, of which time each to be in solitary confinement for one year. William-son, Thompson and Williams to be pardoned on condition of confinement to hard labour for five years each, of which six months each in solitary confinement; Doughty to be confined three years to hard labour, six months of which in solitude.

Day after day, the King confirmed the sentences:

> Weymouth, 15 Aug. 4 P.M. As considerable doubts are en-tertained respecting the legality of the sentence of the Court Martial on James Duncan and John Evans of the *Saturn,* and that the Attorney and Solicitor General have advised that the twelve judges should be consulted upon it, these two cases must be postponed for that purpose, but the law to take its course on George Perry, John Farrel and Thomas Kenyon, whilst J. Goody, Charles Painter and Luke Eardley may be pardoned on condition of confinement to hard labour for seven years, one year of which in solitary confinement; and Simpson and Pilton to be pardoned on condition of three years confine-ment to hard labour, six months of which in solitary confine-ment, and Beedle to be pardoned on condition of forfeiting all pay due him to the time of the Court martial. I desire Earl Spencer will give the proper orders agreable to these directions.—G.R.

The "sick and weak old man," Maurice Fitzgerald, scribe of the *Monmouth* committee, came before the judges. The only evidence against him was the encomium to the executed delegate-captain, Vance, with its hope that the writer's notes on the "nobel exertions" would "be recorded in the annals of Europe . . . of future ages." The court dismissed the indictment against the infirm poet.

In *Standard* mutineer Jonathan Davis's last speech to the court, he said, "I have—or shall, I suppose, *leave*—a wife and three small children which I did the utmost in my power to maintain." He was given death. Of him and the five other Standards sentenced to hang, Captain Parr said to the court, "I am sorry to say that [they] were amongst the best of the ship's company."

In late August a second batch of prisoners from *Standard* came to military justice and one of them renewed public interest in the proceedings. William Redfern, surgeon's assistant, was the highest ranking person of all the accused in the mutiny trials. He was a warrant officer, a gentleman, and a member of the wardroom. He was one of the few defendants who was able to secure counsel.

In addition to belonging to the ship's committee, Redfern had been found with a "suspicious printed paper" and a brace of pistols when he was arrested. He was suspected of circulating seditious matter. The surgeon's assistant was in an unenviable position as the only officer who had accepted to join a mutineer's ring, and dark references to his bruiting suspicious literature seemed to seal the case for hemp.

A defense witness, Seaman Arthur McLoughlan, related how Redfern became involved with the mutiny:

> "All hands was turned up on the forecastle one morning. William Norris and William Holdsworth were standing abaft of the foremast and said to the people that they heard grumbling against Mr. Kirkwood, acting as surgeon. The people all sung out in one voice, 'Turn him ashore!' Then Bill Holdsworth asked if they had any objection against Mr. Redfern doing the duty as surgeon and they all said no, that he had behaved very well to the sick since he had been in the ship. Then Bill Holdsworth said he did not know whether Mr. Redfern would do the duty as surgeon but he said he, Holdsworth, would let us know in the evening. Then the people said, if he would not do it, they would make him do it. Redfern agreed on behalf of the sick. He had previously applied twice for discharge from the navy.

Lancelot Nicholson, foretopman, said he had been in the dispensary for treatment by Redfern when the deposed Kirkwood came in and said, "I have got orders to do no more duty as surgeon."

Redfern told him, "Please do not think I am making any interest to get preferment. I didn't want to have any hand in it, but I was obliged to do it by the consent of the ship's company."

The court asked witness Nicholson, "Did Redfern say 'by the consent' or 'by the order' of the ship's company?"

"To the best of my knowledge it was 'by the consent' of the ship's company."

The verbal distinction damaged Mr. Redfern's hopes for life.

The young officer presented his defense in the form of a curious and impudent address to the court. He began by speculating on military justice:

"As to the difference between a Court Martial and the Old Bailey or any other court which, under the authority of Parliament, meets for the equitable administration of Justice within the Kingdom, I am too young and too ignorant to be sufficiently informed. I suppose, however, that substantial justice is everywhere the same."

But it wasn't:

"If more indulgence is shown to a prisoner at the Old Bailey than at a Court Martial, a conviction of my youth, indiscretion and inexperience induces me to wish that it had been my lot to be tried there. I am, however, by no means dissatisfied in my present judges."

The surgeon's assistant was beginning to sound like John Binns at the Birmingham court. "I am accused of circulating suspicious papers, some printed," Redfern said. "I would remind the court that Algernon Sidney was condemned by Jefferies for writings found upon him without any proof of their emission and this sentence has since been condemned by moral and informed men of all parties." Sidney was a republican leader of the previous century who was convicted of treason before Lord Justice Jefferies and beheaded in the Tower.

"I stand charged with making and encouraging mutiny," Redfern said. "But what kind of a mutiny can a man make by carrying a piece of paper concealed about his clothes? Let whatever you please be contained in it or written upon it. That is indeed a formidable mutiny that is made in a man's pocket, which he can easily suppress with his tobacco box or smother with his handkerchief."

The admiral and the captains sent the defendants below, then readmitted them to be sentenced.

"John Burrows. The court finds the charges proved against you. The court have determined that you shall suffer death . . .

"Joseph Hudson. Whole of the charges proved. . . . However, the court recommends mercy on account of the wounds you have incurred in his Majesty's service and your constant state of drunkenness during the period of the mutiny."

Came the decision on the marine sergeant who had committed to paper one mutinous gesture, which was found among the documents of the *Standard* committee: "Thomas Lunniss. The court have determined that you shall suffer death . . . be accordingly hanged by the neck . . ."

"William Redfern!"

The surgeon's assistant faced it.

"The court finds that the charges against you have been proven. In consideration of your professional situation leading you more among the mutineers than the other officers were obliged to be, the court recommends mercy to his Majesty."

"Bryan Finn. Three hundred lashes . . ."

"Joseph Glaves. Two hundred lashes . . ."

During the trials, his Majesty's sloop-of-war *Stork* pursued and captured the French privateer *Lynx* in the Channel. Seven escaped Nore mutineers were found in the French crew. As they were called on deck to be carried off in chains one of them, an impressed man named Martin, shot himself dead. The body was taken ashore and, according to the law for suicides, it was buried at a crossroads with a stake driven through the heart.

Sir Edward Pellew captured a French corvette bound from Rochefort with political prisoners for the penal colony at Cayenne. Jammed suffocatingly in the bilge were twenty-five Roman Catholic priests. Sir Edward, an irreproachable Protestant—otherwise he would not have been commanding H.M. Ship *Indefatigable*—treated the clergymen with special kindness and sent them off as cabin passengers with a prize crew composed of Irishmen, who knelt to the fathers. Perhaps it was not an accident that the prize crew consisted of the more vocal Irish republicans aboard *Indefatigable*. The French priests started a monastery in Dorsetshire and prayed every day for Sir Edward and Jack Rosbiff.

At the Moot Hall in Northumberland, a lay critic named John Leverit was convicted of sedition for proclaiming, "It is no matter to me who is King or Queen. Damn their eyes. I have no freehold or estate to lose. I may have a chance to get some, and it is a matter of how soon we have a revolution. Blast them. They want to starve the sailors at the Nore; damn their eyes, they have more need to pay their wages: they have four years due, and the blasted government has no money to pay them. The poor fellows are all naked and it is high time for them to get their eyes opened." Such sentiments were common and the populist newspapers took care to repeat them in print when they were privileged as legal evidence. Leverit was sentenced to four years in prison to be paroled at the end of one year upon giving a surety of £140.

At Gravesend, when the Nore mutiny had broken up, 560 men were pointed out and imprisoned as delegates or activists, and 412 of them were held for trial. At least 59 were sentenced to death and at least 36 hanged.* Not more than 200 actually received legal process.

The court itself handed down five results: death, death with a recommendation of mercy, imprisonment, flogging, or acquittal. The Admiralty then interpreted mercy as life transportation to Australia, or various terms at hard labor and solitary confinement, which his Majesty was gracious enough to endorse in all instances. In several cases, the judges found a man innocent but made him forfeit back pay and prize money.

Justice aboard H.M.S. *Neptune* was a changeable muse. From *Monmouth*, 51 men were arraigned, from her sister *Belliqueux* only 3; yet *Belliqueux* was the parliament ship at Yarmouth and *Monmouth* deserted the mutiny. Six Monmouths were executed and no "Bellycues."

Despite the escape of John Blake and eleven committeemen, 41 men from *Inflexible* were tried. None received death, nor did a single man from Bligh's *Director,* the last ship to surrender. Her two delegates, Hulme and MacLaurin, who were captured ashore by Magistrate Graham, got off with their lives. William Bligh knew the value of a good foreman hanging from a yardarm as an example to others, as contrasted to a good foreman with a bit of mutiny on his record, pacing around the forecastle inpiring them.

---

* Prof. Conrad Gill, first to apply scholarly discipline to the mutiny archives, found that 24 were executed. Professor Bonamy Dobrée and his collaborator, G. E. Manwaring, said 29. The present author went over the same sources and found 31 hangings. In 1963, Professor A. Aspinall produced a wonderful volume, *The Later Correspondence of George III,* v. 2, 1793-1797, and outscored us all. Aspinall prints copies of letters in H.M.'s own handwriting, affirming the death sentences of 36 men of the Nore. We must believe that when the King ordered a man hanged, he was hanged. Did others die whose sentences have not been preserved in the Admiralty or royal records?

The most men hanged from a single ship were seven from *Leopard.* (Lord Bridport exceeded this harvest a month later when he swung eight men from H.M.S. *Glory,* at Spithead.) Forty-six Lions went up for their lives and all were spared. Only two men were charged from *Iris* and they vanished before the court-martial. Five other indictments were vacated by the inability of the provost to deliver the accused to the court. Every man in *Lancaster* was pardoned, including her mutineer-captain, James Wilson, who had conferred with Samuel Whitbread, M.P., during the mutiny.

The entire company of the little fireship *Comet* was pardoned.

Approximately three hundred men were interned in the prison hulk *Eagle,* at Gillingham Reach. They included men sentenced to prison and transportation, but most were simply incarcerated at his Majesty's pleasure, with better chances of a flogging than of due process.

As the train of courts-martial in the greatest military mutiny in history passed toward its end in the late days of August, the Lords Commissioners of Admiralty felt a conflict of desires, one for exemplary punishment and the other for professional foremast hands. Orders were sent down to H.M.S. *Eagle* to pick well-behaved mutineers not under court-martial orders and hand them over to needful ships. No two former shipmates were to be sent to the same vessel. Before they were parceled out, Captain Pine of the gunboat *Firm* conducted a short reorientation course in which the prisoners gave a solemn promise not to engage in more mutinies or swear to illegal oaths. These undertakings, however, were not made on a sworn oath. The Admiralty was still incapable of understanding and adopting the most powerful mystique of the delegates: to take a humbled and beaten subject and raise him to manhood and collective strength by administering an oath of fidelity to a cause.

After loyalty class on H.M.S. *Firm,* the successful graduates of the prison hulk were inducted aboard their new ships with impressive rites, the company at general quarters, the marine square glowering, the penitents at the mainmast and the captain extracting more promises that they would shun mutiny and secret oaths and love their King. The whistles sounded. The ex-mutineers took their hammocks below. The Admiralty's remission of sin had another condition: they would receive no arrears of back pay or prize money due. Thus, in a modest way, the mutineers helped sustain the national credit in Britain's blackest year.

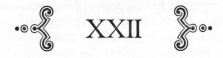

Camperdown

"Aft the most honour; forward the better men."

—British navy proverb

I N PARIS, furious plots and counterplots filled Fructidor, the fruit-ful month. President Carnot's republican grouping regained ground lost to Paul de Barras and brought in Lazare Hoche as Minister of War. Standing on his mountain of loot in Italy, with southern Europe prostrate before his army, Napoleon Bonaparte encouraged Barras's faction to suppress election results in 49 departments of France. On 18 Fructidor (4 September) the rightists staged a *coup d'état* which sent President Carnot fleeing for his life to Switzerland, leaving the contest for power to the two young marshals whose armies he had provided. Hoche was set on stopping Napoleon who had cheated him several times, notably in signing a truce with Austria alone, after Hoche had furnished the decisive victory and Carnot the soldiers. The young Minister of War had too much popularity and too many fighting friends to be easily turned out of power.

Hoche's enlarged powers and the Napoleonic *putsch* sent Lord Malmesbury, Pitt's negotiator, pelting back to London after four months of vain peace talks. On the Royal Exchange, Britain's safest bonds, the bellweather 3 percent consuls, fell to a new low.

In Holland, Wolfe Tone had been cooped up in *Vrijheid* for two months. He sensed that with the end of the Nore mutiny and the restoration of British strength in the approaches to Ireland the Dutch command was looking for an alternate adventure against the British Isles. He went to Paris to propose a new scheme to Hoche: He and Admiral de Winter would issue forth with fighting ships only, no transports, and give battle to Adam Duncan. If victorious, the Dutch could send with impunity 15,000 troops to Edinburgh. Tone was advocating the very tactic he had opposed in previous councils-of-war, but he wanted to move the Batavian republic into action somehow.

While Tone was en route to Paris, two shattering events went against him. At the Texel, rations for the ship-imprisoned Dutch troops became dangerously low and disease approached epidemic rates in the packed holds. General Daendels and Admiral de Winter were forced to disembark the invasion army and, having no billets or means to feed the soldiers ashore, demobilize them. Unknown to Tone, the plan he was taking to Paris was void and meaningless.

And at the moment he was about to make a two-front struggle against Bonaparte and the British, Lazare Hoche was stricken with a ravaging illness. Tone arrived in Hoche's anteroom to see four grenadiers carrying the young minister to his desk. The radiant leader, still only thirty, had been reduced in one week to an emaciated, coughing invalid with "asthmatic convulsions." But Hoche's spirit was not maimed. He encouraged Tone on the new plan and spoke with bold resolution against Bonaparte and Barras.

Tone came from the reunion half sick, noting, "I have the most serious alarms for his life." In five days Hoche was dead. The medical cause was given as galloping consumption. Hoche's army and many Jacobins believed he had been poisoned, despite the autopsy finding of natural death.* Now no republican general stood in the way of Bonaparte's advance to dictatorship.

Wolfe Tone's models for the deliverance of Ireland lay in pieces. The Dutch troops at the Texel were demobilized. President Carnot, who believed in taking the war to British soil, was a fugitive. And Hoche, his comrade, the ever-victorious captain, was a shriveled corpse. Tone, again a penniless émigré, started all over to find Frenchmen who would help his cause.

The crippled and slippery Charles Maurice de Talleyrand became French foreign minister. He was always on the winning side: before the revolution he was a Roman Catholic bishop, afterward celebrated a pagan mass; backed the most radical faction of the revolution, but absented himself in London and Philadelphia during the feud between the Girondists and the Jacobins; and now turned up as a minister in an antirevolutionary regime.** Wolfe Tone had known Talleyrand in Philadelphia and now got his ear on occasion.

---

* The autopsy of Napoleon gave cancer as his fatal ailment. Recent analyses of locks of hair from his head show a high content of arsenic, which may have been systematically fed to the ex-dictator over a long period.

** Talleyrand was only getting in stride. He helped Napoleon overthrow Barras and was made a prince. He helped the allies overthrow Napoleon, and died after inducing the church to give him the last rites of a bishop.

Paris merchants pledged funds to a renewed cross-Channel campaign. Tone's hopes grew as Bonaparte came to Paris to take command of a newly promulgated *armée d'angleterre,* a projected invasion force larger than any Hoche had dreamed. Talleyrand sent Tone to Bonaparte, who received the Irishman in "a small, neat house" in the rue Chanteleine, where he lived "in great simplicity." The general flattered the visitor by opening a folder to Tone's old memoranda on French invasions of Ireland. Tone did not, however, get to examine a special library which Bonaparte was studying in the little house. It consisted of books on the East, stolen from the Ambrosian library in Milan during the Italian campaign. In the volumes the general had set down marginal notes next to passages dealing with Egypt.

In late September, there began the famous horror on H.M.S. *Hermione,* 32, a frigate of the West Indies station. She was cruising the Mona Passage between Santo Domingo and Puerto Rico. Her commander was Captain Hugh Pigot who possessed interest through the commander-in-chief of the West Indies, Admiral Sir Hyde Parker. Pigot was one of the most brutal captains in an age full of them. "All hands aft to witness punishment" was almost a daily cry on his decks. He did not use upended gratings but spread-eagled flagellees over the capstan. One of his able seamen, a twenty-three-year-old Irishman named Martin Steady, one of the most willing and reliable hands on *Hermione,* was flogged eight times in ten months. Pigot killed at least two men with the cat. After three successive whippings, one fatally injured man lingered in pain for eighteen weeks.

Hermione was giving chase to a Yankee schooner from Newport, Rhode Island, when her company reached the explosion point. A tropical storm came up and Pigot sent the topmen aloft to take in canvas. The men on the leaping mizzen topsail yard clutched at the whipping reef points as the gale threatened to tear away the sail. Pigot's bellows through the speaking trumpet unnerved some raw hands on the yard. They heard the dreaded bawl of the captain: "I'll flog the last man down!"

The yard heaved viciously and three youths crashed to the deck at the captain's feet. Two were white boys in their teens, the other a Negro youth named Peter Bascomb. Pigot looked at the dying youngsters and shouted, "Throw the lubbers overboard!" A general moan of disbelief and anger was heard in the tops, over the wind. Pigot looked up and met the hard stares of his crew. "Bosun's mates!" cried the captain. "Start all those men!" Two mates went aloft with their clublike knotted hempen ropes and belabored the men laying across the yardarms. As the ship rode reefed down in the darkness, everyone aboard knew tomorrow would be flogging day.

Next morning Pigot took up another chase on what seemed a privateer and while *Hermione* bounded after the prize, fourteen maintopmen were heavily flogged at the capstan. By nightfall, while *Hermione* was still trying to close on the strange sail, a meeting took place in the forecastle. The proceedings were enlivened by a bucket of rum stolen from the gunroom officers' stores. The group included the captain of the foretop, an Italian maintopman, the gunroom steward, a youngster from Kent, two Irishmen, a Cornishman, and a Dane. Of the 181 members of the ship's company whose national origins were given in the *Hermione* muster book, there were 47 English, 18 Irish, 10 Scots, 4 Americans, 3 Italians, 3 Swedes, and one member of His Britannic Majesty's navy each from Spain, Denmark, Norway, Portugal, Prussia, Nova Scotia, Hanover, France, St. Thomas and Barbados.

At midnight, Marine Private Andrew O'Neill, sentinel at the captain's door, was felled by the flat of a cutlass, and an attacker wrenched away his musket and fixed bayonet. Ten men kicked down the captain's door. Two of them were the bosun's mates Pigot had sent to beat the men on the yards and others were carrying blood-caked stripes from Pigot's second round that morning. As they burst into the cabin, the captain leaped out of bed in his nightshirt and grabbed a two-foot dirk.

Stooping under the beams and slashing out with hangers and tomahawks, the murderers probed for Pigot in the dark. He howled, "Where are my bargemen?" The Dane replied, "Here are your bargemen!" The wild frenzy to hack the tyrant reduced the furniture to wreckage but some blows told. The captain was wounded in a dozen places, but he managed to cut some of his attackers with his dirk. Pigot collapsed over the breech of the twelve-pounder stern chaser and pleaded for his life.

The attackers paused. The deck above was hammering with footfalls. The cries of the general rising sounded outside. Men threw the first lieutenant overboard and gained the wheel.

"You bugger, aren't you dead yet?" an Irish seaman said to Pigot. "No, you villain, I'm not," said the captain, sticking out his dirk. A seaman cut him with a tomahawk and a cutlass swipe knocked him to the blood-slippery deck. Pigot got up again, lurching. "Have mercy, my lads!" The Italian ran him through with the marine sentry's bayonet. "You showed no mercy yourself!" They kicked out the lights in a stern window, took hold of Pigot and swung him into the warm dark sea and heard him shouting in the foamy wake. One of the assassins told the captain's steward, "I just launched your bloody master overboard."

"Hughie's overboard!"

"The ship is ours!"

They took another officer in his dressing gown and tomahawked him and piked him to death on the gratings. They chased a screaming boy midshipman and cut him down for having learned his lessons too well from Captain Pigot; little Mr. Smith had ordered many men flogged. They pitched the midshipman over the side.

"Hand the buggers up!"

"Launch the buggers!"

The mutineers killed six more officers and took *Hermione* into the trades for Venezuela. About one-quarter of the crew had carried the ship with the rest terrified or supine. When the vessel arrived in Venezuela, only a half dozen lower-deck people removed themselves from responsibility by turning themselves over to the Spanish as prisoners-of-war instead of as defectors. Although an Irish crewman took the opportunity to give republican harangues to the company, there appears to have been no political or economic reason behind the *Hermione* mutiny. It was purely Georgian.

For the Hermiones, escape from naval rigors also removed their security, or what little an eighteenth-century seaman had. They were obliged to accept the next thing to convict labor on Spanish rock piles and in the salt pans. Most of them shipped out on American and other neutral vessels under assumed names.

The Lords Commissioners of Admiralty pursued the Hermiones with unsparing relentlessness. The outrage made the transgressions of Richard Parker seem quaint. Lord Spencer believed that no officer could sleep peacefully in his berth if the *Hermione* mutineers were not brought to spectacular execution. In an exchange with the Spanish, his lordship obtained the six men who had surrendered as prisoners-of-war. He collected thirty-five more people from the frigate's company, pardoned the lot and made them King's evidence men with the sole duty of tracking down their shipmates. These privileged characters were distributed to many ports where they could be seen in pairs, walking the front and looking over the men in taverns.

Six months after Captain Pigot's death, the first *Hermione* mutineer was hanged and gibbeted at Port Royal. A week later three more bodies were placed in high strap-iron cages at Cape St. Nicholas

Mole. At home the five surviving officers were court-martialed for losing the ship. The trial was held on *Director,* with William Bligh a member of the court that absolved the officers of blame.

Another group of mutineers was captured and tried. Three were found innocent, including the twelve-year-old son of Captain Pigot's cook. Shocked by the verdict, Sir Hyde Parker demanded that the sea lords remove the President of the Court for letting down "discipline and subordination."

Within a year of the *Hermione* mutiny, eleven men were hanged, one sent to Botany Bay for life, and three acquitted. Soon two more cadavers were on display at Gallow's Point, Jamaica. At Spithead, two were found guilty and three acquitted. Sir Edward Pellew sat on that court and insisted that one of the convicts be hanged immediately because "if delay were allowed, he would meet his fate with hardihood which would destroy the value of the example." The President of the Court demurred on the grounds that the Admiralty warrant of death had to be signed, sealed and delivered before execution. Pellew cited the Act of Parliament outlawing the Nore mutineers. The court summoned the prisoner and told him he was to be hanged in an hour. "You will not allow me a little time to make my peace with God?" he asked. The man was run up outside the court-martial chamber on H.M.S. *Gladiator.* Sir Edward Pellew received the news that "the fleet was appalled when the close of the court-martial was announced to them by the signal for execution."

Some Hermiones with assumed names were impressed from merchantmen at sea but were identified by the King's evidence men. As had been true at Spithead and the Nore, "all the best men were the principals of the mutineers," to quote a *Hermione* officer when they hanged the Dane who had tomahawked Captain Pigot. Two mutineers rejoined the navy under aliases and won coveted oars in a captain's barge. King's evidence men found them in Portsmouth years later. Nine years after the mutiny, the yellow flag was broken out on the *Salvador del Mundo* at Plymouth and the twenty-fourth guilty Hermione was hauled up to the yard. The navy even recaptured the *Hermione* herself in Venezuela. It was a daring cutting-out expedition led by a captain every bit as cruel as Hugh Pigot.

At the Cape of Good Hope, early in October of 1797, a neutral Danish merchantman was leaving St. Simon's Bay for Copenhagen, when a hail came from a boat belonging to H.M.S. *Tremendous,* 74, flagship of Thomas Pringle, Esquire, Rear Admiral of the Red, Com-

mander-in-Chief of His Majesty's Ships & Vessels Employed at the
Cape of Good Hope and the Seas Adjacent. The Danish skipper re-
ceived the boat's officer, who said, "Compliments of Admiral Pringle.
He directs me to request of you whether you should be touching an
English port during your passage."

"It is possible."

"Then, sir, Admiral Pringle desires to know if you would greatly
mind posting a letter to the Lords Commissioners of Admiralty."

The Dane took the letter. It was the only means Pringle could find
to report a general mutiny in his fleet.

A month earlier his seamen at the Cape had received the grand
and long-traveled news of Black Dick Howe's award of better pay
and rations and the removal of cruel officers in the home fleet. They
waited vainly a month for these gains, then formed a fleet parliament,
the third that British seamen instituted in the tumultuous year of
'97. It was led by Andrew Burnett and James Willis, delegates of the
flagship. Eight vessels were involved.

Tremendous collected the grievances of each company:

> The master is much disliked having a most Haughty and con-
> temptuous manner. Had he been on good terms with a supe-
> rior officer he would be a Terror to a ships company. The
> Gunner is cruel and the Purser a thief. —*Imperieuse, 38*

> A vast deal of Mouldy Bread served out and when returned,
> has been re-served out again. . . . Weights and Measures
> in general vastly short of the proper Stipulation . . . very
> unregular hours, both for Work & serving out food for sup-
> port of Our Bodies. . . . One of [our officers] we have turned
> on Shore, He being very Abusive, Haughty and to often
> apt to lifting up his Fist, often without Cause. Query. What
> must be done to others of that Character? —*Braave, 40*
> (Signed by twelve committeemen)

> We agree to keep the Boatswain, Mr. Stenham, on board
> against his further good conduct. We ask for unnecessary work
> to be stopt such as Holy Stoning and washing the Decks.
> The Officers have the prime of meat; We ask that they should
> have mutton every 3rd day like the rest of the Ship. We get
> no greens or vegetables. We want something hot for break-
> fast as well as Burgoo. —*Trusty, 50.*

> Have turned on shore Mr Bayley Master's Mate and Fran-
> cis Crawford Midshipman; the other officers are held in great

respect. We are fully satisfied. —*Chichester,* 44, By John Hicks and George Huggett, delegates.

Turned the master on shore, an infamous character. The beef and bread is bad. The pease is unfit to eat. All measures are short. The people should not be punished for small crimes. —*Star,* 14. By Thomas Pickering (his mark) and John Forton (his mark), delegates.

The company of *Tremendous* put their captain, George Hopewell Stephens, ashore and set up a lower-deck court-martial board of thirteen tars to try him for cruelty. The seamen had begun by complaining against officers, went on to ignore their orders, then put them ashore, afterward held them hostage, and now were proposing to mete out punishment to post-captains with the King's commission.

The grievances of the Cape of Good Hope fleet delegates echoed the Spithead demands, plus the charge that the rum was short and the officers were taking it all. There was no flavor of the Nore in the document. It recognized Admiral Pringle's victualing difficulties and asked that, for condemned bread, "better Bread be substituted in its Room, or a just and sufficient reason why such Bread cannot be procured."

The delegates even extended an excuse to Admiral Pringle for not increasing food and pay:

The People of this Squadron has heard something of the Conduct of His Majesty's Fleet in England and the regulations that has taken place in Consequence with regard to the Extra Allowance of Pay and Provisions, but as we do not expect that you have received any Official Intelligence sufficient to Act on the occasion, We do not expect those Regulations to take place until that time may arrive and we are determined to Patiently Wait the Event.

Admiral Pringle replied promptly:

As I have nothing more at Heart than the Welfare of the People under my Command, I have examined with attention the Nature of the Different Articles of Complaint, some of which had they been quietly represented to the several Captains of the Squadron would by them either have been removed, or the impossibility of it explained, particularly relative to Provisions, for instance the Bread, from the great scarcity of Flour in the Colony has been necessarily made much Coarser for the Fleet, the Army and the Inhabitants.

The admiral ordered a survey of the bread and proposed serving the part found edible as half the daily ration, the other half to be "Biscuit of very superior Quality, which having Lately arrived from India, I have purchased for the Fleet."

He reminded the people that a month earlier he had ordered ships' butchers and an officer from each ship to be present in the Colony slaughterhouse when fleet beef and mutton was butchered, and to reject bad meat. "In respect to Officers having choice pieces, it is improper, although it has long been a Custom in the Navy . . . but Orders shall be given that no such thing be permitted to take place in future in the Squadron," he said.

Admiral Pringle could do little about rum: only *Tremendous* had a stock and it sufficed for only one-fourth of her company. However, he promised to procure tobacco which had disappeared in the Good Hope squadron.

The delegates expressed content with the food concessions. There remained the question of undesirable officers. Pringle made an offer: if the seamen would take all officers back on board, he would immediately arrest those against whom the men would lay charges, and court-martial them "as soon as a sufficient Number of Captains *not concerned* can be assembled." The delegates agreed and Pringle wrote a general amnesty.

In this most distant station, months from orders or support, there was a spirit of moderation and conciliation on both sides. Harmony was restored in Pringle's fleet one week after the business began. Captain Stephens demanded a court-martial, which was duly ordered and convened on *Sceptre*. Several of the Tremendouses who testified against him were accused of "mischievous" and "unruly" behavior while under oath. Shephens was acquitted and they were charged. There was a vociferous protest on *Tremendous*. Admiral Pringle wrote her acting captain:

I am determined that if the Company of the said Ship do not deliver up the Persons who were Promoters of the Riotous and Mutinous behavior so that they may be punished according to Law, I will declare them immediately to be in a state of Rebellion, and cause my Flag to be struck on board said Ship, and will also Order all communication between her and the others Ships, as well as with the Shore, to be cut off.

He gave the Tremendouses two hours to deliver the leaders. There was a scrimmage on board and the main spirits of the new protest were handed over. "The leading offenders were executed or flogged, and discipline was restored," says William Laird Clowes, the navy historian.

Admiral Pringle sent his dispatches on the affair to England by courier—none other than Captain Stephens, thus getting rid of him, honorably and correctly. He recommended that the Admiralty continue to pay Stephens as a post-captain while he was en route and while canvassing the victualing boards for better provisions for the Cape of Good Hope. Stephens was not given another command.

After the Nore mutiny, Adam Duncan cruised his ships off the Texel all summer long, concerned equally with the Dutch and with curing Nore aftereffects by continuous hard work. After nearly four months, scurvy and sprung seams in his ancient craft forced him to return to Yarmouth. He left *Russell, Adamant* and *Circe* to watch the Dutch. At Yarmouth Sands, Duncan told his officers, "I shall not, gentlemen, put foot out of the ship. Your supplies of water and provisions shall be sent to you in the morning, and I hope to be able to sail again in twenty hours, when an early meeting with the enemy will give us cause to rejoice. The caulkers shall go over my ship's bows in the morning and do their best to keep her afloat."

But reality could not match Duncan's fervor. The ships were in Yarmouth for a week. Early on 9 October the lugger *Black Joke* came out of the North Sea under full press of sail with a signal hoist notifying Duncan that the Dutch were out. By noon he got eleven sail-of-the-line under way for a battle that he sought for two years.

Admiral de Winter had emerged two days before with sixteen sail-of-the-line, five frigates and five brigs. Wolfe Tone was ashore and did not know of the sailing. Most of the Dutchmen were converted merchant vessels; although their total firepower approximated that of Duncan, they had no death-dealing carronades and he had ninety. The three British vessels at the Texel shadowed the Dutch and sent a second lugger to Duncan, reporting that de Winter was sailing southwest toward England.

The tall Dutch admiral was on an unwilling sortie. He had no troops aboard for an invasion. There was no French or Spanish naval force available to make a junction with him to outgun Duncan. And October weather was treacherous. Jan de Winter came out because he was ordered to come out by the naval committee of the Batavian republic, and the reason was national pride, which is a dangerous thing for people to entrust to transient governors. His orders were to do battle with the English if there was any chance of victory. He was to be inspired by the great seamen of the past, Maarten Hapertzoon Tromp and de Ruyter, who had humiliated the English. "In case of an approaching engagement," his instructions went, "you are to try to draw the enemy as near the harbors of the republic as will be possible in conformity with the rules of prudence and strategy." Dutch ships, designed for their shallow home waters, were at an advantage over the deepwater English vessels on a foreshore, where de Winter could safely cruise, attracting the impetuous Duncan toward breaking up on the shoals. Moreover, the wind was blowing a fresh northeasterly, carrying Duncan toward his enemy and the shoals.

De Winter was forty miles down the coast when a fisherman told him the British were coming. He turned about and made for the Texel, obeying his orders to pull the enemy toward a Dutch harbor. He was fifteen miles from home, off the village of Kamperduin, when Duncan's two divisions sighted his long battle line. An officer said to Duncan, "How many ships do you propose to engage with this division?" The admiral said, "Really, sir, I can't ascertain, but when we have beat them, we'll count them." Without trying to unify his mismatched fleet with its various rates of speed, Duncan plunged ahead.

The Dutch line was five miles off the dunes. As the King's navy bore in, Duncan's pilot said, "It's awful shallow, sir. I'm afraid we'll go aground." Duncan replied, "Go on at your peril. I'll fight the ships on land if I cannot by sea."

Duncan, in *Venerable,* commanded the northern attacking group in a ragged line abeam. Five of his eight vessels had been out in the Nore mutiny, including *Belliqueux,* the original parliament ship, and *Circe,* the frigate which had conducted a simultaneous mutiny and blockade of the enemy.

To Duncan's right, Vice-Admiral Richard Onslow in *Monarch* led an even more ragged spread of ten ships, half of which had been under the red flag at the Nore. William Bligh in *Director* was in the middle of this force. He logged the clash:

At noon our fleet standing in two divisions for action. The *Monarch, Russell, Director* and *Montagu* the headmost ships. The *Monarch* on our larboard [port] beam, standing toward the Dutch Vice-Admiral. Adm! Duncan nobly leading his division towards the Dutch Command! in Chief . . . . At 12.40 the *Monarch* began to engage the Dutch Vice Adm! in a most spirited manner. At 12.45, we began with the 2nd ship in the rear, the *Russell* just begun before us with the sternmost ship. The rest of our division came on & and on all sides there was a general fireing.

The battle of Camperdown (watched from the dunes by the villagers of Kamperduin) was one of the most fanatical sea fights of the century. It turned into a free-for-all with the Dutch yielding nothing to the English in valor, although their armament was inferior and their officers and gunners not so proficient; Duncan's men fired three shots to de Winter's two.

In this high century of naval sail, an uncompromising sea battle was a horror unsurpassed by modern machine warfare. The compulsion of commanders was to bring the big wooden vessels physically together, forming a compact butcher shop. The grappling of two matched warships was like a collision of overcrowded poorhouses, whose lousy, half-starved and choking inmates fired cannons point-blank through the windows at each other. Men literally shot each other to pieces, and saw the pieces. The carnage did not occur miles away, but where you stood: a messmate suddenly fell headless or a powder boy spun in an uncomprehending annoyance on one leg while an iron ball splattered his other leg along the deck.

The poorhouse roofs were covered with screaming men firing muskets or grenades, the decks often abrawl with men thrusting into each other with cutlasses, pikes and bayonets, slipping and falling in gore. Fires started in various places were attended to by holders and landsmen who passed sea water in leathern buckets, the British ones decorated with His Majesty, God Bless Him. When fires got out of control, the fighting would stop while both crews attacked the flames. The ships ground against each other, fouling yards and rigging. Shot-off spars and masts flung the men in the fighting tops down on those below and great timbers crushed them. Duncan's flagship at Camperdown had a net rigged over the quarterdeck. It was called a *sauve tête.*

After ninety minutes of it, Bligh caught sight, through the rolling smoke, of *Vrijheid.* The Dutch flagship was not engaged. He wrote:

There was no time to be lost! Night was approaching &
and as there were enough ships in our lee division about the
rear of the enemy to take possession of them, for I considered
now the capture of the Dutch Commander-in-Chief's ship as
likely to produce the capture of those ahead of him, and I desired my first Lieu. to inform the officers & men I was determined to be alongside the Dutch Admiral. At 3.5, we began the action with him, lying on his larboard quarter within
20 yds, by degrees we advanced alongside, fireing tremen-
dously at him, & then across his bows almost touching, when
we carried away his foremast, topmast, t.g. mast & soon after
his mainmast together with his mizen mast, & left him nothing
standing. The wreck[age] lying all over his starboard side,
most of his guns were of no use, I therefore hauled up along
his starboard side & there we finished him, for at 3ʰ/55 he
struck and the action was ended.

Bligh's account of conquering de Winter's flagship does not report
what had happened to *Vrijheid* before his attack. He did not see it
and what you do not see you are not required to enter in the ship's
log. In fact Adam Duncan had tackled the Dutchman first, then
Ardent and *Powerful* assailed *Vrijheid. Ardent* must have chipped
away a lot of timber for Bligh to harvest, for she lost 41 killed and
107 wounded, while *Director* sustained merely 3 wounded.

An officer of *Ardent* said, "Our wounded are in general dreadfully
mangled. One of the men's wives assisted in firing a gun where her
husband was quartered, though frequently requested to go below,
but she would not be prevailed on to do so until a shot carried away
one of her legs and wounded the other."

Bligh sent a lieutenant to *Vrijheid,* who found Fleet Admiral de
Winter, the only unwounded officer on board, on his knees on the
quarterdeck, holding a sheet of lead over a hole in a small boat while
the carpenter nailed it on. It was the admiral's hope of escape. He
was taken aboard *Venerable,* where he held out his sword to Adam
Duncan. The massive Scotsman, who did not have to look down on
de Winter, said, "I would much rather take a brave man's hand
than his sword."

The King's navy captured seven battleships, two 50-gun ships, and
two frigates, half the effective strength of the Dutch navy. The battle
of Camperdown was won by men who had been in a state of mutiny
a few months before. On ex-mutinous vessels 89 men were killed in
action and 336 wounded. The total British loss was 228 killed,

812 wounded. The Dutch losses were many times more men, not only swept down by the British carronades and rapid hull-piercing fire, but by drowning in captured hulks that sank during a storm that came up at the close of battle. Lt. Charles Bullen, the enterprising officer who took *Monmouth* out of the Nore mutiny, was in charge of the shattered prize *Delft,* 54, when she went down. Some of the surviving Dutch, a brother officer and part of the prize crew perished. Bullen came out swimming and was picked up alive. Dutch prisoners amounted to 3,775 men.

The riddled Dutch ships were of no use to the British navy. Duncan's ships were scarcely more seaworthy. The Dutch had cannoned the hulls English-style. Part of the victorious fleet went to Great Yarmouth while Duncan took most of the ships and prizes around to the Nore. He and the ex-mutineers had lifted the direct threat of war and enemy occupation from the British Isles for at least the winter ahead. They had saved Pitt's administration.

As he landed at Sheerness, Duncan was notified that he was now Baron Duncan of Lundie and Viscount Duncan of Camperdown, that he was to have the Freedom of the City of London and a 200-guinea sword. The royal theatres put on tableaux of de Winter striking his flag on *Vrijheid,* while a convenient band played "Rule Britannia." Thomas Hardy, founder of the LCS, kept his Piccadilly shoe shop dark during the victory illuminations. A loyal mob arrived to pull the place down. A hundred members of the Corresponding Society successfully defended the shoe shop with cudgels, "in a long-continued and well-conducted" street battle, according to their commander, John Binns.

Charles Dibdin, the Robert Burns of the establishment, hailed Camperdown with a ditty, "A Salt Eel for Mynheer." The last stanza contains the only illusion to lower-deck discontent in the hundreds of navy songs he wrote:

> *Your true honest maxim I've heard 'em commend*
> *Is the nation you live in to sing;*
> *Where your property, children, your wife and your friend,*
> *Are in the care of their father the King.*
> *The man, then, so blest, who disseminates strife,*
> *Deserves, while he sinks in disgrace,*
> *Neither King to protect him, to love him a wife,*
> *Nor children to smile in his face.*

CHORUS

No! While English bosoms boast English hearts,
We'll tip 'em all a round touch,
While with ardour each starts that nothing can quench,
We'll bang the Spaniards,
Belabour the Dutch,
And block up and laugh at the French.

Bulstrode, Friday night, 13 Oct. 1797. The Duke of Portland ventures to hope that your Majesty will forgive his presumption in availing himself of the opportunity of laying before your Majesty his most humble & most sincere congratulations on *the glorious victory* obtained over the fleet from the Texel by your Majesty's squadron under Admiral Duncan's commands, an event which, while it contributes to your Majesty's satisfaction in proportion as it reflects lustre on the national character, the Duke of Portland trusts may also lead your Majesty's more essential happiness by the possibility of its opening a prospect of the restoration of publick tranquillity & order by the convincing & incontrovertible proof it affords of the insuperable superiority under the blessing of Providence of your Majesty's naval power.

When the shouting and the toasts were over and the public had snuffed its heavily taxed candles, Viscount Duncan found that the large sums that had been mentioned as his prize money were not forthcoming; not until the following year did he receive £10,000 as an installment on a vague principal, which was vociferously claimed by all his flag officers and captains, including Bligh, who had never received a piece of prize pudding and wanted the sixpence as well for capturing *Vrijheid*. The squabble went on for years, and few foredeck men got anything from the victory of Camperdown.

And, as was always the case when admirals like Duncan and de Winter closed ships in an embrace of death in clouds of powder smoke, thunderclaps of cannon and showers of blood, there were captains who put the helm up and hung outside hoping to pounce on a cripple or at least not be reported in another captain's log until they ventured into the smoke after the fight was over. Captain John Williamson of the ex-mutineer H.M.S. *Agincourt* was court-martialed for timidity at Camperdown and "rendered incapable of ever serving on board any of his Majesty's ships or vessels" again.

Of Camperdown, Black Dick Howe said, "One benefit I look for from this celebrated victory is that it will eradicate the seeds of discontent which appear ready to vegetate afresh in that northern fleet." Wolfe Tone said, "I fancy I am not to be caught at sea by the English as this is the second escape I have had and by land, I mock myself of them." Pitt paid a strange compliment to the man who saved his administration: "The best service Admiral Duncan has performed for the country was in respect to the Mutiny at the Nore." Duncan had been able to do nothing about the Nore. Some bitter old King's admirals growled about Duncan's softness toward the mutineers. They did not know how he indulged mutiny in *Circe* while she was blockading the Texel.

But the truly great enthusiast for Camperdown and Adam Duncan was his Majesty, who started out for the Nore in blustering weather to meet the returning hero. The King bowled to Greenwich in a four-horse post chaise and boarded the yacht *Royal Charlotte,* which her captain, Henry Trollope, had decorated for the occasion. The forecabin had become a regal sitting room with a crimson velvet and gold-fringed throne. The state bedroom was next aft. To it the King retired early. The wind blew the yacht upstream faster than the tide could take her down. His Majesty was thrown out of bed. The elements continued naughty next day. The King ordered the yacht to take her natural inclination toward London. There he knighted Trollope. The yachtsman inquired whether his Majesty had injured himself during the cruise. "Do not consider my person," said the King, "but, consider, if I cannot get to the Nore, the disappointment of those brave fellows, whom I long to thank for defending me, protecting my people and preserving my country."

His Majesty arranged a London triumph for Adam Duncan and while setting it up showed his versatility by coping with the Fitzgerald Scandal. One of his neighbors at Windsor, Lady Kingsborough, complained that her sixteen-year-old daughter had been enticed by Colonel Henry Fitzgerald of the Foot Guards, and was nesting with him in Kensington. Before the King could fix things, the father, Lord Kingsborough, pistoled Fitzgerald dead. The case called for the wisdom of King Solomon, and King George did rather well. The King decreed that the purchase price of Colonel Fitzgerald's vacated commission in the Foot Guards, now up for sale by Prince Augustus Frederick's mistress, Mrs. Clarke, was to be given the widow Fitzgerald.

His Majesty's autumnal joy was dimmed by the news that Frederick the Great had expired at Sans Souci, and the Camperdown thanks-givings of his subjects were marred by a finding in the Carrickfergus assizes in the case of King *v.* Orr. The government had produced a charge of insurrection against a young farmer, William Orr, for helping fugitive patriots on shadowy journeys. Orr was not permitted to offer a defense. The jury was instructed to find him guilty, but recommended mercy. The judge wept as he followed his orders to sentence Orr to death. The public refused its role in Georgian justice. On the day William Orr was hanged in the marketplace, the entire population of Carrickfergus stayed indoors.

Adam Duncan had a peppery old aunt, Lady Mary Duncan, who was not at all satisfied with his honors. She wrote to Henry Dundas (whom she had never met):

> Report says my nephew is only made a Viscount. But the whole nation thinks the least you can do is to give him an English earldom. Please to recollect what a chicken-hearted way all the nation was in, low-spirited by war, murmuring at taxes (tho' necessary), grumbling and dissatisfied in every country.
>
> Now comes my hero, the first that attempted to quash the rebellious seamen, locks up the Texel for nineteen weeks; when he could no longer remain. They came out. He flies after the Dutch; completely beats them, though they resisted like brave men. I know the little etiquette of not raising gentlemen but by degrees; a very proper distinction for those thirteen gentle lords you made last week. But what has that to do with a conqueror? What a different situation all you Ministers were in at the opening of Parliament. The nation joyful. Not a black democrat dare open his mouth. Even our cowardly allies will be ashamed to have deserted us. All success, under God, owing to my nephew. Lord St. Vincent is a brave man; he merited it; was made an earl. I leave to you the comparison. All my ancestors only rose by their brave actions, both by land and sea. Makes me think this is the only way of rising. Am sure, were this properly represented to our good King, who esteems a brave religious man like himself, would be of my opinion. Therefore, I hope to hear soon of his being made Earl of Lundie, Viscount Texel, and Baron Duncan.

Dundas was not moved. He was looking for a title for himself. Adam Duncan came up to London to submit to the hero's welcome arranged by his Majesty. He brought along a petition for pardon from 180 repentant Nore mutineers imprisoned at Chatham and urged it on the King, saying he would take the men into his fleet. The men prayed for "speedy release to be restored to their country as Useful and Ornamental members to Society." The royal assent was graciously given.

The big sailor went to the House of Peers and was inducted as Viscount Duncan of Camperdown. He began his first speech with, "My Lords. Not accustomed to speak in public—"

The King's reception consisted of a royal procession from Westminster to St. Paul's and a solemn thanksgiving in the cathedral. Owners of buildings overlooking the line of march charged sightseer parties up to fifty guineas.

The great day was clear. At nine o'clock from Westminster Palace yard the procession swung into motion, headed by a division of strutting marines and 200 men-of-wars-men, with three wagonloads of captured naval flags—those Black Dick Howe captured from the French at the Glorious First of June, Spanish *banderola* taken by Old Jarvey at the battle of Cape St. Vincent, and Duncan's yield of Dutch flags from Camperdown.

The lion of the hour followed in a carriage. Duncan received roaring acclaim in the Strand, Fleet Street and Ludgate Hill from throngs held back by lines of Foot Guards and Horse Guards, and militiamen from the City and John Company. It was the first great royal progress since the frightening demonstrations against the King in '95. To reinforce the cordon there were patrols by the Light Horse volunteers that had been formed to save London from Richard Parker and John Binns.

Adam Duncan and a group of admirals went to the rotunda of St. Paul's and waited among the bearers of the captured flags, while the House of Commons division of the parade approached at a deliberate pace in 130 carriages. Near the end of the line was Pitt, who was "very grossly insulted by the populace on his way to the cathedral," said the *Annual Register*. Pitt was followed by a larger and grander coach containing the Speaker. The King had arranged the order of march according to court precedence, but in reverse order, starting with inferior persons and working up through echelons of increasing grace and merit. Fifty coaches wheeled by, carrying the masters in chancery and members of the House of Peers.

Cheering from the west heralded the approach of the royal division. Militia officers trotted ahead, bringing their cordons to the alert. With a noisy clop of hoofs, four of George's sons drove by in four state coaches, each drawn by six horses. Then a stream of crested phaetons, chaises, and carriages with armorial bearings swelled past, bearing dukes, duchesses, earls, viscounts, barons, baronets, knights, and ladies of his Majesty's court. A company of plumed and arrogant Horse Guards rode by. There was a gap in the procession, a long theatrical pause. The people strained forward.

A vision of buff and gold filled the gray street: the sovereign and Queen Charlotte in the golden royal state coach, drawn by eight cream-colored horses.

Unfortunate was the wight who followed that equipage, but the King had allotted some leftover people to form the rear, in descending order of importance. On a chestnut horse, wrapped in a red cloak trimmed with ermine and bearing the Sword of the City, came the Lord Mayor of London. The aldermen and liverymen followed in coaches, and behind them, at the end of the parade, were the coaches of the royal princesses, who wore long purple robes and bandeaux with ostrich plumes stuck in them.

At Temple Bar, the ancient gate to the City, the Lord Mayor overtook the golden coach to defend symbolically his boundary against trespass by the monarch. They each dismounted and handled the city sword before his Majesty was suffered to pass. Meanwhile Adam Duncan and other aged admirals had been standing around on the cold stones of the cathedral for two hours, the cynosure of packed multitudes in the nave, transepts, aisles and balconies. The spectators had paid five guineas a head for the privilege.

The houses of Parliament took appropriate places in the choir, together with the judges on woolsacks, and peeresses, while the royal dukes and their suites lined one side of the nave in order of precedence, facing a line of admirals, similarly sorted out by rank. Duncan was rather low in the order. Amidst the gorgeous manhood on view in the nave, Adam Duncan drew the most attention, and not only because he was the hero of the day or that few Londoners had ever laid eyes on him before. Six feet, four inches tall, with the musculature of a topman, his huge stockinged calves elegantly turned for an age that admired male limbs, a glowing face browned in the heroic campaign, lively blue eyes, and a wreath of tumbling, foam-white hair —his own, ungathered and unpowdered—Duncan was a natural king.

The Bishop of Lincoln, acting as Dean of St. Paul's, and the Bishop of London took either side of his Majesty and the royal party began its entrance, preceded by the herald-at-arms and the prebendaries of the cathedral. They walked between the lines of courage, chivalry and merit. Behind His Nobs came the Queen, robed like her daughters in purple and sporting the biggest ostrich plumes of all.

In the rotunda, the royal family stopped in the ring of enemy flags which screened them from the masses. The bearers dipped their staffs, revealing the Brunswickers to all. With perfect solemn grace, the King, the Queen and the princesses turned and nodded to all four avenues of their subjects. It brought "the loudest acclamations and congratulations ever perhaps heard on any occasion," said the *St. James's Chronicle*. It was an epic moment for his Majesty. Not a stone had been cast at him and not a hiss, and now the crowd was simply holding its mouth open, braying with bliss. That was what one naval victory could do. It is doubtful, however, that his Majesty was thinking of Adam Duncan at that very minute. He led the royal party into the apse.

Under the pipe organ there was a throne, upon which the King placed his strong bottom. Lord Spencer, the ministerial victor of Camperdown, had the honor of bearing the Sword of State and standing at his Majesty's right. To the left stood Pitt's brother, Lord Chatham, by virtue of his presidency of the privy council. The establishment, arranged in the choir in degree of propinquity to his Majesty's ear, looked well upon itself and basked in the eye of God.

The bearers brought them the enemy's colors. Behind them a red curtain swept across the nave, shutting off the choir from the view of the five guinea crowd. This was necessary, because what was to follow constituted a communion of the King with his Maker, assisted only by his family, party, court, clergy and military.

As the flag bearers advanced toward the altar, noon light through stained glass rippled over the shot-torn and bloody banners of conquered ships—*America,* 74, *Impétueux,* 74; *Salvador del Mundo,* 112; and *Vrijheid*. At the altar, Adam Duncan and Black Dick Howe offered the flags to the dean, who ordered the bearers to lay them on the communion table. There the King of England ate the bread of Christ and drank the blood of Jesus over the fallen emblems of atheists, Catholics and republicans.

The Bishop of Lincoln preached a long sermon. It was two-thirty in the afternoon before "God Save the King" was completed. London echoed with twenty-one rounds from the guns in St. James's park, timed by a signalman on the dome of St. Paul's. The thanksgiving service for Camperdown lasted longer than the battle.

The royal planner's hand had not passed lightly over the retreat from St. Paul's. The King took the parade away in reverse order from that of the morning, with his coach first. It was long after dark before Duncan and Black Dick found their carriages and drove through the crowd to a bird and a bottle, their first nourishment in fourteen hours.

After the hostile demonstrations he had received on his way to the ceremony, Pitt abandoned his carriage, dined incognito near St. Paul's, and was escorted home in another coach by the Light Horse.

Camperdown inspired a commemorative verse by a crippled twenty-six-year-old Edinburgh lawyer named Walter Scott. A friend showed it to Pitt, who passed it around among his weekend companions. They thought they could do better, so the Prime Minister set a competition in ballad-writing.

The company judged the best song, superior to theirs and Scott's, was that of Richard Colley Wellesley, the Second Earl of Mornington, elder brother of Colonel Arthur Wellesley, a division commander in India.* Duncan was regaled with Wellesley's ballad at a testimonial dinner by the East India Company. Pitt had a knack for aborting talent. He had delayed the London debut of the Scottish poet, (later Sir) Walter Scott, by several years.

---

* Later, the Duke of Wellington. Old Jarvey said of the family, "The Wellesley's, all powerful, are such a grasping tribe." They were also the champion name-changers of them all. Here is one twig of the genealogy; starting with the Colleys or Cowleys, a plantation Irish tribe coming on record in the sixteenth century.

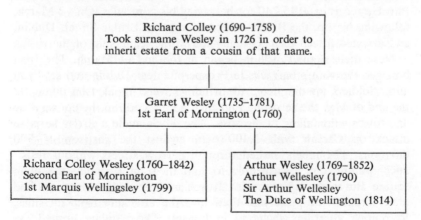

Richard Colley (1690–1758)
Took surname Wesley in 1726 in order to inherit estate from a cousin of that name.

Garret Wesley (1735–1781)
1st Earl of Mornington (1760)

Richard Colley Wesley (1760–1842)
Second Earl of Mornington
1st Marquis Wellingsley (1799)

Arthur Wesley (1769–1852)
Arthur Wellesley (1790)
Sir Arthur Wellesley
The Duke of Wellington (1814)

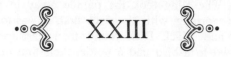

XXIII

The Irish Mutinies

Treason doth never prosper; what's the reason?
Why if it prosper, none dare call it treason.

—SIR JOHN HARRINGTON, *Alcilia* 1613

IN FEBRUARY 1798, Bonaparte visited Brest and inspected the fleet gathered to invade Ireland. He had been getting less and less eager to cross the English Channel. Now he decided to dry his hands of it. Bonaparte took the ships and went to Egypt instead. Wolfe Tone continued to press the Directory not to neglect the hour of decision. The Irish people were ready to rebel: they were only waiting for arms and initiative from France and fresh outbreaks in the British fleet, organized by Irish crewmen.

Thomas Reynolds, one of the rebel inner circle, was in the pay of Pitt. He received £45,740 for betraying his comrades. On 12 March, following his tip, the British raided a house in Bridge Street, Dublin, and arrested fifteen men, virtually the whole leadership of the rising.

Nevertheless, the rebellion began at the end of March. The Irish besieged the King's barracks in Prosperous near Dublin and set them afire. Soldiers jumping from the windows were impaled on pikes. By the end of May the revolt had reached a crescendo in the countryside and towns were falling to the Irish. The rebels made a strong surprise attack on Carlow with 1,400 men against the garrison of 500 dragoons. The rebels dashed through narrow streets without resistance, pulling out townspeople to join them in storming the main square. But it was not a surprise. It was an ambush. The dragoons had a net around the plaza and fired into the attackers from all sides. Retreating guerrillas sheltered in houses. The regulars burned the houses. Concealed dragoons and King's supporters turned every street into a gauntlet of fire. About 60 Irish were killed. Two hundred more were hanged after drumhead courts-martial. For days afterward, corpses of fugitives fell from the chimneys of smoldering houses.

Acts of mercy were rare in the Irish rebellion. On the march the King's troops burned thatch-roofed cottages, which were the dwellings of the Catholic poor. The insurrectionists burned slate-roofed houses in which Protestants usually lived. The regulars had a gigantic executioner called "The Walking Gallows." He knocked his victim to the ground with his fist, tied his hands and feet, and forced him to pray for his Majesty the King. He bent a garrote around the victim's neck and hauled him up on his back, until they were cheek to cheek. The hangman jogged around, jolting the wretch until he was dead.

General Sir David Dundas pledged amnesty to several hundred Irish partisans in Limerick. Troops of the Anglo-Irish general, Sir James Duff, surrounded them and massacred the unarmed men. Those who fled were pursued by Lord Jocelyn's Fencibles, a volunteer horse troop made up of fox hunters. The sportsmen had an enjoyable day chopping down running human beings.

A year after Admiral Pléville-le-Pelley abolished the invasion fleet at Brest, the force had been laboriously reconstructed, even to repurchasing frigates he had disposed of. By summer the squadron had reached invasion capability and a smaller force was ready to sail from Rochefort. But, again the Brest fleet was taken off operations: Paris could not finance the expedition.

Eighteenth-century warfare was often too expensive for the taxing power of the state. Both the British and French naval efforts created enormous deficits which could be stabilized only in part by not paying the seamen. Neither country was productive enough to afford all-out naval warfare. Poverty dictated tactics. Neither side wanted to sink ships; that was much too destructive. They wanted to capture ships. Harsh criticism awaited an officer who captured a ship and then failed to bring it home to join his navy. The frugal French went to the limit of delicacy—they aimed their cannons to bring down British top hamper, not to smash up stout hulls which would be costly to repair. The British, more of a berserker folk, aimed only for the hulls, which accounted for the almost unbelievable disparity in casualties. It was not uncommon in fierce engagements between matched ordnance for ten Frenchmen to fall for one Englishman.

With the Brest force immobilized, the French answered the desperate appeals of the Irish by sending a squadron from Rochefort in August. It consisted of 1,150 troops in four frigates. It was a few days after the Battle of the Nile in which Nelson had erased a large part of the French navy. This result would not be known for six weeks so that any British cruiser that sighted the squadron could not be sure it was not the vanguard of a mighty amphibian effort.

This time the Directory did not send an incapable leader and a parcel of expendable riffraff as it had to Fishguard the previous year. These troops were victors of Italy and the Rhine. They were Hoche's men who had been sleeping in the snow at Metz the winter before. They did not look like soldiers at all, not the kind Frederick the Great would have drilled or George III hired. They tended to be short, sallow fellows dressed in worn-out patched uniforms. They were talkative and nervous, with appraising eyes. But their muskets were pristine; and their bayonets were bright. This was the French citizen-soldier who had whipped every proud professional in Europe.

Their general was the kind of peasant pragmatic that often comes forth in revolutions and civil wars to replace the academy men and rewrite the book of tactics. Jean R. M. Humbert was a rabelaisian, bearlike man, poorly educated, companionable and droll, with a quick, incisive brain and a violent temper. He had been Lazare Hoche's right-hand man in the Vendée antiguerrilla campaign and had helped him throttle the landing at Quiberon Bay. Humbert had been the ranking soldier in the Bantry Bay expedition that the wind defeated in '96. He was enthusiastically hoping to bring about Irish freedom from English rule.

After a two-week voyage unmolested by British vessels, Humbert's thousand landed at Killala on the north coast of County Mayo. They came ashore without opposition or incident and picked Irish flowers and put them in their musket muzzles. The townsmen scuttled for the hills. The Protestant Bishop of Killala remained in his mansion and blandly greeted Humbert with the news that the Irish insurrection had been crushed.

It was true. The King's hundred thousand troops in Ireland had broken both the northern and southern Irish armies at Ballinahinch and Vinegar Hill in one June week. The surviving small bands of fugitives were being hunted down in the mountains of Wicklow. Most of the victorious army was free to deal with Humbert. The peasant general grinned and ran a green flag with *Erin go Bragh* up the episcopal flagpole. He broke open his sealed *Instructions for the March and Operations of General Humbert*. To his surprise, they were for an invasion of England.

G.R.

MUTINIES, INVASIONS, REVOLTS IN 1797-98

NORTH SEA

ATLANTIC OCEAN

SCOTLAND

Edinburgh

BLOODY FORELAND
LOUGH SWILLY
ARAN I.
RUTLAND I.
Londonderry
Killala
Sligo
Carrick-on-Shannon
Belfast
Castlebar
Cloone
Hollymount
Longford
Athlone
Dublin
IRELAND
Carlow
Vinegar Hill
Cork
BANTRY BAY

Liverpool

Birmingham

Norwich
Great Yarmouth

WALES

ENGLAND

Harwich

Fishguard
Haverfordwest
THE SMALLS
BRISTOL CHANNEL
Bristol
Bath
London
Windsor
THE NORE
Sheerness
Chatham
Deal
Dover

Netherstowey
Portsmouth
THE DOWNS

Plymouth
SPITHEAD
ISLE OF WIGHT

→ Humbert's march
→ Cornwallis

0   Miles   100   palacios

ENGLISH CHANNEL
LA MANCHE

It would perhaps be imprudent for you to remain long in Cornwall. It would be more advisable that you should first establish yourself in Devonshire, particularly in that part which lies between the two rivers the Ex and the Tamar. This situation, on account of the passes and mountains, will afford you an easy and safe retreat from the pursuit of the enemy, as well as a more extensive sphere for your operations. With a little enterprize and skill you might easily succeed in cutting off the communication between Dartmouth, Plymouth, and Portsmouth. It would not, however, be advisable for you to approach too near to those places, on account of the numerous garrisons which they contain, unless indeed you had information of any commotion having taken place, which you should labour to promote.

It is therefore of importance that immediately on your debarkation, you should direct your march towards "Dedmana and Newport." Above the latter, and without passing through it, you will cross the Tamar, a river which separates Cornwall from Devonshire, beyond which it will be your object to take up a position.

Humbert was one island and a sea removed from Cornwall. He would have to cross the Tamar when he came to it.

General Humbert put his men to work preparing the long march; first drumming up Irish auxiliaries. They came in readily, starved and half-naked, to croon over the guns, blue uniforms and silver helmets, and gobble the miraculous meat stew the French ate. In fact they enlisted twice and three times to get the clothing and sell it for whiskey. The French soldiers, on their part, refused to act their roles in British ferocity cartoons: they stole nothing and kept aloof from the townspeople. They were not billeted in the houses, did not bother the women, and requisitioned food moderately, paying coin on delivery. It was harvest time.

With all his people and matériel ashore, Humbert released the ships. They sailed away, leaving the nonchalant thousand to their fate. British cruisers under Sir John Borlase Warren arrived to cut off Humbert's escape by sea. Save in this corner of Mayo, all of Ireland was sunk in the peace of blood and ashes.

Humbert sought to impart elements of discipline to his Irish allies, but they did not approve of it. He shot two of them for insubordination. Efficiency was also impaired by a double-language barrier. None of the Irish spoke French and the few French who spoke English found that most of the locals understood only Gaelic. Humbert had two four-pounders and a small ammunition train but couldn't find enough horses, so hitched the unteachable Irish to the cannon and wagons and started his march inland. By this time, 26 August, the King's army had made a leg in Castlebar, 35 miles south, where General Gerard Lake had gathered five times as many troops as the French. Lake, acting on the belief that the French consisted of seven times themselves, held his strength to his bosom and sent out a unit to guard the main bridge between himself and the foe. While this vanguard waited to sell their lives dearly, Humbert's thousand by-passed them on an all-night fifteen-hour rapid flank march on stony hill paths and fell on Lake's main force in Castlebar at seven A.M., next morning. The British were on a hill with superior ordnance and fresh men. Humbert's technicians fired running volleys and trotted up the hill with fixed bayonets. In a few minutes, Lake's soldiers were departing "in wildest terror." The fastest fugitives reached Athlone, 63 miles away, within 27 hours and imparted the news to the King's high commander in Ireland, General Charles Marquis Cornwallis.

Lord Cornwallis sent couriers to Dublin and London, calling for immense reinforcements of troops and guns, fearing that Humbert's stunning blow would reanimate the Irish rising. He had no correct estimate of French strength in front or rear and could not appreciate that Humbert's reserve consisted of three young lieutenants left in Killala as military governors. Their godless ministrations consisted of trying to prevent the Catholics from piking the Protestants and the Protestants from burning the Catholics.

Humbert tidied up at Castlebar, reclaiming British booty that female camp followers had plundered from Lake's baggage train and trying to raise the county. He distributed weapons and slogans, hoping to establish a more secure rear before the thousand plunged on. The French passed out muskets, unaware that most of the recipients were from the Protestant ruling faction who intended to employ the arms against marauding Catholic neighbors and who also wished to deny them to French Catholic atheists in the wicked attempt to overthrow his most Protestant Majesty. Jean Humbert was confronted with internecine hatreds cultured for three centuries, a Vendée soaked with generations of gore. Both branches of Irish Christianity expected Humbert to close the churches and give them all the choice of denying God or being guillotined. He left the churches alone and laughed at their superstitions. During the week of French government in

Castlebar no person was injured or killed in the communal feud. And Humbert won over two hundred trained men from General Lake's Irish militia.

Cornwallis, smarting under quips that the opening French victory was "another Yorktown," marched from Athlone with 20,000 men toward Castlebar, enlarging the battle of Connaught, the province embracing this footwork. It took the King's army six days to cover less than the Castlebar racers had spanned in one. Cornwallis fetched up at Hollymount, fourteen miles south of Castlebar, and spread a long line to interdict French attempts to flood all over counties Limerick, Clare, Kilkenny and Cork.

General Humbert's scouts reported the dispositions of the huge British force. He abandoned Castlebar to its neighborly manslaughters and struck out northeast for Sligo on another lightning march, hoping to link up with a second French invasion group scheduled to land farther north. The French moved according to Hoche's principles learned in the Vendée:

Your march should be conducted with briskness and celerity. You should never keep the high road, but, on the contrary, proceed through the bye-ways and narrow tracks, and especially those that are most remote from the great road. Before you enter a city or town, you should enquire whether it contains any, and what number of troops, whether there is any river in it, and what number of bridges, and whether it has any fortifications; you must then take your measures accordingly. You should frequently change your guides, in order to conceal from the enemy the knowledge of your marches, and never take a fresh guide in the presence of the one whom you dismiss; you should make frequent countermarches; always tell your guides that you have quitted a different road from that which you intend to pursue, and enquire the road to those towns and villages which you mean to leave behind you, or to which at least you do not intend to go.

The better to create surprize and consternation, you must now and then take possession of some little town or harbour, and lay it under contribution. You perceive by this, that all places of any note will apply to Government for troops, which will be in want of them, and will be compelled to divide those which it can spare; this will enable you to destroy a great many of them, by engaging separately with the different detachments sent against you.

The fifty-mile march to Sligo the veterans of the Rhine accomplished in 24 hours, leaving their supply wagons hours behind. Outside of Sligo, their scouts encountered a small detachment of garrison militia from Limerick. Humbert halted his sleepless legion and sent a company in with running fire and cold bayonets. They swept through the militia and fell panting on the grass. They were asleep beside their dead foemen when the main French column came up. Seeing uniformed opponents and learning that they were from another province, Humbert assumed that they were pickets of another British army in or near Sligo.

The town, as it happened, was defenseless and the nearest British troops were a day's march away. Incorrectly thinking that Sligo was now held by the British, Humbert headed east toward the Iron Mountains in Leitrim, where he had heard there were Irish republican redoubts. By this time British reinforcements were landing in Galway Bay and General Lake was on the scent and finding abandoned guns and exhausted allies of the French along the road. Humbert's indefatigibles, nearly fifteen hundred strong, including 500 Irish partisans, crossed the Shannon so well pursued that they did not have time to burn the bridge. They rested briefly at Cloone on 7 September, more than a hundred miles from where they started three days before. The march was made in good order day and night in alien country with vanishing provisions.

During the brief respite, some of the Irish partisans deserted, hearing that General Lake had offered quarter. He had done so. Humbert missed their guns and could not provide for more Irish coming to the French camp. Wolfe Tone's brother Matthew was among them. Most of the Irish were now marching behind a fanatic calling himself "the Champion of the Virgin Mary." Jean Humbert had seen such pious madmen leading Breton farmers against his formations in the Vendée. It was not a good sign.

The next day Humbert's army was surrounded by Cornwallis's enormous force at Ballinamuck a few miles south of Lough Rinn in County Longford. The French general tried to surrender his entire army, but Cornwallis accepted only the 844 Frenchmen. After disarming the Irish, the King's men butchered about four hundred of them where they stood and hunted the rest down on horseback. About a hundred were taken alive to the jail at Carrick-on-Shannon. Matthew Tone was hanged by a military court-martial. Cornwallis ordered the rest to draw lots. Seventeen who picked the black spot were pulled out of the jail and strangled.

This left Humbert's three junior officers still administering French justice in peaceful Killala, scene of the landing. In the meantime they had recruited, armed and drilled several hundred Irishmen. A regiment of 1,200 King's men marched to Killala, burning straw-roofed cottages along the way. The Killala rebels put up a twenty-minute fight, then the militia went in and slaughtered them all. The hasty King's men hanged several townsmen who were on his Majesty's side, but spared the French officers who were later exchanged.

While Humbert's thousand engaged most of the King's troops in Ireland, Irish seamen prepared to seize British men-of-war and go to help the cause. Although Irish separationists were accused of fomenting the Spithead and Nore strikes, it was not until they saw the surprising effectiveness of the mutinies that the United Irishmen began pouring agitators into the King's navy. They went aboard on quota lists to build revolutionary cells of fellow countrymen. They made no recruits among the English, who were not about to turn over his Protestant Majesty's vessels to a wicked alliance of Roman Catholics and French atheists. The old religious feud rendered Irish naval subversion extremely dangerous; high-principled informers surrounded the schemers and not all Irishmen were susceptible, as was to be discovered by Bartholemew Duff, rebel leader of H.M.S. *Caesar,* when he placed trust in Marine Private Edward Brophy.

The Gaelic sea network was too late to carry the ships during the opening of the 1798 outdoor fighting season in Ireland. By midsummer on board *Caesar,* Bartholemew Duff had sworn a much larger cadre than existed on a vessel at Spithead or the Nore prior to seizure, eight committeemen, thirty-seven seamen and eleven marines. They were "constantly in Duff's company" and had a conspicuous sign: Brother A placing his right hand on his left breast, and Brother B taking it with his left hand. One of the committee, Michael Butler, maintained that the English had no right to be in Ireland, that Protestants should be expelled, and that he wished to join the fight ashore, "to recover the title and estate of Ormond, of which my family have been unjustly deprived by the English." Butler said, "I shall never die easy till I swim in English blood."

These doomed romantics planned to take the ship to France or Ireland; Duff had word from home that Bonaparte would soon be there. But *Caesar's* Irish were never able to lift a hand. Marine Brophy gave the captain a complete roster of the cell, which included three seamen described as Frenchmen. A court-martial at Plymouth hanged Duff, Butler and four others, gave two of them 500 lashes, and acquitted the rest.

The disaster to the *Caesar* unit was closely followed by informers' breaking up an Irish combination on *Defiance,* 74, an ex-delegate ship at Spithead. Twenty-four seamen and one marine were court-martialed for holding mutinous assemblies and taking an oath which the prosecutor rendered as:

> I swear to be true to the Free and United Irishmen, who are now fighting our cause against tyrants and oppressors, and to defend their rights to the last drop of my blood, and to keep all secret; and I do agree to carry the ship into Brest the next time the ship looks out ahead at sea, and to kill every officer and man that shall hinder us, except the master; and to hoist a green ensign with a harp on it; and afterwards to kill and destroy the Protestants.

No less than twenty of the defendants were hanged, the largest number from a single vessel in the era of mutiny. On another Spithead mutineer, *Glory,* 98, Captain Brine received a fervent address of loyalty signed by 86 seamen and 26 marines from Ireland. A lower-deck informer told Brine that the letter was a cover for mutinous intent and he obtained court-martial orders on ten men. The testimony against William Regan was that he, as captain-designate, was to take *Glory* to France, where he expected the French would pay prize money for her, then the Irish seamen would enlist with the French invasion army. Regan and seven others were executed, the rest whipped and put in solitary for a year.

Two marines were indicted at the Nore: George Tomms and John Wright of H.M.S. *Diomede* for membership in the Nottingham Corresponding Society. Tomms was accused of trying to administer an oath to others, of threatening to take the ship to an enemy port, and of intending to shoot the officers. Thirteen captains decreed that Tomms would die and Wright would be whipped around the fleet, taking 500 lashes.

H.M.S. *St. George* returned to Spithead from her rebellious period at Cadiz and put up four Irish marine privates for "uttering or making use of mutinous and seditious expressions, or being present without using their utmost endeavours to suppress the same." The testimony merely went to show that "the prisoners had been seen together in their birth [*sic*] on board the said ship," and had been heard to offer a toast, "The tree of liberty to all United Irishmen and damnation to all that are enemies thereto." For that, in the King's navy in 1798, the four marines were sentenced "each and every one of them to receive 300 lashes through the fleet then lying at Portsmouth."

H.M.S. *Marlborough,* 74, whose company had expelled Henry Nicholls, the captain who liked to hit men on the head with a speaking trumpet, got a new commander, Captain Joseph Ellison. A small group of Irish seamen were arrested for mutinous conspiracy and the Admiralty sent the ship to Admiral Lord St. Vincent's disciplinary school in Spain. Old Jarvey did not have to wait for the King's approval to hang people and there were no newspapermen to tell England what was going on.

As *Marlborough* approached, Captain Ellison saw that the fleet was at anchor in two lines and that the flagship, *Ville de Paris,* had hoisted a signal ordering him to come to anchor between them. He reported aboard *Ville de Paris.* Her captain said the admiral was aware of *Marlborough*'s troubles and wanted a list of mutineers to begin immediate trials. Ellison looked around. The quarterdeck was holystoned white. Pitch bubbled in the seams. Officers and middies were assembled to larboard. Eight hundred seamen crowded the forecastle. The marine company with glinting bayonets was standing stiffly behind the poop rail. The men made no sound. Running rigging slatted against the yards. Gulls cried. The great three-decker sloshed peacefully in the sea.

From the great cabin came a squat figure, head beginning to bend with age, pouchy eyes darting around the assembly. Old Jarvey wore full dress, three silver stars upon his golden epaulets, the gold medal to the victor of Cape St. Vincent on a ribbon around his neck, the jeweled starburst of the order of the Bath on his left breast. He advanced to Ellison, lifted his cocked hat and held it poised over his head throughout the interview. His lordship accorded this singular courtesy to every man he spoke with, whatever his rank. The custom had been started in the French revolutionary navy and no one dared ask the old man why he adopted it.

He demanded a list of mutiny charges. Captain Ellison gave him the list and said, "My lord, the ship's company will not permit a man to be hanged on board the *Marlborough.* I request that boat crews from the rest of the fleet attend as usual and that they haul the yard rope."

"Captain Ellison, you are an old officer, sir," said the admiral. "You have lost an arm in action. I should be very sorry that any advantage should now be taken of your advanced years. Not a hand from any other ship in the fleet will touch the rope. You will now return on board, sir." This humbling of a commander was in the hearing of the whole ship's complement.

Lord St. Vincent's nearly continuous court-martial condemned one of the Marlboroughs that day and ordered him executed next morning. *Marlborough* was ordered to house all guns and close her ports. The launches of the fleet were fitted with carronades and a dozen rounds each, and placed under the command of Captain Robert Campbell of *Blenheim,* who brought them into line off *Marlborough*'s bows. Old Jarvey's orders were, "If any symptom of mutiny appears in the *Marlborough,* or any resistance to the hanging, you are to proceed close touching the ship and fire into her, and continue firing until all resistance shall cease. If it becomes absolutely necessary, you shall even sink the ship in the face of the fleet."

Along the double line of warships, the companies were mustered to witness punishment. From *Ville de Paris* came the provost marshal's boat, bristling with arms, bringing the condemned man to *Marlborough.* He was placed on the cathead under the foreyard, his hands and feet tied, a hood placed over his head, the noose adjusted, knot under the left ear. Twelve men told off by a boatswain's mate took the end of the yard rope. The watch bells of the fleet sounded eight. A cannon fired on *Ville de Paris.*

The hanging detail gave a heave. The rope slipped out of their hands and the prisoner swung toward the water.

There was a great sigh. Everyone thought it was defiance. Captain Campbell's carronades were loaded and the slow matches were alight, waiting for orders to rake *Marlborough.*

The hangmen took the rope again and ran. The prisoner arose, swaying and convulsing, toward the block. "Discipline is preserved," said old Jarvey. Day after day, the death sentence was pronounced. Morning after morning, the offender's own messmates ran him up aboard his own ship.

While the Irish rising was being snuffed out, the French made a general out of an old, vainglorious Irish alcoholic named James Napper Tandy and sent him off in a corvette, *Anacreon,* to run guns to his people in Donegal. He landed on the tiny island of Rutland, a satellite of Aran Island, and found the village there newly evacuated. He nailed up revolutionary proclamations, hoisted a green banner, and went into the post office and started reading people's letters. Several of them had news of Humbert's surrender. Napper Tandy was cast down in hopes. He went to the village shebeen, helped himself to whiskey and got drunk. French marines carried their fallen leader back to the ship. After eight hours, he awakened and ordered *Anacreon* to sail to Hamburg. The British government had long been annoyed at neutral Hamburg for harboring all nationalities of haters and plotters against England. Foreign Secretary Lord Grenville threatened an embargo against Hamburg and its senate gave Napper Tandy to the English. This made Bonaparte angry and he declared war on Hamburg. War over Napper Tandy was averted when the Germans groveled to Bonaparte. The English sentenced the old rebel to death, but poor Napper was destined to fail at martyrdom, too. Britain let him go to France in 1801.

With Humbert quelled after marching halfway across Ireland, the second installment of the expedition which was to have landed simultaneously with him obtained funds for the effort and sailed late in September at night from Brest. Commodore J. B. B. Bompart had his flag in the newly renamed 74-gun ship, *Hoche*. He had nine frigates, 3,000 quality troops and a good furniture of field guns. And aboard *Hoche* was Theobald Wolfe Tone, making still another effort to separate his country from Britain.

At daylight three small British vessels detected the departure and one cut away to tell Lord Bridport, who, as was his habit and luck when the French were out, was anchored at Spithead with his fleet. H.M.S. *Ethalian,* 38, and *Sylph,* 18, shadowed the French ships. Commodore Bompart feinted toward Lorient, but could not shake them. He then made course for the West Indies, and noted with satisfaction that the smaller Englishman started north, ostensibly to bring the grand fleet to interdict him on the false track. But the captains of the English reconnaissance had decided that Bompart was going to Ireland and the departing *Sylph* was headed for the west of Ireland to warn Sir John Borlase Warren, who had been standing off the Irish coast since Humbert's landing. Sir John commanded *Foudrayant,* 80, *Canada,* 74, *Robust,* 74, and five frigates.

The French expedition had no idea what had happened to Humbert, but, taking the most optimistic view, decided he had marched north, and accordingly made for Lough Swilly, at the top of Ireland. This happened to be the billet of the English fleet. Bompart sailed on toward Warren past hundreds of miles of undefended Irish coast. The French were very close-hauled as they turned the Bloody Foreland into a brisk north northeast wind. Lookouts shouted "English sail to leeward, off the starboard bow." Admiral Bompart immediately turned about and began running southwest while Admiral Warren hoisted signal for general chase. The pursuit began at nightfall on 11 October and the wind went to gale strength from the northwest quarter. With the ship-eating rocks of Donegal to his port, the wind to his starboard and the British on his stern, Bompart's course was determined for him.

The eve of Wolfe Tone's first battle was not the sort he had expected in his lonely exile's dreams. The masts of *Hoche* began complaining and cracking in the storm. One of the French frigates sprang a serious leak and was obliged to go near the menacing rocks where, in case she filled, the water was shoal. The fore and mizzen topgallant masts of *Hoche* blew down. Then her main-topmast came off. Bompart lost much of his speed. His escorts took in canvas to stay with the flagship. By dawn Admiral Warren's quarry was within easy striking distance. The wind was down.

Before the battle began, Bompart pulled a fast frigate out of the engagement to return to France with dispatches. He urged Wolfe Tone to go aboard her. "Our contest is hopeless. We shall be prisoners of war, but what will become of you?" Tone said, "Shall it be said that I fled while the French were fighting the battles of my country?" He stayed with *Hoche*. The French were in a straggling line with *Hoche* third from the rear, backed by two frigates. At 8:50 the head of the British line, *Robust*, 74, one of the mutineers of Spithead, closed with *Hoche*. The British two-decker reefed sail to stay alongside the crippled Frenchman and the two ships went at it broadside.

The British broke up the French battle line and five more ships went to work on *Hoche,* including *Melampus,* 36, of the Spithead rebellion. Wolfe Tone served a gun on the French flagship, which was now outgunned 346 to 74. The French endured it for 240 minutes before Bompart struck. He had 270 casualties. *Robust* lost 10 killed and 40 wounded and the British total casualty was only 13 killed and 75 wounded. *Robust* herself was a virtual cripple.

Admiral Warren ordered *Robust* to tow *Hoche* to Lough Swilly, an order that nearly lost him the prize. The disabled British two-decker could barely hold steerageway with the tow. Only by the exertions of the French crew and that of H.M.S. *Doris,* 36, was *Hoche* saved from the rocks. (The French flagship was to be taken into the King's navy as H.M.S. *Donegal.*)

Wolfe Tone, in his French officer's uniform, was the first man to step out of the boat on Irish soil. In the reception committee was Magistrate Sir George Hill, a great Tory landowner in Donegal. He had attended Trinity College, Dublin, with Wolfe Tone. Sir George greeted him by name, and Tone politely acknowledged his old schoolmate.

Tone was conducted from Londonderry to Dublin in pomp, the country folk turning out to see what manner of general had come from France to alleviate their wretchedness. He rode in a carriage, escorted by a company of horse, and he wore the full-dress uniform of a *chef de brigade*—a jaunty cocked hat weighted with gold lace and a red, white and blue cockade; a blue frock coat with gold facings and epaulets, blue *pantalons* with gold garters and half boots with gold ornamentation. Out of sight, were the bilboes on his feet.

He was court-martialed in Marshalsea Prison on the charge that, as a subject of his Majesty, he had entered the service of his Majesty's enemy and had borne arms against his King and country.

"Theobald Wolfe Tone, do you plead guilty or not guilty?"

"I presume this is the time when I might read in court a statement I have prepared."

"Do you plead guilty or not guilty?"

"I do not wish to give the court unnecessary trouble. I am ready to admit the whole charge against me. The whole affair is to me a foregone conclusion. I have drawn up my statement as a vindication and not as a defense:

"From my earliest youth I have regarded the connection between Ireland and Great Britain as the curse of the Irish nation and felt convinced that while it lasted the country would never be free nor happy. My mind has been confirmed in this opinion by the experience of every succeeding year. I designed by fair and open war to procure the separation of the two countries.

"In a cause like this, success is everything . . . Washington succeeded and Kosciusko failed."

The military court refused Tone the soldier's right of a firing squad, the ultimate insult to the patriot who tried to be a soldier. He was ordered to be hanged within forty-eight hours. The night before the punishment, Tone cut his throat with a concealed penknife. He did not die but was not in condition to be hanged. A Protestant lawyer named Peter Burroughs petitioned the Court of the King's Bench for habeas corpus, claiming that the court-martial was illegal. He obtained a writ forbidding the military to touch Wolfe Tone. The army provost marshal refused to recognize the court order, declaring that

Lord Cornwallis's orders were supreme. The King's Bench thereupon ordered the army to hand over both the prisoner and the provost. Tone was too weak to move. The chief justice suspended the death sentence. But, like most events in unlucky Wolfe Tone's life, it was too late. He died a week after the court-martial.

XXIV

Repression and Reform

With a host of furious fancies
Whereof I am commander,
With a burning spear, and a horse of air,
To the wilderness I wander.
By a knight of ghosts and shadows
I summoned am to tourney
Ten leagues beyond the wide world's end,
Methinks it is no journey.

—ANON. "Tom O'Bedlam," seventeenth century

LORD SPENCER learned nothing from the great mutinies. Single ship risings continued over the same issues of bad victuals, cruel officers, unpaid wages and various aggravated hardships. Maldistribution of prize money went on as usual and the Admiralty did nothing about it. It was thirty-seven years before the privy council took the initiative and ordered a more equable share of prize money between quarterdeck and forecastle.

In the months following the great mutiny, his Majesty's Jolly Jacks struck *Sovereign,* 100, *Saturn,* 74, *Bedford,* 74, *Ardent,* 74, the storeship *Grampus, Beaulieu,* 40, *Phoenix,* 36 and *Calypso,* 16. Half of them were repeaters. The leaders, however, were not able to attain the formula for success: simultaneous action with sister ships, alliance of the marines, and fleet parliaments. The only redress of grievances they obtained was the Admiralty brand—the halter, the cat, and the solitary dark.

Several of the twice-torn vessels belonged to Lord Bridport, who remained in command of the Channel fleet, complaining of his antiquity, ailments and neglected estates. In March 1799, the old noble received an order from the Lords of Admiralty that practically cured his gout and brought a saintly grin to his gnarled visage. They were putting Sir Edward Pellew under his command. Bridport hated and envied Sir Edward's independence as a frigate squadron leader under direct Admiralty orders. Now, seniority had carried Pellew so high on the list that he could no longer escape promotion and a larger ship.

Pellew despised the great floating Newgates. He was a frigate man. He wanted to chase prizes, get rich, buy an estate, win a peerage, found a line. Nevertheless, he was ordered to carry his flag out of *Indefatigable* into *Impétueux,* 74, under Bridport and Sir Charles Morice Pole, whom he called "old women." The crew of his new ship had an independent and unruly spirit hardly tamed since the big mutiny—the Impétueuxs held a grudge against Pellew for keeping his Falmouth frigates out of the fleet demonstration. Sir Edward knew he was in for trouble and he strongly suspected that Lord Bridport was not going to help him handle it. He requested Lord Spencer to permit him to transfer his officers and foremen from *Indefatigable*. The request was denied, so Pellew enlisted a group of stout-bodied followers from his home town to accompany him aboard the man-of-war as a bodyguard. He also took his son, Pownoll Bastard, and a French émigré nobleman as a tutor and companion for the youth.

The Channel fleet returned to the Brest blockade, and Pellew's gratings were up almost every day as he flogged the Impétueuxs into submission on charges of "insolence," "drunkenness," and "disobedience." The frigate captain ground his teeth at the "old women" as the Channel fleet let the French escape once more from Brest. Bridport decided the enemy was going to Bantry Bay, took his ships there, and waited in ambush. The foe was headed for the Mediterranean.

Bridport kept the fleet at anchor in Bantry Bay for some time, during which the ships' companies held clandestine meetings belowdecks. Pellew's mates one day raised their silver calls and piped all hands on deck to scrub down and clean hawse. There was a roar from the main hatch and the company spilled out, running toward the quarterdeck shouting "One and all!"

"Ship's company aft with a complaint," the first officer informed Sir Edward. He went out half dressed and the clamor increased as the men saw their hard commander.

"A boat!" they demanded.

"One and all!" they shouted.

"A BOAT!"

"What is the matter here?" roared Sir Edward.

". . . a letter to Lord Bridport . . . A boat . . ."

"Give me the letter. I'll carry it to him myself."

"No! No! A boat!"

"I tell you on my honor. I'll carry the letter to Lord Bridport."

"No! A boat of our own."

"We will have a boat, sir. Dammit, we will take one!"

"You will, will you?" Pellew dashed to his cabin and came out with his sword. The carpenter passed out hangers to the officers. Pellew made for the front rank of the crew, followed by his officers and bodyguards and the marine unit with fixed bayonets. He led the naked blades through the unarmed company and down the main hatch. He took nine men captive. The others fell to washing the deck as ordered.

Pellew applied to Bridport for a court-martial order. The old admiral refused to give it. Instead, he placed Pellew under the command of Sir Alan Gardner, detached to take reinforcements to Old Jarvey in the Mediterranean. As soon as he had formally escaped Bridport, Sir Edward applied to Sir Alan for a mutiny court on the nine prisoners. But apparently Bridport had instructed Gardner to deny Pellew his mutiny trials, because he got no orders out of Sir Alan.

The chastening of the proud frigate captain grew more severe when it got out to his crew that the admirals would not permit Sir Edward to try their leaders. He made the cat scream, but even the whipped men sneered at his humiliation. For redress he could only wait until he reported to Hanging Jarvey.

Arriving at Port Mahon, the Mediterranean fleet rendezvous, Pellew hastened to the flagship with his request for a court. Old Jarvey was cocooned ashore, ill and bitter against everyone. Pellew was warned not to bother him, but paid no heed and sent his demand to the sick room. The old admiral knew nothing of Bridport's vendetta. He assumed this was another instance of the Admiralty's evading responsibility and sending miscreants to him for punishment. For two years the home fleet had been sending him disturbed ships to undergo his ritual terror. And this applicant was none other than Sir Edward Pellew!—the proud favorite of fortune with his Admiralty commission to hunt prizes while St. Vincent languished in some forgotten blockade, holding the world together with sick and rebellious seamen, remade spars, rotten rigging and moldering canvas.

Pellew's request was denied. He was fit to be tied. Who now would respect the captain of *Impétueux*? He had been thrice turned down by his superiors on a request that they almost always granted automatically. Pellew now held only the cat-o'-nine-tails and his personal retainers over 500 men who knew how to rush a ship when the chance next came.

Captain Sir George Grey, one of St. Vincent's aides, heard the background of the matter from Pellew, and risked his own career to reopen the question with the old man. St. Vincent hated Bridport. He reversed himself and issued the court-martial order. Three Impétueuxs were hanged. The sailmaker, two carpenter's mates and three others were flogged around the fleet and thrown into different ships. Sir Edward Pellew's magic was restored. The whistle of the lash and the shrieks of the crew continued on *Impétueux*.

In all the single ship rebellions, none fulfilled the desperate last plans of the Nore—to sail for an enemy port—until 1800, when the captain of the foretop of *Danaé,* 20, pulled it off. His name was Jackson and, according to the naval historian William James, he had been Richard Parker's secretary at the Nore. The frigate, under Captain Lord Proby, was chasing a French brig into Camaret Bay near Brest. After nightfall, Jackson and a group of crew members released forty French prisoners and armed them with hangers. Together they made a cutlass charge on the quarterdeck and felled the sailing master. Captain Proby came up the after hatchway but was wounded in the head and driven back. Jackson battened down the main hatch, imprisoning the balance of the crew. The mutineers weighted the gratings with boats filled with shot and shouted appeals below for men to join them. Only a few responded.

The captain and the marine officer found arms for forty men betweendecks and waited for an opportunity to counterattack in the morning. There was a strong easterly wind which would prevent the gang from taking *Danaé* into Brest.

But "King's weather"—the lucky winds that blew her enemies away from Britain and favored her navy on so many occasions—now worked for the mutineers. The wind came round and Jackson took the frigate into the bay and anchored by the Frenchman they had been chasing, the 16-gun corvette *Colombe*. He visited the French vessel and came back with her first lieutenant and an armed party. Lord Proby was called up to the French officer and he said: "I surrender to the French nation but not to mutineers."

The two vessels set out for Brest. His Majesty's frigates *Anson* and *Boadicea* saw the odd pair bound into the bay and made for *Danaé* to offer assistance or at least find what was going on. The French corvette smartly assumed the role of a fugitive and Jackson made flag hoists indicating he was giving chase in water too shoal for the larger frigates. They broke off, satisfied, and the bold mutineer made port and handed over the ship.

Jackson was several years too late. There was no longer a revolutionary government in France. It was the beginning of Bonaparte's autocracy and the French were behaving correctly. They entertained Proby and the officers handsomely and marched Jackson and the British mutineers off to jail in Dinan. The French prisoners, who were legally right to have attempted the English ship, received heroes' welcomes. The *Danaé*'s officers were paroled and Jackson and his crew sank into oblivion.

Although the Spencerian Admiralty took no initiative to alleviate the lot of the sailors, the mutinies awakened individuals in and out of the service to its wrongs and miseries. Minority protests in Parliament and pressure from the reform movement continued. However, with the exception of Tobias Smollett and Tom Paine, British writers did not express lower-deck life until a school of nostalgics led by Captain Marryat began writing of the Nelsonian navy a generation later.

The progress of navy reform, to the extent that it benefited the seamen, went on apace.

—1806, a pay raise of a shilling a week to able seamen and sixpence to ordinaries.

—1815, reduction of navy manpower after Waterloo diminished impressment, although it remains a legal, if disused, method of procurement to this day.

—1825, an Act of Parliament required the navy to pay the seamen more promptly.

—1828, a trend toward reduced strokes of the cat, following descriptive criticism of floggings in the *Times* and other journals.

—1835, a register of seamen reconstituted after a lapse of more than a century.

—1860, articles of war revised to reduce lethal and preposterous penalties.

—1866, Act of Parliament forbids floggings of more than 48 strokes.

—1871, the Admiralty itself institutes a reform, lightening the work of the cat in peacetime.

—1879, flogging legally abolished.

The 1797 mutineers contributed a new practice to the navy through recommendations by Lord Keith and Magistrates Graham and Williams. Keith told Spencer: "I would propose that every seaman who shall voluntarily enter his Majesty's service and receive a bounty, shall sign an attestation similar to that used in the army, and that all seamen in the course of pay should be obliged to take and sign an Oath of Allegiance before they receive either Pay or Prize Money."

This formula would quite probably have produced worse mutinies than the Nore. By omitting to give the oath of allegiance to impressed men or to those who remained unpaid or were bilked of prize money, few ships would have contained a majority sworn to loyalty. What sort of petitions would the outcast majority produce and what plots concert?

Aaron Graham did not exclude anyone. He advised Portland:

> The sailors in general had a very serious sense of the obligation imposed upon them by the [delegates'] oath . . . and [we] are therefore of the opinion that the attesting of seamen . . . might be attended with beneficial effects.

Years passed before the Admiralty adopted this banal advantage to itself and converted the contagious oath ceremonies of the reform societies and mutinous seamen to the improvement of the peace of mind of the sovereign and nation.

Lord Spencer, however, facilitated another change, the most profound of all, because of his urge to cut navy expenses. In 1795 a young Englishman named Samuel Bentham came home on leave from St. Petersburg, where he was employed as an engineer-constructor in the Russian navy, and was amazed at the backward technology of British naval dockyards. Drydocks were still pumped out by horsepower although steam engines had been pumping British mines for seventy-five years. Men labored so hard in the 870-foot ropewalk at Portsmouth that they could not endure more than four hours of it per day. Planks were still made by a top sawyer and his unlucky partner standing in a pit in a rain of sawdust. One of the navy's most expensive handmade items was the wooden block, or pulley, of which the ships required 100,000 a year.

Bentham quit the Russians and became Inspector-General of Naval Works. He patented a machine with rotary planers that would shape several sides of a piece of wood simultaneously. As he was about to introduce this block-making device, a clever French refugee engineer,

Marc Isambard Brunel, arrived from New York with designs for a superior mechanical block-cutter which would make several at the same time. Bentham unselfishly recommended Brunel's invention to the navy.

The engineers tried to bring steam engines into the dockyard to run the new block-shapers, but were beaten back by angry workmen and complacent officials. Bentham appealed to Lord Spencer, who ordered Portsmouth to let him put an experimental twelve-horse-power engine in the yard in 1799. In that modest way, steam entered the maritime world that it was to transform.

The engine pumped docks at night and ran saws by day, drew water from a well and supplied pressure to fire hoses. It was never tired, never demanded pay, and was oblivious to republican propaganda. It cost 30 percent less than the old horse pump and gave ten times the work. Bentham also rigged a steam engine in the ropewalk at Portsmouth.

By 1808 at Portsmouth a Brunel steam block-making plant with forty-three machines was turning out 130,000 pulleys a year, run by ten unskilled men who exceeded the production of 110 master block-makers. It was a very early, if not the first, application of steam-powered tools to mass production and the first machine that built machines—if we may consider the big multiple naval block with its moving parts as a machine. In his father's block-making shop three-year-old Isambard Kingdom Brunel, who was to build the legendary *Great Eastern* steamship, gazed on his first machinery. Some of the 1808-built block-carvers were still functioning at Portsmouth in the mid-twentieth century.

The prayer of the majority of English people in the mutiny year, the dismissal of William Pitt and his cabinet, was answered four years later. The decision was consistently Georgian: after defending Pitt's chronic transgressions against British liberty and his string of military blunders, the King sacked him for backing a liberal proposal—that of restoring the civil rights of Roman Catholics. When he first heard of it, his Majesty raged against the idea and sent Pitt's crony, Henry Addington, the Speaker of the House, to dissuade him. Pitt refused, and of the two stubborn men, the more powerful prevailed. After seventeen years of devoted service, his Majesty sent the Prime Minister away without a title, ribbon, order or pension. The unsuccessful go-between, Addington, became First Minister.

Addington brought in the Earl of St. Vincent to replace Lord

Spencer as First Lord of the Admiralty. Old Jarvey, who had been serving as Bridport's successor in command of the Channel squadron, struck his pendant at Spithead and went up to Whitehall to police the fleet. He arrived in another grave hour of state emergency. Czar Paul (another monarch certified as insane) had made up an alliance of "armed neutrals," consisting of Russia, Sweden, Prussia and Denmark. Britain's obsession with dominating the oceans would not admit of a combined fleet rivaling hers, no matter how pacific in declaration or intent. Before St. Vincent took up the seals, the government had decided to form a Baltic fleet and attack the armed neutrals serially before they could collect an offensive capability. It fell to Old Jarvey to find the ships and men for the northern adventure.

He stirred up the press gang and the shipyards. The civil establishment of the fleet, the Navy Board, goaded the shipwrights to work faster. The underground unions in the royal dockyards deemed the time was right for a long-overdue pay rise. The goblin dreaded in '97 —of shipwright's delegates issuing from the Thames to Whitehall— stalked forth. The men were led by John Gast from the Deptford yard. They demanded higher pay to meet the higher cost of living. The Prime Minister and the cabinet majority were ready to make concessions, but St. Vincent would give them nothing.

The cabinet went over his head and yielded the shipwrights an allowance for bread, without actually raising wages. The union came back with a demand for doubled wages and a guarantee they would not be cut later in peace time. The men demonstrated in the dockyards. Work came to a stop. The government sent militia to guard the yards.

The cabinet nervously entreated Old Jarvey to negotiate. The delegates came upriver again and invaded the waiting room of the Admiralty office. A provost marshal ejected them and, outside, read a proclamation from their lordships. The delegates were discharged from their jobs. The same punishment awaited others who served as committeemen or fund raisers for the illegal combination.

Old Jarvey broke the strike.

Lord Spencer had left another headache for St. Vincent: he had appointed, as commander of the Baltic fleet, Sir Hyde Parker, late of the Jamaica station, a venerable but pusillanimous officer who was newly married to a young woman. To add battle lust to the new fleet, St. Vincent appointed Nelson to command one of the divisions. Early in March the Baltic expedition was ready to sail from Great Yarmouth, but Sir Hyde and Lady Parker were not. They had invited a great many people, including officers of the fleet, to a ball in a week's time. An express rider handed Admiral Parker a personal communication. "Upon consideration of the effect your continuance at Yarmouth an hour after the wind would admit of sailing would produce, I have sent down a messenger purposely to convey to you my opinion, as a private friend, that any delay in your sailing would do you an irreparable injury." It was signed ST. VINCENT. Sir Hyde canceled the ball.

When the necessary diplomatic rift had been accomplished, the Baltic squadron fell upon Copenhagen to destroy the Danish fleet. Halfway through the bloody business, Sir Hyde Parker hoisted signal No. 39—*leave off action*. Nelson turned his blind eye to the flag and took over the operation.* He overcame several Danish warships, but was heavily cannonaded from the shore. He sent a note to the Danish commander: *If the firing is continued on the part of Denmark, I must be obliged to set on fire all the prizes that I have taken, without having the power of saving the brave Danes who have defended them.*

The Danish crown prince sent a note back, asking what Nelson meant by the threat to burn prisoners of war alive. His lordship replied, "It was humanity." He wanted "hostilities to cease." The Danes capitulated to the humanitarian. Nelson went ashore with a heavy guard to protect him from people who had lost relatives and homes in his bombardment of a neutral country without declaring war. Nelson demanded a sixteen-week truce so that he could proceed to the eastern Baltic and deal similarly with the Czar's fleet. When the Danish leader balked, Nelson said to his French interpreter, "Tell him we are ready at a moment! Ready to bombard this very night!" The cannon rattle worked. Shortly thereafter, Czar Paul was assassinated and the Baltic became quiet.

Although Nelson and Old Jarvey were suing each other over prize money, the older man forgave the younger for disobeying orders, intriguing against brother admirals, and conducting his comical affair with Lady Hamilton. St. Vincent knew that Nelson was a winner. So it was that the King's naval fortunes prospered under the wary partnership of an old enemy of the regime and a young danger to the state.

With his first military emergency thus disposed of, Lord St. Vincent turned to internal reforms of the navy. He induced the King to issue

---

* Seven ex-delegate ships fought at Copenhagen. William Bligh was there in a new frigate, the creaky *Director* having been broken up at last. A number of Richard Parker's court-martial, Captain Edward Riou, was torn in half by a cannon ball and his prosecutor, Captain James Robert Mosse, also fell in the action.

a decree dubbing the assault and disciplinary troops the "Royal Marine Corps," and redesigned their uniforms. He promoted marine officers who had been conspicuous in suppressing mutiny. To this point Old Jarvey's disciplinary measures had been in keeping with his policies at sea, but now the old man steered into shoals. He began to turn down influential people who wanted navy and marine commissions for protégés. "Numerous connexions of the Spencer family have contributed to swell the list of post-captains and commanders to an enormous size," he wrote confidentially to a Whig crony, Sir John Carter, the Portsmouth magistrate. He asked Sir John to recommend good officers on half-pay whom his lordship preferred to the gilded relatives of his predecessor. He turned down nominations from royal dukes, loving sisters, Duchesses of This and Marquises of That. And he failed to recommend commemorative medals for the victors of Copenhagen, which sent Nelson into a twitchy rage. Old Jarvey's reasons were a disinclination to celebrate a victory in an unprovoked and undeclared war, to avoid annoying the Danes and to forestall claims for medals from seamen who had participated in seizures of Danish colonies.

The new ministry effected a peace with France at Amiens in 1802, but mutiny continued in the King's navy. In H.M.S. *Téméraire,* 98, whose crew had been confined aboard for years, the end of the war raised no hopes of life and freedom. From Bantry Bay, the three-decker was ordered to the fatal West Indies, where many thousands of H.M. soldiers and sailors died every year of yellow fever. There was a furious revolt of the forecastle, which was put down by officers and marines, and *Téméraire* went round to Spithead for the first trials and punishments of the peace, two floggings and eighteen executions.

St. Vincent reduced the moral strain of the navy by discharging 50,000 sailors and marines after the Peace of Amiens. He decommissioned vessels, sold those he could, and dismantled a small armada of coffin ships. Then he turned his hard stare on the royal dockyards and the navy supply and victualing system. Five years before, when he was running the Cadiz blockade with cranky ships, mutinous men and no dockyards, St. Vincent had written Lord Spencer a memorandum on purging the home establishment when peace arrived:

> Repairs of ships and improvements of dockyards to be set about with vigour, and carried on with perseverance. Much reform necessary in the civil department. If all the clerks in the dockyards were dismissed, with annuities, payable on one con-

dition only, "that they reside fifty miles from any dockyard," the public would benefit exceedingly.

The seat of corruption and complacency was the Navy Board, which controlled all supplies and although a servant of Admiralty and Parliament, had become, through interest and court venality, a power unto itself. Every commander who had taken his vessel into a yard for repair, or had seen a new ship through completion to commission, knew what was wrong, but realized the futility of protest.

If the great families lived like tapeworms in the body politic, the royal dockyards nursed a voracious species of shipworm, boring creatures whose tunnels to the treasury had often been started by a great-grandfather. Samuel Pepys knew them when he was secretary to the Admiralty. They stole navy property. Knowing from the inside what the navy needed, they cornered that article on the outside and bought it from themselves at huge profits. They drew pay for jobs they never went near. They used navy boats and crews in private businesses. They took rebates from contractors and accepted inferior materials. They collected wages for invisible workers. They drew the extra allowance for bread, won by the dismissed union leaders in the names of ficti-tious workmen. In one yard most of the employees consisted of "in-capables, old, infirm, boys, cripples, idiots . . . an asylum for every rogue and vagabond that could not obtain a meal by any other means."

Admiral Sir William James, St. Vincent's biographer, said: "The 3,320 shipwrights in the [royal] dockyards could only repair seven sail-of-the-line per year; 330 shipwrights in merchant yards built seven sail of the line per year."

Continuous investigations had been made of the yards without interrupting corruption and barratry. During the American war, a parliamentary commission made fifteen reports, setting down needed reforms. Pitt appointed another inquiry overlapping it, which studied the plants for seven years. He obliquely started the inquest again in '97 with a select committee on public finances which went over the yards. The result in every case was nil. During hostilities, the Navy Board would block reforms by deeming them interference with the war. In peace, the changes were "impracticable."

Old Jarvey knew the game. He started his attack on navy yard graft by slyly requesting the Navy Board to investigate irregularities and by allowing it to form the inspection group. One of the investigators named to look into the Woolwich situation was the surveyor of the navy, whose regular job was to prevent graft at Woolwich. It was the pretext Old Jarvey needed. He let out a great holler. He suspended the Navy Board, impounded its books, and proposed an Admiralty commission of inquiry. The Navy Board immediately applied its interest in Westminster, where many a white wig had a parcel of the dockyard plunder.

Officials and ministers privately urged the first sea lord to drop the inquiry; and one "spaniel'd him at heels from Downing Street to the Admiralty in the vain hope of inducing him to relent from the Commission." St. Vincent came out of a cabinet meeting and told his secretary, "Excepting my Lord Chancellor, the whole Cabinet has mutinied today! My Commission is rejected! We shall read them a lesson out of the Articles of War tomorrow, sir."

St. Vincent read only one article: he would resign if he did not get his inquiry. The cabinet approved and went to a secondary defensive position—delay in Parliament. Pitt's dismissed and disgruntled cabinet ministers—Spencer, Windham, Canning and Grenville—pounced on the inquiry bill as a club to belabor the new Prime Minister, Addington, and St. Vincent. George Canning led the assault. To Old Jarvey's defense came Charles James Fox, who had ended his vacation from the House of Commons, young Charles Grey, and Richard Brinsley Sheridan. The playwright wrote a death scene for Spencer and Canning:

> I do remember a statement of these abuses made while the late First Lord of the Admiralty was in office, which stated the amount of plunder and embezzlement in his department to be full three million pounds a year. The statement was made professedly for the purpose of applying a remedy; and if Lord Spencer had been still in office the present Bill would have been proposed under his auspices.

Parliament gave Old Jarvey his Navy Abuses Bill. He sent his old ship's surgeon and personal physician, Dr. Andrew Baird, to investigate the hospitals. Baird was an Irishman with a Scottish shingle. He was a most remarkable social physician. He had kept the aged and ill St. Vincent going in his last years at sea and had practically eliminated scurvy in the Channel fleet. Backed by the old disciplinarian, Dr. Baird forced ships to air their bedding regularly, wash clothing, and purge funk holes and bilges. At Baird's recommendation, Old Jarvey issued small stoves to dry out holds and orlops. Despite the traditional morbid dread of fire in the wooden walls, the seamen were so grateful for dry berths that they never permitted one of these stoves to start a fire. Baird substituted hot sand for water to scrub the decks, which absorbed moisture instead of increasing it. He passed out experimental saltwater soaps to commanders and asked them to compare quality. He rid the fleet of infectious ulcers. Baird's campaign culminated in a special naval victory when Old Jarvey took out the Channel fleet that Bridport often could not keep at sea because of epidemics. After 121 days without fresh food, St. Vincent brought back twelve thousand men with only sixteen on the sick list. Alas, there were no medals and promotions for that.

Dr. Baird began his round of hospital inspections with authority to report directly to the first sea lord, bypassing the constituted hospital control, the Navy Board. Old Jarvey received a steady production of coldly documented exposés of hospital practices at East Stonehouse, Haslar at Gosport, Deal, Plymouth, the hospital ship *Le Caton,* and the vaunted Greenwich Hospital itself. The Navy Board had not inspected them for years. Baird found storekeepers diverting the patients' wine, cocoa and sugar to surgeons' and staff's households. Beds were not changed or fumigated between a death and an admission. Payrolls were padded with invisible relatives. Hospital chiefs held contracts to furnish victuals to their own institutions. Operations were made in the open wards, amidst the patients. In one hospital, men with gangrenous limbs refused amputations by the chief surgeon, preferring death to his medical art.

Baird's hospital reforms, enforced by Lord St. Vincent, included separate operating rooms, the bathing of patients regularly, change of bedding every four days, fumigation, and control of drugs and food stores.

St. Vincent's dockyard examiners, also reporting to him instead of to the Navy Board, brought in confirmations of the knavery dominating the shipbuilding industry. When the French war was resumed in the spring of 1803, St. Vincent's inquiry continued by his force of will and growing interest in Parliament. No longer could the Navy Board stop questions by saying they were unpatriotic in time of war. But the general public knew nothing of Old Jarvey's revelations, which were still confidential to the investigating commission. Samuel Whitbread moved in Commons to publish the results so the people could see what St. Vincent had done. A convenient technicality stifled the motion without a vote.

While the exposé was still bottled, Pitt, now leader of the opposition in Parliament, opened fire on Old Jarvey. The former Prime Minister wanted the dockyards to build flat-bottomed gunboats instead of the frigates St. Vincent had ordered. He said, "In the present emergency our navy is not entirely to be trusted." The French were again building alarming invasion forces at Brest, Bordeaux and the Texel.

"Our naval defence, I state from my own knowledge, is very defective," said Pitt. He felt it his duty to call for an investigation of the Admiralty.

The rough fighting man, Admiral Sir Edward Pellew, came in from the seafront off Spain, took his seat in the House, and defended the old admiral:

> "I do not see, in the arrangements of our naval defense, anything to excite the apprehensions of even the most timid among us.
>
> "I see a triple bulwark, composed of one fleet acting on the enemy's coast, another consisting of heavier ships stationed in the Downs, ready to act at a moment's notice, a third close to the beach, capable of destroying any part of the enemy's flotilla."

Pellew called Pitt's gunboats a "most contemptible force."

Fox and Sheridan swung into support of St. Vincent and defeated Pitt's investigation. But Old Jarvey fell ill again, the King was insane once more—his third spell—and Pitt was coming back to power. In 1804, the balance of his Majesty's mind was declared to be restored; again he could issue writs, ministers could kiss hands, Prime Minister Addington could be dismissed with a viscountship, and Pitt could come back to power and turn Old Jarvey out of the Admiralty.

The old man accepted command of the Channel fleet. Ill and frustrated by the King's men, St. Vincent returned uncomplainingly to a wintry quarterdeck. As First Lord of the Admiralty, Pitt named the perennial minister Henry Dundas, now empurpled as Lord Melville and Baron Dunira.

When Parliament gathered, a rumor ran through the lobbies that the reason St. Vincent's investigations were being withheld was that they accused Dundas of mishandling funds when he was treasurer of the navy. The unhappy Prime Minister, with his favorite Dundas spread-eagled on the gratings, maintained that it was Old Jarvey that deserved the beating. At this stage, Parliament forced St. Vincent's exposé into public view. The City of London sent an address of thanks to Admiral St. Vincent. The King's dispatch boxes piled higher, full of petitions to dismiss Dundas. In Commons, Samuel Whitbread offered a resolution that prepared grounds for impeaching Dundas. Pitt admitted that his friend had been careless with public money but had not stolen any. The House split 216 to 216 on Whitbread's motion and looked in silence at the Speaker, who was obliged to decide. He voted against Dundas. The cold emotionless mask of the Prime Minister crumpled. Pitt wept uncontrollably, his friends gathering as a physical curtain around the beaten, proud man. Charles Fox saw his remorseless rival undone but did not exult over the first public shame that had befallen the steward of Georgian plutocracy.

Pitt pulled his mask on again and appointed a new first sea lord, an admiral older than St. Vincent, Sir Charles Middleton, who was in his eightieth year. He was a vice-admiral of the Red, but had passed his career largely as an Admiralty administrator. Middleton harvested St. Vincent's seeds and gave Nelson the means to win at Trafalgar.* After a year, Middleton was replaced by young Charles Grey, the champion of the seamen during the mutiny years. The King's men got rid of Grey by making him Viscount Howick and foreign secretary.

In 1806, William Pitt died of debility and shame over the disgrace of Henry Dundas, followed soon after into the immortal shades by Charles James Fox, dead of dropsy. They lie together in the north transept of Westminster Abbey. Sir Walter Scott wrote:

> *Drop upon Fox's grave the tear,*
> *'Twill trickle to his rival's bier.*

There was so little left of Pitt that a wax effigy was substituted for the corpse in the funeral ceremony. (It is still believed to be stored in the abbey.)

Old Jarvey, who had sailed midshipman before either Fox or Pitt was born, remained on sea duty. He kept a tight blockade on Brest. Nelson's victory at Trafalgar had crippled the enemy fleets and slackened the vigilance of many British seamen. Corrosive tedium, neglect, and hardship brought forth the old unrest between decks.

Old Jarvey wrote a confidant: "How the unaccountably lost spirit of discipline and animation . . . is to be recovered, I cannot tell, but I really think that starvation (*entre nous*) is the only mode. Sure I am that an over-increase of full and half-pay will dish it completely."

---

* One-fourth of Nelson's battleships were ex-mutineers.

Nevertheless, navy pay was raised—by a shilling a week to able seamen and a sixpence to ordinaries.

Placemen had the run of the Admiralty, now that Old Jarvey was gone to sea. He growled about the "great influx of nobility into the navy," and of their transforming "the office of captain into a complete sinecure. . . . All the powers, even punishments, are delegated to the first lieutenants; the captain does not turn out as formerly; seldom comes upon deck, and takes everything upon report. The change is really quite alarming, for the captain now does not think himself responsible for anything."

There was another campaign in Parliament to restore Catholic civil rights. His Majesty expelled a coalition cabinet and brought in the old lineup, this time with the great Jacobin hunter, the Duke of Portland, as Prime Minister. Portland gave the Admiralty to the Baron of Mulgrave, First Viscount Normandy and First Earl of Musgrave— all a single person who had been born Henry Phipps. He was a major general in the army and ran the navy for five years—longer than Howe, Spencer or St. Vincent.

As a first exercise of power, Phipps sent a note to Old Jarvey.

> Whereas we think fit you should haul down your flag and come on shore; you are hereby required to haul down your flag, and come on shore.

St. Vincent hauled down his flag and came on shore. He secured a private audience with the King and said, "Sire, my life ever has been, and ever will be, at your Majesty's disposal, but I am the guardian of my honour, and I could not place it in the hands of your Majesty's present ministers."

The King asked, "What do you think, milord, of the navy? Is it better or worse than when you first joined?"

"It is worse, your Majesty. Though a sprinkling of nobility is desirable to give some sort of consequence to the service, the navy is now overrun by the younger branches of nobility, and the sons of Members of Parliament. They have swallowed up all patronage and so stopped the channels of promotion that the son of an old officer, however meritorious his services, has little or no chance of getting on."

With that Lord St. Vincent closed a navy career of 59 years.

Ever since the mutiny year, the corresponding societies had wobbled along under thickening blows from the home office. E. P. Thompson thinks that the 1797 mutinies split the reform organization, by posing "in the most acute form possible the conflict between the republican sympathies and national loyalties of the members." Government repression deepened the division of the membership.

In 1798 the audacious John Binns, still nominally an LCS organizer, drew frowns from Francis Place for hanging around an action group that met in the cellar of Furnivall's Inn in Holborn. The habitués were mainly militant Irishmen and "Old Jacks," as the scattered Jacobins were now being called. They had a secret handclasp and catechism that the Duke of Portland could have repeated. His spies were all over this naïve little band.

Binns confided to Place that he was working with "Captain Jones," a sort of green pimpernel who was slipping back and forth between France and Ireland via the waist of England. The captain was actually an Irish priest, John James O'Coigly, "of sympathizing mind and indefatigable exertions." Place warned Binns that he would report him to the magistrates if he did not drop "Captain Jones." He advised Binns to leave the country before his activities further endangered the LCS and his own neck. But the mettlesome plumber had pledged aid to O'Coigly and would go through with one more operation. He took O'Coigly and Arthur O'Connor, another hunted Irishman, down to the Kentish coast to find them transportation to France.

Portland's missionaries had been shadowing Binns ever since his acquittal for sedition. They netted him and his two friends and Portland uttered a writ for high treason. Binns was taken in irons to London and brought before the privy council, acting as a kind of grand jury. He was personally interrogated by Mr. Pitt.

This time Portland did not have to invent evidence. O'Coigly was carrying an anonymous memorandum, purportedly drawn up by British republicans, to advise French occupation forces on policy acceptable to British sympathizers:

—Each of the British isles should be a "Distinct republick," allowed to form its own constitution.*

—The French might arm English partisans but should not exact "contributions beyond those necessary for meeting the costs of the invasion."

—Victorious France should take back only her colonies and ships

---

* An earlier and more liberal version of the Union of Soviet Socialist Republics.

that had been captured in the war, and not open a new round of imperial grievances and seizures.

Brought out in the Maidstone assizes, the memorandum cost Father O'Coigly his life. In a quite unexpected side effect, the jury acquitted Binns and O'Connor. Binns decided to take cover. He shook the Duke of Portland's narks and went underground in Nottinghamshire under an assumed name. But Binns could not keep still. He promised the privy council that if it did not pursue him illegally, he would conduct himself legally. For this impudent sally, he was tracked down and seized without a warrant and jailed without charges. By now Pitt had the last dozen officials of the corresponding societies in dungeons without warrant, bail, trial or habeas corpus. Binns was three years in the cage at his Majesty's pleasure, and once the Duke of Portland brought his duchess and daughters on a friendly visit to see the felon.

When released in 1802, John Binns decided that living under His Britannic Majesty was not worth all the trouble—and emigrated to America.

In the panicky days of the great mutiny, Westminster had turned out repressive acts piecemeal and attacked reformers and workmen's combinations in much the same extemporaneous fashion. But all too often, these hasty laws did not hold up in court. In 1798, Pitt's crowd began laying the groundwork for all-purpose suppressive acts against the popular opposition and the unions. To obtain legal pretexts and to prepare the public for a blackout of free speech and the right of organization, Parliament revived the Committee of Secrecy.

This black chamber had been inaugurated four years earlier by Henry Dundas to help crush the corresponding societies. Dundas interviewed government spies and provocateurs. He had one of his Scottish agents plant some pikes in a reformer's house, "discover" them, and turn in drawings which were published by the Committee. The Duke of Portland, who succeeded Dundas during the Committee's labors, contributed his maiden essay in forging evidence, a fantasy about a brass blowgun holding a poison dart, with which the radicals intended to puncture his Majesty. Although people snickered at the Committee's report and called Portland's yarn "the popgun plot," it impressed Parliament, which gave Pitt another suspension of habeas corpus and Portland an opening for the famous 1794 treason indictments against the national reform leaders.

The revived secret committee of 1798 produced a stupendous document, sweeping together a jackdaw's nest of papers including a letter of introduction carried by "Citizens Binns and John Gale Jones" for a tour of the Midlands. "Sweeping" literally applied: Exhibit No. 12 was "Form of Oath, found on the floor of the George, St. John Street, Clerkenwell."

The committee collected symptoms of many forms of resentment and discontent and fashioned them into a diabolical "system" which had been "operating silently and secretly" ever since the "unnatural" French idea came along. The report alleged that:

> At the meetings of the London Corresponding Society, for above two years before this time it had been avowed that the object of the Society was to form a republic, by the assistance of France. Reform in Parliament, or even annual elections, or universal suffrage, were therefore no longer mentioned. Meetings were held, to contribute the means of procuring arms, to enable them to cooperate with a French force in case of invasion. . . . An occasional meeting . . . was held at a cellar in Furnivall's Inn, and was first formed for the purpose of reading the libelous and treasonable publication, called *The Press*.

Here the reformist LCS was charged with the intrigues of a pro-Irish splinter group including John Binns. The secret committee credited the Furnivall's Inn sect with lofty ambitions:

> That of effecting a general insurrection, at the same moment, in the metropolis and throughout the country, and of directing it to the object of seizing or assassinating the King, the royal family, and many members of both Houses of Parliament.

The "system," the parliamentary report went on, "was still further extended by the establishment of clubs, amongst the lowest classes of the community, which were open to all persons paying one penny, and in which songs were sung, toasts given, and language held, of the most seditious nature."

But, the "system" was not content merely to lure laborers to sing-songs. The report found in 1797:

> The mutiny which took place in the fleet, if considered in all its circumstances, will be traced to an intimate connection

with the principles and practices described by Your Committee, and furnished the most alarming proof of the efficacy of those plans of secrecy and concert, so often referred to, and of the facility with which they are applied for inflaming and heightening discontent (from whatever cause it proceeds) and for converting what otherwise might produce only a hasty and inconsiderate breach of subordination and discipline, into the most settled and systematic treason and rebellion. These principles and this concert could alone have produced the wide extent of the mutiny and the uniformity of its operation in so many and such distant quarters. The persons principally engaged in it, even in its early stages, were many of them United Irishmen. The mutineers were bound by secret oaths to the perpetration of the greatest crimes. And attempt was made to give the ships in the mutiny, the name of "The Floating Republic." *

The secret committee held "that whatever were the pretenses and misrepresentations employed to seduce from their duty a brave and loyal body of men; yet a spirit, in itself repugnant to the habits and dispositions of British sailors, must have had its origin in those principles of foreign growth, which the Societies of the conspirators have industriously introduced into this country, and which they have incessantly laboured to disseminate among descriptions of men; but especially among those whose fidelity and steadiness is most important to the public safety."—Crown magistrates Graham and Williams notwithstanding.

The secret committee was at its best when it reprinted, unexpurgated, General Jean Humbert's book of partisan military tactics, devised by Hoche in the Vendée, and which might yet be applied to the British Isles. This was a genuine service to rebel and white wig alike; although the size of the committee report, a crown folio (10 by 15 inches) of 824 pages, discouraged its employment as a field manual by seditious elements.

The fruit of the secret committee was the Seditious Societies Act, which simply outlawed any and all national membership associations. The historian Charles Cestre said, "England was on the eve of a necessary political and social change, and the very behavior of the reform party, even under the provocation of harsh, arbitrary coercion,

---

* The term "Floating Republic" occurs nowhere in the mutineers' papers or in the court-martial transcripts.

is a warrant that the change might have been accomplished gradually by legal stages and peaceful means." That was not to be.

The Whigs and Tories were not affected by the Seditious Societies Act, because they were not parties but rival bands of junkers contesting for power. Their conventions were country house holidays, their caucuses congenial weekend gatherings; their policies anything that retained power and his Majesty's sanction.

Parliament passed a companion bill which proscribed all combinations of workmen to obtain shorter hours and higher wages. This left the newly created industrial worker at the mercy of the factory system, which for most of the following century was the shame of England and produced Marx and Engels. Under the new antitrade union act, a man advocating such reforms as the twelve-hour day could be brought to summary trial before two magistrates, without a jury or opportunity to seek counsel, and be transported to Australia. J. Steven Watson, writing on the Georgian era in the *Oxford History of England,* says the act "simply made the masters judges of their own men in many cases." Mr. Pitt's latest contribution to due process transplanted the naval court-martial to the factory.

The administration also procured the Newspaper Publication Act, which gave magistrates direct supervision of what could and could not be published. Although Pitt had done his best to eliminate his political opposition and close the press to their ideas, their appeals and lampoons still circulated. The Prime Minister went a step further and entered the field of counter-propaganda. (Pitt was a remarkably advanced manipulator of popular sentiment, as has been shown in his handling of the Nore mutiny. He also controlled the two most popular songwriters of the country, Charles and Thomas Dibdin.) Pitt's counterblast to the radical scribblers was a weekly called the *Anti-Jacobin.* It was edited by a crabbed gnome called William Gifford, who, said Robert Southey, "looked upon authors as Isaac Walton looked upon worms." The paper is remembered only as a contraceptive. One of its star contributors was George Canning, the rising junior minister. He wrote a parody of *The Botanic Garden,* which was written in rhymed verse by Erasmus Darwin, M.D., a wonderful thinker-general in the midlands.

Canning ridiculed Darwin's proposals that:

—man evolved from lower forms of life
—electricity would have important uses
—mountains were made much earlier than the Bible says they were.

The *Anti-Jacobin* is credited with damaging Dr. Darwin's reputation to the extent that British science did not take up his glimpse of evolution until his grandson Charles and Alfred Russell Wallace published their independent but similar theories on natural selection as a joint paper sixty years later.

1817

To have fought for so long, and so frequently alone, against half Europe, and the force and vigour of revolutionary peoples and ideas, naturally increased the Englishman's pride, especially so as it had been done without loss of wealth, without economic or social exhaustion. It naturally led to an assumption of arrogance towards the rest of mankind and to the growth of an intense moral vanity."

—J. H. PLUMB
England in the 18th Century

THE WAR against Napoleon ended two years ago with Wellington's triumph at Waterloo. A Greek peasant named Kolokotrones, who is leading a guerrilla band against Turkish occupation of his country, sums up the meaning of the past quarter century. "The French Revolution and the doings, of Napoleon opened the eyes of the world. The nations knew nothing before and the people thought that kings were gods upon the earth and that they were bound to say that whatever kings did was well done. Through the present change it is difficult to rule the people."

In victorious Britain, there is deeper distress than in the hungry, mutinous years when the war against the revolution began. Half of the national income goes to paying interest on the war debt. Parliament last year gave the bondholders further relief by abolishing income taxes, while raising stamp duties on general goods. The newspaper tax was doubled to fourpence a copy. Other wartime measures, such as restrictions of speech and organization, have not been removed, however. Parliament restored habeas corpus for a time, but recently took the right away once more. Prices are high and wages are low.

At the beginning of this year "wheat rose to 103 shillings a quarter and incendiarism was common all over England. A sense of insecurity and terror took possession of everybody. Secret outrages, especially fires by night, chill the courage of the bravest in an agricultural county, when just before going to bed, great lights are seen on the horizon; when men and women collect on bridges or on hilltops, asking, 'Where is it?' or when fire engines tearing through the streets arrive useless at their journey's end because the hose has been cut." *

George III is still alive in the 57th year of his reign and his fourth period of published insanity. The present seizure is regarded as incurable. What may have been the fourth attempt on his Majesty's life was made seventeen years ago by James Hatfield, defended by Lord Erskine who secured the acquittals of Hardy, Tooke and Thelwall in the state treason trials of '94.

Erskine's plea for the intending regicide opened a new tangent in common law. By contending that his client was of unsound mind, Milord gained acquittal and established the precedent plea of "not guilty by reason of insanity." He also skirted *lèse majesté* by omitting to mention the ailment of Hatfield's target.

Rebellious poets still come forth. Twenty-five-year-old Percy Bysshe Shelley has just issued "A Proposal for Putting Reform to the Vote Throughout the Kingdom." He was expelled from Oxford for writing "The Necessity of Atheism" and went on to publish a seditious "Declaration of Rights." This inflamed young man is lucky to enjoy a private income for, as he himself admits, his writings will never be recognized.

Since his Majesty's latest incapacitation, Florizel has been Prince Regent for seven years, while James Monroe, who plotted with Wolfe Tone against Britain, is the newly inaugurated President of the United States. The former Home Secretary, the Duke of Portland, became Prime Minister during 1807–09, and died soon thereafter. Small scribblers and penny poets now refer to Portland's great days with William Pitt as "The English reign of terror."

The country has a vigorous new Home Secretary to curb the reviving reform movement: Viscount Sidmouth, or Henry Addington, a boyhood friend of Pitt's, Speaker of the House of Commons in '97, and the Prime Minister who made Old Jarvey first sea lord. Sidmouth induced Parliament to suspend habeas corpus this year by coming to the front bench with a green bag and proclaiming it full of seditious documents. According to his critics, his lordship has introduced the

---

* *The Revolution in Tanner's Lane.*

"continental spy system." His greatest coup this year is reminiscent of the allegations that Richard Parker was a Jacobin agent sent to debtors' jail and thence to the Nore. Lord Sidmouth released a man named William Oliver from debtors' prison, which cachet helped Oliver to ingratiate himself in the reform movement. The spy worked his way up into the leadership and Sidmouth sent him through the Midlands early this year, making a false call for a national rising. From Lancashire, two hundred fifty unemployed "blanketeers" started marching on London with a petition to the Prince Regent. More deluded men joined along the way and have been ambushed and captured by militia. Thirty-five have been tried for high treason. An unintimidated newspaper, the Leeds *Mercury,* has exposed Oliver's plot, but the court-appointed counsel of the blanketeers secretly agreed with the crown prosecutor not to call Oliver to testify. Thirteen men have been sentenced to transportation and three were to die at Derby in the last exhibition of hanging, drawing and quartering to be given in England. But the Prince Regent has graciously remitted the ancient form of execution and the blanketeers are to be beheaded instead.

As Admiral Lord St. Vincent would say, "Discipline is preserved, sir." Old Jarvey is still alive in great age, bent arthritically over the breastload of jeweled badges on his black velvet coat.

George John the Earl Spencer, first sea lord during the mutinies of Spithead, Nore, Yarmouth, Plymouth, Cadiz, Cape of Good Hope, *Hermione,* and Bantry Bay, is living in studious retirement at "Althorp," a slave to his great book collection. As one of the half dozen claimants to be Nelson's prime patron, Lord Spencer is known as "the organizer of victory." This year the former first sea lord received a royal license to call himself Spencer-Churchill and also succeeded his father as (fifth) Duke of Marlborough.*

The gallant Adam Duncan and his flagship at Camperdown, H.M.S. *Venerable,* perished in the same month in 1804. Duncan came down from retirement in Scotland to offer his services to the Admiralty. He was refused because of age and ill health. On the way home, he died in a country inn. His ship was lost a few weeks later on the rocks near Berry Head, Devon. Wonderful boatwork saved all but thirteen Venerables. The wreck spread over two miles of the coast.

Captain Lord Hugh Seymour, the gold-seeker, died of yellow fever in the West Indies in 1801. The sloop *Hound* of the Nore

---

* He was the great-great-grandfather of Sir Winston Leonard Spencer Churchill (1874-1965).

mutiny, upon which Richard Parker once sailed, was wrecked near Shetland in 1800 and all aboard lost.

Captain Edward Pakenham, of the Plymouth mutiny, was in a new command, H.M.S. *Resistance,* 44, at anchor in the Bangka Strait, Sumatra, in 1798, when his powder magazine exploded. He and 331 others were killed. Thirteen survivors sailed on a raft for Sumatra. A typhoon swept away eight of them. Four others died of maltreatment on the island. Only one survivor returned to England to tell the story.

Captain John Thomas Duckworth, aghast at the ingratitude of his people the day they expelled him at Plymouth, became a model of solicitude for his men. Together they prospered on prizes taken in the West Indies and today Sir John is a Knight of the Bath and a vice-admiral.

Sir Thomas Pasley, who presided at Parker's trial, died ten years ago. Sir Alan Gardner, the marplot at Spithead, was created Baron Gardner of Uttoxeter, and became commander of the Channel fleet in 1807. He died a year later. Admiral Sir John Colpoys, expelled at Spithead by his people and Lord Howe, was not reappointed to a command at sea but is now treasurer of Greenwich Hospital, a desirable shore post in the navy.

Black Dick Howe died in 1799, but Lord Bridport lived until 1814, when he died at the age of eighty-seven. Admiral Sir Peter Parker, the great jobber, died six years ago at the age of ninety. His counterpart at the Nore, Admiral Buckner, was given no further employment after the mutiny.

For several years Magistrate Aaron Graham, the home office investigator of the mutinies, has been incurably ill at his house in Great Queen Street, Lincoln's Inn Fields. A son is a captain in the navy. Graham's contributions to naval history, the depositions of the *Bounty* mutineers and of Richard Parker, have been lost. He closed his career on the bench at Bow Street court and became manager of the Drury Lane Theatre, owned by Samuel Whitbread and Richard Brinsley Sheridan, the archetypes of opposition politicians that the Duke of Portland sent him to Portsmouth and Sheerness to try to connect with the mutineers.

Whitbread committed suicide two years ago and Sheridan died last year.

Commodore William Bligh is dying of cancer in London. Ten years ago, as governor of New South Wales, he experienced his third mutiny. The dominant group in the colony had been trafficking in illegal spirits, and taking their pick of crown lands, bond servants and convict labor. As on the quarterdeck, Bligh enforced the law ashore. The ruling clique sent the New South Wales corps with bayonets to Government House and deposed Bligh. He sent appeals to England for troops to put down the mutiny. Prime Minister Lord Portland replaced Bligh and made no move to punish the mutineers.

In Australia, Bligh encountered seamen transported from the Nore, among them William Redfern, the surgeon's assistant of *Standard,* who was practicing medicine in the colony. The sick, hotheaded delegate, Thomas McCann, whom Bligh had prevented from taking his ship, turned up in Sydney among eight Irish convicts charged with intent to conspiracy. They were acquitted in criminal court, but were hailed before the bench of magistrates, purportedly at Bligh's order. Two men were sentenced to receive one thousand lashes apiece. McCann and the others were found innocent. Nonetheless, Bligh, as if thrusting the Nore republic deeper into oblivion, transported McCann to the wildest part of the colony.

In 1800 Lord Keith, who took the surrender of the Nore mutineers, succeeded Old Jarvey as commander of the Mediterranean fleet, which had reentered the Mediterranean. Keith's flag was in *Queen Charlotte,* parliament ship of the Spithead mutiny. At Leghorn the admiral was ashore for conferences with Britain's Austrian allies when a spark from a slow match, kept alight for the signal gun, fell on hay in the manger on the half deck of *Queen Charlotte.* The ancient, sun-dried, tar-soaked three-decker was soon "one blaze from stem to stern, with her guns going off in all directions from the flames," said her third lieutenant. The second officer sailed a tartan out to the roaring pyre and sent small boats to collect men hanging from the bowsprit and the spritsail yard. From the American merchantman *Castor and Pollux,* three seamen brought a boat alongside the lower gunports. A mad rush of people swamped the boat, drowning the Americans and themselves.

The magazine exploded and *Queen Charlotte* went down by the stern. Her stores rumbled to the surface—bales, casks, boxes, spars and dunnage. The third lieutenant said, "She, for an instant, recovered her buoyant property, and was suddenly seen to emerge her whole length from the deep; and then immediately turning over, she floated on the surface, with her burnished copper glistening in the sun." The hundred-gun queen of the Spithead rising is a charred ruin at the bottom of the Ligurian Sea. Captain Andrew Todd and 673 men went with her. The dead exceeded the combined total of

British seamen killed at the battles of the Glorious First of June, Cape St. Vincent, and Camperdown. In the French wars, the King's navy lost 101 ships by accident and 10 by enemy action.

The spring after the mutinies, the ex-delegate ships from Spithead, *Mars* and *Ramillies,* 74s, and the frigate *Jason* chased a new French 74, *Hercule,* toward Brest. They herded the Frenchman toward the rock-strewn Bec du Raz passage. It was low slack tide and *Hercule* was forced to anchor until the flow could carry her in. Captain Alexander Hood, Lord Bridport's cousin, slid *Mars* in line before *Hercule* and anchored, streaming his ship in the same wind and current, immune to French fire. Eighteenth-century battleships could not fire dead ahead.

Hood's ex-mutineers veered cable on the Frenchman, paying out the anchor hawser until *Mars* was alongside *Hercule,* rolling against her. On the three opposing gun decks, Johnny Crapaud and Jack Rosbiff looked at each other close through the ports, hauled back their pieces to get some firing room, and began thunderous transfigurations. In blinding and smothering smoke, two French boarding parties clashed with the Marses and were repelled. The fight took five lives a minute.

The French captain, mortally wounded, called for his colors to be struck, and gave an officer his sword to deliver to the victor. Captain Hood touched it, as he lay dying. This meaningless one-hour massacre exterminated more than three hundred men, including eighty forgiven Spithead mutineers.

Grampus storeship was wrecked at Barking in 1799, her crew saved. The venerable dilapidations, H.M.S. *Nassau* and *l'Espion* of the Nore, were converted to storeships and both went aground and broke up two years after the mutiny. Nearly all the Nassaus were saved from her finale in Holland and all the Espions got off alive before her demise on the Goodwin Sands. *Repulse,* which eloped with *Leopard* to start the breakdown of the Nore cause, was wrecked at the Ushant in 1800, "nearly all saved," say the annals. The fireship *Comet,* 14, Benjamin of the Nore, was expended at Dunkirk Roads that year, her crew, of course, debarking before she was set adrift in flames.

The frigate *Success* and fireship *Incendiary* of the Spithead breeze were captured in action by the French navy, and their mutinous sister *Jason,* 36, broke up on the rocks at St. Malo, the crew saved.

The gunboat *Calypso,* whose men mutinied in '97, foundered in an Atlantic storm six years later, all hands lost. *Circe,* the frigate that helped Duncan blockade the Texel while in a state of mutiny, was wrecked in the North Sea the same year, her company saved. All her men survived the loss of *Doris,* a Plymouth delegate ship, in shipwreck at Quiberon Bay in 1805. That year *Cleopatra,* 32, of the Spithead mutiny, was captured by the French in American waters. Two years later *Anson,* a cause ship at Plymouth, was wrecked in Mount's Bay, with sixty lost. In 1809 *Agamemnon,* 64, of the Great Nore remonstrance, broke up in Rio de Plata, all saved. A few months later, *Alcmène,* virtuous at Spithead and wicked at Cadiz, was wrecked on the rocks off Nantes, her company delivered. *Nymphe,* 36, of Spithead, came to grief the following December in the Firth of Forth, with a small loss of life.

The 74-gun Spithead ship *Defense* had a violent subsequent history. At Aboukir Bay, in the battle of the Nile, she shot up *Peuple Souverain,* 74, and went to grips with *Franklin,* 80. Although badly shot up, *Defense* dismasted the French man-of-war and brought down the *tricouleur* in surrender. That summer another mutiny broke out on *Defense,* for which nineteen men were hanged and six given 300 strokes. The ship was in the battle of Copenhagen in 1801 and at Trafalgar in 1805. She was finally defeated in Holland, in the heaviest death toll that befell British seamen in the Napoleonic wars. It occurred in 1811 at the Texel, Duncan's old watchful grounds, not in battle but from breaking up on the Haak Sands. The winter before, *Minotaur,* 74, of the Spithead remonstrance, struck the Sands with a loss of the ship and 360 men. *St. George,* 98, of the aborted Cadiz mutiny, *Hero,* 74, and *Defense* were blown to wintry doom on that shoal in December 1811. Of 2,400 men on the three ships, eighteen got ashore alive.

Colonel William Tate, the aged American commander of the French invasion of Wales, was sent to France in 1798 in a prisoner-of-war exchange. The Admiralty kept his commission papers in the French army, which handicapped the old man in regaining rank or pension. Brother officers persuaded the French government to retire him on half pay. Old Bill then took up with a glamorous Parisienne who got him disastrously in debt. Apparently the U. S. colony in Paris contributed to keep him out of jail. The American ambassador arranged his passage home. Tate applied to the French war ministry for an indefinite leave in the United States, a stratagem to retain his pension. He said his native country was probably going to fight England again and would need his services. The ministry gave him the leave but not the pension, so Old Bill went home in 1809 at the age of eighty-two and has been heard of no more.

The shutter telegraph system is abandoned and the stations are falling to ruin. Country people remember where they stood and call the high ground "Telegraph Hill."

Ten years ago the navy began issuing trusses. By now 13,000 have been distributed.

There was a large reform meeting recently at the Crown & Anchor Tavern in London, celebrating the attainment of one million signatures on a petition calling for universal male suffrage, annual parliaments, and vote by secret ballot. At the Three Crowns in Leicester, a "club" was formed. (Corresponding societies and other reform organizations have long been outlawed by name.) The club has 500 members who pay a penny a week dues, which in the case of a farm laborer, may amount to one-tenth of his income. The club organizer, William Scott, a framesmith, sang "Millions Be Free!" which he had sung eighteen years before in the same public house as a church-and-king mob broke in and suppressed the corresponding society.

There is a new law which, if it had obtained in 1797, might have kept Richard Parker from joining the navy. Inmates of debtors' jails are now debited for their upkeep. While receiving punishment for their wrongdoings they sink deeper into wrongdoing.

The House of Lords is firmly opposed to an attempt to repeal the article of the Bloody Code providing death for theft of five shillings or more. "Repeal this law!" shouts Lord Chief Justice Ellenborough, "and no man can trust himself an hour out of doors without the most alarming apprehensions that, on his return, every vestige of his property will be swept away by the hardened robber!" How can a man keep scullery maids, backstairs maids and stableboys on duty sixteen hours a day if he can't threaten 'em with death for pilfering?

Robert Southey, the ex-radical, is now Poet Laureate. He is prominent in the campaign to suppress seditious literature. A mocking reform sheet has reprinted Southey's youthful verse drama, *Wat Tyler,* which is seditious under the present ministerial interpretation. The poet applied to the King's Bench to protect his copyright and force the periodical to pay damages. "Injunction denied," says my Lord Justice Eldon. "The court cannot take notice of property in the unhallowed profits of libellous publications."

Mrs. Ann Parker, widow of the President of the Fleet, is living in extreme poverty in London, often forced to accept charity. Occasionally she receives a banknote from anonymous donors.*

The five sons of George III, the royal dukes, are seeking increases to their incomes from the public purse by threatening Parliament that, without raises, they cannot produce an heir to the throne. The only child of the Prince Regent died this year and Prince Augustus Frederick, his nearest brother, is legally childless thanks to his father's annulment of the fruitful union with Lady Augusta Murray. The third, fourth and fifth sons are unmarried, although the third, the Duke of Clarence, has fathered ten natural children by the deceased actress Mrs. Jordan. The three younger dukes are asking that their incomes be doubled in order that they may take brides. They also demand special state dowries, or "outfit allowances," of £12,000 each. Members of the House of Commons grumble that their "stricken father" could keep the royal dukes in the style to which they aspire from the enormous crown income, grants for upkeep of the royal households now of no utility to the country or the retired King, and from his Majesty's great untaxed personal fortune.

These are hard times in the land, and the hardest times are in the Black Country, where miners' and ironworkers' families are starving. The royal dukes graciously joined in sponsoring a relief fund, but other committeemen offended them by bitter remarks about the royal family. Individual subscriptions include £300 from her Majesty the Queen, £200 from the Duke of Wellington** and £100 from the Archbishop of Canterbury, whose state-provided income is £20,000 per annum. The Marquis of Camden, with a £38,000 annual sinecure, gave £100. The Princess Charlotte of Wales and the Prince of Cobourg, who receive £120,000 a year from the British treasury, subscribed £400 for the relief fund. The City of London livery companies applauded a speaker who denounced these pittances. At provincial relief meetings called by persons of quality, persons of lesser quality are giving voice to uncalled-for outcries: "We don't want subscriptions! Lower the rents! Abolish the sinecures!"

Lord Sidmouth's home ministry recently arranged another high treason trial, King v. Watson, et al, arising from the Spa Fields "insurrection" last year. The chief defendant is Dr. Richard Watson, an Old Jack suspected of a connection with the mutiny at the Nore. A

---

* In 1836 she received some aid from London magistrates. In 1840, Mrs. Parker was still alive, described as "seventy, blind and friendless."—ED.

** Parliament paid Wellington £700,000 for his victories in Spain and at Waterloo.

series of astonishing popular meetings was held last autumn at Spa Fields, the biggest reform demonstrations for twenty years. Before one of them, Committeeman John Castle gave a toast. "May the last of the kings be strangled with the guts of the last priest." This shocked his colleagues. At the meeting, the magistrates seized a cart containing gunpowder and, in a raid on Dr. Watson's privy, came away with some pikes.

Evidence at the treason trial convinced the jury that John Castle was a home office provocateur and had placed the powder in the wagon and the pikes in Watson's jakes. The defendants have been acquitted amidst public rejoicing. Others of Lord Sidmouth's prey are not so lucky. He has the habit of putting reformers in jail for long periods in distant cities, then discharging them. In most cases they must walk home, and when they arrive, they find a summons for a trial in the town they have just left. His jailers place political prisoners in double irons so contrived that they cannot remove their clothes even for acts of nature. A government critic named John Baguley was in double irons for more than three weeks. The prisoners are customarily chained together.

Poor Florizel, after waiting a lifetime to succeed his father, is finding much the same sort of vexations as George III endured. As he coached through the park to open Parliament this year, the Prince Regent was hissed and jeered. Upon his return, "the malcontents had increased in number . . . and they broke out into acts of violence, accompanied by the most foul, shocking, insulting and blasphemous language. Gravel stones and other things were thrown at the royal carriages," said the *Westmorland Advertiser*.

In the provinces, reformers are holding parades on Sundays, carrying banners of "Universal Suffrage"—black flags with devices of hearts and clasped hands inscribed "Love," and unadorned red flags, the first seen in England since the last banner of defiance was lowered at the Nore.*

There is a popular new radical weekly called the *Black Dwarf,* edited by T. J. Wooler. He has just been tried for sedition. The foreman of the jury proclaimed him guilty. "So say you all?" asked the justice. "No!" cried three jurors. "He is *not* guilty." Wooler was acquitted.

A satirist named William Hone recently had the distinction of being

---

* The flag of the English mutineers was later carried by the Paris communards and the Russian revolutionists. Today at British Labour Party meet-

tried for sedition, three times in three days, a trial for each of three
literary contributions cited by the crown. One of Hone's offenses was
a doxology for the King's men in Parliament:

> *Our Lord who art in the treasury, whatsoever be thy name,*
> *thy power be prolonged, thy will be done throughout the em-*
> *pire, as it is in each session. Give us our usual sops, and for-*
> *give us our occasional absences on divisions; as we promise not*
> *to forgive those who divide against thee. Turn us not out of*
> *our places; but keep us in the House of Commons, the land*
> *of Pensions and Plenty; and deliver us from the People. Amen.*

In court, Hone debated cheekily with the Lord Chief Justice and
the jury acquitted him.

The great popular voice of the day, successor to Tom Paine, is
William Cobbett. His *Weekly Register* has been the best-read reform
paper in the country. "His style stuns his readers," says William
Hazlitt. "He is too much for any single newspaper antagonist, 'lays
waste' a city orator or Member of Parliament, and bears hard upon
the government itself. He is kind of a *fourth estate* in the politics of
the country."

Because of the newspaper tax, Cobbett's paper cost one shilling
halfpenny, a day's wage for a seaman of the fleet. He found a tax
loophole: pamphlets are exempted. The first issue of Cobbett's
"Weekly Political Pamphlet" at twopence sold 200,000 copies. The
King's men called it "Tuppenny Trash."

Cobbett served two years in jail for criticizing flogging in the King's
army and navy. Last year he was forewarned that Lord Sidmouth was
going to seize him for treason. Cobbett fled to Philadelphia. He is
planning to return soon and will bring Tom Paine's bones with him

---

ings the assembled nuclear physicists, practitioners in advertising, M.P. and
haut polloi, sing the official party anthem.

> *The People's Flag is deepest red;*
> *It shrouded oft our martyr'd dead,*
> *And ere their limbs grow stiff and cold*
> *Their heart's-blood dyed its every fold.*

> CHORUS

> *So raise the scarlet standard high;*
> *Beneath its shade we'll live or die.*
> *Though cowards flinch and traitors sneer*
> *We'll keep the Red Flag flying here!*

from New Rochelle, New York, where the author of *Rights of Man* died in poverty in 1809.

Cobbett says that Britain's privations and repressions today are "the price of efforts to crush freedom in France, lest the example of France should produce a reform in England. These things are the price of that undertaking."

Francis Place, the tactician of the London Corresponding Society, remains active in the reform cause. He made a modest fortune in the tailoring trade and devotes his time to bringing about repeal of laws restricting trade unions.*

A little man in a white hat is publishing a populist journal called the *Champion*. He is John Thelwall, whom Pitt, Portland and the loyal mobs drove into oblivion twenty years ago. Thelwall stayed alive by working a small farm at Llyswen, Wales, these past decades. John Gales Jones, the LCS field organizer, still goes about speaking for reform, as does Alexander Galloway, who has become the largest engineering employer in London. John Binns, the spunky LCS man, twice acquitted of sedition and treason, then jailed for three years without charges, emigrated to America in 1803. He settled in Northumberland, Pennsylvania, where the aged English émigré scientist Joseph Priestley was spending his last days, and founded a piquant populist newspaper called the *Republican Argus*. He married a local lass and joined the United Brethren Church. Four years later, Binns moved up to Philadelphia and started the *Democratic Press,* which is the best-read newspaper in the Quaker State. It was Binns who suggested that Jefferson's Republican-Democratic Party be called the Democratic Party. He has ten children and is much sought as an orator at patriotic gatherings.**

---

* In 1832, Place dealt the Duke of Wellington his worst defeat since Marshall Soult threw him out of Madrid. Wellington, as Prime Minister, obdurately blocked the reform bill that Place was helping to manage in Parliament. The bill would abolish 56 pocket boroughs, reduce other bogus constituencies to one member, and give seats to cities and counties not represented at all in Parliament. The vote would be extended to male leaseholders and even tenants. Francis Place started a run on the banks by a slogan, "To stop the Duke, go for gold." Wellington was forced to resign. Parliament passed the bill twice, but it was vetoed in the House of Lords where Wellington sat. Public furore grew so hot that Wellington and a hundred diehards in the Upper House did not dare vote against the reform bill a third time. They abstained and it passed.

** For some odd reason, Binns formed an animus toward Andrew Jackson and attacked him stridently as a "tyrant" during the Presidential campaign of 1824. A Jacksonian mob wrecked Binns' house and high public feeling put

General Jean Humbert, who survived the invasion of Ireland, is living in New Orleans, Louisiana, in extreme poverty. He served in Haiti, quarreled with another French general, and was sent home and retired. He took no part in the Napoleonic wars. In 1812, he entered the service of the United States, participated in an Argentine revolution in 1814, and retired again to New Orleans.

General Tadeusz Kosciusko died this year in Poland, after freeing his serfs.

Napoleon, exiled to St. Helena Island, is writing his memoirs. Of the period of the Nore and Spithead mutinies, he says, "On what do the destinies of empires hang! If, instead of the expedition of Egypt, I had made that of Ireland. . . . what would England have been today? And the Continent? And the political world?"

The present distress of the British people has no more melancholy aspect than the plight of the men-of-wars-men who were turned out of the ships two years back and have found no employment. They make up the biggest element of London's street beggars. Idle officers exceed Britain's capacity to provide places for gentlemen of small income and no profession. It is not uncommon to come upon a half-pay midshipman blacking boots in the street.

Hundreds of unemployed ex-soldiers and sailors attend the current reform rallies. One was a discharged Irish seaman named Cashman. This year, he was cooling his heels in the Admiralty waiting room, vainly trying to collect five years' back pay, prize money and the arrears of a pension the navy owed his destitute mother, when another seaman invited him to come along to a Spa Fields protestation. Thirty thousand people there voted a resolution to the Prince Regent to alleviate the distress of the workingman and the discarded warriors who had saved the country. After the demonstration Cashman got drunk with some old messmates and they raided a gunsmith's shop. The constable took Cashman. He was tried and condemned to death.

---

the *Democratic Press* out of business. Nothing daunted, Binns ran for alderman in the Walnut Ward of Philadelphia and was reelected for the rest of his life, which encompassed the American and French revolutions and the stillborn English one, and ended at age eighty-four, within a year of the American Civil War. John Binns called himself a "labourer in the vineyard of liberty." In the antebellum decades it was a Philadelphia tradition to hear Alderman Binns' "mighty feast of eloquence" on Independence Day: he always spoke extemporaneously. In 1842, he published a durable book called *Binns's Justice: The Magistrate's Daily Companion,* which went into a dozen editions, the last dated 1912. In it, he distilled for the benefit of novice jurists his practical experience on both sides of the bench.

As the hangman's cart bore him to Newgate, the sailor indignantly cried to the crowd, "I am not brought to this for any robbery. If I was at my quarters, I would not be killed by the smoke: I'd be in the fire. I have done nothing against my King and Country, but fought for them."

The people pressed toward the cart as if to rescue the seaman. "Hoorah, my hearties, in the cause!" Cashman shouted. "Success! Cheer up!"

Two clergymen came to the gallows to serve Cashman's soul. "Don't bother me. It's no use," said he. "I want no mercy but from God." He shouted to the crowd, "Now, you buggers, give me three cheers when I trip. Hangman, let go the jib boom!"

The lash cracked on the cart horse and the sailor dropped.

The people were silent for a long moment. Then their cheers burst forth:

"Shame!"

"Murder!"

"Shame!"

The navy pay boat is leaving Chatham for the Nore. Pay clerk John Dickens is aboard with his pale, large-eyed son, Charles—a "terrible boy to read," his nurse says. During the passage the small boy reads *Roderick Random,* Tobias Smollett's novel of the Georgian navy. At Sheerness the boat passes under the convict hulk *Eagle,* "roofed like Noah's ark," which will be described for future times in *Great Expectations.*

APPENDICES

APPENDIX I

Author's Interjection

In a sense the great mutiny was an isolated major event in industrial history. Considering the Georgian Admiralty as a major concentrator of wage labor—120,000 men in several "plants"—the cruising squadrons and fleet anchorages—Valentine Joyce and his confederates at Spithead led the first successful mass sitdown strike in history, and Richard Parker the first defeated one. As a horizontal union, the Spithead strikers forced their will twice upon an employer who had the power of death over every man involved. Belaboring the labor analogy, a comparable event did not happen on such a scale again in Britain until the London dock strikes a hundred years later.

Participation of Jacobins, if any, with the mutinies is still conjectural. In 1801, the Admiralty destroyed most of the captured mutineer documents from the Nore as "promiscuous papers." If they contained any clues to republican liaison such would have certainly turned up in that volley of left-wing trivia and right-wing humbug, the Report of the 1799 Committee of Secrecy. The Duke of Portland would not have missed one such paper had it existed.

E. P. Thompson in *The Making of the English Working Class*, thinks "there is some evidence of direct Jacobin instigation" in the great mutiny: "It is foolish to argue that, because the majority of the sailors had few clear political notions, this was a parochial affair of ship's biscuits and arrears of pay, and not a revolutionary movement," says he. "This is to mistake the nature of popular revolutionary crises, which arise from exactly this conjunction between the grievances of the majority and the aspirations articulated by the politically-conscious minority."

The fascination of history's greatest navy mutinies will not down: they have intrigued generations of marine historians and sociologists and, in fact, even the Admiralty, of late. Nearly a century and a half after they occurred, the sea lords became interested in why the mutinies came about and caused a staff study to be made. The investigation was stimulated by the Invergordon mutiny in the Royal Navy in 1931, which was virtually a reprise of Spithead in steel instead of wood. It had the same long-pent miseries of the men, the same ministerial trauma and dithering, and the same utter amazement by the press and public. As a matter of fact, the Bank of England was so scared by Invergordon that it stopped paying gold, as it had in 1797. Some of the mutiny leaders went to Moscow.

APPENDIX II

Copies of Papers found in possession of the Mutineers on board H.M. Fire Ship *Comet* on their return to their Duty after the disgraceful affair at the Nore in May and June 1797. Copied by William P. Cumby 1797.

The Mutineers' Log of the *Comet*

(NOTE: The sailing ship log day was from noon to noon, covering two calendar dates. Below, the *Comet* log is given as midnight-to-midnight on a single day.)

Remarks, Comet, Moor'd in Yarmouth Roads. Tuesday, 30 May 1797. Winds variable. P.M. Hoisted a red flag at the Fore topgnt Masthead seeing his Majesty's ships laying here had the same—viz. the Standard, Lion, Nassau, Inspector, etc, etc, etc.

Wednesday May 31st

AM light airs at 5 the Delegates from HMS Standard came on board & desired to know if we did not mean to go to the Nore in Company with the rest of his Majesty's Ships that were going there with an expectation of being paid their Wages, etc. They told us if we wanted hands, they would send us a gang to assist us round—gave charge of the ship to the Pilot Mr. Williams. Weighed at 7 Captain Duncan desired the hands to come aft and after addressing some time told them if they liked that he Capt. Duncan with the assistance of the rest of the Officers of the Ship would take charge of the ship and carry her round to the Nore, the Ships Company answered him they hoped he & his Officers would not conceive that they had ever meant to take any charges from them—made sail in Company with the Squadron—at 11 fresh breezes & squally with showers of rain—Reefed the Fore & Main Topsails—Opened a cask of Pease 5 Bushels. PM. Fresh Breezes & fair— At 5 brought up at the Great Nore in 7 fms Water found riding here H.M. Ships Sandwich, red at the Main, Montagu, Director, Inflexible, Belliqueux & Repulse—

Grampus, Proserpine, etc, etc. with a Red Flag at the Fore topmast head, joined by the Standard, Lion, Nassau, Brilliant, Iris, Champion, Sisiphone & Inspector with many Merchant Vessels. At ½ past 8 came on board three Delegates from H.M. Ship Sandwich who commanded us to send 2 Seamen to represent our Ship & for them to come on board the Sandwich on hoisting a Union Jack at her fore topmasthead which must be answered by us hoisting a red Jack at the Mizon peak, Light Airs PM.

Remarks—Comet at the Great Nore Thursday 1st June 1797

AM Light breezes—At 8 cheered Ships and ans.ᵈ the Signal for Delegates as ordered from the Sandwich—went on board to represent this Ship Wm. Webb & Robt. Bennington—Out cutter &c—Light Airs & fair Wʳ—Received some Papers or Letters which were ordered to be read to the Ships Company. The Captain & Officers refused to take any charge of the Ship in consequence the Committee of Delegates desired that the Ships Company might appoint certain Persons on board for the better Preservation of H.M. Ship & Stores.

Light Airs & Fair. Moored Ship a Cable each way by an Order from the Delegates of the fleet. Employed People overhauling the Rigging etc, etc. as necessary. Cleaned Ship etc.

Friday 2d June

AM. Fresh Breezes with Rain. At 5 H.M. Sloop Inspector swang foul of us at 6 Cleared us of her with no material damage to either. Read the Instructions Articles, Orders, Memᵐˢ etc, etc. at 10 o'clock to the Ships Company at the same exorting them to pay every respect to their Superior Officers as before, altho' the Officers refused taking any Charge of the Ship—the Ships Company deputed Wm. Webb & Thomas Mills to act as Delegates for this Ship, on their going on board the Sandwich they waited upon the Persons who had charge of the Inspector to desire that they would get a new Birth for her as she had given herself a foul Birth.

PM Fresh Breezes. The Inspector Sloop swang foul of us again, cleared without damage—agreed to assist her by sending a gang of hands on board to have a new birth—the Weather proving too Squally blowing very fresh could not moor the Inspector with any Safety—Received the keys of the Magazine per Order of the Assembly of Delegates on board the Sandwich—who desired that a Committee of not less than 7 or more than 13 men should be chosen by this Company for the better keeping order thro' out the Ship—Arrived here H.M.S. Monmouth with a red flag hoisted Fore topmasthead.

Saturday 3ᵈ June

Fresh breezes & fair Weather. Received an Order from the Delegates of the fleet to discharge Mr. Chalcraft and John Weston Servants to Admiral Frederick and the late Capt. Middleton and to take their Masters' Property with them, as also to discharge the 2ᵈ Lieut. Mᵣ F____ & Mᵣ Chas. Douglas Boatsⁿ—The Ships Company accusing them of being Tyrants without a dissenting Voice. Loos'd Sails to dry—sent a gang of Men to assist in mooring the Inspector. Tried to bring too a Sloop by desire of the Officers one six pounder shotted. Broached a Cask of Rum No. 90 Contents 31 gallons.—

Fresh breezes & squally with Rain—Furled sails—Brought too a Sloop by desire of the Officers of the Ship in Order to get the property of the late Thomas Middleton Esq. & Rear Admˡˡ Frederick's that they might be safely conveyed to London—At 2 o'clock the Sloop sailed hence with the following Persons on Board Viz—Mr. Chas. Douglas Boatswain, Mr. Jnᵒ Chalcroft servant to the late Commander Thomas Middleton Esq deceased. At 7 came on board the gang of men lent to H.M.S. Inspector to assist in mooring her in a new Birth, as also the Delegates for this Ship, who had read the Intelligence of the Day to the Ships Company by order of the Committee of this Ship, agreable to the Orders they had received on having the charge of the proper management of this Ship.

Sunday 4th June

AM Strong Gales & squally with Rain, struck lower Yards & Topgᵗ Masts per Order—At 9 the Delegates went on board the Sandwich per signal—At 10 the following Persons were convicted (by Evidence of the Ships Company) of drunkenness viz. Andrew Moriarty, Martin McCarty, George Neal & Thomas Pantoney & being on duty at the time—Punished by unanimous Consent of the Ships Company—

PM Fresh gales with Rain—Sailed hence two Cutters with Dispatches— More moderate winds—People employed working Junk &c—

Monday 5th June

AM Light Airs & fair winds. At 10 mustered the Ships Company by the Captains Clerk—Light airs & fair winds—Swayed up lower Yards & Top gallent Masts—Cleared hawse &c—Received for the use of this Ship from H.M.S. Sandwich, three Pounds of Candles of ten to the Pound one lb of Mould candles of six in lb. Tried to bring too a Sloop one six & one four Pounder shotted—This day an address was written to the People of England from the seamen of the Fleet at the Nore—

and sent to London to be printed—Fresh breezes & fair weather—At one fired a Royal Salute in Commemmoration of our most gracious Sovereign's Birth Day—Went on Liberty several men—The Captain & Lieut. Caley went to dine on Board H.M.S. Repulse—at ½ past 5 o'clock—Sent the Cutter on board the Repulse by Order of Captain Duncan & Lieut. Caley in order to their coming on board at that time per Request—

Tuesday 6th June

AM D.º W.ʳ—Open'd a Cask of Flour 407 lbs—Open'd a cask of Beef Contents 38 (word indecipherable)

$$\left. \begin{array}{l} 8 \text{ Six lb} \\ 7 \text{ Four lb} \end{array} \right\} \text{Shotted}$$

1 Four Pounder not shotted

PM Moderate Breezes & fair W.ʳ fired several Musquets to bring too Boats & merchant Ships—at 11 MH Ship Sarapis slipped her cables in Order to her getting into the Little Nore, conceiving her People apprehended that his Majesty was not just or merciful to his unfortunate Subjects who might endeavor to support an Application for his Clemency —Fired at sundry times at different Merchant Vessels &c, &c. This 24 hours 15 Guns shotted.

Wednesday 7th June

AM Light Airs—Arrived here hoisting the red flag H.M.S. Ardent, Agammamnon with 2 other ships who had left Yarmouth Roads—AM D.º W.ʳ Address was written to the Seamen of the Fleet at the Nore— Signed a Seaman as also a letter to the Lords of the Admiralty—Winds variable.

PM Light airs & fair. Repeated the Signal for all Committee Men on board H.M.S. Inflexible Exercised Great Guns & small Arms. Lord Northesk Commander of H.M. Ship Monmouth—went on board His Majesty's Ship Sandwich & after a long Conference with the Delegates from the different Ships of the Fleet who layed their grievances before him begging his opinion & to know if he thought them reasonable, he granted they were necessary to be redressed and with permission of the Seamen of the Fleet, he (Lord Northesk) would wait upon His Majesty and would send the Seamen an Answer in 54 hours time from 8 o'clock.

Thursday 8th June

AM D.º W.ʳ Rec.ᵈ 6 lb Candles H.M.S. Sandwich—

PM Light Airs & fair

Friday 9th June

AM at 8 Mr. Cobert came alongside the Sandwich in a Yatch with a flag of truce hoisted—he politely offer'd the use of his Yatch to go into the harbour to accommodate Capt. Knight of His Majesty's Ship Montagu who was expect'd to have returned—at 11 Capt.ⁿ Knight arrived in another Yatch hoisting a flag of truce—He came on board H.M.S. Sandwich to confer with the Delegates of the Fleet—This day an address was sent to His Majesty from the Seamen of the Fleet—

PM Moderate Breezes & fair W.ʳ At 4 o'clock came on board the President of the Committee of Delegates of the Fleet attended by a numerous Procession of Boats with Colours flying the Band playing Martial & Loyal tunes the time he remained on board—Regaled him & the Boats Crews with Bread & Cheese & small grog—having no small Beer on board—Mr. Parker after reading several Papers & Instructions to the Ships Company left the Ship—forming a regular Procession of Boats, Drums Beating &c. as also a Band of Music.—Final determination of the whole fleet this day is to Cruiz of the Texel in pursuit of Dutch Fleet.

Saturday 10th June

AM D.ᵒ W.ʳ The Delegates were instructed to give in a demand for Stores made by the Warrant Officers as also an amount of Provisions wanting to compleat this Ship for 10 Weeks for 96 Men, of all Species— Tried this day to bring too different Vessels 5 Six Pounders Shotted & 4 Four Pounders shotted—Received of the Pursers Stores for making Grog for strange Boats Crews &c, &c. 2 Gallons of Rum—Broached a Cask of Rum—Contents 31, No. 82.

PM Fresh Breezes & fair—At 2 fired a Gun & loosed the Foretopsail as did all the Ships laying here belonging to His Majesty's Service—At 5 Sailed hence His Majesty's Ship Leopard towards the River without advice from any of the other Ships—ran on shore—but soon cleared herself—At 6 H.M.S. Repulse slipped her cables & got on shore—on the Sand—the Ships of the Fleet fired upon her for endeavoring to get away —the Tide being flown she got clear off & got into the Harbour.—At 4 Lieut. Caley with Mr. Carter Midshipman went on board Sloop by Permission on account of Mr. Caley's ill state of health—H.M. Ship Ardent brought too the Sloop & detained Mr. Caley & Master Carter till a Boat was sent from this ship to have them passed—At ½ past 11 H.M.S. Ardent slipped—several Ships fired at her which she returned, she got safe up the River Medway—An Accident happened by a 6 lb Cartridge blowing up & wounded W.ᵐ Ditchburn & W.ᵐ Williams &c.

Sunday 11th June

AM D.° W.ᵣ The Ships of the Squadron with the Red Flag in consequence of Captain Knight's promising (on board the Sandwich) our grievances being redressed by His Majesty—hauled down the Red Flag & hoisted the St. George's Ensign and the Union Jack—& made the Signal for a free Navigation.—

PM Light Breezes & Fair W.ᵣ Went on board H.M.S. Montagu at 2 o'clock to copy off the propositions made by the different Ships of the Squadron with James Fletcher—At ½ past 4 came on board and read the same to the Ships Company—Rec.ᵈ by the Delegates a Copy of the request made to Captain Knight to take to the King—Missing Mr. Watt.

Monday 12th June

AM Light Airs & fair—Ans.ᵈ the Signal for Delegates on board H.M.S. Sandwich went on board different ships to see if we could get Intelligence & find the above mentioned Mr. Watt. H.M.S. Sandwich at 4 brought too a Brig.

PM Light Airs & fair W.ᵣ Saw in Shore a Quarter of Beef under a Union Jack at the Garrison, as also a flag and Bread Bag on board H.M.S. Monmouth at its Mizen Peak.—Rec.ᵈ from H.M.S. Montague two Pounds of candles—H.M.S. Pylades brought too a Galliot richly laden with Bale Goods, Indigo &c, &c. from London & bound to Dieppe in France—six boats.

Tuesday 13th June

AM Light Airs with Showers of Rain—At 10 lowered the Launch down to go on board a fishing smack after which she went on board H.M.S. Inflexible to endeavor to get Candles for present use—the Delegates went as usual on board H.M.S. Sandwich—Expended this day 2 Gallons of Rum for Grog to Ships Company—Broke by accident 4 Launches bars.

PM Light Airs & fair W.ᵣ A Letter was brought on board H.M.S. Montague by a flag of truce said to contain advice from Captain Knight— the Delegates of the whole fleet were assembled on board her to give their answer, which was to the purpose that they wished the Captain of the Montagu (Capt.ⁿ Knight) as being sent to his Majesty to endeavor to reconcile our present affairs, would in person come & give an Answer on the Business. The Union Jack was hoisted at the Main with the Blue Jack at the Mizen Topmasthead—Received from H.M.S. Inflexible 92 lbs of Candles for which Capt.ⁿ Duncan gave a receipt—Capt.ⁿ Duncan requested to go on shore which was permitted by the Delegates of the Fleet if Capt.ⁿ Duncan would take the advantage of going with a flag of truce—as no Ships Boats were allowed to go into Sheerness.

Wednesday 14th June

AM Light Airs & Fair Wᵗ Washed the Ship thro' out.

END OF THE LOG

APPENDIX III

British Naval Vessels Controlled by Delegates of The Fleet in 1797: from Admiralty Records

Ship	Guns	First Spithead	Plymouth	Second Spithead	Nore-Yarmouth	Cape of Good Hope
Advice	Schooner	X		X		
Agamemnon	64				X	
Agincourt	64				X	
Anson	44		X			
Ardent	64				X	
Artois	38		X			
Atlas	98		X			
Belliqueux	64				X	
Bienfaisant	64		X			
Braave	40					X
Brilliant	28				X	
Cambridge			X			
Caton	64		X			
Champion	20				X	
Charon	44		X			
Chichester	44					X
Childers	14		X			
Cleopatra	36	X				
Clyde	38				X	
Comet	14				X	
Concorde	36	X	X			
Defense	74	X		X		
Defiance	74	X		X		
Director	64				X	
Discovery	Bomb				X	
Doris	36		X			
Duke	98	X		X		
Edgar	74		X			
Espion	38				X	
Europe	64		X			
Firm	14				X	
Fly	14	X		X		
Galatea	32		X			
Gibraltar	80		X			
Glory	98	X		X		
Grampus	20				X	
Greyhound	28		X			
Havik	18		X			
Hind	28	X		X		
Hornet	sloop	X		X		
Hound	18				X	

BRITISH NAVAL VESSELS CONTROLLED BY DELEGATES OF THE FLEET IN 1797:
from Admiralty Records

Ship	Guns	First Spithead	Plymouth	Second Spithead	Nore-Yarmouth	Cape of Good Hope
Impérieuse	38					X
Impétueux	74	X		X		
Inflexible	64				X	
Inspector	16				X	
Iris	32				X	
Isis	50				X	
Jason	32	X		X		
Juste	80	X		X		
Lancaster	64				X	
Latona	38	X			X	
Leopard	50				X	
Leviathan	74		X			
Lion	64				X	
London	98	X		X		
Magnanime	44		X			
Majestic	74		X			
Marlborough	74	X		X		
Mars	74	X		X		
Medusa	32	X		X		
Megaera	F.S. 14	X		X		
Melpomene	44	X		X		
Melampus	36	X		X		
Minotaur	74	X		X		
Monarch	74	X		X		
Monmouth	64				X	
Montagu	74				X	
Naiad	38				X	
Nassau	64				X	
Neptune	74				X	
Niger	32	X			X	
Nimble	cutter	X		X		
Nymphe	36	X		X		
Penguin	sloop	X		X		
Plover	sloop	X		X		
Pompée	80	X		X		
Porcupine	24	X	X			
Pomone	40		X			
Powerful	74		X			
Princess	20		X			
Proserpine	28				X	
Prudent	36		X			
Pylades	16				X	
Queen Charlotte	100	X		X		
Ramillies	74	X		X		
Rattlesnake	16					X
Repulse	64				X	
Robust	74	X		X		
Royal George	100	X		X		
Royal Sovereign	100	X		X		

British Naval Vessels Controlled by Delegates of The Fleet in 1797: from Admiralty Records

Ship	Guns	First Spithead	Plymouth	Second Spithead	Nore-Yarmouth	Cape of Good Hope
Sandwich	90				X	
Saturn	74		X			
Scourge	sloop	X				
Serapis	20				X	
Speedwell		X		X		
Stag	32	X		X		
Standard	64				X	
Star	14					X
Swan	16				X	
Success	32	X		X		
Sylph	18		X			
Syren	32	X		X		
Telemachus	cutter	X		X		
Terpsichore	32				X	
Terrible	74	X		X		
Tremendous	74					X
Triton	28	X		X		
Trusty	50					X
Tysiphone	28				X	
Unité	36	X	X			
Venus	32	X		X		
Vestal	28				X	
Vindictive	24					X

The list does not contain vessels of 1797 individually controlled by delegates such as *Circe*, or involved in isolated mutinies such as *Hermione*, or the object of aborted mutinies.

APPENDIX IV

ADMIRALTY DENIES DELEGATES' DEMANDS
Nepean to Bridport, 24 April

After the very liberal additions made to the wages and to the allowance of provisions to the seamen in His Majesty's ships, their Lordships cannot but look upon those further demands to be very unreasonable.

The request that the further issue of a proportion of flour, in lieu of meat, may be discontinued, cannot at this time be complied with, it being impossible to procure a quantity of the last mentioned article of provisions sufficient for the consumption of the fleet; but whenever the present difficulties in that respect can be removed, it has always been their Lordships' intention to cause the full proportion of fresh beef to be supplied.

The quantity of vegetables now served to seamen in port, is much greater than was ever served in any former war, and a proper quantity will always be furnished—but instead of unreasonably asking for more, they ought to be most thankful for that with which, at a great expense to the country, they are now supplied.

With respect to an increase of the out-pensions of the Royal Hospital at Greenwich, I am to state to your Lordship that the present revenues of said Hospital do not admit of a compliance with this request; and when the burthens which must necessarily be laid upon the public, in consequence of the increase of wages, are considered, it cannot be expected that any additional sum can be appropriated to this purpose, or the expedient proposed can be resorted to for removing the difficulty.

On the subject of the complaints which have been made against the different officers, it must be understood that all such complaints ought to be made to the commander in chief, and there can be no doubt should the circumstances appear to justify it, that the officers complained of will be brought to court-martial. Without that mode of inquiry into the merits of the different cases, their Lordships' regard for justice will not admit of their inflicting punishment or censure. But as the characters of officers are not to be lightly attacked, the seamen should be admonished not to prefer any complaint against them without having good cause for so doing.

In consequence, however, of the favourable change that has taken place in the situation of things, their Lordships are inclined to hope that all animosities have ceased, and that the complaints which were brought forward in a moment of ill-humour may now be suffered to drop—more especially when the seamen reflect upon the zealous part which their officers have taken in prevailing on their Lordships to consent to the indulgences which have been granted to them.

APPENDIX V

PITT CONFUSES BUCKNER
Buckner to the Nore Delegates

Sheerness, May 27, 1797

In pursuance of orders communicated to me by the Lords Commissioners of the Admiralty, I am directed to acquaint the crews of his Majesty's vessels at the Nore and Sheerness, that after the very liberal attention of his Majesty in increasing the wages and provisions of the seamen and marines in his Majesty's service, for which they have in general expressed themselves not only satisfied, but highly grateful, their Lordships are extremely surprised to find the seamen and marines of his Majesty's ships at the Nore and Sheerness should be still in a state of disobedience, and bringing forward further requests; their Lordships have therefore commanded me to inform you, that since all that could reasonably be expected by the seamen and marines has already been granted them, their Lordships cannot accede to any such request.

With respect to the first article of the conditions presented by the seamen and marines at this port, their Lordships direct me to inform you, as has already been explicitly declared, that all additional allowances of wages and provisions, and every other regulation announced at Portsmouth, have been established by his Majesty's order in Council, and by Act of Parliament, and extended to all seamen and marines in his Majesty's service. That, with respect to the second article of said conditions, the nature of the service in time of war does not admit of the men having leave to go to their families, except under very particular circumstances, of which the captains, or other superior officer, alone can judge; that with respect to the third and fifth Articles, the ship's company shall be paid in the manner pointed out by the several Acts of

Parliament at present in force for the encouragement of seamen and marines employed in his Majesty's Service, as they always are, unless some very urgent necessity prevents it; but as it ever has been the practice of the Service to show attention to those who, with the true spirit of British seamen, voluntarily stand forth in defence of their country, their Lordships are desirous of giving every possible encouragement to volunteers; and it is not their intention to direct that advance should be paid to impressed men.

With respect to the fourth Article, all arrangements concerning the officers to be employed in the ships of the squadron must be settled by the Admiral or Commanding Officer for the time being, conformably to the instructions of their Lordships, according to the circumstances of each particular place.

With respect to the sixth Article, if it should be his Majesty's pleasure to pardon all who may have deserted from his Service in the Navy, it must be the effect of his Majesty's royal clemency alone, and not of any requisition; that, although their Lordships thought proper to go to Portsmouth for the purpose of obtaining more perfect information of the grievances which the seamen and marines in general might have to represent, and of adopting most expeditiously such measures as might be necessary, and granting such further indulgences as might render their situation more comfortable, and enable them better to provide for the support of their families, no similar reason exists for their taking such a step on the present occasion.

That the representations made at Portsmouth have been fully considered, and the regulations made in consequence have already been extended to the whole fleet, and established by the highest authority. Their Lordships therefore direct that it is to me and to the officers under whom you serve, that ships' companies are to look up, to whom their petitions are always to be presented, and through whom their Lordships' determinations are to be expected.

It is their Lordships' direction that I should also inform you that, notwithstanding all that you have done, his Majesty's most gracious pardon, and their Lordship's order to all the officers to bury in oblivion all that has passed, are now offered to you, which, should you refuse, you will have to answer for all the melancholy consequences which must attend your persisting in the present state of disobedience and mutiny.

When the seamen and marines at the Nore and at Sheerness reflect that the rest of the fleets have returned to their duty, and have proceeded to sea in search of the enemies of their country, their Lordships have no doubt that they will no longer show themselves ungrateful for all that has so liberally been granted to them, but will strive who shall be the first to show his loyalty to his King, and his love to his country, by returning to that state of obedience and discipline, without which they cannot expect any longer to enjoy the confidence and good opinion of their country.

(Signed) CHARLES BUCKNER,
Vice-Admiral of the White, and Commander of his Majesty's ships and vessels in the river Medway and at the buoy of the Nore.

APPENDIX VI

A PROTEST BY M.P.s TO THE KING, 31 MAY 1797

There is at present very great uneasyness in the minds of an extensive number of moderate men concerning the situation of public affairs, and they think the public will not at this moment be satisfied without a change of Administration . . . the moment is critical.

We have occasion to learn the sentiments of many Members of Parliament upon the present situation of the kingdom, who agree with us in their anxiety and earnest wishes that means may be devised for removing those ideas which have of late become prevalent in an extensive manner.

Your Lordship (Moira) cannot have been an indifferent spectator of what has been passing, and we believe, from your character that you cannot be wanting in zeal for the public service. The present state of things admits of no excuse on the part of any individual attached to his Majesty and the Constitution, for neglecting to take such measures as may avert those evils, which seem to menace everything that is valuable.

Without entering into the question of merit or demerit, it is our opinion that the present administration, from the irritation and alarm which now prevail in the public mind, are not likely to extricate the country from the difficulty in which it is involved, and that every hour is pressing for some effectual remedy.

We are authorized by a considerable number of respectable Members of Parliament to signify their concurrence in the sentiments which we have expressed;—a number so considerable as to give the important assurance that a dissolution of the Parliament could not be necessary. We think it right to add that we fear there is but a short interval left for applying the remedy which we have thought it our duty to suggest, believing that it may very speedily be too late to apply any remedy whatever—if, in truth, it be not already too late.

          (Signed) Sir George Shuckburgh-Evelyn
                    Bryan Edwards
                    Sir John Sinclair
                    Sir Christopher Hawkins
                    Joseph Foster Barham

APPENDIX VII

A PROTEST TO THE KING FROM
THE HOUSE OF LORDS, 1797
(date and signatures missing)

This solemn Address which we offer to the Throne, the only measure now left to discharge our duty to ourselves, to the publick and to your Majesty, has induc'd us to lay before you in firm but respectful language our sentiments with regard to the situation of the country.

The enormous and accumulating debt in our opinion will be the principal cause of some convulsion in the Empire.

The continuance of a war (whether in the first instance just and necessary is at present out of the question) presses severely on the country, but as there is no prospect under the measures now adopted of any termination to it, we think its continuance in the highest degree alarming.

Under the present Minister the country can neither treat with dignity or advantage. This opinion, whether the world at large will comment upon it as proceeding from selfish and interested motives, must on our part be hazarded; but this we think it our first duty to point out, and beg leave to state it as such to your Majesty.

If unfortunately for the country a description of men actuated by zeal for its prosperity cannot be selected, and that your Majesty is determin'd at all hazards either to continue the war or to enter into a negotiation with France under the auspices of a Minister whose conduct must have made him peculiarly obnoxious to its Government, our next duty to your Majesty is to advise the means of carrying such a resolution into effect.

It can only be done by a retrenchment of publick and private expence, the burthen of which every individual in the country must endure, especially the higher and richer classes of it, and we offer to your Majesty any support the most sanguine may judge adequate to prevent publick ruin.

But it is our duty to state that your Majesty and family must set the example, except this is done in the most solemn and effectual manner, and that you are pledg'd to carry such retrenchment into execution, we are of opinion the now existing and hourly accumulating burthens of the country will soon be intolerable—perhaps remediless.

These are the leading measures we think it our duty to urge to the Throne, and without the adoption of which we are firmly of opinion the country must be undone. Having thus in the most solemn manner discharg'd our duty as hereditary advisers of the Crown, we leave this Address with your Majesty.

APPENDIX VIII

A ROYAL PROCLAMATION ON THE NORE

By the King—A Proclamation for the Suppression of the mutinous and treasonable Proceedings of the Crews of certain of our Ships at the Nore.

GEORGE R.

WHEREAS, upon the representation of our Lords-commissioners of our Admiralty respecting the proceedings of the seamen and marines on board certain of our ships at the Nore, we were pleased to command our said Lords-commissioners of our Admiralty to signify to the said seamen and marines our gracious intentions, expressed in our royal declaration under our sign manual, bearing date at St. James's the 27th day of May instant; and whereas our right trusty and right well-beloved cousin and councillor, George John, Earl Spencer, our trusty and well-beloved Charles George, Lord Arden, of our kingdom of Ireland, and William Young, Esquire, Rear-Admiral of the White, being three of the lords-commissioners of our Admiralty, did cause our gracious intentions, expressed in such our declaration, to be signified to the crews of our ships at the Nore, and did require such crews to return to their due obedience accordingly; and whereas it has been represented to us, that some of the crews of our said ships have been desirous of returning to their obedience accordingly, but have been prevented from so doing by violence, and others of our ships in the actual discharge of their duty have been fired upon, and attempts have been made to prevent some of our ships from proceeding according to the orders of their commanders; and whereas such continued perseverance in rebellious and treasonable attempts against our crown and dignity, after repeated admonitions and offers of our gracious pardon, render it necessary for us to call on all our loving subjects to be aiding and assisting in repressing the same, we have thought fit, by the advice of our privy council, to issue this our royal proclamation, and we do hereby strictly enjoin all our admirals, generals, commanders, and officers of our forces by sea and land, and all magistrates whatsoever, and all others our loving subjects, that they in their several stations do use their utmost endeavours, according to law, to suppress all such mutinous and treasonable proceedings, and to use all lawful means to bring the persons concerned therein, their aiders and abettors, to justice; and we do hereby strictly enjoin and command all our loving subjects whatsoever not to give any aid, comfort, assistance, or encouragement whatsoever, to any person or persons concerned in any such mutinous and treasonable proceedings, as they will answer the same at their peril; and also to the utmost of their power, and according to law, to prevent all other persons from giving any such aid, assistance, comfort, or encouragement.

Given at our court at St. James's, the 31st day of May, 1797, and in the 37th year of our reign.

God Save the King.

APPENDIX IX

AN UNCONVINCING ADDRESS FROM SPITHEAD TO THE NORE

4 June 1797

BROTHER SAILORS,

It is with the utmost concern we see that several ships' companies continue in a state of disaffection, and illegal proceedings, notwithstanding every demand made by our brethren in Lord Bridport's fleet have been most graciously granted to us, by his Majesty and both Houses of Parliament assembled. We shall lay some outlines of our proceedings before the public view. When we requested Sir Roger Curtis to go from Torbay round to Spithead, we were actuated by no bad principles; there was no disaffection to our king and country—no fresh demands on our side, but what had before been made by our brethren of Lord Bridport's fleet; as we had before been privy to all, we only wished to join our brethren, as in Torbay, where we lay, many reports prevailed which exaggerated matters greatly, and as reports can never be relied on. It was never our intention to distress our country, or leave it exposed to the ravages of the enemy; no, should the enemy have dared to take the advantage of our situation, we were unanimously resolved to chastise their insolence. Our views were honourable, we were perfectly sensible that no state, no body of men could exist without proper subordination and discipline was maintained; our general request was, our wages to be raised, our provisions to be augmented, and our private grievances to be redressed: all this was granted, the king's most gracious pardon given us, and an act of indemnity and total oblivion passed; we returned cheerfully to our duty (which by-the-by we never neglected), and we believe when we say, should the enemies of our country dare to meet us they will be rougher handled than ever they have been yet, we not only speak the sentiments of our own squadron, but the unanimous voice of our brethren in Lord Bridport's fleet.

There is no doubt but evil-minded and designing men wish to take advantage of our honest openness, intending to make us their tools to subvert our most excellent constitution, but we are above their devices— we think ourselves capable of judging for ourselves, without being led by the nose by any set of men from on shore whatever. We will never desert the country which gave us birth, and for which we profess a most sincere esteem. French principles and their agents, under whatsoever mask they may attempt to work upon us, we abhor; and should we ever get any such persons into our hands, we are resolved to bring them to justice. It is therefore our hope that all ships' companies who labour under any grievances will not forget their country, or by continuing in an unsettled state give our enemies any advantage; but should our enemies dare to lift up their heads, and come out of their hiding-holes, we hope our brother seamen will unanimously agree to prefer the public good to their private interests, and unanimously agree to go, meet and chastise the insolence of our enemies, and to preserve the unsullied honour of the British flag.

With this in view we have drawn up this address, hoping it will have a desirable effect upon such of our brethren as are still in an unsettled state, which should it do, will entail a perfect satisfaction upon the sea-man in Sir Roger Curtis's squadron, as likewise upon all our brethren in Lord Bridport's fleet. We have wrote these lines while unmooring, and preparing to go out to sea, to face our enemies, and to protect the com-merce of our country, which as seamen it is our duty to encourage to the utmost of our power. We have a full reliance that all our brother seamen, who labour under any grievances will make no unreasonable demands, nor delay an amicable settlement by standing out for trifling objects.

That all differences may be happily and soon settled, is the sincere wish of the seamen in Sir Roger Curtis's squadron.

Prince
 John Lindsay
 William Horton
Caesar
 William Oliver
 John Gilder
Cumberland
 William Smedley
 Thomas Bridges
Ganges
 Henry Edwards
 John Howe
Bedford
 Robert Berry, X
 Henry Hide, X Their marks

La Juste
 Patrick Rowe
 Michael M'Cue
 William White
Triumph
 Arch. M'Arthur
 James Maddock
Formidable
 George Horser
 David Nicholls
Hector
 Edward Cavenagh
 David Parry

Spithead, 4th June.

APPENDIX X

PICTURE NOTES

1. George III from a portrait c. 1800 by W. Beechey in National Portrait Gallery. 2. William Pitt, from a portrait by J. Hoppner, author's collection. 3. Attempt on King's life, 1795, contemporary engraving, Free Library of Philadelphia.* 4. Thomas Paine, Free Library of Philadelphia. 5. Charles James Fox, 1793, from a portrait by K. Hickel, National Portrait Gallery. 6. Theobald Wolfe Tone, from R. R. Madden, *United Irishmen,* 1858. 7. Louis Lazare Hoche, 1797, engraving from a crayon portrait by Ursule Boze, which Hoche considered the best likeness made of himself. Free Library of Philadelphia. 8. "The Liberty of the Subject," attributed to Thomas Rowlandson, National Maritime Museum. 9. A Ninety Gun Ship at Spithead, from an aquatint by J. Clark and Hamble after D. Serres, published 1806, National Maritime Museum. 10. The Sea Cook, water color by Rowlandson, painted at Spithead, c. 1799, National Maritime Museum. 11. The Purser by Rowlandson, same data as No. 10. 12. "In Port," anon. drawing c. 1799, National Maritime Museum. 13. The Admiralty Board Room, drawn by Rowlandson, engraved by Melville, published 1808, author's collection. 14. Lord Spencer, from a painting by John Singleton Copley, National Maritime Museum. 15. Lord Bridport, after a painting by L. F. Abbott, National Maritime Museum. 16. -Portland, 17. -Thelwall, 18. -Wordsworth, and 19. -Coleridge are c. 1797 portraits from the Free Library of Philadelphia. 20. Richard Earl Howe, from a portrait by J. S. Copley, National Maritime Museum. 21. "Portsmouth Point," etching by Rowlandson, c. 1799. Looking toward Gosport. Spithead offstage left, Dockyard off to right. National Maritime Museum. 22. Sheerness; fort in center, dockyard right, the Great Nore in distance at extreme left. Line engraving by P. C. Canot after R. Paton, published 1803. National Maritime Museum. 23. Richard Parker, published a week after his death, by

---

* Most pictures credited to the Free Library of Philadelphia are from the John Frederick Lewis collection, others from the Rare Book Department.

J. Harrison & Co., from a drawing by W. Chamberlain. National Maritime Museum. 24. Parker hands the grievances to Buckner, anon. mezzotint published three days after the execution by G. Thompson, Old Bailey, and I. Evans, Long Lane, West Smithfield. The artist's somewhat heroic handling of the President is in tune with much populist sentiment of the time. Contrast with the same scene (No. 26) as handled by a loyal satirist, Isaac Cruikshank. National Maritime Museum. 25. Richard Parker, engraving from *The Mutiny at Spithead and the Nore* by W. J. Neale, London 1842, author's collection. An idealized likeness, apparently based on Bailey & Samson's mezzotint of 27 July 1797. Both probably influenced by the death mask. The Neale portrait and his preachy book on the great mutiny show an effort to rehabilitate Parker's reputation at the time of a new reform wave in Britain. 26. "The Delegates in Counsel or Beggars on Horseback," etching by Isaac Cruikshank, published on 9 June 1797, during the last week of the Nore mutiny. National Maritime Museum. The older Cruikshank introduces the Pitt propaganda line into the confrontation scene of Admiral Buckner and President Parker. With "Thelwall's Lecture" under his elbow Parker is saying, "Tell him we intend to be masters. I'll read him a lecture." Irishmen with paddy faces and clay pipes and a Negro are shown among the delegates. On the wall the loyal ditties "True Blue" and "Hearts of Oak" have been defaced and Britannia turned upside down. Under the table, among members of his parliamentary clique, is Charles James Fox, boasting, "Aye, aye, sir, we are at the bottom of it." 27. John Horne Tooke, Free Library of Philadelphia. 28. Samuel Whitbread, from a portrait by James Opie, courtesy Whitbread and Company Ltd. Brewery, Chiswell St., London. 29. John Binns, aged 88, from a daguerrotype, Free Library of Philadelphia. 30. Song "Ward Associations" published 1797. 31. William Bligh in 1814, from a miniature, privately owned. 32. Fox's lair, St. Anne's Hill, contemporary lithograph, author's collection. 33. Lord Keith, mezzotint, author's collection. 34. Admiral Sir Charles Pasley, Free Library of Philadelphia. 35. Parker's death mask, Hunterian Museum, Royal College of Surgeons of England, Lincoln's Inn Fields. 36. Battle of Camperdown from *Admiral Duncan* by the Earl of Camperdown, London, 1898. 37. Admiral Duncan, mezzotint by J. R. Smith after H. P. Danloux, 1800, National Maritime Museum. 38. Earl St. Vincent from painting by J. Hoppner, Greenwich Hospital Collection, National Maritime Museum. 39. "A distressed Sailor" by Rowlandson, 1801, Print Room, British Museum. —British illustrations searched out by Joan St. George Saunders.

BIBLIOGRAPHY

ORIGINAL MANUSCRIPTS

Admiralty documents in the Public Record Office, London

Admiralty 1/56   Cape of Good Hope Mutiny
1/107   Spithead mutinies
1/248   West Indies
1/396   Mediterranean fleet mutinies
1/524   North Sea fleet mutinies
1/727   Nore mutiny
1/728   Nore mutiny
1/811   Plymouth mutiny
1/1022   First Spithead mutiny
1/1023   Second Spithead mutiny
1/3685   Court-martial evidence on the Nore
1/3974   Intelligence reports
1/4172   Royal and government papers relating to the Nore.
1/5125   Seamens' petitions
1/5189   Orders in Council
1/5486   Reports of Courts-martial aboard H.M.S. *Neptune*
—Richard Parker
—Dennis Sullivan *et al*
—William Ross
—William Welch
—James Robertson
—John Habbigan
—John Whitley *et al*
—James Luran *et al*
—George Taylor *et al*
—James Hockless *et al*
—Thomas McCann
—Thomas Jephson
—Richard Brown *et al*
—Andrew Earl *et al*
—Lawrence Vanker *et al*
—William Holdsworth *et al*
—John Burrows *et al*

Admiralty 2/133 — Admiralty Orders & Instructions
2/617 — Secretary's letters to public offices
2/1352 — Admiralty secret orders & letters
Admiralty 3/136 — Rough minutes meetings of the Lords Commissioners of the Admiralty, First Spithead mutiny
3/137 — Rough minutes (cont.) Second Spithead mutiny
Summary of mutineer papers found on Nore ships at end of mutiny
Admiralty 7/343 — Memorials & Reports on the Nore mutiny

Home Office 64/41 — Secret reports relating to the mutiny
CUMBY, William P. — *Copies of Papers found in possession of mutineers on board H.M. fireship* COMET *on their return to duty after the disgraceful affair at the Nore in May and June 1797.* M.S. 1797, 21 pp. folio in vellum. Author's collection.
DUCKWORTH, Thomas, Captain — Correspondence, letter books, account books, etc. Yale University Library

PAMPHLETS

National Maritime Museum
   —Portraits at—
   —H.M.S. *Victory*
   —Dress of the British Sailor
   —Uniform of Naval Officers
   —Concise Guide to National Maritime Museum
Portsmouth Cathedral

PERIODICALS CONSULTED

Gentleman's Magazine
New Annual Register
Boyle's Court Guide
Holden's Triennial Directory
Norfolk Chronicle

BOOKS

Abbott, Charles, *Lord Colchester, Diary & Correspondence of,* 3 volumes, London, 1861.
Anderson, Adam, *Origin of Commerce,* etc, 2 volumes, London, 1764.
Ansted, A., *Dictionary of Sea Terms,* Glasgow, 1880.
Aspinall, A., *Later Correspondence of George III,* Cambridge, 1963.
Barron, John, *Life of Howe,* London, 1888.
Bartholemew, J. G., *Literary and Historical Atlas of Europe,* London, 1941.

496] Bibliography

Beik, Paul H. and Lafore, Laurence, *Modern Europe, a History Since 1500*, New York, 1959.
Berckman, Evelyn, *A Portrait of St. Vincent (Nelson's Dear Lord)*, London, 1962.
Binns, John, *Trial of*, taken in shorthand by Henry Bynner, Birmingham, 1797.
Blake to Byron, From—Pelican books.
Brougham, Henry Lord, *Historical Sketches of Statesmen in the Time of George III*, 2 volumes, London, 1855.
Burke, Thomas, *The Streets of London*, London, 1943.
Campbell, John, *Naval History of Great Britain*, 8 volumes, London, 1813.
Camperdown, Earl of, *Admiral Duncan*, London, 1898.
Carlyle, Thomas, *The French Revolution*, New York, no date.
Cestre, Charles, *Life of John Thelwall*, New York, 1906.
Charles-Edwards, T. and Richardson, B., *They Saw It Happen*, New York, 1958.
Chevalier, *Histoire de la Marine Française sous la Première République*, Paris, 1886.
Childers, Spencer, *A Mariner of England*, London, 1908.
Clowes, G. S. Laird, *Sailing Ships, Their History and Development*, London, 1959.
Clowes, William L., *The Royal Navy, a History*, London, 1899, 6 volumes.
Coleridge, Samuel Taylor, *Poems*, London, 1961.
Committee of Secrecy, *House of Commons Report*, 15 March 1799.
Cook, James, *Journals*, Haklyt Society, 2 volumes.
Desbrières, E., *Projets et Tentatives de Debarquements aux Iles Britanniques*, Paris, 1900.
De Quincey, Thomas, *The English Mail Coach*, London, 1960.
Dibdin, Thomas, Ed., *Songs of the Late Charles Dibdin*, London, 1841.
Dobrée, Bonamy and Manwaring, G. E., *The Floating Republic*, London, 1935.
Drinkwater, John, *Charles James Fox*, New York, 1928.
Duff, Charles, *Handbook on Hanging, A*, London, 1938.
Durand, James, *An Able Seaman of 1812*, New Haven, 1926.
Field, C., *Britain's Sea Soldiers*, 2 volumes, London, 1924.
Geographical Guide, a poetical nautical trip round the Island of Great-Britain, London, 1805.
Gill, Conrad, *The Naval Mutinies of 1797*, Manchester, 1913.
Hargreaves, Reginald, *The Narrow Seas*, London, 1959.
Hazlitt, William, *The Spirit of the Age*, London, 1960.
Hickey, William, *Memoirs*, Quennell, Peter, Ed., London, 1960.
Hobhouse, Christopher, *Fox*, London, 1948.
Hobsbawm, E. J., *The Age of Revolution*, London, 1962.
Hutchinson, J. R., *The Press Gang Afloat and Ashore*, New York, 1914.
James, William, *Naval History of Great Britain*, 6 volumes, London, 1859.
James, William, Admiral Sir, *Old Oak, The Life of John Jervis, Earl of St. Vincent*, New York, 1950.

Kelly, Samuel, *An Eighteenth Century Seaman,* Garstin, C., Ed., New York, 1925.

King-Hele, Desmond, *Erasmus Darwin,* London, 1963.

Koestler, Arthur, *Reflections on Hanging,* London, 1956.

Lewis, Michael, *A Social History of the Navy, 1793-1815,* London, 1960.

Lloyd, Christopher, *St. Vincent & Camperdown,* New York, 1963.

McFee, William, *The Law of the Sea,* Philadelphia, 1950.

Maccoby, S., *English Radicalism, 1786-1832,* London, 1955.

Macintyre, Donald, *Admiral Rodney,* London, 1962.

Mackaness, George, *The Life of Vice-Admiral William Bligh,* London, 1951.

Mahan, Alfred T., *Life of Nelson,* London, 1897, 2 volumes.

Mongan, Roscoe, *British History,* London, 1942.

Musgrave, Richard, *Memoirs of Different Rebellions in Ireland,* 2 volumes, Dublin, 1802.

Neale, W. J., *Mutiny at Spithead and the Nore,* London, 1842.

Paine, Thomas, The Selected Work of, New York, 1943.

Palmer, A. W., *Dictionary of Modern History,* London, 1962.

Parker, Richard, The Trial, Life & Anecdotes of—Anon, Manchester, 1797.

Parkinson, C. Northcote, *Portsmouth Point,* London, 1948.

————— *Edward Pellew, Viscount Exmouth,* London, 1934.

Pelican Book of English Prose 1700-1780.

Pemberton, W. Baring, *William Cobbett,* London, 1949.

Pernoud, Georges and Flaissier, Sabine, *The French Revolution,* London, 1962.

Pevsner, Nikolaus, *London (The Buildings of England),* London, 1952.

Plumb, J. H., *History of England, Eighteenth Century,* Pelican.

Pope, Dudley, *The Black Ship,* London, 1963.

Postgate, R. W., *That Devil Wilkes,* New York, 1929.

Prebble, John, *The Highland Clearances,* London, 1963.

Quennell, Marjorie and C. H. B., *A History of Everyday Things in England,* New York, 1956.

Rosebery, Lord, *Pitt,* London, 1941.

Shore, H. N., *Smuggling Days & Smuggling Ways,* London, 1929.

Stuart Jones, E. H., *The Last Invasion of Britain,* Cardiff, 1950.

————— *An Invasion that Failed,* Oxford, 1950.

Trevelyan, G. M., *English Social History,* Toronto, 1946.

Trevelyan, George Otto, *George III and Charles Fox,* London, 1912.

Thompson, E. P., *Making of the English Working Class,* New York, 1964.

Thompson, J. M., *The French Revolution,* New York, 1945.

Tone, Theobald Wolfe, *Life of,* 2 volumes, Washington, 1826.

Warner, Oliver, *A Portrait of Lord Nelson,* London, 1958.

Watson, J. Steven, *The Reign of George III,* Oxford, 1960.

Werner, J., *We Laughed at Boney,* London, 1943.

White, E. W., *British Fishing-boats and Coastal Craft,* part 1, London, 1957.

White, T. H., *The Age of Scandal,* London, 1963.
Williams, E. N., *Life in Georgian England,* London, 1962.
Young, Art, *Thomas Rowlandson,* New York, 1938.

Index

Theatre of the
N O R E   M U T I N Y
and
B L O C K A D E
1797

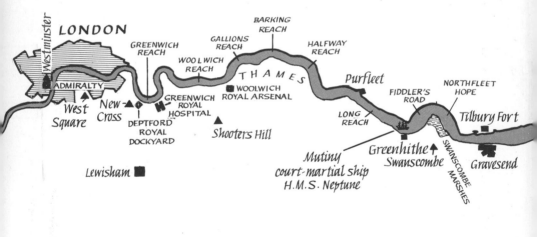

LONDON

BARKING REACH

GALLIONS REACH

GREENWICH REACH

WOOLWICH REACH

HALFWAY REACH

Westminster

THAMES

Purfleet

NORTHFLEET HOPE

ADMIRALTY

WOOLWICH ROYAL ARSENAL

FIDDLER'S ROAD

West Square

New Cross

GREENWICH ROYAL HOSPITAL

LONG REACH

Tilbury Fort

DEPTFORD ROYAL DOCKYARD

Shooters Hill

Mutiny court-martial ship H.M.S. Neptune

Greenhithe

Swanscombe

SWANSCOMBE MARSHES

Gravesend

Lewisham

Croydon

Shoal water and tidal flats

▲ Telegraph station

→ Escape route of H.M.S. Inflexible mutineers

0   Miles   20

map by palacios